Chicago Studies in
POLITICAL
ECONOMY

D0792891

Chicago Studies in
POLITICAL
ECONOMY

Edited by
George J. Stigler

The University of Chicago Press
Chicago and London

George J. Stigler is the Charles R. Walgreen Distinguished
Service Professor Emeritus in the Department of Economics
and in the Graduate School of Business of the University of
Chicago and director of the Center for the Study of the Econ-
omy and the State. Professor Stigler was awarded the Nobel
Prize for economics in 1982.

The University of Chicago Press, Chicago 60637
The University of Chicago Press, Ltd., London
© 1988 by The University of Chicago
All rights reserved. Published 1988
Printed in the United States of America

97 96 95 94 93 92 91 90 89 88   54321

Library of Congress Cataloging-in-Publication Data

Chicago studies in political economy / edited by George J. Stigler.
    p.   cm.
  Includes bibliographies and index.
  ISBN 0-226-77437-6
  ISBN 0-226-77438-4 (pbk.)
    1. Trade regulation—United States. 2. Industry and state—United
States. 3. Chicago school of economics. 4. Political science—
Economic aspects. 5. Crime and criminals—Economic aspects.
I. Stigler, George Joseph, 1911–
HD3616.U47C487 1988
338.973—dc19   87–31218
                                             CIP

Contents

3 STUDIES OF INDUSTRY REGULATION

4 CORRECTIVE POLICIES

Contributors

Gary S. Becker, University Professor of Economics and Sociology, University of Chicago

George J. Borjas, Professor of Economics, University of California, Santa Barbara, and Research Associate, National Bureau of Economic Research

Harold Demsetz, Arthur Andersen Alumni Professor of Business Economics, University of California

Bruce L. Gardner, Professor of Agricultural and Resource Economics, University of Maryland

Gregg A. Jarrell, Senior Vice President and Director of Research, The Alcar Group, Inc., Chicago

Elisabeth M. Landes, Vice-President, Lexecon Inc., Chicago

Peter Linneman, Associate Professor of Finance and Public Policy, The Wharton School, and Director of the Wharton Real Estate Center, University of Pennsylvania

B. Peter Pashigian, Professor of Business Economics, Graduate School of Business, University of Chicago

Sam Peltzman, Sears Roebuck Professor of Economics and Financial Services, Graduate School of Business, University of Chicago

Richard A. Posner, Judge, U.S. Court of Appeals for the Seventh Circuit, and Senior Lecturer, Law School, University of Chicago

George J. Stigler, Charles R. Walgreen Distinguished Service Professor Emeritus, Department of Economics and Graduate School of Business, and Director of the Center for the Study of the Economy and the State, University of Chicago

Preface

> [Herbert] Spencer, during a pause in conversation at dinner at the Athenaeum, said, "You would little think it, but I once wrote a tragedy." Huxley answered promptly, "I know the catastrophe." Spencer declared it was impossible, for he had never spoken about it before then. Huxley insisted. Spencer asked what it was. Huxley replied, "A beautiful theory, killed by a nasty, ugly little fact."
>
> —*Francis Galton, Memories of My Life*

Economic theory is, and should be, always on the move: there are many well-known phenomena we cannot explain satisfactorily—and there are no doubt many more unknown economic phenomena waiting to be discovered. That most fundamental part of economic theory, microeconomics (the study of the allocation of resources and the determination of prices), has been, in recent decades, moving in two directions.

One direction is toward the deepening of the standard theory: the exploration of such concepts as competition, auctions, and dynamic stability, and the recognition of such neglected phenomena as the roles in economics of information and the formation of intelligent expectations by economic actors. This is a fundamental area of economics, and one to which Chicago economists have contributed, but it falls outside the scope of this volume.

The second direction of development has been the widening of the working range of the microeconomist to encompass phenomena previously treated as exogenous in economics. The extension of economic analysis to include the important area of political phenomena is the subject matter of this book. This branch of work is still young— barely three decades old.

The twenty essays in this volume are often subtle and complex in their arguments and sometimes astonishing in their predictions or findings, so I shall not attempt to comment upon them individually. Instead I shall discuss some of the problems they encounter and ideas they suggest.

I. The Political Institutions

Once we raise the question of the nature and functions of the political institutions within which our economy operates, where do we begin and where do we stop? Except for Posner's rich survey of preliterate societies (chap. 5), all the essays in this book and virtually the entire literature of political economy deal with the modern western democratic state. I believe this restriction is due to the youth of the field, and I anticipate that attention will soon be given to a much wider range of political institutions.

Why have the great majority of societies chosen hereditary monarchy (and such lesser variants as the tribal chief and the leader of the highland clan) as the central political decision unit? The monarch will invariably be guided, and largely controlled, by either a hereditary class (the nobles) or a representative assembly, but the monarch will possess substantial autonomy if his post is not purely ceremonial. Why a monarch? Why hereditary?

The monarch has two advantages over the broadly chosen president or prime minister, under certain conditions. The succession is established without (great) controversy, and the monarch can act—for example, declare war—with a minimum of consent. A society whose circumstances often require the making of major decisions, with rapidity, may find a monarchy much more efficient than a democracy. Great and urgent decisions are almost always decisions on the waging of war. Domestic policies usually affect various groups unevenly, and only a deliberative process is likely to find acceptable solutions. Foreign policy is much less divisive—indeed, there is a tradition that asserts that wars unify a nation.

Monarchies rely upon the dice of genetics to produce able leaders, and the phenomenon of regression to the mean is sufficient to guarantee that on average the monarch will not be among the most able people of his time. Still, he can hire them, and it can be immensely costly to resolve the succession by any form of rivalry. Many civil wars, indeed, have been wars of succession, and they impose costs of a magnitude enormously greater than the costs of mediocrity. Indeed, there may be no necessary costs to mediocrity.

Once foreign policy recedes from the center of the political stage and the pace of domestic change accelerates, neither monarch nor nobility becomes appropriate to the tasks of expressing and reconciling the important interests of the society. Traditional societies have no need for democracy, or, if you wish, have already incorporated its desires into the stable social framework. Changing societies must adapt the political framework to economic change and to evolving culture and technology. Ultimately the resulting policies must achieve consent. A Japan can do well enough with an autocracy so long as its social change is slow, but leaps toward explicit democracy when the social change accelerates.

Whatever the governmental form, equilibrium in the political marketplace for legislative goods and harms is determined by the nature and composition of the politically effective coalitions and the size and nature of the programs they achieve. Sensible suggestions are strewn through these essays on the reasons that some coalitions (farmers, the aged) are strong and other groups (small service businesses, the rural poor) are politically weak. The suggestions do not amount to a tight, tested theory, and that is clearly a fundamental goal of future research.

A good deal more has been learned about the policies obtainable by the effective coalitions than about the failures of ineffective groups. The essays in part 3 are a rich sampling of studies of specific regulatory programs, and I shall return to them below. At a more general level, Becker's essay (chap. 2) innovatively develops a calculus of deadweight losses of social policies. Every operative public policy has deadweight losses—costs that have no corresponding benefit to any party directly involved in the policy. Taxpayers end up with larger reductions in income than the treasury receives because of collection costs, constraints imposed by law upon the taxpayers, and the cost of actions taken by taxpayers (e.g., reduced time in the labor force) to reduce taxes. Similarly, the beneficiaries of a public policy receive less than the amount disbursed by the treasury, again because of administrative costs and the regulatory restraints imposed upon the recipients (e.g. inefficient farming practices because of restrictions on the use of land). Becker shows that these deadweight losses impose limits not only upon what beneficiaries can receive but also upon what they seek, and act similarly upon the taxpayers, consumers, or other losers. It becomes the interest of the coalitions to select policies, including sizes of policies, that reduce these losses, and a series of illuminating theorems are deduced from the theory.

The political equilibrium has not been stationary. There was a sustained reduction in the role of the state from 1700 to 1850. More recently, throughout the world and especially in the western world, the growth of the politicized sector of economic life has been immense and similarly sustained. A major study of this development is made by Peltzman (chap. 1). He shows how weak the empirical bases for the traditional explanations for this great change have been. Almost by definition, the growth of the state has been due to the appearance of coalitions or special interest groups (in turn due largely to the changing nature of the society); Peltzman gives a subtle explanation for this development that perhaps paradoxically centers on the diminishing inequality of the distribution of income as well as on the growth of cohesive interest groups. Self-interest rationally pursued is at the center of Peltzman's theory. It is interesting to recall that de Tocqueville found a cumulative tendency toward equality in democratic societies:

> The hatred that men bear to privilege increases in proportion as privileges become fewer and less considerable, so that democratic passions would seem to burn most fiercely just when they have least fuel. . . . When all conditions are unequal, no inequality is so great as to offend the eye, whereas the slightest dissimilarity is odious in the midst of general uniformity; the more complete this uniformity is, the more insupportable the sight of such a difference becomes. Hence it is natural that the love of equality should constantly increase together with equality itself, and that it should grow by what it feeds on. . . .
>
> Every central power, which follows its natural tendencies, courts and encourages the principle of equality; for equality singularly facilitates, extends, and secures the influence of a central power.[1]

De Tocqueville can be interpreted as arguing that the state's aggrandizement is due to either an ideology of equality or a pervasive role of envy in political life. I shall be so bold as to vote with Peltzman, if one must choose between an opaque passion and a rich portfolio of hypotheses.

II. The Theory of Regulation

A distinction is often drawn between the fiscal operations of government, which are constituted by its taxation, borrowing, and spending, and the regulatory operations of government, whose effects on the governmental budget may be negligible at the same time that their effects on the economy are large. This is a distinction of technique rather than of purpose or effect. Fiscal policies have large effects upon the economy, and indeed taxes are often ostensibly used for "regulatory" purposes (e.g., the taxation of liquor and gambling devices). A citizen can be aided or injured equally by a tax or subsidy or by a publicly created cartel of private enterprises such as that of taxicabs or milk marketing authorities. If and when we devise reliable measures of the effects of both public fiscal and regulatory policies, they should be explicable by the same theory of governmental activity.

The paramount role traditionally assigned by economists to government regulation was to correct the failures of the private market (the unconsidered effects of behavior on outsiders), but in fact the premier role of modern regulation is to redistribute income. The farm pro-

---

[1] *Democracy in America* (New York: Alfred A. Knopf, 1945), 2:295. Interestingly, de Tocqueville assigns a role to education directly opposite to Peltzman: "the concentraton of power and the subjection of individuals will increase among democratic nations, not only in the same proportion to their equality, but in the same proportion as their ignorance." *Ibid.*, 299–300.

grams are designed to increase farm incomes, the rent control programs are designed to increase tenants' incomes; tariffs are intended, in Ambrose Bierce's famous definition, to protect producers from the avarice of consumers. This change in the fundamental role of regulation is so widely accepted, and so copiously documented, that it would be pedantic to cite the vast and growing host of supporting studies.

According to one view, the new orientation of regulation courts tautology: one can always find beneficiaries of a policy (Mother's Day for florists) and proceed to ascribe the existence of the policy to that interest group. A more proper view is that conditions favoring the existence of successful interest groups must be determined and the explanations of the existence and tactics of the parties to thousands of regulatory policies must be brought under one general theory. Peltzman's paper and my own (chaps. 7 and 6, respectively) have made beginnings to this challenging work.

Experience has revealed that the task of explaining when and why a regulatory policy was passed is usually much more difficult than the ascertainment of (some) important effects of that policy. This acknowledged difficulty has led some students of regulation to invoke a prevailing ideology to explain the appearance of legislation. An ideology (such as de Tocqueville's) is a commanding set of beliefs, beliefs that are probably not grounded upon self-interest or are related to the interests of the holders in so subtle and obscure a manner as to make it more useful to treat the beliefs as data. Ideology therefore plays the role in analyzing political phenomena that tastes play in analyzing ordinary economic behavior of individuals. The analogy is not satisfying, however, because political activity is conducted by organized coalitions, and a closer economic analogy is to the theory of the firm and associations of firms (cartels)—where tastes commonly play a most modest role overshadowed by the pursuit of profits.

Ideologies are measured in the literature of regulation by such opaque numbers as the ADA ratings of legislators or the state votes for a conservative or liberal candidate. These indices of opinion have received remarkably little study. We do not know how the strategic issues are chosen that govern the ratings, nor whether issues are chosen to obtain favorable ratings for preferred legislators, nor whether the ratings influence elections. These indices are dictated by necessity, and necessity is the mother not only of invention but also of arbitrary decisions. The difficulty that supporters of ideology seek to escape is one which I believe we shall have to address frontally: the construction of a theory of political coalitions.

My own belief is that politically effective groups have used the state to foster their ends in all periods of history. In some periods there was little scope for political actions to benefit important groups. What could Iowa farmers do a hundred years ago to increase their profits when prices were determined in European markets? Whom could they tax when they constituted almost the entire state population? The influence of opportunity upon the scope of and nature of political activity is a fertile ground for historians to till.

III. Specific Regulatory Policies

The studies of individual regulatory policies, of which Harold Demsetz's seminal study of utility regulation and the essays in part 3 of this volume are important examples, serve both scientific and policy ends. They provide us with a rich variety of results, proving that truth can be stranger than theory. They begin to provide us with quantitative estimates of the support for policies and the effects of these policies, tasks no general theory can yet undertake. Finally, they may already begin to have effects upon the regulatory policies. Let us illustrate these services.

Economists have often been accused of cynicism (by people, one wonders, paid to criticize us?). To the important degree that cynicism and realism overlap, the charge is probably true. Consider a public policy that on the surface seemed necessary to deal with a problem which private markets could not handle: the improvement of the air and water of the society. No one polluter, be he a steel mill operator or the owner of a passenger automobile, could justify the costs he would bear in reducing his contribution to pollution by the benefits he alone would receive: most of the benefits of an act of emission control would clearly accrue to the community at large.

The clean air legislation would seem to fit the argument for social controls to deal with the externalities imposed upon the community by unregulated behavior. One would expect public policy to impose stronger restrants on polluters as the society becomes wealthier, for a richer society demands more environmental amenities as well as more private goods and services. No doubt these forces have been important in the development of the clean air policies, but so, too, as Pashigian shows (chap. 17), have the special interests of regions and localities. The areas where the levels of pollution are relatively high (as the New England and North Central regions) have been instrumental in limiting the competition for their industries by the areas (in the South and West) where levels of air purity are high, by imposing a non-degradation rule upon the entire nation. The Clean Air Act has been turned into a device, like the minimum wage, to protect one region at the cost of another—and at the cost of the nation. There is nothing exceptional about this case: it could be duplicated by the rivalries of industries for profit from American grants to relieve foreign distress or from other philanthropic policies.

Some public policies seem to impose substantial costs but have no major beneficiaries. How can the existence of such policies be explained? Perhaps by recognizing that societies, like people, can make mistakes. Any event, no matter how baffling, can be "explained" by the simple statement, "It's a mistake." But what value has such an explanation without a theory about the kinds of mistakes a society can make and how soon they are corrected? Prohibition was an error that fourteen years was required to correct—is that par for national mistakes?

Even more troublesome is the policy which not only lacks important beneficiaries but *persists*. Both of Peltzman's fine studies (chaps. 10 and 11) illustrate this puzzling situation; let us concentrate on the regulation of drugs. The 1962 Drug Amendments added a requirement of efficacy to the previous requirement of safety before a new drug would be licensed by the Food and Drug Administration. The review process for new drugs became extremely long and costly, and the flow of approved "new chemical entities" dropped precipitously. Peltzman employed a variety of approaches to determine whether consumers of drugs benefitted on balance from the protracted review process, and each led to the conclusion that consumers were injured. He found no offsetting benefit for the pharmaceutical firms that supply the drugs (although more recent research suggests that large firms were favored and small firms injured).

Why, then, have only minor improvements in the drug review process been grudgingly allowed in the quarter century since the passage of the Kefauver Act? The bureaucracy of the F.D.A. surely could not withstand the medical professions if they were opposed to the present procedures. The constant efforts to slow down the immense growth of health expenditures in the United States should lead to an examination of the substantial tax the F.D.A. imposes on new drugs. Neither has happened, and the persistence of the program is evidence either of the slowness with which complex public policies are appraised by the community, or of the incompleteness of our understanding of the policy. If the ability of voters to obtain and absorb information is sharply limited, we should explore its effects over a wide range of political activity.

The Chicago students of regulation have usually assumed, explicitly as often as tacitly, that the players who count in regulation are the producers and consumers. Political intermediaries—parties, legislators, administrators—are not believed to be devoid of influence, but in the main they act as agents for the primary players in the construction and administration of public policy. That view is much less popular among political scientists and economists at large than the opposite one that the political machinery has a strong influence on policies. It is easy to guess that the truth lies between these views: when and how much does the political machinery influence the outcomes of policy?

Pashigian's study of the ownership of urban transport facilities (chap. 12) is an interesting case study of this problem. In large American cities, most transport facilities were privately owned as late as 1960, but public ownership grew rapidly in the next decade. To me, his most interesting finding is that public subsidies grew rapidly for the publicly owned systems and served to reduce revenue per vehicle mile in public systems relative to private systems. It was easier to get subsidies for public than for private transit systems; is this generally true?

IV. Effectiveness

The first reaction of almost everyone to a proposed policy is to judge it on the assumption that it will more or less achieve its announced goals. One wonders whether this attitude thrives chiefly in our society and our time. We know all too well that no regulation achieves exactly what it intends. Most policies fall considerably short of goals and some actually move us away from the goals (important examples being found in the clean air programs). Some policies exceed their expectations: could the purpose in assisting convicts to make legal appeals have been to provide legal training during their incarceration?

The discrepancy between purpose and achievement is often due partly to the design of a policy, but it is also due to the problem of enforcement. No statute governing the behavior of many people has ever been spelled out in full detail and enforced with full rigor. Try to imagine the resources that would be required to achieve so unambiguous a goal as preventing everyone from driving more than fifty-five or sixty-five miles per hour for even brief distances. How much more inconceivable the fulfillment of the task of collecting every dollar of taxes due, or of insuring the purity of every bite of food.

Compliance with rules must be achieved by compulsion: sanctions are the heart of the regulatory process. It is for that reason that the calculus of crimes and punishments of Becker (chap. 18) is fully as pertinent to economic regulations as to criminal statutes.

Indeed, the problem of enforcement is equally pervasive in the dealings between private parties. Every contract involves promises whose performance must sometimes be compelled; even a simple exchange of money for a commodity involves implicit warranties such as that the seller has legal possession of the commodity he is selling. I suspect that the recent and extensive increase in attention that economists are paying to principal-and-agent problems and to the role of reputation in private enforcement may have been due partly to the appearance of a growing literature on enforcement in public policy.

The use of a payment system to insure fidelity to contractual obligations, the subject of chapter 19, was noticed as long ago as 1776, when Adam Smith observed that "the wages of labour vary according to the small or great trust which must be reposed in the workmen." This is an instance of what may become a common occurrence: an economic phenomenon long recognized and given casual attention becomes a theoretical corpus with a large and important domain of applicability when subjected to standard economic analysis. The compensation of corporate executives, for example, is clarified by this analysis of the price of fidelity.

V. Conclusion

These and other extensions of economic analysis to political processes, and in particular regulatory processes, support two conclusions. The first is that with traditional theoretical and empirical tools the economists have made substantial progress toward understanding public regulation. The second is that it is reasonably certain that new theories and new methods will be required to unravel some of the major problems we have encountered. Progress and challenge are attractive to the scholar, and they become irresistible when they are joined to a subject of great potential importance in the world of affairs.

The practical applications of these studies will differ for different scholars. The studies will arm some scholars for frontal attacks on policies which are objectionable: the traditional economists' attitude toward restrictions on international trade is an example. Our adherence to free trade despite the perpetual strength of protectionism entitles us to be called practitioners of the optimistic science. For other scholars, it is sufficient to present at higher levels of comprehensiveness and precision the effects actually achieved by a given policy. Then it is for the society at large to make what use it wishes of this new and better knowledge. I believe that putting more accurate price tags on policies will often lead to changes in these policies. The most ambitious goal of these studies reaches farther: it should eventually become possible to offer general advice on the best ways to achieve the goals of policy. We cannot now give general answers to questions such as what is the most efficient way (the way with least deadweight loss) to help declining industry A, or protect workers from danger B, or purify the streams of county C? If—indeed, when—we can give this kind of instruction, in which social goals are accepted and efficiently implemented by the economist, we shall be able to abandon our traditional lament that our advice is given too little attention by our society.

I wish to thank Claire Friedland for seeing the book through publication with her attractive combination of intelligence, care, and wit. Ellen Liebner and Marlo Orlovich were extremely helpful in proofreading.

George J. Stigler

THE POLITICAL SYSTEM

1

The Growth of Government 1

Sam Peltzman

I. Introduction

By conventional budget and gross national product (GNP) measures, government's role in the allocation of resources has increased considerably over the last century, and the growth shows no sign of abating. As a result, governments everywhere in the developed world have moved from a sometimes trivial to a now uniformly considerable role in shaping national expenditures. My task will be to try to explain this growth and size. To do so, I am going to equate government's role in economic life with the size of its budget. This is obviously wrong since many government activities (for example, statutes and administrative rules) redirect resources just as surely as taxation and spending, but the available data leave no other choice. My operating assumption has to be that large and growing budgets imply a large and growing substitution of collective for private decision in allocating resources. But the main intellectual problem I want to explore is the sources of this substitution generally.

I first review the facts about the growth of government and some standard explanations. Since none of the explanations seems very satisfactory, I then present my own explanation, which focuses on the incentives to use a political mechanism to redistribute wealth. Finally, I confront my theory with some relevant data. The main result is counterintuitive: greater equality of private incomes increases the demand for political redistribution.

The author wishes to thank Gerald Dwyer, Bart Taub, and William Pelletier for their valuable assistance. The support of the Walgreen Foundation, the Center for the Study of the Economy and the State, and the National Science Foundation is gratefully acknowledged.
Reprinted with permission from *The Journal of Law and Economics* 23 (October 1980): 209–87. © 1980 by the University of Chicago Law School

II. Trends in the Size and Growth of Government

Table 1 presents a few scraps of historical data on the ratio of government budgets relative to GNP in four developed countries. The data are meant only to illustrate the extent and durability of government growth. Since important sectors of government (for example, social security, local governments) are sometimes excluded, these data cannot

TABLE 1. Trends of Government Spending/GNP, United States and Three European Countries, 1860–1974

Country and Year		Approximate Ratio × 100	Percentage Change from Previous
United States	1870	12	
	1880	8	−30
	1900	8	0
	1920	13	+60
	1940	18	+40
	1960	27	+50
	1974	32	+20
United Kingdom	1860	10	
	1880	10	0
	1900	10	0
	1922	23	+130
	1938	23	0
	1960	30	+30
	1974	45	+50
Germany	1880	3	
	1900	6	+100
	1925	8	+30
	1935	12	+50
	1960	15	+25
	1974	15	0
Sweden	1880	6	
	1900	6	0
	1920	8	+30
	1940	12	+50
	1960	24	+100
	1974	27	+15

Sources: United States and United Kingdom: See Section V *infra.* Germany and Sweden: Brian R. Mitchell, European Historical Statistics: 1790–1970, (1975).

Note: All figures are generously rounded. The numerator for the United States and United Kingdom is spending by all levels of government and for Germany and Sweden *central* government receipts *excluding* social security taxes. For Germany and Sweden 1960 and 1974 total government/GNP ratios are 35, 41 and 32, 49.

be used to compare the size of government across countries. The data do show that government budgets have grown faster than GNPs since at least 1900, and that they may have grown more slowly before. A more precise date for the transition from decline to growth of government would center around World War I and its aftermath. Since then, without any important exception or reversal, the government/GNP ratio in these data has increased on the order of three- or four-fold.

More comprehensive data for two decades ending in the mid-1970s are summarized for the United States and the major developed economies in Table 2. They show the extent and growth of government spending at all levels relative to gross domestic product (GDP) according to international income accounting conventions. While these data are still less comprehensive than we would like (see note to Table 2), they seem to reveal the following broad patterns.

(1) The relative size of the government sector in the typical developed country expanded by over one-third in the two decades, from just over a quarter to around two-fifths of the GDP.

(2) The growth accelerated markedly in the last decade, which accounts for about three-quarters of the total growth.

(3) This accelerated growth is evident both in direct consumption and in transfers. However, transfers have been growing two or three times faster per year than government consumption throughout the period.

(4) The higher recent growth rates also seem slightly more variable across countries, so that the spread among the sizes of their public sectors has widened. The growing importance of transfers, which vary more than consumption, provides an arithmetic explanation for this widening dispersion.

(5) The U.S. government sector has been a comparative laggard. Essentially, the rest of the world has caught up to the United States in public consumption. And despite doubling the share of its GDP going to transfers, the United States has made only a modest dent in the rest of the world's lead in transfers. More specifically, the locus of the United States's lag is its defense sector. By 1974 only Australia and Japan had smaller public sectors than the United States.

III. Some Explanations for the Trends and Their Deficiencies

The literature on the size of government uses two modes of analysis for explaining the trends just described. The first focuses on specific historical events as the primary cause, whereas the second focuses on a market for "public goods." Both types of analysis demonstrate considerable variety which this brief summary cannot hope to reflect adequately. This is especially true of the first type, which prevails in studies of particular countries and time periods where questions of the generality of the analysis tend to be deemphasized.

One widely known example of the historical mode of analysis is Peacock and Wiseman's study of the growth of British government, which develops what has come to be called the "displacement-concentration" hypothesis.[1] Briefly put, the government/GNP ratio tends to be a constant until it is displaced upward by a national crisis— war, in the specific case at hand. This displacement is not completely offset at war's end, first, because the expanded bureaucracy is now better able to assert its interests and, second, because the war concentrates power at the national level. This concentration of power limits the restraint on taxes provided by competition among localities.

A glance at the British and American data underlying Table 1 (see Figures I and II in Section V) indicates some of the attraction of this generalization. The British variable fluctuates around .10 from 1880 to World War I, when it leaps to a high over .5. From 1920 to World War II, the ratio fluctuates around .20 to .25, when it is again displaced upward and then declines only to a range between .3 and .5. The U.S. data also show a ratcheting effect of the two wars, but much less pronounced than for Britain.

This hypothesis has been evaluated critically elsewhere,[2] but a few simple facts can illustrate its problems. Consider the sixteen countries summarized in Table 2. Half were active combatants for most or all of World War II (Australia, Canada, Germany-Austria, Italy, Japan, the United States, and the United Kingdom). The rest did not enter the war or were defeated quickly. The first group ought to have (a) larger public sectors just after the war and/or (b) more rapid growth since then. In fact, the 1953 government/GDP ratios are nearly the same (28.2 for the combatants versus 29.7 for the rest), and the non-combatants' ratios have grown significantly *more* rapidly since then (the difference in mean growth rates to 1974 is 22.2 per cent, $t = 2.09$). From today's vantage, participating in a major war seems ultimately to limit the size of government.

The displacement-concentration hypothesis implies that high and increasing centralization of government produces large and growing governments. This notion plays an important role in Niskanen's interesting contributions to the "specific-event" literature.[3] I put Niskanen

---

[1] Alan T. Peacock & Jack Wiseman, The Growth of Public Expenditure in the United Kingdom (Nat'l Bureau Econ. Research, 1961).

[2] D. Davies, The Concentration Process and the Growing Importance of Non-Central Governments in Federal States, 18 Public Policy (1970).

[3] William A. Niskanen, Bureaucracy and Representative Government (1971); and his Bureaucrats and Politicians, 18 J. Law & Econ. 617 (1975).

in this category because, even though he develops a general model of bureaucracy, he ultimately relies on a few specific events exogenous to his model to explain the size and growth of government.

Niskanen's model contemplates a bureaucracy that values larger budgets and always has some power to extract budget dollars from a legislature that values bureaucratic output. An important constraint on the bureaucracy's ability to gain unproductive budget dollars is competition among bureaucrats and among jurisdictions. Thus, institutional developments that weaken competition imply growing budgets. Among these developments, Niskanen cites centralization of governmental functions, the consolidation of governmental functions into fewer bureaus, and enhancement of bureaucratic tenure (civil service). He gives these factors greater weight than increases in the "rational ignorance" of legislators, another source of a bureau's monopoly power.

A primary difficulty with this theory, one which Niskanen explicitly recognizes, is its treatment of centralization of bureaucratic power as an exogenous event. An obvious alternative is that the same forces generating growth of government generally produce conditions facilitating that growth. This may help explain the temptation to fall back on discrete events, like wars, to rationalize subsequent growth of government. Another difficulty stems from the model's sketchy outline of the relationship between politicians and bureaucrats. Politicians do not benefit directly from bureaucratic budgets, and Niskanen presents evidence that they lose votes from marginal budget expansions.[4] (This is meant to corroborate the model's implication that bureaucracies are able to "overexpand.") But the estimated size of this loss—the elasticity of votes lost by an incumbent president with respect to federal revenues during his term is about .6—is easily large enough so that modest reductions of expenditures would have changed the results of some recent elections. In that case, one has to wonder how "rational" it is for politicians to "ignore" bureaucratic expansion.

However, there are clear factual problems with the general-concentration hypothesis taken on its own terms. The evidence that high or rising concentration of government functions is essential for large or growing government is weak at best. One measure of concentration is the fraction of all government revenues collected nationally. It is, to be sure, imperfect, because national policies can affect incentives to tax locally.[5] For the United States, the broad trend of this

---

[4] Niskanen, Bureaucrats and Politicians, *supra* note 3.

[5] Although Thomas E. Borcherding, The Sources of Growth of Public Expenditures in the United States, 1902–1970, in Budgets and Bureaucrats: The Sources of Government Growth 53-54 (T. E. Borcherding ed. 1977), summarizes evidence that this is unimportant, at least for the United States.

TABLE 2. Size and Growth of Government Expenditures/GDP, U.S. and 16 Developed Countries, 1953–1974

Expenditure Category and Country	Year (Ratio × 100)					Percentage Change from Previous Ten Years	
	1953–54 (1)	1958–59 (2)	1963–64 (3)	1968–69 (4)	1973–74 (5)	1963–64 (6)	1973–74 (7)
Total Government							
United States	27.0	27.5	28.0	31.1	32.2	4%	15%
Avg. of 16 countries	28.9	29.9	31.7	35.8	39.4	10	24
SD of 16 countries	4.1	4.3	4.8	5.9	7.2	9	12
CV of 16 countries	14.1	14.2	15.0	16.6	18.3		
Total Government Less Defense							
United States	14.7	17.6	19.6	22.1	26.5	33	35
Avg. of 16 countries	24.4	26.2	28.2	32.6	36.7	17	30
SD of 16 countries	4.7	4.5	4.6	5.9	7.0	13	14
CV of 16 countries	19.1	17.1	16.3	18.2	19.0		
Government Consumption							
United States	21.5	20.8	20.5	22.4	21.2	−4	3
Avg. of 16 countries	17.2	17.2	18.2	19.8	20.9	7	15
SD of 16 countries	2.7	2.4	2.5	3.4	3.6	12	11
CV of 16 countries	15.8	14.2	13.7	17.4	17.1		

Transfers

	(1)	(2)	(3)	(4)	(5)		
United States	5.5	6.7	7.5	8.7	11.0	36	46
Avg. of 16 countries	11.9	12.9	13.8	16.2	18.8	23	38
SD of 16 countries	4.3	4.2	4.3	4.9	5.9	23	23
CV of 16 countries	36.4	32.5	31.0	30.2	31.6		

Sources of Data: Organization for Economic Cooperation & Development, National Accounts of OECD Countries, various years for all countries except United States. United States data from Council of Economic Advisors, Economic Report of the President (1976).

Notes: Numerator for columns (1)–(5) is current revenue of all levels of government plus net borrowing if any (that is, any net lending to other sectors is not deducted). The data are classified according to the United Nations' new System of National Accounts (SNA) in which receipts and expenditures of separately incorporated nationalized industries are excluded from the government sector. However, subsidies and loans made by governments to nationalized industries are included.

Government consumption includes purchases of goods and services, gross capital formation, and wages paid to government employees. Transfers include subsidies, social security benefits, and interest on debt. (This breakdown is unavailable for Switzerland.)

The sample includes: Australia, Austria, Belgium, Canada, Denmark, Finland, France, Germany, Italy, Japan, the Netherlands, Norway, Sweden, Switzerland, the United Kingdom, and the United States. These countries have adopted the new SNA at different times. Where a particular series could not be reconstructed from the previous SNA, it was spliced to the series from the new SNA.

The denominator is gross domestic product at market prices (that is, includes indirect taxes), which is essentially equal to GNP. The ratios in columns (1)–(5) are averages for the two years indicated. "SD of 16 countries" is the standard deviation of the level or percentage change for the 16 (or 15) country sample, and "CV of 16 countries" is the coefficient of variation.

The years 1975–1976, the last for which I have data, show a marked acceleration of government growth. The first two figures under "Total Government" for these years would be 34.8 (U.S.) and 43.0 (16 country averages). The growth from 1973–1974 is on the order of 40 or 50% that of the entire preceding decade. Although none of the qualitative conclusions is thereby affected, I exclude 1975–1976 because they may atypically bear the brunt of the effects of the most pronounced worldwide recession since the 1930s.

measure supports Niskanen, in that centralization is now higher than in 1900 (about .60 versus .35). However, most of the increase took place in World War II, which is fifteen to twenty years after the persistent growth of the government/GNP ratio began. Growth since 1950 has been accompanied by a mild (about .10) decline in the centralization ratio. A comparison of the developed countries' recent experiences also yields weak support for the role of centralization. What seems most impressive about (measured) centralization is its temporal stability in the face of the considerable worldwide expansion of public sectors in the past two decades. Only Canada has experienced a larger change than the United States (also toward decentralization), and nowhere else has the centralization ratio changed by more than .10. Thus, increased centralization can hardly have played a crucial role in recent growth. The role of centralization is shown a bit more systematically in the regressions of Table 3 which relate the size and growth of the government/GDP ratio to the level and change in centralization. The simple correlation of levels is weakly positive, and in 1973, even significant. However, neither the extent of centralization nor the small changes in centralization seem to explain much of the growth of government. The meager support these results provide for the centralization hypothesis still has to confront the potential endogeneity of both the level and growth of the centralization variable. The "special-event"

TABLE 3.   Regressions of Size and Growth of Government on Centralization Measures, 1953–1973, (16 Developed Countries)

| | Coefficient (*t*-ratio) | | | |
| | Centralization | | Growth of Central- | R^2 |
Dependent Variable	1953	1973	ization	SE
(1) Government Spending/GDP	.097			.09
1953–1954	(1.161)			4.2
1973–1974		.218		.22
		(1.965)		6.7
(2) Growth of Government/GDP	.121		.275	.05
1953–1954 to 1973–1974	(.343)		(.571)	17.1

Source: Organization for Economic Cooperation and Development, National Accounts of OECD Countries. Variables (all × 100):

Centralization: Current Revenues of National Government/Current Revenues of All Levels of Government in year indicated or closest year for which data are available. Series spliced to current SNA where appropriate.

Growth of Centralization: log change of centralization over 20-year period (or extrapolated to 20 years, where required).

Government Spending/GDP: see Table 2.

Growth of Government/GDP: log change of Government Spending/GDP over 20-year period.

explanations of centralization may not be adequate; for example, of the eight full-time combatants in World War II, five rank among the *least* centralized half of our sample in 1953 (or 1973). Centralization of political power can clearly occur without a major war.

In its application to the problem at hand, the "public goods" model is more an analytical framework than the expression of a single widely accepted theory of government expenditure. The common strand of the literature is the treatment of expenditures as the implicit or explicit outcome of a market for government services. That is, demand and cost conditions for publicly provided goods determine expenditures. A vast empirical literature, much of it concentrated on cross-sectional analyses of local government finance,[6] fits this mold, even though much of it is so ad hoc that even this very general categorization is risky. The prototypical procedure goes back at least to Brazer.[7] It consists of regressing aggregate or individual service expenditures on a list of variables which shift the constituents' demand for them (for example, personal income, education) and the government's cost of providing them (for example, wage rates, population densities). A somewhat more theoretically sophisticated branch of this literature tries to take account of the political process that mediates this market or the indivisibilities that the traditional normative theory of government implies will characterize publicly provided services. But these factors have little impact on empirical practice. For example, the well-known collective choice model[8] in which politicians cater to the preferences of the "median voter" is sometimes cited.[9] However, there is no overall consensus that, say, median income is a better proxy for this demand than average income.[10] Similarly, discussions of the "publicness" of government services often serve to rationalize inclusion of, say, a population variable and help in the interpretation of its effect.[11]

[6] See Roy Bahl, Studies in the Determinants of Public Expenditures: A Review, in Sharing Federal Funds for State and Local Needs (F. J. Mushkin & J. F. Cotton eds.) (Brookings Inst., 1968).

[7] Harvey Brazer, City Expenditures in the U.S. (Nat'l Bureau Econ. Research, Occasional Paper No. 66, 1959).

[8] Howard R. Bowen, The Interpretation of Voting in the Allocation of Economic Resources, 58 Q. J. Econ. 27 (1943); Anthony Downs, An Economic Theory of Democracy (1957); Gordon Tullock, Towards a Mathematics of Politics (1967).

[9] See, for example, Theodore C. Bergstrom & Robert P. Goodman, Private Demands for Public Goods, 63 Am. Econ. Rev. 280 (1973); and Thomas E. Borcherding & Robert T. Deacon, The Demand for the Services of Non-federal Governments, 62 Am. Econ. Rev. 891 (1972).

[10] See James L. Barr & O. A. Davis, An Elementary Political and Economic Theory of the Expenditures of Local Governments, 33 S. Econ. J. 149 (1966), for an explicit test of the median voter model.

[11] Again see Bergstrom & Goodman and Borcherding & Deacon, *supra* note 9.

For present purposes, an adequate summary of this literature would be an equation like

$$E = bY + cP + dN + A',$$

where (all variables are logs)

E = real per capita (N) government spending;
Y = real per capita income;
P = relative price of a unit of public services;
A' = all other factors;
b, c, d = elasticities with $b > 0$ if public goods are normal, $d < 0$ if there are "publicness" scale economies, and the sign of c is dependent on the price elasticity of the demand for public goods ($c < 0$ if this elasticity > 1).

It is sometimes argued that government shares with other service industries a labor intensive production function,[12] so P will increase with wage rates. Since wage rates increase with Y over time and cross-sectionally, it is adequate to write this as

$$P = F + hY$$
$$h = \text{constant}, 0 < h < 1$$
$$F = \text{"other factors."}$$

Then, focusing on the government/income ratio, our equation would be

$$e = E - Y = (b + ch - 1)Y + dN + A$$
$$A = A' + cF.$$

It is clear that secular population growth could hardly explain the secular growth of e since d is supposed to be negative. In fact, it turns out that $d \approx 0$ is the better summary of the empirical results, at least for aggregate expenditures.[13] Thus, we have to focus on the coefficient of Y if this model yields insights about e. The simplest explanation, which goes by "Wagner's Law," is that $b > 1$. However, this law remains to be enacted: Borcherding's survey of the empirical literature finds $b = .75$ a more plausible central tendency.[14] If so, there remain the price effects (ch) as a potential source of secular growth in e. Again,

---

[12] See William J. Baumol, The Macroeconomics of Unbalanced Growth: The Anatomy of Urban Crisis, 57 Am. Econ. Rev. 415 (1967).

[13] See the summary in Borcherding, *supra* note 5.

[14] *Id.*

I rely on Borcherding's survey for an estimate of $c \approx +.5$. To get at h, note that real GNP increased at 3.2 per cent annually from 1929 to 1974, the private-goods and services deflator at 2.5 per cent, and the government-goods and services deflator at 3.9 per cent. These percentages imply an h around .4 to .5 $\left(\dfrac{3.9 - 2.5}{3.2}\right)$. Rounding up, we get $ch \approx .25$ and the whole coefficient of $Y \approx 0$. On this admittedly crude summary of conventional income and price effects, e should thus be a constant over time or across space. In fact, simple cross-sectional data are roughly consistent with trivial total income effects. For example, note the following elasticities (t-ratios) from regression estimates of the equation for e for our sixteen-nation sample:

	1953–1954	1973–1974
Income	.035	.059
	(.464)	(.297)
Population	.0003	−.075
	(.0089)	(1.916)

The one result here that is distinguishable from zero (the last population elasticity) makes growing government more rather than less intelligible, given secular population growth.

A cross section of U.S. states yields similar results. In Table 4, per capita budget measures are regressed on per capita income and population for 1942, 1957, and 1972 (lines 1–3). The income elasticities here are a little below unity, but the shortfall seems mainly due to transitory components of income. The temporal transitory components can be reduced by averaging over time. When we do this (lines 4 and 5), the income elasticities move closer to unity. Other income components may be transitory across space: one state may temporarily gain some income lost by another. As a crude correction for this, I aggregated states into census regions. The regressions on the census region data (lines 6 and 7) yield income elasticities of almost precisely unity, just what our crude summary of the literature would lead us to expect and what we found for the cross-nation sample. The state and local data, in whatever form, also yield the negative but numerically trivial population elasticity alluded to above.

The main purpose of this brief summary and extension of the empirical public-goods literature is to establish a foundation for the subsequent empirical work on the size and growth of government relative to income. The main virtue of the "public-goods" framework is precisely its suggestion that the government/GNP ratio is a variable of prime analytic interest. When the framework is given empirical content, it suggests that this ratio ought to be roughly a constant across space and

TABLE 4. Regressions of State and Local Per Capita Expenditures or Receipts on Income and Population (1942, 1957, 1972, U.S. 48 States)

Dependent Variable (Per Capita)	Coefficients/t-ratios of				R^2	SE	N
	Income per Capita	Population	1957	1972			
1. Revenue, includes federal aid	.802[1] 14.87	−.056 −4.49	.382 6.92	.927 9.70	.975	.153	144
2. Revenue, excludes federal aid	.870[1] 16.55	−.035 −2.84	.297 5.53	.696 7.48	.974	.149	144
3. Expenditures	.860[1] 16.40	−.054 −4.41	.540 10.06	.980 10.55	.979	.148	144
4. Revenue, excludes federal aid: average of 3 years' data	.946 9.72	−.035 −2.06			.677	.116	48
5. Expenditures: average of 3 years' data	.897 9.25	−.048 −2.83				.659	.116	48
Census Regions							
6. Expenditures	1.029 12.12	−.046[2] −1.90	.553 6.56	.877 5.97	.994	.092	27
7. Expenditures: average of 3 years' data	1.072 5.54	−.022[2] −.53			.846	.086	9

Sources: Expenditures and Revenue: U.S. Bureau of the Census, Census of Governments; and *id.*, Governmental Finances, various years. Income and Population: *id.*, Statistical Abstracts of the U.S. (1978).

Notes: All variables are in logs, except: 1957 = +1 for 1957, 0 otherwise; 1972 = +1 for 1972, 0 otherwise.

[1] Significantly different from unity.

[2] Population per state in region.

time. This is the happily fortuitous counterpart of the unit income elasticity and near-zero population elasticity. We are then left with the mystery, which we shall try to resolve, of why this ratio has in fact grown over time and varies considerably across space.

A cursory glance at recent history may help explain why "public-goods" models have not resolved that mystery. The public-goods paradigm characteristically is concerned with collective decisions about classically indivisible "community goods." It seems reasonable to expect broad community agreement to expand these provisions with community income. That agreement, however, ought to be less broad for much of what government today in fact does. For example, about half of the typical developed country's public spending today goes for direct transfers, the community-wide benefits of which are dubious. Similar doubts arise about many public-consumption expenditures. For example, the human-capital literature makes clear that there is a large private element in the returns from public provision of education (about one-quarter of government consumption in the United States). And historical evidence indicates that these private returns elicited a considerable private supply which has not clearly been enhanced by subsequent public provision.[15] Whatever the community-good element in public education, a large indirect transfer is clearly involved in the typical public financing arrangements for it.

Such considerations suggest the riskiness of ignoring redistributive elements when analyzing the size or growth of government, and in the remainder of this paper I will focus on these elements. In doing so, I am not denying the importance of the collective-good aspects of public activity. However, my basic working hypothesis is that incentives to redistribute wealth politically are the more important determinants of the *relative* size and growth of the public and private sectors. This hypothesis entails deemphasis of governments' direct cost of collecting and redistributing resources. This does not have the same empirical basis as our deemphasis of public goods, in that evidence on the effect of, for example, modern communications and record keeping on tax-collection costs is lacking. Accordingly, most of the empirical analysis focuses on groups of governments where differences in tax-collection costs are plausibly minor. In the case of less developed countries where such differences may be large, collection costs are given an explicit role in the analysis.

In the next section, I elaborate a model of the incentives to political redistribution of income, which shows how these incentives are re-

---

[15] For example, E. G. West, Education and the State: A Study in Political Economy (Inst. of Econ. Affairs, 1965).

lated to the distribution of income that would prevail in the absence of political redistribution.

IV. Theory of the Equilibrium Size of Government

I treat government spending and taxing as a pure transfer. This is, of course, only meant to focus issues, and the literal-minded reader can interpret spending as an increment over expenditures of a purely public-goods character. I also assume that the amount of spending is determined entirely by majority-voting considerations. This assumption also should not be interpreted literally, since it is meant only to highlight an important difference between political and private resource allocation. What is essential here is simply that popular support contributes to the viability of public policies, so that more such support is better than less. Part of this support may eventually be traded for other goods—monetary gain, relaxed relationships with the bureaucracy, and so forth—but I eschew development of a multifaceted objective function for simplicity. In particular, there is no need to confine the analysis to democratic systems. As long as suppressing dissent is costly to a dictator, he ought to be sensitive to the popular support for his policies. In the empirical work I touch on the question whether redistributive considerations are more important in democratic governments.

My analysis of the democratic case can best be understood as a two-step process. The first consists of a search for a politically "dominant" redistributive program, which, speaking loosely, yields the greatest benefits for the greatest number. Once that policy is described, I take a large second step by assuming that competition among politicians will lead them to converge on that policy in their platforms and implement it upon election. Hence, I brush past the rather formidable problems connected with the uniqueness and stability of political equilibrium.

What then is meant by a "politically dominant" policy? I am going to assume that political preferences are motivated purely by self-interest. A voter will favor only those policies which promise to benefit him; social altruism plays no role. Any redistributive policy creates gainers and losers, and thus, in my scheme, potential supporters and opponents. But we need to know more than who gains or loses from a policy if we want to find the policy that will attain the widest support; the per capita stakes will also be important. To illustrate, consider a proposal whereby all of J. Paul Getty's wealth would be confiscated and redistributed equally to everyone else. This policy would maximize the number of beneficiaries, but it is unlikely to dominate alternative policies. Getty and those closely linked with him would oppose it, since they would do no worse. Perhaps Rockefeller and a few other wealthy individuals would favor it, more out of gratitude for being spared Getty's fate than for the trivial share of Getty's wealth they receive. However, most of the beneficiaries would oppose this proposal, for they could surely do better by waiting for a politician to come along and propose the expropriation of both Getty and Rockefeller. Indeed, they would continue to withhold support until a candidate came along who proposed a policy that maximized their benefits.

Of course, the identity of "they" is changing in this scenario: Rockefeller is converted from a beneficiary to a loser in the second round of this political competition. The outline of a politically dominant policy should, however, be clear. It is the policy that maximizes the difference between the number of beneficiaries perceiving the policy as the best deal and losers perceiving it as the worst deal. In a world of certainty and homogeneous beneficiaries, those perceptions should be identical among individuals. We assume neither certainty nor homogeneity. In the more general case, beneficiaries, for example, are more likely to perceive a policy as "best" the greater the per capita gains it promises, and the policy which receives most support will be the one that maximizes the *product* of the number of beneficiaries and the fraction of these perceiving it to be the best deal.

My first task will be to formalize this description of the politically dominant policy, so that we can say something about its characteristics and, crucially, about the forces which shape it. Given our twin assumptions that political competition leads actual policy to converge on the dominant policy and that incentives to redistribution drive the size of government, we can then derive predictions about the forces that shape the size of government. Important among these, I will argue, is the distribution of income.

A. Full Information

As a convenient starting point, I assume a world of fully informed voters. Each voter understands costlessly the details of a proposed policy and its implications for his well being. He does *not* know with certainty what other proposals may be offered, nor does he necessarily ignore nonredistributive issues (for example, the charisma or ethics of candidates). All that will matter is that, having understood the nature and consequences of a policy, he is more likely to vote for the candidate offering it the more it would materially benefit him. The purpose of assuming full knowledge is both methodological and substantive. It helps to show where the political system is driven when knowledge becomes less costly, and it helps isolate the effects of ignorance, which I consider subsequently.

There are two relevant pools of voters: those whom the policy proposes to tax (let their number be Q) and those who will be paid (P). Let us first focus on the P's, and the political support they will offer for a policy. In line with our previous discussion, this support will be $P \cdot F$, where F is the fraction of the P's who prefer this particular policy to all others that they may possibly face (that is, "pie-in-the-sky" will not be well received). This fraction can, in principle, vary between -1 and $+1$. When F equals -1, every P is sure he can do better by favoring an alternative policy and they all oppose this one, so "support" equals $-P$. When F equals $+1$, every P is sure he can do no better and all support it. One obvious determinant of F is the per capita gain promised by the policy. If the per capita gain is low, as in the Getty expropriation, F will be low also; as the per capita gain increases, so will F.

Thus it appears that F would rise sharply only when a proposed policy moves toward expropriating the wealthiest 49 per cent for the benefit of the poorest 51 per cent. It requires at least 51 per cent support for a policy to dominate, and maximizing the loot with which to buy the favor of beneficiaries requires taxing the rich to pay the poor. While I will immediately consider some forces—the costs of redistribution—that will eliminate this sort of discontinuity, the reader should be forewarned that the Robin Hood feature of this and similar models [16] will be retained. In this stylized democratic process, the rich are taxed to keep down the numerical opposition to redistribution.

The costs of redistribution will limit the appeal of the massive, 49-paying-51, type of redistribution. The costs I focus on are those imposed on private markets by redistribution, rather than, say, the direct costs of running government programs. The P's and Q's deal with each other in goods, labor, and capital markets, so a tax on the Q also decreases the private income of the P. For example, if the Q are major suppliers of capital, a tax on their wealth will discourage saving and so lead to a reduction in the demand for the P's labor services. Thus, any redistribution policy short of pure lump-sum taxes is a mixed blessing for the P; they gain directly but at an indirect cost to their private wealth. This requires two amendments to our story. First, the tax rate levied on the Q to finance any redistributive policy is a political "bad"; the higher it is, *ceteris paribus*, the less attractive the policy is *to the*

---

[16] For example, Thomas Romer, Individual Welfare, Majority Voting, and the Properties of a Linear Income Tax, 4 J. Pub. Econ. 163 (1975); Robert Aumann & Mordechai Kurz, Power and Taxes, 45 Econometrica 1137 (1977); and Alan Meltzer & Scott Richard, The Growth of Government (1979) (mimeographed paper at Carnegie-Mellon Univ., Econ. Dep't).

P's. Thus, extreme Robin Hoodism (tax rate = 1) is not likely to be politically dominant. In fact, it can easily impose net losses on many or
most of the P's.

The second amendment to the story is more technical but helps
motivate the subsequent formalism. Specifically, I argue for the Mar-
shallian mistrust of discontinuities: F, the fraction of P who view a policy as "best," will not suddenly leap from -1 to $+1$ for some critical
change in policy. The P's are never unanimous about a particular policy, because the importance of private-market links to the Q's will vary
among P's. To illustrate, consider a proposed redistributive policy consisting of a per P transfer, g, financed by tax rate R, on Q taxpayers.
Now compare this to a proposal for more redistribution, and trace out
the effects of the change on F. One possible new proposal is to raise
both g and R. Given the varying negative effects of R on the P, some
will favor the new proposal, others the old one; F may rise or fall, but is
unlikely to go to a corner. Or the proposal might be to raise g but not
R. The only way to do this without violating the irrelevance-of-pie-in-
the-sky rule is to raise Q. But this also adversely affects P's generally,
some more than others. So some will prefer the old policy, others the
new. About all we can say at this level of analysis is that, if the old policy involved little redistribution, F (new policy) is more likely to be
higher than if there is already much redistribution (and hence much
deadweight loss).

The different responses among the P to any program play a crucial role in the theory. To elaborate, let us first recapitulate the discussion so far:

1. A politically dominant redistributive policy maximizes

$$M = P \cdot F - \text{numerical opposition,} \tag{1}$$

where

P = number of beneficiaries of the policy
F = fraction of P who prefer this policy over all others.

2. F depends on at least two parameters of the policy; the payment per $P(g)$ and the tax rate levied to raise the funds (R):

$$F = F(g, R)$$
$$F_g > 0, \ F_R < 0. \tag{2}$$

3. Beyond some point, F_g can be < 0, and in general, $F_{gg} < 0$.
The reason, to repeat, is that if g is increased, *given* R, more people
are being taxed. This is a "bad" for the P which can more than offset the

direct benefit of the increased g for at least some of them. Moreover, pushed far enough, proposals to increase g will become too risky for politicians to support even if the proposals would benefit P's on balance. Since such proposals involve adding hostile taxpayers, the politician advocating them increases his risk of losing an election. He or his constituents may prefer to cast their lot with a more modest proposal.

I have argued that any proposal for a dominant policy will involve taxing the rich to benefit the poor. This is because any g can be raised this way at the smallest cost in terms of numerical opposition and at the smallest R for a given numerical opposition. I now want to argue that the income of beneficiaries is also relevant to the likely success of a proposal. One reason for this may be diminishing marginal utility of income, so that the perceived benefits of any g are smaller the higher the private incomes of beneficiaries. But I focus here on the deadweight losses of redistribution borne by the P. These losses are likely to increase with income, at least in absolute dollar terms. Consider, for example, a general reduction in the demand for labor as a result of an increase in R. Surely the dollar loss will be higher the higher the pretax labor income of a P. If the tax discourages nonhuman capital formation, the relative loss to higher income P's will also be greater. If their high income is partly a return on human capital, the rise in the human/nonhuman capital ratio lowers the rate of return to human capital. Those P with a trivial human-capital investment can escape this cost. Put briefly, a P with trivial private income has little at stake in private dealings with the Q and is therefore less resistant to a large tax than a P with substantial income.

This hypothesis requires two further amendments:

1. Equation (2) needs to be expanded to

$$F = F(g, R, Y), F_Y < 0, \tag{3}$$

where Y = per capita income of the P. This says that if Y falls, it has the same effect as if R falls or g rises—it improves the net benefits of any redistributive policy and hence the likelihood of the policy becoming politically dominant.

2. The complement of "tax the richest" is "benefit the poorest." By our logic, if we had to pick 100 individuals from whom to raise any given total tax, they would always be the richest 100. This would minimize R, implying that any proposal to expand the number taxed means adding less wealthy individuals to Q. Similarly, if 100 individuals are to be benefited, they should be the poorest 100. They will bear the lowest indirect cost of the associated tax and so be the least ambivalent about supporting it. The implication is that Y, the per capita income of the P,

is endogenous to the policy: if you propose to increase P, you are proposing to increase Y, because the new members will have higher income than the average of the 100 poorest. So

$$Y = Y(P), \; Y_P > 0. \tag{4}$$

To conclude the analysis, we need to elaborate on the opposition to redistribution from those taxed, the Q's. They face a choice complementary to that of the P's, but simpler: all redistributive policies are bad for the Q's, but some are worse than others. Thus, the degree of opposition from the Q's to any proposed policy will depend on how much the policy would hurt them if adopted *and* how much worse or better off they might be under alternative policies. A simple general statement about the numerical opposition (ϕ) to a proposed policy would be

$$\phi = Q(1 - E), \tag{5}$$

where E = the fraction of the Q who tolerate (that is, do not oppose) the policy. In principle, E could range from zero (the policy is so harmful that no alternative is likely to be worse and all Q's oppose it) to $+2$ (the policy is so mild that *any* alternative is likely to be worse, so all the Q's actually favor it). In practice, we ought to be concerned only about policies for which $0 < E < 1$, since no politician is likely to count on the support of those he proposes to tax as his path to victory. Generally, we expect

$$E = E(R), \; E_R < 0. \tag{6}$$

That is, the higher the proposed tax rate, the larger the proportion of Q's who will conclude that an alternative will be no worse and therefore oppose the proposal.

I now summarize the discussion by rewriting (1) in a modified form, which makes subsequent manipulation more tractable by avoiding inessential complexity. First, express (1) in exponential form

$$M = e^{P+F} - e^{Q-E}. \tag{7}$$

All symbols, except M, are now and henceforth to be understood as natural logs. For example, "P" is now ln P, "E" is a transformation of ln $(1 - E)$, and so on. In doing this, we implicitly focus on policies that the P's support and the Q's oppose. That is, the new F is bounded by $[-\infty, 0]$ and the new E by $[0, \infty]$. In the new notation $E = \infty$ means "none of the Q's oppose the policy," so opposition is $e^{-\infty} = 0$; $E = 0$ means "all the Q's oppose the policy." Next, I write

$$F = F(g, R), \tag{8}$$

where

$g = G - J$,

G = (log of) *total* government expenditures and taxes (recall that we are assuming all expenditures to be on redistribution),

J = (log of) total private income of the P's,

$R = G - I$, the log of the tax rate on Q's total income (I).

In (8), I have simplified (3) to make the critical benefits variable depend on the ratio of the direct transfer to private income rather than on the two separately. This expresses the crucial notion that transfers lose appeal to the P's the higher their private incomes.[17] The discussion leading to (4) implies: $J_P > 1$ (J is determined by P, and the "marginal" P is richer than the average), and $I_Q < 1$ (the "richest-first" tax policy implies that the "marginal" Q is poorer than the average). Finally, with the new notation understood, (6) is left unchanged.

The formal problem emerging from the theory is to find the redistributive policy that maximizes (7) and toward which political platforms will converge, a policy described by specific values of P, Q, and G, and subject to the constraint that benefits equal taxes.[18] The first-order conditions for the solution to this problem ($M_P = M_Q = M_G = 0$) yield the following marginal "revenue-cost" equalities (the gain is on the left-hand side):

$$1 = F_g J_P. \tag{9}$$

This says that the dominant platform pushes P until the direct gain (always a 1 per cent increase in supporters) is balanced by the added cost, which comes from diluting benefits over a wider and wealthier base of beneficiaries.

---

[17]The simplification costs some detail. The theory implies that a simultaneous increase in G and J can, beyond some point, decrease support. This is because, given R, the increase in G increases Q, which is a "bad" for the P's.

[18]Another possible constraint would be something like total voters = beneficiaries + taxed. The motivation for not introducing the constraint is more descriptive than substantive. The subsequent analytical results would hold under such a constraint. However, tax and spending policy are typically kept separate both in political platforms and practice, resulting in a large group which receives substantial benefits and pays large taxes. In terms of the formal model, one can regard a member of this group as facing two decisions—one in the role of a P another as a Q—to which equations like (8) and (6) apply separately.

$$-I_Q[e^{P+F+E-Q} \cdot F_R + E_R] = 1. \tag{10}$$

In (10) the gain from expanding Q by 1 per cent is indirect; the tax base is expanded and permits a lower R, which is valued by both P's and Q's (F_R, $E_R < 0$). The cost is the 1 per cent expansion of numerical opposition.

$$F_g = -[e^{Q-E-P-F} \cdot F_R + E_R]. \tag{11}$$

Here the gain from expanding G is that a larger proportion of P's will support the policy ($F_g > 0$); the cost is that both P's and Q's do not like the resulting higher taxes.[19]

There are two second-order conditions minimally required for (9)–(11) to describe an interior maximum: diminishing returns to benefits and increasing costs to taxation. I have already discussed the economic rationale behind the former ($F_{gg} < 0$).[20] There is also a mechanical rationale; since F cannot be greater than zero (in logs), beyond some point F_g must diminish. With respect to increasing costs, we have a choice: either $E_{RR} < 0$ or $F_{RR} < 0$. Since E has a finite lower bound, it is more convenient to assume $F_{RR} < 0$. This says that a given tax increase leads the Q's to withdraw more wealth from market exchange with the P's at higher than at lower tax rates. There is no strong eco-

---

[19] A more general version of (9)–(11) would begin from something like

$$F = (g', L),$$

where $g' = G - P$ (that is, the per capita benefit instead of the benefit-income ratio)
    L = loss to P from taxation = $L(Y, R, I)$.
This L-function summarizes the P's private interest in trading with the Q; this would be related to the P's private income (Y) as well as R and I (the tax base). Presumably, the same R on a larger base is worse for the P's private welfare. My more tractable specialization already has $F_Y < 0$ implicitly and $F_R < 0$ explicitly, but does not embody a potential offset to the gain in expanding Q (left-hand side of (10)): When Q is expanded it raises I ($I_Q > 0$) as well as reducing R; the former is "bad" for the P, the latter "good." Allowing the ambiguity, (10) would be

$$-I_Q[e^{P+F+E-Q}(F_R - F_I) + E_R] = 1.$$

Note, however, from (9) that $F_g < 1$ ($J_P > 1$) and, consequently, from (11) that $-E_R < 1$. So the term ($F_R - F_I$) must be < 0, to satisfy (10) in spite of $F_I < 0$. In my specialization I assure this by setting $F_I = 0$. All this says is that there has to be some marginal gain for the P from expanding Q to offset the hostility of the Q's. Given this logical necessity, the specialization $F_I = 0$ is only a simplifying detail.

[20] Note that, while this is required for an interior maximum, diminishing returns in logs is not necessarily implied by diminishing returns in natural numbers for this variable.

nomic reason for the deadweight losses to accelerate in this manner. However, if they did not, the model would permit completely confiscatory taxes. To make the subsequent results clear, I do not go beyond these minimal second-derivative conditions.

We can now proceed to derive formally the effects of income distribution characteristics on the equilibrium size of government. First I introduce a variable (X) into the two cumulative income functions $(J(P), I(Q))$ which changes them exogenously in some prescribed way. Then I derive the total effect of this shift on G (that is, dG/dX) from the general relationship

$$[di/dX] = -[M_{iX}][M_{ij}]^{-1}, \tag{12}$$

where

$i, j \quad = P, Q, G,$
$[di/dX] = $ vector of total derivatives,
$[M_{iX}] \quad = $ vector of cross-partial derivative with respect to X,
$[M_{ij}]^{-1} = $ inverse of the matrix of cross-partials.

Consider first an exogenous event that increases every member of P's income by 1 per cent while reducing every Q's income by 1 per cent so $J_X = -I_X = +1$, while $J_{PX} = I_{QX} = 0$. This yields the following sign condition:

$$\text{sgn } dG/dX = \text{sgn } F_{gg}[1 + I_Q F_g] < 0. \tag{13}$$

This is the "Robin Hood" result: as the poor P's get wealthier, the political forces for redistribution weaken. The now wealthier P's have a larger stake in private transactions with the Q's and are therefore less anxious to see the latter's wealth taxed. $J_X > 0$ implies $g_X < 0$; and this lower g reduces support for redistribution, since $F_g > 0$. In effect, the private-market redistribution has substituted for part of the task of the political market.

Now consider what happens when inequality is reduced *within* the beneficiary group, while between-group inequality remains the same. To stylize this event, let the two groups' total incomes remain unchanged $(I_X = J_X = 0)$, but let the marginal (wealthiest) beneficiary's income decline, or, more generally, the slope of the cumulative income function decline $(J_{PX} < 0)$. Application of (12) yields

$$\text{sgn } dG/dX = \text{sgn } \frac{-[F_{RR}I_Q + F_R(1 + E_R I_Q + F_R I_Q)]}{[1 - I_Q F_g]}. \tag{14}$$

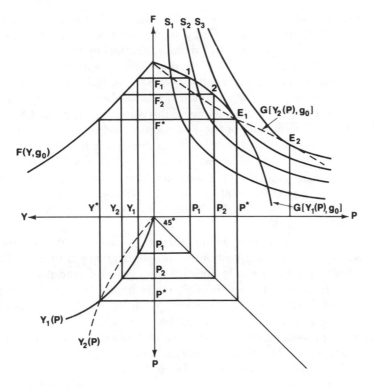

FIGURE I.

Both numerator and denominator are positive, so the right-hand side of (14) is also positive.[21] The former reflects the political costs of taxation and the latter the gains of spending, so (14) is telling us that both are altered in a way favorable to *more* spending when inequality among beneficiaries is *reduced*.

Since this result is important for the empirical work, it deserves some elaboration. A key element of the result is displayed in Figure I, where I have had to suppress parts of the general solution for the sake of exposition, and where, for a similar reason, I temporarily suspend the log notation. Specifically, suppose the per capita transfer to the P's is fixed (at g_0). The political decision in this restricted version of the general problem is the number of P's who will get g_0, so total transfers will be proportional to this number. Recall our crucial assumption that the higher the per capita income of the P's, the less avid their support

[21] Both F_{RR} and $F_R < 0$. The parenthetical expression in the numerator > 0 in equilibrium (see equation (10) and note that $e^{P+F-(Q-E)}$ must > 1 for an interior solution). Since $F_g < 1$ by (9) and $I_Q < 1$, the denominator must be > 0.

for any particular redistributive policy. This is shown as $F[Y, g_0]$ in quadrant II of Figure I: given g_0, a smaller fraction (F) of P's will support a policy that gives each of them g_0 the higher their average income. Recall also that, since high income dulls the appetite for redistribution, any P chosen will be the poorest P in the population. This enables us to express Y as a function of P as displayed by $Y_1(P)$ in quadrant III. If $P = 1$, Y is the income of the poorest person (0); if $P = 2$, $Y =$ the average income of the two poorest, and so on. So $Y_1(P)$ describes the income distribution of P's; as drawn it is meant to describe a relatively [to $Y_2(P)$, which we discuss later] unequal distribution. There are many poor P's, so Y does not increase much if we propose adding P's to a modest set of beneficiaries. However, if we go further and try to add middle class P's, Y starts increasing sharply, for they are much richer than the poor.

These two functions would, except for one difficulty, enable a politician to answer the question: if I proposed giving g_0 to each of P_0, what fraction of them would find this the most preferred policy? The difficulty is that higher levels of P_0 imply higher taxes and/or more people taxed, which, we have argued, are "bads" for P's as well as Q's. One inelegant way around this problem is to imagine that all of the negative effects of taxation are incorporated into the negatively sloped $F(Y, g_0)$ function. That is, the politician says something like: if I widen P, there are more potential votes for redistribution, but I necessarily raise Y *and* increase R and/or Q. *All* of the latter three effects will offset some or all of the potential political gain from widening P. The crucial notion is simply that there is a trade-off between *increasing P* and *reducing* the fraction of the electorate that supports or tolerates redistribution. For expositional purposes, I will ignore parts of this trade-off—the increased opposition and tax effects—and focus on P-income distribution effects.

All of the above understood, the relevant trade-off available in the political market is $G[Y_1(P), g_0]$ in quadrant I, which shows that if a policy proposes a larger set of P a smaller fraction will support it. It is constructed as follows. Suppose benefits are limited to P_1 people. They will have an average income of Y_1, which I find by (*i*) locating P_1 on the vertical axis of quadrant III by means of a 45-degree line and then (*ii*) reading off from $Y_1(P)$. For $Y = Y_1$, I can determine F_1 from $F(Y, g_0)$ in quadrant II. The resulting combination (P_1, F_1), labeled (1), is one point on this political "transformation" locus, $G[Y_1(P), g_0]$. In a similar fashion, point (2) is generated, starting with P assumed $= P_2$, and the locus of all such points is $G[Y_1(P), g_0]$.

The political objective to be sought in a choice of P is maximum numerical support (again read "support" as "support net of all opposition"). Support is simply the product PF. In quadrant I of Figure I, this objective is characterized by a series of rectangular hyperbolae (S_i), each of which collect the P, F combinations consistent with a given support (S_i). The dominant policy is characterized by (P^*, F^*), or point E, where S is maximized, given $G[Y_1]$.

Imagine the sort of exogenous event that occurs in (14). The average income of the P^*, $Y(P^*)$ is unchanged, but it is more equally distributed among them as represented by the new income function, $Y_2(P)$, in quadrant III. It crosses $Y_1(P)$ at P^* and is flatter at P^* and steeper near the origin. Poor marginal beneficiaries now add more and rich marginal beneficiaries less to the average income of the group. This, in turn, implies a new $G[\cdot]$ which cuts the old one from below at the old equilibrium E_1. The dominant policy is now E_2 which implies a higher P^* and, given g_0, a higher level of government spending.

To understand what is involved here, recall why P^* was an equilibrium when $Y_1(P)$ prevailed. There was a positive probability that the $P^* + $ 1st beneficiary would himself favor extra redistribution. But this small expected gain was insufficient to overcome the adverse effects of the added taxes on the remaining P^*. The gain was small because $P^* + 1$ is so wealthy that he bears a heavy indirect cost of the added taxes required to pay him g_0. Now $P^* + 1$ is less wealthy and would bear correspondingly smaller losses to his private wealth if taxes are raised. He is thus more likely to return the favor if a politician proposes to include him among the beneficiaries. Rational politicians will respond by proposing to expand the set of beneficiaries.

The principle that more similar interests in redistribution broaden the support for it could be extended to the direct costs of redistribution, which the formal model ignores. If more diverse interests imply a greater variety of programs (transfers for the poor, state opera for the rich) and each has its own "set-up" costs, the benefits perceived per dollar expenditure will be smaller than otherwise. If we permit benefits to be a fraction of total expenditures to reflect these government "brokerage" costs, it is straightforward to show that the equilibrium expenditure rises as the brokerage costs fall. A corollary to this is that governments will not want to completely offset the effects of divergent within-beneficiary-group interests with different per capita transfers. Equalization of benefit/income ratios among beneficiaries, for example, would be too costly, since it would entail complete exclusion of the poorer beneficiaries from access to some programs. Moreover, even if equalization were feasible, our model implies that an optimal policy redistributes wealth *within* as well as *between* groups.[22] This also has a corollary: the total support produced by any given redistribution is en-

---

[22]This is seen most easily in the following restricted problem (log notation again suppressed): A given G is to be distributed among two equal-sized $(\bar{P})$ groups of bene-

hanced if the pretransfer income differences among beneficiaries narrow.[23] So while we have, for simplicity, ignored problems connected with the distribution of benefits, their resolution reinforces the previous result that homogeneity among potential beneficiaries increases the demand for redistribution.

In any event, the model suggests a distinction between two types of inequality, that *between* beneficiaries and taxpayers and that *within* the former group. It also suggests that a reduction in within-beneficiary-group inequality stimulates the growth of government, whereas reduced inequality between groups retards it. Thus no straightforward connection is implied between any overall measure of income inequality and the size of government. As we shall see, there are formidable empirical problems in disentangling the two types of inequality from the available data.

B. Costly Information

Learning about the effects of a proposed policy or candidate is not, of course, costless, as we have been assuming it to be. There will also be

---

ficiaries, who differ only in their incomes (J), to maximize the political support (S) forthcoming from the two groups. Thus, the objective is to maximize

$$S = \overline{P}[F(g_1) + F(g_2)],$$

where F has the same meaning as before and

$$g_i = G_i/J_i, \quad i = 1, 2.$$

Since $G = G_1 + G_2$, this reduces to selecting the optimum G_1. The solution is to select G_1 such that

$$\frac{F_{g_1}}{F_{g_2}} = \frac{J_1}{J_2}$$

If group 1 is poorer, this ($J_1/J_2 < 1$) and diminishing returns imply $g_1 > g_2$—i.e., the poorer receive higher transfers relative to income.
    [23]To stylize this, let $J_{1X} = -J_{2X} = +1$, and note that

$$\frac{dS}{dX} = \frac{dg_1}{dX} \cdot F_{g_1} - F_{g_2}).$$

Since group 1 is now richer, the optimal response is to reduce g_1. Since $F_{g_1} < F_{g_2}$ in equilibrium, $dS/dX > 0$. So the narrowing of within-group inequality enhances the political payoff to the total transfer expenditure.

costs of organizing groups to support or oppose adoption of a policy. These costs of access to the political mechanism mean that some voters will be ignorant of the effects of a policy. This section discusses the effects of ignorance on the results just derived.

I will continue to assume that all members of Q are fully informed. This simplification is intended to capture a qualitative difference between them and members of P rather than for descriptive accuracy. Any dominant policy will have to keep Q smaller than P, so Q members will have the larger per capita incentive to become informed about the effects of a policy and organize their interests. Therefore, incomplete knowledge should have the strongest impact on the behavior of group P. To get at this differential impact of ignorance, I confine the analytical burden of ignorance to the P group.

I allow for two effects of ignorance. The *direct* effect is simply that only a fraction of the P who would support a policy if all were informed $(P + F$, in logs$)$ will actually know enough to do so. The ignorant remainder either "stay home" or vote randomly. The *secondary* effect is that politicians will try to exclude some of the ignorant from benefits, so as to concentrate benefits on those most likely to reciprocate. To get both effects, I expand (8) as follows

$$F = H(g, R, Z). \tag{15}$$

The added variable, Z, is an "exclusion" parameter, which varies between $(0, 1)$ in natural numbers or $(-\infty, 0)$ in logs. The variable P is now to be interpreted as the maximum number of beneficiaries, that is, the number who would share G under "free" information. If Z is at its lower bound (no exclusion), the "free-information" case obtains: all the P are informed and share in G. An increase in Z represents more ignorance, which means a smaller fraction of the P support a policy and a smaller fraction are rewarded. If Z ever attained its upper bound (total ignorance), $e^F = 0$ and no redistribution policy would be politically viable.

The indirect (concentrated-benefits) effect of ignorance can be expressed as follows. Retain the definition of $g = G - J$, but redefine J to be the total income of those actually receiving benefits. So

$$\begin{aligned} J &= J(P, Z) \\ J_z &< 0. \end{aligned} \tag{16}$$

That is, the more P excluded, the lower the total income of *actual* beneficiaries. For simplicity, assume that those excluded are a random selection of the P's, $J_Z = -1$ (Z in logs); that is, if 1 per cent of the P are randomly excluded, those left have 1 per cent less total income.[24]

If we now combine the indirect with the direct effect of exclusion and examine the overall consequences of increasing the exclusion of P's from benefits, we get for the effects of exclusion

$$F_Z = H_Z + H_g \cdot g_Z = H_Z + H_g \text{ (since } g_Z = -J_Z = +1). \tag{17}$$

The second right-hand side term is the indirect effect of exclusion which states that the more concentrated benefits improve support for any given total expenditure. The H_Z term will be the resultant of two opposing forces. On the one hand, there are fewer potential support- ers, since a subset of the P receives no benefits. This would imply $H_Z = -1$. On the other hand, the remaining beneficiaries are of higher "quality"—that is, more responsive to any benefits, and this implies $H_Z > 0$. Presumably, a rational selection process of excluding the dumbest first will imply diminishing "quality" effects with exclusion, so $H_{ZZ} < 0$. We also know that beyond some point $H_Z < 0$ on balance, since total exclusion implies $e^F = 0$.

As it happens, a first-order condition for the expanded policy choice problem (which now requires selecting Z as well as P, Q, G) is

$$H_g = -H_Z. \tag{18}$$

So $H_Z < 0$ in equilibrium. Exclusion is pushed until its direct effects are negative at the margin and counterbalanced by the favorable effects of concentrated benefits. The remaining first-order conditions carry over intact from the free-information case ((9)–(11)). As a result, the effects of income-distribution changes on the growth of government are the same in both models. The added insight we gain into the size of government concerns changes in the "ability" or quality of voters. The effects of some manifestations of such change can be summarized as follows:

1. An exogenous increase in the average "ability" of the P's ($H_X > 0$ at any Z) increases the equilibrium G.

2. There is no ability counterpart to the within-group income equality effect. Specifically, suppose those individuals at the margin

---

[24] More plausibly $-1 < J_Z < 0$. This would hold if those excluded tend to be a poorer than average subset of the P's, which is what would be implied by the positive correlation between income and likely indicators of the ability to process political infor- mation (education).

A counterforce is that high income implies high time costs of acquiring informa- tion. The optimal included beneficiary is poor and well-educated.

of exclusion suddenly become more able, while average ability is the same. Thus, the difference in ability between the most and least able beneficiary narrows ($H_{ZX} < 0$, $H_X = 0$). This generates two conflicting forces which exactly offset each other: (*i*) the degree of exclusion is reduced, but (*ii*) the maximum set of beneficiaries (P) is contracted. This latter occurs to mitigate the otherwise adverse tax and benefit-dilution effects from a net addition of beneficiaries.

3. Similarly, an exogenous increase in the ability of P's to translate marginal changes in g into political support ($H_{gX} > 0$, while $H_X = 0$) has no effect on G. The temptation to expand P is countered by the negative consequences of higher taxes, which lead to increased exclusion.

In short, G will vary directly with average ability of beneficiaries, but only its distribution among beneficiaries is altered by changes in the distribution of ability. If income and "ability" are positively related, it would no longer necessarily follow that the poor*est* citizens would be prime beneficiaries of redistribution. But the corollary (2, above) to this version of "Director's Law" is that, if the poorest become *relatively more* able, the middle class will lose some of its benefits.

The main theoretical results whose empirical content is the subject of the next section can now be summarized.

1. If potential beneficiaries' incomes increase relative to those of taxpayers, G will fall.

2. But if there is a similar increased equality of the ability of the two groups to recognize their interests, G will increase.

3. Anything which increases the efficiency of G in "buying" support can be put under the "ability" rubric. Thus lower costs of collecting taxes, or of transforming them into benefits, increases the gross G.

4. More equal income among beneficiaries increases G, but more equal ability has no effect.

V. Empirical Analysis

The theory shows how some "pregovernment" distribution of income and ability affects the politically optimal level of government spending. Since no such pristine distributions will ever be found in the world, any attempt to relate empirically the size of government to an actual distribution entails a classic "identification" problem; the distribution can both affect the size of government and be affected by it. Moreover, we would not want to abstract entirely from this feedback effect, even if we could. For example, suppose a progressive income tax is levied and the proceeds are shipped abroad or used to pay for public goods that everyone agrees ought to be bought. Now we want to predict the size of redistributive government spending, the main choice variable in our model. My argument that the stake of potential beneficiaries in private dealings affects optimal redistribution implies that *after*-tax income and its distribution are the relevant variables. On the other hand, it could be argued that the progressive tax is the outcome, not a contributing cause, of the optimal policy. Transfer incomes would seem even more clearly an outcome of the process. But that does not imply that, for example, pretransfer income is the appropriate proxy for the "private" income in our model. Someone with only transfer income might have substituted private income absent the transfer. Government affects the distribution of earned income before as well as after taxes. But how? Presumably progressive taxes lead to more pretax inequality, but egalitarian social policies could offset this, by directly or indirectly shifting demand toward lower wage labor. This listing of the potential crosscurrents in government's effect on any empirical distribution of income or ability could be extended.

I deal with the lack of any real-world counterpart to the theoretical "state-of-nature" distributions in two ways. First, I ignore the complications and use what is available, assuming implicitly that the crosscurrents cancel each other. I focus mainly on income concepts (for example, earned income) where some of the direct effects of government (transfers) are absent, but ultimately there is no obvious income concept that is more nearly "right" for our purposes.[25] Second, I focus on the growth as well as the level of government spending, assuming a lagged adjustment to any target level of G. In this framework, one can explicitly control for the current actual level of G and implicitly for any effects on other determinants of the target G. To elaborate, consider this version of a familiar lagged adjustment model:

$$\Delta G = a(G^* - G), \tag{19}$$

where $*$ = target value and a = fractional adjustment coefficient; and

$$G^* = bX, \tag{20}$$

where b = vector of constants and X = vector of variables determining G^*. For simplicity, assume only one determinant of G^*, say a summary measure of income inequality. However, the measure ought to be one that would prevail in the absence of at least some effects of the

---

[25] Simultaneous equation techniques might appear to offer a way out. But with government spending 40% of GNP and regulating much of the remainder, specifying "exogenous" determinants of, say, the distribution of income involves as much risk as assuming that the distribution is itself exogenous.

current G, and we cannot observe this directly. Instead, we observe Y, which, for simplicity, can be expressed

$$Y = X + cG, \tag{21}$$

where c = coefficient (we do not know its sign). Substituting (21) into (20) and (20) into (19), we get

$$\Delta G = abY - a(1 + bc)G. \tag{22}$$

Here the coefficient of G amalgamates the usual partial adjustment effect, a, and the influence of G on the observed measure of income inequality, c. Empirical implementation of (22) thus entails all the econometric problems of partial adjustment models plus that of collinearity between Y and G (if $c \neq 0$).

The model and the preceding discussion of the empirical literature imply that the target level of G or of the G/income ratio is affected by at least three characteristics: between- and within-group income inequality and some average level of "ability." The available data do not always permit anything like this level of detail. Frequently, nothing more than a crude proxy for overall income equality is available, and the model makes clear that this variable has ambiguous effects on G^*. The initial empirical work is an attempt to see if any of the conflicting forces embedded in an overall equality measure dominate; the refinements are dealt with subsequently. To compensate partly for the crudity of the data, I will examine a few distinct sets of data to see if they yield a consistent story. These include British, American, Canadian, and Japanese time series and cross sections of developed countries, U.S. state and local governments, and less developed countries. Most of these data imply that income inequality, on balance, retards growth of government. We shall see, however, that this connection is more complex than just stated.

A. Time Series

1. Britain and the United States. The historical patterns we seek to explain were described broadly in Section I. In light of our review of the empirical public-goods literature, I focus on the government budget share of GNP as shown in detail in Figures II and III for the United States and Britain. The history of government's share of GNP is similar for both countries: decline or stability in the nineteenth century and growth in the twentieth. The most notable differences between the two countries seem to be: (1) the earlier completion of the British nine-

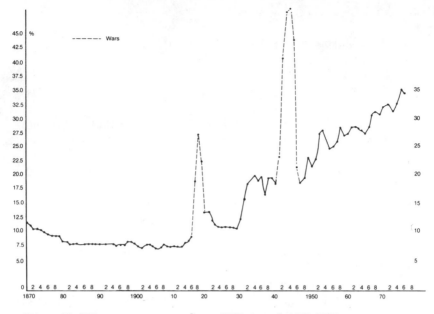

FIGURE II. U.S. government expenditures/GNP. Annual, 1870–1976

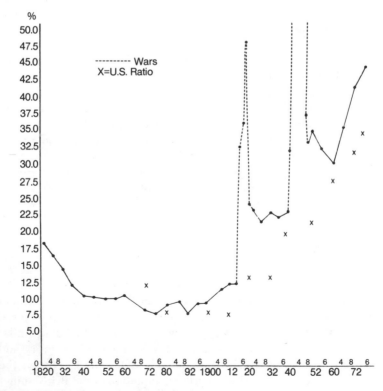

FIGURE III. British government spending/GNP. Five-year intervals, 1829–1974

teenth-century decline, (2) the larger ratcheting effect of the two world wars for Britain, (3) the substantial U.S. growth in the 1930s versus none for Britain, and (4) the sharper recent growth for Britain.

Is there some plausible connection between this history and income inequality? In asking this, I ignore for now a host of potential complicating factors such as, for example, the extent of the franchise and changes in political structure. This leaves a major empirical problem of devising a proxy for income equality that can be matched to the data. Nothing like the standard size distributions is available for most of the period covered by the data, although Kuznets has conjectured they would show inequality following a path opposite to that in Figures II and III, with inequality first widening then narrowing in consequence of the gradual shift of resources from the low-income agricultural sector.[26]

The only inequality-related data of which I am aware that are useful for a long time series concern intra-industry wage dispersion, specifically skill differentials (the ratio of wage rates of skilled to unskilled labor). In a way, this crude measure is better for our purposes than an overall inequality measure, because it should be more closely connected to inequality within the beneficiary group. More recent data, however, imply that it may be difficult to make the sort of distinctions about inequality required by the model. Figure IV illustrates the scattered data we have on U.S. skill differentials over the past 135 years. For the last 60, we also have a series of the share of national income going to the richest 5 per cent of the population. This is labeled "Kuznets," since the pre-1950 data are his.[27] Since 1915, the Kuznets

---

[26] Simon Kuznets, Modern Economic Growth: Rate Structure and Spread (1966). His argument in its simplest form is as follows. Suppose that there are no differences in income within either of the two sectors, but that the nonagricultural incomes are higher. Then the variance of logs (VL) of individual incomes (a standard inequality measure) in the community at a moment in time is

$$VL = a(1 - a)(A - N)^2,$$

where a = fraction of population in agriculture and A, N = log of agricultural and non-agricultural incomes, respectively. If A and N do not change, the change in VL over time is

$$d(VL)/dt = (A - N)^2(1 - 2a)da/dt.$$

Thus if a starts out high ($>1/2$) and declines steadily ($da/dt < 0$), inequality at first rises, then falls (when $a < 1/2$). Kuznets's conjecture assumes that this effect dominates any offsetting changes in $(A - N)$ and within-sector income dispersion.

[27] Simon Kuznets, Share of Upper Income Groups in Income and Savings (Nat'l Bureau Econ. Research, 1953). Post-1950 data are for families—the two series are vir-

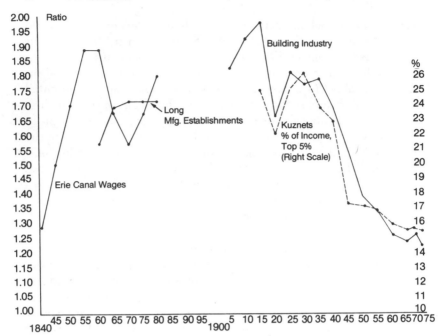

FIGURE IV. Skill differentials, United States 1840–1975, and income share, top 5 percent, 1915–1975

series and the building industry skill differential (journeymen's wages divided by laborers' in union contracts)[28] have followed the same path (their correlation exceeds .8), even though they measure very different aspects of inequality. These data imply that the forces promoting equality have been pervasive.

The skimpy nineteenth-century American data are from Long's study of wages in manufacturing and Smith's study of Erie Canal wages.[29] The pattern emerging from all these data is one of increasing

tually identical where they overlap—from Historical Statistics of the U.S. and Statistical Abstract.

[28] From U.S. Bureau of the Census, Historical Statistics of the U.S. (1975) [hereinafter cited as Historical Statistics]; *id.*, Statistical Abstract of the U.S. (1978); and Harold F. Lydall, The Structure of Earnings (1968).

[29] Clarence Long, Wages and Earnings in the United States, 1860–1900 (Nat'l Bureau of Econ. Research, 1960); and Walter Smith, Wage Rates on the Erie Canal, 1828–1881, 23 J. Econ. Hist. 298 (1963).

Interpolating over the 1885–1905 gap is likely to be as reasonable a procedure as any. For 1890–1900, we know that the ratio of building trades' wages (where skilled labor is important) to manufacturing wages rose.

wage disparity over most of the nineteenth and early twentieth centuries and a long decline from World War I to the present. The two world wars, in particular, have coincided with profound movements toward equality, though some of the change of World War I was offset in the 1920s. These historical patterns are roughly the obverse of the secular path of government. They hint that, on balance and perhaps counter to intuition, income equality stimulates the growth of government. I pursue this hint shortly.

Another kind of inequality deserves mention here, namely, inequality across legislative constituencies. The theoretical discussion abstracts from the legislative mechanism through which conflicting individual interests are actually adjudicated. This is analytically convenient, but risks obscuring some aspects of political choice in a representative system. For one thing, legislators can specialize in collecting and communicating political information and thus a "full-information" model might adequately describe bargaining among legislators. More to the immediate point, bargaining would be more closely focused on the constituencies' average interests than on the interests of income groups who have members everywhere. The legislator will, of course, still have to worry about the disparity of interests within his constituency, but we ought to expect him, all else the same, to more easily ally with a legislator from a district with, for example, a similar average income. Thus, if greater personal income equality facilitates agreement on expanding the size of government, greater interdistrict equality ought to facilitate legislative agreement to implement the expansion.

Given the nature of the American political system at the national level, inequality of average incomes across states can serve as a proxy for the diversity of legislator interests. Figure V shows the relevant history for the available data,[30] which corresponds roughly to the pattern for skill differentials. But the narrowing of disparities began earlier (around 1890 versus 1915), was hardly affected by World War I, and was more profoundly affected by World War II. Also, unlike the relatively small changes in income equality after World War II, a substantial narrowing of interregional disparities continues to this day.

In the empirical work, I investigate whether this narrowing of interregional disparities has contributed to or retarded the growth

[30] Sources of data are as follows: "Taxable Wealth" from U.S. Bureau of the Census, Wealth, Debt, and Taxation (1915). "Easterlin" from estimates by R. Easterlin of per capita personal income by census region relative to U.S. average as reported and updated in Historical Statistics, *supra* note 28. My calculation assigns each state its region's income relative. "Factory Workers' Earnings" from Paul F. Brissenden, Earnings of Factory Workers (U.S. Bureau of the Census, 1929). "Personal Income" from Survey of Current Business (various issues); 1920 figure is from Maurice Leven, Income in the Various States (Nat'l Bureau Econ. Research, 1925).

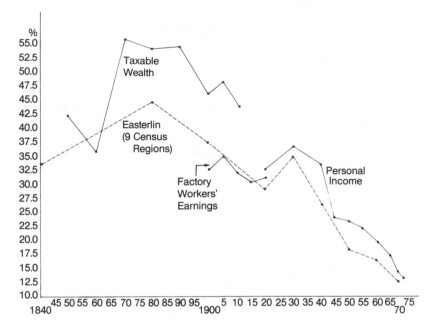

FIGURE V. Coefficients of variation per capita income or wealth. States (United States) 1840–1975

of government.[31] Any connection between the two ought, strictly speaking, to apply only at the federal level, unless disparities among regions within states have tended to follow the same path as interstate inequality.

Table 5 contains regressions of U.S. government expenditures relative to GNP on the two crude inequality measures just discussed. A trend variable is included as a proxy for "other forces" which may have produced secular growth of government. Clearly any comprehensive investigation would have to spell out these "other forces," and several are suggested by the theoretical model (for example, mean education, "between-group" inequality). However the limitations of the time series preclude anything more refined than Table 5. For example, a glance at Figure II indicates that our 105 annual observations are

[31] It is difficult to argue that growth of government is itself responsible for the narrowing, at least directly. For 1970, the coefficient of variation of private income per capita across states is about 18% versus 14.5% for all personal income. This difference is an exaggerated measure of the role of direct government payments, since it assumes that government workers, for example, would earn zero in the private sector. Yet 18% is still half the 1930 figure. Of course, past government activity—World War II—seems to have had a permanent effect on interregional inequality.

TABLE 5.   Regressions of U.S. Government/GNP on Inequality Measures, 1870–1975 (5-Year Intervals, 22 Observations)

	Coefficients (*t*-ratios) of						
Regression	Skill Differ-ential (1)	State Inequality (2)	Trend (3)	Lagged Govern-ment/GNP (4)	R^2	SE	D-W or H
(1)	−21.99	.08	.147		.943	2.28	1.09
	−5.33	.42	3.47				
(2)	−20.90		.132		.942	2.23	1.01
	−6.67		5.82				
(3)	−6.50	.10	1.07	.650	.979	1.48	−2.19
	−1.51	.81	3.24	4.03			
(4)	−5.20		.088	.648	.978	1.46	−1.33
	−1.31		3.74	4.06			
Mean	1.63	30.9		14.85			
SD	.23	9.0		7.92			

Notes: The dependent variable is government spending/GNP × 100. See Figure II and text for sources. The time interval between observations is five years, and each value is a three-year average centered on 1870, 1875, . . . To eliminate effects of wars, 1922 replaces 1920 and 1946 replaces 1945 in this sequence.

The skill differential is the series labeled "Long" in Figure IV for 1870–1880, the "Building Industry" series for 1905–1975, and a linear interpolation of the two for 1885–1900.

State inequality is the "personal income" coefficient of variation (see Figure V) for 1920–1975, the series labeled "factory workers' earnings" spliced to later data at 1920 for 1900–1915, and the series labeled "taxable wealth" spliced to later data at 1900–1910 for 1870–1895. Gaps in this series are eliminated by linear interpolation.

D-W and H are "Durbin-Watson" statistic and Durbin's H. The latter is calculated for regressions (3) and (4) where D-W is inappropriate. For (1) and (2) the D-W test implies positive serial correlation with about 5% risk of error. For (3) H implies negative autocorrelation with risk of <5%.

hardly independent. There are really two or three distinguishable episodes, with a few much less important subcycles. Consequently, I draw observations at five-year intervals, which yield only around twenty degrees of freedom, and even this may overstate the number of independent observations. In addition, the trend variable is itself a proxy for some aspects of inequality. The agricultural share of the labor force, for example, crossed 50 per cent at about our starting point of 1870. Thus, on Kuznets's argument,[32] the subsequent further industrialization would have contributed to equality. Even the two inequality measures in Table 5 are hardly time independent. The correlations with time are −.75 and −.93 for the skill and state measures, respectively.

[32] See note 26 *supra*.

Table 5 thus addresses a limited question: is there any plausible connection between inequality and the size of government?

The answer seems to be a qualified "yes." There is no perceptible effect from the narrowing of cross-state inequality, but in equations (1) and (2) there is a substantial and significant expansionary effect from the narrowing skill differential. To put this effect in perspective, note that from 1870 to 1975, the government/GNP ratio increased by around 23 percentage points, while the skill differential narrowed by about .5. Equation (2) assigns over 40 per cent of this growth (.5 × the 20.9 coefficient = 10.45 percentage points) to the skill differential variable.

The link between inequality and government becomes more obscure, but does not disappear, when we allow for lagged adjustment and the possible effect of government on measured inequality. Equations (3) and (4) in the table are slightly modified versions of (22). The point estimates of the skill-differential effect remain substantial: if we assume no feedback effect ($c = 0$) in (22), then the implied derivative of the target government/GNP ratio with respect to the skill differential—which equals (coefficient of skill differential)/(1 − coefficient of lagged government/GNP)—is on the order of −15 to −20. Indeed, the derivative becomes still larger if we go to the other extreme. Suppose the growth of government is responsible for *all* of the .5 decline in the skill differential since 1870. Then, from (21) and (22), we can estimate c ($\approx -.02$), and the implied derivative (b) is about −30. However, given the relevant standard errors, we cannot attach much confidence to these calculations. They simply encourage examination of other data.

Figure VI shows the history of British skill differentials since the Napoleonic Wars, mainly for the same industry that dominates our U.S. data.[33] The major difference between the two countries seems to be the earlier peak in the British data, around 1850. Skill differentials in the United States do not clearly peak until World War I. Given the U.S. time-series results, this earlier reversal of the Industrial Revolution's trend toward inequality may help explain Britain's earlier completion of the nineteenth-century decline in the size of government. The

[33] The "building industry" series is composed of the following: 1810–1880: weekly or hourly rates for bricklayers relative to helpers at London (or Manchester, if rates for London are unavailable) British Labour Statistics: Historical Abstract (1971). 1880–1950: K. G. J. C. Knowles & D. J. Robertson, Differences between the Wages of Skilled and Unskilled Workers, Bull. of Oxford Inst. Stat. 109 (1951). 1950–1975: the London series, with 1970–75 from British Labour Statistics, *supra* (various years).

The engineering series is also from Knowles & Robertson *supra* for 1880–1950, then spliced to a series of union pay scales for skilled and unskilled labor in London area engineering industry establishments as reported in British Labour Statistics, annual issues and Historical Abstract.

twentieth-century pattern for skill differentials in the two countries is, however, broadly similar—a World War I downward jolt that was incompletely offset in the 1920s and a subsequent downward trend that only recently has flattened. As I point out later, this pattern is characteristic of much of the developed world in the twentieth century.

The British data, summarized in Table 6, show a stronger connection between equality and government than the American data. The effect is numerically larger, completely dominates "trend" effects, and remains significant in the lagged-adjustment formulation. It also holds up in first differences (regression (2), which is motivated by the autocorrelation of the residuals from (1)). Finally, as with the American data, the lagged-adjustment regression implies that, unless growth of government has retarded the decline in skill differentials, the coeffi-

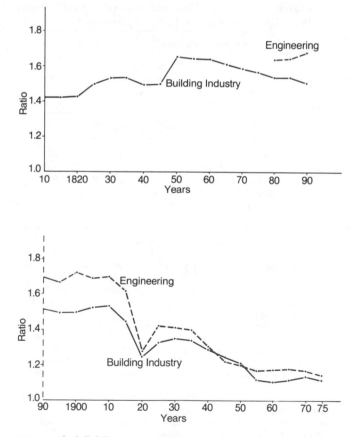

FIGURE VI. British skill differentials, 1810–1975

cients of this variable in (1) and (2) may actually understate the extent of the relevant relationship.

Putting the data in Tables 5 and 6 together would imply that Britain has a larger government sector than the United States because the movement toward equality has gone farther there and because the British political system seems more sensitive to the resulting pressures (that is, the coefficient of the same skill differential is larger). This may be too sweeping a generalization from very crude data. To see if it is, I ask the following question. Do the historical *differences* in the size of the U.S. and British governments have anything to do with the minor *differences* in their histories of inequality? The answer is hardly obvious from the preceding data. The broad movements in both government and inequality in the two countries are more notable for their

TABLE 6.   Regressions of British Government/GNP on Skill Differential, 1820–1975 (5-Year Intervals, 32 Observations)

	Coefficients/t-ratios of					
Regression	Skill Differential (1)	Trend (2)	Lagged Government/GNP (3)	R^2	SE	D-W or H
(1)	−48.63	.001		.898	3.61	.98*
	−9.05	.52				
(2) First	−22.97	.118		.240	3.02	1.83
differences	−3.03	1.08				
(3)	−20.92	.002	.596	.948	2.68	0.76
	−3.03	1.01	5.07			
Mean	1.469		18.27			
SD	.207		10.96			

Sources and Notes: Dependent variable is government spending/GNP × 100 at five-year intervals from 1820–1975. The following replacements are made to eliminate effects of wars: 1898 (instead of 1900), 1913 (1915), 1922 (1920), 1938 (1940), 1947–1948 average (1945); also 1974 (1975) due to data availability.

The numerator is from Organization for Economic Cooperation & Development, National Accounts of OECD Countries for 1955–74. Data for 1820–1950 are from Alan Peacock & Jack Wiseman, The Growth of Public Expenditures in the United Kingdom (1961). They give data at irregular intervals which usually correspond to a year divisible by 5. However, I used their 1822, 1831, and 1841 figures for 1820, 1830, and 1840 respectively. Missing years in the Peacock & Wiseman series were interpolated from percentage changes in British central government expenses (Brian Mitchell & Phyllis Deane, Abstract of British Historical Statistics [1962]).

The denominator is GDP at market prices. Data for 1900–1950 are from The British Economy: Key Statistics, 1900–64 (1965), Organization for Economic Cooperation & Development, National Accounts of OECD Countries; for 1820–1900 from estimates of net national product in Mitchell & Deane, *supra,* spliced to GDP at 1900.

The skill differential is an average of the two series in Figure VI for 1880–1975. The building industry series is spliced at 1880. See text for sources.

* = Significant autocorrelation of residuals.

The coefficient of "Trend" in regression (2) is the annualized constant term in this regression.

TABLE 7.   Regressions of Relative Size of British and U.S. Government Sectors on Skill Differentials, 1870–1975

| | Coefficients/t-ratios of | | | | | |
| | Relative Skill Differential | Trend | Lagged Relative Size | R^2 | SE | D-W |
Regression	(1)	(2)	(3)	(4)	(5)	(6)
			Differences			
1	−10.76	.103		.645	3.01	1.69
	−2.19	5.05				
2	−7.59	.076	.226	.608	3.09	*
	−1.28	2.21	.94			
			Ratios			
3	−3.03	.001		.531	.235	1.23
	−4.04	.86				
4	−3.24			.513	.233	1.21
	−4.59					
5	−1.27		.464	.573	.210	*
	−1.24		2.15			
Mean/SD:						
Differences	−.23		5.21			
	.13		4.80			
Ratios	.86		1.33			
	.07		.33			

* = H statistic cannot be calculated because of large standard error of coefficient in column (3).

similarities than differences, making it more plausible that some common "third" force is pushing on both variables in both countries at any moment. By focusing on relative effects and thereby eliminating this third force, we might easily be left with data reflecting national idiosyncrasies.[34]

This does not, however, appear to be the case. In Table 7 the dif-

[34]To put this more formally, suppose the true relationship is

$$g_i = \beta Y + \varepsilon_i,$$

where g_i = country i's government/GNP ratio; Y = the cosmic force determining both g_i and g_j which we do not observe; and ε_i = random error. We do, however, observe X_i, a country-specific variable (skill differentials) which may be related to Y. For example, suppose

$$X_i = Y + u_i.$$

u_i = country-specific random measurement error. When we estimate the regression

$$g_i = bX_i + v_i,$$

ferences between or ratios of the British and U.S. government/GNP are regressed on differences or ratios of their skill differentials. In either form, the results indicate that any other forces propelling the growth of government seem to be enhanced by more equality. Thus a good part of the differences between the development of British and U.S. government seems explainable by different movements in equality. The main qualification comes from regressions (2) and (5) in the table, which allow for lagged adjustment of relative sizes. Collinearity between the two independent variables makes it hard to separate relative inequality and lagged-adjustment effects, but the direction of the inequality effect is consistent with the other results.[35]

To summarize, the British and American data did not allow the separation of the between-group and within-group components of income inequality as our model requires. Instead, we were forced to use skill differentials, which come closer conceptually to the within-group measure but which are also highly correlated, at least in the U.S. data, with a plausible between-group measure (the share of income going to the top 5 per cent). The empirical results all point in one direction: the within-group effects in the model dominate. More equality appears to stimulate expansion of the government sector.

2. Canada and Japan. These countries are of interest for divergent reasons, Canada for its historical similarities to the United States and Japan for its sharp differences from Canada, the United States, and Great Britain. I review the Canadian history first to see if the preceding findings can be corroborated. The broad pattern of Canadian economic development is so similar to that of the United States, more so than is Britain's, that it provides a strong check on these findings.

---

b will be biased toward zero but will have the same sign as β, because of the correlation between X_i and Y. However, if we estimate

$$g_i - g_j = b'[X_i - X_j] + v_i - v_j,$$

which is akin to what is done in Table 7, we remove the presumed "cosmic force" (Y) and are left with

$$g_i - g_j = b'[u_i - u_j] + v_i - v_j.$$

Our independent variable would be purely random and $E(b') = 0$ (so long as the country-specific components of X_i really do not matter).

[35]The significant trend term in regressions (1) and (2) is better taken as recommending the ratio model than evidence of any unexplained divergence in government growth. The trend term reflects mainly the post-World War II experience, where both government sectors have grown so large that the absolute gap between the two today (about 12 percentage points) is larger than either government sector 100 years ago.

The results in Table 8 generally corroborate and in one respect extend those for Britain and the United States. For Canada, unlike the United States, cross-regional income disparities seem important, and they push in the same direction as personal income equality (column (2), regressions (1)–(3)): both are negatively related to the size of government. This result tends to confirm the importance of the "within-group" inequality effect that has so far dominated the results. Were the "between-group" effect important, large regional inequalities would stimulate rather than retard redistribution in a political system with regional representation. Of course, the inconsistency between the U.S. and Canadian results for this variable ought to give us pause. One possible explanation, elaborated below, is that changes in Canadian regional inequality over the last century have not been nearly as trend-dominated as in the United States, so collinearity problems are less likely to obscure any true effect of regional inequality.

The negative effect of inequality on the size of government persists in the last three regressions, which focus on the relative size of the Canadian and U.S. government sectors. The effect is predictably weaker in these data and seems confined to the personal income-inequality proxy, which again suggests caution in pushing too far the preceding results for regional inequality. But it is more interesting that a negative inequality effect remains in these data, which abstract from the shared history of the two countries.[36]

We gain further insight into these results from Figure VII, which displays the data underlying (4)–(6) in Table 8. Canada has typically had the larger government sector, but the difference tended to be greater up to, say, 1930. Relative skill differentials have moved in the opposite direction; they are higher for Canada in the most recent fifty or so years. These opposing movements are reflected in the negative coefficients of the relative skill differentials in (4)–(6) of Table 8.

Figure VII also raises the possibility of lags in the adjustment of government to equality that the regressions have not captured. The relevant labor market history summarized in Figure VII is that the United States has a ten-to-fifteen year headstart on Canada in the movement toward equality. Up to World War I, skill differentials tend to widen in both countries. They then begin to decline in the United States, but only do so in Canada with the onset of the Great Depression. Notice, however, that, whereas the effects of the U.S. headstart toward equality on relative skill differentials ends around 1930, a major part of the narrowing in the relative sizes of the two government sectors occurs thereafter. Indeed, if the relative skill differentials in equa-

---

[36] Note that the standard errors for regression (4)–(6) in Table 8 are on the order of a fourth smaller than those of the British-U.S. counterparts in Table 7.

TABLE 8.   Canadian Government/GNP Regressions, 1880–1975

Dependent Variable: Government Spending/GNP	Coefficients/t-ratios						
	Skill Differential (1)	Regional Inequality (2)	Trend (3)	G_{-1} (4)	R^2 (5)	SE	D-W
1. Canada:	−12.59	−54.52	.30		.96	2.0	1.08
level	5.02	3.90	16.76				
2. Canada:	−9.06	−39.89	.22	.30	.97	2.0	—
level	2.45	2.25	3.39	1.30			
3. Canada: first	−8.71	−51.24	.31[1]		.41	2.1	2.00
differences	2.01	2.84	3.29				
4. Canada/	−1.01	−.31	.41		.30	.173	1.26
U.S.	1.24	1.02	.70				
5. Canada/	−.47	−.14			.28	.171	1.24
U.S.	2.11	.79					
6. Canada/	−.63	−.76[2]			.27	.172	1.20
U.S.	2.30	.65					

Sources of Canadian Data:

1. *Government spending*

1955–1975. Organization for Economic Cooperation & Development, National Accounts of OECD Countries.

1926–1955. Richard M. Bird, The Growth of the Government Spending in Canada (Canadian Tax Papers No. 51, July 1970).

1870–1926. The annual data are estimates from benchmark data in Bird, *supra*. He gives total government spending for 1870 and decennially from 1890, federal spending annually for 1867–1926, and an "Alternative Series" which includes a part of nonfederal expenditures annually for 1900–26. I use year-to-year percentage changes in these two annual series to estimate annual changes in total expenditures between benchmark years.

2. *GNP*

1926–1975. Same as government expenditures.

1870–1926. Annual estimates from decennial benchmarks for nominal and real GNP, 1870–1910, in Bird, *supra*. I assumed that real GNP grew at a constant rate between benchmarks, and I interpolated annual fluctuations in the GNP deflator from the annual wholesale price index in M. C. Urquhart & K. A. H. Buckley, Historical Statistics of Canada (1965) [hereinafter cited as Historical Statistics]. Nominal GNP in nonbenchmark years is the resulting estimate of real GNP × the estimated GNP deflator. For 1910–1920, the interpolation uses an annual national income series and for 1920–1926 a net domestic product series in Historical Statistics, *supra*.

3. *Skill differentials*. 1920–1975. An average of skilled/unskilled hourly wages in the building and printing industries for five cities (Halifax, Montreal, Toronto, Winnipeg, and Vancouver). The skilled wage for the building industry is an average of wages for carpenters, electricians, and plumbers, and the unskilled wages is for "labourers." The skilled printing occupations are compositors and pressmen and the unskilled "bindery girls." The printing skill differential is set equal to the building industry differential at 1920 and the two are averaged thereafter. Building industry data for 1920–1960 are from Historical Statistics; for 1960–1975, from Canada Year Book (Ministry of Trade & Commerce, various years). Printing industry data are from Wage Rates, Salaries, and Hours of Labour (Dep't of Labour, now Labour Canada, various years).

1901–1920. Building industry differential from data in Historical Statistics (see above).

1880–1900. These are estimates, spliced to and extended backward from the 1901 value, taken from Historical Statistics. For 1890–1900, an Ottawa and Toronto sample of wages for carpenters, masons, painters, and unskilled laborers is used. For 1885–1890, I use immigration agents' reports of carpenters' and laborers' wages at Halifax, Montreal, Toronto, and Winnipeg. For 1880–1885, I use similar 1882–1885 data for Montreal, Ottawa, Hamilton, and Winnipeg.

TABLE 8.   *(continued)*

4. *Regional differentials*. This is a standard deviation of the log of wage rates across cities. The
   cities, except where noted, are Halifax, Montreal, Toronto, Winnipeg, and Vancouver, each of
   which represents an important Canadian region. The sources are the same as for the skill
   differentials. For 1900–1920, the variable is an average of that for the four building occupations. For 1920–1975, an average of the three printing occupations is spliced to the building
   industry average at 1920. For 1885–1890, we have a subsample of the post 1900 building
   industry data (see above—Vancouver and plumber and electrician data are missing). I spliced
   data from this subsample to a similar one drawn from 1901 data and estimate the 1895 value by
   linear interpolation. The 1880 values are set equal to 1885.

Notes:

All variables are, where the data permit, three-year centered averages at five-year intervals from
   1880–1975. To remove effects of the World Wars on government/GNP, the following replacements are made. 1923 for 1920, a linear interpolation of 1910 and 1923 for 1915, 1939 for 1940,
   and 1947 for 1945. In lines 1–3, Canadian data only are used. In lines 4–6, Canadian data are
   divided by the U.S. counterpart. Sample size = 20 (19 for line 3).

[1] Annualized constant term.

[2] Canadian variable *not* divided by United States.

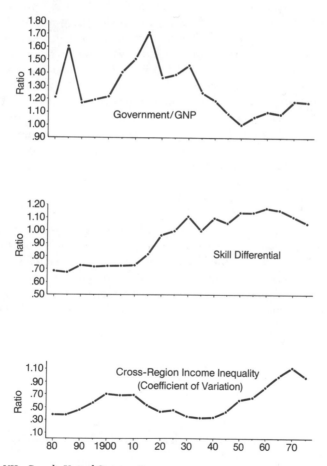

FIGURE VII. Canada-United States ratios

tions (4)–(6) of Table 8 are lagged by twenty years, explained variation roughly doubles. The relevant lag may be even longer. Glancing back at the U.S. data in Figure IV, another kind of lag is apparent, that of the skill differential behind the broader ("Kuznets") measure of inequality.[37] Since all of this implies that movements in the size of government tend to lag behind those of inequality, a model in which the latter "causes" the former gains some credibility. While we cannot pursue the lag structure further with the crude data and small samples, subsequent data reveal lags to be an important part of the story. In fact, the twenty-or-so year lag that is clear in Figure VII is close to the order of the lag magnitudes that these data will reveal.

The bottom panel of Figure VII reflects a substantial recent divergence between Canadian and U.S. movements in cross-regional equality. From 1900 to World War II, regional disparities narrowed in both countries. Whereas this decline accelerated in the United States, it has actually been reversed in Canada in the postwar period, a fact which may help explain the recent centripetal pressures in that country.[38] However, it is evident from Figure VII (and regressions (4)–(6)) that this reversal has not slowed the growth of Canada's government sector. The negative coefficient of regional inequality in regressions (1)–(3) appears to reflect mainly the earlier history. Unlike the United States, Canadian regional disparities widened up to 1900, while its government sector declined or grew slowly. Regional income disparities then narrowed sharply up to about 1930, and this roughly coincides with a period of relatively rapid growth of government.

A Note on the Role of Voting Behavior in the Three Countries

I have so far ignored the role of political institutions in the growth of government in the three basically Anglo countries. Since the theoretical model suggests that they have a role, it is worth asking if the role is sufficiently important to qualify any of the preceding results. In the theory, political institutions would enter under the rubric of "ability." Anything which makes it easier for beneficiaries to return political sup-

---

[37] The relevant regression is

$$\text{Skill differential}_t = \text{constant} + 3.3 \text{ Kuznets}_t$$
$$(t = 4.7)$$

$$+ 2.4 \text{ Kuznets}_{t-1}; \; R^2 = .97.$$
$$(t = 3.4)$$

[38] In fact, it is Quebec and the maritime province wages which have lagged the rest of the country, at least up to 1970.

port ought to stimulate growth of government. Since all three countries have had democratic structures for the periods studied, we must ask whether differences in the administration of these structures have had perceptible effects. One such difference has been the extent of the franchise. Here, there is a sharp division around 1920 when suffrage was extended to women, and the franchise became virtually universal in all three countries. Although the suffrage of women coincided with the beginning of a continuing expansion in the size of government in all three countries, such a crude correlation should be greeted skeptically. Since women represent a roughly random sample from the income distribution, it is unclear that women's suffrage heralded a shift in the demand for redistribution. More to the point, it is doubtful that, with the possible exception of female-headed households, women lacked influence on voting patterns prior to 1920. So we ought to look to the pre-1920 period for unambiguous political effects.

The considerable variety among the three countries prior to 1920 does not seem to explain the role of government.[39] Here we must distinguish voter eligibility from participation. In all three countries, participation rates in national elections have been essentially trendless since at least 1900. They have ranged around 70 to 80 per cent for Canada and the United Kingdom and about 15 points less for the United States.[40] So no change in participation seems connected to the dramatic change in the growth of government experienced by all three countries after World War I. The main differences among the countries occur in pre-1920 eligibility rates (eligible voters/male population over twenty-one). The United States had attained near-universal (90 per cent) male suffrage by 1870. For the United Kingdom, on the other hand, this figure is only one-third. It required an electoral reform in 1884, which doubled eligibility, and another in 1918 for the United Kingdom to close the gap. Canada is the intermediate case. In the immediate aftermath of the British North America Act, it appears that roughly half of Canadian adult males had the franchise. Over the next thirty or so years, most provinces gradually removed property qualifications so that eligibility exceeded three-fourths by 1900. A 1920 federal law made suffrage universal. If the extent of suffrage promotes growth of government, Britain clearly should have had the most rapid growth of government in the nineteenth century, since significant franchise

[39] The data here are from Historical Statistics, *supra* note 28; Howard A. Scarrow, Canada Votes (1962), for Canada; and Stein Rokkan & Jean Meyriat, International Guide to Electoral Statistics (1969), for the United Kingdom.

[40] There was a perceptible, but temporary, decline in all three countries in the decade or so after women's suffrage.

extensions took place in 1832 and 1867 in addition to 1884. But, as we have seen, British government growth was actually negative in the wake of the earlier reforms, and after 1870, all three countries are more notable for their similarities—generally stable government/GNP ratios—than any differences.

These data are too crude to rule out a connection between suffrage and the size of government. They do, however, suggest, that the major changes in the size of government have little to do with extension of the franchise; otherwise the United States would have had by far the largest government sector in 1870.

Japan. Japan provides perhaps a better test of the role of politics than any of the three countries we have looked at so far. The basically democratic institutions that prevailed in these three countries are absent for most of Japan's history. Japanese economic development was also somewhat isolated from the common forces affecting the three At-

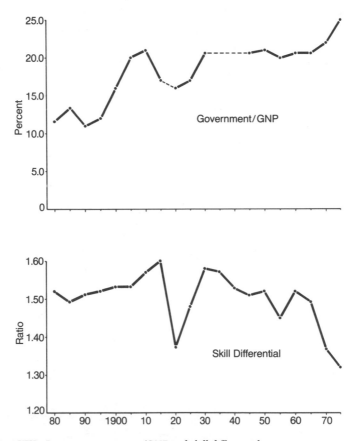

FIGURE VIII. Japanese government/GNP and skill differential

lantic countries. Japan's particularism is mirrored amply in the growth of its government, which is shown in the upper panel of Figure VIII. Unlike any of the Atlantic triad, the major growth in Japan occurs before World War I. It shares virtually none of their subsequent growth and today has the smallest government sector in the developed world.

To what extent can Japan's singular history be reconciled with the previous findings? The first two regressions in Table 9 suggest reconciliation may be difficult. The inequality proxy is positively, rather than negatively, related to the size of government, though the coefficient is of marginal significance. (And we cannot replicate the significant effect of regional inequality found in the Canadian data.) A slightly different perspective is gained by looking at the two series in Figure VIII. Ex-

TABLE 9.   Japanese Government/GNP Regressions, 1880–1975

	Skill Differential (1)	Regional Inequality (2)	Trend (3)	D (4)	D × SK (5)	R^2	SE	D-W
		Coefficients/t-ratios						
1.	11.45	−10.24	.11			.77	1.98	1.22
	1.58	.67	4.75					
2.	11.50		.12			.76	1.95	1.16
	1.68		6.94					
3.	17.87		.14	41.35	−29.66	.82	1.76	1.58
	2.05		6.42	1.89	1.98			

Sources: 1. Data for government spending and GNP 1953–1975, are from Organization for Economic Cooperation & Development, National Accounts of OECD Countries. For 1880–1953, government expenditures are those in the "general account" budgets of national and local governments from Koichi Emi & Yuichi Shinoya, Government Expenditures, vol. 7 Estimates of Long Term Economic Statistics of Japan since 1868 (Kazushi Ohkawa, Miyohei Shinohara, Mataji Umemura eds. 1966). The general account excludes war expenditures which were financed through a "special account" and it excludes operating budgets of, but not subsidies to, nationalized industries. GDP is from Kazushi Ohkawa, Nobukiyo Takamatsu, & Yuzo Yamamoto, National Income, vol. 1 Estimates of Long Term Economic Statistics of Japan since 1868 (Kazushi Ohkawa, Miyohei Shinohara, Mataji Umemura eds. 1965).

2. Skill differential is the ratio of daily wages for skilled workers to day laborers in construction. Data for 1880–1939 are from Ohkawa, et al., *supra;* for 1945–1960 from Koji Taira, Economic Development and the Labor Market in Japan (1970); 1960–1975: Japan Statistical Yearbook (Bureau of Statistics, Office of the Prime Minister, various years).

3. Regional inequality is the coefficient of variation of average wages across 13 cities spliced to series for 46 prefectures at 1940. Data are from Taira, *supra.*

4. $D = +1$ for 1955–1975, 0 otherwise.

5. $D × SK = D ×$ skill differential.

Note: The dependent variable is government expenditures/GNP, constructed in the same way as for Britain, Canada, and the United States. Since Japan was more frequently involved in wars, there is more extensive adjustment for Japan. Specifically, the following substitutions are made: 1895 (average of 1893 and 1896), 1905 (average of 1902 and 1908), 1915 (1913), 1920 (average of 1921 and 1922), 1935 and 1940 are linear interpolations of 1930 and 1945 (which is set at the 1947–1948 average).

cept for the "blip" around World War I, the Japanese skill differential shows remarkable stability at least up to 1960. It is within 10 points of its mean of about 150 for the entire period, when the Western differentials tended to lie between 100 and 200. This lack of any pronounced move toward greater equality, a move which is almost universal in the Western world, seems confirmed by other data.[41] A negative corroboration of the previous results may be that Japanese government did *not* grow in the twentieth century because it lacked the crucial stimulant, a decline in inequality. Of course, this leaves us with the need to explain the rapid growth before World War I. It seems reasonable to raise here the issue of cost of tax collection even if we must postpone explicit analysis of it. The important changes in transportation and communication costs, the size of businesses, the extent of impersonal markets, and so forth, which occurred in the West in the nineteenth century and which presumably reduce tax collection costs ought to have stimulated growth in government's share of national income there. That this did not occur in the West may imply that, once a fairly rudimentary legal and institutional infrastructure is in place, most important tax-collection economies are achieved. But Japan may not have been so endowed immediately following the Meiji restoration. Its per capita income in the late nineteenth century appears to have been on the order of one-fifth or one-tenth that of the United States, and modern local government institutions did not replace the feudal structures of the Tokugawa era until 1878.[42] Thus it seems risky to dismiss tax-collection costs as a factor in the growth of Japan's government in the early Meiji years as easily as we can for the Western countries.

The post-World War II period in Japan is especially interesting for two reasons. The obvious one is the radical change in its political institutions from dictatorship to democracy, a change that permits a sharper test of the role of political institutions than for the three Western democracies. The second reason has to do with changes in income inequality. As in its economic development generally, Japan seems to have lagged behind the Western world by around thirty years. The

---

[41] See, for example, Akira Ono & Tsunehiko Watanabe, Changes in Income Inequality in the Japanese Economy, in Japanese Industrialization and Its Social Consequences 363 (Hugh Patrick ed. 1973). Also Yasukichi Yasuba, Evolution of the Dualistic Wage Structure, in *id.* at 49, calculated coefficients of variation in average wages across operatives in each manufacturing industry for selected years from 1909 to 1951. There is no tendency for the coefficients to decline over time for comparable industries. While such a measure will reflect, *inter alia*, age, sex, and skill mix changes, this stability does seem to conform to the general pattern of comparatively minor changes in inequality before 1960.

[42] Koichi Emi, Government Fiscal Activity and Economic Growth in Japan, 1868–1960, (1963).

bottom panel of Figure VIII shows a sustained narrowing of skill differentials starting in 1960. I would be reluctant to draw firm conclusions from this brief period's data except that they seem to comport well with other data. Ono and Watanabe, after examining a variety of inequality measures, also date the start of a perceptible decline in inequality at about 1960.[43]

From Figure VIII it seems clear that neither the political nor income inequality changes has so far produced any dramatic change in the size of Japan's government. But to determine if there are any symptoms of change, line 3 of Table 9 repeats the basic regression with an intercept and slope dummy variable (columns (4) and (5), respectively) for the period from 1955 (the "democratic" era in Japan). The coefficient of the slope dummy ($D \times SK$) addresses the question: did the process linking inequality to the size of government change when Japan became a democracy? The answer seems to be "yes" and, more interesting, the change is toward the same process that characterized the three other democracies of more equality being associated with bigger government. This regression is, in effect, telling us that the "Robin Hood" motive to redistribution predominates in the nondemocratic era (note the now significantly positive coefficient of the skill differential in column (1), line 3), but that within-beneficiary-group considerations are more important in a democracy.

Moreover, this strengthened importance of within-group equality is predicted by the theory. Refer back to (14), which summarizes the within-group effect. Of the variables in that expression, the one most immediately affected by a shift from dictatorship to democracy would be the variable reflecting the ability of the numerous beneficiaries to give their interests political weight. This is F_g, the marginal political product of the benefit, which should be higher in a democracy. After substitution of some first-order conditions[44] and rearrangement of terms, (14) can be rewritten schematically

$$D = \frac{A + BF_g}{1 - I_Q F_g} > 0, \tag{14'}$$

where A and B are positive expressions not involving F_g, and D is the derivative on the left-hand side of (14). Treating the advent of democracy as an event (X) which raises F_g by a unit, the effect on D is summarized

---

[43] *Supra* note 41.

[44] To eliminate F_R, which may also be affected by the shift to democracy.

$$\text{sgn } \frac{dD}{dX} = \text{sgn}(B + AI_Q) > 0. \tag{23}$$

Note that (23) does *not* say that government will grow if F_g increases, but rather that government growth will be *more responsive* to *changes* in inequality within the beneficiary group, whether the changes push for more government or less. This is precisely what the Japanese findings show: no vast expansion of government, but a larger weighting of the within-group equality effect. Moreover, the model implies no correspondingly unambiguous shift in the importance of the between-group effect, which could have obscured the shift we observe in the Japanese data.[45]

If this analysis is valid (we will subsequently pursue this interaction between equality and political ability), there are profound implications for Japan's future. It appears that the Japanese government sector is on the verge of substantial growth, if its recent move toward greater income equality is as permanent and far-reaching as that experienced in the West some thirty years before. It now has the democratic political structure in which more equality seems to fuel expanding governments. Thus all the conditions now seem in place for Japan to repeat the vast expansion of government which has characterized the Western world since the depression, including perhaps the replacement of its famed intracorporate welfare system with a national social security system.

B. Post-World War II Experience in the Developed World

I now want to see whether the postwar experience among developed countries is consistent with the time-series evidence. While government has grown everywhere, there is enough variety to make the in-

---

[45]The reason for the ambiguity here can be seen most easily by focusing on the marginal political product of numbers of beneficiaries (M_p). This is proportional to $1 - F_g J_p$. An exogenous increase in F_g reduces the marginal product of numbers. When P's become more responsive, the first-order response is to cultivate them more "intensively," with a higher g given to fewer P so that the ambivalence of the highest income P's about redistribution can be economized. (This is analogous to Ricardo's extensive margin shrinking when the marginal product of labor rose.) This is why a rise in F_g, by itself, will not increase the optimal G. However, if the rise in F_g is compensated by a decline in J_p, the ambivalence of the marginal P's is reduced, and the force shrinking the "extensive" margin is attenuated. Now, when there is an increase in between-group inequality, J_p is unaffected, so there is no necessary reason for a rise in F_g to induce a larger rise in G than would otherwise occur; the same rise in G could be optimal if concentrated on fewer P's. But a reduction in within-group inequality *does* lower J_p. When F_g rises in *these* circumstances, it calls for both more intensive *and*

TABLE 10.   The Size and Growth of Government/GDP
              16 Developed Countries Selected Years, 1953–1974

	Government Spending/GDP			Percentage Increase		
Country	1953–54 (1)	1963–64 (2)	1973–74 (3)	(2)/(1)	(3)/(2)	(3)/(1)
Australia	24.2%	25.4%	30.1%	4.8%	18.5%	24.2%
Austria	31.9	34.8	38.3	9.3	10.0	20.3
Belgium	28.1	31.2	39.5	10.9	26.6	40.4
Canada	26.2	28.0	36.4	6.7	30.1	38.7
Denmark	24.4	30.3	46.6	24.4	53.8	91.4
Finland	31.1	31.3	38.4	0.6	22.7	23.5
France	35.6	37.8	38.5	6.2	1.9	8.1
Germany	35.5	36.6	41.9	3.0	14.5	17.9
Italy	27.6	31.5	39.6	14.1	25.6	43.3
Japan	21.0	20.9	24.0	−0.2	14.6	14.3
Netherlands	31.8	36.9	50.7	16.0	37.3	59.3
Norway	30.5	36.5	48.7	19.5	33.5	59.5
Sweden	28.0	36.3	49.0	29.5	35.2	75.0
Switzerland	27.8	28.9	35.2	4.1	21.8	26.8
United Kingdom	32.7	33.7	42.0	2.9	24.8	28.4
United States	27.0	28.0	32.2	3.9	14.8	19.3
Average	28.9	31.7	39.4	9.7	24.1	36.9

Sources: See notes to Table 2 for sources.

vestigation interesting. Table 10 provides some relevant data. The general pattern has been that of rapid growth in Northern Europe, slow growth following high initial levels for France and Germany, and slow growth from low or average levels for the non-European countries. There are, of course, some notable exceptions such as Canada recently, Finland for the whole period, and Britain in the 1950s when it was liquidating its empire. The simple question I try to answer is: can income inequality differences help rationalize this variety?

Comparing inequality across countries poses important problems. The data come from a variety of sources in which income concepts, coverage, and so forth can differ greatly among countries and are susceptible to bias. For example, many income distributions have been compiled from tax returns, which are heavily influenced not only by coverage and income definition differences but by differences in enforcement of the tax laws. I am aware of only two attempts to systematically surmount these comparability problems so that a credible ranking

---

extensive cultivation of the P's and thus an unambiguously larger rise in G than would otherwise occur.

of countries by inequality emerges. The first by Lydall, focuses on pretax wage and salary income.[46] Since it excludes both transfers and property income, this income concept seems like a good proxy for the potential beneficiary-incomes of the theoretical model. Lydall had to rely mainly on tax-based distributions, which he then tried to adjust to a common basis (adult male full-time workers). He is sometimes cryptic about how these adjustments are made, particularly where resolving conflicts among different data for the same country. His ranking, however, can be useful here, since it is independent of this problem.

The more recent study by Sawyer for the Organization for Economic Cooperation and Development (OECD) has the advantage of drawing its data from household budget surveys, rather than tax records, supplemented by unpublished data designed to mitigate comparability problems.[47] The major drawback, for our purposes, is the inclusion of transfers in the basic income concept (household pretax money income). Sawyer is able to estimate income distributions, standardized for household size,[48] for ten countries in Lydall's sample. For six countries, the two studies are in broad agreement about inequality rankings. For four there are clear discrepancies since the countries wind up in different halves of the two rankings. Columns (1) and (2) of Table 11 summarize the findings of the two studies.

The four discrepancies are divided equally in direction. They occur with Australia and Germany (lower OECD ranks), on the one hand, and Japan and the Netherlands, on the other. The following two obvious possible sources of these discrepancies cannot explain them.

1. *Time period.* Lydall's ranking is for the late 1950s, and Sawyer's is for the late 1960s. However, Sawyer provides data for three of the countries in question (Germany, Japan, the Netherlands) which go back to the Lydall period. In no case is there any change in inequality remotely close to explaining the discrepancy. More generally, Sawyer's retrospective data imply that any 1960 ranking would essentially duplicate that for 1970.

2. *Income definition.* The inclusion of transfers in Sawyer's data raises forcefully the issue of the endogeneity of equality. While transfers may affect cardinal measures of inequality, they do not appear

[46] Lydall, *supra* note 28.

[47] Malcolm Sawyer, Income Distribution in OECD Countries, in 19 OECD Economic Outlook, Supp. at 3 (Occasional Studies, July 1976).

[48] The standardization is important. Countries with generous pension and unemployment insurance schemes have many one-person households: more retired and young single people find it feasible to set up their own households. These households typically have below average incomes, so their proliferation tends to increase inequality measured over all households.

to explain the discrepancies in rank. Sawyer provides decile income shares. If the bottom two deciles—where transfers are heavily concentrated—are deleted and the countries re-ranked, the discrepancies remain. Notice that each discrepant couplet contains one country with extensive transfers (Germany, the Netherlands) and one with unusually low transfers (Australia, Japan). Similarly, each couplet has one "big government" and one "small government" country. So government-induced effects on inequality do not appear to resolve the specific discrepancies, though they still may affect the general pattern of the ranks.

The third column of Table 11 shows coefficients of variation in average hourly wages across manufacturing industries from another OECD study. While such a measure will be affected by, for example, differences in skill mix across industries and in national industry defini-

TABLE 11.   Countries Ranked by Income Equality—
Two Comparative Studies and Related Data

	Rank Order (1 = Most Equal)		Coefficient of Variation– Factory Workers
Country	Lydall (1)	Sawyer-OECD (2)	(3)
Australia	1	7	—
Austria	10	—	—
Belgium	8	—	13.5
Canada	7	6	15
Denmark	2	—	—
Finland	12	—	—
France	13	10	19
Germany	5.5	9	15
Japan	14	5	—
Netherlands	11	1	4
Norway	5.5	3	10
Sweden	4	2	11
United Kingdom	3	4	8
United States	9	8	18.5

Notes: See text for income concepts used, years covered, and so on. A dash indicates the country is not in the sample.

Norway is here assigned equal rank with Germany in the Lydall sample, partly on the basis of the OECD data. Lydall is unable to reconcile two sources of data, one of which would place it "near Germany" (1968, p. 161)—that is, relatively high in degree of equality—and another which would place it much lower. Given the OECD findings, the "tie" with Germany may still leave Norway's ranking too low.

Column (3) is the coefficient of variation × 100 of average wage rates for production workers across manufacturing industries *ca.* 1960 from Organization for Economic Cooperation and Development, Wages and Labour Mobility (1965). Industries are approximately two-digit SIC level. Wages are hourly for males, except: United States and Germany (both sexes), France (yearly), and Belgium (daily).

tions, it shares with Lydall the advantage of focusing on income least directly affected by the tax-transfer system. Nevertheless, it would resolve two of the disputed cases (Germany and the Netherlands) in favor of Sawyer. For the remaining seven countries, column (3) basically corroborates both the Sawyer and Lydall rankings.

Since it is beyond the scope of this paper to resolve these differences, I will assume that a "true" ranking of late 1950s earnings inequality is given by: $L + kD$, where L = Lydall rank, k = constant, and $D = -1$ for Japan and the Netherlands and $+1$ for Australia and Germany. Presumably, $k > 0$. The essential question is whether any such ranking scheme can rationalize either the size or growth of government.

The size-growth distinction is especially important in this cross section in light of Lydall's discussion of the recent history of inequality. He finds that the broad outlines of the British, American, and Canadian twentieth-century experience hold almost everywhere in the developed world. Some time around World War I, wage and salary inequality began to decline and some time around 1950, the decline flattened or stopped. Kuznets's data give much the same impression about the upper-tail money incomes.[49] He simply reports what is available in the literature, so comparability across countries is risky. But a clear pattern emerges. Around World War I the top 5 per cent of income recipients in the typical developed country account for around 30 per cent of national income and the fragmentary nineteenth-century data show no clear trend from 1870 to World War I. However, by about 1950 this share falls to just under 20 per cent. Crude interpolation of Sawyer's data for the upper two declines implies that the *circa*-1970 figure is around 17 per cent. In broad outline, the growth of government follows a similar path, in that the aftermath of World War I coincides with a permanent enlargement and sustained growth of government. An important detail, however, is that for many countries a major part of the growth of government has occurred in the last twenty-five years, or after the main force of the trend toward equality had been spent. If equality is indeed a major determinant of the equilibrium size of government, a lagged-adjustment process has been dominating recent experience. Thus recent *growth* of government would be more closely related to the level of inequality than absolute size.

This conjecture is confirmed by the data in Table 12, where the size of government at the time of Lydall's ranking and its subsequent growth are regressed on his ranking and the correction factor from Sawyer's study. Size of government and inequality were essentially un-

---

[49] Kuznets, *supra* note 26.

TABLE 12. Regressions of Size and Growth of Government/GDP on Income Equality Measures, 14 Countries, 1958–1959 to 1973–1974

Dependent Variable	Lydall Rank (L)	OECD Dummy (D)	1958–1959 Government/GDP	R^2	SE
	Coefficients/t-ratios				
Size 1958–1959					
1. Rank (1 = largest)	−.22			.048	4.24
	−.77				
2. Rank	−.47	−3.03		.145	4.19
	−1.32	−1.14			
3. Log (Government/GDP)	.27	2.26		.054	4.80
	.67	.74			
Growth, 1958–1959 to 1973–1974					
4. Rank (1 = most % growth)	.56			.315	3.60
	2.35				
5. Rank	.56		.028	.316	3.76
	2.17		.11		
6. Rank	1.20	7.26	.226	.832	1.95
	6.80	5.55	1.61		
7. Rank	1.10	6.58		.789	2.09
	6.24	4.97			
8. Log Δ (Government/ GDP) × 100	−1.77		.306	.346	11.04
	−2.41		.16		
9. Log Δ	−3.43	−20.17	.151	.816	6.14
	−6.55	−5.06	1.41		
10. Log Δ	−3.31	−18.92		.780	6.41
	−6.14	−4.66			
11. Δ Government/GDP × 100	−1.28	−7.65		.673	3.29
	−4.64	−3.67			
Subcategories of Government/GDP, Log Δ × 100					
12. Nondefense	−3.49	−5.90		.561	12.34
	−3.36	−.76			
13. Government consumption	−2.88	−3.09		.646	8.80
	−3.88	−.55			
14. Government transfers	−4.35	−39.64		.711	12.47
	−4.16	−5.02			

Notes: The 14 countries are listed in Table 11. L = "Lydall" variable in Table 11. D = +1 for Australia and Germany, −1 for Japan and the Netherlands, 0 for all other countries.
Transfers in line 14 include interest on public debt.
The 1958–1959 Government/GDP independent variable is a rank for 5 and 6, and a log for 8 and 9.

correlated in the late 1950s. But there is a very strong negative correlation between inequality then and subsequent growth. Some combination of the Lydall and Sawyer data can explain most of the recent growth no matter how the growth is measured, whether we include or exclude defense spending, or focus on transfers or on consumption.

A major puzzle in the table, however, is lack of evidence of convergence toward equilibrium. None of the coefficients of the government-size variable have the expected negative sign and two (in 6 and 9) suggest an explosive system. The puzzle did not disappear, though the explosive tendency did, when I replicated the relevant regressions for growth in the last ten years instead of the last fifteen. It seems scarcely credible that the governments of, for example, the Scandinavian countries and Holland will continue to grow substantially faster than the rest of the world, yet that is what Table 12 implies.[50]

One way to rescue stability from these data is hinted at by the scheme in (19)–(22). Let X in (17) increase with equality, so $b > 0$. From (22) the whole coefficient of the size of government $[-a(1 + bc)]$ can be zero or even positive while $-a < 0$ if $c < 0$. This would mean that increased government spending *reduces* measured equality. Since our basic equality measure is of pretax earnings, less equality may not be so far-fetched. And the simultaneous slowing of the decline of inequality and growth of government is at least crudely consistent with this sort of process. However, crude extrapolation of prewar-inequality trends hardly provides sufficient evidence.

The broad outlines of the results from the international cross section strongly confirm the time-series evidence. At least for developed democracies, reduced inequality of income stimulates the growth of government. The results also imply, much more strongly than do the Canadian and U.S. time series, a considerable lag in response of the size of government to greater equality.

The international data seem to say something even stronger. Nothing much besides income inequality is needed to explain the growth of government. We are able to pretty much write the history of government growth in the next fifteen years from what we know about income inequality in 1960. In the next section, we show that the rela-

---

[50]The essential results in Table 12 are reproduced if the arguably atypical years, 1975–76, are substituted for 1973–74. Also, if the OECD dummy is replaced by a synthetic OECD ranking of the fourteen countries which uses the Lydall rank to interpolate the missing data; the counterpart to regression (10) gives about twice as much weight to this variable as to the Lydall ranking, though both are significant. If, as column (3) of Table 11 suggests, the Sawyer data more accurately measure inequality, we would expect those data to get the larger weight if there is a negative correlation between growth of government and "true" inequality.

tionship is more complex. Moreover, the complexity is hinted at in the international data. Consider the cases of Finland, France, and Germany which appear not to have been nearly as affected by this century's egalitarian tendencies as, say, Holland or Sweden.[51] Yet, by the early 1950s, their government sectors were all larger than average. To be sure, they have now been surpassed by the more egalitarian countries, but their experience hints that Japan may not be alone in the recent emergence of the stimulative effect of equality on government.

C. State and Local Governments in the United States

An examination of state and local government budgets promises to extend as well as corroborate the previous results. We can employ a fairly extensive sample of comparable data on both government budgets and a diverse set of population characteristics to test parts of the theory that were inaccessible with the preceding data. For example, we can at least hope to exploit cross-sectionally comparable data on income distribution to distinguish "between-" from "within-" group inequality effects.

These virtues are, however, bought at a considerable potential cost. The exigencies of statistical analysis force us to treat the nonfederal jurisdictions as essentially independent observations. Yet they are neither independent of what goes on at the federal level nor of each other. To cite just one problem raised by interdependence, the ability of a local government to serve redistributionist motives is going to be constrained by interjurisdictional competition, both for the tax base and potential supporters. Whereas that possibility did not seem important in the cross-country comparison—small open economies, for example, Denmark, did not appear constrained to have small government sectors—the possibility seems substantially more important across states and localities. Our fears may be partly allayed by data on the actual redistributive impact of governmental tax-spending programs. Reynolds and Smolensky's results indicate that both federal and nonfederal budgets entail substantial rich-to-poor redistribution, and that the nonfederal redistribution is actually the more extensive.[52]

Even if there is considerable redistribution at the local level, a cursory glance at the data suggests another problem. Clearly broad his-

---

[51] For France, this is confirmed by fragmentary skill differential data in Organization for Economic Cooperation and Development, Wages and Labour Mobility (1965). Unlike Britain, the United States, and Canada, these show no narrowing at all since 1930.

[52] Morgan Reynolds & Eugene Smolensky, Public Expenditures, Taxes, and the Distribution of Income: The U.S., 1950, 1961, 1970, (1977).

torical forces producing ubiquitous growth of government dominate any local variety. For the period 1942–1972, the average ratio of state and local spending to personal income across forty-eight states was .15 with a standard deviation of only .02. The average change (standard deviation) between these years is .12 (.02). Variation across states is thus much smaller than across countries (see Tables 2 and 10). This small variation left to be "explained" by local factors poses a substantial constraint on the added insight these data may provide.

In Table 13, I attempt to implement the three main implications of the theory, which are that the size of government responds (*a*) positively to income inequality between prospective beneficiaries and taxpayers, (*b*) negatively to inequality among beneficiaries, and (*c*) positively to the "ability" of beneficiaries to process information. The empirical counterparts to these three notions are:

1. Between-group equality: the share of a state's income accounted for by the richest 5 per cent of the population (SH5).

2. Within-group equality: the standard deviation of the log of income of the group in the twentieth to ninety-fifth percentile of the income distribution in each state (SD2095).

3. Ability: average years of schooling (ED).

The choice of the ninety-fifth percentile as a lower bound for the SH variable was forced by the data. When this bound is lowered, the correlation between the SH and any corresponding SD variable rises dramatically; for example, it is on the order of .8 to .9 if the lower bound of SH is the eightieth percentile and the upper bound of SD is anything up to eighty, compared to .4 when ninety-five is the lower bound. This intercorrelation makes it difficult to distinguish "between-" from "within-" group effects. The motive for excluding the poorest 20 per cent of the population was the model's suggestion of "Director's Law": the very poorest may not have sufficient ability to be included as beneficiaries. The results, however, were basically the same when the lower bound for SD was zero and the upper bound was the sixtieth or eightieth percentile.[53] In light of the results in Table 4, state population is included as an independent variable.

The dependent variable is the ratio of state and local government expenditures to personal income, or its change, for each of forty-eight states. The data are for 1942, 1957, and 1972. The motive for this lengthy time span was to gain insight into the lag process, which the international cross section and some of the time series suggested was an important part of the story. An initial attempt at implementing a

---

[53] Similarly, cutting out either the lower or upper tail of the education distribution made no substantial difference.

conventional partial adjustment model like (19) failed.[54] Therefore, Table 13 shows a range of results. Specifically, the income distribution and ability variables are defined as of *circa* 1940, that is, the start of the thirty-year period.[55] These initial conditions are assumed to determine a target level of the ratio of government spending to personal income. Then a range of adjustment rates to this target is imposed on the data via suitable definition of the dependent variable.[56] The last column of the table departs from the partial adjustment framework in favor of a less specific form: the initial conditions *circa* 1940 simply determine the rate of change over the indefinite future.

The results are uniformly disappointing. None of the coefficients of interest are distinguishable from zero. Some hint of the source of this sharp contrast with previous results is, however, given by the underlying data. The simple correlations between the ability (ED) and within-group inequality (SD2095) variables, on the one hand, and the dependent variable, on the other, always have the "correct" signs (positive and negative, respectively). These correlation coefficients range between .2 and .4 in absolute value, depending on the definition of the dependent variable. While these values are not spectacularly high, they are often significant with only moderate risk of error. (The simple correlation on between-group inequality (SH5) is, however, typically negative, sometimes significant. Yet, when that variable is deleted from the regression, as in column (2) or (6) there is no improvement in the performance of the remaining variables.) There is, how-

[54] Entering the lagged dependent variable as an independent variable always yielded absurdly low adjustment coefficients—on the order of .2 for 30 years. The reason appears to be that "state-specific" effects not captured by the model persist over time—for example, New York had unusually large governments in 1942 as well as 1972. Thus, when a 1972 expenditure variable is regressed on its 1942 counterpart, the coefficient of the latter (1 − adjustment coefficient) tends to have a positive bias.

[55] Usable data on income distributions begin with the 1950 census. (There are some in 1940, but always with a frighteningly large group reporting no or trivial income.) But these data are an implausible proxy for initial conditions around 1940. We have seen that there was a sharp narrowing of income dispersions generally beginning around 1930 and ending around 1940, so the 1950 distribution is more likely to typify the end rather than the beginning of our 30-year period.

The way I took out of this difficulty is as follows. For the early 1920s data are available on several important correlates of SD2095 in 1950. The 1920 counterparts are then weighted and summed to generate an estimate of SD2095 for 1920 (see note to Table 13). This is then averaged with the 1950 value to generate the variable used in the regression. In substance, we are assuming that policy decisions made in 1940 respond to about half of the profound change in inequality that occurred during the depression and World War II.

[56] This procedure confines any state-specific effect to the residual of the regression, thereby avoiding any obvious bias of the coefficients.

TABLE 13.   Regressions of State and Local Government Expenditures/ State Personal Income (48 States, 1942–1972)

Form of Dependent Variable	1942, 1957, 1972 Average		1972	(1972)– ½(1942)	1972–1942	
Model	Complete Adjustment after 15 Years		Complete Adjustment, 30 Years	50% Adjustment, 30 Years	Indefinite Adjustment	
Independent Variables	(1)	(2)	(3)	(4)	(5)	(6)
POP	−.73	−.82	−.41	−.35	−.29	−.14
	2.65	3.21	.31	.29	.25	.12
ED	.35	.47	.35	.35	.34	.13
	.60	.80	.37	.41	.41	.16
SD2095	2.05	2.06	−6.50	−6.56	−6.61	−6.98
	.33	.33	.68	.76	.79	.84
SH5	−8.02		−7.45	1.36	10.18	
	.82		.53	.11	.82	
R^2	.26	.25	.12	.10	.10	.08
SE	1.71	1.71	2.67	2.39	2.32	2.31

Notes: The dependent variables are constructed from the ratio of general expenditures by state and local governments in a state to that state's disposable personal income ($\times$ 100). Government expenditures are from the U.S. Bureau of the Census, Census of Governments (various years), while personal income is from U.S. Bureau of the Census, Survey of Current Business (various years). Columns (1) to (5) are variants of the partial adjustment model:

$$g_{72} - g_{42} = k(g^* - g_{42}),$$

where g_t is this ratio for year t, g^* is its target, and k is a fractional adjustment coefficient. This can be expressed

$$g_{72} - jg_{42} = kg^*, \quad j = (1 - k)$$

and the variables in (2) and (5) are constructed accordingly. In column (1), g_{57}, represented by an average centered on 1957 to reduce error, replaces g_{72} and k is set = 1.

Independent Variables

ED: Mean years of schooling attained by population over 27 in 1940 from U.S. Bureau of the Census, Census of Population. State Volumes. For college graduates, I assume 90% complete 16 years and 10% 17 years.

SD2095: Average of 1950 value and ca. 1920–1930 estimate of the standard deviation of log of income of male heads of households in the 20th to 95th percentile of the income distribution. 1950 data are from Census of Population. State Volumes, supra, which gives a distribution by dollar intervals. For each state, a continuous function was fit to these data by method of cubic splices up to the open-ended upper income interval; this latter was approximated by a Pareto distribution. From this, we were able to estimate income = $f(R)$ where R is an individual's ranking in the distribution. For this purpose, each state's population was set = 1000, and we computed SD2095 from $f(200), f(201), \ldots f(950)$.

The 1920 value is estimated from

$$SD2095_{20} = A + \Sigma \, b_i X_{i, 1920},$$

TABLE 13.   *(continued)*

where the X_i are

1. log of per capita income.
2. $\sqrt{[w(1-w)]}$, w = proportion of population white.
3. $\{\sqrt{[f(1-f)]}|I_f - I_0|\}$, f = proportion farmers, I_f, I_0 is log of per capita income of farmers and other respectively. (The motivation for the square root constructs is that, if the only source of dispersion in the population is, for example, $I_f \neq I_0$, this formula gives the standard deviation of log income in the population.)
4. SH5 (see below).

With the exception of w, which is from U.S. Bureau of the Census, Historical Statistics of the U.S. (various years), all these variables are from Leven, Income in the Various States (1925). The b_i are coefficients from a regression of the 1950 SD2095 on the 1950 counterparts to X_i ($R^2 = .9$ and all coefficients were significant).

(The coefficient of $\sqrt{[w(1-w)]}$ was multiplied by 1.5. In principle, this variable should include an income difference term like that in 3. I had to exclude such a term because the 1920 counterpart does not exist. The 1950 coefficient therefore includes the average racial income difference. For the mid-1930s, when the first racial income data are available, that difference is around 1.5 × that of 1950). A is set so that the mean of the 1920 estimate = .53, which is the value for the first comparable U.S. income distribution (1929).

SH5: share of state income of wealthiest 5%, average of 1950 and 1920. The 1950 value is from $f(R)$, described above, and the 1920 value is from Leven, *supra*. (It is restricted to nonfarm incomes.)

POP: log of state population in 1942, or (columns (3)–(6)) change between 1942 and 1972. From U.S. Bureau of the Census, Statistical Abstract (various years). The means (standard deviations) of the variables are: Average of $g_{72,42,57} = 14.7$ (1.9); $g_{72} - g_{42} = 11.8$ (2.3); ED = 8.40 (.89); SD2095 = .451 (.083); SH5 = .246 (.031).

t-ratios are below coefficients.

ever, a substantial negative correlation (around $-.9$) between ED and SD2095, which may be helping to obscure their independent effects.

The negative correlation between education and inequality may be a systematic outcome of the human-capital accumulation process.[57] If this is so, it raises not only statistical problems but important interpretive problems for our previous results of a fairly consistent negative correlation between inequality and government/GNP. But if inequality and education are also negatively related, could not part of the nega-

---

[57] In what Gary S. Becker, Human Capital (1975), terms the "egalitarian approach" to human capital accumulation, interpersonal differences in the costs of funds are the major determinants of differences in education. So those with a lower cost of funds buy more education and, at least on the margin, earn lower rates of return. *Ceteris paribus*, the income distribution is more equal, the lower the rate of return. Becker cites scattered evidence of a decline over time in rates of return, which, given the simultaneous spread of education, would seem consistent with the "egalitarian approach." Barry R. Chiswick, Income Inequality: Regional Analyses within a Human Capital Framework (Nat'l Bureau Econ. Research, 1974), shows a strong negative correlation between rates of return and mean education across states, which is also consistent with the egalitarian approach. In his work, this rate of return × standard deviation of education is the crucial systematic determinant of income inequality. Since schooling inequality and mean schooling are uncorrelated, the clear implication is that the negative schooling–income inequality relationship which we observe is driven by the tendency for more schooling to lower rates of return.

tive correlation reflect the effects of increased education (political "ability")? To be sure, increased education may have been partially reflected in the typically positive "trend" components of the time-series regression. Our cross-sectional data, however, raise the possibility that inequality is a better proxy for ability than simple trend. A still more subtle possibility, encountered both in the Japanese data and the theory, is summarized by (14') and (23). Perhaps there is no simple relationship between the size of government, on the one hand, and inequality and ability, on the other. Rather, the latter two interact. Explicitly the general scheme estimated in Table 13 is

$$g = a \cdot \text{ABILITY} + b \cdot \text{INEQUALITY} + X, \tag{24}$$

where X = other factors influencing the size of government (g)

a, b = constants, $a > 0$, b?

In spite of our attempt to decompose INEQUALITY, measures like SD2095 tend to be highly correlated with any summary measure of the whole income distribution, like SD0100. So, if SD2095 is our proxy for "INEQUALITY," b will absorb both within- and between-group effects. But if increased ability—whether due to a shift to democracy, as in Japan, or to more education—raises the marginal political impact of g, then (14') and (23) tell us that the weight on the within-group effect is increased. Since this effect is negative, (23) would imply the approximation

$$b = b_0 + b_1 \cdot \text{ABILITY}; \quad b_1 < 0, \quad b_0? \tag{25}$$

The second term here approximates the derivative in (23); it says that an increase in ability enhances the stimulative effect of equality on the size of government. (Since b_0 still contains both within- and between-group effects, its sign remains uncertain.) Substitution of (25) into (24) yields

$$\begin{aligned} g = a \cdot \text{ABILITY} + b_0 \cdot \text{INEQUALITY} \\ + b_1 \cdot (\text{ABILITY} \cdot \text{INEQUALITY}) + X. \end{aligned} \tag{26}$$

The scheme in (26) is estimated in Table 14, and many of the uncertainties evident in Table 13 appear to be clarified. The explanatory power of the regressions in Table 14 (R^2, SE) increases substantially over their counterparts in Table 13, which lends credibility to the interactive scheme in (26). The precision of the coefficients is correspondingly improved, allowing some conclusions:

TABLE 14.   State and Local Government Expenditures/
Personal Income Regressions

Form of Dependent Variable	1942, 1957, 1972 Average		1972	(1972)– ½(1942)	1972–1942	
Model	Complete Adjustment after 15 Years		Complete Adjustment, 30 Years	50% Adjustment 30 Years	Indefinite Adjustment	
Independent Variables	(1)	(2)	(3)	(4)	(5)	(6)
POP	−.71	−.75	−.67	−.60	−.53	−.27
	2.69	3.10	.53	.54	0.49	0.24
ED	4.51	4.71	7.27	7.10	6.92	5.81
	2.39	2.59	2.48	2.74	2.75	2.39
SD2095	72.11	74.50	109.88	107.02	104.17	90.65
	2.33	2.47	2.29	2.53	2.54	2.23
ED × SD2095	−9.01	−9.32	−14.98	−14.62	−14.26	−12.60
	2.30	2.45	2.47	2.74	2.75	2.45
SH5	−4.07		−.01	8.62	17.26	
	0.43		0.00	.71	1.46	
R^2	.34	.34	.23	.24	.23	.19
SE	1.63	1.62	2.52	2.22	2.16	2.19

Notes: See Table 13 and text for definitions and sources of variables.

1. The coefficient of ED is now always significantly positive, as the theory implies, if ED is a proxy for "ability."

2. There is some evidence for a positive between-group inequality effect. Most of this evidence derives from the significantly positive coefficient of SD2095, which is the counterpart to b_0 in (25). This says that, at low levels of ability, more inequality *increases* the size of government. An effort to further isolate this between-group effect in the coefficient of SH5 yields mixed results. The coefficient varies from insignificantly negative to "suggestively" positive, depending on the form of the dependent variable. If SH5 is deleted, none of the other coefficients changes very much.

3. Most important, the significant negative coefficient of the interaction term corroborates what we found in the Japanese data: The within-group effect gets stronger (and eventually outweighs the between-group effect) the more "able" the populace.

4. We are unable to pin down the relevant lag structure. The various lag structures explain the data about equally well,[58] and the pattern of the coefficients provides no further illumination.[59] Some experimentation with different lags than those assumed in Table 14 did, however, suggest that very short lags in response were inappropriate.[60]

Table 14 shows that the concept of "ability" is important both in its own right and on account of its interaction with equality. I therefore try to improve the simple proxy used in Table 14 (education). The theoretical concept can, after all, comprehend any factor facilitating the political repayment of benefits. In Table 15, I consider two additional factors that might have such potential: voter participation and the size of organized interest groups (specifically labor unions and farmer cooperatives). The historical evidence did not imply an important role for voter turnout, but the cross-section data permit a more refined test. There is also a historical motivation for the interest-group variables. The early twentieth-century expansion of government coincides with the emergence of broad-based interest groups, like labor and farm organizations, which successfully exerted influence on the political process. By 1940, the start of our period of analysis for the states, these groups had attained roughly their present size. I want to see if the influence they subsequently exerted at the local level led to a net expansion of local governments. Also, since these groups did not organize primarily for local political action, we can distinguish the impact of organized interests on the growth of government from any stimulus to such organization provided by that growth. (For similar reasons, I use voter participation in presidential, rather than purely local, elections.)

The empirical implementation follows (26) except that an index is the proxy for "ability" instead of a single variable. Specifically,

---

[58] Regressions (3)–(5) of Table 14 purport to explain g_{1972}. When we generate predicted values of this variable and compare them to the actual g_{1972}, we get roughly the same standard errors (2.52, 2.38, and 2.41, respectively). Regression (1) explains a different variable, $\bar{g}_{1942,57,72}$. However, if one (a) assumes that standard deviations of g are proportional to means and then (b) synthesizes a $\bar{g}$ with the same mean and variance as g_{1972}, the standard error of that synthetic variable from regression (1) would also be about the same (2.33) as the others.

[59] In the lagged-adjustment model, the implied coefficient of the target g = regression coefficient/adjustment coefficient. Thus, if the regression coefficients increased roughly in proportion to the assumed adjustment coefficient, we would at least know something about the target g, even if we could not specify how quickly the adjustment proceeded. However, the regression coefficients are largely invariant to the assumed adjustment coefficient.

[60] For example, when the dependent and independent variables were made contemporaneous, the precision of the regression coefficients and the overall fit of the regression tended to deteriorate, though the overall pattern of the results was the same as in Table 14.

$$\text{ABILITY} = \text{ED} + c_1 \text{VPAR} + c_2 \text{FARM} + c_3 \text{LABOR}, \qquad (27)$$

where the c_i are weights, measured as fractions of the weight on ED, and VPAR = ratio of votes cast in the 1940, 1944, and 1948 presidential elections to the population over twenty-one in each state.

FARM and LABOR equal the ratio of membership in farm cooperatives and labor unions respectively to the population of the state.[61] When (27) is substituted back into (26), we get

TABLE 15.   State and Local Government Expenditures Regressions with Added Political Ability Variables

Dependent Variables	1942, 1957, 1972 Average		1972–1942 Change	
Independent Variables (Coefficient Symbol, Equation (28))	(1)	Weights for Ability Index (2)	(3)	Weights for Ability Index (4)
POP	−.69		−1.23	
	2.41		1.10	
	[3.05]			
Ability Index: (a)	.86		1.09	
	3.95		3.78	
	[4.58]		[4.41]	
VPAR (c_1)		−.77		−.97
		3.05		3.60
FARM (c_2)		.73		−.11
		2.03		.37
LABOR (c_3)		.16		.21
		.60		.98
SD2095 (b_0)	186.95		15.50	
	2.24		0.15	
	[4.37]		[2.21]	
SD2095 × Ability (b_1)	−1.78		−2.23	
	2.24		3.51	
	[4.38]		[4.05]	
SH5	12.00		24.67	
	1.24		1.93	
	[1.30]		[2.41]	
R^2	.51			.40
SE	1.46			1.53

Note: See text and Table 13 for sources and definitions of variables.
The numbers in brackets are t-ratios calculated on the assumption that the index weights are known beforehand. They are obtained by computing the ability index for each state and substituting the index for ED in ordinary least squares regressions like those in Table 14.

[61] To avoid distortion by one-party dominance in the South in the 1940s, I calculate VPAR for the 1968 election for the southern states. I then multiply the ratio of

$$g = [a \cdot \text{ED} + \Sigma a \cdot c_i A_i] + b_0 \cdot \text{INEQUALITY} +$$
$$[b_1 \text{ED} \cdot \text{INEQUALITY} + \Sigma b_1 c_i A_i \cdot \text{INEQUALITY}] + X,$$
$$(28)$$

where A_i are the three additional components of the ability index. The resulting overidentified scheme is then estimated by nonlinear least squares, where the restrictions in (28) (that the c_i in the two bracketed expressions be the same) are imposed. To facilitate comparisons, ED and the A_i are each entered as standardized variables with the mean equal to 100 and standard deviation equal to 10. Thus $c_1 = .5$ would mean that if VPAR is one standard deviation above the mean, ability is enhanced by half as much as if ED is a standard deviation above the mean.

The results, for two forms of the dependent variable, the 1942–1972 average level and 1942–1972 change, are summarized in Table 15. There is another substantial improvement in explanatory power and in the precision of the ability and inequality coefficients. Our confidence in the crucial result of Table 14—that ability and within-group inequality interact negatively—is clearly strengthened by Table 15. In addition, the role of the wealthiest citizens as tempting targets for taxation seems better defined here than in Table 14; the coefficient on SH5 is consistently positive. All this is compatible with the notion that changes in the political process, as well as in personal capabilities of voters, play a role in the growth of government. But the nature of this role seems peculiar. The role of organized interest seems generally weak, statistically and numerically. The one exception of the large and significant impact of farm cooperatives on the level of government (column (2)) does not carry over to the change (column (4)). The unexpected result of a consistent and strong *negative* effect of voter participation on expenditures deserves more study than I can give it here. It is broadly consistent with certain nineteenth-century historical facts. Recall that Britain had a rapidly expanding franchise in the nineteenth century, while the United States did not, and apparently experienced a sharper contraction in the size of government. The result is also consistent with the spirit of bureaucratic-monopoly models, such as Niskanen's or Peacock and Wiseman's,[62] which have at their

---

VPAR in a state to the national average in 1968 by the national average for the 1940 elections to get es'imates of the "true" VPAR in the South for those years.

    Data on membership in labor unions and farm cooperatives are unavailable for the early 1940s, so I use the earliest available dates (1960 for cooperatives and 1964 for unions). All data are from Statistical Abstract.

    [62] Niskanen, *supra* note 3; and Peacock & Wiseman, *supra* note 1.

core the notion of government expansion being antithetical to the interest of the broad mass of citizens. Our result implies that when the masses indicate they have sufficiently overcome their "rational ignorance" to come to the polls, the political process pays more heed to their interest.

There would then remain the question of just whose interest the political process is serving. It could not plausibly be just the bureaucracy's, given the empirical importance of broad measures of education and income equality. But our theory does not require that everyone in a specific income-education range be a beneficiary either. In fact, the technology of government, in which benefits are conferred through specific programs, rather than per capita grants, pretty much rules this out. One plausible interpretation of Table 15 is that government expands when specific programs attract a sufficiently broad constituency, but this constituency is always smaller than a majority of voters. However, a bigger potential coalition is better than a smaller one, and the chances for forming a successful coalition would be greater the larger the pool of voters who are prime potential beneficiaries. In our analysis, the size of this pool is larger the more educated voters with similar economic interests there are.

I now address the issue of the quantitative, as opposed to the statistical, significance of the ability-inequality nexus uncovered in Tables 14 and 15. Specifically, do the results explain any substantial part of the recent growth of government, or are the ability-inequality effects merely a sideshow on how spending is distributed among locales? This question is relevant for two reasons. First, even if ability, inequality, and their interaction help explain variation in the size and growth of local government, we have already noted there is not much variation to explain. Since the similarity among states is more notable than their differences, our regression can be measuring empirically trivial deviations from an all-important average. Second, the results imply that changes in inequality or ability, standing alone, have no clear-cut empirical implications for the size or growth of local government. This is most clear in Table 13 and confirmed by measuring the partial effects of either inequality or ability in Table 14 or 15 at the sample means (they are essentially nil). The issue of empirical significance thus rests on the importance of the interaction effect when there are substantial changes in *both* inequality and ability. Even at this level, the issue has no clear *a priori* answer. The differential form of (26) is

$$\Delta g = \Delta \text{ABILITY} \, [a + b_1 \cdot \text{INEQUALITY}] \\ + \Delta \text{INEQUALITY} \, [b_0 + b_1(\text{ABILITY} + \Delta \text{ABILITY})].$$

$$(26')$$

Since we find a, $b_0 > 0$ and $b_1 < 0$, there is no obvious prediction even for the direction of Δg.

To get at the empirical import of the results, I use the coefficients in Tables 14 and 15 to estimate the effects of the sorts of changes that have characterized the relevant history, namely an increase in education or ability coupled with a decrease in income inequality. Specifically, for Table 14 I ask: what is the predicted effect on the level (column (1) is the relevant regression) or the change (column (6)) in the size of government if education increases two standard deviations while inequality (SD2095 and SH5) decreases two standard deviations from the sample mean: The effect on the level is +4.28 percentage points and on the change +6.57 percentage points. For Table 15, we can perform a similar exercise in which the ability index, is also increased by two standard deviations. The results are +8.05 for level and +7.36 for change.

There are three points to note about these results.

1. The effects are substantial by any measure, running between 2.6 and 5.5 times the relevant regression standard errors. The effects on the level are between 30 and 60 per cent of the sample mean, and on the change about 60 or 70 per cent of the mean. Put differently, the level regressions purport to describe the change over the fifteen years from 1942 to 1957, while the change regressions pertain to 1942–1972. The 1942–1957 actual change is around +6.0 and the 1942–1972 change around +12.0. If our simulated ability-inequality changes accurately describe what went on in the interwar period, the regression parameters account for over half of the subsequent growth of government.

2. Our simulation roughly corresponds to the relevant historical change. For example, the simulated change in education is a little less than +2 years. Whereas we do not have pre-1940 data on ED, we know that mean schooling has been rising at over one year per decade subsequently (from 8½ years in 1940 to over 12 in 1970). We also know that prior to World War I no more than 5 per cent of seventeen-year olds were graduating from high school and that secondary school enrollment was also only 5 per cent of elementary school enrollment. So extrapolating the post-1940 experience back to around 1920, as done in the simulations, could not be far off the mark. Our assumed changes in inequality and the ability index are also reasonably accurate caricatures of the relevant history.[63]

---

[63] For SD2095 and SH5 our simulations entail decreases of .16 and .06, respectively. The former roughly corresponds to the actual change between 1930 and 1950, so we may be overstating the pre-1940 change. The latter figure describes roughly what occurs between 1930 and 1942; this series is shown in Figure IV. We have almost surely understated the historical change in the ability index. The relevant history is a change of around +2 SD for ED and unionization, +1 for farm cooperatives, and 0 for

3. The driving force behind our results is the negative effect of the interaction between education-ability and inequality. The combination of increasing education-ability and decreasing inequality decreases their product and thereby accounts for the bulk of the historical growth in government that the cross-section results can rationalize. Consequently, considerable weight must be given to the confluence of these two forces, rather than to either separately, in any explanation of the growth of government.[64]

D. The Less Developed Countries (LDCs)

The less developed countries (LDCs) pose a severe test of our model, perhaps too severe. Quite apart from the data problems, which are discussed subsequently, one can be skeptical whether the same processes that affect the size of government in the developed countries (DCs) carry over more or less intact to societies with markedly different economic and political structures. Yet the severity of the test is also an attraction, one that is enhanced by the diversity of LDCs. While they differ on average from the DCs in most measures of political and economic development, they also span a much wider range—from countries with living standards only moderately below the DCs to those with virtually all the population in subsistence agriculture, from democracies to dictatorships, from income distributions more equal than those in the DCs to inequality far exceeding any recorded in the DCs over the last century. This enormous diversity creates a special opportunity to clarify the relative impact of political institutions and personal "abilities" on the growth of government. So far we have been able to treat this issue only in the context of isolated events (for example, the

---

VPAR. If we sum these changes with the weights in columns (2) or (4) of Table 15, we would get changes in the index of around $+30$ or $+20$, respectively. The simulations entail changes only two-thirds as large.

[64] I attempted unsuccessfully to replicate the results in Tables 14 and 15 for the developed country cross section. I first constructed an inequality index $= L + 6 \cdot \varnothing$ which seems to be roughly the weighting scheme implied by the regressions in Table 12. Then I constructed an ability index: a simple average of standardized indices of newspaper circulation per person over 25 and school attendance per person under 15. When these two variables and their interaction were entered in a regression like 10 in Table 12, none of the coefficients was significant. However, when the interaction term was dropped, both of the remaining variables had significant *negative* coefficients and the R^2 increased from .8 in Table 12 to about .9. This implies that the "ability" index may be improving our inequality measure: as in our state and local data, "ability" and inequality are negatively $(-.5)$ correlated in this sample. If our ability measure is partly a proxy for inequality, detection of the interaction effect would be difficult, since inequality would interact with itself rather than with "ability."

advent of Japanese democracy) or fairly homogeneous populations (for example, education differences across American states).

The basic facts about the size of government in the LDCs can be summarized succinctly. They are neither as large nor growing as rapidly relative to GDP as those in the DCs.

1. In the sample we will analyze (42 LDCs in the decade 1960–1970), the average government/GDP ratio is 17.6 per cent, or about half that of our DC sample (see Table 2).

2. There is substantially more diversity among the LDCs, at least relative to the lower mean. The standard deviation of government/GDP for the LDCs is 5.1 per cent, which is comparable to that for the DCs, so the coefficient of variation is about double that of the DCs.

3. The average 1960–1970 growth in government/GDP in the LDCs tends to be smaller than for the DCs; the mean change (standard deviation) is +3.4 (2.2) percentage points.

This combination of small and slowly growing governments is somewhat reminiscent of the pre-1920 history of the Western DCs (and of Japan for most of the twentieth century). And the crude data on LDC income distributions seem compatible with the explanation offered for DC history. A within-group measure of inequality which we subsequently exploit is the ratio of eighth to third decile incomes. This exceeds 3, on average, for the LDCs versus 2+ for the DCs. (The same sort of difference holds for the upper tail: the average share of income for the tenth decile is 39 per cent for the LDCs and 25 per cent for the DCs.) But there is considerable overlap in the two samples, and, of course, much more than differences in income inequality distinguish them. So the crude consistency ought to be greeted cautiously. We are on even slipperier ground with the changes in inequality in the LDCs. The earlier history of the DCs, the more recent experience of Japan and Kuznets's elaboration of the conflicting implications of development for inequality are all we have to create a presumption that nothing like the pervasive shrinking of inequality in the DCs has gone on in the LDCs.

My strategy in analyzing the LDC data is to replicate the analysis of the U.S. state and local government data, thereby forcing a comparison between the most and least homogeneous samples. Analogues to the variables in (26) (namely, ABILITY, INEQUALITY) are required, thus entailing considerable compromise with the poor quality of LDC data. For example, while there are published income distributions for most LDCs, there is none of the refinement of their conceptual differences as in the Lydall-Sawyer data for the DCs.[65] Nevertheless, I take from these raw data the ratio of income in the 70–80

---

[65] Sawyer, *supra* note 47; Lydall, *supra* note 28.

percentile of the distribution to income in the 20–30 percentile (R83) as a proxy for "within-group" inequality. (See notes to Table 16 for details on this and the other variables discussed below.) In preliminary work, I also used the tenth decile share as a proxy for between-group inequality. Since this variable proved even less helpful than its analogue in the state and local data (SH5), none of the results reported here use it.

I supplemented R83 with the same sort of nonmonotonic transform $\sqrt{x(1-x)}$ of the agricultural share of the population that proved useful in estimating U.S. income distributions and is suggested by Kuznets's work.[66] Here some facts about LDCs are useful. Most have substantial agricultural population shares (about 50 per cent on average), but they span virtually all of the relevant range. In addition, a large share of the typical LDC's farmers are in a "traditional" or subsistence sector where income differences with the rest of the economy are especially great. Accordingly, I use for "x" above the share of the population in this traditional sector as estimated by Adelman and Morris.[67] I then simply average indexes of this variable and R83 to construct an index of INEQUALITY (see below for refinements).

An ABILITY proxy for the LDCs should make use of the considerable variety of their political institutions as well as of relevant population characteristics. Therefore, I constructed an ABILITY measure which weights the two kinds of ability equally. "Political ability" is an average of two indexes constructed by Adelman and Morris of the "strength of democratic institutions" and of the "degree of freedom of political opposition and press."[68] These indexes contain large subjective elements but are at least independent of this study and may shed light on a major unresolved question: does more active representation of broad groups of potential beneficiaries ("democracy") stimulate the growth of government? Data on educational attainment, the personal-ability proxy used in Table 14, are too fragmentary to permit a direct analogue. Accordingly, I used an average of two proxies for personal ability, the fraction of the literate population and an Adelman-Morris index of the "effect of mass communication" (essentially a weighted average of newspaper circulation and radio ownership per capita).[69] The ABILITY measure is the average of the "political" and "personal" ability indexes.

[66] See text at note 26 *supra*.

[67] Irma Adelman & Cynthia Taft Morris, Society, Politics, and Economic Development: A Quantitative Approach (1971). Data on income differences between sectors are unavailable.

[68] See *id.*

[69] In the subsample of countries where median schooling attainment is available, the simple correlation with either proxy is about .9.

TABLE 16. Government Expenditures/GDP Regressions
42 Less Developed Countries, 1960–1970

Form of Dependent Variable	1960–70 Average	1970	1970–½(1960)	1970–1960
Model	Complete Adjustment, 5 Years	Complete Adjustment, 10 Years	50% Adjustment, 10 Years	Indefinite Adjustment
Independent Variables	(1)	(2)	(3)	(4)
POP	−.28	−.30	−.17	−.05
	.69	.67	.58	.20
MODERN	.18	.18	.10	.01
	2.61	2.40	1.88	.21
MODERN 2	−.10	−.10	−.05	−.01
	.93	.86	.69	.10
ABILITY	−.06	−.04	.01	.05
	.56	.30	.07	.78
INEQUALITY	−.26	−.32	−.22	−.13
	2.90	3.23	3.37	2.47
R^2	.54	.55	.54	.30
SE	3.66	4.08	2.72	2.08

Notes:
Definitions and Sources of Variables
Independent variables are derived from the 1960 and 1970 ratios × 100 of current government
revenue from domestic sources to GDP, from United Nations Yearbook of National Account
Statistics (various years). Revenue rather than expenditures is used, because data on capital
expenditures are sketchy and, where available, they imply that capital expenditures are financed mainly from current revenues. In the rare case where current expenditures exceeded
current revenues, the former is used.
For some countries, either 1960 or 1970 government revenue data are unavailable. If data over an
interval of at least 5 years are unavailable, the country is excluded. Otherwise, I computed the
ratio of government revenue to government consumption in the first or last available year and
multiplied government consumption in the terminal year by this ratio. In two cases (Israel and
South Vietnam), I extrapolated the 1960–1966 growth in government/GDP to 1970 to elimi-
nate the effects of post-1966 wars.
Independent Variables
POP: Log of 1960 population. Statistical Yearbook, *supra*.
ABILITY: Average of four indexes, each normalized to mean = 100, standard deviation = 10. The
components are:
  1) *Democracy:* An index of the "strength of democratic institutions" which ranges 0–100 from
  I. Adelman & C. T. Morris, Society, Politics, and Economic Development: A Quantitative
  Approach (1971) (hereinafter cited as AM). Their sample covers about three-fourths of mine.
  For the remainder (non-AM countries) I first regressed the AM index on a set of dummy
  variables which were based on my reading of each country's political history in Political
  Handbook of the World: 1975, (Arthur S. Banks ed. 1975).
    (a) Degree of party competition: +1 if, *ca.* the early 1960s, a democratically elected parlia-
    ment wielded effective political power; −1 if power was held by one person or party and
    rivals were outlawed; 0 for intermediate cases.
    (b) Post-World War II history of party competition: +1 if a multiparty democracy had pre-
    vailed for the whole period; −1 if the country had always been a dictatorship; 0 if some
    party rivalry had occurred for some of the period.
    (c) Press freedom: +1 if, up to the early 1960s, the press was largely free of government
    control; −1 if the press was government controlled; 0 for intermediate cases.
    (d) Military coups: −1 if a military coup had been attempted since World War II; +1 if a
    military coup had never been attempted up to 1965; 0 for doubtful cases (for example,
    civilian disturbances with military participation).

TABLE 16.   *(continued)*

   (e) Coups in one-party states: -1 if a coup had *not* been attempted in a one-party state, 0
       otherwise. The notion here is that military opposition to a dictator means more "democ-
       racy" than a totally unopposed dictatorship.
   (f) Log of GDP per capita in 1963 in U.S. dollars, to capture any positive income elasticity
       of democracy. The regression ($R^2 = .7$) coefficients were then used to generate an esti-
       mate of the "democracy index" for non-AM countries.
2) *Freedom of Political Opposition and of Press:* Index from AM with estimates for non-AM
   sample from regression technique described above. The independent variables for the estimating regression are the same as above ($R^2 = .5$).
3) *Extent of Mass Communication:* Index from AM, for non-AM countries a regression estimate of the AM index is used. The independent variables in the estimating regression ($R^2 =$
   .95) were the logs of per capita newspaper circulation and radio ownership (from UNESCO,
   Statistical Yearbook, various years)—that is, the AM index is essentially a weighted average
   of newspaper and radio use.
4) *Literacy:* Percentage of population literate *ca.* 1960 (UNESCO, Statistical Yearbook, various
   years).
MODERN: Weighted average of two AM indexes. The level of modernization of techniques in
(1) agriculture and (2) industry. The weights are the percentage of population in agricultural
and nonagricultural sectors. For non-AM countries, a regression estimate of the AM index (on
log per capita GDP, $R^2 = .6$) is used.
MODERN 2: MODERN-$\overline{\text{MODERN}}$ if this difference > 0; 0 otherwise.
INEQUALITY: This is an average of two standardized (Mean = 100, S.D. = 10) indexes based on:
1) R83, the ratio of the share of income in the 8th to the share in the 3rd decile of the income
   distribution. The main data source is Shail Jain, Size Distribution of Income: A Compilation
   of Data (World Bank, 1975), which gives decile share estimates for most published income
   distributions. Where possible, I use a national household distribution *ca.* 1960. (Alternatives
   in order of preference are national population, urban households, national income recipients. For the latter 0.3% is added to the 3rd decile share, because this was the average
   (significant) difference between income recipient and household 3rd decile shares where
   both are available for the same countries. No other similar difference among distributions
   was found.) For some countries data are from a similar, partly overlapping, compendium in
   Irma Adelman & Cynthia T. Morris, Economic Growth and Social Equity in Developing
   Countries (1973) (hereinafter cited as AM2). They provide five points on the cumulative
   income distribution, rather than decile shares. To estimate the relevant decile shares, I first
   regressed the logs of the shares in Jain on the logs of the five values in AM2 for the 16 cases
   where both summarize the same distribution ($R^2 > .9$, SE $< .05$ for both decile shares),
   then I used the regression coefficients as weights to estimate 3rd and 8th decile shares from
   the AM2 data for other countries. The Jain and AM2 data cover about three-fourths of our
   sample. For the remainder, I averaged available estimates of R for countries in the same
   region at roughly the same level of per capita GDP.
2) $\sqrt{[t(1-t)]}$, where t = percentage of population in traditional agriculture, as estimated by
   AM. For non-AM countries, estimates are based on weights from a regression of the AM
   estimate (on the percentage of the population in agriculture and log per capita GDP, $R^2 =$
   .8). The sample comprises the following 42 countries:

Argentina	Israel	Singapore
Barbados	Jamaica	South Africa
Bolivia	Jordan	South Vietnam
Burma	Korea (Republic of)	Southern Rhodesia
Chile	Malaysia	Spain
Colombia	Malta	China (Taiwan)
Costa Rica	Nicaragua	Tanzania
Dominican Republic	Nigeria	Thailand
Ecuador	Panama	Togo
Greece	Paraguay	Trinidad
Guatemala	Peru	Tunisia
Guyana	Philippines	Turkey
Honduras	Portugal	Uruguay
India	Sierra Leone	Venezuela

My only substantive departure from the analysis of U.S. local governments is to add variables reflecting the level of economic development and, implicitly, tax collection costs. The motive is to use this diverse sample to elaborate on two aspects of the earlier data: Japan's atypical pre-World War I growth of government and the general absence among DCs and U.S. states of any correlation between per capita income and the relative size of governments. Taken together, these two factors seemed to imply that major income-related reductions in revenue-raising costs occur only fairly early in the development process. To verify the implication, I use two variables. One is an index of the extent to which the economy has adopted "modern" techniques,[70] which presumably entail monetary exchange, modern record keeping, and so forth and hence serve as a proxy for tax collection costs. The second is simply this variable less its sample mean for countries with above average modernization. If tax-collection-cost economies diminish with development, the first variable should have a positive partial correlation and the second a negative partial correlation with the size of government.

All of these variables are defined *circa* 1960 and are used to explain the size and growth of govern.nent in the subsequent decade, which is about as long a period as the data permit.[71] Our sample consists of forty-two LDCs for which government budget data are available and which were substantively independent political entities around 1960.[72] The analogues to the regressions in Table 13, which implement equation (24), are in Table 16. One notable difference from Table 13, where essentially nothing but population worked,[73] is the consistently negative correlation between inequality and either the size or growth of government. We also find a pattern of coefficients for

[70] This is a weighted average of two Adelman-Morris indexes, *supra* note 67: the "level of modernization of industry" and of agriculture, with urban-rural population shares as weights.

[71] Pre-1960 budget data are unavailable for most LDCs, and the gaps and reporting lags get more serious the closer we approach the present. In addition, the sharp rise in oil prices post 1973 leads to major departures from trend for revenues of some of the governments in our sample.

[72] That is, if the country was *de jure* a colony for a substantial part of the period, it had to have been granted at least local autonomy by around 1960 to be included in the sample. The *de facto ca.*-1960 status was determined from the country narratives in Political Handbook of the World: 1975 (Arthur S. Banks ed. 1975).

[73] The role of population here is less clear-cut than for U.S. states. In the public goods framework, there are both "set-up-cost" and density economies, and among U.S. states population and density are positively correlated. However, in this sample the smallest entities include some of the most densely populated (Barbados, Malta, Singapore). I include the population variable here only for the sake of completeness.

the tax-collection-cost proxies (MODERN, MODERN 2) consistent
with the hints in the Japanese, DC, and state data. That is, lower collection costs stimulate the growth of government (the coefficient of
MODERN is positive), but at what appears to be a diminishing rate
(the negative coefficient of MODERN 2 is insignificant). Table 16 duplicates the insignificant ABILITY effect of Table 13.

We learned from Table 14, however, to mistrust the too easy inference that effects of ability play no role in determining the size or
growth of government. Accordingly, Table 17 implements the interaction model of equation (26) on the LDC data, yielding a remarkable consistency with the results for U.S. states in Table 14: (1) The
ABILITY and INEQUALITY variables both tend to have significantly
positive coefficients as in Table 14. (2) The interaction effect (coefficient
of ABILITY × INEQUALITY) tends to be significantly negative as in
Table 14. (3) There is a substantial improvement in the fit of the Table
17 regressions over their Table 16 counterparts, again duplicating the
pattern for U.S. states.

TABLE 17.   LDC Government/GDP Regressions, with
             Ability-Inequality Interaction

Form of Dependent Variable	Average, 1960–70	1970	1970–½(1960)	1970–1960
Model	Complete Adjustment, 5 Years	Complete Adjustment, 10 Years	50% Adjustment, 10 Years	Indefinite Adjustment
Independent Variables	(1)	(2)	(3)	(4)
POP	.06	.04	−.00	−.05
	.16	.09	.01	.19
MODERN	.18	.19	.10	.01
	3.06	2.72	2.03	.21
MODERN 2	−.13	−.14	−.07	−.01
	1.40	1.25	.93	.10
ABILITY	3.29	3.31	1.68	.05
	3.29	2.89	2.09	.08
INEQUALITY	3.16	3.10	1.48	−.12
	3.10	2.65	1.82	−.18
ABILITY × INEQUALITY	−.034	−.034	−.017	−.001
	3.37	2.93	2.09	.01
R^2	.65	.64	.59	.30
SE	3.23	3.71	2.60	2.11

Note: See notes to Table 16 for definitions and sources of variables.

The only exception to these conclusions is in column (4) of Table 17, where the interaction model clearly fails to work. However, the indefinitely long adjustment process implied by column (4) seems to be an inappropriate characterization of the growth of LDC governments.[74] And this, too, appears reasonable. The rationale for a long drawn-out adjustment process is strongest when the determinants of the size of government have changed profoundly over a relatively short interval. This was true of the developed world, especially with respect to inequality, up to about 1950, but it is not obviously true of the LDCs. Although Table 17 does not permit pinning down the adjustment lag for the LDCs to anything closer than a five- to twenty-year range, it does rule out much longer lags. The LDCs thus appear to have adjusted faster to their smaller gap between actual and "desired" size of government than the DCs.

Finally, note that Table 17 is slightly more emphatic about the diminishing effect of tax collection costs. If we take the results for the MODERN variables at face value, they imply the marginal impact of "modernization" is only about one-fourth as great for the more developed LDCs as for the least developed. The implication for the historical experience is that Japanese government grew rapidly prior to World War I while Western governments did not, because Japan was then developing the sort of revenue-raising infrastructure that the others had achieved much earlier.

The results in Table 17 raise two questions:

(1) What is the relative importance of political ability (democracy, and so on) and personal ability (literacy, and so on)? An attempt to use the technique of Table 15 failed for the LDC data.[75] However, experimentation with different weights on the "political" and "personal" components of the ABILITY index revealed that both are important and that it is tolerably accurate to give them equal weight.[76] So these

[74] We can use the same test as for the state data (see note 58 *supra*). Note that columns (2)–(4) of Table 17 purport to explain Government/GDP for 1970. When we compute the standard error of the value of this variable predicted by each of these regressions we get 3.70 for (2), 3.87 for (3), and 4.82 for (4). So (2) and (3) do about equally well in explaining the data, but (4) is clearly inferior. Column (1) describes a different dependent variable (1960–70 average). To compare that regression with the others, we compute the standard error of this regression after adjusting the dependent variable to the same mean and variance as the 1970 variable. This turns out to be 3.93, or about the same as for (2) and (3).

[75] In an attempt to estimate the weights of the components of ABILITY and INEQUALITY, the nonlinear-least-squares regression failed to converge.

[76] For example, consider the following weighting schemes for the political (average of "democracy" and "freedom" indexes) and personal (average of "literacy" and "mass communications") components and the resulting R^2s for regressions otherwise identical to (2), Table 17.

LDC results are consistent with both the Japanese results, which isolated a political ability effect (the shift to democracy), and the U.S. state results, which isolate personal ability effects (education).

(2) Is the ability-inequality nexus important empirically? The LDC data suggest an even more positive answer than the state data. One useful formulation of the problem is to see if the results in Table 17 can rationalize any of the substantial difference in size of government between LDCs and DCs. Recall that the average DC government sector spends fully twice as large a fraction of GDP as the average LDC government. Therefore, I plugged values of the independent variables appropriate to the DCs into Table 17 regressions to obtain estimates of what the size of the average LDC government sector would be if these countries had the characteristics of DCs.[77]

For regression (1) Table 17, the results of this exercise were:

1) Average government/GDP, 1960–70, for LDCs   17.62%
2) Predicted change, if LDC industry became
     as modernized as DCs
     (MODERN = 100, MODERN 2 = 42)   +3.55
3) Predicted change, if LDC ABILITY and
     INEQUALITY = DC average   +12.49
4) Predicted government/GDP for LDC with
     DC characteristics (1 + 2 + 3)   33.7%
5) Actual average for 16 DCs, 1960–70   33.4

ABILITY =	
j POLITICAL + k PERSONAL	R^2
$j = 0$, $k = 1$	.607
$j = \frac{1}{4}$, $k = \frac{3}{4}$	.628
$j = \frac{1}{2}$, $k = \frac{1}{2}$ (as in Table 17)	.644
$j = \frac{3}{4}$, $k = \frac{1}{4}$	.648
$j = 1$, $k = 0$	.641

They suggest only that very low weights on the political variables are inappropriate. I conducted a similar exercise for the components of INEQUALITY (see note to Table 16). Here, too, nothing much improved on the equal weighting in Table 17, and only low weights on the R83 component could be ruled out.

[77] Specifically, the characteristics assumed for a DC are: (1) A fully modernized industrial structure. MODERN = 100. (2) A democratic society with no restraints on opposition or the press, that is, "democracy" and "freedom" indexes = 100. (3) A fully literate society. (4) A "mass communications" index as implied by the AM index and the average values of radio ownership and newspaper circulation for the DC sample of Table 12 (see note to Table 16). This index = 106. (5) A nominal .01 share of the population in subsistence agriculture. (6) The average value of R83 for the DCs in Sawyer's data (supra note 47).

For regression (2), which describes 1970 data, the counterparts to lines (1), (4), (5) above were:

1) Average government/GDP, LDCs, 1970		19.2%
4) Predicted 1970, DC characteristics		36.9
5) Actual average, 1970, DCs		36.7

(The relative magnitudes of the counterparts to lines (2) and (3) were roughly the same as above.)

The essential result is that we are able to rationalize *all* of the differences between DCs and LDCs, virtually to the decimal point. These remarkable[78] results suggest that the large behavioral differences between these two groups are really the outcomes of precisely the same process, one which is dominated by the ability-inequality nexus (compare lines (2) and (3) on previous page).

If that is so, there are some strong implications for the future growth of government in the LDCs. As (if) the LDCs' overall level of economic development, their degree of income inequality, and the "personal" characteristics of their populations approach those of contemporary DCs, the recent slow growth of LDCs' government sectors will accelerate. Whether the gap between them and contemporary DC governments closes completely depends on political developments that are difficult to predict. If there is no corresponding move toward more democratic political institutions at all, a nontrivial gap will remain.[79]

VI. Concluding Remarks

The broad conclusion to which our diverse data point is that governments grow where groups which share a common interest in that growth *and* can perceive and articulate that interest become more numerous. The view that sharp differences are (should be?) an important source of government sponsored redistribution seems to carry less weight. Our results do detect a stimulative role of inequality but only where the population is least capable of articulating support for more government spending.[80] As this capability increases, homogeneous in-

---

[78] There is one catch. The predicted values, line (4), are for an *equilibrium* size of government. But our analysis of DCs suggested that the *actual* values around 1970 or 1965 were subequilibrium.

[79] If one carries out the extrapolation above keeping the levels of "democracy" and "freedom" at the LDC sample mean, the predicted size of government is on the order of 5 percentage points less than on line (4).

[80] In both the U.S. state and LDC data, the net effect of more inequality on the size of government is positive only at below average levels of ability.

terests become a more important source of government growth. Our results imply that the *leveling* of income differences across a large part of the population—the growth of the "middle class"—has in fact been a major source of the growth of government in the developed world over the last fifty years. On our interpretation, this leveling process, which has characterized almost every economically developed society in the latter stages of industrialization, created the necessary conditions for growth of government: a broadening of the political base that stood to gain from redistribution generally and thus provided a fertile source of political support for expansion of specific programs. At the same time, these groups became more able to perceive and articulate that interest (as measured by, for example, educational attainment). On our interpretation, this simultaneous growth of "ability" served to catalyze politically the spreading economic interest in redistribution.

The counterintuitive result that, on balance, more equality breeds a political demand for still more income equalization runs through virtually all our data and proves capable of rationalizing a wide variety of experience—for example, why Britain's government declined in the early nineteenth century and grew in the twentieth, why Sweden's government has grown faster than ours, why the developed world has larger and more rapidly growing government sectors than the underdeveloped. The role we assert for "ability" as a catalyst for equality-induced growth also has a broad base of support, and the concept appears to comprehend attributes of both the political system and its constituency. We were able to see the catalyzing process at work in Japan, when it became a democracy, in the U.S. states with above average levels of education, and in less developed countries that were both more democratic and had better educated populations than is typical of that group. It is, in fact, the enormous diversity of experience that the ability-equality nexus proves capable of rationalizing, rather than any single result, that provides the main empirical message of this paper. This common process seems capable of rationalizing a substantial part of the differences among and between constituencies as diverse as local school boards, European welfare states, and traditional agricultural societies.

A caveat is in order, lest my conclusion be read as implying that all or even most members of groups which contribute support to growth of government have benefited from that growth. The "bourgeoisification" of Western societies widened the political base from which support for expansion of government could be drawn. But the particular programs that expand will, at least in each instance, benefit a subgroup. It is at least arguable, and compatible with "rational ignorance" in politics, that the net result is for a minority of the population to receive large per capita net benefits at the expense of the majority. Our one result relevant to this issue—that large voter turnout retards the growth of government—tends to support this view.

If the foregoing analysis is correct, it points to a future somewhat different from the recent past. In developed countries, the leveling process in the labor market has been far more gradual in the last quarter century than the preceding. At the same time, the scope for increased educational attainment of their population, at least in the United States (and Canada, Australia, and—to some extent—Britain) has narrowed. A high school education has become the norm, and the waves of the unschooled immigrants who produced the high school and college graduates of a subsequent generation have long since crested. If the twin forces of increased equality and increased education are indeed petering out, our analysis implies that the pressure for further growth of government is likely to abate in the developed world. It would be imprudent to try to be precise about this prediction, especially in light of our evidence that these forces can take considerable time to work themselves out and of our lack of success in pinning down just how long it is before they are spent. Nevertheless, it would be fair to infer from the evidence here that the next quarter century will witness a perceptible, perhaps substantial, deceleration of the relative growth of government in the developed world. If anything, this ought to be more profound in the United States than in Continental Europe, where there still may be some scope for the spread of education. The one exception is Japan, where the emergence of a broad middle class as a concomitant of a mature industrial economy seems to be a comparatively recent phenomenon, and where, in consequence, we are led to predict a narrowing in the gap between the size of its government sector and that of the Western democracies. With less confidence, we can also predict a narrowing of differences between the developed and less developed worlds.

The larger message of this paper is that there is nothing inevitable or inexorable about the growth of government, nor is there some arbitrarily limiting ratio of government to GNP.[81] Instead, our argument is that the size of government responds to the articulated interests of those who stand to gain or lose from politicization of the allocation of resources. The balance of those interests can make for declining governments, as they appear to have done in the last century, as well as for the growth we have experienced more recently.

[81] Not even 100 per cent. Government transfers, for example, can be taxed, retransferred, retaxed, and so on, so that the annual government budget can be a multiple of GNP. In fact, this ratio exceeds 1 in Israel currently.

Public Policies, Pressure Groups, and Dead Weight Costs

2

Gary S. Becker

I. Introduction

The activities of governments have grown remarkably rapidly in all Western countries during the twentieth century, especially during the last fifty years. This growth cannot be entirely explained by benevolent governments that maximize social welfare because subsidies to agriculture, restrictions on entry into the airline, trucking and other industries, duties on Japanese imports, and many other regulations and public activities are not consistent with any traditional social welfare function.

This failure of theories of benevolent government induced economists to join political scientists in searching for alternative ways to analyze actual government behavior. The usual alternative is a model of majority rule voting, either among the electorate or the legislature, as best illustrated by median voter theory. Another approach assumes that bureaucrats have the power to determine the enactment and implementation of many regulations and other legislation.

A third approach stresses the capacity of pressure groups to influence political outcomes as they jockey for political power. This approach received an early and vigorous formulation by Arthur Bentley (1908) that greatly affected the thinking of political scientists. I recently [Becker (1983)] published a paper that tries to model the competition among pressure groups for political influence in a more rigorous way.

Prepared for the Nobel Symposium on the Growth of Government, 15–17 August, 1984. Let me express appreciation to the commentators, James Mirrlees and Ingemar Ståhl for excellent comments, and to other participants at the Symposium for a lively discussion. I had valuable assistance from Gale Mosteller, and useful comments from Robert Barro, Michael Munger, Richard Posner, and George Stigler. My research was supported by the Center for the Study of the Economy and the State at the University of Chicago.

Reprinted with permission from the *Journal of Public Economics* 28 (1985): 329–47. © 1985 by Elsevier Science Publishers B.V. (North-Holland)

This paper extends the analysis and develops many implications. To concentrate on pressure groups, I ignore bureaucrats and politicians, and do not give much attention to voters, although, of course, I recognize that bureaucrats must be induced to implement policies, and votes and politicians are necessary to pass legislation.

The next section presents a generalized version of this model that permits pressure groups to be altruistic and envious as well as selfish. The 'representative' member of a group maximizes his utility by spending resources on political activities to create pressure that affects his subsidies or taxes. These expenditures compete with expenditures by other pressure groups because of the budget constraint that the total amount collected in taxes (including taxes on future generations) must equal total government expenditures.

The optimal pressure by a group is determined by the effect of its political expenditures on the utility of members. The effect on utility is crucially related to the dead weight (or social) costs and benefits of taxes and subsidies. Section III uses this relation between utility and dead weight costs and benefits to reformulate the 'Compensation Principle' of welfare economics as a major tool in the analysis of actual, as opposed to normative, public policies.

Sections IV and V consider various examples of the effect of dead weight costs and benefits on public policies. These include the deregulation and privatization 'movements' in the United States and other countries, the effects of recessions and declines in demand on tariffs and trade barriers, the *apparent* lower efficiency of public firms than of private firms, the taxation of farmers in developing countries and their subsidization in rich countries, and the effect of altruism and envy on taxes and subsidies. Section VI contains a summary, and a brief discussion of the role of pressure groups in democracies and other political systems.

II. The Model

Any relevant model of the political sector must incorporate a political budget constraint because subsidies are obviously limited by taxes. Indeed, if all taxes (T) were explicit levies, as with property and income taxes, and if all subsidies (S) were explicit transfers, as with welfare payments and veterans' bonuses, the political budget constraint would simply be

$$S = T. \tag{1}$$

Implicit taxes and subsidies due to regulations of activities are also related, but less simply. Still, equality between taxes and subsidies provides a convenient point of departure to begin the formal analysis. If n_s *identical* persons are subsidized and n_t *identical* persons are taxed, this political budget constraint can be written as

$$S = n_s\sigma = n_t\tau = T, \tag{2}$$

where σ and τ are the subsidy per member of s, and the tax per member of t.

The term τ should be interpreted as the tax collected per member of t, *net* of any subsidy to t; similarly, σ is the subsidy per member of s, *net* of any tax paid by t. Since τ and σ can be negative as well as positive, I need not specify a priori which group on balance pays taxes or receives a subsidy. However, I do assume at this stage that the characteristics defining membership in a group—such as age, location, or occupation—are exogenously determined, so that a member of t cannot convert into a member of s, and vice versa.

Taxes and subsidies are influenced, but not fully determined, by constitutions and other aspects of political systems. A crucial assumption of my approach is that they are also influenced by taxpayers and recipients who exert pressure on voters, legislators, and others involved in political decisions to further their own interests through the political process. A simple way to incorporate political pressure is to relate the taxes levied and subsidies transferred to political pressure by different groups (and other variables):

$$S = T = I\left(p_s, p_t, \frac{n_s}{n_t}, x\right), \tag{3}$$

where I is the 'influence function', p_s and p_t are pressures by recipients and taxpayers, n_s/n_t is the relative number of recipients, and x refers to the political system and other relevant considerations. My earlier paper [Becker (1983)] started with separate influence functions for taxes and subsidies, and showed that the equality between taxes and subsidies reduces these to a single influence function.

Since selfish taxpayers only exert pressure to lower taxes, and selfish recipients only exert pressure to raise subsidies, pressure from selfish groups would be positive only in regions where

$$\frac{\partial S}{\partial p_s} = \frac{\partial I}{\partial p_s} = I_s \geq 0 \quad \text{and} \quad \frac{\partial T}{\partial p_t} = \frac{\partial I}{\partial p_t} = I_t \leq 0. \tag{4}$$

The influence function presumably also directly depends on the ratio of recipients to taxpayers because an increase in that ratio would raise the number of votes in favor of subsidies to s. That is,

$$\frac{\partial I}{\partial (n_s/n_t)} \geqq 0. \tag{5}$$

However, this does not guarantee that an increase in the relative number of s raises subsidies because pressure exerted by s is negatively related to their relative number of members (see section V).

More detailed properties of the influence function are determined by constitutions, judicial traditions, and other aspects of political structures. Fortunately, for the limited purposes of this paper, it is not necessary to examine further the 'black box' of political structure. I only need to assume that the influence function, especially the derivatives specified in eqs. (3) and (4), is stable over time, so that the 'contest' between s and t has a stable foundation. Even riots and other violence are permitted as a form of political pressure [see Mirani (1985)], as long as political outcomes are stably related to violence as well as to other kinds of pressure.

If payoffs from political activities do not distinguish between identical members of s and identical members of t, subsidies and taxes would be public goods. Recipients (and payers) then have strong incentives to share costs by exerting pressure collectively. To model the group exertion of pressure, I introduce a pressure production function for each group that depends on its total political expenditures and the number of members:

$$\left. \begin{array}{l} p^i = p^i(m_i, n_i), \quad \text{with} \quad m_i = a_i n_i, \\[2mm] \dfrac{\partial p^i}{\partial m_i} = p^i_m \geqq 0 \quad \text{and} \quad p^i_n \leqq 0, \end{array} \right\} i = s, t, \tag{6}$$

where m_i is total expenditure of money, time, and effort by the ith group on campaign contributions, lobbying, advertisements, and other political activities, and a_i is their expenditure per member.

Free riding and shirking increase the cost of producing pressure. If the incentive to free ride increases with the number of members, the pressure produced by a given total expenditure (m) would decline as the number of members increased because the cost of 'collecting' m would rise. The second inequality in (6) captures the effect of numbers on free riding and the cost of producing pressure.

The utility function of each person depends on his tax or subsidy, and his expenditure on the production of pressure:

$$
\left.
\begin{array}{ll}
U^s = U^s(\sigma, \tau, a_s) & \text{with } \dfrac{\partial U^s}{\partial a_s} = U^s_a < 0 \\[1.5em]
& \text{and } \dfrac{\partial U^s}{\partial \sigma} = U^s_\sigma > 0 \\[1.5em]
U^t = U^t(\tau, \sigma, a_t), & \text{with } U^t_a < 0 \\[1.5em]
& \text{and } \dfrac{\partial U^t}{\partial \tau} = U^t_\tau < 0
\end{array}
\right\} .
\tag{7}
$$

Clearly, taxes hurt and subsidies benefit. Moreover, with altruism toward the other group, U^t also depends positively on σ, and U^s also depends negatively on τ; with envy, these signs would be reversed.

I assume that each group chooses its expenditure on political pressure to maximize the utility of its members, where optimal expenditures are conditional on the political budget equation and pressure production functions, including incentives to free ride. The interaction between groups is modeled simply as a Cournot–Nash noncooperative game in expenditures. Equilibrium for this game is determined by the utility maximizing condition for each group with respect to its expenditures on political pressure, that take as given expenditures by the other group:

$$
\left.
\begin{array}{l}
\dfrac{dU^t}{da_t} = 0 = U^t_a + U^t_\tau \dfrac{\partial \tau}{\partial p_t} p^t_m n_t \\[1.5em]
\dfrac{dU^s}{da_s} = 0 = U^s_a + U^s_\sigma \dfrac{\partial \sigma}{\partial p_s} p^s_m n_s
\end{array}
\right\} ,
\tag{8}
$$

or

$$
\left.
\begin{array}{l}
-F(\tau, \sigma a_t) = -\dfrac{U^t_a}{U^t_\tau} = I_t p^t_m \\[1.5em]
G(\sigma, \tau a_s) = -\dfrac{U^s_a}{U^s_\sigma} = I_s p^s_m
\end{array}
\right\} .
\tag{9}
$$

The optimal expenditures on pressure, and hence the optimal levels of pressure, are determined by these equations [see Becker (1983) for a discussion of second-order and stability conditions]. The equilibrium level of taxes and subsidies is then determined by the influence function in eq. (3). Optimal expenditures on pressure by a group would be zero, and the group would not organize politically, if the gain in lower taxes or higher subsidies were less than the cost of exerting pressure; one or both of these equations would then be replaced by inequalities.

The right-hand side of (9) measures the effect on influence of additional expenditures on pressure, while the left-hand side is determined by the monetary value of the change in utility from changes in taxes and subsidies, respectively. If s and t were both selfish, and if taxes and subsidies adversely affected the allocation of resources, the monetary value of the utility cost of taxes would exceed the amount paid ($F < 1$), and the monetary value of subsidies would be less than the amount received ($G > 1$). If taxes or subsidies improved the allocation of resources—perhaps by promoting public goods, reducing pollution, or because t were sufficiently altruistic toward s—then either $F > 1$, $G < 1$, or both.

The effect of taxes and subsidies on the allocation of resources can be brought out explicitly by writing

$$F = 1 - d^t(\tau, \sigma), \quad G = 1 + d^s(\sigma, \tau), \tag{10}$$

where d^t is the marginal dead weight or social cost to taxpayers from taxes equal to τ and subsidies equal to σ, and d^s is the marginal social cost to recipients from subsidies equal to σ and taxes equal to τ. If marginal taxes or subsidies raised efficiency, then d^t, d^s, or both would be less than zero. These functions depend on the level of taxes and subsidies because marginal distorting effects tend to rise, and marginal improving effects tend to fall, as the rate of taxation and subsidization increase. With altruism, envy, public goods, or externalities, d^t may depend on subsidies as well as taxes, and d^s may depend on taxes as well as subsidies.

Substitution of eq. (10) into the optimality conditions in eq. (9) immediately shows that expenditures on political pressure by taxpayers tend to be greater when the social cost of taxes is greater. This seems surprising and counterintuitive when taxpayers are selfish and not concerned about society as a whole. However, since pressure by taxpayers is assumed to reduce tax *collections* [by eqs. (3) and (4)], the effect of additional pressure on the utility of selfish recipients depends on the effect of lower taxes on their utility, which is positively related to the dead weight costs of taxation. Similarly, optimal expenditures on pressure even by selfish recipients are smaller when the social cost of subsidies is greater because the effect of subsidies on the utility of selfish recipients depends negatively on the dead weight cost of subsidies.

Since marginal social costs of subsidies tend to rise, and any marginal social benefits tend to fall, as subsidies increase, recipients would be discouraged from exerting additional pressure as subsidies increased, *even without any reactions by taxpayers.* Moreover, increased subsidies and taxes would encourage taxpayers to exert additional pressure by raising the marginal social cost of taxes. That is, higher subsidies and taxes tend to raise the 'countervailing political power' of taxpayers.

If all taxes and subsidies adversely affect efficiency, taxing and subsidizing each group would involve inefficient 'cross-hauling' because both could be made better off by equal reductions in their taxes and subsidies until one group were only subsidized and the other only taxed. Fortunately, a group does have an incentive to reduce the amount of cross-hauling because the incentive to exert pressure to lower taxes tends to exceed the incentive to exert pressure to raise subsidies. The reason is that the monetary equivalent of a dollar reduction in taxes paid exceeds a dollar because of the dead weight cost of taxes, whereas the monetary equivalent of a dollar increase in subsidies received is less than a dollar because of the dead weight cost of subsidies. If, as a result of the incentive to eliminate taxes first, s exerted enough pressure to eliminate its taxes, cross-hauling would be eliminated since the subsidy to t would also be eliminated. Cross-hauling could remain only if pressure by *both* groups were more productive in obtaining subsidies than in reducing taxes.[1]

Aggregate efficiency should be defined not only net of dead weight costs and benefits of taxes and subsidies, but also net of expenditures on the production of political pressure $(m_s + m_t)$ since these

---

[1] Formally,

$$n_s \sigma_s = n_t \tau_t = I^t(p_s^0, p_t^1),$$

$$n_t \sigma_t = n_s \tau_s = I^s(p_s^1, p_t^0),$$

where σ_j and τ_j are the subsidies and taxes to each member of the jth group $(j = s, t)$, p_j^0 and p_j^1 are the pressures by j to raise its subsidies and lower its taxes, respectively, and I^t and I^s are the influence functions for subsidies to s and t. Equilibrium conditions for t are

$$\frac{\partial I^t}{\partial m_t^1} \frac{\partial U^t}{\partial \tau_t} \lesseqgtr \frac{-\partial U^t}{\partial a_t^1}$$

and

$$\frac{\partial I^s}{\partial m_t^0} \frac{\partial U^t}{\partial \sigma_t} \lesseqgtr \frac{-\partial U^t}{\partial a_t^0},$$

with similar conditions applying to s. Since $-\partial U^t/\partial \tau_t > \partial U^t/\partial \sigma_t$ because of the dead weight cost of taxes and subsidies, expenditures to reduce taxes are more productive than expenditures to raise subsidies unless $-\partial I^t/\partial m_t^0$ is sufficiently larger than $\partial I^t/\partial m_t^1$.

expenditures are only 'rent-seeking' inputs into the determination of policies. Therefore, efficiency would be raised if all groups could agree to reduce their expenditures on political influence. Restrictions on campaign contributions, registration of and monitoring of lobbying organizations, limitations on total taxes and public expenditures, and other laws may be evidence of cooperative efforts to reduce 'wasteful' expenditures on cross-hauling and political pressure. Unfortunately, little is known about the success of different kinds of political systems in reducing the waste from competition among pressure groups.

Cournot–Nash behavior is especially wasteful because each group is assumed to believe that pressure by other groups is fixed and independent of its own pressure, whereas in the model, increased pressure by one group tends to stimulate countervailing pressure from other groups by raising their taxes or reducing their subsidies; see the positively sloped reaction curves in Becker (1983). A more realistic model of behavior would be Cournot–Nash in *strategies,* and would permit each group to consider these reactions when determining its own 'strategy' (its own reactions). A noncooperative equilibrium incorporating such reactions appears to have less pressure than a Cournot–Nash equilibrium in expenditures because each group would be discouraged from raising its pressure by the positive reactions of other groups. If so, fewer resources would then be wasted on the production of pressure. Mutually beneficial reductions in pressure might be expected also if competition among groups were modeled as repeated games. Such repetition may explain how even large groups manage to limit free riding by members (see section V), and why groups may prefer to spread their subsidies and taxes over time [see Smith (1985)].

Although the equilibrium level of taxes and subsidies depends on how the interaction between groups is modeled, social costs of subsidies appear to discourage pressure by subsidized groups, and social costs of taxes encourage pressure by taxed groups, in very different models of this interaction. The apparent robustness of these effects suggests that costs and benefits are important determinants of *actual* taxes, regulations, and other public policies.

III. The Compensation Principle and Public Policy

The new welfare economics developed the compensation principle to determine whether public policies are socially beneficial. Some of the pioneers even claimed[2] that a policy is beneficial as long as gainers

---

[2] For example, Kaldor wrote: 'Whether the landlords, in the free-trade case, should in fact be given compensation or not, is a political question on which the economist, *qua* economist, could hardly pronounce an opinion. The important fact is that,

could compensate losers, regardless of whether compensation were actually paid. This view is untenable except when the political process has equalized the marginal social 'worths' of gainers and losers, which begs the question of what determines *actual* policies. Nevertheless, distribution continues to be neglected by most assessments of the harm from monopoly and other 'market failures', and by most evaluations of public policies; these essentially consider only whether gainers *could* compensate losers.

Yet, somewhat paradoxically, the potential to compensate is an important determinant of *actual* political behavior in a model of competing interest groups. To show why, assume that taxes on t are positive even when neither s nor t exert pressure, ($I^0 = I(0, 0) > 0$), and that both must decide whether to exert pressure to change taxes by say $100. Clearly, s would not be willing to spend more than $100/(1 + d_0^s)$ on pressure because this amount measures their monetary gain from an additional subsidy of $100; for the same reason, t would not be willing to spend more than $100/(1 - d_0^t)$. Hence, the maximum that s would spend exceeds, equals, or is less than the maximum that t would spend as

$$\frac{100}{1 + d_0^s} \gtreqless \frac{100}{1 - d_0^t}, \quad \text{or as } d_0^s + d_0^t \lesseqgtr 0. \tag{11}$$

The second inequality is precisely the condition that determines whether gainers (s) could compensate losers (t). If both taxes and subsidies were socially costly (d_0^s and $d_0^t > 0$), gainers could not compensate losers, and the maximum expenditure by losers to block an increase in taxes would exceed the maximum expenditure by gainers to support the increase. Similarly, if both taxes and subsidies were socially beneficial (d_0^s and $d_0^t < 0$), gainers could compensate losers, and the maximum expenditure by gainers would exceed that by losers. More generally, the sign of $d_0^t + d_0^s$ determines whether gainers could compensate losers, and whether the maximum expenditure by gainers would exceed or would be less than that by losers.

Therefore, the maximum expenditure by gainers to support a policy would exceed the maximum expenditures by losers to oppose the policy if, and only if, the sum of the monetary equivalents of the gains and losses to all persons were positive. An increase in the sum of

---

in the argument in favour of free-trade, *the fate of the landlords is wholly irrelevant:* since the benefits of free-trade are by no means destroyed even if the landlords are fully reimbursed for their losses' [Kaldor (1939, pp. 550–551), my italics]. I owe this reference to Chipman and Moore (1978), who have an excellent review of the issues.

these monetary equivalents will be called an increase in 'social output'. The link between social output and incentives to exert pressure does not presume that pressure groups are altruistic, nor that compensation is paid to losers, nor that any social welfare function is politically relevant, for they are linked even in a noncooperative game without side payments between competing and selfish pressure groups.

I have been careful to refer to the *maximum* expenditure on political pressure because actual expenditures depend also on the right-hand side of eq. (9): on the cost of producing pressure and the effect of pressure on political influence. If both groups were equally efficient at producing pressure when they spent equal amounts, recipients would spend more to raise subsidies (and taxes) than payers spend to reduce them if additional subsidies (and taxes) raised social output. If gainers did spend more, the value of the influence function would increase above its initial level, and subsidies and taxes would increase; conversely, the value of the influence function would decrease below its initial level if losers spent more because social output had been reduced by subsidies to s.

The equilibrium conditions for both groups given by eqs. (9) and (10) imply that if the productivity of s and t in producing influence were equal, only policies that raised social output would be supported by pressure of s and t, although some policies that raised social output might be blocked by the countervailing pressure of t. Clearly, however, the effect on social output of some implemented policies could be negative *net* of the supporting and opposing (rent-seeking) expenditures by s and t.

Some policies might raise social output because of altruism by taxpayers or envy by recipients. Redistributions are Pareto-improving when altruistic taxpayers also benefit. Although altruists would be harmed by redistributions beyond the Pareto-efficient point, social output would be increased as long as the monetary value of the gains to beneficiaries exceeds the monetary value of the loss to altruists. If beneficiaries were no less efficient at producing political influence than altruists, expenditures by beneficiaries to support further redistribution would exceed the opposing expenditures by altruists. The amount redistributed would then go beyond the Pareto-efficient point [the same conclusion is reached by Roberts (1982)]. A similar argument leads to the expectation of political redistributions to envious groups even when they are no more efficient at producing influence than envied groups.

Of course, policies that reduced social output would be supported if gainers were sufficiently effective at producing influence to offset their relatively small gains. Yet despite the complaints of economists and others about the social cost of various regulations and programs, policies with high social cost would not survive competition among pressure groups unless those benefiting were *exceedingly* powerful politically. More commonly, surviving policies have low social cost *relative* to the millions of proposals that fail to gain political support. Similarly, public goods with large social benefits, such as protection against crime, tend to survive the competition among pressure groups, but public goods with modest social benefits do not survive when those opposing are politically powerful.

The compensation principle also suggests some tendency for the political sector to use the most efficient methods available to redistribute to beneficiaries. However, a satisfactory analysis of the choice of methods must consider whether the influence function itself depends on the methods used—perhaps because some methods hide private and social costs. Moreover, apparently inefficient taxes and subsidies may be used to reduce free riding on the political expenditures of others; for example, acreage restrictions are used in agriculture to limit entry of additional farmers [see Gardner (1983) and the discussion at the end of section V], or subsidies may be spread over time rather than paid as a lump sum to permit retaliation against free-riding members [see Smith (1985)].

If the *intent* of public policies were fully known, I am confident that the public sector would be revealed to be a far more efficient producer and redistributor than is popularly believed. For example, casual impressions and systematic evidence [see Borcherding (1982)] both indicate that public and regulated enterprises appear to be less efficient than private enterprises producing the same products. Yet, since employees (and other inputs) in public and regulated industries are paid relatively well [see the evidence on earnings in regulated industry in Moore (1978) and Pergamit (1983); the evidence in Robinson and Tomes (1984) on public enterprises is somewhat mixed], these enterprises may only *appear* to be less efficient because they are used to raise the income of employees (or others). Redistribution should be included among the measured 'outputs' of public and regulated enterprises before one can conclude that they are less efficient than private enterprises.

IV. Regulation and Deregulation

Subsidies that affect prices of outputs and inputs cause small dead weight loss when supply elasticities are low, say because capital and labor are not very mobile. Short-run mobility is lower when more is invested in human and physical capital specific to a firm or industry.

Therefore, workers and firms with sizable specific investments tend to have relatively large gains from lobbying for government protection against temporary and unexpected declines in demand because the dead weight cost of subsidies to them is relatively small. Several studies have found, indeed, that tariffs and other import restrictions do increase during recessions and at other times when output of domestic industries declines [see, for example, Hillman (1982) and Marvel and Ray (1983)]. This explanation of why depressed firms and industries are often successful at obtaining political assistance does not require irrationality (or even altruism), and meets Bernholz's (1984) challenge to find an explanation consistent with rational political choice.

Workers and firms with specific investments are also vulnerable to taxes, such as 'excess profits' taxes, when demand for their services rises temporarily or unexpectedly, since they have relatively small gains from lobbying against these taxes. The relatively low dead weight cost of taxes on factors with permanently inelastic supplies makes them good sources of revenue to finance public good and other public expenditures that raise social output because they offer less political resistance.[3] However, they are as likely to be subsidized, at the expense of other groups, as taxed to finance subsidies to others, unless they are more or less productive at political lobbying than others.

Small open economies have little international monopoly power because they face elastic supplies of imports and elastic demands for exports. Since the dead weight cost to countries imposing tariffs or export taxes is greater when these elasticities are greater, industries and consumers who benefit from tariffs and export taxes should have less political power in small open economies than in large self-sufficient economies, and less power in open regions of an economy than in self-sufficient regions [see Maloney, McCormick and Tollison (1984)]. Krueger (1983) uses a related argument to explain why Hong Kong, Taiwan, Singapore, South Korea, and some other small developing countries were among the earliest to reject the emphasis prevailing in the 1950s on import substitution and self-sufficiency in favor of international specialization.

Protection to firms and workers from adverse conditions is likely to be incomplete because marginal dead weight costs rise as the degree of protection increases. In my approach, rising dead weight costs curtail the power of firms and other subsidy recipients *even when* the political power of consumers and other *taxpayers* is *unchanged*. Although taxpayers are more likely to organize and exert pressure when dead

---

[3] I am indebted to Robert Barro for reminding me of the literature on the optimal taxation of factors with inelastic supplies.

weight costs are greater, additional pressure by subsidy recipients is discouraged by higher dead weight costs even when taxpayers remain unorganized (see section II).

I have assumed active pressure groups with stable influence functions, but I have not restricted the analysis to democracies, or to societies that permit easy formation of pressure groups. Consequently, the analysis implies that regulations and other public programs are moderated by their social cost in *any* political system, no matter how totalitarian, where groups lobby for political influence. In particular, the trend in Communist countries away from collective farms to private plots, and away from 'sharing the same rice bowl' to 'eating out of separate bowls' appears to be a response to the large (and perhaps growing) social cost of collectivization and sharing. Large social costs reduce the political feasibility of programs even when farmers, consumers, and others have no political power, as long as the incentive to exert pressure by bureaucrats, party members, and other beneficiaries declines as the social cost of their subsidies increases.

Dead weight costs of regulations and other policies often rise over time as labor and capital become more mobile, as substitutes develop for products that have been made more expensive, and as other costly methods of evading and avoiding the effects of particular regulations are discovered. For example, the dead weight cost of regulating security transactions rose significantly as institutional investors with elastic demands became important [see Jarrell (1984)], the cost of regulating airline travel rose as airline travel expanded into new and diverse markets [see Spiller (1983)], the cost of banking regulations grew as interest rates became higher and more variable, and new methods of intermediation were invented [Carron (1983)], and the cost of high marginal income tax rates grew as tax shelters, the underground economy, and other 'loop-holes' were expanded.

Therefore, the recent deregulation of airlines, banks, security firms, and other industries in the United States—see the catalog in Noll and Owen (1983, table 1.1)—is consistent with the implication of my analysis that political support for a regulation withers when its dead weight cost becomes large. However, this catalog cannot yet be called a 'movement' because the total amount of regulation in the United States has not declined appreciably. Expanded environmental, energy, safety, civil rights, labor, import, and other social regulations replaced the reduced regulation of particular industries.

I suspect that the appearance of a deregulation 'movement' is partly an echo of the regulatory 'movement' of the 1930s (itself a response to the Great Depression), when the securities, airline, banking, and many other industries became regulated. If dead weight costs in these industries grew over time at not very different rates, their political influence would wane at similar times. The deregulations and privatizations in recent years are also related, I believe, to the rapid expansion of transfer payments during the 1960s and 1970s. This expansion raised the marginal dead weight burden of income and other taxes,[4] which stimulated pressure by taxpayers to prune more socially costly programs that could not muster enough political support after tax burdens rose.

V. Many Pressure Groups

Many countries have hundreds, and some have thousands, of active pressure groups; for example, over 3000 Political Action Committees (PACs) are active in the United States [U.S. Federal Election Commission (1982)]. The influence function that determines taxes and subsidies with only two pressure groups can be generalized to separate influence functions for the taxes and subsidies of each of many groups:

$$\left. \begin{array}{l} T^i = I^{t_i}(p_1, \ldots, p_k, n_1, \ldots, n_k) \\[2mm] S^i = I^{s_i}(p_1, \ldots, p_k, n_1, \ldots, n_k) \end{array} \right\}, \quad i = 1, \ldots, k, \quad (12)$$

where T^i and S^i are the taxes collected from and subsidies given to the ith group, and p_i is the pressure exerted by the ith group with n_i identical members. Cross-hauling of taxes and subsidies tends to increase as the number of distinct groups increases because a group may sometimes be subsidized along with some other groups, and taxed along with still different groups. An example is the subsidy to railroad conductors as a 'by-product' of regulation that raises the price of air travel, and the tax on conductors as a 'by-product' of subsidies to build highways.

Although taxes and subsidies need not be equal for each group, the total amount collected in taxes would be related to the total paid in subsidies. If taxes and subsidies are explicit levies and transfers, total taxes collected would equal total subsidies paid out:

$$\sum S^i = S = T = \sum T^i. \tag{13}$$

This government budget equation implies that one of the influence functions in eq. (12) can be determined from the others, and that lower

---

[4] See, for example, estimates by Browning and Johnson (1984) and Stuart (1984) of the sizable burden of income taxes in the United States, and by Lindbeck (1983) of the huge burden of income taxes and transfer payments in Sweden.

taxes or higher subsidies to one group would raise the taxes or lower the subsidies of all other groups.

If groups did not cooperate, pressures exerted by each, including perhaps no pressure, would be determined from conditions similar to those in eq. (9) that depend on utility functions, pressure production functions, influence functions, and a government budget equation. Some groups may cooperate, however, through coordinated lobbying or log-rolling in the legislature to raise their subsidies and lower their taxes. I do not try to model political cooperation because the main implication of noncooperative behavior used in this paper—the effect of dead weight costs on subsidies, taxes, and political pressure—appears to be highly relevant also to cooperating groups who do not use side payments. Even when cooperating with other groups, the gain to a group from additional pressure is greater when the dead weight cost of its subsidies is smaller and when the dead weight cost of its taxes is larger.

Small groups might seem to have especially strong incentives to cooperate with others because they do not have enough members to support favorable referenda and legislation. This apparent disadvantage of small groups motivates models of the median voter, of legislative log-rolling [see Buchanan and Tullock (1962)], and of competition for votes in cooperative political games [see, for example, Aumann and Kurz (1977)].

I believe, however, that the political handicaps of small groups are exaggerated by models that assume voters are well informed and automatically vote in favor of their interests. As is well known, the same majority rule that motivates these models implies rational voters would not become well informed, and may be misled to vote against their interests [see, among others, Becker (1983), and Brennan and Buchanan (1984)]. Therefore, small groups may be able to acquire political support by persuading misinformed voters to vote in their favor [Denzau and Munger (1983) develop an explicit model combining unorganized voters and expenditures on pressure]. If many voters are vulnerable to persuasion, the size of a group would be less important than its capacity to persuade others.

Moreover, small groups have certain political advantages that may swamp any adverse effects of fewer voters.[5] They may control more easily free riding and shirking by members. In addition, if groups taxed to finance subsidies are much larger, those subsidized face less countervailing political pressure. An increase in the number of tax-

---

[5] A recent model of the politics of tariff formation by Wellisz and Wilson (1984) also implies (for somewhat different reasons) that small groups have political advantages.

payers lowers taxes per payer, and hence also lowers the marginal dead weight loss to each payer, which discourages countervailing pressure [see the proof in Becker (1983, pp. 384–385)]. Note that this conclusion is another example of the effect of dead weight costs, and does not assume small taxes and subsidies are neglected.

That *relatively* small groups are effective competitors for political influence is consistent with the evidence that farmers are more likely to be subsidized in countries where farming is less important, and are more likely to be taxed in countries where farming is more important [see Bates (1981), Binswanger and Scandizzo (1983), and Miller (1985)]. This view also implies that the rapid aging of Western populations will *reduce* rather than raise social security and other subsidies to older persons, even though the old will have more voters.

Fear of universal suffrage has essentially been a fear that the numerous poor will out-vote the rich and middle classes, and tax away much of their wealth. Yet the *net* redistribution to the poor appears to be modest, at least in the United States [see Reynolds and Smolensky (1977)]. My analysis claims that the number of poor is also a political handicap because large redistributions to them impose a sizable excess burden on the less numerous middle class and rich.

Even without envy, the wealth of the rich is also a political handicap because a given amount collected in income or wealth taxes per person has a smaller dead weight cost when the payer is rich. The middle classes could provide an effective political compromise between numbers and wealth since they are less numerous than the poor and less wealthy than the rich. Perhaps this is the explanation of 'Director's Law' of redistribution to the middle classes from the rich and poor [see Stigler (1970)].

Although I have assumed throughout that the size of each group is fixed, politically successful groups do attract additional members, e.g. farming became more attractive after being subsidized, or work became less appealing after welfare payments grew. Subsidized groups try to limit the entry of additional members because that dilutes the gains of established members. One way to limit entry is to lobby for subsidies that are less vulnerable to entry. For example, acreage restrictions encourage fewer new farmers than output subsidies do [see Gardner's (1983) comparison], and the Civil Aeronautics Board did not certify a single new trunk airline between 1938 and 1976 [see Meyer and Oster (1984)].

VI. Summary and Discussion

A model has been presented of competition among special interest groups for political influence. Each active group exerts pressure to affect its subsidies and taxes, where activities of different groups are related by the equality between total tax collections and total subsidy payments. A group's political effectiveness depends on its control over free riding by members, as stressed in the extensive literature on collective choice.

This paper argues that political effectiveness is also determined by the dead weight (or social) costs and benefits of taxes and subsidies. An increase in the dead weight cost of taxation encourages pressure by taxpayers because they are then harmed more by tax payments. Similarly, an increase in the dead weight cost of subsidies discourages pressure by recipients because they then benefit less from subsidies received.

The 'Compensation Principle' of welfare economics turns out to be a significant part of this theory of actual political policies. If the gain to groups that benefit exceeds the loss to groups that suffer, and if access to political influence were otherwise the same for all groups, gainers would exert more political pressure than losers, and a policy would tend to be implemented. Note that the criterion is whether gainers *could* compensate losers; actual compensation need not be paid to losers.

If gainers could not compensate losers, a policy would not be implemented unless gainers had much better access to political influence. Therefore, the Compensation Principle combined with an analysis of the production of political influence provides a unified approach to the political feasibility both of public goods and other policies that raise social output (where gainers could compensate losers), and of policies that redistribute to favored groups (where gainers could not compensate).

The emphasis in the theory on dead weight costs is reminiscent of Ramsey pricing and the theory of optimal taxation, where marginal dead weight costs are related to marginal 'social worths'. However, optimal tax theory uses dead weight costs to prescribe *optimal* public policies, whereas my analysis uses dead weight costs to explain *actual* policies in a world of competing and possibly selfish pressure groups. Still, if dead weight costs (and benefits) are important determinants of actual policies, the many calculations of dead weight cost in the applied welfare literature, and many analytical results of welfare economics and optimal tax theory, are relevant also to positive theories of political behavior.[6]

The almost universal condemnation of special interest groups includes the recent allegation by Olson (1982) that they are responsible

---

[6] For example, Barro (1986) uses optimal tax theory to explain actual government deficits.

for sluggish growth and the eventual decline of nations. Most of the condemnation is based on the many redistributions to special interest groups that reduce social output because of dead weight costs of taxes and subsidies.

Clearly, actual political systems do not have social welfare functions, benevolent dictators, or other political procedures that *automatically* choose the optimal production of public goods, optimal effluence taxes, and other public policies that raise output and efficiency. Therefore, the condemnation of special interest groups is excessive because competition among these groups contributes to the survival of policies that raise output: favorably affected groups tend to lobby more for these policies than unfavorably affected groups lobby against. Indeed, no policy that lowered social output would survive if all groups were equally large and skillful at producing political influence, for the opposition would always exert more influence than proponents. The condemnation of special interest groups is more justified when there is highly unequal access to political influence. Powerful groups then can secure the implementation of policies that benefit them while reducing social output, and can thwart policies that harm them while raising output.

If special interest groups are crucial to the political process, political systems would be largely defined by their activities and opportunities. Democracies have competition among groups with relatively equal political strength, while totalitarian and other nondemocratic systems have restricted competition among groups with highly unequal strength. Redistribution in democracies (and other systems) would be guided not by social welfare functions or other measures of social fairness, but mainly by the altruism, selfishness, envy, and morality of the more powerful interest groups.

In democracies so defined, a few pressure groups cannot easily obtain very large subsidies (although many groups may each obtain relatively small subsidies), since I have shown that large subsidies stimulate countervailing pressure by those taxed to finance the subsidies. In totalitarian systems, on the other hand, a few groups can more readily use the state to raise substantially their well-being because other groups are not permitted to form effective opposition.

I conclude by considering briefly the implications of the analysis in this paper for the theme of the [Nobel] Symposium: the expansion of government in Western democracies during the last hundred years. More efficient taxes (such as the income tax) and subsidies, and improved methods of collecting and distributing them, encouraged expansion by reducing the resistance of taxpayers and raising pressure from potential recipients. Industrialization and the accompanying division of labor multiplied separate interests, which permitted some special interests to acquire political influence because they were small relative to the number of taxpayers. The development of radio, television, and other methods of communication widened the opportunities to influence the revealed 'preferences' of voters and legislators. Undoubtedly, the decline in laissez faire ideology contributed to the growth in government, but most of the decline was probably *induced* by the arguments and propaganda of the many groups seeking public largess.

These changes facilitated government growth in all countries, but can they explain the details of growth documented in the papers by Bernholz (1984), Borcherding (1984), Lindbeck (1984), Musgrave (1984), and others, especially the rapid increase in transfer payments during the last twenty years? Although an answer is beyond the goals of this paper, I believe an important part of the answer is found in changes in the access to political influence of the old, ill, and other beneficiaries of transfer payments.

References

Aumann, Robert J. and Mordecai Kurz, 1977, Power and taxes, Econometrica VL, 1137–1161.

Barro, Robert J., 1986, The behavior of U.S. deficits, in: R. Gordon, ed., The American business cycle: Continuity and change (University of Chicago Press, Chicago).

Bates, Robert H., 1981, Markets and states in tropical Africa (University of California Press, Berkeley).

Becker, Gary S., 1983, A theory of competition among pressure groups for political influence, The Quarterly Journal of Economics XCVIII, 371–400.

Bentley, Arthur F., 1908, The process of government (University of Chicago Press, Chicago).

Bernholz, Peter, 1984, Growth of government, economic growth and individual freedom, Nobel symposium on the growth of government, Stockholm.

Binswanger, Hans P. and Pasquale L. Scandizzo, 1983, Patterns of agricultural protection (World Bank Discussion Paper No. ARU15, Washington, D.C.).

Borcherding, Thomas E., 1982, Toward a positive theory of public sector supply arrangements, in: R. Prichard, ed., Public enterprise in Canada (Butterworth, Toronto).

Borcherding, Thomas E., 1984, A survey of empirical studies about causes of the growth of government, Nobel symposium on the growth of government, Stockholm.

Brennan, Geoffrey and James M. Buchanan, 1984, The logic of levers: The pure theory of electoral preference, Paper delivered at a conference on the Political Economy of Public Policy, Stanford Center for Policy Research.

Browning, Edgar K. and William R. Johnson, 1984, The trade-off between equality and efficiency, Journal of Political Economy 92, 175–203.

Buchanan, James M. and Gordon Tullock, 1962, The calculus of consent (University of Michigan Press, Ann Arbor).

Carron, Andrew S., 1983, The political economy of financial regulation, in: Roger G. Noll and Bruce M. Owen, eds., The political economy of deregulation (American Enterprise Institute, Washington, D.C.) 69–83.

Chipman, John S. and James C. Moore, 1978, The new welfare economics, 1939–1974, International Economic Review 19, 547–584.

Denzau, Arthur T. and Michael C. Munger, 1983, Legislators and interest groups: How unorganized interests get represented, Working Paper No. 81, Center for the Study of American Business, Washington University.

Gardner, Bruce, 1983, Efficient redistribution through commodity markets, American Journal of Agricultural Economics 65, 225–234 (chap. 16 of this volume).

Hillman, Arye L., 1982, Declining industries and political-support protectionist motives, American Economic Review 72, 1180–1187.

Jarrell, Gregg A., 1984, Change at the exchange: The causes and effects of deregulation, Journal of Law and Economics 27, 273–312.

Kaldor, Nicholas, 1939, Welfare propositions of economics and interpersonal comparisons of utility, Economic Journal 49, 549–552.

Krueger, Anne O., 1983, The developing countries' role in the world economy, ITT Key Issues Lecture Series, University of Chicago.

Lindbeck, Assar, 1983, Interpreting income distributions in a welfare state, European Economic Review 21, 227–256.

Lindbeck, Assar, 1984, Redistribution policy and the expansion of the public sector—The political economy of the welfare state, Nobel symposium on the growth of government, Stockholm.

Maloney, Michael T., Robert E. McCormick and Robert D. Tollison, 1984, Economic regulation, competitive governments, and specialized resources, Journal of Law and Economics 27, 329–338.

Marvel, Howard P. and Edward J. Ray, 1983, The Kennedy round: Evidence on the regulation of international trade in the United States, American Economic Review 73, 190–197.

Meyer, John R. and Clinton V. Oster, Jr., 1984, Deregulation and the new airline entrepreneurs (Massachusetts Institute of Technology, Cambridge, MA).

Miller, Tracy C., 1985, A political interest group model of agricultural price policy in developing countries, Agricultural Economics Workshop, University of Chicago.

Mirani, S. Kaveh, 1985, Collective political violence and the redistribution of political income, Ph.D. dissertation, University of Chicago.

Moore, Thomas Gale, 1978, The beneficiaries of trucking regulation, Journal of Law and Economics 21, 327–343.

Musgrave, Richard, 1984, Excess budget: norms, hypotheses, and performance, Nobel symposium on the growth of government, Stockholm.

Noll, Roger G. and Bruce M. Owen, eds., 1983, The political economy of deregulation (American Enterprise Institute, Washington, D.C.), chapter 2.

Olson, Mancur, Jr., 1965, The logic of collective action (Harvard University Press, Cambridge, MA).

Olson, Mancur, Jr., 1982, The rise and decline of nations (Yale University Press, New Haven).

Pergamit, Michael R., 1983, Wages and employment in regulated industries, Ph.D. dissertation, University of Chicago.

Reynolds, Morgan and Eugene Smolensky, 1977, Public expenditures, taxes, and the distribution of income (Academic Press, New York).

Roberts, Russell, 1982, A positive model of private charity and public transfers, University of Rochester.

Robinson, Chris and Nigel Tomes, 1984, Union wage differentials in the public and private sectors: A simultaneous equations specification, Journal of Labor Economics 2, 106–127.

Smith, Rodney T., 1985, An economic theory of coalition formation, Claremont Graduate School.

Spiller, Pablo T., 1983, The differential impact of airline regulation on individual firms and markets: An empirical analysis, Journal of Law and Economics 26, 655–689.

Stigler, George J., 1970, Director's law of public income redistribution, Journal of Law and Economics 13, 1–10 (chap. 3 of this volume).

Stuart, Charles, 1984, Welfare costs per dollar of additional tax revenue in the United States, American Economic Review 74, 352–362.

U.S. Federal Election Commission, 1982, Reports on financial activities, 1979–1980 (U.S. Government Printing Office, Washington, D.C.).

Wellisz, Stanislaw and John D. Wilson, 1984, A theory of tariff formation, Columbia University.

Director's Law of Public Income Redistribution

3

George J. Stigler

Almost a decade ago Aaron Director proposed a law of public expenditures: Public expenditures are made for the primary benefit of the middle classes, and financed with taxes which are borne in considerable part by the poor and rich. The law was empirical, and the present essay seeks not only to present and illustrate the law (which its inventor refuses to do) but to offer an explanation for it.

The philosophy of Director's Law is as follows. Government has coercive power, which allows it to engage in acts (above all, the taking of resources) which could not be performed by voluntary agreement of the members of a society. Any portion of the society which can secure control of the state's machinery will employ the machinery to improve its own position. Under a set of conditions to be discussed below, this dominant group will be the middle income classes.

I. Director's Law Illustrated

A reasonably rigorous demonstration that the state redistributed income in favor of the middle income classes would require vast empirical studies of the distribution of public revenues, non-revenue burdens, and benefits, by income class. We are content here to defend the plausibility of Director's Law.

The distribution of incomes of parents of students in California institutions of higher education is highly skewed toward larger incomes (see Table 1). California is a relatively wealthy state so somewhat lower incomes would be received by parents in other states, but no defensible adjustments of the data would qualify the assertion that the colleges of America are populated by the children of the middle and upper classes. The rough estimates of the distribution of state and local taxa-

Reprinted with permission from *The Journal of Law and Economics* 13, no. 1 (April 1970): 1–10. © 1970 by The University of Chicago.

TABLE 1.   Distribution of Parents of Students in California Colleges and
Universities by Income, 1964, and Related Data

Income Class	1964 Percentage of Parents		1964 Percentage of all U.S. Families	1965 State and Local Taxes as Percent of Income	1961 Share of Total State and Local Taxes Paid
	State Colleges	University of California			
Under $4,000	4	5	26	11	17
$ 4,000–$ 8,000	27	19	38	10	46
$ 8,000–$14,000	48	38	27	9	27
$14,000 and over	21	39	9	8	9

Sources: Parents' income: J. Edward Sanders and Hans C. Palmer, The Financial Barrier to Higher
Education In California; A Study Prepared for the California State Scholarship Commission
(1965). Family income: U.S. Bureau of the Census, Statistical Abstract of the United States,
Table 472, at 324 (1968) [approximate]. Taxes as Per cent of Income and Share of Total Taxes:
Tax Burdens & Benefits of Gov. Expenditures by Income Class, 1961 and 1965, Tables 7, B-9
(Tax Foundation, 1967) [approximate].

tion by income classes are persuasive: public provision of higher education redistributes income from the poorer to the higher income classes.

The same redistributive effect, one may conjecture, was achieved
in equal degree by the public provision of high school education thirty
years ago, and even today the parents of high school *graduates* are primarily in middle and upper income classes. In the nineteenth century
the same analysis would apply to elementary public schools; the *graduates* of elementary schools in 1900 were probably largely from middle
income class families.

The main beneficiaries of several other traditional governmental
functions appear to be much the same. Fire and police activities, for
example, are clearly middle-income oriented to the extent that they
protect property, and it would be interesting to investigate the extent
to which such activities are provided more liberally in middle than in
lower income areas of cities. But the major examples of the use of the
state by the middle classes lie elsewhere:

1. *Farm policy.* The basic method of assisting farmers has been
to raise prices by restricting output, and the restriction of output has
been based upon the use of land. The beneficiaries of the policy have
therefore been the farm land owners, not the poorer farm laborers and
tenants. The burden of the system has been placed upon the consumers of farm products—a regressive excise tax, in effect—as well as on
the public treasury. The redistribution of income has therefore much
exceeded direct governmental expenditures.[1]

[1] See John E. Floyd, The Effects of Farm Price Supports on the Returns to Land
and Labor in Agriculture, 73 J. of Pol. Econ. 148 (1965).

2. *Minimum wage laws.* The main beneficiaries of minimum wage legislation have been two types of workers. The first is the higher paid Northern worker (in textiles, for example) who received some measure of protection from the Southern, low-wage branch of the industry. The second class of beneficiaries has been the better-paid workers, for whom the lower-paid workers are an important substitute. The income redistribution, which is not part of the public budget, is financed by the workers who are displaced by the minimum wage statute and the consumers who purchase the products of low-wage industries.

3. *Social security.* The social security system taxes most heavily, relative to the benefits they will receive,

    a. Those who begin work early, as compared with those who continue in school.

    b. Those who die early, as compared with those who live longer.

    c. Those families in which the wife works, relative to those in which she does not.

    d. Those who were young, as compared to those who were old, when first covered by the law.

All of these effects are in favor of the middle classes. There are other effects which run in favor of lower income classes (for example, benefits are a lower fraction of average wages as wages rise), but it is quite possible that the system on balance redistributes income to the middle classes.[2]

4. *Public housing.* The public housing program has had for its primary purposes the reduction in the density of population and improvement in the quality of structure, with the implicit rise in housing costs offset to some extent by public subsidies. Even when the new housing is made available to those displaced, many of the displaced cannot be rehoused in the area, and of course the more attractive housing attracts the competition of those who are better off. The public housing has therefore at a minimum injured many of the poor, and in good measure benefited the non-poor.[3]

5. *Tax exempt institutions.* One form of subsidy is tax exemption, and if we examine the classes of institutions which were given tax exemption, we find that they were primarily those which served the middle classes. Churches are the largest of the tax exempt institutions, but educational and medical institutions are equally directed to the middle classes.

---

[2]This argument implicitly assumes that workers bear the tax; if consumers bear a portion, the conclusion is even more likely.

[3]See Martin Anderson, The Federal Bulldozer, A Critical Analysis of Urban Renewal, 1949–1962 (1964).

6. *Welfare expenditures.* Public charitable expenditures in the nineteenth century could be viewed as the transfer to the state of burdens otherwise necessarily borne by the well-to-do. The great modern programs presumably involve net transfers to the poor and are therefore apparently contradictory to Director's Law. We shall return to this category of state expenditures.

There remains that enormously expensive social activity, war. Have the middle classes been the special beneficiaries of war? Possibly some wars, such as the American Revolution, could be viewed as levying a highly progressive tax on the wealthy loyalists. Modern wars, however, are not easily viewed as profitable to any income class (although by devices such as conscription the middle classes reduce the costs to *them*). Simply to put aside a large subject which should not be dismissed simply as pathological, wars will be adduced neither as support nor counter-evidence on Director's Law.

II. The Bases for Voter Coalitions

A majority coalition of voters may be formed upon any of a variety of bases: religion, nationality, region, industry, or income, to mention only a few historically important bases. If the coalition of voters is to make effective use of the political machinery of the state to redistribute income, it must find a state activity (expenditure) whose benefits flow to the coalition in greater proportion than the taxes which will finance the activity.

In the nineteenth century there were relatively few available tax bases or functions (expenditure categories) which were closely related to income. The federal governmental revenues (the Civil War period aside) were either custom duties or excises upon liquor and tobacco, and of course the burden of commodity taxes is only loosely related to income. The overwhelming preponderance of state and local governmental revenues came from the general property tax, which again bore only a loose relationship to income. (The tax on land, indeed, would be capitalized and have no necessary relationship to even property incomes at later times.) In the nineteenth century, in summary, only unconcealable assets (real property) and commodities which passed through bottlenecks (a port, or large production processes) and were inelastic with respect to taxes were feasible objects of taxation.[4]

---

[4] The elasticity of supply with respect to taxes is determined by both demand and supply elasticities. Let $f(q)$ be the demand price and $h(q)$ the supply price, so before tax $f(q_0) = h(q_0)$. After a unit tax of t, the equilibrium is given by

$$f(q_0 + \Delta q) + t = h(q_0 + \Delta q),$$

If the state is to be used to redistribute income, the activities it undertakes are also limited. Normally it will not be possible to give any commodity (or sell it at subsidized prices) to a particular class, unless the allotments of the commodities to individuals can be effectively rationed, because the members of this class will simply resell the commodity to other classes. Redistribution is a form of discrimination, and is subject to the usual limitation that the classes discriminated against not be able to deal with the classes who are favored. Services are generally non-transferable, and on reflection it is a remarkable fact that the state has almost never supplied anything but services.[5]

In the nineteenth century there were relatively few services which the state could supply only to favored income groups. The protective functions (the courts and police functions, in particular) and a measure of transportation and educational services were of special value to the upper income classes, but as with taxes the relationship to income was not close.

With both expenditures and taxes largely unrelated to income in the nineteenth century, we are not surprised that relatively little use was made of the state as an instrument of income redistribution. One may conjecture that other bases of classes (regional, urban v. rural) entered largely into the determination of public activities.

Increasingly in the twentieth century income has become a more important basis of political classes. Income taxes and an almost unlimited variety of excise taxes gradually became feasible, that is collectible at tolerable costs. A modern state is by no means unrestricted in its ability to assign tax liabilities to various income classes—in fact

---

and expanding in a Taylor series,

$$\Delta q = \frac{t}{h'(q_0) - f'(q_0)}$$

and the elasticity of output with respect to the tax is

$$\frac{\Delta q}{q} \bigg/ \frac{t}{p} = \frac{1}{\dfrac{1}{\varepsilon} - \dfrac{1}{\eta}}$$

where ε is the elasticity of supply and η the elasticity of demand.

[5] When a commodity producing industry seeks governmental benefits, it generally prefers output or entry restriction because the benefits of direct subsidies are likely to be dissipated by competition of firms in the industry. Hence the opposition of farm groups to the Brennan plan: the supply of poor farmers is more elastic than the supply of farm land.

even the ability of families to divide income among members is an important restriction. Nevertheless changes in economic organization (for example, employment by large organizations rather than self-employment) and in the recording of economic information have greatly increased the power and flexibility of taxation.

There has been a corresponding enlargement of the eligible expenditure programs. Services have increased generally as a part of modern living—education and health services are examples. Direct transfer payments have also become practicable, although many such payments are still unrelated to income (for example, the subsidies to sugar and other farm products).

As income has become a widely usable basis for tax and expenditure programs, we conjecture that both the extent of governmental activities and their income redistribution effects grow.

III. Notes on a Theory

Let us henceforth assume that income is the strategic basis for the formation of voting coalitions. The actual income distribution of a society may be presented as a conventional frequency distribution, which is shown in Figure I.

In each income interval there is also a given number of possible voters (adults). The number of possible voters increases with income: low income families are often single persons, and high income families will also contain more grown children and dependents. If every adult were to vote, we would have a distribution of voters by income of the type (labelled "100 per cent Vote") illustrated in Figure I.

The actual number of votes cast will differ from the maximum possible votes for two reasons. The first is that the dominant coalition can impose a variety of restrictions upon voters which decreases the voter participation of other income classes. In particular, upper income classes increase their share of votes if they impose literacy requirements, poll taxes, and residence requirements (which affect most the more migratory persons). Registration requirements have recently been shown to have a substantial influence upon the fraction of eligible voters who actually vote.[6] The second reason for differential voting is that individuals outside the majority coalition will receive smaller benefits from voting. The distribution of actual voters will be skewed to the right; it is labelled "Actual Vote" in Figure I.

When only excises and real property were feasible bases of taxa-

---

[6]See Stanley Kelley, Jr., Richard E. Ayers, & William G. Bowen, Registration and Voting: Putting Things First, 61 Amer. Pol. Sci. Rev. 359 (1967).

tion, the distribution of tax revenues by income class would be relatively regressive—perhaps similar to the tax revenue curve displayed in Figure II. The distribution of benefits of eligible expenditures (education, justice) might be that shown in the same figure; other potential public functions would be excluded because they put a larger tax than benefit upon the majority coalition of voters. The net redistribution of income by income class would be obtained by subtracting the tax distribution from the expenditure distribution (assuming budget balancing). There would be as many possible income redistribution curves as there were possible combinations of tax and expenditure programs.

Each income class would of course prefer that income redistribu-

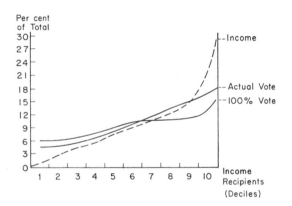

FIGURE I. *Source:* U.S. Bureau of the Census, Statistical Abstract of the United States, income, 1966 in table 472, at 324 (1968).

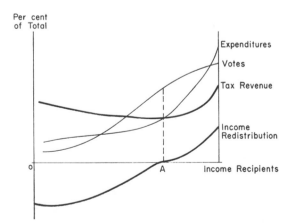

FIGURE II

tion which benefited it the most, and if a single income redistribution met this requirement for 51 per cent of the voters, it would be chosen. As a rule, however, different fiscal programs would be preferred by different income classes, and then the program to be chosen must represent a compromise. The program displayed in Figure II would be chosen only if the area under the votes curve to the right of A contained a majority, and if no alternative program offered more to some majority.

At the present time both taxes and expenditures can be much more closely assigned to particular income classes. Suppose now that taxes could be made strictly proportional to income, and expenditures consisted of uniform family subsidies. Then the difference between the income curve and a uniform curve ($\frac{1}{10}$ of subsidies received by each income decile) would represent the gains or losses to an income class from recourse to the political machinery.

Under these restrictive conditions—proportional taxation and uniform subsidies—the gain to any decile income *class* from a K per cent tax would be readily calculated:

1. Let its pre-tax income be $(s_i N)$, where N is national income.
2. The tax upon it would be $Ks_i N$.
3. The uniform income class subsidy would be one-tenth of the total tax receipts, or $KN/10$.
4. Hence the subsidy to the class would exceed its tax if

$$\frac{KN}{10} > Ks_i N$$

or

$$\frac{1}{10} > s_i.$$

Hence all income deciles with less than one-tenth of income would gain. If they contained a majority of the votes, they would vote for redistribution, and if they had less than a majority, the government would not engage in redistributive activities. Since the gain to an income decile from redistribution is

$$KN \left(\frac{1}{10} - s_i \right) \qquad \left(s_i < \frac{1}{10} \right),$$

it rises with the tax rate until $K = 1$. Absolute leveling of income would have self-defeating disincentive effects upon the rich, so that a rate of taxation would be imposed which maximized the present value of a perpetual stream of redistributions, taking account of the effects of taxes upon the supply of large incomes. A variant of this scheme is analyzed in the mathematical notes to this paper.

The fiscal machinery of government is not limited to such simple policies as proportional taxation and uniform subsidies. Tax systems may be made regressive in certain regions and progressive in others, not only by income tax rate schedules but by deductions (costs of owned homes) and by excises on suitably chosen commodities. Expenditures, as we have seen, can be concentrated on certain income classes by subsidizing goods and services which primarily these income classes consume.

The increase in the flexibility of taxes and expenditure programs works toward a larger role for government, and toward programs which redistribute income increasingly toward lower income classes. As the amount that can be collected from upper income classes increases, and the amount that can be given directly to the lower income classes increases, the potential rewards from redistribution rise for the lower income classes. In the long run the middle classes may have been beneficiaries of this process because they were in coalition with the rich in the nineteenth century, and are entering into coalition with the poor today.

Mathematical Notes

1. Let families be ranked over the interval $(0,1)$ by income. At any point x on the interval,

$v(x)$ is the number of votes of family x

$y(x)$ is the income of family x.

The votes in the successful coalition are given by

$$V_c = \frac{1}{V_t} \int_{x_0}^{x_1} v(x)dx > 1/2, \tag{1}$$

where V_t is the total number of votes.

Let us consider a case in which taxes are levied at a uniform rate t on families *outside the coalition*, and the receipts distributed only to members of the majority coalition. The tax receipts will be

$$T = t \left\{ \int_0^{x_0} y(x)dx + \int_{x_1}^1 y(x)dx \right\}. \tag{2}$$

Suppose we add a small increment of wealthier families to the coalition: they will possess

$v(x_1)(\Delta x)_u$ votes.

Correspondingly we must subtract an equal number of votes from the lower incomes to maintain a minimum majority:

$v(x_0)(\Delta x)_L$ such that

$$v(x_1)(\Delta x)_u = v(x_0)(\Delta x)_L. \tag{3}$$

This reconstitution of the coalition will reduce aggregate taxes (and hence benefits for the members of the coalition) if

$$t\{y(x_1)(\Delta x)_u - y(x_0)(\Delta x)_L\} < 0,$$

or, using equation 3, if

$$y(x_1)(\Delta x)_u - y(x_0)(\Delta x)_u \frac{v(x_1)}{v(x_0)} < 0$$

or

$$\frac{v(x_0)}{y(x_0)} < \frac{v(x_1)}{y(x_1)}. \tag{4}$$

But $v(x)/y(x)$ is a decreasing function of x for all x, so (4) holds for all x. Hence the successful coalition is that for which $x_0 = 0$, and x_1 is given by (1). This conclusion ignores the question of marginal incentives, to which we turn.

2. The system of uniform taxation of the non-members of the coalition founders on the problem of marginal incentive, that is, the families with income above x_1 have after tax incomes of $(1 - t) y(x)$, $x > x_1$, and this may be less than x_1. If one exempted $y(x_1)$, the tax would become $t'[y(x) - y(x_1)]$, where t' is the new rate. The reconstitution of the coalition by adding $(\Delta x)_u$ and deleting $(\Delta x)_L$ must be such that the limits set by disincentives be taken into account.

An Economic Interpretation of the History of Congressional Voting in the Twentieth Century

4

Sam Peltzman

This paper interprets historical change in the U.S. Congress in terms of the simplest principal-agent model. I will show that profound changes in congressional voting patterns over the course of the twentieth century can be traced mainly to corresponding changes in the economic interests of their constituents. This claim may appear, at once, modest and extravagant. Modest, because the notion that agents by and large serve their principals' interests is so familiar in nonpolitical contexts. Extravagant, because economists have found the notion difficult to apply to the behavior of political agents. I begin by outlining the empirical source of this difficulty. Then I describe the main trends in twentieth-century economic history and congressional voting behavior that are the focus of subsequent empirical analysis. The analysis reveals a much closer connection between economic and political history than might be suggested by much contemporary empirical literature on the economics of voting. I conclude by attempting to reconcile these apparently divergent results.

I. The Questionable Connection Between Congressmen and their Constituents

Economists and political scientists have adduced a variety of explanations for why congressmen might rationally choose *not* to vote consistently for the interests of a majority of constituents (see, for example, Anthony Downs, 1957; James Buchanan and Gordon Tullock, 1962; George Stigler, 1971; Morris Fiorina, 1974). A more recent literature

I thank Kenneth Carl and John Markson for research assistance and anonymous referees for valuable criticism and suggestions. The financial support of the Center for the Study of the Economy and the State, University of Chicago, and the Procter and Gamble Foundation is acknowledged gratefully.

Reprinted with permission from *The American Economic Review* 75, no. 4 (September 1985): 656–75. © 1985 by American Economic Association.

emphasizes the difficulty of linking empirically congressional voting patterns and constituent economic interests (James Kau and Paul Rubin, 1979, 1982; Joseph Kalt, 1981; Kalt and Mark Zupan, 1984; Edward Mitchell, 1979). Because my focus is also empirical, I attempt in Table 1 to provide the general reader with a sense of that difficulty.

Consider first who gains and who loses from federal tax-spending policy. This is summarized in panel A of the table. Here two measures of benefits and costs from federal programs are regressed on some state economic characteristics.[1] Each is scaled so that higher values imply more per capita "net benefits" (or lower tax rates). Neither measure is perfect,[2] but the regressions tell a similar story: the federal budget tends to redistribute wealth away from states with high incomes and large manufacturing sectors. Urbanization has a less clear-cut effect. City dwellers pay more taxes (line 2a), but perhaps those who dwell in small cities (i.e., outside SMSAs) receive net benefits (line 1b).

Panel B describes voting patterns in the Senate. The two dependent variables here, like those in panel A, are scaled so that higher values imply more support for federal taxing and spending. Again, despite their imperfections,[3] both measures tell a similar story: apart from the tendency for Democrats to vote for more spending/taxes (col. 7),[4] there is either no connection or a *perverse* connection between the interests of constituents and the votes of their senators. For example, holding party constant, pro-tax/spending voting is either uncorrelated (line 1a) or *negatively* correlated (1b, 2a, 2b) with the direction of benefits from those policies. Further, the characteristics most clearly *negatively* cor-

---

[1] The particular characteristics—income, urbanization and the state's industrial mix—are chosen pragmatically. They can explain these data fairly well, and they are readily available for the much longer historical period which is this paper's main concern.

[2] Both numerator and denominator of line A.1 are estimates based on sometimes arbitrary assumptions—for example, that the burden of the deficit is proportional to taxes paid. Apart from its neglect of benefits, some of the taxes attributed to a state in line A.2 are in fact paid by residents of another.

[3] The variable NTUA is derived from an unweighted count of a senator's votes for increased spending or taxes on *all* roll calls dealing with taxing and spending. Thus, a vote to increase total taxes is weighted the same as a vote to increase the budget of the Battle Monuments Commission. The variable ADA is derived from votes for the Americans for Democratic Action (ADA) position on a selected sample of 20 issues deemed "important" by that organization. These issues are not limited to tax-spending matters, as with NTUA. However, they will usually include the more important tax-spending issues in a Congress, since the ADA has traditionally favored expansion of federal spending, especially on domestic programs.

[4] My 1984 article shows that in popular elections, Democrats tend to draw votes from lower-income voters. Thus, since federal tax-spending policy appears "progressive," the tendency for Democrats to be pro-spending/taxing is consistent with a simple principal-agent story.

TABLE 1. Federal Tax-Spending Patterns, Senate Voting Patterns, and State Economic Characteristics

| | Coefficients of[a] | | | | | | | | |
Dependent Variable	HH INC (1)	MFG (2)	URB (3)	METRO (4)	SPEND/TAX (5)	1 − TAX (6)	DEMS (7)	R^2 (8)	SEE (9)
A. Measures of Benefits									
1. SPEND/TAX × 100									
a	−11.8 (5.5)	−1.22 (3.8)	.20 (.8)					.58	17.5
b	−12.3 (5.8)	−.88 (2.2)	.79 (1.6)	−.36 (1.4)				.60	17.3
2. 1 − TAX									
a	−1.36 (4.2)	−.15 (3.2)	−.09 (2.4)					.64	2.66
b	−1.42 (4.4)	−.11 (1.7)	−.01 (.1)	−.05 (1.3)				.65	2.64
B. Pro-Spending or Pro-Liberal Voting Measures									
1. NTUA									
a					−.01 (.2)		18.4 (3.7)	.24	11.4
b						−.68 (1.8)	18.9 (3.9)	.30	10.9
c	.48 (.3)	.03 (.1)	−.25 (.8)	.18 (1.0)			16.0 (2.9)	.28	11.4

2. ADA

a	.65 (3.4)	.88 (2.4)	.03 (.1)		−.28 (2.7)		26.3 (3.4)	.34	17.5
b				−2.08 (3.6)			30.7 (4.2)	.40	16.7
c			−.13 (.5)				29.5 (3.9)	.51	15.7
Mean	13.5	22.2	65.7	57.6		83.9	106.7	.59	
S.D.	1.6	8.2	14.6	26.1		4.3	26.1	.33	

Notes: Dependent Variables:

1. *SPEND/TAX*: Estimate of federal government expenditures in a state/estimate of federal tax burden in the state. The tax "burden" includes allocation of various nonpersonal taxes (for example, corporation income taxes) to citizens of each state: average for 1975, 1976, 1979 × 100.

2. $(1 - TAX)$: One minus ratio of Internal Revenue Service collections from individual income and payroll taxes in each state to total personal income in the state (taxes may be collected in one state from residents in another). Average for 1977–79 × 100.

3. *NTUA*: 100-average rating by National Taxpayer's Union (NTU) of senators from state for 1979–80. The *NTUA* rating is the percentage of a senator's votes that favored reduced taxes or spending, or opposed increases, so higher values of *NTU* imply more support for taxes/expenditures. The NTU uses all votes on tax-spending issues to construct its index.

4. *ADA*: Average rating by Americans for Democratic Action (ADA) of senators from a state for 1979–80. The *ADA* rating is percentage of times a senator votes for the ADA position on a selected sample of 20 issues. The ADA counts absence or abstention as opposition; I recalculated the *ADA* rating by ignoring these nonvotes.

Independent Variables: Col. 1. *HH INC*: Median Household Income in state (thousands), 1975; col. 2. *MFG*: Percent of nonagricultural labor force in manufacturing, 1978; col. 3.*URB*: Percent of state population in urban areas, 1970; col. 4. *METRO*: Percent of state population in standard metropolitan statistical areas (SMSAs), 1978; cols. 5, 6: see lines A.1, A.2; col. 7. *DEMS*: Number of Democrat senators from state/2, 1979–80.

Sources: SPEND/TAX, $(1 - TAX)$, and independent variables: *Statistical Abstract of the United States; NTUA* and *ADA* from data supplied by NTU and ADA, respectively.

[a] The *t*-ratios are shown in parentheses below coefficients.

related with net spending benefits—income and manufacturing—are either uncorrelated (line 1c) or *positively* correlated (2c) with voting for larger federal spending.

The results in Table 1 are only a suggestive introduction to the empirical literature on congressional voting.[5] But I believe that the reader will find Table 1 consistent with an important broad conclusion of that literature, namely that there is a large "inertial" component (often labelled "ideology") in congressional voting: "liberal" or "conservative" voting patterns tend to persist from issue to issue, whether or not they seem consistent with constituent interests.

My task here will be to see if this sort of inertia is evident in a much longer historical perspective: is it just a recent anomaly or a main feature of the history of legislation? Have long-period changes in economic circumstances had any substantial connection with historical changes in congressional voting patterns? If so, is the connection consistent with changes in economic interests? In answering these questions, I shall try to disentangle the economic analysis of legislation from some of the idiosyncracy of American history. A clear regional pattern underlies data such as those in Table 1: southern congressmen tend to be more conservative than northerners (Kau and Rubin, 1979), while per capita income in the South is also lower than the North. If "economic interest" is supposed to be *all* that matters, this positive correlation between income and liberalism appears perverse. But it can be consonant with a world in which economic interest is either *important* or *unimportant*. There is a long American history of regional political division, as well as of regional economic differences, and any cross-section correlation between income and liberal voting will reflect a mix of historical and economic forces. Accordingly, we cannot tell from the positive correlation we observe today whether economic interest and other factors (like the legacy of the Civil War) tug strongly in opposing directions, or whether economic interest matters little next to "history," or whether history matters little and political redistribution is merely a "normal" consumer good "bought" most heavily by rich constituencies. A major goal herein is to sort these possibilities out.

The paper is organized as follows. Section II sets out the basic

---

[5] The regressions in panel A do not, for example, capture the within-state variance of benefits or costs. For example, if taxes are sufficiently concentrated within a state, a high tax-income ratio or low spending-tax ratio for a state may still leave a majority of residents with net benefits from the federal budget. Also, note that even if the *total* impact of the federal budget is progressive, this need not be true of the *additions* to the budget at issue in congressional votes in 1980. Hence a positive correlation between "pro-spending" votes and income is not necessarily "perverse" from the standpoint of the economic interests of constituents.

economic and political history that underlies the subsequent empirical analysis. Section III describes how I measure both economic interest and voting behavior and what I think these measures tell us. Sections IV and V use these measures in empirical analyses designed to gauge the importance of economic forces in shaping the history of congressional voting. The main findings of this analysis are that: 1) voting patterns in a typical Congress reveal an interplay of economic forces and often conflicting regional cultural preferences, but these preferences seem remarkably stable over time. More importantly: 2) this "historical inertia" has not prevented a profound change in voting patterns over the course of the twentieth century; and 3) this change seems entirely attributable to a corresponding change in economic interests in redistributive legislation. Section VI reexamines some puzzles such as those in Table 1 in light of these findings.

II. The Historical Background

One fact dominates the twentieth-century American economic history which is relevant to this paper: states and regions have become economically more homogeneous. Figure 1 illustrates this for three characteristics.[6] The solid lines track dispersion across states. They begin turning down c. 1920 (over a period centered on 1920) or earlier, and by 1980, have fallen by about 25 percent (urbanization) to about 70 percent (income) from their peak values. The same movements are evident when states are grouped into the nine census regions (broken lines). The generally small vertical distances between these roughly parallel lines imply that the homogenization process has been mainly a regional phenomenon.

Any economic explanation of congressional voting has to come to grips with this profound narrowing of regional economic differences and, presumably, of economic interests. However, if this would seem to imply a similar narrowing of political differences, the crude data belie such similarity. Figure 2 portrays the history of a few measures of state and regional political difference. The top panels focus on party membership in Congress. Any detectable narrowing of sectional differences in party membership seems confined to the most recent two decades or so, or thirty years after the onset of the economic homogenization. In addition, there is much more intraregional variability in party membership than in the economic data. Because the heterogeneity of American parties may make party membership too crude a measure of political difference, the bottom panels of the figure focus directly on

[6] See the notes to Table 3 for explanation and sources of these variables.

voting behavior. The specific measure underlying these panels is the average frequency with which a state's or region's congressmen voted with the northern Democrat majority on successive samples of 25 votes taken in a session of each House. (The sample and the voting variable are described more fully in the next section.) The bottom panels of Figure 2 show time-series of the standard deviation of these frequencies

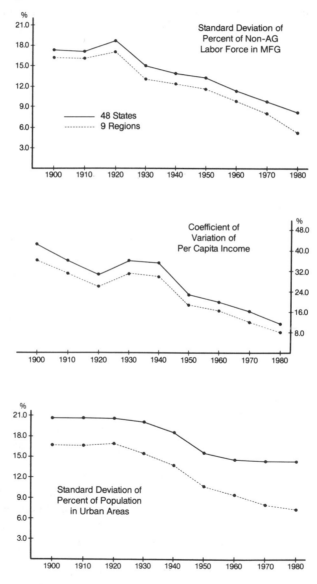

FIGURE 1

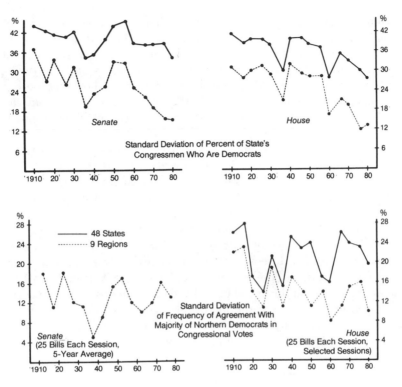

FIGURE 2

across states and regions. They appear trendless. As with party membership, agreement between these political data and the economic data in Figure 1 escapes the naked eye.[7]

I will attempt to bridge this apparent disjunction between economic and political differences in Section VI.

III. The Calibration of Economic Interest and Congressional Voting

Are the data discussed in the two previous sections hiding some historically durable connection between the way congressmen vote and their constituencies' economic stake in that vote? I want to answer this with conventional, easily replicable statistical analysis, and this de-

[7]We cannot, of course, rule out the possibility that increased homogeneity has affected the content of proposed legislation. For example, rural congressmen will oppose either a 1 percent tax or a 10 percent tax on farm incomes, but the former clearly entails a smaller difference between urban and rural interests.

mands plausible empirical summaries of both the votes and the economic interests. This is a formidable demand. The dramatic growth of
the size and scope of the federal government implies that the menu of
issues facing Congress and the nature of the stakes may be much different today than in 1900. My first task, therefore, is to show that there is
enough historical consistency in both the nature of the "stakes" and the
pattern of voting to motivate the reader's interest in the subsequent
empirical analysis.

To get at the consistency of the stakes, I focus on the redistributive element in federal policies. I showed earlier that contemporary
budget policy redistributes wealth away from high-income, manufacturing-intensive, and, possibly, large urban areas. Unfortunately, a
long history of the redistributive effects of federal spending and taxes is
unavailable. However, the income-progressivity feature of the redistribution seems to go back at least to 1950 (Morgan Reynolds and Eugene
Smolensky, 1977). Moreover, there are enough income tax collection
data for replication of the sort of regression on line A.2a in Table 1 for
most of the relevant historical period and they also show a fairly consistent pattern. I regressed the log of the income taxes/income ratio in
each state in the years 1920, 1930, . . . , 1970 on the same three variables as in Table 1 plus time dummies and obtained:

$$\text{Log}(Tax/Income)_{it}$$

$$= \text{Constant} + \text{coefficients} \times YEAR \text{ dummies}$$

$$+ \underset{(5.0)}{.59} \left(\frac{Per\ Capita\ Income_{it}}{US\ Per\ Capita\ Income_{t}} \right) \tag{1}$$

$$+ \underset{(5.4)}{.011}\ URB_{it} + \underset{(3.8)}{.006}\ MFG_{it}$$

$$R^2 = .95,\ SEE = .32,$$

where i = state, t = 1920, 1930, . . . , 1970.[8]

When the regression is estimated separately for each of the six
years, the coefficients are not always significant, but 17 of the 18 are
positive and all 18 simple correlations are significantly positive. Thus,
the few available pieces of data give at least a broad hint about the nature of the stakes in political redistribution: the constituents from high-
income, manufacturing-intensive, and urban areas have *generally* been

---

[8]The sample is the 48 continental states, except Delaware, which is an extreme
outlier in the earlier years. Tax data are from U.S. Internal Revenue Service and comprise personal income and employment taxes. See Table 1 for definition of *URB* and
MFG, and see Table 3 for sources. The *t*-ratios are shown in parentheses.

asking for opposition by their congressmen to expansion of the federal budget for at least the last sixty years.[9] Accordingly, in the subsequent analysis I use the income, urbanization, and manufacturing measures to summarize the diversity of interest in redistribution across congressional constituencies.

I will compare these interests with an equally simple summary measure of congressional voting behavior: the extent of support for the position taken by the majority of northern Democrats. While the details of my treatment of the Senate and House differ, nothing essential is lost if I first describe my procedure for senators and then explain why I think it results in an historically consistent measure of voting behavior.

From each Congress, from the 63rd (when popularly elected senators began sitting) to the 96th (1980), I drew a sample of 25 bills on which record votes were taken.[10] I included only votes on "economic" (i.e., non-defense budgetary and economic regulatory) issues where the winning side had less than a 2–1 margin and where over half the senators voted.[11] These criteria were meant to limit the analysis to controversial issues with potentially significant redistributive elements. Each senator's vote on each bill was then coded +1 if he voted in favor of the position taken by the majority of northern Democrats or 0 if he voted the other way. Call the dichotomous variable liberal (*LIB*). I then extracted the *regional*[12] elements of *LIB* on each vote from the regression

[9]The qualifications to this conclusion would include: 1) Non-income taxes—customs and excises—were far more important revenue sources prior to World War II than today, and there is no presumption that their geographical distribution followed that of income taxes. In addition, customs duties provided net *benefits* to protected industries. 2) Other forms of federal government activity (for example, regulation) could have different distributional implications than spending and taxes, so general opposition to expansion of government economic activity need not be in the interest of, for example, a high-income constituency. 3) One could surely lengthen the list of variables potentially related to the interest in redistribution—I intend my short list as a plausible summary, not an exhaustive summary.

[10]The voting data are from tape files compiled by the University of Michigan Inter-University Consortium for Political and Social Research (ICPSR). The files give a brief narrative description of each record vote and the position taken by each congressman.

[11]Today a record vote almost always attracts substantial participation, but prior to the 1930's it was not uncommon for a majority of Senators to be absent without declaring a preference on a vote. I counted any expression of support or opposition—paired votes and announced positions—as a "vote."

[12]Since the economic data are available by state, my goal of relating political to economic behavior suggests extracting the state, rather than regional, regularities in *LIB*. However, with no more than two senators from a state voting on a bill, the "standard error" of the "state" regularity is rather high. Also, the dominant role of regional differences in the interstate variance of economic variables suggests that "region" is a sensible level of aggregation for my purpose.

$$[LIB_{ij} - \overline{LIB_j}] = \sum_k B_{kj} \cdot D_{ik} + \text{error term}, \tag{2}$$

where $LIB_{ij} = i$th senator's vote on the jth bill, $\overline{LIB_j} = $ average value of LIB on the jth bill, ($i = 1, \ldots, 96$ senators; $j = 1, \ldots, 25$ bills in each session of Congress), $D_{ik} = $ dummy variable $= +1$ if senator i represents a state in census region k; 0 otherwise; $k = 1, \ldots, 9$ census regions, $B_{kj} = $ bill-specific regression coefficient of D_{ik}.

For each bill, I also estimated a regression with the same left-hand side variable as (2) and right-hand variables:

$$\text{regional dummies} + C_j\,(P_i - \overline{P_j}) \tag{3}$$

where $P_i = +1$ if senator i is a Democrat,[13] 0 if Republican; $\overline{P_j} = $ average value of P on bill j; $C_j = $ bill-specific regression coefficient.

An important motivation for holding party effects constant, as in (3), is to control for some of the effects of the intraconstituency diversity of economic interest.[14]

The measure (denoted B_{kt}) of a region's liberal voting tendency for a session which I use in subsequent analyses is the average of each region's B_{kj} across the 25 sample votes in that session. In substance, each B_{kt} is just a count of the relative frequency of agreement with the northern Democrat majority. For example, suppose that the typical New England senator voted LIB 30 percent more frequently than the average senator and 20 percent more frequently than the average of his party colleagues in 1920. Then B_{kt} from (2) $= +.3$, while B_{kt} from (3) $= +.2$ for $t = 1920$. Since the average of the B_{kt} across regions is roughly zero[15] in every session, any B_{kt} measures the liberalism (LIB) of a region's senators *relative* to all senators in that session.

---

[13] Senators who belonged to neither major party were assigned to one of the two main parties as follows. For each of the 25 bills in each session, I calculated the average value of LIB for Democrats and for Republicans. Then I correlated the third-party senator's LIB with the difference between the Democrat and Republican average. If the correlation was significantly positive (negative), I called the senator a Democrat (Republican). In virtually every case these correlations were so high (on the order of $\pm.8$) that there was little doubt about where to put the ostensibly maverick senator.

[14] See fn. 4. More generally, a senator's constituency is not his "state," but those parts of the electorate relevant to putting him in office and keeping him there. See Richard Fenno (1978) for a discussion of this point. My earlier article shows that the economic characteristics of this "supporting electorate" differ systematically according to a senator's party. Thus, for example, the typical constituency of Democrats from rich states gains less from redistribution than that of Democrats from poor states, but not necessarily less than that of Republicans from poor states.

[15] More precisely, since the number of states per region varies, a state-weighted average of B_{kt} across regions is zero. At the same time, my procedure induces a purely statistical bias in favor of positive B's for the North and negative B's for the South. The nature and size of the bias is discussed in fn. 18 below.

My *LIB* measure and its derivatives are replicable, but are they measuring any historically consistent political behavior? I want to suggest that they measure just what the *LIB* acronym might suggest: a propensity to support progressive redistribution. This is not a controversial suggestion for the period since the New Deal, since Democrats, especially in the North, have been in the vanguard of support for expansion of the progressive tax-spending structure. But I want to argue that the same interpretation is plausible for the pre-New Deal period as well. In my sample of bills from the pre-New Deal Congresses, I found two issues recurring often enough to permit meaningful generalization. These were bills to change 1) the level or degree of progressivity of federal income tax rates, and 2) tariff rates on imports of manufactured goods. For each such bill in my sample, I computed the difference between the percentage of northern Democrat and Republican votes in favor of increased taxes or progressivity or of increased tariffs on manufactured goods. The results, summarized in Table 2, indicate the clear preference of northern Democrats for higher/more-progressive income taxes and lower tariffs on manufactured goods. The distributive implications of the northern Democrats' income tax policy are reasonably clear. I am unaware of any evidence on the incidence of tariffs in this period. However, the first-order protective effects of tariffs in the early twentieth century would appear to be regressive: they raised incomes of individuals (owners and workers in manufacturing) who, in a society with a large, low-income agricultural sector, had

TABLE 2.   Differences between Northern Democrat and Republican Positions on Income Tax and Tariff Issues, Vote Samples for 61st–74th Congresses

	Number of Votes	
Issue and Position	Senate	House
A. For Higher Income Taxes or More Progressivity		
1. Total Bills	21	11
a. % Northern Dems (*ND*) For > % Republicans (*GOP*)	14	10
b. % *ND* < % *GOP*	3	0
c. No significant difference	4	1
B. For Higher Mfd. Good Tariffs:		
1. Total Bills	32	21
a. % *ND* > % *GOP*	0	0
b. % *ND* < % *GOP*	30	20
c. No significant difference	2	1

Source: ICPSR File.

above-average income. So, with some uncertainty, it seems plausible to characterize the economic policy favored by northern Democrats as consistently pro-redistributive for all of this century.

The main conclusions from this brief tour of twentieth-century economic and political data are: 1) high values of B (or LIB) connote congressional support for a progressive redistributive economic policy; 2) the main beneficiaries of such policies should be found in poor, non-urban, non-manufacturing-intensive areas.

IV. Empirical Results: The Historical Connection Between Economics and Politics

In light of previous discussion, I analyze the link between economics and politics in terms of three models of the process:

1. Only economic forces matter in politics.

2. Economic forces don't matter at all, that is, historical regional political differences persist in spite of economic change.

3. Both economics and history matter. Operationally, this entails estimating regressions which are variants of the general form

$$B_{kt} = K + \Sigma M_i \cdot ECON_{ikt} + \Sigma N_k \cdot R_k, \tag{4}$$

where B_{kt} = the relative LIB of region (or state) k's congressmen in year t; $ECON_{ikt}$ = proxies for k's economic ($ECON$) interest in liberal (LIB) votes in t; R_k = a set of time-invariant regional (or state) dummies; K, M, N = parameters.

The overall fit and the accuracy of the parameters of regressions on various subsets of the $ECON$ and R variables will be used to draw inferences about which of the three models best describes the voting behavior summarized by the B_{kt}.

For the Senate, I have estimates of each region's B_k for each session of Congress from the 63rd through the 96th (1913–80). The $ECON$ variables suggested by the preceding discussion (income, urbanization, manufacturing intensity) are consistently available only every decade. As a compromise between the rich political data and lean economic data, I computed (a) 5-year averages of the B_k and (b) semidecadal values of the economic variables (by interpolation of the decade-end values). The economic variables, like the political variables, are each measured relative to their period means. This yields 126 observations on relative political behavior and relative economic conditions: one for each of nine regions in each of 14 periods ending 1915, 1920, . . . , 1980. Table 3 summarizes the results of implementing the three models with this body of data. There are two dependent variables: relative liberalism of a region's senators without regard to party in columns 1–3 and adjusted for party (i.e., the average deviation of a region's Democrats and Republicans from their party's average) in columns 4–6. Each triplet implements the three models successively. The clear result is that the eclectic model which includes both *ECON* variables and regional dummies yields the most adequate description of the voting history. The eclectic model has greater explanatory power (as measured by *SEE*), and coefficients of both the economic and regional variables tend to be estimated more precisely than in the special-purpose models. Thus, these data suggest that economic forces have combined with persistent regional differences to produce the observed Senate voting patterns.

The same conclusion emerges from analysis of voting in the House of Representatives. Here, to economize on computation costs, I sampled votes only from sessions ending in year 0 and year 6 of each decade from 1910 through 1980. However, with over 400 representatives, there are sufficient degrees of freedom to allow the state, as well as the region, to be the unit of analysis. Accordingly, for each House vote,[16] I estimated equations like (2) and (3) except that 48 state dummy variables, rather than just 9 regional dummies appear in them. Then, as with the Senate, I averaged the coefficients of the dummies over the 25-vote regressions in each session to provide my measure of the liberalism of a state's House delegation for that session. This yielded a sample of 720 observations on the measure of political behavior—one for each of 48 states in each of 15 sessions ending 1910, 1916, 1920, 1926 . . . 1980. The results of implementing the same three models as for the Senate are shown in Table 4. Again, the eclectic models (cols. 3 and 6) fit the data significantly better than either the "economics only" or "history only" models.[17]

---

[16] As with the Senate, I drew samples of 25 votes—on criteria like those for the Senate vote samples—from each of the sessions included in the analysis.

[17] The economic variables appear to have less marginal explanatory power over the "location only" model for the Senate (compare the change in *SEE* from cols. 2 to 3 or cols. 5 to 6 in the two tables). However, this is due to the larger number of locational dummies in the House regressions, and the consequent ability to better "explain" state idiosyncrasies. If the House data are, like the Senate data, grouped into regions and the Table 3 regressions replicated exactly (i.e., with regional economic and dummy variables), the *SEE*'s are as follows:

col. 1: .116   col. 2: .124   col. 3: .087

col. 4: .086   col. 5: .075   col. 6: .057.

Here the gain in *SEE* from col. 2 to 3 or col. 5 to 6 is around twice that in Table 4 and almost identical to that in Table 3 for the Senate.

TABLE 3. Regressions of Political Liberalism in the Senate on Economic Characteristics and Regional Dummies; 5-Year Periods: 1910–15 to 1975–80, 9 Regions

| | Dependent Variable and Model, Liberalism (B_{kl}) | | | | | |
| | No Adjustment for Party | | | Net of Party Effect | | |
Independent Variables	ECON (1)	Region (2)	Both (3)	ECON (4)	Region (5)	Both (6)
Economic						
1. MFG	-.281 (2.2)		-.576 (1.5)	-.199 (1.9)		-.436 (1.8)
2. PCI	-.319 (3.3)		-.501 (5.1)	.018 (.2)		-.374 (5.9)
3. URB	.288 (1.3)		-.467 (1.5)	.232 (1.3)		-.195 (1.0)
Regional Dummies						
4. New England (NE) (ME, NH, VT, MA, RI, CT)		-.071 (2.2)	.138 (2.9)		.029 (1.4)	.171 (5.6)
5. Mid-Atlantic (MA) (NY, NJ, PA, DE, MD)		-.060 (1.9)	.227 (5.9)		.037 (1.8)	.223 (8.9)
6. EN Central (ENC) (OH, IN, IL, MI, WI)		-.022 (.7)	.180 (4.8)		.032 (1.5)	.166 (6.9)
7. WN Central (WNC) (MN, IA, MO, ND, SD, NE, KS)		-.064 (2.0)	-.193 (5.6)		.040 (1.9)	-.042 (1.9)
8. S Atlantic (SA) (VA, WV, NC, SC, GA, FL)		.039 (1.2)	-.128 (2.4)		-.103 (4.9)	-.207 (6.0)
9. ES Central (ESC) (KY, TN, AL, MS)		.074 (2.3)	-.210 (3.7)		-.037 (1.8)	-.222 (6.1)
10. WS Central (WSC) (AR, LA, OK, TX)		.047 (1.5)	-.148 (4.2)		-.084 (4.0)	-.219 (9.6)
11. Mountain (MT) (MT, ID, WY, CO, NM, AZ, UT, NV)		.007 (.2)	-.077 (1.3)		-.002 (0.1)	-.060 (1.5)

12. Pacific (PAC) (WA, OR, CA)	.24	.050 (1.6)	.209 (4.9)	.085 (4.1)	.188 (6.9)
R^2	.112	.17	.57	.38	.69
SEE		.119	.087	.078	.057
			.09		
			.093		

Notes: Dependent Variables: For cols. 1–3, the variable is derived from regression estimates of equation (2) (see text). Coefficients of the regional dummies in those vote regressions are averaged over the 25 votes in each session. Then these regional averages are further averaged over 5-year periods as follows. Since each session of Congress ends in an even-numbered year, let $\bar{B}_{k2}, \bar{B}_{k4}, \ldots, \bar{B}_{k10}$ represent the average coefficient for region k in the 25 vote regressions for a session ending in year 2, year 4, etc., of a decade. The dependent variable for the first 5-year period in a decade is $1/2.5\,(\bar{B}_{k2} + \bar{B}_{k4} + .5\bar{B}_{k6})$ and that for the second 5-year period is $1/2.5\,(.5\bar{B}_{k6} + \bar{B}_{k8} + \bar{B}_{k10})$. (For the period ending 1915, the calculation is $(1/1.5)\,(\bar{B}_{k4} + .5\bar{B}_{k6})$, because I exclude data from Senates without popularly elected senators.) The variable for cols. 4–6 is constructed in the same way except that it is based on regression coefficients from equation (3) which includes a party dummy. The vote data on which these variables are based come from the ICPSR files.

Independent Variables: Economic—each of these has the form $(X_{kt} - \bar{X}_t)$ where X_{kt} is an average over the states in a region in year t and $\bar{X}_t$ is a 48-state average for t (Alaska and Hawaii are excluded), and t is every 5 years from 1915 through 1980. The definition and sources of the state data are

1. MFG = percent of nonagricultural labor force in manufacturing. For 1940, see the U.S. Bureau of Labor Statistics, *Handbook of Labor Statistics*; for 1910–40, I use (gainful workers in manufacturing/all nonfarm gainful workers) from Everett S. Lee et al. (1957). I regressed the BLS data on the Lee et al. data for 1940 and 1950 ($R^2 > .95$) and used the regression coefficients and the Lee et al. data to generate estimates of the BLS measure for years prior to 1940.

2. PCI = Log of per capita personal income. For 1930–80, from U.S. Bureau of the Census, *Historical Statistics of the United States* and *Statistical Abstract* . . .; for 1920, Maurice Leven (1925); for 1910, Lee et al.

3. URB = Percent of state population in urban areas from *Historical Statistics* . . . and *Statistical Abstract*. . . .

For the middle year of each decade, each variable is a linear interpolation of the value at the beginning and end of the decade. Regional dummies each = +1 if the dependent variable is for region k, 0 otherwise. The regions are as defined by the Census Bureau, except that, as in Lee et al., Delaware and Maryland are moved from the South Atlantic to Middle Atlantic region. All variables except dummies are in fractions of 100, for example, the coefficient of MFG in col. 1 means: "in a region where MFG is 10 percent above the national average, senators will vote LIB 2.81 percent less frequently than the average senator." The coefficients of the regional variables in col. 3 are given for $MFG = PCI = URB = 0$, for example, the coefficient for New England in col. 3 means "if New England had the national-average economic characteristics, its senators would have voted LIB 13.8 percent more frequently than the average senator." For cols. (4)–(6), these statements apply to the deviation of the average senator in a region from the average of all his party colleagues. The residuals from the regressions in cols. 3 and 6 are both serially correlated ($r = .35$). (This is partly induced by the averaging process used in generating the data, in that the dependent variable for adjacent periods shares the common term $.5\bar{B}_{k6}$ (see above). Accordingly, I reestimated these regressions via GLS. The results were virtually identical to those reported here, except that t-ratios were smaller than those reported here (shown below the averaging coefficients in parentheses). For example, the GLS t-ratios for MFG, PCI, and URB were 1.1, 4.2, and 1.4 for the col. 3 regression, and 1.0, 4.6, and 1.1 for col. 6.

TABLE 4. Regressions of House Voting Patterns on Economic Characteristics and State Dummies, 15 Congresses (1910–80), 48 States

| | Dependent Variable and Model Liberalism (B_{kt}) | | | | | |
| | No Adjustment for Party | | | Net of Party Effect | | |
Independent Variables	ECON (1)	State (2)	Both (3)	ECON (4)	State (5)	Both (6)
Economic						
1. MFG	−.134		−.273	−.042		−.151
	(2.1)		(1.7)	(1.1)		(1.5)
2. PCI	−.323		−.327	.093		−.163
	(7.5)		(5.4)	(3.5)		(4.4)
3. URB	.234		−.878	.070		−.483
	(3.2)		(6.6)	(−1.6)		(6.0)
State Dummies: Regional Averages (and standard deviations)						
4. New England		−.085	.104		.042	.144
		(.12)	(.35)		(.02)	(.12)
5. Mid-Atlantic		−.002	.297		.042	.201
		(.08)	(.13)		(.01)	(.07)
6. EN Central		−.060	.124		.026	.125
		(.05)	(.09)		(.02)	(.05)
7. WN Central		−.087	−.213		.058	−.010
		(.12)	(.22)		(.05)	(.06)
8. S Atlantic		.100	−.082		.093	−.189
		(.04)	(.09)		(.06)	(.06)
9. ES Central		.115	−.144		−.057	−.193
		(.05)	(.11)		(.09)	(.12)
10. WS Central		.150	−.006		−.066	−.148
		(.02)	(.09)		(.03)	(.04)
11. Mountain		.025	.081		−.017	−.048
		(.11)	(.16)		(.04)	(.06)
12. Pacific		−.011	.168		.059	.154
		(.04)	(.14)		(.02)	(.06)
R^2	.09	.30	.45	.02	.31	.43
SEE	.205	.185	.165	.126	.109	.099

Notes: See Table 3 and text for definitions and sources of variables. Each of the 720 observations is on a state in a session. The sessions are at 4- or 6-year intervals 1910, 1916, 1920, 1926 . . . 1980. The dependent variable is the average coefficient on a state dummy variable from 25 vote regressions like equations (2) and (3) estimated in each session. The regressions used for estimating the dependent variable for cols. 4–6 include a party dummy. The Economic variables are deviations of state variables from a 48-state average for each session. (District-level data are unavailable for the whole period.) The regressions in cols. 2, 3, 5, and 6 include 48 state dummies. Their coefficients are summarized here by region: the standard deviations of the state coefficients in a region are shown in parentheses below the regional mean of these coefficients. These means have the same interpretation as their counterparts in Table 3—i.e., they show the difference between frequency of liberal voting in a region and in whole House (cols. 2, 3) or within a party (cols. 5, 6). I reestimated the regressions using weighted least squares, with (number of congressmen)$^{-1/2}$ as the weight, because analysis of the residuals revealed some heteroscedasticity. But the coefficients and *t*-ratios of the economic variables were virtually identical to those reported here.

It is, at this point, only convenient shorthand to describe the preceding results as showing that economic change modifies historical inertia. These results are conceptually similar to those of the previously cited literature on contemporary voting in that "noneconomic" variables—here regional dummies—have important marginal explanatory power. So, one could allude to regional differences in ideology as easily as to "historical inertia" (or "tastes" or "unmeasured variables"). Later, I provide some motivation for my shorthand by showing that there is in fact considerable inertia in the history—that is, that the coefficients of the regional dummy variables in cols. 3 and 6 of Tables 3 and 4 are stable. But, however they are labeled, the statistical significance and large magnitudes of these regional differences are a challenge to future research:[18] can we find measurable regional characteristics with histo-

---

[18] A very small part of these differences is due to the statistical bias alluded to in fn. 12. The bias arises because my *LIB* measure is, in part, regionally based. Since northern Democrats are a subset of northern senators, measures of how the average northern senator and the northern Democrat majority vote will tend to agree even if there are no substantive regional differences. Thus, the coefficients of the northern regional dummies will tend to be positive. However, the *magnitude* of this bias is much too small to account for the regional differences observed in cols. 3 and 6 of Tables 3 and 4.

To isolate the magnitude of the bias, assume that every one of 100 senators votes randomly on every bill, so there are no substantive regional differences at all. My procedure would then select the X Democrats among the 70 (in round numbers) northern senators and use their randomly generated majority position to define a *LIB* vote. The random process generating this majority produces a mean of $.5\,X + .399\sqrt{X}$ votes in favor of that position among northern Democrats (under a normal approximation). This implies the following differences between the mean probability ($\bar{P}$) of a vote favorable to the northern Democrat majority and the corresponding regional probability;

$$P_{NORTH} - \bar{P} = .399\sqrt{X}\,[(1/70) - (1/100)]$$

$$P_{SOUTH} - \bar{P} = -.399\sqrt{X}\,/100.$$

These differences (or, equivalently, regression coefficients on regional dummies) are as follows for various values of X which span the range of twentieth-century political experience:

X	$P_{NORTH} - \bar{P}$	$P_{SOUTH} - \bar{P}$
10	.005	−.013
30	.009	−.022
50	.012	−.028
60	.013	−.031

Thus, statistical bias implies coefficients of regional dummies which average only one-tenth or so of those in cols. 3 and 6 of Tables 3 and 4.

ries much different from those already in my analysis whose inclusion would reduce the explanatory power of the regional dummies?[19]

In the next section, I use the results in Tables 3 and 4 to analyze historical *changes* in voting patterns, but they also reveal interesting regularities in the average "levels" of political behavior:

1. The coefficients of the economic variables in columns 3 and 6 are "sensible" (unlike their contemporary counterparts in Table 1): these variables, all of which we have seen to be negatively correlated with benefits from redistribution, are also negatively correlated with voting for redistribution.

2. Economics and history have tended to be opposing forces. This is revealed by comparing the regional coefficients in columns 2 and 5 (of either Table 3 or 4) with their counterparts in columns 3 and 6. The latter isolate the effect of history, because economics is separately accounted for in these regressions. The coefficients in columns 2 and 5 show the *net* impact of history and some average of economic forces. Note that these "net" measures range less broadly (±.10, very roughly) than the "pure history" measures (the range in cols. 3 and 6 is around ±.20). Thus, economic forces have typically dampened the effects of history. In particular, they have dampened the South's conservatism and the North's liberalism.[20]

3. Economic forces affect both the behavior of congressmen from

[19] My earlier paper argues that differences among senators in sources of electoral and financial support can explain much of the apparent ideological inertia in contemporary voting. For example, senators from the same state will vote differently because they drew votes and funds from systematically different groups within the state. This finding suggests that we look to persistent regional differences in these sources of electoral and financial support for an economic explanation of historical inertia—for example, senators from historically conservative regions may have drawn support from the upper end of their state's income distribution. On this argument, the low voting participation of low-income blacks in the South for most of the twentieth century may help explain that region's historical conservatism. If so, the size of the regional coefficients would be reduced if we could substitute something like income per voter for income per capita in the regressions.

[20] The same dampening also shows up within regions. In table 4, note the smaller intraregional variation (the entries in parentheses) of the net coefficients in cols. 2 and 5 vs. their pure history counterparts in cols. 3 and 6. Yet another indication of the opposition of economics and history is revealed by subtracting the coefficients in col. 3 (or col. 6) from their counterparts in col. 2 (or col. 5). This operation shows the average direction of the effect of regional economic forces in modifying history, and it almost always yields a number opposite in sign to the impact of history. For example, line 4, col. 6 of Table 3 tells us that, *holding economic forces constant*, the typical New England senator votes liberal 17 percent more frequently than his party colleagues. But when economics is not held constant (col. 5), this excess liberal frequency is only 3 percent. The implication is that economics has, on average over the twentieth century, pulled against these senators' "natural" liberalism.

the same party and the party composition of Congress. To see this, compare the coefficients of the economic variables in column 6 (which describe intraparty behavior) with those in column 3 (where interparty differences are not removed). The former have the same signs but are smaller absolutely than the latter. This says that, for example, higher income in a region makes both Democrats and Republicans in that region more conservative (col. 6, line 2) but it makes the average congressman still more conservative (the absolute value of col. 3, line 2 exceeds that of col. 6, line 2 in both tables). This implies an increase in the number of more conservative Republicans representing that region.[21] Apparently congressmen are at least partly constrained by the central position of their party: they move away from it to accommodate the economic interests of their constituencies but not always far enough to remain in office. This finding helps explain why narrowing of interregional differences in party composition (for example, the breakup of the "Solid South") lags behind the narrowing of economic differences: the initial changes in economic interest can be accommodated by shifts in position within a party, but their cumulation over time eventually breaks a party's hold on a region.

V. The Economic Basis of Historical Change in Congressional Politics

Thus far I have shown that voting patterns in a typical Congress can be described by the interaction of economic forces and persisting regional differences, rather than by the working of economic forces alone. In this section, I examine critically the logical corollary of that description—that the only source of historical *change* in voting patterns is economic change. How well does this corollary describe the changes that have occurred over the course of the twentieth century? Are the political changes attributable to economic change substantial or trivial? Are they substantial enough to overcome or just slightly modify the otherwise persisting regional differences?

The answers are summarized in Table 5 (for the Senate) and Table 6 (House). These tables reveal a profound change in regional voting patterns over the course of the century, and they show that

---

[21] Compare also the sizes of the differences between the regional coefficients in cols. 2 and 3 on the one hand, with those between cols. 5 and 6 on the other. These measures of the impact of economic forces in modifying history tend to be smaller absolutely within parties (col. 5–col. 6) than within the Senate or House as a whole (col. 2–col. 3), though they go in the same direction. Again, the implication is that if economics impels toward, for example, more conservative voting, part of the impulse is reflected in the replacement of members of the more liberal party.

TABLE 5.   Change in Frequency of Liberal Voting in the Senate, c. 1920–c. 1975, Regions

Liberal Voting Measure	Region and Voting Measure × 10³									SD Across Regions (10)
	NE (1)	MA (2)	ENC (3)	WNC (4)	SA (5)	ESC (6)	WSC (7)	MT (8)	PAC (9)	
A. Within Senate (No Party Adjustment)										
1. Actual c.1920	-225	-118	-75	-71	206	188	171	0	-58	152
2. Actual c.1975	154	89	148	-6	-136	-139	-119	-90	135	128
3. Change (2.-1.) (Col. 3, Table 3)	379	207	223	65	-342	-327	-291	-90	193	273
					($r = .95$)					
4. Predicted Change	290	189	109	-121	-214	-274	-230	-63	115	204
5. Residual (3.-4.)	89	18	114	186	-128	-53	-61	-27	78	100
B. Within Parties (Net of Party Effect)										
1. Actual c.1920	-44	-30	18	50	-12	-22	-51	-13	48	37
2. Actual c.1975	151	212	107	25	-198	-175	-167	-64	141	159
3. Change (2.-1.) (Col. 6, Table 3)	195	242	89	-25	-186	-153	-116	-51	93	153
					($r = .96$)					
4. Predicted Change	182	121	66	-85	-147	-192	-148	-26	79	134
5. Residual (3.-4.)	13	121	23	60	-39	39	-13	-25	14	49

Note: The entries in the table are based on the measure of liberal voting analyzed in Table 3—i.e., the frequency of agreement with the majority position of northern Democrats, for example, the -225 on line A.1, col. 1, means that New England senators voted with the northern Democrat majority 22.5 percent less frequently than the average senator (over a period centered on 1920). The entries on lines A.1 and A.2 are the average of the dependent variable in Table 3, cols. 1–3 (×10³) for the 1915, 1920, and 1925 periods, and 1970, 1975, and 1980 periods, respectively. Lines B.1 and B.2 use the dependent variable in Table 3, cols. 4–6. The entries on lines A.4 and B.4 are the changes in the predicted values over the relevant period from the regressions in cols. 3 and 6 of Table 3, respectively. These are found by multiplying the change in each economic variable by its coefficient from the indicated Table 3 regression and summing. The r = coefficient of correlation between actual and predicted change.

TABLE 6.   Change in Frequency of Liberal Voting in the House, c.1920–c.1975, Regions

Liberal Voting Measure	NE (1)	MA (2)	ENC (3)	WNC (4)	SA (5)	ESC (6)	WSC (7)	MT (8)	PAC (9)	SD Across Regions (10)
				Region and Voting Measure × 10^3						
A. Within House (No Party Adjustment)										
1. Actual c.1920	-227	-108	-90	-13	171	230	231	-35	-144	169
2. Actual c.1975	183	108	-54	-85	-80	-91	-35	-117	73	105
3. Change (2.-1.)	410	216	36	-98	-252	-321	-266	-82	217	253
					(r = .98)					
4. Predicted Change	340	210	121	-84	-187	-195	-247	-90	143	207
5. Residual (3.-4.)	70	6	-85	-14	-65	-126	-19	8	74	67
B. Within Parties (Net of Party Effect)										
1. Actual c.1920	-65	-13	2	73	-23	25	-5	-28	20	39
2. Actual c.1975	170	120	45	-10	-183	-130	-180	-58	65	129
3. Change (2.-1.)	235	133	43	-83	-160	-155	-175	-30	45	142
					(r = .98)					
4. Predicted Change	182	115	66	-46	-103	-107	-136	-50	78	114
5. Residual (3.-4.)	48	18	-23	-37	-67	-48	-39	20	-33	36

Note: See Table 5. The same techniques used to generate data in that table are used here. Predicted and actual values come from regressions like those in Table 3 rather than Table 4, i.e., the House data are grouped into regions and regressions like those in Table 3 (using 9 regional dummies) are used to generate the coefficients of the economic variables which are then used to calculate the predicted changes on lines A.4 and B.4. The data are from 4-period averages with 1910, 1916, 1920, and 1926 comprising the first period, and 1966, 1970, 1976, and 1980 the second.

nearly all this change can be attributed to changed economic interests. The basic facts about voting patterns are on the first three lines of each panel of each table (positive values denote support for liberal policies). In the early part of the century, support for liberal economic policy came mainly from the South, and opposition from the Northeast and Pacific states. Today, these alignments are exactly reversed (see panel A). Party alignments changed similarly: the number of northern Democrats grew and victory for southern Republicans became conceivable. But a profound change in the same direction also occurred within each party. This is shown on the first three lines of panel B in the tables. In the early twentieth century, regional differences within parties were relatively small (line B.1).[22] But in the sixty years after World War I, the northern members of both parties grew more liberal and the southerners more conservative (B.3). These within-party changes have accounted for a substantial part of the overall change in Congress (compare the standard deviations in col. 10 for lines A.3 and B.3) and have produced considerable regional differences within parties today.

I think that the most noteworthy finding of this paper is the remarkably close degree to which these profound political changes can be attributed to changes in economic interest. This is seen by comparing lines 3 and 4 of each panel in both Tables 5 and 6. The "predicted changes" on line 4 are obtained from the coefficients of the economic variables in the regressions in col. 3 or col. 6 in Table 3 or 4, and the change in those variables from the early to late twentieth century. There are 36 predicted changes in Tables 5 and 6 (two voting measures for each House for each of nine regions). Only 1 of these 36 disagrees with the sign of the actual change. Only 2 deviate from the actual change by more than half the standard deviation of the actual change. None of the correlation coefficients between these actual and predicted changes is below .95.[23]

---

[22] But economic differences were relatively large. The explanation for this strange pairing which is consistent with my previous results rests on the opposition of history and economics. Prior to World War I, the strong northern economic interest in conservative economic policy and southern interest in liberal policy clashed with opposite historical tendencies (see the pattern of the dummy variables in Tables 3 and 4, cols. 3 and 6). At the level of Congress as a whole (line A.1) the economic interest dominated, but within parties the two forces offset each other (B.1).

[23] The regressions in Table 4 and associated data permit comparison of actual and predicted changes across the 48 states. These state-level data are also highly correlated (.82 for both the within-House and within-party measures). In spite of the greater "noise" in these state-level data, the positive correlation holds even after the very large regional elements are removed: the correlation of the actual with predicted *deviations* of state changes from the regional means is .37 for within-House data and .49 within-party (both are significant).

The results are similar if the longer period is divided into two subperiods of roughly equal length centered on the end of World War II. This is done in Table 7. These subperiods have somewhat different characteristics—more stable regional party alignments and slower erosion of regional economic differences in the pre-World War II period—but the simple economic model is able to rationalize most of the political change in both subperiods: of the 72 pairs of actual and predicted changes in Table 7, the signs agree in 63 cases. The correlation coefficient between these two variables never falls below .80 in the eight series in the table, and averages .86. The substantive message of Table 7 is that the South's move away from liberal policies and the North's move toward them is not compressed into the recent period when regional party alignments began changing. The economic forces underlying these shifts and the political response to them are palpably evident long before this and continue to work essentially up to the present.

So far I have forced on the data a model in which economic change is the only source of political change. An alternative story would be that the noneconomic regional preferences, which I have so far assumed to have remained unchanged, have in fact changed as well. That alternative cannot be ignored in light of the seemingly massive and long-lasting political realignments engendered by the New Deal. Could not, for example, the post-New Deal rise of labor unions and ethnic and racial constituencies in the North have been responsible for the shift toward liberal politics in that region? Table 7 provides part of the answer—the shift was going on before the New Deal. But I sought a more formal test. Instead of *assuming* that the regional effects in the columns 3 and 6 regressions of Tables 3 and 4 never changed, I added a set of post-New Deal regional dummies; each = 1 for an observation on a particular region for 1940 and after, 0 otherwise. The coefficients of these post-New Deal regional dummies show the extent to which regional voting patterns (net of the effects of the economic variables) *changed* from the pre- to the post-New Deal period. Test of the null hypothesis (that the set of regional coefficients changed) generates statistics with an F-distribution as follows: [24]

$$F(\text{Senate}) = 0.85 \qquad (d.f. = 9,105)$$
$$F(\text{Senate, within parties}) = 2.09 \qquad (9,105)$$
$$F(\text{House}) = 1.64 \qquad (9,114)$$
$$F(\text{House, within parties}) = 2.30 \qquad (9,114)$$
$$F_{.05} \approx 2.0 \qquad F_{.01} \approx 2.6$$

[24] For the House, I am testing the hypothesis that coefficients of *regional* dummies in regressions using *regional* data changed over time. My computer program could not perform a similar test on the coefficients of the 48 state dummies.

TABLE 7. Actual and Predicted Changes in Frequency of Liberal Voting in Congress, Two Subperiods (c.1920–1945, 1945–1975) Regions

Type of Change and Period	Region and Voting Measure × 10^3									Correlation of Actual and Predicted (10)
	NE (1)	MA (2)	ENC (3)	WNC (4)	SA (5)	ESC (6)	WSC (7)	MT (8)	PAC (9)	
A. Within House of Congress										
1. Senate, 1920–45										
a. Actual Change	194	136	–10	–80	–156	–61	–138	74	77	.92
b. Predicted Change	114	34	–12	–45	–103	–42	–49	–15	67	
2. Senate, 1945–75										
a. Actual Change	185	71	233	145	–187	–266	–153	–164	116	.82
b. Predicted Change	175	155	121	–76	–11	–232	–180	–48	48	
3. House, 1915–45										
a. Actual Change	112	83	–6	–102	–63	–154	–91	128	252	.84
b. Predicted Change	131	46	–34	–38	–101	–45	–102	8	127	
4. House, 1945–75										
a. Actual Change	341	164	84	59	–274	–246	–268	–239	11	.93
b. Predicted Change	227	168	147	–49	–106	–168	–160	–81	23	

B. Within Parties

1. Senate, 1920–45										
a. Actual Change	104	63	4	−80	−51	45	−23	31	31	.80
b. Predicted Change	76	15	−11	−30	−71	−27	−25	−4	38	
2. Senate, 1945–75										
a. Actual Change	92	179	85	55	−134	−196	−92	−82	62	.90
b. Predicted Change	107	107	77	−56	−77	−165	−124	−22	41	
3. House, 1915–45										
a. Actual Change	116	63	54	−6	−120	−143	−93	83	97	.82
b. Predicted Change	73	26	−18	−21	−55	−24	−56	3	70	
4. House, 1945–75										
a. Actual Change	120	67	3	−57	−73	−23	−110	−107	−37	.86
b. Predicted Change	126	92	81	−27	−58	−92	−89	−46	12	

Note: Actual and predicted changes are computed in the same manner as in Tables 5 and 6 (see their Notes), but for two subperiods. Three-term averages of the relevant data are computed for an "early," "middle," and "current" period as follows. The early period is an average of 1910, 1916, and 1920 data for the House and 1915, 1920, and 1925 data for the Senate. The middle period is an average of 1940, 1946, and 1950 data for the House and 1940, 1945, 1950 for the Senate. The current period is 1970, 1976, and 1980 for the House and 1970, 1975, and 1980 for the Senate. The changes shown above as 1920–45 or 1915–45 are middle minus early data; the 1945–75 changes are current minus middle data.

These numbers imply rejection of the null hypothesis at the 1 percent level for all four regressions, but acceptance at 5 percent for two of them. So, the evidence for ("noneconomic") shifts in regional political preferences is weak, and this provides justification for the restricted model in which economic change alone drives political change.

Shifts in regional preferences seem quantitatively, as well as statistically, insignificant. We already know that the restricted model (i.e., only economic change matters) explains virtually all of the change in political behavior. So, the only way that changes in regional preferences could plausibly be an important source of political change would be for the unrestricted model to "reapportion" explanatory power from the economic variables to those measuring the shift in regional preference. However, Table 8 shows that this is not what the unrestricted model does. The data are based on the two separate elements of the change in voting behavior predicted by the unrestricted model—the *ECON* element (the sum of coefficients of the economic variables times the changes in these variables over time) and the change in histori-

TABLE 8.   Measures of Relative Impact of Economic and Historical Change on Political Change in Congress, World War I to Present

	Correlation Coefficient Actual Change vs. Components of Predicted Change		*Beta* Coefficients for Components of Predicted Change	
Type of Change	ECON (1)	HIST (2)	ECON (3)	HIST (4)
A. Within Houses				
1. Senate	.92	.43	.92	.22
2. House	.93	−.30	1.17	.39
B. Within Parties				
1. Senate	.95	.08	.99	.30
2. House	.93	.74	.71	.47

Note: Data are from the unrestricted model (see text) in which changes in both economic and historical forces are permitted to affect voting behavior; this model permits the coefficients of the regional dummies to change between the pre- and post-1940 periods. Accordingly, the predicted (*PRED*) change in voting behavior for any region has two components in this model: (a) *ECON* = change due solely to changes in economic variables (i.e., holding constant any shift in the coefficient of the regional dummy). (b) *HIST* = change in the coefficient of the regional dummy.

Cols. 1 and 2 show the correlation coefficient between actual change and each component of *PRED*. Cols. 5 and 6 show the contribution of each component to *PRED* in standard deviation (*SD*) units. For example line A.1 says "a region where *ECON* is 1 *SD* above the mean will have a *PRED* .92 *SD* above the mean," etc. These *beta* coefficients are calculated by dividing *SD* of *ECON* and of *HIST* by *SD* of *PRED*. Panel A data are for changes in behavior across all congressmen without regard to their party. Panel B refers to changes within parties.

cal (*HIST*) preferences (the change in the coefficients of the regional dummies from the pre- to post-1940 period). The first two columns show that, standing alone, *ECON* is the much more *reliable* guide to the data than *HIST;* indeed the correlations in column 1 are not much lower than those previously reported for the restricted model. The last two columns show that *ECON* is quantitatively the much more important element in the change in behavior predicted by the unrestricted model.

All of this implies that what I had before merely labeled the "persistent historical" element in political behavior (i.e., the coefficients of the regional dummies in Table 3 and 4) really is persistent. This focuses more sharply my earlier challenge to future research: an economic explanation of these regional differences will have to uncover economic differences among regions that *have not changed much since the beginning of the century*. The regional homogenization evident in so many dimensions of economic activity makes this a formidable challenge.

VI. A Reexamination of Previous Puzzles

I showed (Section II) that political differences among regions in Congress have not declined along with economic differences. That seeming anomaly is restated in panel A of Table 9. This shows simple correlations between the *dispersions* of the economic and the various congressional voting measures I have been analyzing. If there is a simple connection between narrowing economic and political differences among states, these should be consistently positive, and they obviously are not. However, if there are persistent regional elements in political behavior, there should be a positive correlation over time between the dispersions of economic variables and of voting measures *net of the persistent regional element*. Accordingly, I subtracted the appropriate coefficient of the regional (or state) dummy in Table 3 and 4 from each measure of voting behavior and recomputed the simple correlations between the dispersions of the adjusted political and economic variables. These are in panel B of Table 9 and they are all strongly positive.

The persistent regional element has to be removed to reveal this tandem decline of political and economic differences because the conflict between history and economics described in Section IV has abated over time. Early in the century, the South's historical conservatism and the North's liberalism (see the regional coefficients in cols. 3 and 6 of Tables 3 and 4) clashed sharply with the redistributive interests entailed by southern poverty and northern affluence. This clash made regional differences in political behavior smaller than otherwise. However, the clash and its restraining influence on regional political differ-

TABLE 9.   Correlation Coefficients between Standard Deviations of
            Liberal Voting Measures in Congress and of Economic
            Variables; 1910 or 1915 to 1980; Across Regions or States

| | Correlation Coefficient with SD of | | |
Standard Deviation of Liberal Voting Measure	MFG (1)	PCI (2)	URB (3)
A. Unadjusted (for Persistent Regional or State Differences)			
1. Within			
a. Senate	.10	−.14	.03
b. House: Regions	.48	.45	.53
States	.01	−.01	.01
2. Within Parties in			
a. Senate	−.86	−.85	−.80
b. House: Regions	−.67	−.74	−.67
States	−.74	−.66	−.73
B. Adjusted for Persistent Regional or State Differences			
1. Within			
a. Senate	.82	.76	.75
b. House: Regions	.87	.85	.84
States	.83	.87	.82
2. Within Parties			
a. Senate	.77	.86	.76
b. House: Regions	.82	.83	.85
States	.71	.76	.79

Note: Each entry is a simple correlation coefficient between a time-series of standard deviations of an economic variable across regions or states and a time-series of a SD of one of the political liberalism measures analyzed previously (see Tables 3 and 4 Notes). Each House time-series has 15 observations and each Senate time-series has 14 observations. See text for method of calculating voting measures used in panel B.

ences, has diminished with the relative economic rise of the South.[25] Interestingly, my data imply that regional political differences will *grow* in the future even as the economic element of these differences diminishes.[26]

TABLE 10.   Regressions of Senate Voting Patterns, on Economic and Political Characteristics, States, 1979

					Coefficient of				
Dependent Variable	HH INC (1)	MFG (2)	URB (3)	MET (4)	SPEND/ TAX (5)	DEMS (6)	HIST (7)	R^2	SE
1. NTUA									
a					.13	20.8	39.8	.41	10.1
					1.8	4.6	3.4		
(Table 1)					(−.01)	(18.4)		(.24)	(11.4)
c	−5.96	−.46	−.59	.27		16.0	92.3	.59	8.7
	3.7	2.1	2.2	2.0		3.9	5.4		
(Table 1)	(.48)	(.03)	(−.25)	(.18)		(16.0)		(.28)	(11.4)
2. ADA									
a					.08	32.3	95.0	.68	12.4
					.8	5.8	6.6		
(Table 1)					(−.28)	(26.3)		(.34)	(17.5)
c	−3.85	.08	−.52	.02		28.6	148.7	.80	10.2
	2.1	.3	1.7	.1		6.1	7.5		
(Table 1)	(.65)	(.88)	(.03)	(−.13)		(29.5)		(.51)	(15.7)

Note: The regressions follow the same format as counterparts in Table 1, panel B, except for the addition of *HIST* as an independent variable. *HIST* is a vector of the coefficients of the state dummy variables in the regression in col. 6, Table 4. That is, *HIST* measures the historical liberalism of a state's representatives (I have no state-specific data for senators) relative to their party mean over the whole 1910–80 period after accounting for economic variables. For comparison, the regression coefficients and summary statistics from the corresponding Table 1 regression are shown in parentheses on the lines labeled (Table 1). See Table 1 for definitions and sources of all variables other than *HIST*. *t*-values are shown below coefficients.

[25]To see formally why the variance of political behavior (S^2) across regions need not decline along with the variance of the economic (+ any random) element (E^2) of that behavior, note that $S^2 = E^2 + H^2 + 2rEH$, where H^2 = variance of the historical (i.e., time-invariant) element across regions, and r = correlation between the historical and economic (+ random) elements across regions at time t. Then

$$\frac{dS}{dt} = \frac{1}{S}\left[\frac{dE}{dt}(E + rH) + \frac{dr}{dt}\cdot EH\right].$$

For most periods in the data, $dE/dt < 0$, but $r < 0$, so the sign of dS/dt is indeterminate.

[26]In the notation of fn. 25, E^2 is now so small that, with $r < 0$, $(E^2 + 2rEH) < 0$ and $S^2 < H^2$. Therefore, if E continues to approach zero, over time S^2 will rise toward H^2. For the Senate, in the period 1970–80, $S = .128$ while $H = .185$. The latter figure is about equal to the maximum S observed in this century.

The weak or even perverse relationship between voting and economic interest often found in contemporary Congresses (see the discussion surrounding Table 1) can also be clarified by my results. They suggest that, for example, wealthy areas sometimes produce liberal congressmen because the pull of history can overcome the push of interest. This is more likely today, when differences in interest are smaller, than it has been in the past. If this explanation is correct, then some adjustment for history should bring the role of interest in contemporary voting into sharper focus. This adjustment is made in Table 10 which adds history, in the form of a vector of the coefficients of state dummy variables from the column 6, Table 4 regression, to some of the regressions in Table 1.[27] The coefficient of this *HIST* variable (col. 7) is uniformly positive and significant, which is further testimony to the durability of these sectional differences. More important, with the addition of *HIST*, the coefficients of the economic variables change in the "right" direction from their Table 1 values (shown in parentheses); that is, income, manufacturing and urbanization, which are negatively correlated with the benefits of redistribution, have algebraically smaller and usually negative coefficients in Table 10.[28] Similarly, the partial correlation of liberal voting with the benefits from redistribution (lines 1a and 2a) is positive in Table 10, while it was strangely negative in Table 1.

VII. Summary and Conclusions

The evidence in this paper is consistent with a model in which congressional agents act as if they are maximizing a utility function like

$$U = F(L,W), \tag{5}$$

where L = the number or frequency of liberal votes cast,[29] and W = their principals' wealth per capita.

The agent's choice of L affects W via the political redistribution process, and the usual first-order conditions are

---

[27] These coefficients describe historical preferences in the *House* and the regressions in Table 10 describe voting in the *Senate*. This is done because I do not have comparable state-level data for the Senate. I also ran the regressions in Table 10 with the relevant regional *HIST* of the Senate. These were qualitatively similar to those in Table 10, but none explained the data as well as its Table 10 counterpart.

[28] The coefficient of *MET*, however, moves in the "wrong" direction, in that the crude evidence in Table 1 implies that residents of SMSAs lose from redistribution.

[29] At this level of generality, one has to be agnostic about whether L generates utility for the agents or principals or both.

$$F_L/F_W = -dW/dL, \tag{6}$$

the "price" of a liberal vote in terms of W. That price depends on the nature of redistribution—it will be positive in some constituencies and negative in others. Accordingly, (6) has an interior solution only where liberalism is a costly good (F_L, $-dW/dL$; both > 0) or a productive bad. My data imply that where liberalism seems to be a good (the North) it has historically been costly, and where it is a bad (the South) it has been productive. This amounts to invoking a "tastes" category to permit F_L to be nonzero in the same way that, say, an analyst of the market for rock music might have to invoke tastes to "explain" why some pay to hear it and others pay to avoid it. But to invoke tastes is also to challenge future research. In this case, the challenge is to uncover objective forces which can reduce the importance of my particular tastes category.

Meanwhile, I have followed the traditional path in utility analyses of choice, that of focusing on the effects of changes in constraints. The characteristics of American political redistribution suggest that, in general, the shadow price of a liberal vote ($-dW/dL$) rises with relative wealth, and, when that price rises, we expect fewer such votes to be "bought." That expectation is strongly confirmed by my data, as is the underlying assumption that the tastes in question are stable. I have shown that this conventional economic model is powerful enough to explain substantially all of the major political realignments among regions in this century. The economic convergence of congressional constituencies has gradually lowered the price of a liberal vote to northern congressmen and lowered the price of a conservative vote to southerners. This elemental fact is sufficient to explain 1) why the once conservative North has become liberal and why the opposite occurred in the South; 2) why once more-or-less homogeneous parties have become regionally divided, with northern members of either party now more liberal and southerners now more conservative than their party average, and 3) why Democrats have gained "market share" in the North and lost it in the South. Since the process of economic convergence appears not to have run its course, the strong suggestion of my results is that these political trends will continue. The seemingly paradoxical result predicted by my data is that Congress will become more sharply divided regionally as their constituencies converge economically.

References

Buchanan, James and Tullock, Gordon, *The Calculus of Consent*, Ann Arbor: University of Michigan Press, 1962.

Downs, Anthony, *An Economic Theory of Democracy*, New York: Harper & Row, 1957.

Fenno, Richard, *Home Style: House Members in their Districts*, Boston: Little Brown, 1978.

Fiorina, Morris, *Representatives, Roll Calls & Constituencies*, Lexington: Lexington Books, 1974.

Kalt, Joseph, *The Economics and Politics of Oil Price Regulation*, Cambridge: Harvard University Press, 1981.

———— and Zupan, Mark, "Capture and Ideology in the Economic Theory of Politics," *American Economic Review*, June 1984, *74*, 279–300.

Kau, James and Rubin, Paul, "Self-Interest, Ideology and Logrolling in Congressional Voting," *Journal of Law and Economics*, October 1979, *22*, 365–84.

———— and ————, *Congressmen, Constituents and Contributors*, Boston: Nijhoff, 1982.

Lee, Everett S. et al., *Population Redistribution and Economic Growth, United States, 1870–1950*, Vol. I., Philadelphia: American Philosophical Society, 1957.

Leven, Maurice, *Income in the Various States*, New York: National Bureau of Economic Research, 1925.

Mitchell, Edward J., "The Basis of Congressional Energy Policy," *Texas Law Review*, March 1979, *57*, 591–613.

Peltzman, Sam, "Constituent Interest and Congressional Voting," *Journal of Law and Economics*, April 1984, *27*, 181–210.

Reynolds, Morgan and Smolensky, Eugene, *Public Expenditures, Taxes and the Distribution of Income*, New York: Academic Press, 1977.

Stigler, George, "The Theory of Economic Regulation," *Bell Journal of Economics*, Spring 1971, *2*, 3–21 (chap. 6 of this volume).

U.S. Department of Commerce, Bureau of the Census, *Historical Statistics of the United States*, Washington: USGPO, 1975.

————, *Statistical Abstract of the United States*, Washington: USGPO, various years.

U.S. Department of Labor, Bureau of Labor Statistics, *Handbook of Labor Statistics*, Washington: USGPO, 1967.

U.S. Internal Revenue Service, *Annual Report of the Commissioner*, Washington: USGPO, various years.

A Theory of Primitive Society, With Special Reference to Law

5

Richard A. Posner

Introduction

This paper uses economic theory to explain some of the characteristic social, including legal, institutions of primitive and archaic societies. The literary remains of a number of early civilizations contain detailed descriptions of the preliterate societies out of which modern Western civilization evolved. (The poems of Homer, the Old Testament, and the Norse Sagas are examples of such literary records.) We may call these "archaic" societies. In the nineteenth century anthropologists and colonial administrators began compiling detailed descriptions of primitive societies—African, North American Indian, Polynesian, and many others. The strong similarity of the social, including legal, institutions of primitive and archaic societies justifies discussing them together. For want of a better term, and with no pejorative intent, I shall refer to both types as "primitive." My working definition of primitive is not poor, by modern standards, but preliterate (thus I exclude, for example, the Roman Empire). Because most preliterate societies lack either a complex economy or an effective government, and most literate societies have both, literacy is a good criterion for distinguishing primitive from more advanced societies. Why this should be so will be considered later.

The applicability of the economic model of human behavior to

I am grateful to Gary Becker both for his comments on a previous draft and for discussions of the subject matter of this paper; to Robert Bourgeois, Dennis Carlton, Ronald Coase, Frances Dahlberg, Arthur DeVany, David Friedman, Amyra Grossbard, Anthony Kronman, Arthur Leff, Douglass North, Frederic Pryor, James Redfield, Steven Shavell, George Stigler, and participants in the Industrial Organization Workshop of the University of Pennsylvania, for comments; to Robert Bourgeois, for research assistance; and to the Center for the Study of the Economy and the State at the University of Chicago, for financial support.

Reprinted with permission from *The Journal of Law and Economics* 23, no. 1 (April 1980): 1–53. © 1980 by The University of Chicago Law School

primitive man has been debated extensively by anthropologists, with occasional joinder in the debate by economists such as Frank Knight.[1] One group of anthropologists, the "formalists," have argued that the economic model is fully applicable to primitive man, and have sought to prove this by studying the explicit markets which are sometimes found in primitive societies. The other group, the "substantivists," argue that the conventional economic categories are largely inapplicable to primitive society—that what appear to be counterparts to Western markets have mainly a different, and noneconomic, function in primitive society.

It is a sterile debate. The contending groups share an excessively narrow view of what is economic. The formalists equate the domain of economics with the explicit market and hence focus on what is, after all, not the most distinctive feature of primitive society. (However, their work is useful in demonstrating, though in a rather restricted sphere, that primitive man is capable of rational maximizing behavior.) The substantivists make the same equation as the formalists and hence conclude that the distinguishing features of such societies—such as the greater emphasis placed on reciprocal gift exchange than on strictly contractual market exchanges—lie outside the range of economic understanding.[2] Yet, despite their hostility to economic theory, the substantivists have contributed to the literature not only a wealth of valuable detail regarding the distinctive institutions of primitive society but also valuable, if unsystematic, insights into the economic function of those institutions.[3] Some of the writings of economic historians on ar-

---

[1] For the flavor of the debate see the essays in the first half of Economic Anthropology (Edward E. LeClair, Jr. & Harold K. Schneider eds. 1968); and for a brief summary Harold K. Schneider, Economic Man 2–17 (1974). Knight's contribution is Anthropology and Economics, 49 J. Pol. Econ. 247 (1941), reprinted in Melville J. Herskovits, Economic Anthropology 508 (rev. ed. 1952).

[2] Thus George Dalton, a leading substantivist, has written: "Primitive economy is different from market industrialism not in degree but in kind. The absence of machine technology, pervasive market organization, and all-purpose money, plus the fact that economic transactions cannot be understood apart from social obligation, create, as it were, a non-Euclidean universe to which Western economic theory cannot be fruitfully applied. The attempt to translate primitive economic processes into functional equivalents of our own inevitably obscures just those features of primitive economy which distinguish it from our own." Economic Theory and Primitive Society, 63 Am. Anthropologist 1, 20 (1961). To similar effect see, e.g., Karl Polanyi, The Great Transformation, ch. 4 (1944); Karl Polanyi, The Livelihood of Man (Harry W. Pearson ed. 1977). The grandparent of this point of view seems to be Max Weber.

[3] An outstanding example of substantivist writing is Marshall Sahlins, Stone Age Economics (1972), especially chs. 1, 2, and 5. Melville J. Herskovits, Economic Anthropology (rev. ed. 1952), is the largest compendium of substantivist description of primitive economies. A good anthology in which the substantivist viewpoint is dominant is Tribal and Peasant Economies (George Dalton ed. 1967). Some more eclectic works of

chaic economies, such as that depicted in the Homeric poems, resemble (in character, not quantity) the work of the substantivists in combining excellent description with a denial of the applicability of the economic model.[4]

With economists devoting increasing attention to the study of nonmarket activities and institutions—including the family, information, and the law[5]—the foundation is now in place for the thoroughgoing and unapologetic application of economic theory to the full range of primitive social institutions. Such application has, indeed, begun. Clifford Geertz's recent article applying the economics of information to trading in bazaars shows how the pervasive ignorance regarding qualities of goods and reliability of traders is mitigated by "clientalization" (the pairing off of buyers and sellers in repetitive transactions) and also by each buyer's bargaining intensively with one seller in lieu of shopping among many.[6] Geertz's emphasis on the costs of information

---

economic anthropology are Manning Nash, Primitive and Peasant Economic Systems 1–57 (1966); Markets in Africa (Paul Bohannan & George Dalton eds. 1962); Themes in Economic Anthropology (Raymond Firth ed. 1967); LeClair & Schneider, *supra* note 1. A recent review of the economic anthropology literature is George Dalton, Economic Anthropology, 20 Am. Behavioral Scientist 635 (1977). An important recent addition to economic anthropology should be mentioned: Frederic L. Pryor, The Origins of the Economy (1977). The main content of the book is a series of statistical tests of various hypotheses concerning primitive economic behavior. I discuss Pryor's book in Anthropology and Economics, 88 J. Pol. Econ. 608 (1980).

Herskovits generously reprints Frank Knight's scathing review of a previous edition of Herskovits's book, in which Knight stated: "The first essential weakness of Professor Herskovits' opus is that it explicitly sets out to make anthropological data 'intelligible to economists' in the absence of any clear grasp on his part of *any* of the principles in which economists are interested and with which they deal. . . ." Herskovits, *supra* note 1, at 510. For other sharp criticism of substantivism see, e.g., Scott Cook, The Obsolete "Anti-Market" Mentality: A Critique of the Substantivist Approach to Economic Anthropology, 68 Am. Anthropologist 323 (1966).

[4] See especially M. I. Finley, The World of Odysseus (2d rev. ed. 1978), the standard (and best) discussion of the society and economy described by Homer. Other economic historians reject a Polanyi-esque view of the ancient economy. See, e.g., Chester G. Starr, The Economic and Social Growth of Early Greece, 800–500 B.C. (1977). See generally, S. Todd Lowry, Recent Literature on Ancient Greek Economic Thought, 17 J. Econ. Lit. 65 (1979).

[5] See, e.g., Gary S. Becker, The Economic Approach to Human Behavior (1976); J. Hirshleifer, Where Are We in the Theory of Information?, 63 Am. Econ. Rev. 31 (Papers & Proceedings, May 1973); Richard A. Posner, Economic Analysis of Law (2d ed. 1977). Lack of familiarity with these new branches of applied economics is the reason why Schneider's book, see note 1 *supra*, fails to deliver on its promise of applying economic theory to the entire range of primitive behavior.

[6] See Clifford Geertz, The Bazaar Economy: Information and Search in Peasant Marketing, 68 Am. Econ. Rev. 28 (Papers & Proceedings, May 1978). Geertz anticipated his own analysis by many years. See his Social Change and Economic Moderni-

in primitive society and on the social responses to those costs is, I shall argue in this paper, extremely fruitful for a general understanding of the institutions of primitive society.[7] Among other recent work, Gary Becker and his student Amyra Grossbard have discussed the marital arrangements of primitive society, including polygamy and brideprice, from an economic standpoint;[8] Harold Demsetz, Douglass North, and others have related the mixture of individual and communal property rights in primitive societies to the scarcity of the resources involved;[9] William Landes and I, and also David Friedman, have discussed several aspects of primitive law from an economic standpoint;[10] and (independently of Geertz) I have discussed several aspects of primitive society, including the prevalence of gifts and the formality and de-

---

zation in Two Indonesian Towns: A Case in Point, in On the Theory of Social Change 385 (Everett E. Hagen ed. 1962). The bazaar is not, of course, an institution limited to primitive society, although it is a characteristic market form in such a society. See, e.g., Markets in Africa, *supra* note 3, *passim*. This illustrates the important point, which I do not attempt to pursue in this paper, that the study of primitive society may cast light on the institutions of more advanced societies—"peasant societies," for example, which appear to have many features in common with primitive societies. See generally Peasant Society (Jack M. Potter, Mary N. Diaz, & George M. Foster eds. 1967).

[7] I am indebted to Gary Becker for having directed my attention to Geertz's paper and for having emphasized in conversation the importance of information costs to an understanding of primitive society. And see Gary S. Becker, Imperfect Information: Marriage, Divorce, and Kinship (Jan. 1979) (unpublished manuscript, Univ. of Chi., Dep't of Econ.); a later version appears in his *A Treatise on the Family* (1981).

[8] See Gary S. Becker, *supra* note 5, at 238–41; Gary S. Becker, Marriage: Monogamy, Polygamy, and Assortative Mating (Oct. 1978) (unpublished manuscript, Univ. of Chi., Dep't of Econ.), and see Becker (1981) in note 7; Amyra Grossbard, Toward a Marriage between Economics and Anthropology and a General Theory of Marriage, 68 Am. Econ. Rev. 33 (Papers & Proceedings, May 1978); An Economic Analysis of Polygyny: The Case of Maiduguri, 17 Current Anthropology 701 (1976); and The Economics of Polygamy, vol. 2 (Julie DaVanzo & Julian L. Simon eds. 1980) in Res. in Population Econ.

[9] See Harold Demsetz, Toward a Theory of Property Rights, 57 Am. Econ. Rev. 347, 351–53 (Papers & Proceedings, May 1967); David E. Ault & Gilbert L. Rutman, the Development of Individual Rights to Property in Tribal Africa, 22 J. Law & Econ. 163 (1979); Vernon L. Smith, The Primitive Hunter Culture, Pleistocene Extinction, and the Rise of Agriculture, 83 J. Pol. Econ. 727 (1975); Douglass C. North & Robert Paul Thomas, The First Economic Revolution, 30 Econ. Hist. Rev. 229 (2d ser. 1977). And see North's interesting economic criticism of the substantivist view of the ancient economy. Douglass C. North, Markets and Other Allocation Systems in History: The Challenge of Karl Polanyi, 6 J. Euro. Econ. Hist. 703 (1979).

[10] See William M. Landes & Richard A. Posner, Salvors, Finders, Good Samaritans, and Other Rescuers: An Economic Study of Law and Altruism, 7 J. Legal Stud. 83, 106–08 (1978); William M. Landes & Richard A. Posner, Adjudication as a Private Good, 8 J. Legal Stud. 232, 242–45 (1979); David Friedman, Private Creation and Enforcement of Law: A Historical Case, *id.* at 399.

corum of primitive speech and manners, from an information-cost standpoint.[11]

The original interest that sparked the present paper was in seeing whether and how far the theory that law is an instrument for maximizing social wealth or efficiency—a theory that has proved fruitful in studies of modern law—could be extended to primitive law. That question cannot be answered, however, without pushing the economic analysis of primitive society further than has been done to date. Accordingly, the first part of the paper sketches a general economic theory of primitive society. It argues that many of the distinctive institutions of primitive society, including gift-giving and reciprocal exchange, customary prices, polygamy and brideprices, the size of kinship groups, and the value placed on certain personality traits, such as generosity and touchiness, can be explained as adaptations to uncertainty or high information costs. Part I is ambitious in scope but far from complete— warfare, religion, and slavery are among the omitted topics.

Part II extends the analysis in Part I to the characteristic legal institutions of primitive society,[12] involving contracts, property, inheritance, marriage, and other legal concepts. Most of these areas are discussed quite briefly; however, one especially striking feature of primitive law, the merger of our modern categories of tort and crime in a system of private strict liability, is examined in some detail.

Because an effort to explain the behavior of primitive people in economic terms is likely to be misunderstood by noneconomists, I emphasize at the outset that I do not believe that primitive people consciously calculate costs and benefits of alternative courses of actions, any more than the modern consumer engages in conscious utility maximization when buying one good instead of another. The rationality of

[11]See Richard A. Posner, The Homeric Version of the Minimal State, 90 Ethics 27 (1979); The Right of Privacy, 12 Ga. L. Rev. 393, 402 (1978); and Privacy, Secrecy and Reputation, 28 Buff. L. Rev. 1 (1979). See also Posner, Anthropology and Economics, *supra* note 3; Reuven Brenner, A Theory of Development, or Markets and Human Capital in Primitive Societies (mimeographed paper, N.Y.U. Dep't of Econ., Jan. 1980)—the latter a recent paper which builds in part on an earlier draft of the present paper; and Richard A. Posner, Retribution and Related Concepts of Punishment, 9, J. Legal Stud. 71 (1980).

[12]The line between legal and other social institutions is often unclear in primitive society because many of the features which we conventionally use to distinguish law from custom, order, habit, rule, moral precept, and other regulatory devices which may or may not be "law" are absent. Since I am not interested in taxonomy, I will not worry about whether some of the social institutions discussed in Part I would be better classified as legal and discussed in Part II and vice versa. Certainly much of the discussion of family law in Part II could have been merged with the discussion of the family as a primitive social institution in Part I.

"economic man" is a matter of consequences, not states of mind.[13] I return to this theme briefly in the conclusion to the paper.

I. An Economic Model of Primitive Society

A. *Information Costs*

The fact that primitive people do not understand the laws of nature well (belief in magic and sorcery is almost universal among primitive peoples), have no system of writing and consequently no records,[14] and lack modern communications technology—with all that these lacks imply—suggests that the costs of obtaining information are higher in primitive than in advanced societies: that more inputs of time or other resources are required to obtain the same amount of information. This is trivially true of information concerning the many scientific and technical principles unknown to the primitive world, but it is also true of information concerning the probability that the other party to a contract will perform (there are no courts to coerce his performance) or that the quantity delivered in a sale is the quantity bargained for (there are no scales in primitive markets), the cause of a death (there are no police or autopsies, and the possibility that death was caused by witchcraft cannot be rejected out of hand), or the marginal product of a farm laborer's work.

To be sure, some sources of ignorance or uncertainty are more characteristic of modern than of primitive life. One is specialization of knowledge, which in the twentieth century has advanced to the point where each of us is an ignoramus regarding most areas of human knowledge. The other is the conditions of life and work in an urbanized society—whose anonymity, impersonality, and privacy result in our knowing less about neighbors, co-workers, and even friends and family members than we would in primitive societies. Both sources of ignorance, however, far from reflecting the high costs of information in modern society, are actually the product of low information costs, which have enabled the advancement of knowledge to the point where specialization in knowledge has become efficient, and have enabled social order to be maintained without continuous surveillance of the population.

---

[13]Thus, animals have been found to be "rational maximizers." See, e.g., John H. Kagel *et al.*, Experimental Studies of Consumer Demand Behavior Using Laboratory Animals, 13 Econ. Inquiry 22 (1975).

[14]Like most generalizations about primitive society, this one is not universally valid. Some primitive societies developed ingenious systems of record-keeping not involving writing. See A. S. Diamond, Primitive Law, Past and Present 203 (1971).

The second point (surveillance) requires amplification. No matter what the ratio of territory to inhabitants is (and often it is very high), primitive people tend to live in crowded conditions where they are denied the preconditions of privacy—separate rooms, doors, opportunities for solitude or anonymity, a measure of occupational or recreational mobility.[15] The lack of privacy has a number of implications for primitive values and institutions. For example, it helps explain why crime rates in primitive societies are, as we shall see, apparently moderate despite the absence of either formal investigative machinery (public or private) or compensatingly heavy penalties. This very example suggests, however, that the absence of privacy in primitive societies may itself be an adaptive response to the high costs of information in a society that lacks (also, as we shall see, because the costs of information are so high) public or private investigatory institutions, any form of press, etc. One way of reducing information costs is to create living conditions in which everyone knows everything about everyone else. The denial of privacy in a primitive society serves to enlist the entire population as informers and policemen.[16]

While the denial of privacy increases the production of information in one respect, it reduces it in another that helps explain why the accretion of knowledge, and hence economic development, proceed very slowly in primitive societies. Some measure of privacy is necessary both to create the peace and quiet that sustained and effective mental activity (which might lead to an improved understanding of the world) requires and to enable people to appropriate, by concealing their ideas from other people, the social benefits of their discoveries and inventions. In the absence of either formal rights to intellectual property (such as patent laws create) or public subsidization, concealment is the only method of obtaining a reward for developing a new productive technique. The costs of defining and enforcing intellectual-property rights are high even in our society (and trade secrets remain, therefore, an important method of appropriating the benefits of inno-

---

[15] For evidence, see references in privacy articles cited in note 11 *supra*.

[16] Sahlins, *supra* note 3, at 204, remarks on the "publicity of primitive life" as a mechanism for preserving public order. With the growth of privacy, which reduces the effectiveness of surveillance as a method of social control, we find the emergence of another, and curiously related, mode of social control—conscience. The idea of conscience is historically associated with being watched, but with being watched by God rather than neighbors and other associates. The idea persists in the "impartial spectator" ethics of Adam Smith and others. See Adam Smith, The Theory of Moral Sentiments ([1759] 1959 ed.). The difference between a "guilt" and a "shame" culture (see E. R. Dodds, The Greeks and the Irrational 17 (1951)) is perhaps the difference between a culture in which people have a lot of privacy and one in which they have little or none.

vation), and presumably even higher in primitive societies.[17] Public subsidization of inventors is ruled out by the rudimentary public finance in primitive societies, a factor itself traceable, as we shall see, to the high costs of information in such societies. That leaves secrecy—something the lack of privacy in a primitive society makes difficult to obtain.

The costs of information that result from the lack of a system of writing require special mention. Complicated mental activity is possible without literacy, including subtle analysis of character and prodigious feats of memorization, both illustrated by the circumstances in which the Homeric poems were composed and originally performed. But what is generally not possible without a system of writing is large-scale organization for production or governance. Bureaucracy is closely associated with record-keeping. This is as true of the Mycenaean palace state depicted in the Linear B tablets and the even earlier Egyptian and Sumerian kingdoms as of the modern state.[18] Among preliterate peoples government is generally weak[19] and sometimes nonexistent.[20] The absence of effective government, which I tentatively attribute to nonliteracy,[21] has, as we shall see, profound consequences for the structure of primitive social institutions.

[17]To be sure, one often finds property rights to a song, a spell, a crest, or a name (see e.g., Diamond, *supra* note 14, at 188; Harold E. Driver, Indians of North America 268, 285 (2d rev. ed. 1969); Herskovits, *supra* note 3, at 390–91)—but, so far as I am aware, not to a productive idea or invention.

[18]The link between literacy and government is occasionally noted. See Diamond, *supra* note 14, at 39; Jack Goody, Introduction, in Literacy in Traditional Societies 1, 2 (Jack Goody ed. 1968); Jack Goody & Ian Watt, The Consequences of Literacy, in *id.* at 27, 36; Maurice Bloch, Astrology and Writing in Madagascar, in *id.* at 277, 286.

[19]An exception, but one that proves the rule, is the Ashanti Kingdom in eighteenth-century Africa, which developed a system of record-keeping that did not involve writing. See Herskovits, *supra* note 3, at 420.

[20]On government in primitive societies see, e.g., Driver, *supra* note 17, at ch. 17; Herskovits, *supra* note 3, at 399–405, 416–38; Lucy Mair, Primitive Government (1962); Max Gluckman, Politics, Law, and Ritual in Tribal Society (1965); African Political Systems (M. Fortes & E. E. Evans-Pritchard eds. 1940); Posner, The Homeric Version of the Minimal State, *supra* note 11. I. Schapera, Government and Politics in Tribal Societies (1967), argues that previous writers exaggerated the weakness of primitive government, at least in African tribal society, but he gives examples of very weak governments in such societies. See *id.* at 38, 85–87, 88.

[21]The causation could, however, go the other way, as stressed in Brenner, *supra* note 11. Primitive societies lack large-scale institutions because they are illiterate, but lacking such institutions they have no need for the kind of record-keeping which requires literacy. For other communicative needs, even extremely subtle ones, an unwritten language may be quite adequate, as the Homeric poems attest.

B. The Model: Assumptions, Implications, Evidence

1. Assumptions. I shall propose a simple, nonformal model ("ideal type") of primitive society, deduced from the conditions of information in such societies. Economists (and Weberian sociologists) will not need to be reassured, but some anthropologists and lawyers may, that the purpose of such a model is not to deny the variety and complexity of primitive societies or to provide a realistic description of a particular society, but to explain those fundamental institutions and values that are common to most such societies. Weak government, ascription of rights and duties on the basis of family membership, gift-giving as a fundamental mode of exchange, strict liability for injuries, emphasis on generosity and honor as high ethical norms, collective guilt—these and other features of social organization recur with such frequency in accounts of primitive and archaic societies[22] as to suggest that a simple model of primitive society, which abstracts from many of the particular features of specific societies, may nonetheless explain much of the structure of primitive social institutions. Finally, although I view all of the threads in the model as derived from the assumed high information costs of primitive society, the model can equally well be viewed, and defended, as an inductive generalization from the descriptive anthropological literature on primitive societies, unrelated to any underlying premise concerning the conditions of information in such societies.

The specific assumptions of my model are as follows:

(1) There is no (effective) government. This exaggerates the anarchy of primitive life, but, for most primitive societies, not critically.[23]

---

[22] For archaic societies, the best general account of social institutions remains Henry Sumner Maine, Ancient Law (1861), though some of its conclusions are no longer accepted. On the current standing of Maine in light of the findings of modern anthropology see Robert Redfield, Maine's *Ancient Law* in the Light of Primitive Societies, 3 W. Pol. Q. 574 (1950), especially at pp. 585–87. Finley, *supra* note 4, is very good on the society depicted in the Homeric poems. On the Norse Sagas, see sources referenced in Friedman, *supra* note 10. The literature of modern social anthropology is of course vast. Some examples of this literature are Driver, *supra* note 17, on the North American Indian societies; Herskovits, *supra* note 3; Robert H. Lowie, Primitive Society (2d ed. 1947); Lucy Mair, African Societies (1974); Carleton S. Coon, The Hunting Peoples (1971); African Systems of Kinship and Marriage (A. R. Radcliffe-Brown & Darryll Forde eds. 1950); Elman R. Service, Primitive Social Organization (2d ed. 1971). There are innumerable highly readable studies of particular societies, such as E. E. Evans-Pritchard, The Nuer (1940); Bronislaw Malinowski, Crime and Custom in Savage Society (1926); Leopold Pospisil, Kapauku Papuans and Their Law (1958).

[23] For those primitive societies, and there are some, which have strong governments this assumption will not hold even as a reasonable approximation and we can expect the model to have less explanatory power—a caveat equally applicable, of course, to the other assumptions of the model.

There may be a chief who is the leader in wartime but has no functions in peacetime and elders who exercise some intermittent authority, but generally there will be no courts, legislatures, police, prosecutors, tax collectors, or other familiar public officials. At the level of abstraction at which I am operating here, the difference between no government and slight government is too small to matter. As mentioned earlier, I attribute the lack of government to nonliteracy, although the possibility that the causation runs in the opposite direction cannot be excluded.

(2) The state of technical knowledge in the society is such that only a limited variety of consumption goods can be produced, where variety is measured both by the number of separate goods and by quality variations within a single good. Admittedly, however, lack of standardization may generate considerable random quality variation, and variety is to a considerable extent in the eye of the beholder.

(3) The goods produced in the society are assumed to be traded on only a limited basis for goods produced in other societies. Unlimited trade would allow for unlimited variety. In fact the costs of transportation, plus (other) transaction costs created by language differences, lack of currency, and lack of contract-enforcement mechanisms, make foreign trade generally a small, though often an important, part of the primitive economy.

(4) The consumption goods produced in the society are assumed not to be durable or storable but instead to be perishable goods that are consumed in the period in which they are produced. This is again an exaggeration. Yet food preservation is a serious problem, and food is the most important product of such societies.[24]

A fifth assumption is necessary to keep the society from adopting more productive techniques:

(5) The private gains from innovation—from reducing the costs of production (including transportation) or increasing the variety of goods produced—are assumed to be negligible, either because such gains cannot be appropriated (the privacy problem) or because scarcity of natural resources or other exogenous conditions make cost reduction

---

[24] Sahlins, *supra* note 3, at 11–12, 31–32, explains the interrelationship, in a hunting economy, of lack of variety and lack of storability. Hunting bands must rove widely in search of game. Possessions, including preserved meat, would hamper their mobility, so one observes that the members do not have many possessions and do not preserve meat. Primitive cultivation societies are in a similar situation where, as is commonly the case, most of their energies are devoted to crop production and the crops cannot readily be stored or converted into storable food products. Herding societies produce the most durable consumption goods and, as we shall see, their institutions are somewhat different—and in the direction the model predicts.

or product improvement unattainable goals at any feasible scale of investment.

2. *The Insurance Principle and Its Implementing Institutions and Values.* The model described above (which, I emphasize, is designed to capture general tendencies and not to describe literally) implies the strong if somewhat misnamed "redistributive" ethic that has been noted in innumerable studies of primitive society.[25] One expects insurance—specifically, against hunger—to be a very important product in such a society. The conditions of production, in particular the difficulty of storing food, create considerable uncertainty with regard to the future adequacy of an individual's food supply and hence considerable variance in his expected wealth.[26] In these circumstances a transaction whereby A, who happens to produce a harvest that exceeds his consumption needs, gives part of his surplus to B in exchange for B's commitment to reciprocate should their roles some day be reversed will be attractive to both parties. Notice that the alternative of self-insurance is not open to A, because of the assumption that food is not storable.

The attractiveness to A of insurance is further enhanced by the assumed scarcity of alternative goods for which to exchange his surplus food. If the variety of consumption goods available in the society is limited, A will not be so "tempted" as he otherwise might be to exchange his food surplus for other consumption goods rather than to buy hunger insurance with it. To be sure, it may be possible to exchange one's extra food for production or capital goods, of which the most important are women (there is of course a consumption aspect as well). Women are another form of "crop insurance," as are children, which they also

[25] Redistribution as used in economic and ethical discourse implies an effort, through the state, to bring about more *ex post* economic equality than the free market would. Anthropologists generally assume that primitive societies are redistributive in approximately this sense (that is, in wanting to equalize *ex post* wealth beyond what the market would do or what would be efficient in strict economic terms), but tend to reserve the word "redistribution" for the allocation of a tribe's surplus agricultural production by the tribe's chief. See, e.g., Nash, *supra* note 3, at 32; Sahlins, *supra* note 3, at 209.

[26] For a good introduction to the economics of uncertainty, risk, and insurance see Kenneth J. Arrow, Essays in the Theory of Risk-Bearing, ch. 5 (1971). The idea that institutions other than explicit insurance contracts perform an insurance function is, of course, not a new one. See, e.g., Arrow, *supra*, ch. 8; Steven N. S. Cheung, The Theory of Share Tenancy, ch. 4 (1960); and McCloskey papers cited in note 42 *infra*. Nash, *supra* note 3, at 22, speaks of the "precariousness" of primitive life. For a succinct description of the hazards of primitive agriculture see M. Fortes, The Political System of the Allensi of the Northern Territory of the Gold Coast, in African Political Systems, *supra* note 20, at 239, 249.

produce, because of kinship obligations to be discussed shortly. However, apart from other economic reasons that, as we shall see, limit the incidence of polygamy even in societies which permit it (as most primitive societies do), there is the disparity in value between one good harvest or one good kill—limited and evanescent goods—and a highly durable and valuable good such as a woman. It is therefore difficult to accumulate the purchase price. One is led to predict that, other things being equal, polygamy will be more common in herding than in other primitive societies, because a herding society has a durable good to exchange for women.[27]

In short, without assuming that primitive people are any more risk averse or less individualistic than modern people, one can nonetheless give an economic explanation for the importance of insurance as a product demanded and supplied in primitive society. Indeed, primitive people might be less risk averse than modern people yet still desire more insurance, both because of their riskier circumstances and because of the dearth of alternative goods. However, we have yet to consider the institutional form in which the insurance will be provided. The first assumption of the model—the absence of a government—is important here. It rules out the possibility that the food surplus will be taxed away and redistributed by the state to the needy. Also, in combination with the underlying conditions of information in primitive society, which as we shall see are likely to retard the emergence of formal markets, the absence of an effective government impedes the emergence of a formal (private) insurance market in which food would be exchanged for an enforceable promise to reciprocate when and if necessary in the future. The problem is that there is no state to enforce promises.[28] Even without formal sanctions for breach of promise,

---

[27] Some evidence relevant to this prediction can be found in Pryor, *supra* note 3. Eliminating from his sample societies—not primitive in my sense—which he classifies as "economically oriented" or "politically oriented," and then comparing the incidence of polygamy in societies in which animal husbandry yields at least 10 per cent of all foods with societies in which it yields less than 10 per cent, yields the following results:

Type of Society	Number of Societies	
	Polygyny Common	Polygyny Not Common
Animal husbandry > 10%	13	7
Animal husbandry < 10%	9	11

Source: Calculated from Pryor, *supra* note 3, at 328 (variable 5), 333–34 (59, 61, 69), 336–39.

[28] To be sure, as we shall see in Part II, there is rudimentary contract law in primitive societies; but formal contracts of insurance are not within its scope. The "drafting" (if one can use the word with respect to a preliterate society) and administration of formal insurance contracts would involve heavy information costs in the setting

most promises will still be honored simply because the promisor wants the promisee to deal with him in the future. But not all will be: an old man might renege on his promise to share his surplus if it was unlikely that he would live long enough to be "punished" for his breach of contract by the refusal of anyone else to sell him hunger insurance in the future.[29]

Uncertainty as to whether sharing one's surplus food will be reciprocated can be expected to make people want to confine their sharing to (or at least concentrate it within) a group to which they belong whose members know and continually interact with one another and have broadly similar abilities, propensities, character, and prospects. The institution most likely to satisfy these requirements for a satisfactory informal "mutual insurance company" is the family. The family as we know it, however, is too small to constitute an adequate risk pool for insurance purposes. This may be one reason (another—the protection or law-enforcement function of kinship—is discussed in Part II) why primitive societies devote so many of their linguistic, legal, and informational resources to delineating kinship groups much larger than the modern family or, for that matter, the primitive household.[30] The primitive concern with careful definition and determination of the kinship group is based not on some idle genealogical curiosity but on the fact that in a primitive society the kind of legal and moral obligations which

---

of primitive society. But there is again a chicken-and-egg problem: formal insurance may not be found in primitive societies because of the adequacy of the alternative informal arrangements.

[29] In fact, in at least one primitive society it is reported that the young are reluctant to share their food with the old because it is unlikely that the old will be there to reciprocate in the future. See Allan C. Holmberg, Nomads of the Long Bow 151–53 (1969).

[30] The most common system of kinship among primitive peoples is the patrilineal, wherein descent is traced through the male line. Thus, in a patrilineal system a man, his sons, their sons, and so on belong to the same descent group, while his daughters' sons will become members of the descent group of the men the daughters marry. But kinship ties often cross the line between different descent groups. For example, a woman upon marriage may remain a member of her father's descent group, entitled to seek assistance from him, albeit living with another descent group. See text at note 136 *infra*. The important point, however, is that the primitive kinship group is larger than the modern or primitive *household*, and where kinship ties cross descent groups may achieve a measure of geographical diversification. These characteristics of the kinship group are obviously related to its insurance functions, as are the rigid and demanding obligations among kin—for example, a brother's son might be entitled to take a cow from the brother without asking permission, let alone paying. See, e.g., I. Schapera, A Handbook of Tswana Law and Custom 219–21 (1938). For excellent introductions to the complexities of kinship definitions and structures in primitive society see A. R. Radcliffe-Brown, Introduction, in African Systems of Kinship and Marriage, *supra* note 22, at 1; Robin Fox, Kinship and Marriage (1967).

we moderns have to support our very close relatives (sometimes only our children) extend to all of the members of one's kinship group. I attribute this to a lack of alternative insurance mechanisms in primitive society.

The argument so far establishes only why people might want to limit their insurance arrangements to kinsmen—not why they should be *required* to enter into such arrangements with them. Recent work in the economics of information suggests an answer to this question. Consider modern life insurance. If we assume that the individual knows his personal life expectancy better than the insurance company, there will be a tendency for the better risks to withdraw from the insurance pool (they do not wish to pay premiums based on average life expectancies, which are lower than theirs) and the pool will shrink, conceivably to the vanishing point.[31] One solution to this problem is employee life insurance, whereby insurance is provided as a condition of employment and no one can withdraw from the insurance pool without giving up his job.[32] A similar problem and solution are found in primitive society. If a man knows better than anyone else how likely he is some day to need food from a kinsman, the better risks will tend to select themselves out of the insurance system. This problem would disappear if the customary insurance premium (for example, a nephew can demand one cow from his uncle during the nephew's lifetime) could be varied by a negotiation in which the parties could adequately communicate to each other any respects in which their prospects differed from the average. But if this alternative to selection out is assumed to be infeasible because of the high costs of information, then we have a reason to expect the obligations of sharing to be made compulsory within the kinship group. To be sure, this leaves open the possibility that the better risk will simply forswear his kinship membership. But this is a very costly step to take because of the protective functions of the kinship group discussed in Part II of this paper.

What determines how broadly the kinship group within which an obligation to share is recognized will be defined? On the one hand, the larger the group is, the smaller will be the covariance in the food production of the individual members and hence the more insurance will be provided. It is essential that the kinship group be larger than the household, since the covariance within the household is likely to be very high; and the more geographically scattered the kinship group

---

[31] See George A. Akerlof, The Market for "Lemons": Quality Uncertainty and the Market Mechanism, 84 Q. J. Econ. 488 (1970).

[32] See Yoram Barzel, Some Fallacies in the Interpretation of Information Costs, 20 J. Law & Econ. 291, 303 (1977).

is, the better that is from an insurance standpoint.[33] On the other hand, the smaller and geographically more concentrated the kinship group is, the less serious will be the "moral hazard" or incentives problem— the temptation of a man to work less and live off his kinsmen.[34] Presumably, then, there is some optimum size and dispersion of the kinship group depending on the particular circumstances of the society. The optimum size is presumably larger the more primitive the society is, because in a very primitive society, the disincentive effects of insurance on both givers and takers are probably small. The less variety, and storage possibilities, of consumption goods, the less the wealthy man gives up by producing a surplus that will be shared in part with his poor kinsmen. The effects on his incentives may be trivial indeed if, as is plausible, the precise amount of the surplus produced is beyond his control. And given the nonstorability of food and the uncertainty of the harvest, the poor kinsman who relaxed his own productive effort in reliance on sharing in a wealthy kinsman's harvest would be acting recklessly.[35]

The obligation of sharing with kinsmen is not the only device by which primitive society, lacking formal insurance contracts or public substitutes therefor, provides hunger insurance for its members. Generosity—toward other members of one's village or band as well as toward kinsmen—is a more highly valued trait in primitive than in modern society and the reason appears to be that it is a substitute for formal insurance.[36] The fact that a man obtains prestige in primitive societies by giving away what he has rather than by keeping it (the potlatch of the Northwest Indians is only the most dramatic example of "buying" prestige by giving away one's goods on a seemingly extravagant scale[37])

[33] On the insurance effects of geographical dispersal of production see also text at note 42 *infra*.

[34] Cf. S. F. Nadel, Dual Descent in the Nuba Hills, in African Systems of Kinship and Marriage, *supra* note 22, at 333, 358.

[35] The optimal size of the group within which income is shared is discussed in another context in John Umbeck, A Theory of Contract Choice and the California Gold Rush, 20 J. Law & Econ. 421 (1978).

[36] Compare E. E. Evans-Pritchard, *supra* note 22, at 85: "This habit of share and share alike is easily understandable in a community where every one is likely to find himself in difficulties from time to time, for it is scarcity and not sufficiency that makes people generous, since everybody is thereby insured against hunger. He who is in need to-day receives help from him who may be in like need to-morrow."

[37] See Stuart Piddocke, The Potlatch System of the Southern Kwakiutl: A New Perspective, in LeClair & Schneider, *supra* note 1, at 283. There are also informational and political objectives of dissipating surpluses, discussed later in this paper, which in primitive societies that have the technological capacity to store food may interfere with storage of surpluses and thus with the provision of insurance against hunger. For an example see Siegfried F. Nadel, The Nuba 49–50 (1947).

has been thought evidence of the inapplicability of the economic model to primitive society. But since, in a society where consumption goods are limited in variety and durability, giving away one's surplus[38] may be the most useful thing to do with it, at least from society's standpoint, one is not surprised that it should earn the prestige that in a different kind of society is bestowed on a great inventor, scientist, captain of industry, or entertainer.[39]

If prestige is the carrot which encourages generosity, an extreme illustration of the stick is the occasional Eskimo practice of killing ungenerous rich people.[40] Such behavior in our society would be shortsighted: a productive individual, however selfish, produces consumer surplus for others to enjoy. But consumer surplus reflects the benefits of division of labor, specialization, and exchange of the resulting output, features largely absent from primitive society. The principal good exchanged in the simplest societies (such as that of the Eskimos) is insurance, and the rich man's refusal to share his surplus with others manifests his refusal to engage in this exchange. So he really is of little or no use to the rest of the society and killing him does not impose the social costs that it would in an advanced society.

The insurance perspective may also help to explain why some primitive societies do not allow interest to be charged on a loan. A "loan" in primitive society is often just the counterpart to the payment of an insurance claim in modern society—it is the insurer's fulfillment of his contractual undertaking and to allow interest would change the nature of the transaction. Also, custom may *require* a man to make a loan when requested.[41] The involuntary loan is another dimension of

[38] By "surplus" I mean simply production of food above normal consumption.

[39] The fact that in primitive as in modern society prestige is related to social productivity is (inadvertently) brought out in a passage quoted in Herskovits, *supra* note 3, at 121, to illustrate his contention that "the prestige drives that have been seen to afford so strong a motivation for labor in the other groupings is at a minimum" in nomadic society. The quoted passage reads: "When the immediate needs for food have been supplied, a person is neither much criticized for doing nothing, nor much praised for occupying his time in constructive labor. . . . No prestige is gained by building a better house or a larger garden, both of which may have to be abandoned in the next move." But in these circumstances building a better house or a larger garden is *not* constructive. The society is better off if people conserve their energies (and hence food needs) rather than make investments whose fruits cannot be reaped.

[40] See E. Adamson Hoebel, The Law of Primitive Man 81 (1954). Little emphasis is placed on kinship in Eskimo culture, probably because their environment forces them to live in very small, widely scattered bands which have little regular contact with one another. See *id.* at 68. In these circumstances the emphasis placed on generosity (or its absence) to unrelated individuals within the band provides a substitute for kin insurance.

[41] See R. F. Barton, The Kalingas 132 (1949); Herskovits, *supra* note 3, at 373.

the duty of generosity noted earlier. Since a man's surplus is assumed in my model to have relatively little value to him (because of storage problems and lack of goods for which to exchange a surplus), the ordinary resistance that rich people would feel at being required to make loans—perhaps without being allowed to charge interest—is attenuated.

The insurance function of loans in primitive society is especially pronounced in the cattle lending which is so prominent a feature of African tribal society. The main purpose of such "loans" is not to earn interest but to disperse one's cattle geographically so as to reduce the risk of catastrophic loss because of disease.[42]

A loan without interest resembles a gift, especially where (as is common) the society does not provide remedies for default.[43] Yet the moral duty to repay a loan is recognized in primitive societies and is enforced in various ways. Similarly, gifts in primitive society are explicitly reciprocal: a man is under a strong moral duty to repay a gift, when he can, with a gift of equivalent value.[44] In these circumstances the term "gift" is a misnomer. Gifts, non-interest-bearing loans (sometimes involuntary), feasts,[45] generosity, and the other "redistributive" mechanisms of primitive society are not the product of altruism; at least, it is not necessary to assume altruism in order to explain them. They are insurance payments.[46] The principle of reciprocity, which commands a

[42]See, e.g., E. H. Winter, Livestock Markets among the Iraqw of Northern Tanganyika, in Markets in Africa, *supra* note 3, at 457, 461; Elisabeth Colson, Trade and Wealth among the Tonga, in *id.* at 601, 607; Nash, *supra* note 3, at 50–51. The resemblance to the "open fields" policy in medieval English agriculture, discussed by McCloskey in similar terms, is evident. See Donald N. McCloskey, English Open Fields as Behavior Towards Risk, 1 Res. in Econ. Hist. 124 (1976), and The Persistence of English Common Fields, in European Peasants and Their Markets 73 (William N. Parker & Eric L. Jones eds. 1975). McCloskey remarks the presence of open-field policies in some primitive societies. See *id.* at 114. He also notes the possibility of the family as an insurance institution. See *id.* at 117.

[43]The absence of such remedies appears to explain why, where interest is permitted, the interest rate is often very high: the probability of default is very high. See Herskovits, *supra* note 3, at 228.

[44]The literature on gift-giving in primitive and archaic societies is immense. For some examples see Finley, *supra* note 4, at 62; Herskovits, *supra* note 3, ch. 8; B. Malinowski, Tribal Economics in the Trobriands, in Tribal and Peasant Economies, *supra* note 3, at 185; Marcel Mauss, The Gift (Ian Cunnison trans. 1954); Valentin A. Riasanovsky, The Customary Law of the Nomadic Tribes of Siberia 144–45 (1965); Sahlins, *supra* note 3, at ch. 5.

[45]The feast is not only a means of providing food to many people; it is also a form of "forced saving"—the giver of the feast must accumulate food in order to give it. Of course, the feast may dissipate the accumulated food prematurely. See note 37 *supra*.

[46]Cyril S. Belshaw, Traditional Exchange and Modern Markets 38 (1965), describes a practice in one tribe which illustrates this point nicely. A creates a gift-

man to repay a loan when he can or a gift when he can, or to feast his benefactors when he can, provides some protection against the free-riding or moral-hazard problems that so inclusive and informal a system of insurance as is found in primitive societies would otherwise create.

It is sometimes argued that the exchange of gifts in primitive society, however reciprocal, cannot be a form of trade because so often what is exchanged is the same sort of good and because there is no time limit on when reciprocation is due. But these points show only that the exchange of gifts in primitive society is not the same kind of trade that arises in a more complex society out of the division of labor and resulting specialization of production. Its purpose is to even out consumption over time rather than to exploit the division of labor. It would utterly defeat this purpose if the gifts were exchanged simultaneously. (The simultaneous exchange of gifts does occur in primitive societies but it has, as we shall see, a different function from either insurance or exploiting the division of labor.)

Nor is it correct to argue, as in the following passage from a discussion of gift exchange in early medieval society, that the absence of "profit motive" distinguishes such exchange from modern commercial transactions:

> This mutual exchange of gifts at first sight resembles commerce, but its objects and ethos are entirely different. Its object is not that of material and tangible "profit," derived from the difference between the value of what one parts with and what one receives in exchange; rather it is the social prestige attached to generosity, to one's ability and readiness to lavish one's wealth on one's neighbours and dependents. The "profit" consists in placing other people morally in one's debt, for a counter-gift—or services in lieu of one—is necessary if the recipient is to retain his self-respect—.[47]

The author writes as if the typical modern commercial transaction were one-sided—A sells B a good or service knowing that it is worth less than B thinks. Rather, the usual transaction is mutually advantageous because it enables both parties to exploit the division of labor. Giving in the expectation that the gift will some day be reciprocated involves

---

exchange relationship by making a gift to B. B is not free to refuse the gift. Thereafter A can demand reciprocation of the gift from B at any time. This "on demand" reciprocity gives A a hedge against uncertainty.

[47] Philip Grierson, Commerce in the Dark Ages: A Critique of the Evidence, in Studies in Economic Anthropology 74, 79 (George Dalton ed. 1971).

the same "profit motive" as the modern commercial transaction, although its basis is the desire for insurance rather than to exploit the division of labor. For reasons discussed earlier, the fact that the gift is not repaid with interest does not make the gift exchange a one-sided or commercially unreasonable one.

Another example of the insurance mechanisms of primitive society is the pair of principles that (a) debts never expire—there is no statute of limitations, though in an oral society it would be a considerable convenience—and (b) people inherit their fathers' debts even when the debts exceed the estate.[48] These principles increase the scope of the insurance principle. If you lend money to an old and poor man, you are not permanently out of pocket; his heirs remain obligated to you. Yet the inheritance of debts is not a crushing burden on them. They will be obligated to repay the loan only if and when they have a good year and so can afford to repay it without lowering their own consumption below its normal level.

The system of reciprocal exchange, as we may describe the network of institutions described above for allocating a food surplus in a primitive society, would appear to be a fragile one because there are no legal sanctions for failure to reciprocate promptly and adequately for benefits received.[49] Perhaps, therefore, a sixth assumption should be added to the model:

(6) The population is immobile, in the sense that the member of one village, band, or tribe cannot readily join another and distant unit. Mobility would make the incentive to free ride and the reluctance to share without an enforceable promise to reciprocate very great. Mobility is in fact quite limited in most primitive societies, as the conditions of information in such societies would lead one to expect. Where it is great, the system of reciprocal exchange tends to break down.[50]

Some quantitative evidence bearing on the above analysis of primitive society is presented in Table 1, which is adapted from a table in Pryor's recent book. Table 1 shows that the less developed a primi-

---

[48] See, e.g., Barton, *supra* note 41, at 126; Max Gluckman, The Ideas in Barotse Jurisprudence 195 (1965); R. S. Rattray, Ashanti Law and Constitution 370–71 (1929). The saying is: "debts never rot." See Walter Goldschmidt, Sebei Law 62, 188, 204 (1967).

[49] For some examples of attempts to evade the obligations of reciprocal exchange see Sahlins, *supra* note 3, at 125, 128, and note 29 *supra*.

[50] For evidence of this in an Eskimo village see Pryor, *supra* note 3, at 91. A similar point is made in the biological literature on reciprocal altruism. See David P. Barash, Sociobiology and Behavior 314 (1977). The biological concept of reciprocal altruism seems, in fact, indistinguishable from the economic concept of self-interested but reciprocal exchange that this paper uses to explain primitive social institutions.

TABLE 1.   Relative Frequency of Modes of Distribution at Different
Levels of Economic Development

Type of Distribution	Relative Frequency in the Different Development Groups	
	The 15 societies at the lowest level	The 15 societies at the highest level
Goods		
Market exchange	7	14
Sharing	13	3
Reciprocal exchange	13	3
Centralized redistribution	3	10
Labor		
Market exchange	2	14
Reciprocal exchange	10	9
Centralized redistribution	0	5
Other types of distribution		
Presence of interest	2	9.5

Source: Pryor, *supra* note 3, at 309 (tab. 11.1).

tive society is—and the more, therefore, its economy is likely to approximate the conditions of my model—the more likely it is to rely on gift exchange, non-interest-bearing loans, and sharing, and the less likely it is to rely on market exchange, for the distribution of goods. Pryor also found that reciprocal exchange is more important in hunting, fishing, and agricultural societies than in gathering and herding societies. Consistently with the spirit of my model, he noted that there is greater uncertainty of food supply in the first three types of society and this increases the demand for a principle of reciprocal exchange.[51]

[51] See Pryor, *supra* note 3, at 195. For other recognition in the literature of the insurance function of reciprocal exchange in primitive societies see Sahlins, *supra* note 3, at 211–17; Marguerite Dupire, Trade and Markets in the Economy of the Nomadic Fulani of Niger (Bororo), in Markets in Africa, *supra* note 3, at 335, 344; Paul Einzig, Primitive Money 338–88 (2d ed. 1966); Leonard Joy, One Economist's View of the Relationship between Economics and Anthropology, in Themes in Economic Anthropology, *supra* note 3, at 29, 37; T. Scarlett Epstein, Production Efficiency and Customary Systems of Rewards in Rural South India, in *id.* at 229; Daryll Forde & Mary Douglas, Primitive Economics, in Tribal and Peasant Economies, *supra* note 3, at 13, 23; Henry J. Rutz, Ceremonial Exchange and Economic Development in Village Fiji, 26 Econ. Dev. & Cultural Change 777, 801–02, 805 (1978); and note 36 *supra*. Cf. Ralph L. Beals, Gifting, Reciprocity, Savings, and Credit in Peasant Oaxaca, 26 Sw. J. of Anthropology 231, 239 (1970); Allen W. Johnson, Security and Risk-Taking among

The rows in Table 1 labeled "centralized redistribution" refer to redistribution by a public authority such as a chief or king. The paucity of centralized redistribution among the least developed societies is a clue to the weakness of government in those societies,[52] the subject to which I now turn.

3. *Political Aspects of Insurance and of Polygamy.* One effect of insurance is to tend to equalize the *ex post* distribution of wealth, and there is evidence that this is an effect of the insurance arrangements of primitive society.[53] But equality of wealth is not only a by-product of insurance; it is also a precondition of the maintenance of a pregovernmental political equilibrium. A man who had a food surplus year after year—a wealthy man—would be an inviting target to other members of the society. He could use his wealth to hire retainers to protect him, trading part of his surplus for their loyalty. But other members of society could try to undermine the retainers' loyalty by promising them more of his surplus if they turned against him. In the resulting struggle, either the wealthy man or someone else might emerge with such a following that he could overawe the other individuals and families in the society—that he could, in short, establish a state with himself as its head. Hence, observing a society that has little or no government despite the limited variety of consumption goods (and hence great incentive to use any surplus to hire thugs and henchmen), one may assume that there are institutions that limit the ability of the abler or more energetic people to use their surplus food for political ends. The insurance institutions of primitive society have this effect by tending to dissipate surpluses.[54]

In discussing the institutions that support a pregovernmental equilibrium in primitive society, I make no judgment as to whether

---

Poor Peasants: A Brazilian Case, in Studies in Economic Anthropology, *supra* note 47, at 151; and James C. Scott, The Moral Economy of the Peasant, chs. 1–2 (1976).

[52] Pryor's sample includes peasant as well as primitive societies. The predominance of market exchange and public redistribution in the second column suggests that the columns are comparing primitive (column 1) with what in my terminology would be nonprimitive societies (column 2).

[53] Pryor finds reciprocal exchange to be positively correlated with socioeconomic equality. See Pryor, *supra* note 3, at 200–01. See also *id.* at 261, 276.

[54] Consistently with this analysis, Pryor, *supra* note 3, at 426–27, finds a negative correlation between socioeconomic equality and amount of government, as do several earlier studies referenced in Edwin E. Erickson, Cultural Evolution, 20 Am. Behavioral Scientist 669, 673 (1977). And Robert A. LeVine, The Internalization of Political Values in Stateless Societies, 19 Human Organization 51, 53 (1960), finds a negative correlation between equality and sharing on the one hand and the possession of political values on the other hand.

those institutions are efficient in an economic sense. Probably government is more efficient than alternative institutions of public order. I am interested simply in describing those institutions, and in particular in noting the dual economic-political functions of the pervasive insurance arrangements of primitive society. But I return in the conclusion of this paper to the issue of the efficiency of primitive social organization.

The political function of the insurance institutions in primitive societies is illuminated by comparison with the feudal system. Feudalism is one response to a situation in which some people are able to produce an agricultural surplus but there are few goods to buy with it. They use the surplus to hire retainers and thus enhance their political power.[55] Most primitive societies are not feudalistic. The poor man has rights to the goods of his (wealthy) kinsmen without corresponding duties to serve them. This one-sided relationship would be intolerable under conditions of great and persistent inequality of wealth—a class system. But the emergence of such a system is forestalled by the vagaries of the harvest and the hunt, which are extreme in the primitive economy, and by the difficulty of storing an agricultural surplus or an animal's carcass without decay, or of exchanging these things for durable goods. Because of these factors everyone in the society has a large variance in his expected wealth and is therefore willing to subscribe to an elaborate set of insurance arrangements despite his current wealth position. The result is to equalize wealth *ex post*.

Polygamy, superficially a source of great inequality, may actually promote the economic equality and resulting political stability of primitive society. To be sure, in its usual form, polygyny (many wives), polygamy presupposes some inequality of wealth.[56] For, given diminishing returns (not offset by opportunities for greater division of labor) from having additional wives, a supply of women more or less fixed at the number of men, and a strong desire of most men to have at least one wife, one man would have to be much wealthier than another to be willing and able to pay more for his second, third, or *n*th wife than a rival suitor seeking his first. The generally low incidence of polygyny even where it is freely permitted[57] thus indicates that the inequality of wealth is not great (as appears to be true in most primitive societies) and/or that the returns from having a second wife are indeed much lower than those from the first. In any event, while polygyny presup-

---

[55]This is (approximately) Adam Smith's theory of feudalism. See The Wealth of Nations Bk. III, ch. IV (1776). Cf. Mair, *supra* note 20, at ch. 4, especially p. 67. On the importance of armed retainers in at least the early stages of medieval European feudalism see 1 Marc Bloch, Feudal Society 154, 156, 169 (L. A. Manyon trans. 1961).

[56]See Becker, *supra* note 8, at 240.

[57]See, e.g., Diamond, *supra* note 14, at 246 n. 2.

poses some inequality in wealth, it need not increase it, for where polygyny is common generally the bridegroom (or his kin) must pay a substantial brideprice to the bride's kin.[58] More important, polygyny actually has a tendency to reduce inequality over time by increasing the number of dependents (wives and children) who must be provided for when the husband dies.[59] Because his estate is divided in more ways than if he had one wife,[60] the inequality of wealth in the next generation is less. Where polygamy is not permitted, inheritance in accordance with the principle of primogeniture would tend to perpetuate inequalities of wealth across generations, so we would expect to find rules of equal inheritance or other equalizing departures from primogeniture in primitive societies where polygamy is forbidden. There is some evidence for such a correlation.[61]

To be sure, polygyny tends to increase inequality across families, assuming that the polygynous offspring remain within the father's family, as would be true of the male offspring in a patrilineal society. Be-

---

[58] Since the brideprice is divided among the bride's kin, this is a further example of the insurance principle at work. Lucy Mair, Marriage, ch. 4 (2d ed. 1977), is a good introduction to the complex subject of brideprice. Polygyny seems strongly associated with payment of substantial brideprice. See Grossbard, Toward a Marriage between Economics and Anthropology and a General Theory of Marriage, *supra* note 8, at 36; Pryor, *supra* note 3, at 364 (tab. B3). Incidentally, Pryor's statistical study of brideprices (see *id.* at 348–68) goes some way toward resolving the old debate over whether the payment of brideprice is a real exchange or merely some kind of symbolic gesture—in favor of the exchange model. On the prevalence of bride purchase in archaic societies see Diamond, *supra* note 14, at 57, 69. For further discussion of primitive marriage customs see pp. 36–42 *infra*.

[59] See M. Fortes, *supra* note 26, at 250; Jack Goody, Bridewealth and Dowry in Africa and Eurasia, in Jack Goody & S. J. Tambiah, Bridewealth and Dowry 1, 13, 17–18, 32 (1973); Robert A. LeVine, Wealth and Power in Gusiiland, in Markets in Africa, *supra* note 3, at 520, 522–23; Frederic L. Pryor, Simulation of the Impact of Social and Economic Institutions on the Size Distribution of Income and Wealth, 63 Am. Econ. Rev. 50, 54 (1973). See also Jack Goody, Production and Reproduction (1976), arguing for an association between polygamy, brideprice, equality of wealth, and weak government, on the one hand, and monogamy, dowry, inequality of wealth, and strong government, on the other. And for some evidence that monogamy is positively and polygamy negatively correlated with strong government see Mary Douglas, Lele Economy Compared with the Bushong, in Markets in Africa, *supra* note 3, at 211.

[60] See discussion of inheritance laws at note 109 *infra*.

[61] Of the 17 societies classified by Pryor, *supra* note 3, at 327–39, as ones in which a positive political orientation was lacking but in which polygyny was also uncommon, information contained in the Human Relations Area Files indicates that only one had primogeniture as the method of inheritance, one had no inheritance at all, and the other 15 divided property more or less equally on death (though sometimes only male offspring inherited). In contrast, primogeniture is common in primitive polygynous societies. See note 109 *infra*.

cause of the important role of the family in the maintenance of public order (discussed in Part II-B), such a disequalizing force could upset the political equilibrium of a primitive society. If, however, as seems generally the case in primitive societies, authority in kinship groups is not tightly centralized and, moreover, the groups tend to fission when they grow large,[62] beyond some point an increase in number of members may not significantly increase the group's power—the added strength may be offset by reduced cohesion. The contrast with the hierarchical structure of feudalism (or of the modern corporation) is evident.

Polygyny disperses political power in another way, by increasing the opportunity costs of retainers.[63] Wealth is thereby diverted into a politically harmless channel, because women are useless as fighters in primitive societies.[64] (The value of additional wives, it should be noted, is not only or mainly to provide sexual variety; it is also to provide additional insurance, especially by increasing the number of sons to whom, as members of his kin group, the father can look for support in his old age.[65]) Consistently with this analysis, Schapera reports that in one African tribe where government had emerged to the extent that the chief was claiming a monopoly of the right to redistribute the tribe's food surplus to the needy members of the tribe, the chief encouraged the wealthy men of the tribe to buy additional wives. He was concerned that if they did not use their wealth in that way they might use it to feed the needy and thus undermine his position.[66]

Table 2 cross-tabulates two of Pryor's variables: polygyny, and

[62] See, e.g., Daryll Forde, Double Descent among the Yakö, in African Systems of Kinship and Marriage, *supra* note 22, at 285, 294.

[63] An alternative use of wealth would be to rent one's extra land or hire laborers to work it. But this alternative appears to encounter information costs greater than primitive society can cope with. See note 107 *infra*.

[64] Thus is it completely accidental that feudalism flourished in medieval Europe, which was strongly monogamous, and that an approximation to feudalism is found in the Greek society—also strongly monogamous—depicted in the Homeric poems? My analysis predicts that, other things being equal (obviously a vital qualification), feudalism is less likely to emerge in a society where polygamy is permitted than in one where it is forbidden. Diamond, *supra* note 14, at 376–77, states that brideprice diminished with the growth of feudalism. This finding makes sense because the opportunity cost of a wife is higher in a feudal than in a prefeudal system.

[65] Where women are the principal capital good in a society, it is understandable why a man who sells women for other goods should be despised—as he is among the Tiv, for example (see Paul Bohannan, Some Principles of Exchange and Investment among the Tiv, in LeClair & Schneider, *supra* note 1, at 300, 304): he is dissipating his capital.

[66] See I. Schapera, Economic Changes in South African Native Life, in Tribal and Peasant Economies, *supra* note 3, at 136, 142.

TABLE 2.   Political Orientation and Polygyny

	Number of Societies	
Type of Orientation	Polygyny Common	Polygyny Uncommon
Positive Political Orientation*	4	12
Negative Political Orientation**	7	1

Source: Calculated from Pryor, supra note 3, at 318, 333–34 (variables 6, 69), 336–39.
 *Marked 1 in col. 61, p. 339 of Pryor.
**Marked −1 in id.

whether the society is "politically oriented." Table 2 shows that polyg-yny is more common in a society that is negatively politically oriented than in one that is positively so oriented. This evidence is consistent with the suggestion that polygamy operates to disperse political power and thus to support the pregovernmental political equilibrium of a primitive society.

4. Other Primitive Adaptations to High Information Costs. The model from which I have attempted to deduce the fundamental social institu-tions of primitive people is based, it will be recalled, on the high costs of information, and resulting uncertainty, in primitive society. I turn now to other ways in which primitive societies adapt to the costs of information.

(1) Concerning the most conspicuous primitive institution expli-cable by reference to the high costs of information—the belief in and practice of magic, sorcery, and witchcraft—I shall content myself with noting the frequency with which primitive superstitions appear to pro-mote the economic well-being of the society. For example, in many so-cieties a man who gets too wealthy—who fails, in other words, to carry out his social duty of sharing his surplus when he has one—is likely to be considered a witch.[67] This result may be thought an example of the primitive's envious resentment of anyone who lifts himself above the average—and envious resentment may in fact describe his feelings—but it can equally well be viewed as a rational[68] response to the demand for insurance in primitive societies and the lack of the conventional modern mechanisms of supplying it. Or consider the belief of one tribe that misfortune will befall anyone who sells his goods on the way to the market.[69] This seems a silly belief—until it is remembered that a mar-

[67] See, e.g., Driver, supra note 17, at 444.
[68] On the meaning of "rational" see text at note 13 supra & note 174 infra.
[69] See Herskovits, supra note 3, at 205.

ket's efficiency is increased if as many buy and sell offers as possible can be pooled in it. Or consider the common practice in primitive and archaic societies of burying people with their personal possessions, or destroying those possessions at their death.[70] These are methods of equalizing wealth in the next generation,[71] yielding benefits already discussed.[72]

(2) Age grading—the assignment of tasks or roles on the basis of age—is more common in primitive than in modern societies. For example, all males 7–10 years of age in a primitive community might be assigned as herdsmen, all 11–14 year olds as junior warriors, all 15–30 year olds as senior warriors, and all those above 30 as tribal elders. Sex is also used more than in modern societies to determine work assignments.

One possible explanation for age and sex grading in primitive society is simply that the tasks in such societies are so simple that individual differences are unimportant to the quality of performance. Another is that since many primitive societies do not have good data on ages, assignment to one or another age group may in fact reflect individual fitness rather than chronology. A third explanation draws on recent work in the economics of information. Age and sex are proxies for individual fitness for a particular job. They economize on information by avoiding an assessment of individual strength, skill, and character.[73] Despite the better knowledge of each other's character that primitive people possess because of their lack of privacy, difficulties of evaluation and supervision may make the measurement of an individual's marginal product more costly in primitive than in modern societies, leading the former to rely more heavily on crude but cheap proxies of individual capacity.[74]

(3) As mentioned earlier, gifts play a larger role in primitive than in advanced societies. While their role is partly to be explained in terms of mutual insurance, they also have a direct informational aspect.[75] A gift is a way of communicating information about one's wealth,

---

[70] See, e.g., Herskovits, *supra* note 3, at 491–92.

[71] See T. Scarlett Epstein, Capitalism, Primitive and Modern 31 (1968).

[72] Another example of the economic function of superstition is offered at p. 47 *infra*. See also Smith, *supra* note 9, at 742.

[73] See, e.g., Edmund S. Phelps, The Statistical Theory of Racism and Sexism, 62 Am. Econ. Rev. 659 (1972).

[74] This analysis suggests the general point, which cannot be pursued in this paper, that the apparent secular growth in tolerance in Western culture may result from a secular trend toward lower costs of measuring individual performance.

On the costs of labor markets in primitive societies see further note 107 *infra* and accompanying text.

[75] I discuss this aspect of gifts in the context of archaic society in The Homeric Version of the Minimal State, *supra* note 11, at 41–42. The distinction between gifts as

tastes, and attitudes more credibly than by a statement, especially in circumstances where a statement would be difficult to verify and guarantees of its truth would not be enforceable. Gifts have this function today, though the abundance of other and cheaper substitutes in communication renders them less important than in primitive societies. Yet, gift-giving remains a custom in visits between heads of state; the lack of supranational government prevents the formal enforcement of promises and so makes the assessment of character and intentions more critical than in transactions enforceable by a public judiciary. Gifts in primitive society within the kin group or village are generally an aspect of the insurance system described earlier, for within the small group all is known about everyone's character and nothing remains to be communicated by gift. But where the gift is between strangers, as where an exchange of gifts accompanies betrothal to the member of another kin group living in another village,[76] it probably has an informational function instead. (These betrothal gifts, it should be noted, are distinct from the brideprice, which is not a gift but the purchase price.) Gifts are to be distinguished from trade in the ordinary sense of an exchange of unlike goods to take advantage of the division of labor. Gift exchange is not motivated by the division of labor and resulting opportunities to reduce the costs of production through specialization, but by either the costs of information in, or the insurance needs of, primitive society.

Notice that, viewed as a signaling device, a gift need not actually be received or enjoyed by the donee. The form of Northwest Indian potlatch, sometimes regarded as pathological, in which goods are destroyed rather than given away can be interpreted as an especially credible method of signaling the possession of wealth, and of whatever qualities are correlated with the possession of wealth.[77]

(4) With regard to trade in the ordinary sense—trade of unlike articles between strangers—in primitive society, transaction costs are presumably high because of the costs of information regarding the reliability of the seller, the quality of the product, and trading alternatives (that is, the market price). However, institutions have arisen which reduce these transaction costs.

---

assistance and as a means of "cementing a relationship" is of course not new. See, e.g., Günter Wagner, The Political Organization of the Bantu of Kanirondo, in African Political Systems, *supra* note 20, at 206–08.

[76] See, e.g., Barton, *supra* note 41, at 40. The principle of exogamy (see pp. 41–42 *infra*), the size of the kinship group, and the likelihood that most of the people in the village are kin combine to create a situation in which a spouse often must be sought in another village—which is likely to mean among strangers.

[77] See Edward O. Wilson, Sociobiology 561 (1975).

(a) One is gift-exchange, viewed as a means of communicating information about one's character and intentions. The exchange of gifts is a common accompaniment to primitive trade.[78] For example, the *kula* ring of the Trobriand Islanders, an elaborate system of gift-exchange between members of different communities, although not trade in the usual sense (it consisted essentially of the exchange of like ornamental objects) facilitated trade. As Belshaw explains:

> The *kula* itself was not oriented to individual trade in its ceremonial activities. But alongside the *kula* persons visiting their partners took advantage of the opportunity to engage in trade. Malinowski makes the point that *kula* partners would exchange gifts of a trade character in addition to *vaygu'a* [the ornamental objects exchanged in the *kula* ring], and that the security afforded by the partnership would make it possible for the visitor to make contact with other persons in the village and trade with them.[79]

(b) Many primitive societies have "customary" prices for the goods involved in trade rather than prices determined by negotiation between the parties.[80] Customary prices do not change as quickly as the conditions of demand and supply and are therefore a source of inefficiency. But given the high costs of markets in primitive societies, such prices may be less inefficient, on balance, than freely bargained prices. The efficiency of customary prices is reinforced by the fact, noted earlier, that people have claims on the goods of their kin.[81] Multi-party transactions are generally more costly than transactions between just two parties; this is presumably one reason why trade is relatively rare in primitive societies.[82] To the extent that there is trade, however, it can be facilitated by customary prices. These reduce trans-

[78] See, e.g., Herskovits, *supra* note 3, at 196. A related practice is the solemnization of a formal debt by the exchange of gifts. See Gluckman, *supra* note 48, at 197–98.

[79] Belshaw, *supra* note 46, at 16.

[80] See examples in Herskovits, *supra* note 3, at 206–10; Sahlins, *supra* note 3, at 295, 299–300, 308–09; and Pospisil, *supra* note 22, at 121–22. Notice that both haggling (see Geertz, *supra* note 6) and fixing of customary prices, though seemingly at opposite ends of the spectrum of price flexibility, are explicable in terms of the high information costs in primitive societies. Neither method of price setting is as common in advanced societies.

[81] This is the reason why, in at least one society, it is customary for the buyer of a good to give gifts to the seller's kin. See Barton, *supra* note 41, at 107.

[82] See *id.* at 110–11; Maine, *supra* note 22, at 271 (Beacon ed. 1970); and Table 1, *supra* p. 18.

action costs by eliminating the need for a many-sided negotiation over price.[83]

(c) Another response to market transaction costs is the transformation of an arms-length contract relationship into an intimate status relationship. In some primitive societies if you trade repeatedly with the same man he becomes your blood brother and you owe him the same duty of generous and fair dealing that you would owe a kinsman.[84] This "barter friendship" resembles the pairing of buyers and sellers in bazaars that Geertz noted. It is a way of bringing reciprocity into the exchange process and thereby increasing the likelihood that promises will be honored despite the absence of a public enforcement authority.[85]

(d) Sahlins has noted still another device by which security of primitive trade is enhanced—what he calls economic "good measure," that is, a buyer's deliberately overpaying a seller in order to induce the seller to deal fairly with him in the future.[86] The overpayment increases the cost to the seller of a breach of trust that would induce the buyer to withdraw his patronage.[87] Finally, the bazaar itself may be viewed as an adaptation to the high costs of information and communication. Those costs make it difficult to pool offers to buy and offers to sell other than by bringing all of the buyers and sellers face to face with each other.

(5) Certain behavioral traits of primitive man are illuminated by reference to the conditions of information in primitive society. Generosity, its connection with prestige, and the concomitant hostility toward people who accumulate rather than give away wealth have already been noted. The sense of honor—less grandly, touchiness—which is so pronounced a character trait in primitive and ancient societies[88] may be related to the importance of the threat to retaliate as a device for

[83] For further analysis of the role of custom in reducing transaction costs see pp. 37–38 *infra*.

[84] See Gluckman, *supra* note 48, at 174. Raymond Firth speaks of the "personalization" of economic relations in primitive society. Primitive Polynesian Economy 315 (1939). See also Malinowski, *supra* note 22, at 39–40 (1951 ed.); Goldschmidt, *supra* note 48, at 192–93. Nash, *supra* note 3, at 49, describes the use of an "idiom of fictive kinship" in market transactions.

[85] See Nash, *supra* note 3, at 31. On pairing, or reciprocal buying, as a modern response to high costs of formal contract enforcement see Benjamin Klein, Robert G. Crawford, & Armen A. Alchian, Vertical Integration, Appropriable Rents, and the Competitive Contracting Process, 21 J. Law & Econ. 297, 304–05 n. 18 (1978).

[86] See Sahlins, *supra* note 3, at 303. Cf. *id.* at 304.

[87] Cf. Gary S. Becker & George J. Stigler, Law Enforcement, Malfeasance, and Compensation of Enforcers, 3 J. Legal Stud. 1, 6–13 (1974) (chap 19 of this volume).

[88] See, e.g., Gluckman, *supra* note 48, at 232; Evans-Pritchard, *supra* note 22, at 151; Mair, *supra* note 20, at 40. The *locus classicus* of touchiness in archaic society is Achilles' conduct in the *Iliad*.

keeping order in a society lacking (for reasons based on information costs) formal institutions of law enforcement. The sense of honor increases the probability that a man will retaliate for a wrong to him or to his kin and it thereby increases the credibility of threatened retaliation as a deterrent to antisocial behavior.[89]

(6) The formality and decorum of primitive speech and manners are well documented, and in other papers I have related these traits to the lack of privacy in primitive societies.[90] The argument in those papers, briefly, is that people who lack conversational privacy must learn to express themselves very precisely and circumspectly since many of their conversations are bound to be overheard, creating all sorts of possibilities for recrimination and misunderstanding. The economic analysis of primitive rhetoric can be carried further, though in this paper I shall only sketch the argument.

The art of rhetoric, so highly developed in primitive and early cultures, so neglected (except by politicians) in modern ones, appears to be a response to high costs of information. In the words of one of the few modern textbooks on the subject:

> In dealing with contingent human affairs, we cannot always discover or confirm what is the truth. . . . But frequently, in the interests of getting on with the business of life, we have to make decisions on the basis of uncertainties or probabilities. The function of rhetoric is to persuade, where it cannot convince, an audience. And in matters where the truth cannot be readily ascertained, rhetoric can persuade an audience to adopt a point of view or a course of action on the basis of the merely probable. . . .[91]

Take the familiar rhetorical device known as the "ethical appeal." This refers to a speaker's trying to ingratiate himself with his audience. As Corbett points out, "All of an orator's skill in convincing the intellect and moving the will of an audience could prove futile if the audience did not esteem, could not trust, the speaker."[92] However, if the truth of the speaker's words were readily verifiable, there would be no interest in his character, no occasion for trust. Character is a proxy for credibility which becomes important only where the costs of information are high. Thus, I conjecture that the importance attached to rhetorical skill in primitive and early cultures reflects not only the absence of privacy

[89] For some evidence see LeVine, *supra* note 54, at 54, finding a negative correlation between possession of political values and of a strong sense of honor. The basis of public order in the primitive state is discussed further in Part II-B *infra*.

[90] See privacy papers cited in note 11 *supra*.

[91] Edward P. J. Corbett, Classical Rhetoric for the Modern Student 73 (2d ed. 1971).

[92] *Id.* at 35.

in those cultures, but also the high costs of information, which make it necessary for speakers to use rhetorical techniques in order to make their utterances credible.

(7) Lack of privacy may explain why primitive people often seem more tolerant of certain forms of mendacity and (less consistently) of defamation than modern people.[93] Where everything is known about people's lives, the opportunity to use lies (including false aspersions) to mislead and manipulate the people with whom one transacts is more limited than in a modern impersonal society, where one is apt to know very little about most of one's transacting partners. The analysis is complicated in the case of defamation by (a) the emphasis on honor, which implies a high degree of sensitivity to slights, (b) the importance of reputation in a society that lacks effective sanctions for dishonoring promises, and (c) the costs of information that result from ignorance of scientific principles. These costs may exceed the reduction of information costs that is made possible by the lack of privacy. A false accusation that a person is a witch is a very serious charge in a primitive society. But many other forms of mendacity are harmless and are more likely to be adopted for dramatic or diplomatic effect than to mislead.

II. Legal Aspects of Primitive Society

A. In General

This part of the paper considers the extent to which the characteristic legal institutions of primitive and archaic societies are economically rational responses to the conditions of primitive life. I begin with brief examinations of the systems of procedure, property law, contract law, and family law in primitive society.[94] I then examine in somewhat

---

[93] See Posner, Privacy, Secrecy, and Reputation, *supra* note 11, at 31–32.

[94] For archaic societies my major sources are Maine, *supra* note 22; Diamond, *supra* note 14, at pt. I. See also Harold J. Berman, The Background of the Western Legal Tradition in the Folklaw of the Peoples of Europe, 45 U. Chi. L. Rev. 553 (1978). For primitive societies my major sources are Barton, *supra* note 41; Gluckman, *supra* note 48, and his Politics, Law, and Ritual in Tribal Society (1965); Goldschmidt, *supra* note 48; P. H. Gulliver, Social Control in an African Society (1963); Hoebel, *supra* note 40; P. P. Howell, A Manual of Nuer Law (1954); Leopold Pospisil, Anthropology of Law (1971); Riasanovsky, *supra* note 44; John Phillip Reid, A Law of Blood (1970); Schapera, *supra* note 30; Ideas and Procedures in African Customary Law (Max Gluckman ed. 1969); Law and Warfare (Paul Bohannan ed. 1967); Readings in African Law (E. Cotran & N. N. Rubin eds. 1970). For detailed literature reviews and bibliographies, unfortunately a bit out of date, see Sally Falk Moore, Law and Anthropology, 1969 Biennial Rev. Anthropology 252 (Bernard J. Siegel ed. 1970); Laura Nader, The Anthropological Study of Law, 67 Am. Anthropologist (Spec. Publication), no. 6, pt. 2, at 3 (1965); Laura Nader, Klaus F. Koch & Bruce Cox, The Ethnography of Law: A Bibliographical Survey, 7 Current Anthropology 267 (1966).

greater detail the system of strict liability in primitive society, covering the area which in our system is parcelled out between tort and criminal law.

1. The Legal Process in Primitive Societies. "Legal process" as I shall use the term has two broad aspects—the promulgation of substantive rules of law and the resolution of disputes arising under these laws. In a society that has no government worth speaking of—no legislature, executive branch, or public judiciary—the answer to the question how these functions are carried out is not obvious.

Let us begin with dispute resolution. Suppose there is a rule (we won't worry for the moment where it comes from) that a man may not take his neighbor's yams without the neighbor's permission, but he does so, or at least the neighbor alleges that he has done so. How is the dispute between them to be resolved and a sanction applied if the rule is found to have been violated? One possibility is simply retaliation by the neighbor for the theft. But that may be a costly procedure given the organization of primitive society into kin groups that provide mutual protection to their members (the "collective responsibility" of the kin group is examined in greater detail in Part II-B).[95] In these circumstances the aggrieved neighbor may wish to engage a passer-by, village elder or wise man, or other presumptively impartial and (perhaps) competent third party, to adjudicate his dispute.[96] The alleged violator also has an incentive to submit to adjudication—or "arbitration" as we should probably call it in view of its private nature—lest his refusal to do so trigger retaliation by the neighbor. To be sure, the alleged thief who is clearly guilty and expects to be so adjudged by an impartial arbitrator may prefer not to submit to arbitration at all or not to comply with the arbitrator's (adverse) judgment. But his kin group are a restraining influence here. They may urge him to submit to arbitration lest they get involved in a feud over his deed, as they are apt to do given the principle of collective responsibility. He will probably submit to their urging, for otherwise they may desert him when the neighbor or the neighbor's kin retaliate for his refusal to submit to arbitration or to comply with the arbitrator's award.[97]

Turning briefly to the factfinding procedures used in primitive adjudication, we find high information costs reflected in the reliance on

[95] On the limitations of retaliation as a means of maintaining order see Richard A. Posner, Retribution and Related Concepts of Punishment, *supra* note 11; also p. 43 *infra*.

[96] See, e.g., Maine, *supra* note 22, at 364 (Beacon ed. 1970).

[97] For a more detailed analysis of primitive arbitration see Landes & Posner, Adjudication as a Private Good, *supra* note 10, at 242–45.

oaths, ordeals, and other dubious or irrational methods of factual determination that are sometimes used in primitive adjudication. Yet the
superstitious element in primitive factfinding is easily exaggerated.
There is less reliance in African tribal society than there was in medieval European adjudication on the ordeal, the wager of battle, and
similarly bizarre methods of finding facts.[98] Observers of tribal justice
have been generally well impressed by the competence of the tribunal
and by the distinctions it makes—sometimes more intelligently than
under modern American rules of evidence designed to guide and control juries—among hearsay, circumstantial, direct, and other categories of evidence.[99] Yet the ability of primitive tribunals to find the facts
remains limited in many important respects because of the absence
of police and other investigatory machinery and techniques (autopsies,
etc.) and because of the possibility of assigning supernatural causes to
natural phenomena (as where a death from natural causes is ascribed to
the witchcraft of an enemy). These costs of information appear to have
shaped primitive substantive law in important ways.[100]

The remaining question is the source of the norms applied in a
primitive adjudication. Two of the common sources of legal norms, legislation and executive decree, are ruled out by the assumption of no
state. Since the arbitrators, though private, are a sort of judge, it may
seem that the third common source of law—judicial decisions viewed
as precedents guiding future conduct—could operate in primitive society. But even putting aside the problems that illiteracy would create
for any system of precedent similar to the Anglo-American common
law (but that primitive man's ingenuity might be able to overcome[101]),
one has still to ask what incentive the arbitrator has to issue opinions
that will stand as precedents. Even our society does not attempt to
create property rights in rules or precedents and certainly primitive
societies do not. Our judges receive salaries from the state and, if
appellate judges, are expected to write opinions setting forth their
grounds of decision; such opinions are precedents. But the typical
primitive judge, like the modern arbitrator, must look to the disputants

----

[98] See Diamond, *supra* note 14, at ch. 21. Even the bizarre methods can perhaps
be understood in a setting of transaction costs so high that people are unwilling to
attempt factual determinations on their own, that is, without divine assistance.

[99] See Max Gluckman, The Judicial Process among the Barotse of Northern Rhodesia, ch. III, 107–08 (1955); Max Gluckman, Reasonableness and Responsibility in
the Law of Segmentary Societies, in African Law: Adaptations and Development 120
(Hilda Kuper & Leo Kuper eds. 1965); Pospisil *supra* note 94, at 236–38.

[100] See pp. 49–50 *infra*.

[101] See discussion of "remembrancers" in I. Schapera, The Sources of Law in
Tswana Tribal Courts: Legislation and Precedent, 1 Afr. Law 150 (1957).

rather than to the society at large for his compensation, since he is a private citizen.[102] And just as modern arbitrators usually do not write opinions, because the parties to a dispute typically obtain only a trivial fraction of the benefits generated by a precedent (those benefits accruing to all whom the precedent enables to shape their future conduct better) and hence are unwilling to pay for the arbitrator's creating precedent, so primitive judges are unlikely to provide (oral) opinions usable as precedents.

The remaining source of law, and the one that dominates primitive law, is custom. It is custom that prescribes the compensation due for killing a man, the formalities for making a contract, the rules of inheritance, the obligations of kinship, the limitations on whom one may marry, and so forth. Custom (including customary law) resembles language in being a complex, slowly changing, highly decentralized system of highly exact rules. The exactness or detailedness of customary rules is a substitute for a system of broad standards particularized by judges through the creation of precedents. The exactness of those customary rules that are designed to price an act (like killing) can also be explained in terms of the high costs of negotiation where, as is typically the case, an entire kin group (or more likely two) is affected by the negotiation, thus making it a multi-party transaction.

The more exact a rule is, the less adaptable it is to changing circumstances. We would therefore expect a system of exact rules to have some method for changing the rules quickly. A system of customary law has none, but this is not a serious problem in a static society. In such a society there is little danger that legal change will lag behind social change, producing the sorts of anachronisms which in the case of English common law (as in that of Roman law) created the demand analyzed by Maine for legal fictions, equity, and legislation to keep the law up to date. These devices are found less often in primitive legal systems.[103] Evidently Roman and English society were changing faster

---

[102] See, e.g., Barton, *supra* note 41, at 164–67. A famous example is the "shield scene" in Book XVIII of the *Iliad*. Maine's interpretation that the two talents of gold referred to in the scene are a fee for the judges is now widely accepted. See Maine, *supra* note 22, at 364 (Beacon ed. 1970); Robert J. Bonner & Gertrude Smith, The Administration of Justice from Homer to Aristotle 38–40 (1930). Even where a primitive society has some rudimentary government, the judges tend to be at best quasi-official figures and to be paid, if at all, out of litigant fees. See, e.g., Riasanovsky, *supra* note 44, at 12.

[103] On legal fiction in Roman and English law see Maine, *supra* note 22, ch. 2. Equity and legislation require a more elaborate governmental structure than is found in the usual primitive society. Legal fictions, too, appear to be rare in primitive societies. For a good discussion see T. O. Beidelman, Kaguru Justice and the Concept of Legal Fictions, 5 J. Afr. Law 5 (1961). However, fictive kinship is sometimes found. See,

than a system of purely customary law (no fictions, no equity)—could keep up with—which means faster than the typical primitive society changes.

2. *Property.* Demsetz's study of the property rights systems of North American Indians pointed out that the appropriateness of recognizing a property right in a resource is a function of the scarcity and hence market value of the resource relative to the costs of enforcing such a right. [104] Where land is so abundant relative to population that its market price would be less than the cost of fencing the land or otherwise enforcing a property right to it, individual rights will not be asserted to the land; it will be treated as common property. As land becomes scarcer—because of a rise in the ratio of population to land due to the introduction of Western medicine, or a rise in the demand for some crop or animal grown on the land due to access to Western markets—a system of individual property rights will tend to develop. [105] But even in a very primitive agricultural society, some land is bound to be much more valuable than other land because of superior fertility, workability, or location (for example, proximity to the camp or village, making it safer from enemy attack), and so would command a positive market value if it could be bought and sold. And enforcement of a property right to such land should not be costly if it is a purely possessory right (a "usufruct") which allows the possessor to exclude people from the land only so long as he is actually working it. In fact, such possessory rights are common in primitive law. They have two additional elements: (1) the possessor can transfer his right to members of his family or pass it to his heirs, but (2) he cannot sell the land and, of course, he cannot establish rights in land that he is not actually working—that is what a purely possessory right or usufruct means. [106]

The model of primitive society developed in Part I is helpful in

---

e.g., note 80 *supra.* And one often finds artificial, "legalistic" reasoning. For example, in one African tribe if a man kills a member of his clan he pays a smaller composition (compensation) than if he kills a stranger, on the ground that as a member of the clan he is entitled to share in any composition which it receives. See Robert Redfield, Primitive Law, in Law and Warfare, *supra* note 94, at 3, 12. The reasoning is absurd but the rule makes economic sense. Where killer and victim are members of the same clan, the probability of detection is higher and hence the optimal penalty lower. But this is not an example of legal fiction in the sense, relevant to the discussion in the text, of a device for getting around an anachronistic, dysfunctional rule.

[104] See Demsetz, *supra* note 9.

[105] See, e.g., Ault & Rutman, *supra* note 9.

[106] See, e.g., Herskovits, *supra* note 3, at 68–70; Barton, *supra* note 41, at 89–98; Schapera, *supra* note 30, at 201, 205, 207; and Maine, *supra* note 22, at ch. 8.

explaining this structure of property rights. The benefits of such a system of rights are both political and narrowly economic. (1) The man who has a good harvest is not permitted to use his surplus to buy another's land and reduce the other to dependency on him—which would be a politically destabilizing transaction in a pregovernmental society—but is led instead to give the surplus to the other. The effective demand for land is thereby reduced as well, making it more likely that a poor man will be able to find tolerably good land somewhere else in the community. (2) Possession, in the sense of actually working a piece of land or killing and seizing a wild animal, provides clear evidence of the fact and extent of ownership. The alternative is either fencing or a record system. The former could be quite costly in a society that has only simple tools. The latter is ruled out by the assumption of illiteracy.

Turning to the costs of a possessory system, we find they are lower than they would be in an advanced society. To begin with, the sale of land would be difficult in any event because of the network of kinship obligations. A man cannot sell land on whose output some kinsman may depend, or cows that are needed to buy his younger brother a wife, without consulting the affected kinsmen or at least allocating the proceeds of the sale among them. But either step would increase the effective number of transacting parties and so the costs of transacting. And all the other obstacles that plague the primitive market, discussed in Part I, likewise plague the market in land. Thus, the primitive land market would probably operate poorly even if land were in principle freely alienable.

Furthermore, while in an advanced society inalienability would prevent the concentration of land into holdings large enough to enable economies of large-scale production to be exploited, such exploitation is largely infeasible in primitive society in any event, because it entails a capacity for organization—for coordinating the work of many people under central direction—that is precluded by the high costs of information.[107] The social benefits of allowing a man to assemble more land

---

[107] Some empirical support for this proposition is provided by Pryor's findings that land-rental and labor contracts generally emerge late in the development of a society, relative to markets in goods. See Pryor, *supra* note 3, at 126–27, 141. And notice how strongly in Table 1, *supra* p. 18, reciprocal exchange of labor persists after reciprocal exchange of goods has largely given way to market exchange of goods. Presumably the costs of market transactions in the rental of land or the hiring of labor (to work the land or do any other work) are higher than the costs of simply selling goods, because of the difficulty of either determining the tenant's or worker's marginal product or monitoring his effort. Cf. M. I. Finley, The Ancient Economy 65 (1973).

than he could personally work would therefore be slight. Moreover, some opportunity for expanding one's holdings is created by polygamy, which enables a man to buy several wives to work a large estate.[108] The potentially destabilizing effect of polygamy on the equality of wealth and power is counteracted, as we have noted, by the increased number of children, which leads to a greater division of the land in the next generation.[109]

Another cost of a purely possessory rights system that is relatively unimportant in a primitive economy is the distortion that such a system creates in the temporal pattern of resource exploitation. When one can obtain ownership rights in a resource only by capture or use, there is a tendency to take too much too soon; but again this is not a frequent problem in a simple society. It is cheaper for a band of hunters to move on when the game in an area is depleted than to regulate the game population by creating fee-simple rights to hunting territories, and cheaper to abandon worn-out land for several years until its fertility is naturally restored than to enforce fee-simple rights in the hope of encouraging the owners to regenerate the land more quickly (the techniques for doing so are unknown). Where investment preparatory to use is feasible in primitive society—the setting of traps is an example—it is often protected by the grant of a nonpossessory property right. The man who sets a trap is entitled to the trapped ani-

[108] Consistently with this suggestion, Pryor found a negative correlation between the existence of land rentals and the presence of polygyny. See Pryor, *supra* note 3, at 137. Given the limitations on the sale of land, the question arises how one would obtain a large estate in the first place; one answer might be inheritance of several plots of land from different people. Another question is why the costs of supervising wives should be thought lower than those of supervising (other) field hands. The answer is that the food that the wife grows in part to feed her son is a form of joint consumption of husband and wife; the feeding of his son is a benefit to the husband that the latter doesn't have to exert himself in supervising the wife to obtain.

[109] Under South African tribal law, for example, the land worked by each of a polygamist's wives is a separate estate which on his death passes to the eldest son of that marriage, so that his total holdings are broken up on his death. See A. J. Kerr, The Native Law of Succession in South Africa 35, 54 (1961); 4 N. J. van Warmelo, Venda Law 815, 899 (1949). Notice that the combination of polygamy and primogeniture achieves similar results to a rule of equal inheritance, which would be less efficient because it would often force the division of estates into inefficiently small units. However, where as among nomads the principal wealth is almost perfectly divisible (herds), a rule of equal inheritance is often found. See Austin Kennett, Bedouin Justice, ch. 10 (1925). Cf. Manning Nash, The Social Context of Economic Choice in a Small Society, in LeClair & Schneider, *supra* note 1, at 311, 320. On the equalizing tendencies of primitive inheritance law see also Lowie, *supra* note 22, at 248–55; Charles Douglas, The Organization and Laws of Some Bantu Tribes in East Africa, 45 J. Royal Anthropological Inst. 234, 294 (1915).

mal even if someone else finds it in the trap and thus "possesses" it first.[110]

To summarize, analysis of the benefits and costs of a possessory system of rights in land indicates that it may well be the efficient system under the conditions prevailing in primitive society. As additional, admittedly oblique, evidence of this, notice that the modern appropriation system of water rights, a possessory system that has close counterparts in primitive law,[111] emerged in an area and time widely regarded as lawless, or at least lacking settled legal institutions—California, in the period immediately following the Gold Rush of 1849.[112]

3. Contracts. In primitive as in modern law, exchange and contract are not synonymous. And because the formation of marriage, exchanges within the household or kin group, and gift-giving are the most important forms of exchange in primitive society (or, the same point, because the role of explicit markets in organizing production and distribution is smaller in primitive than in modern economies), the potential domain of the law of contracts in primitive society—the law, that is, governing trade with strangers—is limited.

Several features of primitive contract law recur with sufficient frequency to be regarded as typical: (1) executory contracts (contracts which neither party has begun to perform when the breach occurred) are not enforced; (2) damages are not awarded for loss of the expected profits of the transaction—the standard remedy is restitution; (3) a breach of contract where the other party has completed performance—that is, breach of a half-executed as distinct from an executory contract—will often be treated as a form of theft from the promise; and (4) the seller is liable for any defect in the product sold (*caveat venditor*).

These features taken together suggest that contract law barely

[110] See, e.g., Diamond, *supra* note 14, at 189; Goldschmidt, *supra* note 48, at 157. Cf. Smith, *supra* note 9, at 742–43.

[111] See Barton, *supra* note 41, at 103; Hoebel, *supra* note 40, at 108.

[112] See Charles W. McCurdy, Stephen J. Field and Public Land Development in California, 1850–1866: A Case Study of Judicial Resource Allocation in Nineteenth Century America, 10 Law & Soc'y Rev. 235, 253–62 (1976); John Umbeck, *supra* note 35. The analysis in this section has been of land rights, with special reference to agricultural land. The position with respect to other kinds of property is closer to that of modern law—always subject to the "cloud over title" that is cast by the rights of kinsmen. One of the few goods to which a kinsman usually cannot assert a claim is a man's wives (though he may, if in need, be able to claim a share of her or her children's agricultural surplus which might otherwise go to the husband-father). Women's (comparative) immunity from the claims of kinsmen is another reason why they are such a highly valued good in primitive societies, as measured by the brideprice which they command.

exists even in the limited sphere in which it applies. A law of contracts is not needed to generate the rule that a buyer who refuses to pay for goods of which he has already taken possession must return them to the seller, yet apart from liability for defective products that seems to be the only important duty that primitive contract law imposes. The reason becomes apparent once it is realized that the economic function of modern contract law is to facilitate transactions in which the performance of one or both parties takes considerable time.[113] Such an interval opens up the possibility both that unforeseen events will disrupt performance and that one of the parties will be tempted to exploit the strategic opportunities that nonsimultaneous contractual performance may create. The interval over which contract performance occurs is presumably a positive function of the complexity of the economic activity being regulated by the contract. The economic activity of primitive societies is simple; and if therefore it can be assumed that the transactions governed by the law of contracts in primitive society usually involve simultaneous (or virtually simultaneous) performance, the scope for that law is reduced to assigning liability for defects that show up later. If we assume just one element of nonsimultaneity, namely that payment sometimes follows transfer of the good sold, then only a principle of restitution that will make the buyer return the good to the seller is needed. This would not be good enough in a modern economy, where prices may change rapidly and where an important purpose of contracts is to assign the risk of such changes to one party or the other.[114] But prices change slowly in primitive societies, partly because so many of the prices are customary.

The rule of *caveat venditor* in primitive sales law can be derived from Geertz's observation concerning the costs of information in primitive markets. To be sure, the products tend to be simple, and this fact in isolation would suggest that the costs of inspection to buyer and to seller would be the same. Such reasoning has been used to explain the rule of *caveat emptor* in nineteenth-century Anglo-American common law, a rule now giving way to *caveat venditor,* presumably under pressure of growing complexity of products and hence increasing costs of inspection to buyers relative to sellers. An important difference between nineteenth-century markets and primitive markets, however, is the infrequency of trading in the latter. Because exchange with strang-

---

[113] See The Economics of Contract Law 1, 3–4 (Anthony T. Kronman & Richard A. Posner eds. 1978).

[114] For example, if I agree to sell you widgets for $2 apiece, I make delivery as agreed, and you then refuse to pay me because immediately after delivery the price of widgets falls to $1, a purely restitutionary remedy (namely, I get my widgets back) would not carry out the risk-shifting function of the contract.

ers is exceptional, individuals may not develop the skills of the experienced and knowledgeable consumer. In these circumstances the relative costs of inspection to the buyer compared to the seller may be high despite the simplicity of the product. In addition, the seller is the superior insurer of a product defect because he can spread its costs over his entire output. Although this argument is also made in modern discussions of the relative merits of *caveat venditor* and *caveat emptor,* it is superficial in the modern context because the buyer has a variety of insurance options open to him which may be as good as or better than seller self-insurance or seller market insurance. The insurance options of the primitive consumer are more limited.

4. Family Law. The law relating to marriage and divorce, obligations within the family, and inheritance is, judging by the number and detail of the rules,[115] the most important branch of primitive law. This is not surprising. The rules governing relations within the household correspond in function and importance to the law of corporations and of agency in modern societies; and since women are the principal goods exchanged in most primitive societies the rules governing marriage and divorce overshadow the contract law of these societies. I will discuss four general issues in primitive family law: (1) the level of detail in that law, (2) brideprice, (3) the liberality of primitive divorce law, and (4) exogamy.[116]

(1) One could imagine a system of primitive family law that consisted of a few fundamental principles (the right of kin to payment for giving a girl in marriage, the right to buy more than one wife, and so forth) but left the details to negotiation among the affected parties. That is not the typical pattern in primitive society. Commonly a vast number of family transactions are regulated by custom in minute detail, often including prices, and the scope for individual variation whether by testamentary will or by agreement is quite limited and sometimes nonexistent. Among the reasons suggested earlier for the characteristic exactness of primitive law the one that seems most important in the family-law context is the high costs of voluntary transactions where a large number of parties—often all of the members of two kinship groups—are involved. For example, since brideprice is the property of the bride's kinship group, if the price and its allocation among the kin were not specified by custom but were left to negotiations within the kin group, the transaction with the bridegroom would

---

[115] For a sense of the complexity of primitive family law see N. J. van Warmelo, Venda Law (4 vols., 1948–1949).

[116] Polygamy and inheritance were discussed earlier. See pp. 21, 33–34 *supra.*

be extremely costly. Protracted negotiations are in fact reported where the brideprice and its allocation are not fixed by custom.[117] Primitive family law often seeks to avoid these costs by specifying not only the brideprice but how it is to be split up among the bride's kin. My analysis predicts that, other things being equal, the level and allocation of brideprice among the bride's kin are more likely to be fixed by custom, rather than left to negotiation, the larger the average size of the kinship group that is entitled to share in the brideprice.[118]

The relationship between the communalizing of property rights and the fixing of price or shares by custom is a general one. For example, where hunting is done in groups, or (an even closer parallel to the brideprice case) where the insurance principles of the society require that the kill be shared among the kin group or in some cases the entire band or village, primitive law often prescribes the exact division, thus avoiding a multi-party negotiation.[119] It would also be avoided if each kin group or village had a chief who negotiated on behalf of the group and distributed the proceeds among the members. Such figures do emerge in primitive societies, but when this happens it may mean that the society is on its way to becoming a state. Where leadership is weak even on the kinship-group and village levels, customary prices and shares have an important allocative role to play.

(2) More often than not in primitive society one finds (a) a positive brideprice (rather than no price, or a negative price—dowry) (b) paid to the bride's kin rather than to the bride herself. This pattern may be related to the (conjectured) three-stage historical evolution in methods of obtaining a wife from capture or stealing to payment to the modern system of promising to cherish and support.[120] The reason why in each stage the male takes the initiative appears to be genetic.[121] Be-

---

[117] See Mair, *supra* note 58, at 57.

[118] For some evidence bearing on this point compare Radcliffe-Brown, *supra* note 30, at 17 (large kin group and fixed compensation and shares), with Max Gluckman, Kinship and Marriage among the Lozi of Northern Rhodesia and the Zulu of Natal, in *id.* at 166, 194 (flexible brideprice and small number of involved kin), and Nadel, *supra* note 34, at 341–42. Cf. Wagner, *supra* note 75, at 222–23 (optimal clan size).

[119] See Barton, *supra* note 41, at 85–86; Forde & Douglas, *supra* note 51, at 19.

[120] The first stage is speculative; for some evidence regarding it see Mair, *supra* note 58, at 110–11. Several forms of nonpecuniary exchange generally precede brideprice, including sister exchange, working for one's prospective father-in-law, and going to live with the bride's kin. And some marriages involve payment of dowry (generally a preinheritance distribution to the bride by her kin) without brideprice. Some of these variants will be taken up later.

[121] See, e.g., Barash, *supra* note 50, at 147–50; Edward O. Wilson, On Human Nature 125–26 (1978).

cause of the female's limited reproductive capacity, submission to sexual intercourse imposes a substantial opportunity cost on her from the standpoint of perpetuating her genes. Male fecundity is so great that the corresponding opportunity cost to the male is trivial. Hence the woman tries to conserve her reproductive capacity through careful screening of eligible mates but the man does not try to conserve his. Where wives are obtained by capture, the woman's effort to elude capture operates to screen out the less enterprising males (who may also be less likely to produce numerous and viable offspring). Brideprice is an alternative screening device, less costly in real resources than fighting yet effective from the female's standpoint if there is a good correlation between willingness and ability to pay for a wife on the one hand and the likelihood of producing and protecting her children on the other.[122] Since this paper is premised on the assumption that human beings were rational throughout prehistory, I attribute the transition from capture to barter to growing wealth rather than to growing rationality: bride purchase requires production sufficiently beyond subsistence needs to yield a stock of goods that can be exchanged for women.

Consistently with this analysis, we find that the man who is too poor to raise the brideprice can in some societies obtain a bride by going to work for her father for a period of time.[123] The man demonstrates by his habits of work his fitness to marry the girl. One can see how brideprice might be the cheaper screening method when there is greater affluence. A related solution is "matrilocal" marriage, where the husband remains with the wife's family without payment of brideprice.[124] The bride's family have less need to screen his fitness for the marriage in this case; they are present to help protect the offspring and thus do not leave the entire protective function to the husband and his kin, as in patrilocal marriage.

This analysis does not explain why brideprice is used as a screening device rather than, as today, dating or courtship. Where, however, as is generally the case in primitive societies, girls are married at puberty—at an age when they lack mature judgment—dating may not be an efficient method of choosing among suitors. Of course, the marriage could instead be arranged by the girl's parents, without brideprice. But it may not be easy for the parents to inform themselves about the qualities of a stranger, often from a different village,[125] save as his capacity to make a substantial payment may convey information about his qualities.

[122] Cf. Barash, *supra* note 50, at 294.
[123] See, e.g., Driver, *supra* note 17, at 225.
[124] See Schneider, *supra* note 1, at 145.
[125] See note 76 *supra*.

Another way of interpreting brideprice, one also based on the costs of information, is as a device for compensating the wife in advance for her services in the household. A wife in a primitive society may have limited ability to enforce fair compensation by her husband for her services, so she demands payment for them in advance, in the form of brideprice. However, this explanation is plausible only where the brideprice is paid to the bride. More commonly it is paid to her kin. One possible reason why this is so is that girls are the slaves of their kinsmen, in the sense that the latter can appropriate a part of the product of their services while they are unmarried and hence demand compensation for giving up their rights. Two explanations that do not involve "sex discrimination" are also possible. One is that payment of brideprice to the bride's kin is a security device.[126] The bride's kin have an incentive to encourage her satisfactory performance as a wife (as by refusing to harbor her should she run away from her husband), because if she misbehaves the husband may have a claim to the return of the brideprice. He has an incentive to treat her well because if he mistreats her she may have a right to leave him without her kin being obliged to return the brideprice. Another explanation is that the brideprice compensates the girl's kin either (1) for the costs of administering the screening process for her, since, as mentioned, she will normally be a young girl not obviously competent to compare the offers she receives, or (2) for their investment in training her to be a good wife.

The payment of dowry, or negative brideprice, remains unexplained by this analysis. Perhaps dowry is often simply a gift to the bride by her (well-to-do) parents. This is consistent with the fact that payment of dowry is associated with wealthier societies than payment of brideprice is.[127] But much more work is needed on this question.

Notice, finally, that there is a tension between wanting to have a detailed and exact family law and wanting to use brideprice as a device for screening suitors. If brideprice is fixed by custom, the costs of the multi-party negotiation between the suitor and the girl's kin group are reduced but the use of brideprice as an allocative device is weakened because direct bidding of the suitors against one another is prevented.

(3) Primitive law is on the whole more liberal toward divorce by either husband or wife than Western law was until very recently,[128] and

[126] See Becker, Marriage: Monogamy, Polygamy, and Assortative Mating, *supra* note 8, at 33.

[127] See Pryor, *supra* note 3, at 357, 364–66.

[128] See Diamond, *supra* note 14, at 183, 249; Mair, *supra* note 58, at ch. 11. It must be remembered that until well into the nineteenth century divorce was possible in England only by act of Parliament. In Roman Catholic countries divorce on any ground was traditionally impossible though annulment was sometimes available as a substitute.

divorce is common in many primitive societies.[129] The liberality of primitive divorce law may reflect the fact that the cost of divorce to the children is less where, as in primitive society, there are alternative child-rearing institutions to the nuclear family. The children of primitive people grow up amidst numerous kin who have an interest (based on having common genes) in protecting the children to whom they are related. This ready-made "day-care center" reduces the importance of having both parents attend to the raising of the child.[130]

The frequency of divorce in primitive society may also reflect the inferiority of brideprice as a sorting device relative to courtship of a mature woman who makes her own choice of husband.[131] The costs of information may be so high in primitive society that there is no good way of sorting the females to the males, so that matching is poor and marital instability high. Alternatively, because the parents spend less time with their children (since other kin share in the rearing of the children) there is less demand for a sorting device that will mate people with similar genetic endowments (positive assortative mating). One value of positive assortative mating is in reducing the variance of traits between parent and child, thereby promoting a harmonious household.[132] If such harmony is relatively unimportant in primitive society, so will be a sorting device designed to produce it, and a crude and cheap sorting device such as brideprice may be an efficient substitute.[133] Furthermore, positive assortative mating fosters inequality between families,[134] which could undermine the primitive social equilibrium. Hence the fact that brideprice may not be a very efficient method of positive assortative mating may be, not a shortcoming, but an advantage.[135]

---

[129] See, e.g., *id.* at 189; Pryor, *supra* note 3, at 430.

[130] See Barash, *supra* note 50, at 295, 308.

[131] Another factor is that since women in primitive societies usually do some work outside the home (especially agricultural work), they are in a better position to fend for themselves than many women in modern societies.

[132] See Becker, *supra* note 5, 225–26.

[133] Brideprice is not cheap to the groom's kinship group, of course, but it is cheap to society as a whole because it is simply a transfer payment between the two kinship groups—the loss to one is the gain to the other. Notice that brideprice, where it takes the form of cattle or some other edible food product, serves the incidental purpose of inducing the accumulation of such products, which in turn provides an important form of hunger insurance. See Dupire, *supra* note 51, at 338–39, 359 (cattle "hoarding" as insurance).

[134] See Becker, *supra* note 5, at 241.

[135] As a detail, there is no reason to expect brideprice to be the sole sorting device used in primitive marriage. A mixture of brideprice and courtship might be optimal, depending on the shape of the function that relates the costs of obtaining

Another possible factor in the relative instability of primitive marriage is that the insurance function of marriage is less important than at later stages of social development. This insurance function arises from the fact that the correlation of spouses' health and other welfare factors is less than one, so given a mutual obligation of support and assistance, marriage serves as a form of health, hunger, and even life insurance (since if one spouse dies the other will take care of the children). The network of primitive kinship obligations makes this particular form of insurance less important, and hence marital dissolution less costly, than at a later stage of social development when kinship obligations have receded but market and social insurance is not yet common. In principle, the insurance function of marriage is compatible with consensual (though not with unilateral) divorce, because a spouse will agree to a divorce only if he or she is fully compensated for any forgone benefits, including insurance, of the marriage. However, if we assume that at this intermediate stage of social development the costs of monitoring the voluntariness of a woman's agreeing to a divorce are great, we can see why requiring grounds for divorce, or even forbidding divorce altogether, might be a rational social measure. Moreover, stringent divorce laws reduce marital instability, and hence increase the insurance function of marriage in another way. They increase the optimal level of investment in screening prospective marriage partners for compatibility, since the costs of incompatibility are greater than when divorce is easily available.

(4) Exogamy—requiring a man to marry outside his group, normally his kinship group—is practised in most primitive societies. Unlike the incest taboo, exogamy appears to be cultural rather than genetic. This is shown by the facts that (1) the rules of exogamy vary greatly across cultures—and some cultures encourage endogamy, whereas none to speak of encourage incest; (2) often the rules prohibit marriage with relatives who are quite remote in a genetic sense and sometimes with nonrelatives (namely, adopted members of the kinship group), while some incestuous unions (for example, between a man and his sister's daughter) may not be forbidden by the rules of exogamy although contrary to the tribe's incest taboo; (3) the incest taboo prohibits sexual intercourse within or outside marriage, while exogamy is a limitation on marriage rather than on intercourse as such.

A cultural explanation of exogamy thus seems indicated. One explanation is that exogamy serves an insurance function in those cases,

---

information through courtship to its benefits at various levels of inputs of time and other resources into courtship.

which are common, where kinship obligations cross the boundary between the intermarrying kinship groups. Thus, in a patrilineal kinship
system, a man is not a member of his mother's kinship group but
he may still have a claim for assistance from her relatives.[136] Exogamy
thus broadens the insurance pool. This effect is particularly important
where, as is again common, each kinship group resides in a compact
area, so that exogamy enables geographical diversification of risk.[137] Exogamy also facilitates trade and alliances by creating personal relationships between families and villages. Finally, it may reduce the ferocity
of retaliation for wrongs done by a member of one kinship group
against a member of another.[138]

B. The System of Strict Liability in Primitive Law

1. Tort Law. The tort law of advanced societies embraces a variety of
accidental and intentional injuries—killing, wounding, taking property, slandering, and so on. Generally, for liability to be imposed the
injury must have been inflicted intentionally or negligently; if the accident could not have been avoided by the exercise of reasonable care
there is no liability. The intentional injurer may be guilty of a crime as
well as of a tort. Primitive law deals with this class of harms in a broadly
uniform way that is quite unlike the approach of the advanced societies. It may be summarized in the following propositions:[139]

(1) *Virtually the entire burden of deterrence is placed on the tort
(that is, private) law.* There is no criminal law to punish acts such as
murder or theft,[140] because there is no state. Criminal law as we know
it is a branch of public law.

(2) *The remedy for a wrong evolves from retaliation to compensation.* The earliest remedy for tort—retaliation, often leading to a
feud—yields in time to a system of compensation ("bloodwealth,"

---

[136] See, e.g., Fox, *supra* note 30, at 132–33 ("complementary filiation"); Forde,
supra note 62, at 329.

[137] See note 42 *supra* and accompanying text.

[138] This point is explored in Posner, Retribution and Related Concepts of Punishment, *supra* note 11, at 83.

[139] For sources, besides those listed in note 94 *supra*, see L. T. Hobhouse, Development of Justice, in 2 Evolution of Law 128 (Albert Kocourek & John W. Wigmore
eds. 1915); Richard R. Cherry, Primitive Criminal Law, in *id.* at 122; Kennett, *supra*
note 109, at ch. 6; T. P. Ellis, Welsh Tribal Law and Custom in the Middle Ages (1926);
Friedman, *supra* note 10; 1 Bloch, *supra* note 55, at 123–30; The Lombard Laws 7–11
(Katherine Fischer Drew trans. 1973). Of course, not every primitive society has all of
the features in my sketch of the system of strict liability in primitive law.

[140] But see pp. 51–52 *infra.*

"composition," "wergelds") paid to the victim or his kin by the injurer or his kin. Acceptance of compensation is at first optional and the right to refuse it and instead to retaliate against the injurer is recognized. But eventually it becomes customary to accept compensation and improper to retaliate. Compensation is a cheaper remedy from the standpoint of society as a whole than retaliation, because it involves simply a transfer payment rather than the destruction of a person or his property. As before, I attribute the transition from retaliation to compensation not to growing rationality, diminishing blood-thirstiness, or other factors that assume fundamental differences in intelligence or tastes between primitive and modern man, but simply to growing wealth. A system of compensation will not work unless injurers and their kin have a sufficient stock of goods in excess of their subsistence needs to be able to pay compensation for the injuries they inflict on others.[141]

An intermediate stage between the feud and compensation is the duel, a means of redress that economizes on the expenditure of resources on fighting.[142] The duel is to the feud in the liability law of primitive societies what matrilocal marriage is to marriage by capture in their family law.

(3) *Responsibility is collective.* If one person kills another, in the retaliation stage of social order the victim's kinsmen have a duty to him which they can discharge by killing either the killer or one of *his* kinsmen. In the compensation stage the killer's kinsmen must come up with the required compensation if the killer himself cannot or will not do so. If neither the killer nor his kinsmen pay the required compensation, the killer's kinsmen then have a duty to retaliate against the killer—or his kinsmen—to punish them for their refusal to compensate.

The importance of the kin group in the enforcement of primitive tort law derives, as suggested earlier, from the absence of effective government. Where threat of retaliation is the only deterrent to misconduct, it is important that the threat be credible and often it would not be if there were only one potential retaliator. Even after compensation is substituted for retaliation there must still be a credible threat of retaliation in the background to coerce payment of the compensation. The need to maintain a credible retaliatory capability is another reason, besides the need for a risk pool discussed in Part I, why the (recognized) kin group is larger in primitive than in modern societies.

The principle of collective responsibility—so abhorrent to mod-

---

[141] Thus, in some societies an injurer who cannot afford the wergeld is allowed to give a child instead. See Diamond, *supra* note 14, at 265. The question of the deterrent adequacy of a purely monetary sanction is addressed below.

[142] See Redfield, *supra* note 103, at 9.

ern sensibilities—may be efficient in the conditions of primitive society. The fact that any of a killer's kinsmen is fair game to the victim's kinsmen avenging his death, or, in the later stage of development, that the killer's kinsmen are collectively liable to the victim's kinsmen should the killer fail to pay the compensation that is due from him, gives the killer's (or potential killer's) kinsmen an incentive to control his conduct. They may decide to kill him themselves to avert the danger to them. More generally, they have an interest in weeding out the potential killers in their midst in order to avoid the costs in retaliation or compensation should they be harboring a killer.[143] Thus the fact that the killer may not be the initial target of retaliation, rather than reducing the probability that the sanction will ultimately come to rest on him, increases it by giving his kinsmen an incentive to "turn him in."[144] Collective responsibility is another ingenious device, like denying people privacy, by which a primitive society creates substitutes for the public investigatory machinery that it lacks.[145]

(4) *The relevant collectivity is the kin group.* The preceding discussion simply assumed that the collective rights and duties in the primitive tort system should be kinship rights and duties. This assumption has now to be examined. Why do we not find instead of kinship groups voluntary groups—the protective associations discussed by Nozick?[146] First, the transaction costs of organizing a large group of people for common ends are presumably lower where the members are (*a*) relatively homogeneous and (*b*) already bound together in a system of reciprocal rights and duties by virtue of the insurance function of the kinship group; self-defense becomes just another one of these rights and duties. Second, use of kinship as the organizing principle limits the size of the self-defense group. A purely voluntary system of protective associations would be unstable because of the great advantages that would accrue to any association that, by overcoming the problem of internal coordination and control, grew to where it over-

---

[143] See, e.g., Barton, *supra* note 41, at 244; Diamond, *supra* note 14, at 264–65; Sally F. Moore, Legal Liability and Evolutionary Interpretation: Some Aspects of Strict Liability, Self-Help, and Collective Responsibility, in The Allocation of Responsibility 51, 88–93 (Max Gluckman ed. 1972); Reid, *supra* note 94, at 83–84; Wagner, *supra* note 75, at 218–19.

[144] There are analogies in modern law. For example, under the doctrine of *respondeat superior,* an employer is liable for the torts committed by his employees in the furtherance of their employment. The economic explanation of this liability is that it will give the employer an incentive to monitor the employees' behavior carefully. See Richard A. Posner, A Theory of Negligence, 1 J. Legal Stud. 29, 42–43 (1972).

[145] Cf. J. C. Vergouwen, The Social Organization and Customary Law of the Toba-Batak of Northern Sumatra 365 (1964).

[146] See Robert Nozick, Anarchy, State, and Utopia 118–19 (1974).

shadowed any other association. Such an association would become the state. This is a reason to expect self-defense to be a kinship obligation in a society that has managed to survive without effective government. Third, when an individual is injured or killed, all of the members of the kinship group within which a duty to share is recognized are injured, since they have a claim on his income which has now been reduced. They are therefore the proper parties plaintiff.

What form of kinship is optimal for law enforcement? Compare a unilineal kinship system, such as the patrilineal system, with an ambilineal or cognatic system. In a patrilineal system a man's kinship group includes his relatives in the male line for some designated number of generations. This system automatically assigns every individual to a nonoverlapping kin group. A cognatic kinship group, where a man is the kin of his relatives in both the male and female line, does not yield a neat pattern of nonoverlapping kinship groups. This creates problems in using the kinship group as a basis for assigning collective responsibility for law enforcement.[147] If A kills B, a relative of A's wife, in a patrilineal system B's kinship group would not include A and would have a duty to take action against A or A's kin. But in a cognatic system A and B would be kinsmen and there would be no clear basis for action against A. This point may conceivably be relevant in explaining the rise of feudalism (and later the state) in medieval Europe, where the compensation system was based on cognatic kin groups.[148] In tribal Africa, in contrast, the compensation system was based on patrilineal kin groups and was more stable.

But as noted in Part I a patrilineal kinship group is not ideal from the insurance standpoint. There is likely to be a high covariance in the wealth of the members where, as is common, they live in the same village. Exogamy with complementary filiation, or some similar concept of obligation to relatives by marriage,[149] provides a solution. The insurance principle is broadened to embrace groups living in different locales and therefore having a lower covariance of wealth, but the kinship groups remain distinct for purposes of law enforcement.

(5) *The compensation due for killings and other injuries is prescribed in an exact schedule.* The customary law will specify, for example, that 40 head of cattle is the compensation required for killing a freeman, 20 for killing a slave, two for putting out a man's eye, and so forth.[150] This pattern is different from that of modern tort law, where

---

[147] See Fox, *supra* note 30, at 47–49, 150.

[148] See 1 Bloch, *supra* note 55, at 137–38, 142.

[149] See text at notes 136–37 *supra*.

[150] See, e.g., Diamond, *supra* note 14, at 58–59, 65, 66, 269–70; Howell, *supra* note 94, at 70; Douglas, *supra* note 109, at 279–83.

damages are assessed on an individual basis in every case. At the stage of social development where acceptance of compensation by the victim's kin is optional, it is easy to see why a fixed, customary level of compensation would be preferred to a costly, multi-party transaction involving the membership of both kin groups. Even later, when acceptance of compensation becomes compulsory, the information costs of an individualized determination of damage may make adherence to the fixed-compensation approach optimal for the primitive society.

Exclusive reliance on monetary penalties may seem questionable because many of the people in a primitive society must be too poor to pay a sum equal to the value of a life in such a society, even if that value is rather low because of short life expectancy or other factors. However, the principle of collective responsibility enables the society to set a level of compensation higher than the average individual can pay since his kinsmen are liable for the judgment debt.[151] Moreover, even if solvency limitations make it inevitable that monetary punishments will be less severe than the physical punishments inflicted in the retaliation stage of primitive tort law, it does not follow that the expected cost of punishment to offenders will be lower. The severity of punishment is less but the probability that it will be imposed is greater, for compensation gives the kinsmen of the slain man (or the victim himself if he survives) an incentive besides revenge for seeking to punish the injurer.

Thus far I have assumed that the fine is adequate if it is equal to the cost of the violation. However, if the probability of punishment is less than one, the fine must be raised so that the expected cost of punishment will remain equal to the cost of the violation.[152] And since primitive societies have no police or other public investigatory agencies and since the costs of information in primitive society are generally high anyway, we might expect that the probability of punishment would be very low and hence the optimal "bloodwealth" very high. Yet, from what (little) evidence we have, penalties in primitive societies are not on average higher than in modern societies,[153] proba-

---

[151] There is once again an analogy here to the modern tort principle of *respondeat superior*. See Posner, *supra* note 144.

[152] See Gary S. Becker, Crime and Punishment: An Economic Approach, 76 J. Pol. Econ. 169 (1976) (chap. 18 of this volume).

[153] Especially where compensation has replaced retaliation as the characteristic sanction. For some evidence see Friedman, *supra* note 10, at App. I. An unresolved question in my mind is the economic interpretation of those primitive liability systems, which are fairly common, in which the required compensation is less where the injury is accidental than where it is intentional. See, e.g., Howell, *supra* note 94, at 42. The most straightforward interpretation would be that the required compensation is raised in the intentional case in order to discourage people from substituting coercion for voluntary transactions. See Posner, *supra* note 5, at 120–22, 165–66. But this would imply that the compensation required in the unintentional case would be approxi-

bilities of punishment are high,[154] and crime rates—where comparison is possible—seem comparable to those found in advanced societies.[155] A number of factors appear to compensate for the lack of a police force and related institutions of public law enforcement:

(a) The lack of privacy makes it difficult to conceal wrongdoing.

(b) The principle of collective responsibility creates incentives for the kin group to identify and eliminate members of the group showing dangerous criminal proclivities.

(c) Efforts to conceal a crime are often punished separately.[156]

(d) Religious belief often discourages concealment of crime. For example, it may be considered unlucky to eat with either the kinsman of a man you have slain or the killer of one of your kinsmen. If you kill a stranger you will not know who his kin are. The only way to be sure of never eating with one of them is by announcing your deed so that the victim's kinsmen—who of course know who they are—will avoid eating with you.[157] Devices for inducing the killer to reveal his identity are especially important because if the killer's identity is unknown there is no basis for bringing the collective responsibility of his kin group into play—the identity of the responsible kin group is also unknown.

(e) The widespread "social insurance" of primitive society reduces the gains from acquisitive crimes and so presumably their incidence. If I am free to take the food I need from my kinsmen and forbidden to "hoard" more than I need, there is no purpose in stealing food unless none of my kinsmen, or anyone I might beg from, has any food to spare. Theft seems in fact an unimportant crime in many primitive societies.[158]

---

mately equal to the value of the life taken, and in the intentional case higher. Some evidence to the contrary is that the required compensation in cases of deliberate homicide (the price from which discounts for unintentional homicide would be made) is often set equal to the customary brideprice. See, e.g., Mair, *supra* note 58, at 54. However, in at least one society, damages are doubled in the case of an intentional homicide as a deliberately punitive device. See Wagner, *supra* note 75, at 216. See also C. R. Moss, Nabaloi Law and Ritual, 15 Am. Archaeology & Ethnography 207, 263–65 & n. 225 (1920).

[154] See Gulliver, *supra* note 94, at 127–34.

[155] See African Homicide and Suicide 237, 256 (Paul Bohannan ed. 1960).

[156] See Diamond, *supra* note 14, at 63–64, 76.

[157] See Barton, *supra* note 41, at 241; Gluckman, *supra* note 48, at 219. In another society, it is believed that a person who does not submit to a (public) ritual cleansing after killing someone will develop an itch which he will scratch until he dies. See Goldschmidt, *supra* note 48, at 97.

[158] See Diamond, *supra* note 14, at 222. Of course, this appearance may be an artifact of the communal nature of much of the property in primitive societies: the loss to any one co-owner is too slight to move him to vigorous efforts to apprehend and punish the thief.

The interrelationship between primitive tort law and the model of primitive society sketched in Part I deserves emphasis. The lack of privacy in primitive life helps keep probabilities of punishment high and so the required level of compensation down to a level where offenders can afford to pay. The solvency problem is also reduced by the system of kinship obligation, and the demand for acquisitive crime by the communalization of property rights within the kinship group.

The combination of high probabilities of punishment with only moderately severe penalties makes economic sense, as a combination of high probabilities of punishment with very severe penalties would not. But whether it is the *optimal* combination is a different question. Economic analysis suggests that a combination of low probabilities with very severe penalties will frequently be optimal because, assuming the costs of collecting fines or damages are low, a reduction in the probability of punishment, which enables a saving of resources devoted to investigation and prosecution, can be offset at low cost by increasing the severity of the punishment for those (few) offenders who are caught.[159] However, solvency problems to one side, the low probability-high severity approach would probably not be optimal in the conditions of primitive society. Such an approach would increase the variance of punishment compared to systems which combined high probabilities of punishment with low severity. Variance or risk is a cost to people who are risk averse, and the prevalence of insurance arrangements in primitive societies suggests that primitive people, like modern people, are indeed risk averse. The risk factor in a high severity-low probability punishment scheme would be especially pronounced in a primitive society because, as we are about to see, primitive tort law rests on the principle of strict liability. This means that at least some of the people who are punished for torts bear a risk of punishment which they cannot eliminate simply by behaving carefully.

(6) *Liability is strict.* The term "strict liability" denotes attaching liability to the mere act of injuring another regardless of the state of mind of the injurer or the care he took to try to avoid the injury. Strict liability is the characteristic response of primitive society to acts causing death or injury. If a man kills another, even in an accident that could not have been prevented by the exercise of due care, he must pay compensation to the kin of the victim. In some primitive legal systems the specified compensation is lower if the killing or injuring is accidental, in others not, but invariably some compensation must be paid whether or not the injurer was "at fault" in the sense of modern tort law. One common explanation for the prevalence of strict liability in

[159] See Becker, *supra* note 152.

primitive law is the existence of an "irrational belief in the ubiquity of guilt, which presumed a will behind all causation."[160] The economist, however, asks whether strict liability might not have been the most efficient system in the conditions of primitive society.

The economic literature identifies four factors bearing on the choice between a strict and a fault approach to liability questions that might be important here:[161]

(a) *The costs of information.* The determination of fault is more costly—because it involves the consideration of more factors—than the determination simply whether the defendant injured the plaintiff.

(b) *The ratio of avoidable to unavoidable injuries.*[162] If this ratio is very low, a rule of strict liability will be unattractive because it will require a lot of (costly) legal activity having no allocative effect. The threat of a judgment awarding damages to the victim of an unavoidable injury will not affect the conduct of potential injurers, because, by definition, the judgment cost is lower than the cost of accident avoidance in such a case.

(c) *The cost of accident avoidance to the victim.* If we are confident that the injury could not have been avoided by the victim at lower cost than the injurer, then we need not worry that strict liability will create the wrong incentives or that it will have to be supplemented by a defense of contributory negligence to take care of cases where the victim is the cheaper accident avoider.

(d) *The relative cost of insurance to injurer and injured.* Strict liability makes the injurer the insurer of the injured. This may or may not be a cheaper method of insurance than a scheme of liability under which the injured is induced to obtain insurance because he can claim against the injurer only if the latter is at fault.

All four factors suggest that strict liability is probably more efficient than fault liability in the conditions found in primitive society.

(a) The costs of adjudicating fault issues would be high in a society lacking both a professional judiciary and a clear idea of how the natural world works (though a factor pushing in the opposite direction is the simpler technologies in use in primitive societies). Lacking a clear understanding of natural phenomena, a primitive arbitrator would often have difficulty distinguishing intentional from accidental (let

---

[160] Izhak Englard, The System Builders: A Critical Appraisal of Modern American Tort Theory, 9 J. Legal Stud. 27, 28 (1980).

[161] See Posner, *supra* note 5, at 137–42, 441–42.

[162] By an "avoidable" injury I mean one that could have been prevented at lower cost than the expected cost of the injury. Either an intentionally or a negligently inflicted injury would be avoidable in this sense.

alone negligent from unavoidable) conduct.[163] Suppose A and B are members of the same hunting party. They shoot their arrows at a wild boar but A's arrow is deflected off the boar's back and hits B. It looks like an accident—but A may have procured this "accidental" result by casting a spell. The primitive arbitrator cannot reject such possibilities out of hand.

To be sure, uncertainty may bedevil the ascription of causal responsibility as well. This may explain the curious rule of archaic law that makes the punishment more severe if the violator is caught in the act than if he is apprehended later on.[164] The rule is usually explained in psychological terms: the victim or his relatives feel less vengeful after some time has elapsed from the commission of the offense.[165] However, an economic explanation is possible. The probability that the wrong man has been apprehended is greater where apprehension occurs as the result of an after-the-fact investigation, because of the difficulty in primitive society of determining causal relationships when the act and the injury are not observed at the same time. The reduction in the severity of the penalty when the offender is not caught in the act is thus a method of reducing the punishment costs borne by innocent people.

The widespread use of irrebuttable factual presumptions is further evidence that the costs of factual determination in primitive society are high. For example, in some tribes the fact that sexual intercourse occurred is conclusively presumed from proof that a man and woman were alone together for however brief a time.[166] In another tribe, if extramarital intercourse occurs in an inhabited area and the woman is not heard to scream, her rape complaint is conclusively presumed to be unfounded.[167] The reliance of primitive law on strict liability may likewise have an information-cost rationale.

This analysis may help to explain why, in some societies, if the person killed is a member of the killer's own kinship group there is no liability for the killing.[168] A rule of no liability resembles one of strict

---

[163] See, e.g., J. Walker Jones, The Law and Legal Theory of the Greeks 261 (1956).

[164] See Diamond, *supra* note 14, at 78; Maine, *supra* note 22, at 366 (Beacon ed. 1970).

[165] See *id.* at 367.

[166] See Gluckman, *supra* note 48, at 223.

[167] See A. L. Epstein, Injury and Liability in African Customary Law in Zambia, in Ideas and Procedures in African Customary Law 292, 300–01 (Max Gluckman ed. 1969).

[168] See, e.g., Goldschmidt, *supra* note 48, at 91, 98, 107–08. This result may also follow simply from the kinship basis of primitive law enforcement.

liability in dispensing with the need to determine nice questions of motive, duty, and care. There is a presumption that the intrafamilial killing is justifiable—for example, to weed out a killer in the family's midst who might subject the family to retaliation or liability—and a costly factual determination is avoided by making this presumption irrebuttable. And in an intrafamilial killing or wounding case liability is unnecessary for insurance. The victim and his family already have a claim for assistance on their kinsmen by virtue of the kin relation.

(*b*) The second factor bearing on the choice between strict and fault liability, the ratio of avoidable to unavoidable injuries, also points toward strict liability in the primitive setting. Judging from the reports of anthropologists, most serious injuries in primitive society are avoidable in the economic sense—most in fact are deliberately inflicted. In these circumstances a rule of strict liability will rarely shift losses without an allocative gain, for rarely will the injurer's costs of avoidance exceed the expected injury costs.

(*c*) The large proportion of deliberate injuries also suggests that avoidance costs are higher to victims than to injurers (though no doubt many of the fights that lead to injuries among primitive people involve an element of avoidable provocation). In these circumstances it is efficient to place all the costs on the injurer and strict liability does this.

(*d*) The final factor, insurance, exists in some tension with the last two. If *all* of the accidents subject to a rule of strict liability were culpable in the sense that they would also give rise to liability under a fault system, strict liability would provide no additional insurance. The case for strict liability would still be compelling: the costs involved in making a determination of fault would be completely wasted from a social standpoint since they would not serve to screen out a set of accidents where imposing liability on the injurer would serve no allocative purpose. Assuming that a small but significant fraction of accidents in primitive society are not due to fault, the system of strict liability does perform a modest insurance function beyond what a fault system would provide. Whether it is an *efficient* insurance mechanism depends on whether the injurer is a better insurer than the victim. Under either of two plausible conditions, the answer is probably yes. First, if injurers are on average wealthier than victims, injurer liability will make sense from an insurance standpoint (provided that utility functions are uncorrelated with wealth). Probably injurers are on average wealthier than victims—the man who is stronger, more active, who owns more dogs and cattle and tools, is more likely to be an injurer than a victim (we are speaking of purely accidental injuries here). Second, if compensation is less than completely adequate, injurer liability serves in effect to divide the loss between the injurer and victim rather than shift it entirely from the victim to the injurer.[169] For serious injuries, which are the relevant ones from the insurance standpoint, the evidence from our society is that damage awards undercompensate victims.[170] The same thing is probably true in primitive society: a man is not indifferent between losing his life and gaining 40 head of cattle for his kin group.

2. *Criminal Law.* I said earlier that primitive peoples have no criminal law because there is no state. But this is an overstatement in two respects. First, even societies that do not have any governmental organs will often regard a few acts, principally witchcraft and incest, as offenses against the community to be punished even if the victim or his kin does not take action against the offender.[171] The reason for a public sanction seems clear in the case of incest, a "victimless" crime which is harmful to the community. Perhaps witchcraft is deemed a practice whose potential magnitude and difficulty of detection justify a sanction greater than the compensation remedy used in (ordinary) killing and wounding cases.

Second, with the rise of the state, the criminal law in the strict sense just referred to—that is, a system of punishments separate from the compensation system—tends to expand to embrace murder, assault, theft, and the other acts that we conventionally deem criminal.[172] Why does the sovereign consider acts of violence directed against private citizens an offense against him? A possible reason is that the sovereign in effect sells protection to the citizens in exchange for the taxes he collects from them, but this overlooks the fact that the citizens are already protected—not badly on the evidence of prepolitical societies—by the compensation system. A reason more solidly grounded in economic theory is that a killing or wounding imposes a cost on the sovereign by reducing the tax revenues he can collect from the victim. The sovereign "owns" an interest in his subjects which is impaired by acts that reduce their wealth. This economic interest is not taken into account by the purely private compensation system so the sovereign establishes a system of criminal punishment as a method of internalizing this externality.

---

[169] One tribe splits the cost of an accident 50-50 between injurer and victim. See Riasanovsky, *supra* note 44, at 146–47.

[170] See U.S. Dep't of Transportation, Motor Vehicle Crash Losses and Their Compensation in the United States 90 (1971); Alfred F. Conard, *et al.*, Automobile Accident Costs and Payments 178–79 (1964).

[171] See, e.g., Diamond, *supra* note 14, at 260.

[172] See *id.* at 74–75, 85, 92, 273, 293.

Conclusion

This paper has developed an economic theory of primitive society and applied it to a number of the social, including legal, institutions commonly found in such societies. I have argued that these institutions are best understood as adaptations to the pervasive uncertainty and high information costs of primitive life, which create a demand for insurance that cannot be supplied through formal insurance markets and which in other ways directly and indirectly shape the values and institutions of primitive society. In focusing on social characteristics common to many societies, I have downplayed the many significant differences among primitive societies. A task for future research is to study whether these differences, too, are explicable in economic terms; some specific hypotheses (and in a few cases some confirming evidence) have been suggested in this paper. Another challenge for future research is to integrate into the analysis important primitive social institutions such as religion, war,[173] and slavery ignored in my analysis.

Should further study confirm the suggestion in this paper that the legal and other social institutions of primitive society are economically rational,[174] the question would arise what mechanism drives primitive society to that surprising result. The same question has been discussed with regard to the finding that the Anglo-American judge-made law evinces an implicit concern with promoting efficiency, and no very satisfactory answer has thus far been offered.[175] However, it is actually easier to explain why efficiency would have great social survival value in the primitive world than to explain this for our world. The efficient society is wealthier than the inefficient—that is what efficiency means—and a wealthier society will support a larger population. This effect of greater wealth can be decisive in the competition among primitive societies, where the methods of warfare are simple and numbers of people count for much more than in modern warfare. Archaic societies sufficiently durable to have left substantial literary or archaeological remains and primitive societies sufficiently durable to have survived into

---

[173] Elsewhere I have stressed the importance of external security in explaining the rise of the state. See The Homeric Version of the Minimal State, *supra* note 11.

[174] The suggestion will not surprise all anthropologists. See, e.g., Nash, *supra* note 3, at 49. I emphasize once again that, in suggesting that primitive people are economically rational, I am not making any statement about their conscious states. Rational behavior to an economist is a matter of consequences rather than intentions, and in that respect resembles the concept of functionality in traditional anthropology. See, e.g., Radcliffe-Brown, *supra* note 30, at 62, 83; A. R. Radcliffe-Brown, Structure and Function in Primitive Society, ch. IX (1965).

[175] See discussion and references in Landes & Posner, Adjudication as a Private Good, *supra* note 10, at 259–84.

the nineteenth century (when serious anthropological study began) are likely, therefore, to be societies whose customs are efficient.

An additional factor is that a primitive society is one that by definition has had a long time to adapt to its environment. The interval within which adaptation occurs is a function of the rate of change of the environment to which the society is adapting. If that rate of change is very slow, the society has plenty of time to evolve efficient adaptations to the environment.

Clearly, however, the primitive social equilibrium is less efficient, at least in the long run, than that of advanced societies: consider the very small proportion of the world's population that lives in primitive societies today. This situation is due in some part to coercion, rather than peaceful competition, from the advanced societies (dramatically so in the case of the North American Indians, for example), but in greater part to the adaptive responses of primitive society to its economic environment. These responses include practices, such as denying people privacy and preventing them from amassing wealth, which are inimical to economic progress and in turn to population growth. This is a point to give the romantic anarchist pause.

THE THEORY OF REGULATION

2

The Theory of Economic Regulation

George J. Stigler

6

The state—the machinery and power of the state—is a potential resource or threat to every industry in the society. With its power to prohibit or compel, to take or give money, the state can and does selectively help or hurt a vast number of industries. That political juggernaut, the petroleum industry, is an immense consumer of political benefits, and simultaneously the underwriters of marine insurance have their more modest repast. The central tasks of the theory of economic regulation are to explain who will receive the benefits or burdens of regulation, what form regulation will take, and the effects of regulation upon the allocation of resources.

Regulation may be actively sought by an industry, or it may be thrust upon it. A central thesis of this paper is that, as a rule, regulation is acquired by the industry and is designed and operated primarily for its benefit. There are regulations whose net effects upon the regulated industry are undeniably onerous; a simple example is the differentially heavy taxation of the industry's product (whiskey, playing cards). These onerous regulations, however, are exceptional and can be explained by the same theory that explains beneficial (we may call it "acquired") regulation.

Two main alternative views of the regulation of industry are widely held. The first is that regulation is instituted primarily for the protection and benefit of the public at large or some large subclass of the public. In this view, the regulations which injure the public—as when the oil import quotas increase the cost of petroleum products to America by $5 billion or more a year [1970]—are costs of some social goal (here, national defense) or, occasionally, perversions of the regulatory philosophy. The second view is essentially that the political process defies ra-

Reprinted with permission from *Rand Journal of Economics*; from the *Bell Journal of Economics and Management Science* 2, no. 1 (Spring 1971): 1–21. © 1971 by American Telephone and Telegraph Company

tional explanation: "politics" is an imponderable, a constantly and unpredictably shifting mixture of forces of the most diverse nature, comprehending acts of great moral virtue (the emancipation of slaves) and of the most vulgar venality (the congressman feathering his own nest).

Let us consider a problem posed by the oil import quota system: why does not the powerful industry which obtained this expensive program instead choose direct cash subsidies from the public treasury? The "protection of the public" theory of regulation must say that the choice of import quotas is dictated by the concern of the federal government for an adequate domestic supply of petroleum in the event of war—a remark calculated to elicit uproarious laughter at the Petroleum Club. Such laughter aside, if national defense were the goal of the quotas, a tariff would be a more economical instrument of policy: it would retain the profits of exclusion for the treasury. The non-rationalist view would explain the policy by the inability of consumers to measure the cost to them of the import quotas, and hence their willingness to pay $5 billion in higher prices rather than the $2.5 billion in cash that would be equally attractive to the industry. Our profit-maximizing theory says that the explanation lies in a different direction: the present members of the refining industries would have to share a cash subsidy with all new entrants into the refining industry.[1] Only when the elasticity of supply of an industry is small will the industry prefer cash to controls over entry or output.

This question, why does an industry solicit the coercive powers of the state rather than its cash, is offered only to illustrate the approach of the present paper. We assume that political systems are rationally devised and rationally employed, which is to say that they are appropriate instruments for the fulfillment of desires of members of the society. This is not to say that the state will serve any person's concept of the public interest: indeed the problem of regulation is the problem of discovering when and why an industry (or other group of like-minded people) is able to use the state for its purposes, or is singled out by the state to be used for alien purposes.

I. What Benefits Can a State Provide to an Industry?

The state has one basic resource which in pure principle is not shared with even the mightiest of its citizens: the power to coerce. The state can seize money by the only method which is permitted by the laws of

---

[1] The domestic producers of petroleum, who also benefit from the import quota, would find a tariff or cash payment to domestic producers equally attractive. If their interests alone were consulted, import quotas would be auctioned off instead of being given away.

a civilized society, by taxation. The state can ordain the physical movements of resources and the economic decisions of households and firms
without their consent. These powers provide the possibilities for the
utilization of the state by an industry to increase its profitability. The
main policies which an industry (or occupation) may seek of the state
are four.

The most obvious contribution that a group may seek of the government is a direct subsidy of money. The domestic airlines received
"air mail" subsidies (even if they did not carry mail) of $1.5 billion
through 1968. The merchant marine has received construction and
operation subsidies reaching almost $3 billion [1970] since World War
II. The education industry has long shown a masterful skill in obtaining
public funds: for example, universities and colleges have received federal funds exceeding $3 billion annually in recent years, as well as sub-
sidized loans for dormitories and other construction. The veterans of
wars have often received direct cash bonuses.

We have already sketched the main explanation for the fact that
an industry with power to obtain governmental favors usually does not
use this power to get money: unless the list of beneficiaries can be limited by an acceptable device, whatever amount of subsidies the industry can obtain will be dissipated among a growing number of rivals. The
airlines quickly moved away from competitive bidding for air mail contracts to avoid this problem.[2] On the other hand, the premier universities have not devised a method of excluding other claimants for
research funds, and in the long run they will receive much-reduced
shares of federal research monies.

The second major public resource commonly sought by an industry is control over entry by new rivals. There is considerable, not to say
excessive, discussion in economic literature of the rise of peculiar price
policies (limit prices), vertical integration, and similar devices to retard
the rate of entry of new firms into oligopolistic industries. Such devices
are vastly less efficacious (economical) than the certificate of convenience and necessity (which includes, of course, the import and production quotas of the oil and tobacco industries).

The diligence with which the power of control over entry will be
exercised by a regulatory body is already well known. The Civil Aeronautics Board has not allowed a single new trunk line to be launched
[1970] since it was created in 1938. The power to insure new banks has
been used by the Federal Deposit Insurance Corporation to reduce the
rate of entry into commercial banking by 60 percent.[3] The interstate
motor carrier history is in some respects even more striking, because

[2] See Keyes (1951), pp. 60 ff.
[3] See Peltzman (1965).

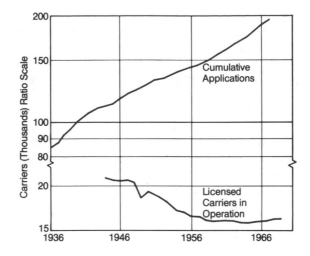

FIGURE 1. Certificates for interstate motor carriers. *Source:* Table 5

no even ostensibly respectable case for restriction on entry can be developed on grounds of scale economies (which are in turn adduced to limit entry for safety or economy of operation). The number of federally licensed common carriers is shown in Figure 1: the immense growth of the freight hauled by trucking common carriers has been associated with a steady secular decline of numbers of such carriers. The number of applications for new certificates has been in excess of 5000 annually in recent years [1970]: a rigorous proof that hope springs eternal in an aspiring trucker's breast.

We propose the general hypothesis: every industry or occupation that has enough political power to utilize the state will seek to control entry. In addition, the regulatory policy will often be so fashioned as to retard the rate of growth of new firms. For example, no new savings and loan company may pay a dividend rate higher than that prevailing in the community in its endeavors to attract deposits.[4] The power to limit selling expenses of mutual funds, which is soon to be conferred upon the Securities and Exchange Commission, will serve to limit the growth of small mutual funds and hence reduce the sales costs of large funds.

One variant of the control of entry is the protective tariff (and the corresponding barriers which have been raised to interstate move-

---

[4]The Federal Home Loan Bank Board is the regulatory body. It also controls the amount of advertising and other areas of competition.

ments of goods and people). The benefits of protection to an industry, one might think, will usually be dissipated by the entry of new domestic producers, and the question naturally arises: Why does the industry not also seek domestic entry controls? In a few industries (petroleum) the domestic controls have been obtained, but not in most. The tariff will be effective if there is a specialized domestic resource necessary to the industry; oil-producing lands is an example. Even if an industry has only durable specialized resources, it will gain if its contraction is slowed by a tariff.

A third general set of powers of the state which will be sought by the industry are those which affect substitutes and complements. Crudely put, the butter producers wish to suppress margarine and encourage the production of bread. The airline industry actively supports the federal subsidies to airports; the building trade unions have opposed labor-saving materials through building codes. We shall examine shortly a specific case of inter-industry competition in transportation.

The fourth class of public policies sought by an industry is directed to price-fixing. Even the industry that has achieved entry control will often want price controls administered by a body with coercive powers. If the number of firms in the regulated industry is even moderately large, price discrimination will be difficult to maintain in the absence of public support. The prohibition of interest on demand deposits, which is probably effective in preventing interest payments to most non-business depositors, is a case in point. Where there are no diseconomies of large scale for the individual firm (e.g., a motor trucking firm can add trucks under a given license as common carrier), price control is essential to achieve more than competitive rates of return.

A. Limitations Upon Political Benefits

These various political boons are not obtained by the industry in a pure profit-maximizing form. The political process erects certain limitations upon the exercise of cartel policies by an industry. These limitations are of three sorts.

First, the distribution of control of the industry among the firms in the industry is changed. In an unregulated industry each firm's influence upon price and output is proportional to its share of industry output (at least in a simple arithmetic sense of direct capacity to change output). The political decisions take account also of the political strength of the various firms, so small firms have a larger influence than they would possess in an unregulated industry. Thus, when quotas are given to firms, the small firms will almost always receive larger quotas than cost-minimizing practices would allow. The original quotas under

TABLE 1.   Import Quotas of Refineries as Percent of Daily Input of
            Petroleum (Districts I–IV, July 1, 1959–Dec. 31, 1959)

Size of Refinery (Thousands of Barrels)	Percent Quota
0–10	11.4
10–20	10.4
20–30	9.5
30–60	8.5
60–100	7.6
100–150	6.6
150–200	5.7
200–300	4.7
300 and Over	3.8

Source: Hearings Select Committee on Small Business, U.S. Congress, 88th Cong., 2nd Sess., Aug.
10 and 11, 1964, p. 121.

the oil import quota system will illustrate this practice (Table 1). The
smallest refiners were given a quota of 11.4 percent of their daily consumption of oil, and the percentage dropped as refinery size rose.[5] The
pattern of regressive benefits is characteristic of public controls in industries with numerous firms.

Second, the procedural safeguards required of public processes
are costly. The delays which are dictated by both law and bureaucratic
thoughts of self-survival can be large: Robert Gerwig found the price of
gas sold in interstate commerce to be 5 to 6 percent higher than in in-
trastate commerce because of the administrative costs (including delay)
of Federal Power Commission reviews (Gerwig 1962).

Finally, the political process automatically admits powerful outsiders to the industry's councils. It is well known that the allocation of
television channels among communities does not maximize industry
revenue but reflects pressures to serve many smaller communities.
The abandonment of an unprofitable rail line is an even more notorious
area of outsider participation.

These limitations are predictable, and they must all enter into
the calculus of the profitability of regulation of an industry.

B. An Illustrative Analysis

The recourse to the regulatory process is of course more specific and
more complex than the foregoing sketch suggests. The defensive power
of various other industries which are affected by the proposed regula-

[5]The largest refineries were restricted to 75.7 percent of their historical quota
under the earlier voluntary import quota plan.

tion must also be taken into account. An analysis of one aspect of the regulation of motor trucking will illustrate these complications. At this stage we are concerned only with the correspondence between regulations and economic interests; later we shall consider the political process by which regulation is achieved.

The motor trucking industry operated almost exclusively within cities before 1925, in good part because neither powerful trucks nor good roads were available for long-distance freight movements. As these deficiencies were gradually remedied, the share of trucks in intercity freight movements began to rise, and by 1930 it was estimated to be 4 percent of ton-miles of intercity freight. The railroad industry took early cognizance of this emerging competitor, and one of the methods by which trucking was combatted was state regulation.

By the early 1930's all states regulated the dimensions and weight of trucks. The weight limitations were a much more pervasive control over trucking than the licensing of common carriers because even the trucks exempt from entry regulation are subject to the limitations on dimensions and capacity. The weight regulations in the early 1930's are reproduced in the appendix (Table 6). Sometimes the participation of railroads in the regulatory process was incontrovertible: Texas and Louisiana placed a 7,000-pound payload limit on trucks serving (and hence competing with) two or more railroad stations, and a 14,000-pound limit on trucks serving only one station (hence, not competing with it).

We seek to determine the pattern of weight limits on trucks that would emerge in response to the economic interests of the concerned parties. The main considerations appear to be the following:

(1) Heavy trucks would be allowed in states with a substantial number of trucks on farms: the powerful agricultural interests would insist upon this. The 1930 Census reports nearly one million trucks on farms. One variable in our study will be, for each state, trucks per 1000 of agricultural population.[6]

(2) Railroads found the truck an effective and rapidly triumphing competitor in the shorter hauls and hauls of less than carload traffic, but much less effective in the carload and longer-haul traffic. Our second variable for each state is, therefore, length of average railroad haul.[7] The longer the average rail haul is, the less the railroads will be opposed to trucks.

---

[6] The ratio of trucks to total population would measure the product of (1) the importance of trucks to farmers, and (2) the importance of farmers in the state. For reasons given later, we prefer to emphasize (1).

[7] This is known for each railroad, and we assume that (1) the average holds within each state, and (2) two or more railroads in a state may be combined on the basis of mileage. Obviously both assumptions are at best fair approximations.

(3) The public at large would be concerned by the potential damage done to the highway system by heavy trucks. The better the state highway system, the heavier the trucks that would be permitted. The percentage of each state's highways that had a high type surface is the third variable. Of course good highways are more likely to exist where the potential contribution of trucks to a state's economy is greater, so the causation may be looked at from either direction.

We have two measures of weight limits on trucks, one for 4-wheel trucks (X_1) and one for 6-wheel trucks (X_2). We may then calculate two equations,

$$X_1 \text{ (or } X_2) = a + bX_3 + cX_4 + dX_5,$$

where

X_3 = trucks per 1000 agricultural labor force, 1930,
X_4 = average length of railroad haul of freight traffic, 1930,
X_5 = percentage of state roads with high-quality surface, 1930.

(All variables are fully defined and their state values given in Table 7 on page 231).

The three explanatory variables are statistically significant, and each works in the expected direction. The regulations on weight were less onerous; the larger the truck population in farming, the less competitive the trucks were to railroads (i.e., the longer the rail hauls), and the better the highway system (see Table 2).

The foregoing analysis is concerned with what may be termed the industrial demand for governmental powers. Not every industry will have a significant demand for public assistance (other than money!), meaning the prospect of a substantial increase in the present value of the enterprises even if the governmental services could be obtained gratis (and of course they have costs to which we soon turn). In some economic activities entry of new rivals is extremely difficult to control—consider the enforcement problem in restricting the supply of domestic servants. In some industries the substitute products cannot be efficiently controlled—consider the competition offered to bus lines by private car-pooling. Price fixing is not feasible where every unit of the product has a different quality and price, as in the market for used automobiles. In general, however, most industries will have a positive demand price (schedule) for the services of government.

TABLE 2.   Regression Analysis of State Weight Limits on Trucks
(t-Values under Regression Coefficients)

Dependent Variable	N	Constant	X_3	X_4	X_5	R^2
X_1	48	12.28	0.0336	0.0287	0.2641	0.502
		(4.87)	(3.99)	(2.77)	(3.04)	
X_2	46	10.34	0.0437	0.0788	0.2528	0.243
		(1.57)	(2.01)	(2.97)	(1.15)	

X_1 = Weight limit on 4-wheel trucks (thousands of pounds), 1932–33
X_2 = Weight limit on 6-wheel trucks (thousands of pounds), 1932–33
X_3 = Trucks on farms per 1,000 agricultural labor force, 1930
X_4 = Average length of railroad haul of freight (miles), 1930
X_5 = Percent of state highways with high-type surface, Dec. 31, 1930

Sources: X_1 and X_2: *The Motor Truck Red Book and Directory*, 1934 Edition, p. 85, 102, and U.S.
Dept. of Agric., Bur. of Public Roads, Dec. 1932.
X_3: *Census of Agriculture*, 1930, Vol. IV.
X_4: A.A.R.R., Bur. of Railway Economics, *Railway Mileage by States, Dec. 31*, 1930 and
U.S.I.C.C., *Statistics of Railways in the U.S.*, 1930.
X_5: *Statistical Abstract of the U.S.*, 1932.

II. The Costs of Obtaining Legislation

When an industry receives a grant of power from the state, the benefit
to the industry will fall short of the damage to the rest of the community. Even if there were no deadweight losses from acquired regulation, however, one might expect a democratic society to reject such
industry requests unless the industry controlled a majority of the
votes.[8] A direct and informed vote on oil import quotas would reject
the scheme. (If it did not, our theory of rational political processes
would be contradicted.) To explain why many industries are able to
employ the political machinery to their own ends, we must examine
the nature of the political process in a democracy.

A consumer chooses between rail and air travel, for example, by
voting with his pocketbook: he patronizes on a given day that mode of
transportation he prefers. A similar form of economic voting occurs with
decisions on where to work or where to invest one's capital. The market
accumulates these economic votes, predicts their future course, and invests accordingly.

[8] If the deadweight loss (of consumer and producer surplus) is taken into account, even if the oil industry were in the majority it would not obtain the legislation
if there were available some method of compensation (such as sale of votes) by which
the larger damage of the minority could be expressed effectively against the lesser
gains of the majority.

Because the political decision is coercive, the decision process is fundamentally different from that of the market. If the public is asked to make a decision between two transportation media comparable to the individual's decision on how to travel—say, whether airlines or railroads should receive a federal subsidy—the decision must be abided by everyone, travellers and non-travellers, travellers this year and travellers next year. This compelled universality of political decisions makes for two differences between democratic political decision processes and market processes.

(1) The decisions must be made simultaneously by a large number of persons (or their representatives): the political process demands simultaneity of decision. If A were to vote on the referendum today, B tomorrow, C the day after, and so on, the accumulation of a majority decision would be both expensive and suspect. (A might wish to cast a different vote now than last month.)

The condition of simultaneity imposes a major burden upon the political decision process. It makes voting on specific issues prohibitively expensive: it is a significant cost even to engage in the transaction of buying a plane ticket when I wish to travel; it would be stupendously expensive to me to engage in the physically similar transaction of voting (i.e., patronizing a polling place) whenever a number of my fellow citizens desired to register their views on railroads versus airplanes. To cope with this condition of simultaneity, the voters must employ representatives with wide discretion and must eschew direct expressions of marginal changes in preferences. This characteristic also implies that the political decision does not predict voter desires and make preparations to fulfill them in advance of their realization.

(2) The democratic decision process must involve "all" the community, not simply those who are directly concerned with a decision. In a private market, the non-traveller never votes on rail versus plane travel, while the huge shipper casts many votes each day. The political decision process cannot exclude the uninterested voter: the abuses of any exclusion except self-exclusion are obvious. Hence, the political process does not allow participation in proportion to interest and knowledge. In a measure, this difficulty is moderated by other political activities besides voting which do allow a more effective vote to interested parties: persuasion, employment of skilled legislative representatives, etc. Nevertheless, the political system does not offer good incentives like those in private markets to the acquisition of knowledge. If I consume ten times as much of public service A (streets) as of B (schools), I do not have incentives to acquire corresponding amounts of knowledge about the public provision of these services.[9]

[9] See Becker (1958).

These characteristics of the political process can be modified by having numerous levels of government (so I have somewhat more incentive to learn about local schools than about the whole state school system) and by selective use of direct decision (bond referenda). The chief method of coping with the characteristics, however, is to employ more or less full-time representatives organized in (disciplined by) firms which are called political parties or machines.

The representative and his party are rewarded for their discovery and fulfillment of the political desires of their constituency by success in election and the perquisites of office. If the representative could confidently await reelection whenever he voted against an economic policy that injured the society, he would assuredly do so. Unfortunately virtue does not always command so high a price. If the representative denies ten large industries their special subsidies of money or governmental power, they will dedicate themselves to the election of a more complaisant successor: the stakes are that important. This does not mean that every large industry can get what it wants or all that it wants: it does mean that the representative and his party must find a coalition of voter interests more durable than the anti-industry side of every industry policy proposal. A representative cannot win or keep office with the support of the sum of those who are opposed to: oil import quotas, farm subsidies, airport subsidies, hospital subsidies, unnecessary navy shipyards, an inequitable public housing program, and rural electrification subsidies.

The political decision process has as its dominant characteristic infrequent, universal (in principle) participation, as we have noted: political decisions must be infrequent and they must be global. The voter's expenditure to learn the merits of individual policy proposals and to express his preferences (by individual and group representation as well as by voting) are determined by expected costs and returns, just as they are in the private marketplace. The costs of comprehensive information are higher in the political arena because information must be sought on many issues of little or no direct concern to the individual, and accordingly he will know little about most matters before the legislature. The expressions of preferences in voting will be less precise than the expressions of preferences in the marketplace because many uninformed people will be voting and affecting the decision.[10]

The channels of political decision-making can thus be described

[10]There is an organizational problem in any decision in which more than one vote is cast. If because of economies of scale it requires a thousand customers to buy a product before it can be produced, this thousand votes has to be assembled by some entrepreneur. Unlike the political scene, however, there is no need to obtain the consent of the remainder of the community, because they will bear no part of the cost.

as gross or filtered or noisy. If everyone has a negligible preference for policy A over B, the preference will not be discovered or acted upon. If voter group X wants a policy that injures non-X by a small amount, it will not pay non-X to discover this and act against the policy. The system is calculated to implement all strongly felt preferences of majorities and many strongly felt preferences of minorities but to disregard the lesser preferences of majorities and minorities. The filtering or grossness will be reduced by any reduction in the cost to the citizen of acquiring information and expressing desires and by any increase in the probability that his vote will influence policy.

The industry which seeks political power must go to the appropriate seller, the political party. The political party has costs of operation, costs of maintaining an organization and competing in elections. These costs of the political process are viewed excessively narrowly in the literature on the financing of elections: elections are to the political process what merchandizing is to the process of producing a commodity, only an essential final step. The party maintains its organization and electoral appeal by the performance of costly services to the voter at all times, not just before elections. Part of the costs of services and organization are borne by putting a part of the party's workers on the public payroll. An opposition party, however, is usually essential insurance for the voters to discipline the party in power, and the opposition party's costs are not fully met by public funds.

The industry which seeks regulation must be prepared to pay with the two things a party needs: votes and resources. The resources may be provided by campaign contributions, contributed services (the businessman heads a fund-raising committee), and more indirect methods such as the employment of party workers. The votes in support of the measure are rallied, and the votes in opposition are dispersed, by expensive programs to educate (or uneducate) members of the industry and of other concerned industries.

These costs of legislation probably increase with the size of the industry seeking the legislation. Larger industries seek programs which cost the society more and arouse more opposition from substantially affected groups. The tasks of persuasion, both within and without the industry, also increase with its size. The fixed size of the political "market," however, probably makes the cost of obtaining legislation increase less rapidly than industry size. The smallest industries are therefore effectively precluded from the political process unless they have some special advantage such as geographical concentration in a sparsely settled political subdivision.

If a political party has in effect a monopoly control over the governmental machine, one might expect that it could collect most of the benefits of regulation for itself. Political parties, however, are perhaps an ideal illustration of Demsetz' theory of natural monopoly (Demsetz 1968). If one party becomes extortionate (or badly mistaken in its reading of effective desires), it is possible to elect another party which will provide the governmental services at a price more closely proportioned to costs of the party. If entry into politics is effectively controlled, we should expect one-party dominance to lead that party to solicit requests for protective legislation but to exact a higher price for the legislation.

The internal structure of the political party, and the manner in which the perquisites of office are distributed among its members, offer fascinating areas for study in this context. The elective officials are at the pinnacle of the political system—there is no substitute for the ability to hold the public offices. I conjecture that much of the compensation to the legislative leaders takes the form of extrapolitical payments. Why are so many politicians lawyers?—because everyone employs lawyers, so the congressman's firm is a suitable avenue of compensation, whereas a physician would have to be given bribes rather than patronage. Most enterprises patronize insurance companies and banks, so we may expect that legislators commonly have financial affiliations with such enterprises.

The financing of industry-wide activities such as the pursuit of legislation raises the usual problem of the free rider.[11] We do not possess a satisfactory theory of group behavior—indeed this theory is the theory of oligopoly with one addition: in the very large number industry (e.g., agriculture) the political party itself will undertake the entrepreneurial role in providing favorable legislation. We can go no further than the infirmities of oligopoly theory allow, which is to say, we can make only plausible conjectures such as that the more concentrated the industry, the more resources it can invest in the campaign for legislation.

A. An Empirical Application: Occupational Licensing

The licensing of occupations is a possible use of the political process to improve the economic circumstances of a group. The license is an effective barrier to entry because occupational practice without the license is a criminal offense. Since much occupational licensing is performed at the state level, the area provides an opportunity to search for the characteristics of an occupation which give it political power.

[11] The theory that the lobbying organization avoids the "free-rider" problem by selling useful services was proposed by Thomas G. Moore (1961) and elaborated by Mancur Olson (1965). The theory has not been tested empirically.

Although there are serious data limitations, we may investigate several characteristics of an occupation which should influence its ability to secure political power:

(1) *The size of the occupation.* Quite simply, the larger the occupation, the more votes it has. (Under some circumstances, therefore, one would wish to exclude non-citizens from the measure of size.)

(2) *The per capita income of the occupation.* The income of the occupation is the product of its number and average income, so this variable and the preceding will reflect the total income of the occupation. The income of the occupation is presumably an index of the probable rewards of successful political action: in the absence of specific knowledge of supply and demand functions, we expect licensing to increase each occupation's equilibrium income by roughly the same proportion. In a more sophisticated version, one would predict that the less the elasticity of demand for the occupation's services, the more profitable licensing would be. One could also view the income of the occupation as a source of funds for political action, but if we view political action as an investment this is relevant only with capital-market imperfections.[12]

The average income of occupational members is an appropriate variable in comparisons among occupations, but it is inappropriate to comparisons of one occupation in various states because real income will be approximately equal (in the absence of regulation) in each state.

(3) *The concentration of the occupation in large cities.* When the occupation organizes a campaign to obtain favorable legislation, it incurs expenses in the solicitation of support, and these are higher for a diffused occupation than a concentrated one. The solicitation of support is complicated by the free-rider problem in that individual members cannot be excluded from the benefits of legislation even if they have not shared the costs of receiving it. If most of the occupation is concentrated in a few large centers, these problems (we suspect) are much reduced in intensity: regulation may even begin at the local governmental level. We shall use an orthodox geographical concentration measure: the share of the occupation of the state in cities over 100,000 (or 50,000 in 1900 and earlier).

(4) *The presence of a cohesive opposition to licensing.* If an occupation deals with the public at large, the costs which licensing imposes upon any one customer or industry will be small and it will not be economic for that customer or industry to combat the drive for li-

---

[12] Let n = the number of members of the profession and y = average income. We expect political capacity to be in proportion to (ny) so far as benefits go, but to reflect also the direct value of votes, so the capacity becomes proportional to $(n^a y)$ with $a > 1$.

censure. If the injured group finds it feasible and profitable to act jointly, however, it will oppose the effort to get licensure, and (by increasing its cost) weaken, delay, or prevent the legislation. The same attributes—numbers of voters, wealth, and ease of organization—which favor an occupation in the political arena, of course, favor also any adversary group. Thus, a small occupation employed by only one industry which as few employers will have difficulty in getting licensure; whereas a large occupation serving everyone will encounter no organized opposition.

An introductory statistical analysis of the licensing of select occupations by states is summarized in Table 3. In each occupation the

TABLE 3.   Initial Year of Regulation as a Function of Relative Size of Occupation and Degree of Urbanization

| | | | Regression Coefficients (and t-Values) | | |
| | | | Size of Occupation (Relative to Labor Force) | Urbanization (Share of Occupation in Cities over 100,000*) | |
Occupation	Number of States Licensing	Median Census Year of Licensing			R^2
Beauticians	48	1930	−4.03 (2.50)	5.90 (1.24)	0.125
Architects	47	1930	−24.06 (2.15)	−6.29 (0.84)	0.184
Barbers	46	1930	−1.31 (0.51)	−26.10 (2.37)	0.146
Lawyers	29	1890	−0.26 (0.08)	−65.78 (1.70)	0.102
Physicians	43	1890	0.64 (0.65)	−23.80 (2.69)	0.165
Embalmers	37	1910	3.32 (0.36)	−4.24 (0.44)	0.007
Registered Nurses	48	1910	−2.08 (2.28)	−3.36 (1.06)	0.176
Dentists	48	1900	2.51 (0.44)	−22.94 (2.19)	0.103
Veterinarians	40	1910	−10.69 (1.94)	−37.16 (4.20)	0.329
Chiropractors	48	1930	−17.70 (1.54)	11.69 (1.25)	0.079
Pharmacists	48	1900	−4.19 (1.50)	−6.84 (0.80)	0.082

Sources: The Council of State Governments, "Occupational Licensing Legislation in the States," 1952, and U.S. Census of Population, Various Years.
*50,000 in 1890 and 1900.

dependent variable for each state is the year of first regulation of entry into the occupation. The two independent variables are

(1) the ratio of the occupation to the total labor force of the state in the census year nearest to the median year of regulation,

(2) the fraction of the occupation found in cities over 100,000 (over 50,000 in 1890 and 1900) in that same year.

We expect these variables to be negatively associated with year of licensure, and each of the nine statistically significant regression coefficients is of the expected sign.

The results are not robust, however: the multiple correlation coefficients are small, and over half of the regression coefficients are not significant (and in these cases often of inappropriate sign). Urbanization is more strongly associated than size of occupation with licensure.[13] The crudity of the data may be a large source of these disappointments: we measure, for example, the characteristics of the barbers in each state in 1930, but 14 states were licensing barbers by 1910. If the states which licensed barbering before 1910 had relatively more barbers, or more highly urbanized barbers, the predictions would be improved. The absence of data for years between censuses and before 1890 led us to make only the cruder analysis.[14]

In general, the larger occupations were licensed in earlier years.[15] Veterinarians are the only occupation in this sample who have a well-defined set of customers, namely livestock farmers, and licensing was later in those states with large numbers of livestock relative to rural population. The within-occupation analyses offer some support for the economic theory of the supply of legislation.

---

[13] We may pool the occupations and assign dummy variables for each occupation; the regression coefficients then are:

size of occupation relative to labor force: -0.450 $(t = 0.59)$
urbanization   : -12.133 $(t = 4.00)$.

Thus urbanization is highly significant, while size of occupation is not significant.

[14] A more precise analysis might take the form of a regression analysis such as:

Year of licensure = constant
$+b_1$ (year of critical size of occupation)
$+b_2$ (year of critical urbanization of occupation),

where the critical size and urbanization were defined as the mean size and mean urbanization in the year of licensure.

[15] Lawyers, physicians, and pharmacists were all relatively large occupations by 1900, and nurses also by 1910. The only large occupation to be licensed later was barbers; the only small occupation to be licensed early was embalmers.

A comparison of different occupations allows us to examine several other variables. The first is income, already discussed above. The second is the size of the market. Just as it is impossible to organize an effective labor union in only one part of an integrated market, so it is impossible to regulate only one part of the market. Consider an occupation—junior business executives will do—which has a national market with high mobility of labor and significant mobility of employers. If the executives of one state were to organize, their scope for effective influence would be very small. If salaries were raised above the competitive level, employers would often recruit elsewhere so the demand elasticity would be very high.[16] The third variable is stability of occupational membership: the longer the members are in the occupation, the greater their financial gain from control of entry. Our regrettably crude measure of this variable is based upon the number of members aged 35–44 in 1950 and aged 45–54 in 1960: the closer these numbers are, the more stable the membership of the occupation. The data for the various occupations are given in Table 4.

The comparison of licensed and unlicensed occupations is consistently in keeping with our expectations:

(1) the licensed occupations have higher incomes (also before licensing, one may assume),

(2) the membership of the licensed occupations is more stable (but the difference is negligible in our crude measure),

(3) the licensed occupations are less often employed by business enterprises (who have incentives to oppose licensing),

(4) all occupations in national markets (college teachers, engineers, scientists, accountants) are unlicensed or only partially licensed. The size and urbanization of the three groups, however, are unrelated to licensing. The inter-occupational comparison therefore provides a modicum of additional support for our theory of regulation.

III. Conclusion

The idealistic view of public regulation is deeply imbedded in professional economic thought. So many economists, for example, have denounced the ICC for its pro-railroad policies that this has become a

[16]The regulation of business in a partial market will also generally produce very high supply elasticities within a market: if the price of the product (or service) is raised, the pressure of excluded supply is very difficult to resist. Some occupations are forced to reciprocity in licensing, and the geographical dispersion of earnings in licensed occupations, one would predict, is not appreciably different than in unlicensed occupations with equal employer mobility. Many puzzles are posed by the interesting analysis of Arlene S. Holen (1915), pp. 492–98.

TABLE 4.   Characteristics of Licensed and Unlicensed Professional Occupations, 1960

Occupation	Median Age (Years)	Median Education (Years)	Median Earnings (50–52 wks.)	Instability of Membership*	Percent not Self-employed	Percent in Cities Over 50,000	Percent of Labor Force
Licensed							
Architects	41.7	16.8	$ 9,090	0.012	57.8%	44.1%	0.045%
Chiropractors	46.5	16.4	6,360	0.053	5.8	30.8	0.020
Dentists	45.9	17.3	12,200	0.016	9.4	34.5	0.128
Embalmers	43.5	13.4	5,990	0.130	52.8	30.2	0.055
Lawyers	45.3	17.4	10,800	0.041	35.8	43.1	0.308
Prof. Nurses	39.1	13.2	3,850	0.291	91.0	40.6	0.868
Optometrists	41.6	17.0	8,480	0.249	17.5	34.5	0.024
Pharmacists	44.9	16.2	7,230	0.119	62.3	40.0	0.136
Physicians	42.8	17.5	14,200	0.015	35.0	44.7	0.339
Veterinarians	39.2	17.4	9,210	0.169	29.5	14.4	0.023
Average	43.0	16.3	8,741	0.109	39.7	35.7	0.195

Partially Licensed							
Accountants	40.4	14.9	6,450	0.052	88.1	43.5	0.698
Engineers	38.3	16.2	8,490	0.023	96.8	31.6	1.279
Elem. School Teachers	43.1	16.5	4,710	(a)	99.1	18.8	1.482
Average	40.6	15.9	6,550	0.117(b)	94.7	34.6	1.153
Unlicensed							
Artists	38.0	14.2	5,920	0.103	77.3	45.7	0.154
Clergymen	43.3	17.0	4,120	0.039	89.0	27.2	0.295
College Teachers	40.3	17.4	7,500	0.085	99.2	36.0	0.261
Draftsmen	31.2	12.9	5,990	0.098	98.6	40.8	0.322
Reporters and Editors	39.4	15.5	6,120	0.138	93.9	43.3	0.151
Musicians	40.2	14.8	3,240	0.081	65.5	37.7	0.289
Natural Scientists	35.9	16.8	7,490	0.264	96.3	32.7	0.221
Average	38.3	15.5	5,768	0.115	88.5	37.6	0.242

(*) 1-R, where R = ratio: 1960 age 45–54 to 1950 age 35–44.

(a) Not available separately; teachers N.E.C. (incl. secondary school and other) = 0.276

(b) Includes figure for teachers N.E.C. in note (a)

Source: U.S. Census of Population, 1960.

cliché of the literature. This criticism seems to me exactly as appropriate as a criticism of the Great Atlantic and Pacific Tea Company for selling groceries, or as a criticism of a politician for currying popular support. The fundamental vice of such criticism is that it misdirects attention: it suggests that the way to get an ICC which is not subservient to the carriers is to preach to the commissioners or to the people who appoint the commissioners. The only way to get a different commission would be to change the political support for the Commission, and reward commissioners on a basis unrelated to their services to the carriers.

Until the basic logic of political life is developed, reformers will be ill-equipped to use the state for their reforms, and victims of the pervasive use of the state's support of special groups will be helpless to protect themselves. Economists should quickly establish the license to practice on the rational theory of political behavior.

Appendix

TABLE 5.   Contract and Passenger Motor Carriers, 1935–1969[1]

Year Ending	Cumulative Applications			Operating Carriers	
	Grandfather	New	Total	Approved Applications[3]	Number in Operation[2]
Oct. 1936	82,827	1,696	84,523	—	—
1937	83,107	3,921	87,028	1,114	—
1938	85,646	6,694	92,340	20,398	—
1939	86,298	9,636	95,934	23,494	—
1940	87,367	12,965	100,332	25,575	—
1941	88,064	16,325	104,389	26,296	—
1942	88,702	18,977	107,679	26,683	—
1943	89,157	20,007	109,164	27,531	—
1944	89,511	21,324	110,835	27,177	21,044
1945	89,518	22,829	112,347		20,788
1946	89,529	26,392	115,921		20,632
1947	89,552	29,604	119,156		20,665
1948	89,563	32,678	122,241		20,373
1949	89,567	35,635	125,202		18,459
1950	89,573	38,666	128,239		19,200
1951	89,574	41,889	131,463		18,843
1952	(89,574)[4]	44,297	133,870		18,408
1953	—	46,619	136,192		17,869
1954	—	49,146	138,719		17,080
1955	—	51,720	141,293		16,836
June 1956	—	53,640	143,213		16,486
1957	—	56,804	146,377		16,316
1958	—	60,278	149,851		16,065
1959	—	64,171	153,744		15,923
1960	—	69,205	158,778		15,936
1961	—	72,877	162,450		15,967
1962	—	76,986	166,559		15,884
1963	—	81,443	171,016		15,739
1964	—	86,711	176,284		15,732
1965	—	93,064	182,637		15,755
1966	—	101,745	191,318		15,933
1967	—	106,647	196,220		16,003
1968	—	(6)	(6)		16,230[5]
1969	—	(6)	(6)		16,318[5]

Source: U.S. Interstate Commerce Commission Annual Reports.

[1] Excluding brokers and within state carriers.

[2] Property carriers were the following percentages of all operating carriers: 1944—93.4%; 1950—92.4%; 1960—93.0%; 1966—93.4%.

[3] Estimated.

[4] Not available; assumed to be approximately constant.

[5] 1968 and 1969 figures are for number of carriers required to file annual reports.

[6] Not available comparable to previous years; applications for permanent authority disposed of (i.e., from new and pending files) 1967–69 are as follows: 1967—7,049; 1968—5,724; 1969—5,186.

TABLE 6.   Weight Limits on Trucks, 1932–33*, by States (Basic Data for Table 2).

State	Maximum Weight (in Lbs.) 4-Wheel[1]	Maximum Weight (in Lbs.) 6-Wheel[2]	State	Maximum Weight (in Lbs.) 4-Wheel[1]	Maximum Weight (in Lbs.) 6-Wheel[2]
Alabama	20,000	32,000	Nebraska	24,000	40,000
Arizona	22,000	34,000	Nevada	25,000	38,000
Arkansas	22,200	37,000	New Hampshire	20,000	20,000
California	22,000	34,000	New Jersey	30,000	30,000
Colorado	30,000	40,000	New Mexico	27,000	45,000
Connecticut	32,000	40,000	New York	33,600	44,000
Delaware	26,000	38,000	No. Carolina	20,000	20,000
Florida	20,000	20,000	No. Dakota	24,000	48,000
Georgia	22,000	39,600	Ohio	24,000	24,000
Idaho	24,000	40,000	Oklahoma	20,000	20,000
Illinois	24,000	40,000	Oregon	25,500	42,500
Indiana	24,000	40,000	Pennsylvania	26,000	36,000
Iowa	24,000	40,000	Rhode Island	28,000	40,000
Kansas	24,000	34,000	So. Carolina	20,000	25,000
Kentucky	18,000	18,000	So. Dakota	20,000	20,000
Louisiana	13,400	N.A.	Tennessee	20,000	20,000
Maine	18,000	27,000	Texas	13,500	N.A.
Maryland	25,000	40,000	Utah	26,000	34,000
Massachusetts	30,000	30,000	Vermont	20,000	20,000
Michigan	27,000	45,000	Virginia	24,000	35,000
Minnesota	27,000	42,000	Washington	24,000	34,000
Mississippi	18,000	22,000	West Virginia	24,000	40,000
Missouri	24,000	24,000	Wisconsin	24,000	36,000
Montana	24,000	34,000	Wyoming	27,000	30,000

*Red Book (1934) Figures are reported (p. 89) as "based on the states' interpretations of their laws [1933] and
on physical limitations of vehicle design and tire capacity." Public Roads (1932) Figures are reported
(p. 167) as "an abstract of state laws, including legislation passed in 1932."

[1]4-Wheel: the smallest of the following 3 figures was used:

(A) Maximum gross weight (as given in Red Book, p. 90–91).

(B) Maximum axle weight (as given in Red Book, p. 90–91), multiplied by 1.5 (see Red Book, p. 89).

(C) Maximum gross weight (as given in Red Book, p. 93).

Exceptions: Texas and Louisiana—see Red Book, p. 91.

[2]6-Wheel: Maximum gross weight as given in Public Roads, p. 167. These figures agree in most cases with those
shown in Red Book, p. 93, and with Public Roads maximum axle weights multiplied by 2.5 (see Red
Book, p. 93). Texas and Louisiana are excluded as data are not available to convert from payload to
gross weight limits.

TABLE 7.   Independent Variables (Basic Data for Table 2—cont'd)

State	Trucks on Farms per 1,000 Agricultural Labor Force	Average Length of Railroad Haul of Freight (Miles)	Percent of State Highways with High-type Surface
Alabama	26.05	189.4	1.57
Arizona	79.74	282.2	2.60
Arkansas	28.62	233.1	1.72
California	123.40	264.6	13.10
Colorado	159.50	244.7	0.58
Connecticut	173.80	132.6	7.98
Delaware	173.20	202.7	21.40
Florida	91.41	184.1	8.22
Georgia	32.07	165.7	1.60
Idaho	95.89	243.6	0.73
Illinois	114.70	207.9	9.85
Indiana	120.20	202.8	6.90
Iowa	98.73	233.3	3.39
Kansas	146.70	281.5	0.94
Kentucky	20.05	227.5	1.81
Louisiana	31.27	201.0	1.94
Maine	209.30	120.4	1.87
Maryland	134.20	184.1	12.90
Massachusetts	172.20	144.7	17.70
Michigan	148.40	168.0	6.68
Minnesota	120.40	225.6	1.44
Mississippi	29.62	164.9	1.14
Missouri	54.28	229.7	2.91
Montana	183.80	266.5	0.09
Nebraska	132.10	266.9	0.41
Nevada	139.40	273.2	0.39
New Hampshire	205.40	129.0	3.42
New Jersey	230.20	137.6	23.30
New Mexico	90.46	279.0	0.18
New York	220.50	163.3	21.50
No. Carolina	37.12	171.5	8.61
No. Dakota	126.40	255.1	0.01
Ohio	125.80	194.2	11.20
Oklahoma	78.18	223.3	1.42
Oregon	118.90	246.2	3.35
Pennsylvania	187.60	166.5	9.78

TABLE 7.   (*continued*)

State	Trucks on Farms per 1,000 Agricultural Labor Force	Average Length of Railroad Haul of Freight (Miles)	Percent of State Highways with High-type Surface
Rhode Island	193.30	131.0	20.40
So. Carolina	20.21	169.8	2.82
So. Dakota	113.40	216.6	0.04
Tennessee	23.98	191.9	3.97
Texas	62.48	180.5	1.67
Utah	101.70	235.7	1.69
Vermont	132.20	109.7	2.26
Virginia	71.88	229.8	2.86
Washington	180.90	254.4	4.21
West Virginia	62.88	218.7	8.13
Wisconsin	178.60	195.7	4.57
Wyoming	133.40	286.7	0.08

(1) *Average length of RR haul of (revenue) freight* = Average distance in miles each ton is carried = ratio of number of ton miles to number of tons carried. For each state, average length of haul was obtained by weighting average length of haul of each company by the number of miles of line operated by that company in the state (all for class I RR's).

(2) *Percentage of state roads with high-quality surface:* where high quality (high-type) surface consists of bituminous macadam, bituminous concrete, sheet asphalt, Portland cement concrete, and block pavements. All state rural roads, both local and state highway systems, are included.

References

Association of American Railroads, Bureau of Railway Economics. *Railway Mileage by States.* Washington, D.C.: December 31, 1930.

Becker, G. S. "Competition and Democracy." *Journal of Law and Economics,* October 1958.

The Council of State Governments. "Occupational Licensing Legislation in the States." 1952.

Demsetz, H., "Why Regulate Utilities?" *Journal of Law and Economics,* April 1968 (chap. 8 of this volume).

Gerwig, R. W. "Natural Gas Production: A Study of Costs of Regulation." *Journal of Law and Economics,* October 1962, pp. 69–92.

Holen, A. S. "Effects of Professional Licensing Arrangements on Interstate Labor Mobility and Resource Allocation." *Journal of Political Economy,* Vol. 73 (1915), pp. 492–98.

Keyes, L. S. *Federal Control of Entry into Air Transportation.* Cambridge, Mass.: Harvard University Press, 1951.

Moore, T. G. "The Purpose of Licensing." *Journal of Law and Economics,* October 1961.

Olson, M. *The Logic of Collective Action.* Cambridge, Mass.: Harvard University Press, 1965.

Peltzman, S. "Entry in Commercial Banking." *Journal of Law and Economics,* October 1965.

The Motor Truck Red Book and Directory, 1934 Edition, pp. 85–102.

U.S. Congress, Select Committee on Small Business. *Hearings*, 88th Congress, 2nd Session, August 10 and 11, 1964.

U.S. Department of Agriculture, Bureau of Public Roads. *Public Roads*. Washington, D.C.: U.S. Government Printing Office, December 1932.

U.S. Department of Commerce, Bureau of the Census. *United States Census of Agriculture, 1930*, Vol. 4. Washington, D.C.: U.S. Government Printing Office, 1930.

————. *United States Census of Population*. Washington, D.C.: U.S. Government Printing Office, appropriate years.

————, Bureau of Foreign and Domestic Commerce. *Statistical Abstract of the U.S., 1932*. Washington, D.C.: U.S. Government Printing Office, 1932.

U.S. Interstate Commerce Commission. *Annual Report*. Washington, D.C.: U.S. Government Printing Office, appropriate years.

————. *Statistics of Railways in the United States, 1930*. Washington, D.C.: U.S. Government Printing Office, 1930.

Toward a More General Theory of Regulation   7

Sam Peltzman

George Stigler's work on the theory of regulation is one of those rare contributions—rare for the rest of us, though not for him—which force a fundamental change in the way important problems are analyzed. Stigler's influence will be clear in this article. There is perhaps no more telling evidence of this influence than that its basic motivation was my dissatisfaction with some of Stigler's conclusions. (It was a dissatisfaction that Stigler shared, since I can report that we simultaneously reached one of the conclusions elaborated here—that regulatory agencies will not exclusively serve a single economic interest.) My intellectual debt to Stigler is so great that this article emerges as an extension and generalization of his pioneering work.

What Stigler accomplished in his *Theory of Economic Regulation* was to crystallize a revisionism in the economic analysis of regulation that he had helped launch in his and Claire Friedland's work on electric utilities.[1] The revisionism had its genesis in a growing disenchantment with the usefulness of the traditional role of regulation in economic analysis as a *deus ex machina* which eliminated one or another unfortunate allocative consequence of market failure. The creeping recognition that regulation seemed seldom to actually work this way, and that it may have even engendered more resource misallocation than it cured, forced attention to the influence which the regulatory powers of the state could have on the distribution of wealth as well as on al-

This study has been supported by a grant from the National Science Foundation to the National Bureau of Economic Research for research in law and economics. The views expressed herein are those of the author and do not necessarily reflect the views of the National Bureau of Economic Research.

Reprinted with permission from *The Journal of Law and Economics* 19, no. 2 (August 1976): 211–40. © 1976 by The University of Chicago
[1] George J. Stigler, The Theory of Economic Regulation, 2 Bell J. of Econ. & Man. Sci. 3 (1971) (chap. 6 of this volume); and George Stigler & Claire Friedland, What Can Regulators Regulate? The Case of Electricity, 5 J. Law & Econ. 1 (1962).

locative efficiency. Since the political process does not usually provide the dichotomous treatment of resource allocation and wealth distribution so beloved by welfare economists, it was an easy step to seek explanation for the failure of the traditional analysis to predict the allocative effects of regulation in the dominance of political pressure for redistribution on the regulatory process. This focus on regulation as a powerful engine for redistribution shows clearly in such works as Jordan's *Producer Protection* and Posner's *Taxation by Regulation*.[2] The common role of regulation in this literature is as a fulcrum upon which contending interests seek to exercise leverage in their pursuit of wealth. A common, though not universal,[3] conclusion has become that, as between the two main contending interests in regulatory processes, the producer interest tends to prevail over the consumer interest.

In one sense, Stigler's work provides a theoretical foundation for this "producer protection" view. However, its scope is much more general. It is ultimately a theory of the optimum size of effective political coalitions set within the framework of a general model of the political process. Stigler seems to have realized that the earlier "consumer protection" model comes perilously close to treating regulation as a free good. In that model the existence of market failure is sufficient to generate a demand for regulation, though there is no mention of the mechanism that makes that demand effective. Then, in a crude reversal of Say's Law, the demand is supplied costlessly by the political process. Since the good, regulation, is not in fact free and demand for it is not automatically synthesized, Stigler sees the task of a positive economics of regulation as specifying the arguments underlying the supply and demand for regulation.

The way he does this abstracts almost completely from pure allocation questions. The essential commodity being transacted in the political market is a transfer of wealth, with constituents on the demand side and their political representatives on the supply side. Viewed in this way, the market here, as elsewhere, will distribute more of the good to those whose effective demand is highest. For Stigler, the question of which group will have the highest effective demand translates very quickly into a question of numbers. In this view, "producer protection" represents the dominance of a small group with a large per capita stake over the large group (consumers) with more diffused inter-

---

[2] William A. Jordan, Producer Protection, Prior Market Structure and the Effects of Government Regulation, 15 J. Law & Econ. 151 (1972); and Richard A. Posner, Taxation by Regulation, 2 Bell J. of Econ. & Man. Sci. 22 (1971).

[3] Richard A. Posner, *supra* note 2, is an important exception.

ests. The central question for the theory then becomes to explain this regularity of small group dominance in the regulatory process (and indeed the political process generally). The way the question is posed already foreshadows one of the results of the theory. For in Stigler's model, unlike most market models, there are many bidders, but only one is successful. There is essentially a political auction in which the high bidder receives the right to tax the wealth of everyone else, and the theory seeks to discover why the successful bidder is a numerically compact group. The answer lies essentially in the relationship of group size to the costs of using the political process.

To summarize the argument briefly, the size of the dominant group is limited in the first instance by the absence of something like ordinary-market-dollar voting in politics. Voting is infrequent and concerned with a package of issues. In the case of a particular issue, the voter must spend resources to inform himself about its implications for his wealth and which politician is likely to stand on which side of the issue. That information cost will have to offset prospective gains, and a voter with a small per capita stake will not, therefore, incur it. In consequence the numerically large, diffuse interest group is unlikely to be an effective bidder, and a policy inimical to the interest of a numerical majority will not be automatically rejected. A second major limit on effective group size arises from costs of organization. It is not enough for the successful group to recognize its interests; it must organize to translate this interest into support for the politician who will implement it. This means not only mobilizing its own vote, but contributing resources to the support of the appropriate political party or policy: to finance campaigns, to persuade other voters to support or at least not oppose the policy or candidate, perhaps occasionally to bribe those in office. While there may be some economies of scale in this organization of support and neutralization of opposition, these must be limited. The larger the group that seeks the transfer, the narrower the base of the opposition and the greater the per capita stakes that determine the strength of opposition, so lobbying and campaigning costs will rise faster than group size. The cost of overcoming "free riders" will also rise faster than group size. This diseconomy of scale in providing resources then acts as another limit to the size of the group that will ultimately dominate the political process.

In sum, Stigler is asserting a law of diminishing returns to group size in politics: beyond some point it becomes counterproductive to dilute the per capita transfer. Since the total transfer is endogenous, there is a corollary that diminishing returns apply to the transfer as well, due both to the opposition provoked by the transfer and to the demand this opposition exerts on resources to quiet it.

Stigler does not himself formalize this model, and my first task will be to do just this. My simplified formal version of his model produces a result to which Stigler gave only passing recognition, namely that the costs of using the political process limit not only the size of the dominant group but also their gains. This is, at one level, a detail, which is the way Stigler treated it, but a detail with some important implications—for entry into regulation and for the price-output structure that emerges from regulation. The main task of the article is to derive these implications from a generalization of Stigler's model.

I. A Stiglerian Model of Regulation

I begin with the presumption that what is basically at stake in regulatory processes is a transfer of wealth. The transfer, as Stigler points out, will rarely be in cash, but rather in the form of a regulated price, an entry restriction, and so on. I shall ignore that detail here, and the resulting model applies to any political wealth redistribution. A particularization to price and entry regulation comes later. I treat the relevant political process as if control of the relevant taxing power rests on direct voting, though this too is meant only for simplification. Though appointment of a regulatory body may lie effectively with a legislature, a committee thereof, or an executive, the electorate's receptivity to these intermediaries ought to be affected by the performance of their appointees. With Stigler, I assume that beneficiaries pay with both votes and dollars. However, again as a simplification, I assume that the productivity of the dollars to a politician lies in mitigation of opposition. A more general model might make "dollars" (broadly defined to include, for example, employment of former regulators) a source of direct as well as indirect utility to the regulator. In this model, though, direct political support—"votes"—is the object sought directly by the regulator. More particularly, he seeks to maximize net votes or a majority in his favor. There is no presumption that the marginal utility of a majority vanishes at one. Greater majorities are assumed to imply greater security of tenure, more logrolling possibilities, greater deference from legislative budget committees, and so on. The crucial decision that the regulator (or would-be regulator) must make in this model is the numerical size of the group to which he promises favors, and thus implicitly the size of the group he taxes. At this stage, I retain Stigler's presumption that the agency confers benefits on a single victorious group, and the essential purpose of the model is to elaborate the limits on this group's size.

To put this formally, the regulator wants to maximize a majority M, generated by

$$M = n \cdot f - (N - n) \cdot h, \tag{1}$$

where

    n = number of potential voters in the beneficiary group
    f = (net) probability that a beneficiary will grant support
    N = total number of potential voters
    h = (net) probability that he who is taxed (every non-n) opposes.

Note that, because both gainers and losers face transaction and information costs, f and h are not either zero or unity, but depend on the amount of the group member's gain or loss. There are similar costs facing the regulator, so he cannot exclude nonsupporting beneficiaries. At this stage, I assume that gains and losses are equal per capita within groups. This nondiscrimination assumption serves both to simplify the problem and to force Stigler's result of a single politically dominant economic interest, but the assumption is subsequently dropped. I also assume that ignorance does not lead to perverse or biased voting. If a beneficiary, for example, does not know enough to vote for his benefactor, his voting decision is not biased for or against the benefactor. Either he does not vote, or he decides how to vote by tossing a fair coin. In either case, the f in equation (1) will be zero, and M will be the (same) difference between votes for and votes against. With nonparticipation by the ignorant, f (or h) is simply the probability that a beneficiary (or loser) votes, while with random voting by the ignorant f is the difference between the probability of a favorable and unfavorable vote by the beneficiary.

The probability of support may now be specified as

$$f = f(g), \tag{2}$$

where g is the per capita net benefit, and is

$$g = \frac{T - K - C(n)}{n}, \tag{3}$$

with

    T = total dollar amount transferred to the beneficiary group
    K = dollars spent by beneficiaries in campaign funds, lobbying, and so on, to mitigate opposition
    $C(n)$ = cost of organizing both direct support of beneficiaries and efforts to mitigate opposition. This organization cost increases with n, but we place no restrictions on the shape of the marginal cost curve.

It is assumed that equation (2) holds for any subset of the electorate, in the sense that any coalition of size n faces the same costs of organization and has members with the same responsiveness to benefits. Thus, the number of votes in support depends on n in two offsetting ways: a larger n provides a broader base for support, but dilutes the net gain per member and so the probability of a member's support.

As a further simplification I assume that the regulator chooses K as well as T. The process could be modeled with the benefited group itself determining the appropriate K, but in doing so it would be motivated by the same forces affecting a regulator who would ask K as a price for conferring the benefit. Thus, I treat it as a detail whether the beneficiaries "bid" a K and "ask" a T, or whether the regulator asks a K and bids a T.

The transfer is assumed generated by a tax at the rate t on the wealth (B) of each member outside the benefited group, so

$$T = t \cdot B(N - n), \text{ or } t = \frac{T}{B(N - n)}. \tag{4}$$

For application to problems of regulation, B can be thought of as a typical consumer's surplus and t a regulated price if producers are beneficiaries, or B might be a producer's surplus and t the difference between the surplus maximizing price and the regulated price where consumers are beneficiaries. At this level of generality, though, I simply treat B as a negative function of t.[4] Opposition is assumed generated by the tax rate and mitigated by voter education expenditures per capita (z), so

$$h = h(t, z), \tag{5}$$

$$z = K/(N - n). \tag{6}$$

In keeping with Stigler's model, I assume that, in the relevant range, benefits are subject to decreasing returns so that

$$f_g > 0, f_{gg} < 0 \tag{7}$$

---

[4]This treatment is less innocent than it appears. It implicitly rules out a "pure" transfer—that is, one with no allocative effects. There may be forms of wealth whose supply is totally inelastic with respect to taxes, but, as a general matter, these cannot be presumed to suffice the demands of the political process—or even yield costless taxes, once tax administration and evasion costs are allowed for. The general proposition that every tax affects the wealth base being taxed has important implications for the evaluation of the whole range of government redistributive policies. See Gary Becker's comments on this article in 19 J. Law & Econ. 245 (1976).

(unless specified otherwise subscripts will denote partial or, where appropriate, total derivatives from here on). A complementary assumption is made for z:

$$h_z < 0, \ h_{zz} > 0 \tag{8}$$

(opposition is measured in positive units), and there are assumed to be increasing political costs to taxation:

$$h_t > 0, \ h_{tt} > 0. \tag{9}$$

In this characterization of the political process, then, officeholders or candidates to replace them must pick the size (n) of the group they will benefit, the amount (K) they will ask that group to spend for mitigating opposition, and the amount (T) they will transfer to the beneficiary group. The necessary conditions for these choices to yield the maximum majority, the presumed goal for the office seeker, are

$$M_n = 0 = -(g + m)f_g + f - h_t \left(\frac{tB}{B + tB_t} \right) - h_z \cdot z + h, \tag{10}$$

$$M_T = 0 = f_g - h_t \left(\frac{1}{B + tB_t} \right), \tag{11}$$

$$M_K = 0 = -f_g - h_z, \tag{12}$$

where
$m = C_n$, the marginal cost of group organization.

Combining equations (10)–(12) and making use of the definitions yields the following solution for n:

$$\frac{n}{N} = 1 - \left[\frac{f_g(g + a)}{f + h - f_g(m - a)} \right] \tag{13}$$

where
a = average cost of organization (C/n).

If there are no organization costs ($a = m = 0$), the ratio is less than one because of diminishing returns ($f_g g < f$). Diseconomies of scale in organization ($m > a$) tend to reduce the ratio further. Since we have ruled out net gains to regulation, it is hardly a surprise that a political wealth maximizer must benefit a subset of the population, so subsequent analysis will deal more formally with the forces affecting the size of this subset.

Before some of these forces are elaborated it is worth dwelling on equation (11) for a moment. This condition—essentially that the marginal political return from a transfer must equal the marginal political cost of the associated tax—has an important subsidiary implication. Since both f_g and h_t are positive, an interior maximum can occur only if the term $(B + tB_t)$ is also positive. This term is the marginal product of t in raising revenue from a member of the losing group. That it must be positive implies that these losers must be taxed less than the interests of the winners would dictate (a revenue maximizing tax—that is, $B + tB_t = 0$).

This result is portrayed in figure I. The function $R(t)$ is (h_t/f_g). With diminishing returns in g and increasing costs in t, R_t is positive and increasing in the relevant range. The marginal revenue from t, $(B + tB_t)$, is decreasing in t, and the revenue maximizing tax is t_m where this marginal revenue is zero. However, with $R(t)$ positive at *any* $t > 0$, t_m cannot be a political equilibrium. The equilibrium, from equation (11), must occur at something like $t_a < t_m$.

Thus we have an important first principle of regulation: even if a single economic interest gets all the benefits of regulation, these must be less than a perfect broker for the group would obtain. The best organized cartel will yield less to the membership if the government organizes it than if it were (could be) organized privately. This principle is independent of organization or campaigning costs, but rests on the heed the political process must pay to marginal position. (Condition (11) holds even if K and C are assumed zero.) It suggests that what the "capture" literature treats as an ad hoc detail—that "the political process automatically admits powerful outsiders to the industry's councils"[5]—is in fact integral to regulatory processes. The principle also suggests that failure of regulation to maximize cartel profits need not, as Posner has suggested, arise as an efficient substitute for other forms of taxation.[6] Even if more efficient substitutes exist and are used, a rational regulator will still tax cartel profits to secure his own position.

This logic may be pushed a step further. It will pay the rational regulator to exploit differences within the group that, taken as a whole, either wins or loses. The ability to do this may be constrained by "due process" considerations, but not typically to the point that a uniform tax must be levied or gain transferred to each member of a group. Therefore, the regulator's-choice problem is not limited to selecting

[5] George J. Stigler, *supra* note 1, at 7.
[6] Richard A. Posner, *supra* note 2.

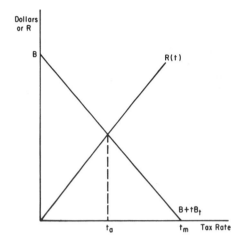

FIGURE I

the appropriate size of an interest group to benefit or tax; it includes selection of an appropriate structure of benefits and costs. Once we drop the simplification of uniform taxes (prices), the identification of regulation with any single economic interest can no longer be maintained as a general proposition.

To see this, consider the following restricted problem: the regulator has decided on the total wealth that must be transferred to one economic interest (say producers) from another, so that both T and n are data. However, he desires minimization of opposition (O) from consumers by exploiting differences among them in per capita wealth or the responsiveness of wealth to taxes (that is, differences in the height and elasticity of their demands) or in their voting sensitivity to taxes. Assume that the $(N - n)$ consumers can be separated into 2 groups of size P_1 and P_2 respectively so that the last term in equation (1) may be written

$$O = P_1 h_1 + P_2 h_2. \tag{14}$$

(Subscripts denote groups here.) To simplify still further, treat z as fixed and equal for both groups. Minimization of equation (14) then involves forming the Lagrangian

$$L = P_1 h_1 + P_2 h_2 + \lambda(T - t_1 B_1 P_1 - t_2 B_2 P_2), \tag{15}$$

where the term in parentheses is the constraint that the sum of subgroup taxes is fixed, and setting the first partials with respect to t_1, t_2

and λ equal to zero. The resulting expression for the opposition minimizing t_1 is

$$
t_1 = \frac{B_2 + \dfrac{TB_2'}{P_2 B_2} - \dfrac{h_2'}{h_1'} B_1}{B_1'\left(\dfrac{h_2'}{h_1'}\right) + B_2'\left(\dfrac{P_1 B_1}{P_2 B_2}\right)}. \tag{16}
$$

(Primes denote derivatives.) The denominator is negative, but only the last two terms in the numerator are negative. This means that a negative t_1 cannot be ruled out. Thus if one group of consumers has sufficiently large per capita demand (B_2), sufficiently low demand elasticity (B_2') and tax responsiveness (h_2') relative to the other group, the latter may become part of the winning group (get a subsidized price). On a similar argument, some producers may be taxed even if most are benefited. The regulator's constituency thus cannot in general be limited to one economic interest.

The structure of equation (16) shows that t_1 is affected not only by some obvious characteristics of that group (its wealth and voting response to t_1) but also by characteristics of the other group. I shall return to this subsequently, for equation (16) hints at some important implications for the structure of prices emerging from regulation—for example, that this will be the result of forces pushing both for and against profit-maximizing price discrimination.

I want now to return to equations (10)–(13) and discuss some forces affecting the size of the winning group. The Stigler model leads, after all, to more than the near truism that n/N is less than one; it more nearly asserts that the ratio is close to zero. So let us examine the effect of three variables whose importance the Stigler model asserts—support, opposition, and organization costs.

In general, if x represents a variable affecting choice of n (and T and K), we want to determine the vector of total derivatives: [dn/dx, dT/dx, dK/dx]. This can be found by solving

$$
[M_{ij}][di/dx] = -[M_{ix}], \tag{17}
$$

where
$[M_{ij}]$ = matrix of cross partial derivatives, $i, j = n, T, K$
$[M_{ix}]$ = vector of the cross-partials of M_i w.r.t. x.

I now treat three simple cases:

1. A parametric shift in the support function, f, (which leaves f' unaffected). From equations (10)–(12) we obtain

$$\begin{bmatrix} M_{nf} \\ M_{Tf} \\ M_{Kf} \end{bmatrix} = \begin{bmatrix} 1 \\ 0 \\ 0 \end{bmatrix}, \tag{18}$$

and from equation (17) and the second order condition for a maximum M (that $[M_{ij}]$ be negative definite), we obtain the following sign condition:

$$\text{sign } dn/df = \text{sign } C_{nn}, \tag{19}$$

where

$$C_{ij} = \text{cofactor of } M_{ij}.$$

Since $C_{nn} > 0$ by a second-order condition for a maximum, $dn/df > 0$—that is, an increase in the probability of support for a given g increases the size of the winning group. Or, as Stigler might wish to put it, the difficulty of translating the transfer into votes leads the regulator to concentrate benefits. For the other variables we have

$$\text{sign } dT/df = \text{sign } C_{nT}, \tag{20}$$

and

$$\text{sign } dK/df = \text{sign } C_{nK}, \tag{21}$$

which are uncertain and negative respectively. The underlying reasons may be seen by writing out the co-factors

$$C_{nT} = [M_{TK} \cdot M_{nK} - M_{Tn} \cdot M_{KK}], \tag{22}$$

$$C_{nK} = [M_{Tn} \cdot M_{TK} - M_{nK} \cdot M_{TT}]. \tag{23}$$

$M_{TK} > 0$, because an increase in K reduces opposition and makes an increase in T more attractive. $M_{nK} < 0$, because an increase in K also dilutes the net gain and makes concentration of the transfer on a smaller group more attractive. M_{TT}, M_{KK} are both negative, because of diminishing returns. This leaves M_{Tn}, whose sign is ambiguous: an increase in n dilutes the gain to the winners, which would induce an increase in T. But the increase in n also concentrates the opposition, and this pushes for a reduction in T. The only restriction that can be imposed (from the second-order conditions) is $(M_{Tn} + M_{Kn}) < 0$, which is enough to imply $C_{nK} < 0$ and $dK/df < 0$, but is insufficient to predict the sign of C_{nT}. If buying off a more concentrated opposition is sufficiently important to render $M_{Tn} \leq 0$, then $dT/df < 0$.

2. A parametric shift in the opposition function, h. This yields precisely the same result as a shift in support (the vector of the relevant cross-partials is the same as the right-hand side of equation (19)), and this symmetry between the effects of support and opposition is perhaps one of the chief insights of Stigler's model. If a more effective political support technology (a rise in f) induces a more numerous winning group, a more effective opposition technology must lead the regulator to permit a larger group to *escape* taxation as well. Some losers will then be made winners when there is a rise in opposition. This is better stated in the reverse. The difficulty of translating a tax into political opposition (a low h) induces the regulator to tax the many and thus to concentrate his favors on a few. Hence the filtering of information through the noise of a political process that forces consideration of many programs simultaneously acts unambiguously, as Stigler intuited, to restrict the size of the winning group. This filtering must be done by both winners and losers, and this makes it simultaneously unattractive to spread the benefits and attractive to spread the losses over large numbers.

3. A parametric shift in the cost of organizing a group for political support. Stigler argues that the cost of organizing support (for example, the cost of overcoming the "free rider" problem) also restricts n. However, on closer inspection, this is not obvious. Consider a rise in the $C(n)$ of (3) which, for simplicity, leaves marginal cost unchanged. Then, focusing only on dn/dC, we obtain

$$\text{sign } dn/dC = \text{sign}(M_{nC} C_{nn} + M_{TC} C_{Tn} + M_{KC} C_{nK}). \tag{24}$$

This will be ambiguous for reasons apart from ambiguity about C_{Tn}. Stigler's argument focuses essentially on M_{nC}, which is indeed negative and induces a smaller n. However, because of diminishing returns to per capita gains, a rise in C will lead to an offsetting decrease in K ($M_{KC} < 0$). On balance, this fall in K requires a rise in n ($C_{nK} < 0$). That is, if K is reduced, restoring optimum effectiveness of lobbying and education efforts requires concentration of these efforts on a smaller group of losers. To obtain Stigler's result, one must conjecture that this sort of secondary effect is outweighed by the initial impulse to concentrate gains to offset the effect of increased organization costs.

It is well to summarize the results of this formalization of Stigler's model:

1. With a few ambiguities, the thrust of imperfect information about both the gains and losses of regulatory decisions and of costs of

organizing for political favors is to restrict the size of the winning group.

2. But this winning group will not obtain even a gross gain through political action as great as is within the power of the political process to grant it.

3. Moreover, even if groups organize according to an economic interest (producers v. consumers), political entrepreneurship will produce a coalition which admits members of the losing group into the charmed circle.

I now apply these principles specifically to price-entry regulation and derive implications for the price-profits outcome and the demand for new regulation.

II. The Politics of Price-Entry Regulation

A generalization of the Stiglerian model of political transfers just discussed would be to write the politician's objective function as:

$$M = M(W_1, W_2), \tag{25}$$

where W_i = wealth of group i, and where $M_i > 0$, but where we assume no intergroup dependencies, so that $M_{12} = 0$. This is then maximized subject to a constraint on total wealth (V):

$$V = W_1 + W_2 = V(W_1, W_2), \tag{26}$$

where $V_i > 0$, but where $V_{12} < 0$. That is, the total wealth to be distributed is limited: market failures aside, one group's wealth can be increased only by decreasing the other's. Let us now suppose that the two groups vying to achieve benefits or mitigate losses from the political process are consumers and producers, and that the process is constrained to provide these gains and costs through the setting of a maximum or minimum price together with control of entry. In this case, we can specialize the majority generating function (25) as

$$M = M(p, \pi), \tag{27}$$

where

   p = price of the good
   π = wealth of producers, $M_p < 0$ and $M_\pi > 0$.

The implicit assumption here is that the powers of the state are sufficient to, on the one hand, enforce competition, so that any $\pi > 0$

translates into political support, and on the other, to ban sale of the good or price it out of existence, so that any consumer surplus provides some votes or stills some opposition. A somewhat more elegant, though not necessarily more insightful, formulation would define equation (27) with respect to an anarchistic reference point. I retain the Stiglerian assumption that the political returns to higher π or lower p are diminishing ($M_{pp} < 0$, $M_{\pi\pi} < 0$).[7] I will also assume no intergroup political effects (such as envy or vindictiveness), so $M_{\pi p} = 0$. The relevant constraint here is given by cost and demand conditions, summarized by the profit function

$$\pi = f(p, c), \tag{28}$$

where $c = c(Q)$ = production costs as a function of quantity (Q), and where over the range we shall be interested in, $f_p \geq 0$ and $f_{pp} < 0$, and, of course, $f_c < 0$. The formal problem for a successful regulator then is to maximize (I assume sufficient competition for the regulator's office) the Lagrangian

$$L = M(p, \pi) + \lambda(\pi - f(p, c)), \tag{29}$$

with respect to p, π and λ, which yields

$$-\frac{M_p}{f_p} = M_\pi = -\lambda. \tag{30}$$

This says that the marginal political product of a dollar of profits (M_π) must equal the marginal political product of a price cut ($-M_p$) that also costs a dollar of profits (f_p is the dollar profit loss per dollar price reduction). This result requires $f_p > 0$ (since $-M_p$, $M_\pi > 0$); which is merely

---

[7] $M_{pp} < 0$ is not, of course, strictly implied by diminishing returns, and we shall see later that so strict a condition is unnecessary. If we have the simple function $M = M(S)$, where S = consumer's surplus, rather than p, and $S = \int_p^{p'} Q(p)dp$, where $Q(p)$ is the demand curve, and $Q(p') = 0$, then diminishing political returns requires $M_{SS} < 0$. However, this is related to M_{pp} by

$$M_{pp} = M_S \cdot S_{pp} + S_p^2 \cdot M_{SS}$$

where

$$S_p = -Q < 0 \text{ and } S_{pp} = -Q_p > 0.$$

Thus M_{pp} may be positive even if $M_{SS} < 0$, but $M_{pp} < 0$ is sufficient for $M_{SS} < 0$.

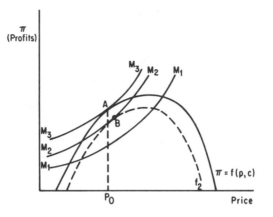

FIGURE II

a concrete application of the result in equation (11). That is, political equilibrium will not result in the monopoly or cartel-profit maximizing price ($f_p = 0$). The solution is shown graphically in Figure II, where equation (27) is represented as a series of iso-majority curves ($M_i M_i$) obeying the assumed signs for first and second derivatives. Political equilibrium occurs at tangency (A) between the profit hill and an iso-majority curve. On this formulation, pure "producer protection" can be rational only in the absence of any marginal consumer opposition to higher prices ($M_i M_i$ are all horizontal) and pure "consumer protection" requires no marginal support for higher profits.

This analysis says nothing about whether A in Figure II is anything more than trivially different from either the top or bottom of the profit hill. To make the analysis meaningful, we must either derive the appropriate political power function (the shape of the $M_i M_i$) or focus on the effects of changes in the underlying economic constraints. In the remainder of the article I take the latter tack. That is, I set aside the question of who gets what share of the spoils to focus on the implications of the result that the spoils will in fact be shared. For example, note one implication of equation (30) for entry in regulation. *Either* naturally monopolistic or naturally competitive industries are more politically attractive to regulate than an oligopolistic hybrid. The inducement to regulate is the change in the level of $M_i M_i$ occasioned thereby. For an oligopoly with a price already intermediate between the competitive and monopoly price, the political gain from moving to A will be smaller in general than if the pre-regulation price is either at the top or bottom of the profit hill. This may help explain such phenomena as the concurrence of regulation of ostensible "natural monopolies" like railroads, utilities and telephones with that of seemingly competitive industries like trucking, airlines, taxicabs, barbers, and agriculture. It may also rationalize the twin focus of antitrust on reducing concentration and protecting small businessmen, and the delay until comparatively recent times in applying the Sherman Act to less than the most concentrated industries. However, the model does not explain the dilatoriness of the government in regulating a gamut of unconcentrated retail and manufacturing markets.

There is also implicit here a connection between regulation and productivity and growth. Reduction in costs or growth in demand will increase the total surplus (the height of the profit hill in Figure II) over which a regulator might have control and, pari passu, the political payoff for its redistribution.[8] I have seen this point made before only in connection with welfare programs,[9] and it deserves a systematic test. However, the association of new regulation with industries where demand and/or productivity is growing rapidly is frequent enough to be suggestive (electricity and telephones in the early 20th century, trucking and airlines in the 1930's and 1940's, natural gas in the 1950's, automobiles and drugs in the 1960's).

Some interesting implications for the pattern of regulatory choice can be derived from a more formal treatment of the interaction between productivity and growth and rational political choice. Consider a market already subject to regulation and in a political equilibrium such as A in Figure II. Then consider the effects on this equilibrium of a parametric shift, dx, in either the cost or demand function. To obtain the effect of the shift on the $p = \pi$ configuration generated by regulation, we must solve

$$[L_{ij}] \begin{bmatrix} dp/dx \\ d\pi/dx \\ d\lambda/dx \end{bmatrix} = -[L_{ix}], \tag{31}$$

where i, j denotes p, π or λ. In the case of a (marginal) cost shift, we obtain

$$\frac{dp}{dx} = \frac{-\lambda f_{px} + f_x \cdot f_p \cdot M_{\pi\pi}}{-(M_{pp} - \lambda f_{pp}) - f_p^2 M_{\pi\pi}}. \tag{32}$$

[8] This is easiest to see for a constant cost competitive industry where demand increases. In that case, the no-regulation majority is unaffected by the increased demand (p and π are the same) but the gain to regulating the industry and moving to a majority maximizing (p, π) is increased. I demonstrate below that a similar result obtains for more complicated cases.

[9] See W. Allen Wallis, Causes of the Welfare Explosion, in Welfare Programs: An Economic Appraisal 33, 54 (1968).

The denominator is positive by a necessary condition for a maximum, so the sign of equation (32) depends on that of the numerator, which is positive.[10] This is hardly surprising, since a rise in marginal cost leads to the same result without regulation. However, the insight provided by equation (32) is that the price increase has distinct "political" and "economic" components. The first term in the numerator $(-\lambda f_{px})$ is essentially a "substitution effect" akin to that facing an unregulated firm. A rise in marginal cost makes a higher price profitable. The second term is a "political wealth" effect: the surplus to be disposed of has shrunk, and this forces the regulator to reduce his purchases of political support. However, the usual marginal conditions familiar from consumer theory are applicable here. The regulator will, in general, not force the entire adjustment onto one group. In particular, consumers will be called on to buffer some of the producer losses. To see this more clearly, abstract from the substitution effect by assuming a change in fixed cost only, so $f_{px} = 0$. Then the profit hill in Figure II shifts down by a constant to f_2, leaving the profit-maximizing price unchanged, but increasing the political-equilibrium price and buffering the fall in profits that would otherwise occur. Of course, as is the case in consumer choice, one cannot rule out "inferiority" of price decreases or profit increases.[11] But the "normal" purely political component of the response to cost changes involves consumers shielding producers from some of the effects of cost increases and producers sharing some of their gains from cost reductions.

The case of a shift in demand is more complex, because the de-

---

[10] $\lambda < 0$, from (30); $f_x = -c_x < 0$; $f_p > 0$, since profits are below a maximum; $M_{\pi\pi} < 0$ by assumption; and

$$f_{px} = -Q_p c_{Qx} > 0.$$

[11] Such inferiority is in fact essentially ruled out here by the absence of intergroup dependencies. This plays the same role here as utility independence does in ruling out inferior goods in consumer choice theory. The closest analogy to the conventional consumer choice problem would be where the regulator always sets a marginal price equal to (a constant) marginal cost and then merely allocates the resulting surplus among producers and consumers by fashioning a suitable two-part or declining-marginal price scheme. In this case, the surplus is the regulator's "income" which can be used to purchase the "goods" producer or consumer support at a price of $1. If the utility (votes) of the two goods is independent, declining marginal utility will assure that both are normal.

This analogue helps illuminate the attraction of regulation to markets with growing productivity and demand. The increased surplus, which is the regulator's income, generates a larger utility (vote) gain from moving from either corner (monopoly or competition) to the vote maximum, again so long as there are diminishing political returns to both producer and consumer wealth.

mand function enters indirectly into the M function: M_p depends on the relationship between price and consumer surplus, which depends on the height of demand. Formerly, a change in demand, dy, yields

$$\frac{dp}{dy} = \frac{-\lambda f_{py} + M_{py} + f_y \cdot f_p M_{\pi\pi}}{-(M_{pp} - \lambda f_{pp}) - f^2 M_{\pi\pi}}. \tag{33}$$

Again, the first term of the numerator is a profit-maximizing "substitution" effect which is positive,[12] and the last term a political wealth effect which is, in this case, negative ($f_y > 0$). The middle term represents the effect of the demand shift on political "tastes"—that is, on the slope of the $M_i M_i$ in Figure II, but this effect is ambiguous.[13] For example, if a rise in consumer income raises the payoff to price reductions, $M_{py} < 0$, and the political-wealth effect is reinforced. Ignoring this taste change, the results are symmetric with those of a cost change. Consider a rise in demand such that $f_{py} = 0$.[14] The political wealth effect will nevertheless induce a price reduction because the diminishing political returns to both profit increases and price decreases make a combination of the two the best strategy for political "spending" of more wealth.

What emerges from this discussion is more a working hypothesis than an a priori conclusion about the nature of price and profit adjustment under regulation. *If* the political wealth effect is empirically important, it will be manifested in attenuation of price changes when demand changes and in their amplification when costs change and vice versa for profit changes. In the case of the latter, the wealth-effect components of the counterparts to equations (32) and (33) may be written

---

[12] Ignoring, as usual, any offsetting changes in the slope of demand.
[13] In particular

$$M_p = M_S \cdot S_p = -Q M_S$$

where S again denotes the underlying consumer surplus. So

$$M_{py} = -Q M_{SS} S_y - M_S Q_y.$$

Since M_S, Q_y and $S_y > 0$, while $M_{SS} < 0$, the sign of M_{py} is ambiguous.
[14] This requires an appropriate change in the slope of the demand curve, since

$$f_{py} = (P - C_Q) \cdot Q_{py} + Q_y.$$

So some $Q_{py} < 0$ is required for $f_{py} = 0$.

$$\frac{d\pi}{dx} = \frac{f_x}{1 + f_p^2 \left(\dfrac{M_{\pi\pi}}{M_{pp} - \lambda f_{pp}} \right)}, \tag{34}$$

$$\frac{d\pi}{dy} = \frac{f_y}{1 + f_p^2 \left(\dfrac{M_{\pi\pi}}{M_{pp} - \lambda f_{pp}} \right)}. \tag{35}$$

These are both smaller absolutely than what would obtain under pure producer protection (which yields simply f_x or f_y). We can then summarize the interaction between cost and demand changes and regulatory utility maximization as follows: Define variables π' and p' as the *difference* between regulated and profit maximizing profits and prices respectively. The purely political effects of changes in underlying economic conditions are then for dp'/dx and $d\pi'/dx > 0$; dp'/dy and $d\pi'/dy < 0$. Among the empirical implications of these forces would be:

1. Regulation will tend to be more heavily weighted toward "producer protection" in depressions and toward "consumer protection" in expansions. Thus, for example, it is not useful to view events like the Robinson-Patman Act and the National Recovery Act (NRA) as "inconsistent" with the intent of antitrust legislation; this intent is endogenous. Similar arguments apply to the structure of taxes (the corporate-personal tax mix should offset changes in the share of GNP earned by capital), tariffs (more free trade when demand grows or costs fall), and so on.

2. Government intervention and regulation are both normal goods. Though this generalization has exceptions, the difference between the no-regulation iso-majority curve and the regulatory equilibrium (that is, the incentive to regulate) grows with the level of demand. As a further generalization, the income elasticity of producer protection ought to be less than that of consumer protection. This follows from the negative wealth effect of demand growth on equilibrium price, which makes for an increased consumer share of the total surplus as demand (income) increases.

3. The tendency of regulation to change prices infrequently, sometimes called "regulatory lag," ought to be stronger when demand changes than when costs change. This follows from the opposing wealth and substitution effects in the case of a shift in demand (but not in the case of a cost change). Here failure to change a price can be interpreted to mean that the opposing effects offset one another.

4. Some reexamination of studies, such as Stigler and Friedland's, which show regulation to be ineffective, is called for. In the first place the result ought to be sensitive to the dynamics of supply and demand.

In a growing, technologically progressive industry, producer protection ought to yield to consumer protection over time, even if, on average, there is no effect. (Stigler and Friedland's data do show some secular trend toward lower prices.)[15] Secondly, deviations about the zero mean effect should be systematic: high-cost, low-demand markets will have prices elevated by regulation and low-cost, high-demand markets will have prices reduced. Finally, as a generalization of 2. above, entry of regulation is not exogenous. It should occur first in the low-cost, high-demand markets. This last point indicates some of the complexity engendered by the interaction of the static and dynamic aspects of the model: whether entry of regulation into any market raises or lowers prices depends on whether the market was initially competitive or monopolistic. Once that initial adjustment has been made, subsequent cost and demand changes will govern any redistribution from the initial position.

5. If regulation is evaluated against a zero-profit (fair rate of return) benchmark, we might be tempted to conclude that positive profits imply a "captured" regulator and thereby expect a positive correlation between prices and profitability. In fact the observed correlation ought to be negative. Whatever its source—increased demand or lower costs—an increase in the profit hill of Figure II generates a political incentive to move toward a combination involving higher profits and lower prices. Thus, quite apart from any private profit-maximizing incentives toward this configuration, the most profitable regulated firms ought to have the lowest prices. More precisely, the gap between the profit-maximizing and regulated price will be positively correlated with the gap between the former and the "fair-rate-of-return" price.

6. The model also yields predictions on the bias of regulation. Briefly, elastic demand and economies of scale create a bias favorable to consumers. The reason is that these sorts of demand and cost conditions enhance the consumer surplus gained while mitigating the producer surplus lost due to a price reduction. To see this formally, first introduce a parameter, w, into the slope of the demand curve at equilibrium, so that a positive dw implies a less elastic demand. By appropriate reformulation of the right-hand side of equation (31), we obtain the vector

$$
-\begin{bmatrix} L_{pw} \\ L_{\pi w} \\ L_{\lambda w} \end{bmatrix} = -\begin{bmatrix} M_{pw} - \lambda f_{pw} \\ M_{\pi w} \\ -f_w \end{bmatrix} = -\begin{bmatrix} M_{pw} - \lambda f_{pw} \\ 0 \\ 0 \end{bmatrix}, \tag{36}
$$

[15] George J. Stigler & Claire Friedland, *supra* note 1, at 7. Their estimate is that regulation had no effect on electricity rates in 1912 and lowered prices by about 10 per cent in 1937.

where we set $f_w = 0$ (that is, assume that the less elastic demand passes through the initial price quantity combination). Both M_{pw} and $-\lambda f_{pw}$ are positive: a less elastic demand reduces the consumer surplus and vote productivity of a price reduction, while it enhances the profitability and vote productivity of a price increase.[16] The signs of the relevant total derivatives then become

$$\text{sign } dP/dw = \text{sign } L_{pw} > 0, \tag{37}$$

$$\text{sign } d\pi/dw = \text{sign } f_p \cdot L_{pw} > 0. \tag{38}$$

That is, a less elastic demand induces the regulator to "relocate" toward the northeast on any iso-majority curve in Figure II.

For the scale-economies case, introduce a parameter, v, into marginal cost and assume that a negative dv leaves profits at the old equilibrium unchanged. That is, if there is a lower marginal cost in the neighborhood of equilibrium, it is sufficiently higher at lower outputs to leave total costs unchanged. This sort of characterization of increased scale economies implies the vector

$$-\begin{bmatrix} L_{pv} \\ L_{\pi v} \\ L_{\lambda v} \end{bmatrix} = -\begin{bmatrix} M_{pv} - \lambda f_{py} \\ M_{\pi v} \\ -f_v \end{bmatrix} = -\begin{bmatrix} \lambda Q_p \\ 0 \\ 0 \end{bmatrix} \tag{39}$$

The term λQ_p is positive. The diseconomies of smaller outputs when $dv < 0$ make a price increase less profitable (and so a price decrease more attractive politically). This renders the derivatives, dP/dv and $d\pi/dv$, both positive, so more scale economies induce a move to the southwest on any iso-majority curve.

Pending a systematic test of the empirical relevance of these propositions, I point out potential pitfalls. The long history of "producer" regulation of agriculture (price supports, marketing restrictions, and so on) seems consistent with the model, given the conventional wisdom about low supply and demand elasticities in this sector. However, the cartelization of airlines, trucking, railroads, and taxi-

---

[16] Again starting from $M_p = -QM_S$, we get $M_{pw} = -QM_{SS} \cdot S_w$, and $S_w > 0$, so with $M_{SS} < 0$, $M_{pw} > 0$. Since

$$f_p = (P - C_Q)(Q_p + w) + Q$$

$$f_{pw} = (P - C_Q) > 0,$$

and with $\lambda < 0$, $-\lambda f_{pw} > 0$.

cabs where there are either constant or decreasing costs is obviously troublesome. A more general problem is how to distinguish the political incentives here from corresponding profit-maximizing incentives which push in the same direction if we want to use the result to predict the behavior of established regulators rather than the entry pattern in regulation.[17]

7. Finally, I note an implication for the theory of finance. Regulation should reduce conventional measures of owner risk. By buffering the firm against demand and cost changes, the variability of profits (and stock prices) should be lower than otherwise. To the extent that the cost and demand changes are economy-wide, regulation should reduce systematic as well as diversifiable risk.

There is no obvious risk pattern among currently regulated firms: electric, gas, and telephone utility stocks rank among the least risky while airline stocks are among the most risky. However, in one case of *new* regulation (of product quality), I found that both total and systematic risk of drug stocks decreased substantially after regulation.[18] A crude test on railroad and utility stock prices shows the same pattern, though the effect is weak. I correlated annual (December to December) changes in the log of the Standard and Poor's or Cowles indexes of railroad and utility stock price indices[19] with those of the industrial index (which I treat as a diversified portfolio of stocks of unregulated firms) for equal periods spanning the onset of regulation. I took 1887 as the first year of railroad regulation and 1907 as the start of utility regulation. (New York began regulating that year.) The indexes of systematic risk (estimated as the regression coefficient on industrial stock price changes) were, with standard errors in parentheses,

	Before Regulation	After Regulation
Railroads	.74	.56
(1871–86, 1887–1902)	(.24)	(.17)
Utilities	.67	.60
(1871–1906, 1907–42)	(.12)	(.10)

[17] As an example of the kind of entry pattern that can be predicted, consider a competitive industry with inelastic demand and supply. The political equilibrium here is closer to the monopoly equilibrium than it is with elastic demand and supply. Hence such an industry is more likely to attract regulation than one with elastic demand and supply. Similarly a natural monopoly with elastic demand and supply makes an inviting target for regulation.

[18] See Sam Peltzman, The Benefits and Costs of New Drug Regulation, in Regulating New Drugs 205-206 (Richard L. Landau ed. 1973).

[19] Standard and Poor's Trade and Securities Statistics: Security Price Index Record (1971).

The total risk of these stocks relative to industrials (the ratio of standard deviations of annual changes) was

	Before Regulation	After Regulation
Rails	1.16	.85
Utilities	.97	.84

All of the differences go in the right direction, but none are significant. The main point of this exercise is simply to hint what further research might be useful.

III. The Structure of Regulated Prices

I have argued that the rational regulator will not levy a uniform tax nor distribute benefits equally. Rather, he will seek a structure of costs and benefits that maximizes political returns. This search for political advantage will in turn lead the regulator to suppress some economic forces that might otherwise affect the price structure. For example, the cost of serving a group of customers or their elasticity of demand will have a different impact under regulation than it will in an unregulated market because of the absence of political constraints in the latter case. The substitution of political for economic criteria in the price formulation process has several interesting implications which I shall elaborate. It is at the heart of the pervasive tendency of regulation to engage in cross-subsidization—that is, the dissipation of producer rents on sales to some customers by setting below-cost prices to others. We shall see that this cross-subsidization follows a systematic pattern in which high-cost customer groups are subsidized by low-cost customers. Further, this pattern of price discrimination emerges from a process in which conventional profit maximizing price discrimination as well as other economic forces leading to price differences are attenuated.

A convenient starting point for this analysis is the problem first set out in equations (14)–(16), where the regulator seeks a tax structure to minimize opposition. Here I want to consider the effect on the resulting tax structure when a change occurs of the type that would ordinarily lead the gainers to seek a change in only one of the two tax rates. As an example, suppose per capita wealth rises for one group only. In the price-regulation analogue of this problem, this would lead to a rise in one group's demand, and a profit-maximizing monopolist might then raise that group's price, but not the other group's price. Under regulation, however, no such specialization of a tax increase will be tolerated, because this would violate the basic principle that opposition from the two groups must be equated at the margin.

This point can be demonstrated formally with the same framework used previously. Specifically let there be a parameter shift, dx, in the wealth of group 1 only. Then trace the effects of this shift on t_1 and t_2. These effects are obtained by solving

$$
\begin{bmatrix} dt_1/dx \\ dt_2/dx \\ d\lambda/dx \end{bmatrix} = - [L_{1x}, L_{2x}, L_{\lambda x}] \begin{bmatrix} L_{11} L_{12} L_{1\lambda} \\ L_{21} L_{22} L_{2\lambda} \\ L_{\lambda 1} L_{\lambda 2} L_{\lambda \lambda} \end{bmatrix}^{-1}
\tag{40}
$$

where the subscripts 1, 2 on the right-hand side refer to t_1 and t_2. This has the following relevant solutions:

$$
\text{sign } \frac{dt_1}{dx} = \text{sign } [- L_{1x} \cdot L_{2\lambda}^2 - L_{\lambda x} \cdot L_{22} \cdot L_{\lambda 1}],
\tag{41}
$$

$$
\text{sign } \frac{dt_2}{dx} = \text{sign } [L_{1x} \cdot L_{\lambda 1} \cdot L_{2\lambda} - L_{\lambda x} \cdot L_{11} \cdot L_{\lambda 2}].
\tag{42}
$$

The sign of equation (41) is ambiguous, since the first term in brackets is positive while the second is negative. The first term reflects the ability of the regulator to both maintain revenues and limit opposition by raising taxes on the now wealthier group 1 individuals, while the second term is a political wealth effect which induces lower tax rates. The more interesting result is that the sign of equation (42) is unambiguously negative. This occurs first because of the incentive to substitute higher taxes on group 1, which creates the ambiguity in equation (41) and which in equation (42) requires an offsetting decrease in t_2 to maintain equilibrium. This incentive to a lower t_2 is reinforced by the political wealth effect. The analysis assumes no interdependencies between the two groups' political responsiveness or wealth (that is, L_{12} is assumed to be zero). Thus what emerges here is that the regulator's striving for minimum opposition by equating opposition at the margin leads him to spread effects of economic forces which are local to all groups. This common element in the tax structure is provided by the wealth effect which leads the regulator to buy more of both relevant "goods" (less opposition from group 1 and from group 2).

This result can be applied to the regulation of prices by suitably generalizing the analysis of a single price summarized in Figure II. That is, assume that there are two separable groups of buyers, so that the majority generating function (27) is

$$
M = M(p_1, p_2, \pi),
\tag{43}
$$

with M_1, $M_2 < 0$. The distinction between the two groups is economic rather than political, in that I assume only that there are cost and/or demand differences. Thus customers whom the regulator might wish to single out for benefits can be scattered among both groups, and p_1 and p_2 can be regarded as averages from another price structure conditioned by political forces. I suppress this structure here only to highlight the difference between a regulated and unregulated market's response to common economic forces. The cost/demand differences also give rise to the new profit function

$$\pi = f(p_1, p_2, c). \tag{44}$$

With no loss of generality, I assume that it costs nothing to produce the product for group 2, so $c = $ cost of production for group 1. Otherwise the properties of equation (44) and its simpler counterpart (28) are the same (f_1, $f_2 \geq 0$, f_{11}, $f_{22} < 0$, $f_c < 0$). Again, to make the problem nontrivial, I rule out cross-group effects, so

$$M_{12} = M_{1\pi} = M_{2\pi} = f_{12} = 0.$$

We may now proceed to trace out the implications for the structure of regulated prices if there is a change of the sort that would lead, in an unregulated market, to a change solely of one group's price. As an example, let group 1's demand increase, so that, with independent demands and costs, the profit-maximizing or short-run competitive price would rise for that group alone. The general problem now facing the regulator is to choose the set (p_1, p_2, π, λ) which maximizes the Lagrangian

$$L = M(p_1, p_2, \pi) + \lambda[\pi - f(p_1, p_2, c)]. \tag{45}$$

(Note that we are dropping the restriction in equations (14)–(16) and (40)–(42) of fixed "tax receipts"—here profits—transferred to winners.) The first-order conditions for a maximum here are similar to equation (30); specifically

$$-\frac{M_1}{f_1} = -\frac{M_2}{f_2} = M_\pi = -\lambda. \tag{46}$$

So both p_1 and p_2 will be held below the profit-maximizing level (f_1, $f_2 > 0$). Now let there be a parameter shift, dy, in group 1's demand, and let us see what effect this has on p_1 and p_2. Consequently, we solve

$$\left[\frac{d_i}{d_y}\right] = -[L_{iy}][L_{ij}]^{-1},\qquad(47)$$

where $i, j = p_1, p_2, \pi, \lambda$. The left-hand side of equation (47) is a vector of total derivatives; the first term on the right is a row-vector of partial derivatives, and the second term is a matrix of partial derivatives. To present the results in a manageable fashion, I define the following variables, and indicate their signs:

$$A = [(\lambda f_{22} - M_{22}) - f_2^2 \cdot M_{\pi\pi}] > 0$$

(by second-order conditions for a maximum);

$$B = f_1 \cdot M_{\pi\pi}(M_{22} - \lambda f_{22}) > 0$$

(by second-order conditions and $f_1 > 0$);

$$C = f_2 \cdot M_{\pi\pi}(M_{11} - \lambda f_{11}) > 0$$

(by second-order conditions and $f_2 > 0$). I then show the results for the signs of dP_1/dy and dP_2/dy by components.

$$\text{sign } \frac{dP_1}{dy} = \text{sign:}$$

$$
\begin{array}{lll}
M_{1y} \cdot A? & \text{(``taste'' shift)} & \\
-\lambda f_{1y} \cdot A > 0 & \text{(``substitution'')} & (48) \\
-f_y \cdot B < 0 & \text{(``political wealth''),} &
\end{array}
$$

$$\text{sign } \frac{dP_2}{dy} = \text{sign:}$$

$$
\begin{array}{lll}
-M_{1y} \cdot f_2? & \text{(taste shift)} & \\
+\lambda f_{1y} \cdot f_2 < 0 & \text{(substitution)} & (49) \\
-f_y \cdot C < 0 & \text{(political wealth).} &
\end{array}
$$

The results in equation (48) are similar to those in equation (33), where we analyzed the effects of a shift in demand on a single price. There is a change in consumer surplus with ambiguous effects on the responsiveness of group 1 to price reductions (that is, its "tastes" for price reductions). There is a substitution effect, showing that it is "cheaper" for the regulator to collect transfers in the form of higher prices to the higher demand group. Finally there is a political wealth effect, showing that the regulator will use the expanded opportunity locus to shield group 1 from the full substitution effect.

The more interesting result is equation (49), since group 2 would be unaffected in an unregulated market. Apart from the ambiguous "taste" effect, there are two forces under regulation leading this group to benefit from the higher demand of group 1. First, there is the converse of the substitution effect. If it is now more attractive to tax group 1, then for any given tax receipt, the price to group 2 will be lower. Second, there is the same wealth effect that assists group 1. The regulator distributes the gains made possible by the higher demand partly in the form of higher profits,[20] partly in the form of a lower price to group 1 *and* partly in the form of a lower price to group 2. *All* the margins in equation (46), not just one or two, require adjustment when one group's demand increases and thereby increases the wealth available to the regulator.

This result is illustrated in Figure III, where I focus on the structure of prices. Each of the curves labeled M_i is a locus of price combinations consistent with a constant level of support or opposition from consumers. These are negatively sloped, indicating that the regulator can maintain the fixed support level by trading lower prices to one group for higher prices to another. The M index increases toward the origin, since lower prices are preferred by both groups. For simplicity, I assume diminishing political returns to price reduction, so the M are convex from above. The point A is the combination of profit-maximizing prices, but the rational regulator wishes to set lower prices than these. The frontier DGC shows the p_1, p_2 combinations which yield the desired level of producer wealth. It is negatively sloped since f_1 and f_2 are both positive (or zero at D and C respectively), and concave from above, since both f_{11} and f_{22} are negative. The equilibrium at G is defined by the first two conditions in equation (46). Consider now the special case where the regulator desires to keep profits fixed and the group 1 demand increases. If p_1 at G exceeds marginal cost, the profit frontier will shift outward over a range of prices in the neighborhood of G. That is, with 1's higher demand, the same profit can be generated by a lower p_1 holding p_2 constant, or by a lower p_2 holding p_1 constant. (For simplicity, I have assumed that the p_1 at C also exceeds marginal cost, so that the frontier shifts out over the entire relevant range.) It is this shift to $EHG'F$ that produces a "wealth effect" toward a lower p_1, p_2 set, though there will also be a change in the slope of the frontier which will offset the incentive toward a lower p_1.

---

[20]The result for the wealth component of $d\pi/dy$ is a more complex analogue to equation (35) with the same properties.

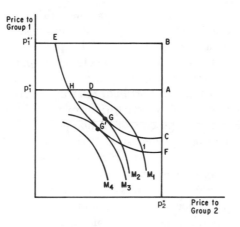

FIGURE III

The implication here is that, not only will the average level of prices under regulation be below what it would be in pure monopoly, but the structure of relative prices will depart from that in either pure monopoly or competition. The important contribution of politics is to suppress economically important distinctions and substitute for these a common element in all prices. On the demand side, this means that regulators will tax profits by attenuating profitable price discrimination. Discrimination is not eliminated, because there is a force—the substitution effect—unifying the interests of a discriminating monopoly and the regulator.[21] It is countered by the wealth effect, so the empirical importance of this effect will determine that of the unique political effect on the price structure. Equations (48) and (49) do shed this further light: the term f_y is proportional to the difference between price and marginal cost. So, the political element in pricing should be more prominent the more profitable the regulated firm.

Except that this last result does not hold, the case of a change in costs is similar to that of a change in demand. Specifically, a rise in the marginal cost of serving group 1 leads, in addition to the conventional substitution effect raising p_1/p_2, to a wealth effect raising both p_1 and p_2.

This incentive to reward or tax all customers for the peculiar characteristics of some has interesting implications for the structure of regulated prices. Not only will profit-maximizing price discrimination be discouraged, but a peculiar form of price discrimination will replace it. This is usually referred to as "cross-subsidization" and, to the extent

---

[21] In the case of a pure change in 1's elasticity of demand—that is, a change in the slope but not the height of demand—the relevant total derivatives of P_1 and P_2 are opposite, because only a substitution effect is at work.

that this is not just another name for ordinary price discrimination, it connotes a structure in which an unprofitably low price for some is paid for from profits on sales to others. This sort of phenomenon seems difficult to reconcile with the producer protection view of regulation. Why, after all, would a surface transportation cartel wish to perpetuate unprofitable passenger train or short haul rail freight service? So far such questions have received no satisfactory answer, and the phenomenon tends to be viewed as "a process of ad hoc pacification" of vocal consumer groups.[22] Our model suggests that the process is in fact systematic: holding demand constant, the higher-cost customers will receive the lower price-marginal cost ratios. Their peculiarly high costs will be spread among all customer groups by a rational regulator. Thus we need not appeal to ad hoc judgments about the political power of, say, train passengers or short haul freight users to explain the pattern of cross-subsidization. Instead, the model implies that we should observe either a higher level of costs (say for short hauls compared to long hauls) or more rapid increases in costs (for passengers compared to freight) for the subsidized group. More generally, the model sheds light on the tendency of regulation to produce rate "averaging" across dissimilar customer groups—for example, charging similar electricity rates to rural and urban customers (which benefits the former) or similar auto insurance rates to rural and urban customers (which benefits the latter). The common element in these price structures is their suppression of cost differences.

I used this sort of model to rationalize differences in the price structure under government ownership and regulation. This required an assumption that purely political forces will be more prominent in the former regime.[23] It will take further empirical work to show whether the political impulse to uniform treatment of customers also affects regulated rates systematically. I can illustrate some of the promise and pitfalls by application to the airline rate structure. Keeler estimated price-marginal cost ratios for standard coach service in 29 regulated city-pair markets as of 1968.[24] He found that the most prominent cost difference in airline service is distance-related. Since major elements of cost are constant per flight, the per mile marginal cost falls continuously with a flight's distance. My model would imply that effective Civil Aeronautics Board (CAB) regulation would convert this cost structure into a

[22] George W. Hilton, The Basic Behavior of Regulatory Commissions, 62 Am. Econ. Rev. pt. 2, at 47, 49 (Papers & Proceedings, May 1972).

[23] Sam Peltzman, Pricing in Public and Private Enterprises: Electric Utilities in the United States, 14 J. Law & Econ. 109 (1971).

[24] Theodore E. Keeler, Airline Regulation and Market Performance, 3 Bell J. of Econ. & Man. Sci. 399 (1972).

price structure whereby price/marginal cost rises continuously with distance—that is, the fare-distance taper would be less severe than the cost-distance taper. One immediate problem is that profit-maximizing discrimination would imply a similar price structure, since ground alternatives are more competitive over shorter distances. However, especially for standard coach service, where individual business travel tends to predominate over family and vacation travel (for which airlines offer discounts), the viability of ground alternatives is restricted. Gronau estimates that, for plausible values of time, airlines will essentially monopolize the relevant market for distances over 600 miles.[25] This implies that a profit-maximizing fare structure would have price/marginal cost ratios rising substantially more sharply with distances up to 600 miles than beyond. My model implies no such break, or at least a continual increase in this ratio in the over-600-mile segments.

To sort these forces out, I regressed the log of Keeler's estimate of price/marginal cost $(P - MC)$ on two distance variables: the log of distance if the city pair is less than 600 miles apart and zero (that is, one mile) otherwise (D_1), and log of distance if the distance exceeds 600 miles, zero otherwise (D_2). From Gronau's results, profit maximization implies that the coefficient of D_1 is positive, while that of D_2 is zero. Political support maximization implies that both coefficients are positive, and, in the extreme, equal. The result is

$$P - MC = -.66 + .17D_1 + .17D_2$$
$$(3.71) \quad (4.49)$$

$$R^2 = .69 \quad \text{S.E.} \times 100 = 8.46$$

(t-ratios in parentheses). If the log of per-mile cost is regressed on D_1 and D_2, the corresponding coefficients are both $-.26$. This association of a continuous increase in $P - MC$ with a continuous distance economy is strong support for the political-support maximization model against simple profit maximization. The CAB essentially ignores the strength of ground competition for a particular flight and simply spreads the same part (about ⅔) of *any* flight's distance-related economy among all fares.

Now the pitfall: Keeler has recently updated his cost estimates to 1974.[26] There has been no important change in airline technology: per-

[25] Reuben Gronau, The Effect of Traveling Time on the Demand for Passenger Transportation, 78 J. Pol. Econ. 377 (1970).

[26] See Staff of the Subcomm. on Administrative Practice and Procedure of the Senate Comm. on the Judiciary, 94th Cong., 1st Sess., Civil Aeronautics Board Practices and Procedures 58 (Comm. Print 1975).

mile costs still fall continuously with distance (the 1974 elasticity is
$-.22$). There has been, though, a major change in the fare structure.
For the 1974 data, the $P - MC$ distance relationship is

$$P - MC = .41 - .01D_1 - .01D_2$$
$$\quad\quad\quad\quad (.23) \quad\quad (.68)$$

$$R^2 = .33 \quad S.E. \times 100 = 4.17.$$

The CAB has recently espoused the desirability of cost-based fares,
and, more importantly, it has implemented them: the fare and cost-
distance gradients are now essentially identical. To get there, the CAB
has permitted fares on the longest flights in the sample to rise by under
30 per cent between 1968 and 1975, while those on the shortest have
more than doubled. By 1974, much of the price discrimination, at least
on coach service, had vanished.[27] This implies that the CAB has been
sacrificing producer and, in terms of my model, political wealth to the
ghost of Pareto. I will not pretend that my model offers any insight into
this recent behavior, however well it seems to explain matters up to
1968.[28] Perhaps, though, it does help explain recent congressional and
executive initiatives to reduce the CAB's regulatory powers.[29]

[27] The range of the $P - MC$ variable was .47 in 1968 and .16 in 1974.

[28] The promise and pitfalls of the model are also illustrated by surface freight
rates. The cost structure here is similar to air—a negative cost/mile-distance taper.
This is most pronounced for rails, and they have experienced the most profound effects
of the resulting political incentives: short-haul rates sometimes below marginal cost,
regulatory inhibitions on elimination of such services and, recently, bankruptcies
among short-haul specialists. This all appears consistent with the basic model, except
that a simple extension should have firms and consumers treated similarly. That is, the
firms in this industry happen to be crudely separable by an economic criterion—average length of freight haul. Maximization of political support from producers would then
appear to require spreading some of the profit effects of high-cost short-haul service to
the long-haul specialists. Indeed the Interstate Commerce Commission (ICC) has the
power to do this by regulating divisions of joint rates. However, it has obviously not
been sufficiently diligent in its use of the power to prevent striking differences in the
prosperity of long- and short-haul specialists, differences which appear superficially
greater than those that might be expected without regulation of rates and exit. This
suggests two problems: (1) Why are the ICC's incentives to weld a coalition so much
stronger in the case of consumers and producers? (2) What accounts for the difference
between the ICC and CAB willingness to endanger the consumer coalition by permitting economic efficiency criteria to intrude in the rate structure?

There is finally a problem of appropriate units. A prime example of cost-based
cross subsidization is first-class postage. The rate here ignores distance-related costs
entirely and so results in price/marginal cost *declining* with distance. The model can
only hint at why weight happens to be the relevant unit for the Postal Service and
distance for the ICC and CAB. One way by which a regulator can suppress cost differences is to ignore them entirely. However, in deciding which kinds of differences to

The intra-group equilibrium aspects of the model reveal some implications for entry—both of regulators and of regulated firms. First there is a clear incentive for regulators to limit entry (or seek the power to do so) quite apart from considerations of the producer interest. This stems directly from the fact that the politically appropriate price structure is invariably discriminatory (in the economic sense) when costs differ among customers. The proverbial "cream skimming" entrant must be prevented from serving the low-cost customers and thereby preventing the regulator from spreading the low costs to others. On the other hand, we can expect the regulator to be more tolerant of entry which dampens the enthusiasm of producers for demand-based price discrimination. The regulator seeks to suppress the full effects of differences in the elasticity of demand, and his way can be eased by permitting entry into low-elasticity market segments. This last argument has more force in industries, like banking, where the primary regulatory control is over entry rather than price. In these cases, the regulator uses the entry control to produce indirectly the desired price structure. A testable implication would be that more entry is permitted in banking, say, the larger the gap between interest rates on small and large loans.

The obverse of the previous argument is that entry of regulation is more attractive the more disparate the price structure. This is independent of the pre-regulatory market structure. Competitively determined, cost-based price differentials create an opportunity for political gain through entry and/or price regulation designed to suppress the effects of cost differences, just as discriminating monopoly invites political suppression of the effects of demand elasticity differences.

In summary, the same forces that make regulators seek a broad-based coalition operate on the price structure. Opportunities for increasing producer wealth by price discrimination are not ignored, but they are never fully exploited. To do this would narrow the consumer base of the coalition. The uniquely political contribution to a price structure is to force a more uniform treatment of consumers than the unregulated market by weakening the link between prices and cost and demand conditions.

---

ignore, he must also take account of the implications for profits. Hence my conjecture would have to be that weight-related costs are more important than distance-related costs in determining first-class postal service profits and vice versa for transportation. A further implication would then be that price/marginal cost in first-class postal service would be negatively related to marginal cost/pound, holding distance constant.

[29] See Staff, *supra* note 26; and U.S. President, [proposed] Aviation Act of 1975, H. R. Doc. No. 94-278, 94th Cong., 1st Sess. (1975).

IV. Concluding Remarks

This article is concerned more with the design than the implementation of a research strategy. Much of the recent work in the theory of regulation has focused on political power relationships: which groups will have the muscle to extract gains from their regulatory process. I have largely begged this issue. In my general model, every identifiable group contains winners and losers, and even where all the winners are in one group they end up short-changed. This sort of result can hardly illuminate the nature of the underlying power relationships, but that shortcoming is purposeful.

In the way I have chosen to model the regulatory process, these power relationships play a role analogous to tastes in consumer choice theory. They shape the regulator's utility function. It has proved a highly rewarding research strategy for consumer choice theorists precisely to beg questions of taste formation and concentrate instead on the behavioral effects of changes in constraints in a regime of stable tastes. With some qualification, there is an analogous history in production theory. I am suggesting here that the theory of politics has something to learn from this experience. Even if we can do no more than derive the most general properties of political power functions, there is much to learn about political behavior in a world where the constraints do change. And the specific contribution of economics to this venture will be enhanced if the constraints are those already familiar to economists. I have tried to show here how the most familiar sort of supply-demand apparatus can be converted into a constraint on regulatory behavior. Once this is accomplished the equally familiar analytics of supply-demand changes yield refutable implications about a wide range of regulatory behavior: when regulation will occur, how it will modify the unregulated price structure, even how it will change the division of the gains over time (with no change in relative political strengths).

Of course, no student of George Stigler can view the derivation of refutable implications as more than a first step. The usefulness of the model developed here awaits tests of these implications, of which the present article is nearly devoid. The limited progress we have made in exploring political "tastes" is my main ground for optimism about the fruitfulness of a return to a more familiar theoretical mode.[30]

---

[30] Some specification of power relationships is unavoidable. It is implicit, as Stigler has pointed out to me, in the choice of groups for which the model's regulator acts as broker. For example, why not posit a political redistribution between electricity producers and peanut vendors? Also, most of the results of the model are driven by "normality" of the political-wealth effect. Normality, in this context, is a specific assumption about power (inter)relationships.

Why Regulate Utilities?

Harold Demsetz

8

Current economic doctrine offers to its students a basic relationship between the number of firms that produce for a given market and the degree to which competitive results will prevail. Stated explicitly or suggested implicitly is the doctrine that price and output can be expected to diverge to a greater extent from their competitive levels the fewer the firms that produce the product for the market. This relationship has provided the logic that motivates much of the research devoted to studying industrial concentration, and it has given considerable support to utility regulation.[1]

In this paper, I shall argue that the asserted relationship between market concentration and competition cannot be derived from existing theoretical considerations and that it is based largely on an incorrect understanding of the concept of competition or rivalry. The strongest application of the asserted relationship is in the area of utility regulation since, if we assume scale economies in production, it can be deduced that only one firm will produce the commodity. The logical validity or falsity of the asserted relationship should reveal itself most clearly in this case.

Although public utility regulation recently has been criticized because of its ineffectiveness or because of the undesirable indirect effects it produces,[2] the basic intellectual arguments for believing that

The author is indebted to R. H. Coase, who was unconvinced by the natural monopoly argument long before this paper was written, and to George J. Stigler and Joel Segall for helpful comments and criticisms.

Reprinted with permission from *The Journal of Law and Economics* 11 (April 1968): 55–65. © 1968 by The University of Chicago

[1] Antitrust legislation and judicial decision, to the extent that they have been motivated by a concern for bigness and concentration, *per se*, have also benefited from the asserted relationship between monopoly power and industry structure.

[2] Cf., George J. Stigler and Claire Friedland, What Can Regulators Regulate? The Case of Electricity, 5 J. Law & Econ. 1 (1962); H. Averch and L. Johnson, The Firm under Regulatory Constraint, 52 Am. Econ. Rev. 1052 (1962); Armen Alchian and

truly effective regulation is desirable have not been challenged. Even those who are inclined to reject government regulation or ownership of public utilities because they believe these alternatives are more undesirable than private monopoly, implicitly accept the intellectual arguments that underlie regulation.[3]

The economic theory of natural monopoly is exceedingly brief and, we shall see, exceedingly unclear. Current doctrine is reflected in two recent statements of the theory. Samuelson writes:

> Under persisting decreasing costs for the firm, one or a few of them will so expand their q's as to become a significant part of the market for the industry's total Q. We would then end up (1) with a single monopolist who dominates the industry; (2) with a few large sellers who together dominate the industry . . . or (3) with some kind of imperfection of competition that, in either a stable way or in connection with a series of intermittent price wars, represents an important departure from the economist's model of "perfect" competition wherein no firm has any control over industry price.[4]

Alchian and Allen view the problem as follows:

> If a product is produced under cost conditions such that larger rates . . . [would] mean lower average cost per unit, . . . only one firm could survive; if there were two firms, one could expand to reduce costs and selling price and thereby eliminate the other. In view of the impossibility of more than one firm's being profitable, two is too many. But if there is only one, that incumbent firm may be able to set prices above free-entry costs for a long time. Either resources are wasted because too many are in the industry, or there is just one firm, which will be able to charge monopoly prices.[5]

At this point it will be useful to state explicitly the interpretation of natural monopoly used in this paper. If, because of production scale

---

Reuben Kessel, Competition, Monopoly, and the Pursuit of Pecuniary Gain, in Aspects of Labor Economics 157 (1962).

[3] Thus, Milton Friedman, while stating his preference for private monopoly over public monopoly or public regulation, writes:

However, monopoly may also arise because it is technically efficient to have a single producer or enterprise. . . . When technical conditions make a monopoly the natural outcome of coompetitive market forces, there are only three alternatives that seem available: private monopoly, public monopoly, or public regulation.

Capitalism and Freedom 28 (1962).

[4] Paul A. Samuelson, Economics 461 (6th rev. ed. 1964).

[5] Armen Alchian and William R. Allen, University Economics 412 (1st ed. 1964).

economies, it is less costly for one firm to produce a commodity in a given market than it is for two or more firms, then one firm will survive; if left unregulated, that firm will set price and output at monopoly levels; the price-output decision of that firm will be determined by profit maximizing behavior constrained only by the market demand for the commodity.

The theory of natural monopoly is deficient for it fails to reveal the logical steps that carry it from scale economies in production to monopoly price in the market place. To see this most clearly, let us consider the contracting process from its beginning.

Why must rivals share the market? Rival sellers can offer to enter into contracts with buyers. In this bidding competition, the rival who offers buyers the most favorable terms will obtain their patronage; there is no clear or necessary reason for *bidding* rivals to share in the *production* of the goods and, therefore, there is no clear reason for competition in bidding to result in an increase in per-unit *production* costs.

Why must the unregulated market outcome be monopoly price? The competitiveness of the bidding process depends very much on such things as the number of bidders, but there is no clear or necessary reason for *production* scale economies to decrease the number of *bidders*. Let prospective buyers call for bids to service their demands. Scale economies in servicing their demands in no way imply that there will be one bidder only. There can be many bidders and the bid that wins will be the lowest. The existence of scale economies in the production of the service is irrelevant to a determination of the number of rival bidders. If the number of bidders is large or if, for other reasons, collusion among them is impractical, the contracted price can be very close to per-unit production cost.[6]

The determinants of competition in market negotiations differ from and should not be confused with the determinants of the number of firms from which production will issue after contractual negotiations have been completed. The theory of natural monopoly is clearly unclear. Economies of scale in production imply that the bids submitted will offer increasing quantities at lower per-unit costs, but production scale economies imply nothing obvious about how competitive these prices will be. If one bidder can do the job at less cost than two or more, because each would then have a smaller output rate, then the bidder with the lowest bid price for the entire job will be awarded the

[6] I shall not consider in this paper the problem of marginal cost pricing and the various devices, such as multi-part tariffs, that can be used to approximate marginal cost pricing.

contract, whether the good be cement, electricity, stamp vending machines, or whatever, but the lowest bid price need not be a monopoly price.[7]

The criticism made here of the theory of natural monopoly can be understood best by constructing an example that is free from irrelevant complications, such as durability of distributions systems, uncertainty, and irrational behavior, all of which may or may not justify the use of regulatory commissions but none of which is relevant to the theory of natural monopoly; for this theory depends on one belief only—price and output will be at monopoly levels if, due to scale economies, only one firm succeeds in producing the product.

Assume that owners of automobiles are required to own and display new license plates each year. The production of license plates is subject to scale economies.

The theory of natural monopoly asserts that under these conditions the owners of automobiles will purchase plates from one firm only and that firm, in the absence of regulation, will charge a monopoly price, a price that is constrained only by the demand for and the cost of producing license plates. The logic of the example does dictate that license plates will be purchased from one firm because this will allow that firm to offer the plates at a price based on the lowest possible per-unit cost. But why should that price be a monopoly price?

There can be many bidders for the annual contract. Each will submit a bid based on the assumption that if its bid is lowest it will sell to all residents, if it is not lowest it sells to none. Under these conditions there will exist enough independently acting bidders to assure that the winning price will differ insignificantly from the per-unit cost of producing license plates.

If only one firm submits the lowest price, the process ends, but if two or more firms submit the lowest price, one is selected according to some random selection device or one is allowed to sell or give his contracts to the other. There is no monopoly price although there may be rent to some factors if their supply is positively sloped. There is no regulation of firms in the industry. The price is determined in the bidding market. The only role played by the government or by a consumers' buying cooperative is some random device to select the winning bidder if more than one bidder bids the lowest price.

---

[7] The competitive concept employed here is not new to economics although it has long been neglected. An early statement of the concept, which was known as "competition *for* the field" in distinction to "competition *within* the field" is given by Edwin Chadwick, Results of Different Principles of Legislation and Administration in Europe; of Competition for the Field, as compared with the Competition within the Field of Service, 22 J. Royal Statistical Soc'y. 381 (1859).

There are only two important assumptions: (1) The inputs required to enter production must be available to many potential bidders at prices determined in open markets. This lends credibility to numerous rival bids. (2) The cost of colluding by bidding rivals must be prohibitively high. The reader will recognize that these requirements are no different than those required to avoid monopoly price in any market, whether production in that market is or is not subject to scale economies.

Moreover, if we are willing to consider the possibility that collusion or merger of all potential bidding rivals is a reasonable prospect, then we must examine the other side of the coin. Why should collusion or merger of *buyers* be prohibitively costly if an infinite or large number of bidding rivals can collude successfully? If we allow buyers access to the same technology of collusion, the market will be characterized by bilateral negotiations between organized buyers and organized sellers. While the outcome of such negotiations is somewhat uncertain with respect to wealth distribution, there is no reason to expect inefficiency.

Just what is the supply elasticity of bidders and what are the costs of colluding are questions to be answered empirically since they cannot be deduced from production scale economies. There exists more than one firm in every public utility industry and many firms exist in some public utility industries. And this is true even though licensing restrictions have been severe; the assertion that the supply of potential *bidders* in any market would be very inelastic if licensing restrictions could be abolished would seem difficult to defend when producing competitors exist in nearby markets. The presence of active rivalry is clearly indicated in public utility history. In fact, producing competitors, not to mention unsuccessful bidders, were so plentiful that one begins to doubt that scale economies characterized the utility industry at the time when regulation replaced market competition. Complaints were common that the streets were too frequently in a state of disrepair for the purpose of accommodating competing companies. Behling writes:

There is scarcely a city in the country that has not experienced competition in one or more of the utility industries. Six electric light companies were organized in the one year of 1887 in New York City. Forty-five electric light enterprises had the legal right to operate in Chicago in 1907. Prior to 1895, Duluth, Minnesota, was served by five electric lighting companies, and Scranton, Pennsylvania, had four in 1906. . . . During the latter part of the nineteenth century, competition was the usual situation in the gas industry in this country. Before 1884, six competing companies were operating in New York City. . . . Competition was common and especially persistent in the telephone industry. According to a special report of the Census in 1902, out of 1051 incorporated cities in the United States with a population of more than 4,000 persons, 1002 were provided with telephone facilities. The independent companies had a monopoly in 137 of the cities, the Bell interests had exclusive control over communication by telephone in 414 cities, while the remaining 451, almost half, were receiving duplicated service. Baltimore, Chicago, Cleveland, Columbus, Detroit, Kansas City, Minneapolis, Philadelphia, Pittsburgh, and St. Louis, among the larger cities, had at least two telephone services in 1905.[8]

It would seem that the number of potential bidding rivals and the cost of their colluding in the public utility industries are likely to be at least as great as in several other industries for which we find that unregulated markets work tolerably well.

The natural monopoly theory provides no logical basis for monopoly prices. The theory is illogical. Moreover, for the general case of public utility industries, there seems no clear evidence that the cost of colluding is significantly lower than it is for industries for which unregulated market competition seems to work. To the extent that utility regulation is based on the fear of monopoly price, *merely because one firm will serve each market*, it is not based on any deducible economic theorem.

The important point that needs stressing is that *we have no theory that allows us to deduce from the observable degree of concentration in a particular market whether or not price and output are competitive*. We have as yet no general theory of collusion and certainly not one that allows us to associate observed concentration in a particular market with successful collusion.[9]

It is possible to make some statements about collusion that reveal the nature of the forces at work. These statements are largely intuitive and cannot be pursued in detail here. But they may be useful in imparting to the reader a notion of what is meant by a theory of collusion. Let us suppose that there are no special costs to competing. That is, we assume that sellers do not need to keep track of the prices or other activities of their competitors. Secondly, assume that there are some costs of colluding that must be borne by members of a bidders' cartel. This condition is approximated least well where the government subsidizes the cost of colluding—for example, the U.S. Department of Agriculture. Finally, assume that there are no legal barriers to entry.

Under these conditions, new bidding rivals will be paid to join

[8] Burton N. Behling, Competition and Monopoly in Public Utility Industries 19–20 (1938).

[9] However, see George J. Stigler, A Theory of Oligopoly, 72 J. Pol. Econ. 44 (1964).

the collusion. In return for joining they will receive a pro rata share of monopoly profits. As more rivals appear the pro rata share must fall. The cartel will continue paying new rivals to join until the pro rata share falls to the cost of colluding. That is, until the cartel members receive a competitive rate of return for remaining in the cartel. The next rival bidder can refuse to join the cartel; instead he can enter the market at a price below the cartel price (as can any present member of the cartel who chooses to break away). If there is some friction in the system, this rival will choose this course of action in preference to joining the cartel, for if he joins the cartel he receives a competitive rate of return; whereas if he competes outside the cartel by selling at a price below that of the cartel he receives an above-competitive rate of return for some short-run period. Under the assumed conditions the cartel must eventually fail and price and output can be competitive even though only a few firms actually produce the product. Moreover, the essential ingredient to its eventual failure is only that the private per-firm cost of colluding exceeds the private per-firm cost of competing.

Under what conditions will the cost of colluding exceed the cost of competing? How will these costs be affected by allowing coercive tactics? What about buyer cartels? What factors affect how long is "eventually"? Such questions remain to be answered by a theory of collusion. Until such questions are answered, public policy prescriptions must be suspect. A market in which many firms produce may be competitive or it may be collusive; the large number of firms merely reflects production scale diseconomies; large numbers do not necessarily reflect high or low collusion costs. A market in which few firms produce may be competitive or it may be collusive; the small number of firms merely relects production scale economies; fewness does not necessarily reflect high or low collusion costs. Thus, an economist may view the many retailers who sell on "fair trade" terms with suspicion and he may marvel at the ability of large numbers of workers to form effective unions, and, yet, he may look with admiration at the performance of the few firms who sell airplanes, cameras, or automobiles.

The subject of monopoly price is necessarily permeated with the subject of negotiating or contracting costs. A world in which negotiating costs are zero is a world in which no monopolistic inefficiencies will be present, simply because buyers and sellers both can profit from negotiations that result in a reduction and elimination of inefficiencies. In such a world it will be bargaining skills and not market structures that determine the distribution of wealth. If a monopolistic structure exists on one side of the market, the other side of the market will be organized to offset any power implied by the monopolistic structure. The organization of the other side of the market can be undertaken by members of that side or by rivals of the monopolistic structure that prevails on the first side. The co-existence of monopoly *power* and monopoly *structure* is possible only if the costs of negotiating are differentially positive, being lower for one set of sellers (or buyers) than it is for rival sellers (or buyers). If one set of sellers (or buyers) can organize those on the other side of the market more cheaply than can rivals, then price may be raised (or lowered) to the extent of the existing differential advantage in negotiating costs; this extent generally will be less than the simple monopoly price. In some cases the differential advantage in negotiating costs may be so great that price will settle at the monopoly (monopsony) level. This surely cannot be the general case, but the likelihood of it surely increases as the costs imposed on potential rivals increase; legally restricting entry is one way of raising the differential disadvantages to rivals; the economic meaning of restricting entry *is* increasing the cost of potential rivals of negotiating with and organizing buyers (or sellers).

The public policy question is which groups of market participants, *if any,* are to receive governmentally sponsored advantages and disadvantages, not only in the subsidization or taxation of production but, also, in the creation of advantages or disadvantages in conducting negotiations.

At this juncture, it should be emphasized that I have argued, not that regulatory commissions are undesirable, but that economic theory does not, at present, provide a justification for commissions insofar as they are based on the belief that observed concentration and monopoly price bear any necessary relationship.

Indeed, in utility industries, regulation has often been sought because of the inconvenience of competition. The history of regulation is often written in terms of the desire to prohibit "excessive" duplication of utility distribution systems and the desire to prohibit the capture of *windfall* gains by utility companies. Neither of these aspects of the utility business are necessarily related to scale economies. Let us first consider the problem of excessive duplication of facilities.

Duplication of Facilities

Communities and not individuals own or control most of the ground and air rights-of-way used by public utility distribution systems. The problem of excessive duplication of distribution systems is attributable to the failure of communities to set a proper price on the use of these scarce resources. The right to use publicly owned thoroughfares is the right to use a scarce resource. The absence of a price for the use of these resources, a price high enough to reflect the opportunity costs of such alternative uses as the servicing of uninterrupted traffic and unmarred views, will lead to their overutilization. The setting of an appropriate fee for the use of these resources would reduce the degree of duplication to optimal levels.

Consider that portion of the ground controlled by an individual and under which a *utility's* distribution system runs. Confront that individual with the option of service at a lower price from a company that is a rival to the present seller. The individual will take into consideration the cost to him of running a trench through his garden and the benefit to him of receiving the service at lower cost. There is no need for excessive duplication. Indeed, there is no need for any duplication of facilities if he selects the new service, provided that one of two conditions holds. If the *individual* owns that part of the distribution system running under his ground he could tie it in to whatever trunk line serves him best; alternatively, once the new company wins his patronage, a rational solution to the use of that part of the distribution system would be for the utility company owning it to sell it to the utility company now serving the buyer.

There may be good reasons for using community property rather than private property to house the main trunk lines of some utility distribution systems. The placement of such systems under or over streets, alleyways, and sidewalks, resources already publicly owned (a fact taken as datum here), may be less costly than routing them through private property. The failure of communities to charge fees for the use of public property, fees that tend to prevent excessive use of this property, can be explained in three ways.

(1) There was a failure to understand the prerequisities for efficient resource use. Some public officer must be given the incentives to act as a rational conservator of resources when these resources are scarce.

(2) The disruption of thoroughfares was not, in fact, costly enough to bother about.

(3) The setting of fees to curtail excessive use of thoroughfares by utility companies was too costly to be practical.

The first two explanations, if true, give no support to an argument for regulating utility companies. The third explanation may give support to some sort of regulation, for it asserts that the economic effects that are produced by the placing of distribution systems are such that it is too costly to economize through the use of a price system. The costs of taking account of these effects through some regulatory process must be compared with the benefits of realigning resource use, and if the benefits are worth the costs some regulation may be desirable. Note clearly: scale economies in serving a market are not at issue. To see this, imagine that electrical distribution systems are thin lines of a special conducting paint. The placing of such systems causes no difficulties. They are sprayed over either public or private property.

Nonetheless, suppose that the use of each system is subject to scale economies. Clearly, the desire to regulate cannot now be justified by such problems as traffic disruption, even though scale economies are present. "Excess" duplication is a problem of externalities and not of scale economies.

Let us suppose that it is desirable to employ some sort of regulation because it is too costly to use the price system to take account of the disruptive effects of placing distribution systems. Regulation comes in all sizes and shapes, and it is by no means clear what type of regulation would be most desirable.

A franchise system that allows only a limited number of utility companies to serve a market area was employed frequently. A franchise system that awarded the franchise to that company which seemed to offer the best price-quality package would be one that allowed market competition between bidding rivals to determine that package. The restraint of the market would be substituted for that of the regulatory commission.

An alternative arrangement would be public ownership of the distribution system. This would involve the collection of competing bids for installing the distribution system. The system could then be installed by the bidder offering to do the specified job at the lowest price. This is the same process used by communities to build highways and it employs rival bidding and not commissions to determine that price. The community could then allow its distribution system to be used by that utility company offering to provide specified utility services at lowest cost to residents. Again the market is substituted for the regulatory commission. Public ownership of streets may make public ownership of distribution systems seem desirable, but this does not mean that the use of regulatory commissions is desirable.

The Problem of Windfalls

We must now consider a last difficulty that has sometimes been marshalled to support the regulation of utilities. This argument is based on the fact that events in life are uncertain. The application of this observation to the utility business goes like this. After a buyer enters into an agreement with a utility company for supplying utility service, there may be changes in technology and prices that make the agreed upon price obsolete. In such cases, it is asserted, the price should be changed to reflect the current cost of providing utility services. The regulation by commission of prices on the basis of current costs is needed in the utilities industries because of the durability of original investments in plant and distribution systems. This durability prohibits the use of recontracting in the market place as a method for bringing about appropriate changes in price.

Problems of uncertainty create a potential for positive or negative windfalls. If market negotiations have misjudged the development of a better technology and if there is some cost to reawarding contracts to other producers once they are agreed upon, then an unexpected improvement in the technology used by those who are awarded the contracts may generate a price that is higher than per-unit cost, but higher by an amount no greater than the cost of reawarding contracts. In such cases, the firms now holding the contracts may collect a positive windfall for a short-run period. Or, if input prices increase by more than is expected, these same firms may suffer from a negative windfall. But the same thing is true of all markets. If a customer buys eggs today for consumption tomorrow, he will enjoy a positive windfall if the price of eggs is higher tomorrow and a negative windfall if the price is lower. The difference in the two cases is that, where long-term contracts are desirable, the windfalls may continue for longer periods. In such cases it *may* be desirable to employ a cost-plus regulatory scheme or to enter a clause that reserves the right, for some fee, to renegotiate the contract.

The problem faced here is what is the best way to cope with uncertainty. Long-term contracts for the supply of commodities are concluded satisfactorily in the market place without the aid of regulation. These contracts may be between retailers and appliance producers, or between the air lines and aircraft companies, all of whom may use durable production facilities. The rental of office space for ninety-nine years is fraught with uncertainty. I presume that the parties to a contract hire experts to provide relevant guesses on these matters and that the contract concluded resolves these issues in a way that is satisfactory to both parties. Penalties for reopening negotiations at a later date can be included in the contract. I presume that buyers and sellers who agree to contract with each other have handled the problem of uncertainty in a mutually satisfactory way. The correct way to view the problem is one of selecting the best type of contract. A producer may say, "if you agree to buy from me for twenty-five years, I can use facilities that are expected to produce the service at lower costs; if you contract five years, I will not invest much in tooling-up, and, hence, I will need a higher price to cover higher per-unit costs; of course, the longer-run contract allows more time for the unexpected, so let us include an escape clause of some kind." The buyer and seller must then agree on a suitable contract; durability of equipment and longer-term commitments can be sacrificed at the cost of higher per-unit costs, but there is no reason to expect that the concluded contract will be biased as to outcome or nonoptimal in other respects.

Cost-plus rate regulation is one way of coping with these problems, but it has great uncertainties of its own. Will the commission be effective? Does a well defined cost-plus arrangement create an inappropriate system of incentives to guide the firm in its investment and operating policies? Do the continual uncertainties associated with the meaning of cost-plus lead to otherwise avoidable difficulties in formulating investment plans? Rate regulation by commissions rather than by market rivalry may be more appropriate for utility industries than for other industries, but the truth of this assertion cannot be established deductively from existing economic theory. We do not know whether regulation handles the uncertainty-rent problem better or worse than the market.

The problem of coping with windfalls must be distinguished from the problem of *forecastable* rents. Suppose that it is known that buyers will incur considerable recontracting cost if they decide to change sellers after they are part way through an awarded contract. It would appear that the seller who wins the initial contract will be able to collect a rent as large as this recontracting cost. But this is not true if this recontracting cost is forecastable, that is, if it is not a windfall. The bidding for the initial contract will take account of the forecastable rent, so that if the bidding is competitive the rent will be forfeited by the lower bid prices to which it gives rise.

To what degree should legislation and regulation replace the market in the utilities or in other industries and what forms should such legislation take? It is not the objective of this paper to provide answers to such questions. My purpose has been to question the conventional economic arguments for the existing legislation and regulation. An expanded role for government can be defended on the empirical grounds of a documented general superiority of public administration in these industries or by a philosophical preference for mild socialism. But I do not see how a defense can be based on the formal arguments considered here; these arguments do not allow us to deduce from their assumptions either the monopoly problem or the administrative superiority of regulation.

In the case of utility industries, resort to the rivalry of the market place would relieve companies of the discomforts of commission regulation. But it would also relieve them of the comfort of legally protected market areas. It is my belief that the rivalry of the open market place disciplines more effectively than do the regulatory processes of the commission. If the managements of utility companies doubt this belief, I suggest that they re-examine the history of their industry to discover just who it was that provided most of the force behind the regulatory movement.

The Social Costs of Monopoly and Regulation

9

Richard A. Posner

When market price rises above the competitive level, consumers who continue to purchase the sellers' product at the new, higher price suffer a loss (L in fig. 1) exactly offset by the additional revenue that the sellers obtain at the higher price. Those who stop buying the product suffer a loss (D) not offset by any gain to the sellers. This is the "deadweight loss" from supracompetitive pricing and in traditional analysis its only social cost, L being regarded merely as a transfer from consumers to producers. Loss D, however, underestimates the social costs of monopoly. The existence of an opportunity to obtain monopoly profits will attract resources into efforts to obtain monopolies, and the opportunity costs of those resources are social costs of monopoly too (Tullock 1967). Theft provides an instructive analogy. The transfer of wealth from victim to thief involves no artificial limitation of output,[1] but it does not follow that the social cost of theft is zero. The opportunity for such transfers draws resources into thieving and in turn into protection against theft, and the opportunity costs of the resources consumed are social costs of theft (Tullock 1967; Becker 1968, p. 171, n. 3).

This sort of analysis has long been familiar in a few special contexts. Plant's criticism of the patent system, made more than a generation ago, was based on the effect of the patent monopoly in drawing greater resources into invention than into activities that yield only

Research on this paper was supported by a grant from the National Science Foundation to the National Bureau of Economic Research for research in law and economics. I am grateful to William F. Baxter, Gary S. Becker, Harold Demsetz, Victor R. Fuchs, William M. Landes, Sam Peltzman, and George J. Stigler for helpful comments on previous drafts of the paper. This version of the paper corrects the computational error pointed out by Göran Skogh.

Reprinted with permission from the *Journal of Political Economy* 83, no. 4 (August 1975): 807–27. © 1975 by The University of Chicago

[1] If a thief took three radios from a home and on the way out dropped one, which broke, the resulting loss would correspond to the deadweight loss of monopoly.

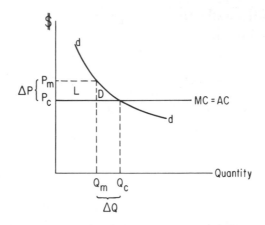

FIGURE 1. Social costs of supracompetitive pricing

competitive returns (Plant 1934). Telser's theory of resale price maintenance is in the same vein (Telser 1960), as is the literature on nonprice
competition among members of a cartel (Stigler 1968, pp. 23–28;
Douglas and Miller 1974). But, while the tendency of monopoly rents
to be transformed into costs is no longer a novel insight, its implications both for the measurement of the aggregate social costs of monopoly and for a variety of other important issues relating to monopoly and
public regulation (including tax policy) continue for the most part to be
ignored. The present paper is an effort to rectify this neglect.[2]

Part I presents a simple model of the social costs of monopoly,
conceived as the sum of the deadweight loss and the additional loss resulting from the competition to become a monopolist. Part II uses the
model to estimate the social costs of monopoly in the United States and
the social benefits of antitrust enforcement. The estimates are crude;
their primary value may simply be to induce skepticism about the
existing empirical literature on the social costs of monopoly. Part III
considers the implications of the analysis for several qualitative issues
relating to monopoly and public regulation.

I. A Model of the Social Costs of Monopoly

A. Assumptions

The critical assumptions underlying the model are the following:

1. Obtaining a monopoly is itself a competitive activity, so that,
at the margin, the cost of obtaining a monopoly is exactly equal to the

[2] See Krueger (1974) for a parallel approach to the measurement of the social
costs of import licenses in India and Turkey.

expected profit of being a monopolist. An important corollary of this assumption is that there are no intramarginal monopolies—no cases, that is, where the expected profits of monopoly exceed the total supply price of the inputs used to obtain the monopoly. If there were such an excess, competition in the activity of obtaining the monopoly would induce the competing firms (or new entrants) to hire additional inputs in an effort to engross the additional monopoly profits.

2. The long-run supply of all inputs used in obtaining monopolies is perfectly elastic. Hence, the total supply price of these inputs includes no rents.

3. The costs incurred in obtaining a monopoly have no socially valuable by-products.

The first two assumptions assure that all expected monopoly rents are transformed into social costs, and the third that these costs do not generate any social benefits.[3] But how reasonable are such assumptions?

1. The first is a standard assumption of economics and, pending better evidence than we have, seems a reasonable one in the present context. Anyone can try to obtain a patent, a certificate of public convenience and necessity, a television license, a tariff, an import quota, or a minimum-wage law; and anyone can try to form a cartel with his competitors or, if he is a member of a cartelized industry, try to engross a greater share of the monopoly profits of the industry.[4] Nonprice competition in the airline industry illustrates the last point. If the Civil Aeronautics Board places a floor under airline prices that exceeds the marginal cost of providing air transportation under competitive conditions, the situation initially is as depicted in figure 2 and is unstable. Since nonprice competition is not constrained, the airlines will expend resources on such competition (better service, etc.) until the marginal costs of air transportation rise to the level (P in fig. 2) where the industry is earning only a normal return (see Douglas and Miller 1974). The result will be the transformation of the monopoly profits initially generated by the regulatory price floor—the shaded rectangle—into higher costs for the industry. The demand curve shifts to the right because the increased expenditures on service improve the product from the standpoint of the consumer. But the additional consumer surplus is not great enough to offset the higher costs—otherwise the higher level of service would have been provided without the spur of monopoly pricing.

If nonprice competition were forbidden (say, at zero cost) or were

---

[3] Another assumption, but one that does not affect the analysis, is that the monopoly is enjoyed for one period only; otherwise the optimum expenditures on obtaining a monopoly could not be compared directly with L in fig. 1.

[4] Other than by reducing price, a method of obtaining a larger share of the cartel's profits that would not involve a socially wasteful use of resources.

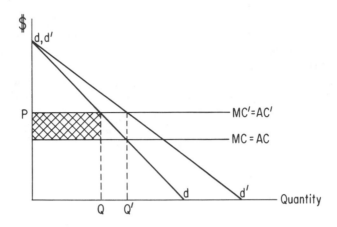

FIGURE 2. Nonprice competition when market price exceeds competitive level

somehow not feasible, it would not follow that our assumption that monopolizing is a competitive activity would be overthrown. It would mean simply that the expected profits of the airline business would be greater than if the airlines could expect those profits to be dissipated in nonprice competition. Hence, more resources would be devoted to obtaining a license from the CAB in the first place. The expected profits from monopoly pricing of air transportation would still be zero.

2. Although the assumption that obtaining monopolies involves constant costs seems plausible as a first approximation—there seems little reason to think that it involves using resources whose long-run supply is inelastic—a more important point is that the assumption may not be a crucial one. Assume that suppliers of inputs into monopolizing do obtain rents. In the long run, the availability of such rents will attract additional resources into the production of those inputs, and these resources will be wasted from a social standpoint. Some possible exceptions are considered in part III(7). Clearly, however, the production function of monopolies requires greater attention that I give it in this paper. The assumption of a perfectly elastic long-run supply may fail for an input as foreign to conventional economic analysis as political power.

3. In the airline example, the expenditures on monopolizing had a socially valuable by-product (improved service), although the value was less than its cost. However, the possibility that expenditures on monopolizing will yield such by-products will be ignored in the development of the model, and its principal relevance, therefore, is to methods of monopolizing that have little or no social value. The formation of a cartel, the procuring of a tariff or other protective legislation, and the

merging of competing firms in a market to produce a monopoly (where the merger does not enable economies of scale or other efficiencies to be realized) are examples of such methods. (Even in these cases, there will be some socially valuable by-products [e.g., information] if, for example, the cartel agreement fails to limit nonprice competition.) At the opposite extreme, obtaining a monopoly by cutting costs or prices or by innovation will normally yield social benefits greater than the expenditures on monopolizing.

Several more preliminary points should be noted briefly.

1. Legal and illegal monopolies must be distinguished. The threat of punishment can be used to increase the expected costs of monopolizing and thereby reduce the amount of resources invested in the activity. To the extent that enforcers' resources are merely substituted for monopolizers', there will be no social savings (see Becker 1971, p. 101); but the literature on punishment (e.g., Becker 1968) suggests that activities such as monopolizing can be deterred at low social cost by combining heavy monetary penalties (i.e., transfer payments) with modest resources devoted to apprehending and convicting offenders.[5] Hence, under an optimum system of penalties, the social costs of *illegal* monopolies might be quite low.

2. As an extension of the last point, note that the observed monopoly profits in an industry may actually underestimate the social costs of monopoly in that industry. Considerable resources may have been expended by consumers or enforcers to reduce those profits. Monopoly profits in an industry could be zero, yet the social costs of monopoly in that industry very high, if enforcement of antimonopoly measures were both expensive and effective.

3. Given uncertainty, the expected monopoly profits of any firm seeking a monopoly may be much smaller than the actual monopoly profits, and so will its expenditures. If 10 firms are vying for a monopoly having a present value of $1 million, and each of them has an equal chance of obtaining it and is risk neutral, each will spend $100,000 (assuming constant costs) on trying to obtain the monopoly. Only one will succeed, and *his* costs will be much smaller than the monopoly profits, but the total costs of obtaining the monopoly—counting losers' expenditures as well as winners'—will be the same as under certainty. If the market for monopoly is in fact characterized by a high degree of uncertainty, this would explain why the costs of obtaining monopoly have largely eluded detection. Most of the costs are incurred in unsuccessful

---

[5]This could, to be sure, merely shift the problem to a new level: the opportunity to obtain substantial rents from apprehending and convicting monopolists will induce enforcers to pour resources into enforcement activities. This problem is analyzed in Landes and Posner (1975).

efforts to obtain a monopoly—the lobbying campaign that fails, the unsuccessful attempt to obtain a bank charter or form a cartel.

    4. It might seem that where monopoly is obtained by bribery of
government officials, the additional loss of monopoly with which this
paper is concerned would be eliminated, since a bribe is a pure transfer. In fact, however, bribery merely shifts the monopoly profits from
the monopolist to the officials receiving the bribe and draws real resources into the activity of becoming an official who is in a position to
receive these bribes (Krueger 1974, pp. 292–93).

B. The Model

Given the assumptions explained above, the total social costs of mo-
nopoly prices in figure 1 are simply $D + L$, and since $D \simeq \frac{1}{2}\Delta P\Delta Q$
and $L = \Delta P(Q_c - \Delta Q)$, the relative sizes of D and L are given by

$$\frac{D}{L} \simeq \frac{\Delta Q}{2(Q_c - \Delta Q)}. \tag{1}$$

This ratio can also be expressed in terms of the elasticity of demand for
the product in question at the competitive price and the percentage
increase in price brought about by monopolization (p):

$$\frac{D}{L} \simeq \frac{p}{2(1/\varepsilon - p)}. \tag{2}$$

The partial derivatives are

$$\frac{\partial(D/L)}{\partial\varepsilon} \simeq \frac{2p}{(2 - 2p\varepsilon)^2} > 0;$$

$$\tag{3}$$

$$\frac{\partial(D/L)}{\partial p} \simeq \frac{2\varepsilon}{(2 - 2p\varepsilon)^2} > 0.$$

In words, the ratio of D to L is smaller, the less elastic the demand for
the industry's product at the competitive price and the smaller the percentage price increase over the competitive level. At moderate elasticities and percentage price increases, D is only a small fraction of L
(and hence of the total costs of monopoly). For example, at an elasticity
of one[6] and a price increase over the competitive level of 10 percent, D
is only 5.6 percent of L.

---

    [6]Throughout this paper, ΔQ is treated as a positive number. Therefore, ε
$[= (\Delta Q/\Delta P)/(Q/P)]$ is also positive.

Observe that the model does *not* assume that the actual supra-competitive price being charged (P_m in fig. 1) is the optimum monopoly price for the industry (otherwise the supracompetitive price increase would not be determined independently of the elasticity of demand, as in [2]). The rationale of this procedure is that perfect monopoly is presumably rare; it will, however, be considered as a special case later.

Using R_c to denote total sales revenues at the competitive price, C, the total social costs of monopoly, is approximated by

$$D + L = pR_c - \tfrac{1}{2}\Delta P \Delta Q \qquad (4a)$$

$$= R_c(p - \tfrac{1}{2}\varepsilon p^2). \qquad (4b)$$

The partial derivatives of C are (approximately)

$$\frac{\partial C}{\partial R_c} = p - \tfrac{1}{2}\varepsilon p^2 > 0 \text{ iff } \varepsilon p < 2;$$

$$\frac{\partial C}{\partial p} = R_c(1 - \varepsilon p) > 0 \text{ iff } \varepsilon p < 1; \qquad (5)$$

$$\frac{\partial C}{\partial \varepsilon} = -\tfrac{1}{2}p^2 R_c < 0.$$

In words, the social costs of monopoly will usually—not always—be higher, the larger the industry's sales revenues at the competitive price and output and the greater the percentage price increase over the competitive level. And they will always be higher, the less elastic the demand for the product at the competitive price—the costs of monopoly being greatest when demand is totally inelastic at the competitive price.

Formulas (2) and (4b) are accurate only for small changes in the price level. Yet monopolization might result in large price increases. Hence (1) and (4a) remain useful. For purposes of empirical estimation, it is helpful to derive two additional formulas: one for the case where data on the deadweight loss, the elasticity of demand, and the monopoly price increase are available and the elasticity of demand is assumed to be constant, and the other for the case where data on the monopoly price increase, the monopoly output, and the elasticity of demand at the monopoly price are available and the demand curve is assumed to be linear.

1. For the case of constant elasticity, let $k \equiv P_c/P_m$ and $R_m \equiv$ total sales revenue at the monopoly price and output. Then, since $Q_c \equiv$

$\alpha P_c^{-\varepsilon}$ and $Q_m = \alpha P_m^{-\varepsilon}$, and therefore $\Delta Q = \alpha(P_c^{-\varepsilon} - P_m^{-\varepsilon})$, D/L and C are approximately

$$\frac{D}{L} = \frac{(kP_m)^{-\varepsilon} - P_m^{-\varepsilon}}{2P_m^{-\varepsilon}} = \frac{k^{-\varepsilon} - 1}{2}; \tag{6}$$

$$C = D + L = D\left(1 + \frac{2}{k^{-\varepsilon} - 1}\right) = R_m(1 - k)\left(\frac{k^{-\varepsilon} + 1}{2}\right).^{\,7} \tag{7}$$

The partial derivatives of D/L are (approximately)

$$\frac{\partial(D/L)}{\partial k} = \frac{-\varepsilon}{2k^{\varepsilon+1}} < 0;$$

$$\frac{\partial(D/L)}{\partial \varepsilon} = \frac{-k^{-\varepsilon} \ln k}{2} > 0. \tag{8}$$

In words, the ratio of the deadweight loss of monopoly to the additional loss is smaller, the smaller the monopoly price increase (k, the ratio of the competitive to the monopoly price, is larger, the smaller the relative price increase) and greater, the more elastic the demand.

2. For the case where the elasticity of demand at the monopoly price (as well as the monopoly price increase and the quantity sold at

---

[7] For the special case where the firm is able to charge the optimum monopoly price for the industry, so that $P_c = MC = P_m(1 - 1/\varepsilon)$, equation (6) becomes

$$\frac{D}{L} = \frac{(1 - 1/\varepsilon)^{-\varepsilon} - 1}{2} \tag{6'}$$

and equation (7) becomes

$$C = \frac{R_m[(1 - 1/\varepsilon)^{-\varepsilon} + 1]}{2\varepsilon}. \tag{7'}$$

Since a demand curve of constant elasticity is nonlinear, the question arises whether the linear approximation of the deadweight loss used in equations (6) and (7) (and [6'] and [7']) introduces a source of serious inaccuracy. It appears not to, at least in the simple case where $\varepsilon = 1$ and therefore

$$\frac{D}{L} = \frac{\int_{Q_m}^{Q_c} P\, dQ - P_c\, \Delta Q}{(P_m - P_c)Q_m} = \frac{\ln(1/k) - 1 + k}{1 - k}. \tag{6''}$$

Table 1, which compares D/L as calculated from equation (6) (with $\varepsilon = 1$) and from equation (6''), shows that the linear approximation overestimates the deadweight loss, but not seriously.

TABLE 1.

P*	D/L†	
(%)	Eq. (6)	Eq. (6″)
5	.025	.025
10	.050	.049
15	.075	.072
20	.100	.094
50	.250	.216

*Monopoly price increase.
†Ratio of deadweight to additional loss.

the monopoly price) is known or can be computed, and the demand curve can be approximated by a straight line, we begin by determining the slope of the demand curve at the monopoly price:

$$\frac{\Delta Q}{\Delta P} = \frac{\varepsilon Q_m}{P_m}. \tag{9}$$

Since the slope of a linear demand curve is constant, this equation can be used to find ΔQ and hence C and D/L:

$$C = R_m(1 - k)[1 + \tfrac{1}{2}\varepsilon(1 - k)]; \tag{10}$$

$$\frac{D}{L} = \frac{\varepsilon(1 - k)}{2}. \tag{11}$$ [8]

The estimates produced by our two formulas for the ratio of the deadweight to the additional loss from monopoly—equations (6) and (11)—turn out not to be very different for price increases of less than 25 percent, and even for much larger price increases if the elasticity of demand is no greater than one (see fig. 3).

[8] In the special case where the firm is able to charge the optimum monopoly price,

$$C = \frac{3R_m}{2\varepsilon}; \tag{10'}$$

$$\frac{D}{L} = \frac{1}{2}. \tag{11'}$$

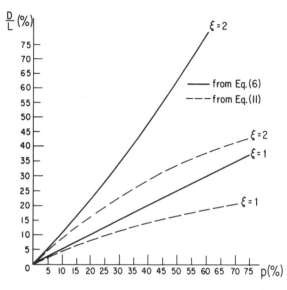

FIGURE 3. Ratio of deadweight to additional loss of monopoly, for different price increases and demand elasticities.

II. Empirical Estimates

The formulas developed in the preceding part can be used to derive, from the estimates of the deadweight loss of monopoly made by Arnold Harberger and others, an estimate of the total social cost of monopoly. Harberger (1954), estimating an average monopoly price increase of about 6 percent and assuming that the elasticity of demand was constant and equal to unity, found the deadweight loss from monopoly in the manufacturing sector to be equal to (at most) 0.1 percent of GNP. Harberger's (implicit) k is 0.9434, and from equation (6) the ratio of D to L in Harberger's analysis is, therefore, 0.03. Hence, if D is 0.1 percent of GNP, L is about 3.3 percent and C about 3.4 percent of GNP. Schwartzman (1960) used similar methods and found D equal to about 0.1 percent of GNP too. But he assumed a price increase of 8.3 percent and an elasticity of demand of 1.5. Plugging these values into equation (6) yields $D/L = 0.06$. Hence, if $D = 0.1$ percent of GNP, $L = 1.7$ percent and $C = 1.8$ percent.

Neither estimate can be given much credence, however, because of the method that both Harberger and Schwartzman employed to determine the monopoly price increase. Persistently above average rates of return were used both (1) to identify the monopolized industries and (2) to calculate the monopoly price increase. If the approach of this paper is correct, such a procedure is improper, especially the second step. Because of uncertainty, many monopolists may enjoy supernormal rates of return ex post, but those rates will understate the percentage of the monopolist's revenues that is attributable to monopoly pricing, unless no cost whatever was incurred in obtaining (or maintaining) the monopoly.[9]

A better method of calculating the social costs of monopoly (deadweight plus additional loss) is to obtain from industry studies estimates of the monopoly price increase and of the elasticity of demand at the relevant points along the demand curve. An independent estimate of the elasticity of demand would be unnecessary if we could assume that, after the price increase, the price charged was the optimum monopoly price; and where an independent estimate of ε is available, it can serve as a check on that assumption. To illustrate, there have been a number of estimates of the percentage by which CAB regulation has increased the price of airline travel. The simple average of these estimates is .66 (computed from Caves 1962, p. 372; Jordan 1970, pp. 110–11, 124–25; and Yale Law Journal 1965, pp. 1435–36). If a 66 percent price increase over competitive levels is assumed to raise the price of air travel to the optimum monopoly level, then the elasticity of demand at the monopoly price can be calculated, from the formula which equates marginal cost to marginal revenue,[10] to be 2.5 at the monopoly price. An independent estimate of the long-run elasticity of demand for air travel made by Houthakker and Taylor (1966, p. 124) is 2.36,[11] which is virtually identical to my calculation.

If we assume a constant elasticity of 2.5 and solve for D/L using equation (6'), $D = 1.29L$, and (from equation [7']) it is readily calculable that the total social cost of the airline monopoly is equal to 92 percent of the total revenue of the industry at the monopoly price. However, the assumption of a linear demand curve seems more plausible than the assumption of constant elasticity, especially for large

[9]This point is distinct from the (also valid) objections to Harberger's procedure raised by Stigler (1956)—that monopoly profits are often capitalized into the valuation of a firm's assets and that some of the profits may be received as rents by suppliers of the firm's inputs.

[10]This was essentially the procedure used by Kamerschen (1966) to estimate the deadweight loss from monopoly in manufacturing. He has been criticized, rightly, for assuming that firms in concentrated industries subject to the Sherman Act's prohibition of collusive pricing are typically able to charge the profit-maximizing monopoly price. The assumption is more plausible with regard to a regulated industry in which entry and price competition are limited by the regulatory agency and the Sherman Act is inapplicable.

[11]This is presumably the elasticity of demand at the regulated price, since only a small part of the airline industry is exempt from CAB regulation.

relative price increases, which one expects to find associated with a rising elasticity of demand as substitutes become increasingly attractive. If, therefore, equations (10′) and (11′) are used instead of (6′) and (7′), $D = 0.5L$ and $C = 0.6R_m$—still a very large social loss from the regulation-induced airline monopoly. (These estimates ignore, however, the partially off-setting benefits of excessive nonprice competition in the airline industry.)

All of the previous studies of the cost of monopoly to the economy have been based on supposed monopoly pricing in manufacturing alone. Yet the ability of firms to maintain supracompetitive prices must be greater in industries in which a regulatory agency limits entry and price competition than in the manufacturing sector, where express collusion is forbidden by the Sherman Act. Table 2 collects estimates of the regulation-induced price increase and the elasticity of demand at the current price for several industries for which these data are available. Two estimates of elasticity are given: one (ε_1) is derived from the price-increase data, on the assumption that the industry is charging the optimum monopoly price; the other (ε_2) is an independent estimate of elasticity. The estimates of the total social costs of the regulation in question (C_1, where ε_1 is the estimate of elasticity used, and C_2, where ε_2 is used) are based on the assumption that the industry's demand curve is linear in the relevant region and are expressed as a percentage of the total revenues of the industry.

TABLE 2.   Social Costs of Regulation

Industry	Regulatory Price Increase (%)	Elasticity ε_1	Elasticity ε_2	Costs (as % of Industry's Sales) C_1*	Costs (as % of Industry's Sales) C_2*
Physicians' services	.40†	3.500	0.575‡	.42	.31
Eyeglasses	.34§	0.394	0.450‖	.39	.24
Milk	.11#	10.000	0.339**	.15	.10
Motor carriers	.62††	2.630	1.140‡‡	.57	.30
Oil	.65§§	2.500	0.900§§	.60	.32
Airlines	.66	2.500	2.360	.60	.19

*C_1 based on ε_1; C_2 based on ε_2.
†Kessel 1972, p. 119.
‡Houthakker and Taylor 1966, p. 99 (short run).
§Benham 1973, p. 19.
‖Benham 1973, p. 30 (simple average).
#Kessel 1967, p. 73.
**Houthakker 1965, p. 286. This estimate is for all food; an estimate limited to dairy products in the Netherlands was not significantly different (Ayaynian 1969).
††Average estimates in Department of Agriculture studies cited in Moore (1972) and Farmer (1964).
‡‡Simple averages of various estimates for transportation in Scandinavia (see Frisch 1959 and Parks 1969, p. 649).
§§Cabinet Task Force on Oil Import Control 1970.

These estimates are, of course, very crude, but they do suggest that the total costs of regulation may be extremely high, given that about 17 percent of GNP originates in industries—such as agriculture, transportation, communications, power, banking, insurance, and medical services—that contain the sorts of controls over competition that might be expected to lead to supracompetitive prices.[12] Indeed, the costs of regulation probably exceed the costs of private monopoly. To be sure, a higher percentage of GNP—30 percent—originates in manufacturing and mining, a highly concentrated sector of the economy, and the conventional wisdom associates high concentration with supracompetitive pricing. But only about one-fifth of the output of this sector comes from industries in which four firms account for 60 percent or more of sales, and there is little theoretical basis for believing that the sellers in less concentrated industries could collude effectively without engaging in behavior prohibited by the Sherman Act.[13] Not all violations of the Sherman Act are detected and punished, but the secret conspiracies that escape detection are probably not very effective— even the great electrical conspiracy, an elaborate and relatively durable conspiracy among a very small group of firms, apparently succeeded in raising prices by less than 10 percent on average (see U.S. Congress 1965, p. 39). It would be surprising if the price level of the manufacturing and mining sector as a whole were more than about 2 percent above the competitive level.[14] Assume that it is 2 percent, and that the average elasticity of demand for the products of this sector, at current prices, is 1.1607.[15] Then the total social costs of monopoly in this sector are 1.9 percent of the total revenues generated in the sector (from

[12] Of course, not all of the markets in the regulated industries are in fact subject to the relevant regulatory controls (almost half of the trucking industry, for example, is exempt from regulation by the Interstate Commerce Commission). On the other hand, tariffs and similar restrictions (e.g., the oil import quota) are excluded from the estimate of the percentage of GNP affected by regulation.

[13] Thus, Kessel's study of underwriting costs (1971, p. 723) shows that an increase beyond eight in the number of bids does not reduce those costs substantially—and an industry where the four largest firms have less than 60 percent of the market is apt to contain at least eight significant competitors.

[14] If we assume that only in industries where the four-firm concentration ratio exceeds 60 percent is effective, undetected collusion likely, and that collusion allows these industries to maintain prices, on average, 5 percent above the competitive level while in the rest of the manufacturing and mining sector the average price level is only 1 percent above the competitive level, then average prices for the entire sector would be only 1.83 percent above the competitive price level. (Statistics on the distribution of output among industries in different four-firm concentration ratio groups are from the 1963 Census of Manufactures.)

[15] This figure is a simple average of the long-run price elasticities for nine product groups within the manufacturing and mining sector estimated in Houthakker and Taylor (1966, pp. 72, 74, 83, 112–14, 116, 128–31).

equation [10]). This amounts to a total dollar loss substantially smaller than that generated in the regulated sector.[16] And this is true even if we assume that prices in the manufacturing and mining sector are, on average, 4 percent above the competitive level, rather than 2 percent.[17]

This comparison excludes, of course, both the relative costs of regulation and of antitrust enforcement and the relative benefits of monopoly in the two sectors.[18] Were these additional factors included, however, it is doubtful that the comparison would become more favorable to the regulated sector. In particular, while there are theoretical reasons for believing that concentration in unregulated markets is associated with economies of scale and other efficiencies (Demsetz 1973), there is no accepted theory or body of evidence that ascribes social benefits to regulation limiting entry and price competition.

The analysis developed here can also be used to estimate the social benefits of the antitrust laws. Table 3, which is constructed on the same basis as table 2, presents estimates of the social costs of several well-organized (mainly international) private cartels.[19]

Presumably, collusive price increases of this magnitude and the attendant very substantial social costs are deterred by current enforcement of the American antitrust laws. A complete cost-benefit analysis of the antitrust laws would, however, also require estimation of (1) the costs of administrating those laws[20] and (2) the large social costs imposed by the many perverse applications of antitrust laws that are, perhaps, an inevitable by-product of having such laws.

A very large disclaimer concerning the accuracy of the estimates presented in this part of the paper needs to be entered at this point.

[16]The simple average of the social-cost estimates presented in table 2 is 34.9 percent of the total revenues of the regulated industry. Assuming that 50 percent of the output of that sector is produced in markets that are regulated in a manner similar to the industries in table 2 and that the average social cost of regulation in each such market is 34.9 percent of total revenue, the social costs of regulation would be equal to 3.0 percent of GNP, while the social costs of monopoly in manufacturing and mining would be equal to 0.6 percent of GNP.

[17]In which event the social costs of monopoly in that sector would be about 1.2 percent of GNP.

[18]To recur to an earlier point, the assumed monopoly price increase in the manufacturing and mining sector may underestimate the social costs of monopoly in that sector. Those costs may be reflected in expenditures by consumers and enforcers in preventing monopoly pricing.

[19]As distinct from the sorts of covert conspiracies that might escape detection under present enforcement of the Sherman Act (see Stigler 1968, pp. 268–70).

[20]A point to be kept in mind is that, while these costs are incurred annually, private—unlike governmentally protected—cartels eventually collapse (although they often re-form later). Hence, table 3 gives an exaggerated picture of the *average* annual costs of cartelization as it would exist in the absence of the Sherman Act.

TABLE 3.   Social Costs of Cartelization

Industry	Cartel Price Increase (%)	Elasticity		Costs (as % of Industry's Sales)	
		ε_1	ε_2	C_1	C_2
Nitrogen	0.75*	2.3256	1.4493†	.62	.30
Sugar	0.30‡	4.3276	0.3390§	.36	.22
Aluminum	1.00‖	2.0000	—	.75	—
Aluminum	0.38#	3.6311	—	.42	—
Rubber	1.00**	2.0000	—	.75	—
Electric bulbs	0.37††	3.7023	—	.42	—
Copper	0.31‡‡	4.2499	—	.36	—
Cast-iron pipe	0.39§§	3.5641	—	.42	—

* Stocking and Watkins 1946, p. 163.
† Stocking and Watkins 1946, p. 166.
‡ Stocking and Watkins 1946, p. 46.
§ Houthakker 1965, p. 286; obviously a much too low estimate for one food product sold at a cartel price!
‖ Stocking and Watkins 1946, p. 228.
Stocking and Watkins 1946, p. 251.
** Stocking and Watkins 1946, p. 64–65.
†† Stocking and Watkins 1946, p. 343.
‡‡ Stocking and Watkins 1946, p. 127.
§§ United States v. Addyston Pipe & Steel Co., 85 F. 271 (6th Cir. 1898).

Quite apart from any reservations about the realism of the assumptions on which the model used to generate these estimates is based, the crudeness of the data on price increases and elasticities of demand precludes treating the estimates of the costs of the monopoly and regulation as anything more than suggestive. The suggestions are, however, interesting ones: (1) previous studies of the costs of monopoly may have grossly underestimated those costs; and (2) the costs of monopoly are quite probably much greater in the regulated than in the unregulated sector of the economy, despite the greater size of the latter sector.

III. Other Applications

1. In a recent paper Comanor and Smiley (1975) attempt to show that a large part of the inequality in the distribution of wealth in contemporary America is attributable to monopoly. They use studies such as Harberger's (1954) to determine the aggregate wealth transfer from consumers to the owners of monopoly firms and, by a series of additional assumptions concerning the incomes of consumers and shareholders, family size, the savings rate, etc., derive an estimate of the distributive impact of monopoly. Many of the assumptions are questionable, but even if their correctness were conceded the conclusion

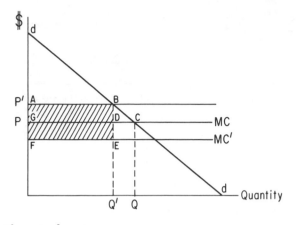

FIGURE 4. The costs of mergers

would be highly doubtful. There is no reason to think that monopoly has a significant distributive effect. Consumers' wealth is not transferred to the shareholders of monopoly firms; it is dissipated in the purchase of inputs into the activity of becoming a monopolist.

2. Oliver Williamson (1968) has argued that the refusal of the courts to recognize a defense of economies of scale in merger cases under the Clayton Act is questionable because, under plausible assumptions concerning the elasticity of demand, only a small reduction in the merging firms' costs is necessary to offset any deadweight loss created by the price increase that the merger enables the firms to make (see fig. 4).

This analysis is incomplete, however. The expected profits of the merger (*ABEF*) will generate an equivalent amount of costs as the firms vie to make such mergers or, after they are made, to engross the profits generated by the higher postmerger price through service competition or whatever. As a first approximation, the total social cost of the merger is *ABEF* + *BCD* and exceeds the cost savings (*GDEF*) made possible by it. The curves could, of course, be drawn in such a way that the merger would generate net cost savings; the point is only that there is no presumption that anticompetitive mergers generate net savings. This consideration, together with the high cost of litigating issues of cost savings, may provide a justification for refusing to recognize a defense of efficiencies in merger cases where the merger is likely to produce a substantial increase in monopoly power.

3. It has been argued (e.g., Bowman 1973) that the antitrust laws should not concern themselves with practices that are merely methods of price discrimination, since there is no basis for thinking that discrim-

ination increases the deadweight loss of monopoly, and it may reduce it (it will reduce it to zero if discrimination is perfect). The conclusion may be justifiable by reference to the costs of administering anti-discrimination rules, but the basis on which it has been defended by its proponents is incorrect. Even when price discrimination is perfect, so that the deadweight loss of monopoly is zero, the total social costs of a discriminating monopoly are greater than those of a single-price monopoly.[21] Under perfect price discrimination, C is the entire area between the demand curve and the marginal (= average) cost curve, and it is greater than $D + L$ at any single price (see fig. 1).

4. It is occasionally suggested that the case for antitrust enforcement has been gravely weakened by the theory of the second best. Since the elimination of one monopoly in an economy containing other monopolies (or other sources of divergence between price and marginal cost, such as taxation) may reduce the efficiency of resource allocation, antitrust enforcement may increase, rather than reduce, D. The true economic basis for antitrust enforcement, however, is not D but $D + L$, and we have seen that, under plausible assumptions as to the elasticity of demand, D is only a small fraction of $D + L$, at least for moderate increases in price above the competitive level. The social costs measured by L, like the social costs of theft (i.e., the opportunity costs of thieves' and policemen's time and of the labor and capital inputs into locks, burglar tools, etc.), are unaffected by the existence of second-best problems (cf. Markovits 1972).

5. The analysis in this paper suggests a possible explanation for the positive correlation that has been found between concentration and advertising.[22] It may be easier to collude on price than on the amount of advertising. Although there is no great trick to establishing an agreed-upon level of advertising and detecting departures from it, the incentives to violate any such agreement are strong, because the gains from a successful advertising campaign may be difficult to offset immediately and hence offer promise of a more durable advantage than a price cut would. In that event the situation is similar to nonprice competition in the airline industry. If price is fixed by the cartel but the level of advertising is not, or at least not effectively, the monopoly profits generated by the cartel price will be transformed into additional expenditures on advertising. Cartelization is presumably more common in concentrated industries.

[21] I abstract from the costs of administering the price-discrimination scheme; these increase the costs of discriminating monopoly relative to those of nondiscriminating monopoly.

[22] The finding has been questioned, however (e.g., Ekelund and Gramm 1970).

This analysis suggests, incidentally, a possible difficulty in distinguishing empirically between Telser's theory of resale price maintenance (1960) and an alternative explanation which stresses cartelization by dealers. In Telser's theory, manufacturers impose resale price maintenance in order to induce dealers to provide services in connection with the resale of the manufacturer's brand. If Telser's theory is correct, we would expect to find resale price maintenance imposed where the efficient merchandising of a product involved the provision of extensive point-of-sale services. However, a dealer's cartel might also result in the dealers' competing away the cartel profits through service competition.

6. Discussions of the "social responsibility" of large corporations generally assume that a firm (or group of firms) having some monopoly power could, without courting bankruptcy, decide to incur somewhat higher costs in order to discharge its social responsibilities. Thus, in figure 1, even if MC rose to P_m the firm would still be covering its costs. However, if the analysis in this paper is correct and the expected profits of monopolizing are zero, it follows that the entire area L in figure 1 will represent fixed costs to the firm unless the monopoly was obtained under conditions of uncertainty. In the latter case the fixed costs will be somewhat lower, but in the former *any* increase in MC will jeopardize the firm's solvency.

7. Assuming that the decision to create or tolerate a monopoly has been made, it may still be possible to prevent the expected monopoly profits from being completely transformed into social costs. The basic technique is to reduce the elasticity of supply of the inputs into monopolizing. (Thus, the present discussion modifies my original assumption of perfect supply elasticity.) Consider, for example, a market that is a natural monopoly. If the monopolist is permitted to charge a monopoly price—and suppose that he is—he may set a price that exceeds the average costs of new entrants, albeit those costs are higher than his; and new entry will presumably occur. The resulting increase in the average costs of serving the market is an example of the social costs of monopoly (independent of the welfare triangle). These costs can be reduced, however, by a rule limiting entry. Such a rule will reduce the responsiveness of a key input into monopolizing—capacity to produce the monopolized product—to increases in the expected value of the monopoly. But the rule is not very satisfactory. Prospective entrants will have an incentive to expend resources on persuading the agency to change or waive the rule—and the monopolist to expend them on dissuasion. Moreover, the more efficient the rule is at keeping out new entrants at low cost to the monopolist, the greater will be the expected value of having a natural monopoly—and, hence, the greater

will be the resources that firms expend on trying to become the first to occupy a natural-monopoly market.[23]

As another example, consider the recurrent proposal to replace the present method of assigning television licenses (now awarded to the applicant who convinces the Federal Communications Commission in a formal hearing of his superior ability to serve the public interest) by an auction system. This proposal is frequently supported on distributive grounds—why should the licensee, rather than the public, receive the rents generated by the limited allocation of electromagnetic spectrum for broadcasting? But there is also an efficiency justification for the proposal. The auction would substitute a transfer payment for a real cost, the expenditures on the hearing process by competing applicants. To be sure, these expenditures might simply be redirected into rigging the bidding. But this could be discouraged, possibly at low cost, by appropriate legal penalties. The objective would be to increase the expected costs of obtaining the license (other than by an honest bid), which include any expected punishment costs, to the point where the applicants are induced to make the costless transfer rather than to expend real resources on trying to obtain the license outside the auction process. As mentioned earlier, in an optimum system of penalties the resources expended on enforcement would be slight.

The patent laws embody a somewhat similar economizing technique. In their absence inventors would expend substantial resources on preserving the secrecy of their inventions. Their efforts in this direction would generate indirect as well as direct social costs, by retarding the spread of knowledge. By providing a legal remedy against "stealing" inventions, the patent laws reduce the level of such expenditures in much the same way as the existence of legal penalties for theft reduces the level of resources that people devote to protecting their property from thieves.

An interesting method of reducing the social costs of monopoly is used by labor unions. The existence of a monopoly wage might be expected to induce the expenditure of more and more resources by workers seeking entry into the union, until the expected benefits of union membership were reduced to zero. However, unions traditionally have rationed membership in a way that greatly reduces the marginal benefits of expenditures on obtaining membership, and hence the resources expended in that pursuit, by conditioning membership on a status that is difficult or impossible for the job seeker to buy at any price—such as

[23]This is the obverse of the situation discussed in Demsetz (1968), where competition to become a monopolist results in a competitive price level.

being white or the son of a union member.[24] In the limit, this method of rationing would reduce the elasticity of the supply of inputs into obtaining union membership, and hence the social costs of labor monopolies (excluding the welfare triangle), to zero, disregarding the costs resulting from the exclusion of possibly better qualified workers who do not meet the membership criterion. Yet even this method may not be ultimately effective in preventing the transformation of monopoly rents into social costs. The more profitable union membership is, the greater are the resources that workers will be willing to invest (e.g., in forgone earnings due to being on strike) in union-organizing activities.

8. One reason why most students of tax policy prefer income to excise taxes is that the misallocative effect of an income tax is believed to be less than that of an excise tax: the cross-elasticity of demand between work and leisure is assumed to be lower than that between a commodity and its substitutes. Even if correct, this does not mean that the total social costs of collecting a given amount of revenue by means of an income tax are lower than those of an excise tax. The amount of the tax transfer represents potential gain to the taxpayer, and he will expend real resources on trying to avoid the tax until, at the margin, cost and gain are equated. A critical question in comparing the costs of income and excise taxation is therefore the shape and location of the supply curves for avoiding income tax liability and excise tax liability, respectively. In the case of a highly progressive income tax system in which expenses for the production of income are deductible, the comparison is likely to be unfavorable to income taxation. Were the marginal income tax rate in the highest bracket 90 percent (as it once was in this country), the taxpayer would continue expending resources on tax avoidance until the expected value of a dollar so expended fell below 10 cents. Thus, he might spend as much as 10 times his marginal tax liability in order to reduce that liability to zero. (How much he would actually spend would depend on the location and shape of the supply curve for avoidance and on his resources and attitude toward risk.) This analysis is not conclusive against the income tax. It might be possible to increase the private marginal costs of avoidance by punishment or by disallowing the deduction of expenses on avoidance. The main problem would be to distinguish legitimate from illegitimate avoidance efforts.[25] Still, no general presumption that excise taxation is less costly than income taxation can be derived from an analysis limited

---

[24]The use of these methods by unions is being increasingly limited by government regulations designed to eliminate racial discrimination.

[25]It would make no sense to punish everyone who believed that some provision of the Internal Revenue Code was not intended to apply to his activity.

to the allocative costs of taxation, corresponding to the deadweight loss of monopoly.

References

Ayaynian, Robert. "A Comparison of Barten's Estimated Demand Elasticities with Those Obtained Using Frisch's Method." *Econometrica* 37 (January 1969): 79–94.

Becker, Gary S. "Crime and Punishment: An Economic Approach." *J.P.E.* 76, no. 2 (March/April 1968): 169–217 (chap. 18 of this volume).

———. *Economic Theory.* New York: Knopf, 1971.

Benham, Lee. "Price Structure and Professional Control of Information." Mimeographed. Univ. Chicago Graduate School Bus. (March 1973).

Bowman, Ward S., Jr. *Patent and Antitrust Law: A Legal and Economic Appraisal.* Chicago: Univ. Chicago Press, 1973.

Cabinet Task Force on Oil Import Control. *The Oil Import Question.* Washington: Government Printing Office, 1970.

Caves, Richard E. *Air Transport and Its Regulators.* Cambridge, Mass.: Harvard Univ. Press, 1962.

Comanor, William S., and Smiley, Robert H. "Monopoly and the Distribution of Wealth." *Q.J.E.* 89 (May 1975): 177–94.

Demsetz, Harold. "Why Regulate Utilities?" *J. Law and Econ.* 11 (April 1968): 55–65 (chap. 8 of this volume).

———. "Industry Structure, Market Rivalry, and Public Policy." *J. Law and Econ.* 16 (April 1973): 1–9.

Douglas, George W., and Miller, James C., III. "The CAB's Domestic Passenger Fare Investigation." *Bell J. Econ. and Management Sci.* 5 (Spring 1974): 204–22.

Ekelund, Robert B., Jr., and Gramm, William P. "Advertising and Concentration: Some New Evidence." *Antitrust Bull.* 15 (Summer 1970): 243–49.

Farmer, Richard N. "The Case for Unregulated Truck Transportation." *J. Farm Econ.* 46 (May 1964): 398–409.

Frisch, Ragnar. "A Complete Scheme for Computing All Direct Costs and Cross Demand Elasticities in a Market with Many Sectors." *Econometrica* 27 (April 1959): 177–96.

Harberger, Arnold C. "Monopoly and Resource Allocation." *A.E.R.* 44 (May 1954): 77–87.

Houthakker, H. S. "New Evidence on Demand Elasticities." *Econometrica* 33 (April 1965): 277–88.

Houthakker, H. S., and Taylor, Lester D. *Consumer Demand in the United States, 1929–1970.* Cambridge, Mass.: Harvard Univ. Press, 1966.

Jordan, William A. *Airline Regulation in America.* Baltimore: Johns Hopkins Univ. Press, 1970.

Kamerschen, David. "Estimation of the Welfare Losses from Monopoly in the American Economy." *Western Econ. J.* 4 (Summer 1966): 221–36.

Kessel, Reuben A. "Economic Effects of Federal Regulation of Milk Markets." *J. Law and Econ.* 10 (October 1967): 51–78.

300   *Richard A. Posner*

———. "A Study of the Effects of Competition in the Tax-exempt Bond Market." *J.P.E.* 79, no. 4 (July/August 1971): 706–38.

———. "Higher Education and the Nation's Health: A Review of the Carnegie Commission Report on Medical Education." *J. Law and Econ.* 15 (April 1972): 115–27.

Krueger, Anne O. "The Political Economy of the Rent-seeking Society." *A.E.R.* 64 (June 1974): 291–303.

Landes, William M., and Posner, Richard A. "The Private Enforcement of Law." *J. Legal Studies* 5 (January 1975): 1–46.

Markovits, Richard S. "Fixed Input (Investment) Competition and the Variability of Fixed Inputs (Investment): Their Nature, Determinants, and Significance." *Stanford Law Rev.* 24 (February 1972): 507–30.

Moore, Thomas Gale. *Freight Transportation Regulation.* Washington: American Enterprise Inst., 1972.

Parks, Richard W. "Systems of Demand Equations: An Empirical Comparison of Alternative Functional Forms." *Econometrica* 37 (October 1969): 629–50.

Plant, Arnold. "The Economic Theory Concerning Patents." *Economica* 1 (n.s.) (February 1934): 30–51.

Schwartzman, David. "The Burden of Monopoly." *J.P.E.* 68, no. 6 (November/December 1960): 627–30.

Stigler, George J. "The Statistics of Monopoly and Merger." *J.P.E.* 64, no. 1 (January/February 1956): 33–40.

———. *The Organization of Industry.* Homewood, Ill.: Irwin, 1968.

Stocking, George W., and Watkins, Myron W. *Cartels in Action.* New York: Twentieth Century Fund, 1946.

———. *Cartels or Competition?* New York: Twentieth Century Fund, 1948.

Telser, Lester. "Why Should Manufacturers Want Fair Trade?" *J. Law and Econ.* 3 (October 1960): 86–105.

Tullock, Gordon. "The Welfare Costs of Tariffs, Monopolies, and Theft." *Western Econ. J.* 5 (June 1967): 224–32.

U.S. Congress, Joint Committee on Internal Revenue Taxation. *Staff Study of Income Tax Treatment of Treble Damage Payments under the Antitrust Laws.* Washington: Government Printing Office, 1965.

Williamson, Oliver E. "Economics as an Antitrust Defense: The Welfare Tradeoffs." *A.E.R.* 58 (March 1968): 18–36.

Yale Law Journal. "Is Regulation Necessary? California Air Transportation and National Regulatory Policy." *Yale Law J.* 74 (July 1965): 1416–47.

STUDIES OF INDUSTRY REGULATION

3

An Evaluation of Consumer Protection Legislation: The 1962 Drug Amendments

10

Sam Peltzman

I. Introduction

The 1962 Kefauver-Harris Amendments to the Food, Drug, and Cosmetics Act are a landmark of the modern consumer movement. While they continued a tradition of legislative attempts to improve product safety, their primary aim of preventing economic loss by regulation of product quality still has few counterparts.

The initial impetus to the 1962 amendments came from hearings begun in 1959 by Senator Kefauver's Antitrust and Monopoly Subcommittee. A major theme developed there was that many new drugs of dubious efficacy were being marketed at unusually high prices. New chemical formulas qualify for patent protection, and information about them had to be obtained by most physicians outside their formal training in pharmacology. The only legal restriction then placed on the marketing of new drugs was that the Food and Drug Administration (FDA) could, within a statutory maximum period of 180 days, deny approval of a new drug application (NDA) and thereby prevent sale of a new drug if the NDA did not adequately demonstrate that the drug was "safe" for use as suggested in proposed labeling. It was alleged in the Kefauver hearings that these circumstances provided powerful incentives for drug companies to develop minor variants of existing drugs and capitalize on their patent protection with expensive promotion in which exaggerated claims of the new drugs' effectiveness would be im-

This article is based on a larger study of the costs and benefits of new-drug regulation (Peltzman, 1974) prepared under a grant from the Center for Policy Study, University of Chicago. I am indebted to Harold Demsetz, Milton Friedman, James Jondrow, Richard Landau, George Stigler, and Lester Telser for helpful comments and criticism. Joyce Iseri provided diligent research assistance. I am grateful to Richard Burr, of R. A. Gosselin, Inc., and Paul de Haen, of Paul de Haen, Inc., for providing me with essential data.

Reprinted with permission from the *Journal of Political Economy* 81, no. 5 (October 1973): 1049–91. © 1973 by The University of Chicago

pressed upon physicians (and, sometimes, their patients). Physicians, in part because they did not directly bear the cost of the drugs, would treat these claims with insufficient skepticism. The resulting demand for the new drugs would thus be sufficiently large for sellers to more than recoup their promotion and development expenses, and the net result would be that patients paid far more than the true worth of the new drugs. This view of the drug market was summarized well at the Kefauver hearings by a former drug-company medical director:

> . . . industry spokesmen would have us believe that all research is on wonder drugs or better medicinal products. They stress that there are many failures for each successful drug. This is true. . . . The problem arises out of the fact that they market so many of their failures. . . . Most [industries] must depend on selling only their successes. . . . [But] with a little luck, proper timing, and a good promotion program a bag of asafetida with a unique chemical side chain can be made to look like a wonder drug. The illusion may not last, but it frequently lasts long enough. By the time the doctor learns what the company knew at the beginning it has two new products to take the place of the old one. [U.S., Congress, Senate, Judiciary Committee 1961, p. 127; see also chaps. 6–15]

Senator Kefauver concluded that government regulation of manufacturer claims for new drug effectiveness would be a cheaper source of information about new drugs than hindsight. It is, however, doubtful (see Harris 1964) that such regulation would have been enacted without the intervention of the thalidomide episode of 1961 and 1962. Thalidomide was, in fact, kept from the U.S. market by the FDA under the then-existing law, but the drug had been distributed to some physicians for experimental purposes. Such distribution was lightly regulated, and reports of births of deformed babies to European mothers who had taken the drug raised concern here that, in their rush to market new drugs, manufacturers were egregiously exposing humans to potentially harmful drugs during clinical testing. This concern served as a catalyst for the enactment of the 1962 drug amendments.

This paper focuses on the provisions of the amendments related to new drugs, and only the most important of these are summarized here:

1. A "proof-of-efficacy" requirement was added to the existing proof-of-safety requirement, and the time constraint on FDA disposition of NDAs was removed. This meant that no new drug could be marketed unless and until the FDA determined that the drug was both safe and "effective" in its intended use. In this context, an effective drug is one which the FDA determines will meet the claims made for it by the manufacturer. In its promotion of the drug, the seller can claim only

those effects established before the FDA, and the promotion must include a summary of "side effects, contraindications and effectiveness."

2. The testing procedure a manufacturer employed to produce information for an NDA was made subject to FDA regulation. Under this regulation, a manufacturer must submit a plan for any clinical tests to the FDA along with information from preclinical tests. The FDA may, at any point, terminate or order changes in the clinical investigation if the drug is deemed unsafe or ineffective.

These provisions were meant to spare ignorant consumers from wasting money on drugs which could not live up to exaggerated claims, first, by subjecting the claims to premarket evaluation by the FDA and, second, by assuring that the FDA could have sufficient information to make the evaluation. This system of premarket evaluation and regulation of clinical testing would also, it was hoped, reduce human exposure to drugs like thalidomide before and after marketing.

This paper seeks to determine whether, and to what degree, consumers have succeeded in obtaining a more valuable flow of new drugs under the regulatory system engendered by the 1962 amendments. Their specific effects on drug safety are not treated here. (See Peltzman [1974] for a fuller discussion of drug safety.) I begin by estimating the effects of the amendments on the sheer size of this flow. If the amendments are more than well-intentioned verbiage, they could be expected to have reduced the flow of new drugs directly (eliminating those deemed ineffective by the FDA but not by the manufacturer) and indirectly (through reaction to costs associated with the expanded information requirements of the amendments). While I show in the next section that the amendments have indeed substantially reduced the flow of new drugs, this only focuses the question of their effects on consumer welfare more sharply. A large reduction in the flow of new drugs, unless it is offset by increased consumption per new drug, can be consistent with large net benefits or large net costs, depending on the magnitude of the preamendment cost of ineffective drugs and the selectivity with which the amendments operate against ineffective drugs. Section III shows how consumer surplus analysis can be adapted to measure the relevant benefits and costs; Section IV carries out the estimation and then checks the results against some "expert" drug evaluations. The principle conclusion is that the amendments have generated substantial net costs for consumers, and the conclusion is not altered if "expert" judgment is substituted for that of the marketplace.

II. Introduction of New Drugs

A glance at table 1 indicates that there has been a precipitous decline in the flow of new drugs since 1962. The post-1962 flow is less than half

TABLE 1.   Average Annual Number of New Drugs Introduced,
1951–70, Selected Subperiods

Period	New Chemical Entities	Other New Drugs
1951–54	39.0	303.0
1955–58	42.0	351.5
1959–62	43.5	239.3
1963–66	17.0	120.0
1967–70	15.3	68.8
1951–62	41.5	297.9
1963–70	16.1	94.4
Ratio (1963–70/1951–62)	0.389	0.317

Source: Paul de Haen, Inc., New York.

Note: "New chemical entities" are drugs containing a single chemical formula not previously marketed. "Other new drugs" are new combinations of previously marketed chemical entities and
duplicates of chemical entities marketed under a new brand name (usually by a new manufacturer, sometimes for a new therapeutic indication). About 80 percent of "other new drugs" are
combinations. Data on new dosage forms, e.g., a tablet form of a liquid, are omitted. Their
flow has paralleled that of other new drugs, falling from 104.5 per year in 1951–62 to 26.4
annually for 1963–70.

that prior to 1962, and there was no obvious downward trend prior to
1962. However, I want to allow for the possibility that some, all, or
even more than all[1] of this decline was due to fundamental change, unrelated to the amendments, in factors underlying the demand or supply of new drugs. Therefore, I first develop a model for the "unregulated" introduction of new drugs, and then estimate its parameters
on pre-1962 data. These parameter estimates are then used to project post-1962 drug flows. A comparison of these projections with actual
post-1962 flows provides an estimate of the effects of the amendments.

My model treats each drug formula as a homogeneous bit of nondepreciable therapeutic information. I assume that the demand for
these bits by drug producers is derived from the expected size of the
drug market. Specifically,

[1] That is, it might be argued that the 1962 amendments were in the nature of
a "public good" for the drug industry which could have raised the demand for new
drugs. If many ineffective drugs were being marketed prior to 1962, there would have
been a large demand for independent evaluation and certification of new drugs. However, costs of detecting and excluding free riders may have deterred direct sale to
consumers of such evaluations by a private producer, while their sale to drug companies may have engendered skepticism which would reduce their value. If the resultant private underproduction of new drug evaluations is corrected by the amendments, the demand price of new drugs would be increased more than the costs of
complying with the amendments, and new-drug output would rise.

$$N_t^* = f(X_t^*), \tag{1}$$

where N_t^* = number of drug formulas producers wish to have available for marketing in year t and X_t^* = output of drugs producers anticipate in year t. Producers must anticipate the size of the drug market, because production of new drugs entails a lengthy research-and-development process. I assume that these anticipations are based on naïve extrapolation of current levels of drug output and current output of an important complement, physicians' services. That is, if drug producers observe, say, a decline in output of drugs or a decline in output of physicians' services, they will revise downward their estimate of future drug output and reduce the resources committed to the new-drug development process. This reduced R & D commitment then translates into a reduced N^* in the future. This may be expressed:

$$X_t^* = g(X_{t-j}, P_{t-j}), \tag{2}$$

and, from (1),

$$N_t^* = h(X_{t-j}, P_{t-j}), \tag{3}$$

where P = output of physicians' services and j = gestation period for a new drug.

One would expect the cost of producing drug formulas, as well as their demand, to affect N^*. For example, since much of this cost is labor expense for R & D personnel, the relative wage of R & D to production personnel ought to influence the extent to which changes in X^* are met from existing or new drug formulas. Unfortunately, construction of an empirical counterpart to this relative wage variable is precluded by lack of continuous data on wages of R & D personnel, so the variable is omitted here. However, based on fragmentary data, this omission will not seriously bias the subsequent estimate of the effects of the 1962 amendments. There is no apparent upward trend or post-1962 increase in the relative wages of R & D and production personnel.[2]

---

[2]The Bureau of Labor Statistics (BLS, *b*) reports that, from 1961 to 1970, the average annual salary of chemists (a prototypical form of research labor) rose by 50.2 percent. This corresponds closely to the 52.6 percent rise in average hourly earnings of drug-industry production workers (BLS, *a*). Data from the U.S., Bureau of the Census, *Census of Population* show that, from 1949 to 1959, median annual income of chemists rose by 63.8 percent while that of "natural scientists" rose 74.0 percent. In the same period, BLS data show a 55.8 percent increase in drug-production worker average hourly earnings (BLS, *a*). Taken together, then, the data imply a slightly more favorable labor-cost environment for research after 1962 than before. However, annual earn-

It remains then for us to specify how producers react to the demand for drug formulas in supplying *new* formulas in any marketing period (1 year). The annual flow of new drugs may, in this context, be regarded as an attempt by producers to close the gap between the number of formulas they wish to have on the market and those already developed and marketed. I assume that the cost of closing this gap will rise with the rate at which it is closed, so that producers may not wish to eliminate the gap entirely in one marketing period. If this adjustment process is linear, we may then write:

$$n_t^* = k(N_t^* - N_{t-1}), \tag{4}$$

where $n^* =$ number of *new* drug formulas producers wish to market, $N_{t-1} =$ number of formulas available for marketing at the start of year t, and $k =$ a constant coefficient of adjustment between zero and unity.

To implement (4), I assume that producers attain n^* on average, with deviations being random. I also assume that (3) is linear in form, so that when its right-hand side is substituted for N^* in (4) we get

$$n_t = a + bX_{t-j} + cP_{t-j} - kN_{t-1} + u, \tag{4'}$$

where $a, b, c =$ constants and $u =$ random variable.

The empirical counterpart to the dependent variable will be new chemical entities (NCEs), that is, single chemical formulas not previously marketed (as opposed, e.g., to new combinations of existing formulas). The motivation for this focus will become clear subsequently. Suffice it to say here that NCEs include almost all important therapeutic breakthroughs and have triple the development expense of a combination product (Schnee 1970, p. 77). I use Schnee's (1970, p. 77) estimate that mean development time of a (pre-1962) NCE was about 2 years with standard deviation of 1 year in constructing empirical counterparts to X_{t-j} and P_{t-j}.[3] To conserve degrees of freedom, these counterparts employ three-term moving averages centered about $t - 2$.

The least-squares estimate ($E =$ estimate) of (4') on pre-1962 data is:

---

ings of research personnel could have been unduly depressed by the 1949 recession, and the safest conclusion would be that no obvious labor-cost inducement to substitute production for research activity can explain any of the post-1962 decline in new drug innovation.

    [3] Development time comprehends the period from clinical testing of a chemical entity with desirable biological activity to approval of an NDA.

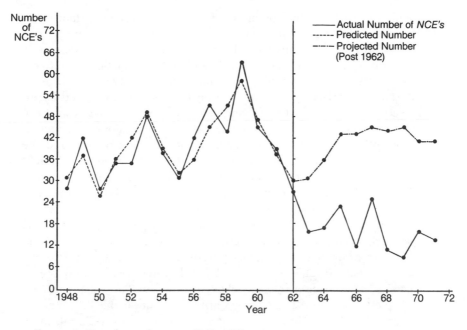

FIGURE 1. New chemical entities, 1948–1971

$$n_t = -2990.016 + 471.352\bar{X}_{t-2} + 45.590\bar{P}_{t-2} - .672N_{t-1}, \quad (E1)$$
$$(75.616) \qquad (32.142) \qquad (.113)$$

where coefficient of determination $= .800$; standard error of estimate $= 4.969$; sample period is 1948–62 (15 observations); standard errors of coefficients are in parentheses; n_t = number of NCEs introduced in t (data provided by Paul de Haen, Inc., New York); $\bar{X}_{t-2}$ = log of 3-year moving average of total number of out-of-hospital prescriptions sold (millions) centered about $t - 2$ (*American Druggist*); $\bar{P}_{t-2}$ = log of 3-year moving average of personal consumption expenditures on physicians' services (million dollars) deflated by price index (1958 = 100) for these services and centered about $t - 2$ (U.S., Office of Business Economics 1966a, 1966b); and N_{t-1} = cumulative number of NCEs introduced through $t - 1$ (Paul de Haen, Inc., New York).[4] The regression

[4] The cumulation is begun from 1945, so that N_{t-1} is, in fact, the "true" number of chemical entities developed to $t - 1$ minus a constant (the number developed to 1945). This difference between N_{t-1} and the "true" value will affect only the intercept of the regression estimate of equation (4′). The cumulation procedure assumes no "depreciation" of the stock of chemical entities. In fact, old chemical entities are sometimes withdrawn from the market, but this does not imply that the knowledge embodied in them has "worn out." That knowledge is nondepreciable, and so we treat each NCE as a net addition to the stock of knowledge.

implies that size of the drug market is by far the more important of the two demand variables[5] and that roughly two-thirds of the gap between $N*$ and N is closed in any annual marketing period. This rather simple model is, given the size of the coefficient of determination, able to explain most of the variation in NCE flows in the postwar period up to 1962. The satisfactory performance of the model is confirmed by inspection of figure 1, where actual values of n are plotted against the values predicted by (E1). There were at least two major cycles (beginning 1948 and 1955) in NCE flows in the pre-1962 period, and the model "tracks" both of them closely. It is especially important, in light of post-1962 experience, to note that the decline from the postwar peak (63 NCEs in 1959) to the trough (27) just prior to passage of the 1962 amendments is virtually all accounted for by the variables in (E1).

We next use (E1) to predict annual NCE flows in the post-1962 period and compare these predictions with actual flows. The predicted flows are estimated by plugging post-1962 values of $\bar{X}$ and $\bar{P}$, along with the implied values of N, into (E1);[6] they may be regarded as estimates of n in the absence of any change in the law. These estimates are also plotted in figure 1, and they imply that, but for the 1962 amendments, there would have been a gradual recovery in NCE introductions from the 1962 trough to a level in excess of 40 per year for most of the 1960s. Although the model predicts that post-1962 NCE flows would not have attained the peak pre-1962 levels, the average post-1962 predicted flow is 41 per year which is virtually identical with the average pre-1962 flow (40). The mean difference between the predicted and actual post-1962 annual flows (25) is over 10 times its standard error and only in the transition year, 1963, is the difference much smaller (15) than this average. I conclude from these data that (*a*) the 1962 amendments significantly reduced the flow of NCEs and, what is perhaps more interesting, (*b*) *all* of the observed difference between pre- and post-1962 NCE flows can be attributed to the 1962 amendments.[7] While this conclusion appears strong, it tends to be supported

----

[5] A given percentage change in X increases the demand for chemical entities by more than 10 times that of the same percentage change in P.

[6] That is, N is computed by adding the post-1962 predicted values of n to N_{1962}.

[7] To check the reasonableness of these conclusions, I replicated a variant of (4′) on cross-sectional data. The data are for drug submarkets in 1960–62 and will be described more fully later. Because of data limitations it is necessary to assume continuously complete adjustment of N to $N*$. Therefore, n is regressed on the change in X for each submarket; the level of X is retained because the larger submarkets should have more NCEs. The regression is

$$n_i = .394 + 1.901\,\dot{\bar{X}}_{i,\,t-2} + .195\bar{X}_{i,\,t-2}, \qquad\qquad (E1')$$
$$(.884)\phantom{\,\dot{\bar{X}}_{i,\,t-2} +} (.098)$$

by a simple comparison of U.S. and British NCE flows. Data reported by Wardell (1972) show that, for 1960–61, the U.S. flow was 1.13 times the British, while, for 1966–71, this ratio was only 0.52, or 0.46 of its pre-1962 value. This last figure is already roughly comparable in magnitude to the ratio of U.S. NCEs to the number predicted by (E1) for 1966–71 (0.34). However, simple enumeration of British post-1962 NCE flows probably understates the amount of innovation to be expected in a pre-1962 regulatory environment and, correspondingly, understates the effect of the amendments in the United States. Most of the British NCEs are produced by firms with substantial sales in the United States, and the British NCE flow is reduced whenever the cost of complying with the U.S. law is sufficiently great to deter development of an NCE for both markets. While a detailed study of this transnational effect of the amendments is beyond the scope of this paper, the simple comparison of American and British experience lends credence to the large effects I have attributed to the amendments.

To the extent that some of the costs of complying with the amendments are "fixed"—that is, unrelated to the size of a new drug's market—one might expect that output of new drugs has declined less than their number. However, there is no strong evidence that drug manufacturers have been successful in achieving larger output per NCE than prior to 1962, though there is some indication that they have tried to do so. In subsequent analysis I use a sample consisting of "important" NCEs. These are NCEs which account for 1 percent or more of prescriptions sold in a submarket which itself typically accounts for over a million new prescriptions annually. Number of prescriptions is, to be sure, a rather crude output measure, and the criteria defining submarkets (therapeutic categories) may not always correspond to relevant economic criteria. I shall, however, tolerate these imperfections in order to be able to work with disaggregated data.[8] The percentage of

---

$R^2 = .14$, $i = 1, 2, \ldots, 42$ submarkets where n_i = average annual number of NCEs in submarket i for 1960–62 and $\bar{X}$ = average annual change in $\bar{X}$. I next used (E1′) to extrapolate forward and backward in time on the aggregate data. Since the scale of the dependent variables in (E1) and (E1′) differ, it is convenient to express the results as an index. For 1948–59, (E1′) predicts an average n equal to 109 percent of the 1960–62 average. The actual average using aggregate data is identical to this. For the period 1963–70, the average predicted value for n is 106 percent of the 1960–62 average. The actual value, however, is only 43 percent. Extrapolation from the cross-sectional results, then, leads to the same conclusions as that from the time series: all of the large post-1962 decline in drug innovation must be attributed to extramarket forces, such as the amendments.

[8] The data to be used here are from R. A. Gosselin, Inc., NPA. The NPA uses a sample of prescriptions filled at a panel of pharmacies to estimate national dollar and

all drug prescriptions accounted for by these important NCEs 1 year after introduction fell from 1.58 in the period just prior to the amendments (1960–62) to 0.57 subsequently (1964–69, the transition year 1963 is excluded). This decline roughly parallels that in the number of NCEs introduced, so that each NCE captures about the same share (0.1 percent) of total prescriptions in each period.[9] Manufacturers have, perhaps in response to fixed costs of compliance with the amendments, concentrated innovation on larger submarkets since 1962.[10] An explanation for their failure to achieve thereby an increase in sales per NCE is provided in subsequent analysis of the demand for new drugs.

III. Costs and Benefits of the 1962 Amendments: Analytical Framework

The preceding analysis establishes only that the 1962 amendments have had a substantial effect on the new-drug market, but not whether the amendments have benefited or failed their intended beneficiaries. Some of the 200 or so new drugs that would have been introduced in

---

prescription sales for each drug sold by prescription. Drugs are grouped by two-, three-, and four-digit therapeutic categories according to chemical similarity (e.g., penicillins) and/or similarity of the symptoms for which the drugs are prescribed (e.g., analgesics). Four-digit categories are employed here. The data are limited to new prescriptions, since the NPA began collecting data on refills only after 1962. I exclude from my sample of the NPA data those therapeutic categories in which the major innovation (50 percent or more of dollar or prescription sales) took place in a single year during or up to 3 years prior to the period being sampled. The motivation for these exclusions derives from the subsequent analysis of the relative output of new and old drugs. Where a category has, in effect, just been invented, it will not contain a reliable sample of old drugs. The categories remaining in my sample account for about 80 percent of all prescriptions sold in a typical year.

[9] These data, however, exclude two important drug categories (diuretics and oral contraceptives) which were essentially invented just prior to 1960, but where substantial post-1962 innovation took place (see above, n. 8). Their inclusion would bring the post-1962 annual NCE share up to 1.18 percent compared to 1.77 percent for the pre-1962 period. It would be risky, though, to conclude from this last comparison that there is a persistent tendency to increased output per NCE. The effect of these few major innovations is concentrated in the first triplet of the post-1962 years, which implies that they are a "spin-off" of preamendments innovation. The average annual NCE share for 1967–70 is a mere 0.36 percent. More important, perhaps, no wholly new drug category has appeared since 1962 which has produced innovations that now seem capable of duplicating the impact of diuretics and oral contraceptives. The safest conclusion to draw here would be that the decline in number of new drugs has been roughly matched by a decline in their output.

[10] The average submarket penetrated by one or more important NCEs in a post-1962 year accounted for 3.49 percent of all drug prescriptions compared with 1.82 percent before 1962. The difference is significant.

the absence of the amendments may have been "worthwhile," and their potential consumers are made worse off by their unavailability. Others may have been "inefficacious" (or unsafe) and their potential consumers are benefited by their unavailability. I shall attempt here to outline a procedure for determining how these gains and losses, and, thereby, the net impact of the 1962 amendments, can be estimated.

The 1962 amendments will be treated here as an attempt to reduce the costs to the consumer (doctor-patient unit) of obtaining information about new drugs. This treatment leads me to estimate the resulting benefits and costs from evaluation of new drugs manifested in the marketplace by well-informed consumers. I am thus taking at face value the view adumbrated at the Kefauver hearings that the major problem requiring a regulatory solution was the underproduction of reliable consumer information on new drugs. One might wish to view the amendments in a somewhat more paternalistic light, namely, as an attempt simply to substitute "expert" judgment for that of even the best-informed consumer. My conjecture, which I subsequently test, is that differences in judgment between these groups should not be pervasive, because, unlike, say, cigarettes and rich food, there appears to be little room for conflict between experts and most consumers over what the desirable characteristics of new drugs are.

The 1962 amendments seek to reduce the cost of new-drug information to the consumer by substituting FDA-produced information for drug-company promotion and information obtained from actual usage. That is, the NDA today restricts what the drug company may claim, but provides the user with independent assurance about the accuracy of what is claimed. This independent assurance is produced by preventing actual usage until the FDA has what it considers sufficient clinical test evidence to make the assurance valuable. I next outline the circumstances in which this substitution of information would benefit drug consumers.

First, consider a pre-1962 consumer of a drug X that has just been placed on the market. He evaluates the benefits of X in the light of the information available to him (the fact of NDA approval plus information provided by, e.g., the manufacturer). This perceived evaluation is summarized by his demand curve for X, ADM in figure 2. If the consumer is faced with a per unit price of OB, his evaluation leads him to purchase OC units, on which he perceives a net benefit of BDA. Now suppose that, in the light of his initial experience with the drug, the consumer discovers that X was not as valuable as he had originally thought—the manufacturer's claims overstate what he discovers to be the drug's effects. Having discovered the drug's genuine value, he then reduces his demand to $GHEN$. He buys only OF units, and his genuine net surplus is BHG dollars per unit of time. He also discovers that,

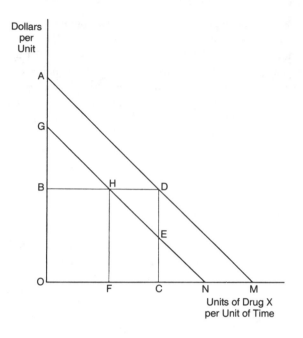

previously, he wasted money. Before he discovered the genuine merits of the drug, he was consuming an extra *FC* units of the drug per unit of time, the true value of which was *HECF*, but for which he paid *HDCF*. These extra *FC* units, therefore, entailed a net loss of *HDE* dollars per period until the consumer learned the drug's true value. Put differently, if an alternative information source had, from the outset, provided the consumer with all the information he obtained by experience, the consumer would have been willing to pay up to *HDE* dollars to this source in each period that he would otherwise have consumed *OC* units. If this source had provided the consumer with this information at a cost less than the value of the stream of his *HDE* losses, the consumer would have been left with a net benefit.

The 1962 amendments established an additional source of information. In this context, the rationale for the amendments would be that, by relying on the information gathering and evaluation expertise of the FDA, the consumer could frequently avoid losses like *HDE*. He may, to be sure, have to pay something for this information, since the costs of the added testing required of drug manufacturers may be reflected in a price above *OB*. This higher price would cause net benefits to be less than *BHG* per unit of time. But, so long as the present value of these reduced benefits fell short of that of his prospective *HDE* losses, the 1962 amendments would yield the consumer a net gain.

The preceding analysis raises important problems if we try to generalize its characterization of the incompletely informed consumer in the pre-1962 environment. Specifically, what consumers have learned about some new drugs from their market experience should affect their evaluation of other new drugs. If, for example, they find that they have consistently overestimated the benefits of a particular manufacturer's new drugs, their evaluation of claims for his future new drugs will be discounted—the initial and "true" demand curves will come together. We must, however, minimize the empirical importance of this more general learning-from-experience process if we wish to entertain the possibility that the 1962 amendments have conferred net benefits on consumers. Similarly, we must judge empirically unimportant any other private source of information which would reduce quickly the difference between *ADM* and *GHEN*. I shall assume that in the pre-1962 drug market such differences may have been numerous and persistent. I will also treat the pre- and post-1962 drug markets as mutually exclusive and exhaustive states of the world.

To estimate the social gains and losses produced by the 1962 amendments we would want, in this context, to compare estimates of the initial and "true" consumer evaluations of the same new drugs. We cannot, of course, know what both of these are at the time a drug is introduced, since, prior to 1962 at least, the true evaluation depended to a greater extent than now on market experience. Therefore, we shall have to infer this true evaluation from consumer behavior at some time after the drug has been introduced. Further, since we cannot observe evaluations by the same set of consumers of the same drugs marketed under alternative regulatory environments, we will have to compare consumer evaluations of different drugs. This would pose no problem if we could assume that the only important difference between pre- and post-1962 drugs is that the latter have passed through a more extensive review process which unambiguously provides more information. However, the 1962 amendments try to change both the composition and amount of consumer information. Specifically, they regulate the amount of privately produced information which is tied to a new drug. While it is convenient to speak of the consumer as buying pills or prescriptions, he values these for their expected effects on his health. The consumer may wish to spend something to learn these expected effects, and some of this expenditure, most notably that for drug-industry-produced information, will be tied to his purchases of pills and prescriptions. Therefore, the valuations manifested in the market are those for a tied product: pill-*cum*-information. Because the 1962 amendments were designed to change the information component of this package, they may have changed consumer evaluations of the package. Drug manufacturers may no longer advertise effects other than those claimed and certified by the FDA in its approval of an NDA. While this stricture may not prevent all consumption of new drugs for nonsanctioned purposes, it will raise the cost of, and presumably decrease the amount of, privately produced information sold with each new drug.

The amendments may also have reduced the amount of new-drug information unintentionally. Consumers cannot form an evaluation of products of whose existence they are ignorant, and some consumers will learn about a new type of drug when brand A is introduced to them. If the potential seller, faced with the cost and uncertainty of complying with the amendments, never markets brand A, a consumer may remain ignorant about the new drug type, and he will, therefore, not seek out brand B. In this way, the decision not to market A reduces information about and the demand for the new drug type generally. More to the point, perhaps, if neither brand A nor brand B is marketed, the consumer cannot express an evaluation of the drug type, so demand for it will be operationally nonexistent. It was shown previously that essentially all of the drastic post-1962 decline in the number of new drugs can be attributed to the amendments, so this source of reduced new-drug information may well be more important than the explicit restrictions on promotion.

However, the essential motive to the amendments is the possibility that much of this privately produced information may be worthless, so a lower initial demand for new drugs-*cum*-private information following the amendments cannot be interpreted unambiguously. This may be seen with reference to figure 2. Let us suppose that a drug exactly like X is marketed after 1962, but that we observe an initial demand curve for it like *GHEN* instead of *ADM*. This different initial demand could reflect the elimination of exaggerated claims for the drug by the 1962 amendments. It could also reflect the elimination of worthwhile information because manufacturers could not demonstrate the worth of the drug to the FDA's satisfaction at an acceptable cost or because there are fewer sellers of X. One cannot choose between these alternative possibilities simply by observing the lower initial demand curve.[11]

I shall make the choice by comparing changes over time in demand

---

[11] If the initial demand curve had been above *ADM*, one could conclude that government produced information is more valuable than any privately produced information it displaces, but there would remain the question of whether this improvement in value exceeds the extra costs of obtaining it.

curves for drugs introduced before 1962 with changes in post-1962 demand curves. My procedure can be most readily understood by assuming, for simplicity, that the true demand never changes and that the rate of interest is zero. Assume, again for simplicity, that there are only two periods, one before (BL) and one after (AL) any learning from experience is completed, and that prices are unaffected by the amendments. Now we compare two somewhat simplistically labeled states of the world: I, amendments are right, and II, amendments are wrong. In State I, the pre-1962, BL-period demand curve is ADM, but the "true" demand curve, which we observe in period AL, is $GHEN$. The true surplus in period BL is $BGH - HDE$, that in the subsequent period is BGH. Total surplus is $2BGH - HDE$. After 1962, in this state, consumer overoptimism is dispelled by FDA testing so the true demand is revealed instantly. True surplus is BGH in each period, and the net benefit of the amendments is the HDE loss suffered in pre-1962 period BL. In State II, pre-1962 consumers learn from experience that their initial evaluation of the new drug was correct, so the true demand is ADM, and it is observed in period BL as well as period AL. The true pre-1962 surplus is, thus, $2ABD$. The post-1962 consumer is, in this state, simply deprived of valuable information about new drugs, so his demand for the new drug is lower than ADM, say, for expositional convenience, $GHEN$. The OF units purchased yield net benefits of BGH in each period. The net cost of the amendments is then $2AGHD$ or the difference between pre-1962 net benefits ($2ABD$) and post-1962 net benefits ($2BGH$).

Finally, consider the mixed case where the true pre-1962 demand lies above $GHEN$ but below ADM. Here, true pre-1962 benefits exceed post-1962 benefits by something less than $2AGHD$, and there is a pre-1962 loss but smaller than HDE. Whether the amendments confer net benefits or costs must then be determined empirically.

To implement this approach, I shall have to estimate new-drug demand curves before and after 1962. Further, for pre-1962 new drugs, I will want to estimate the demand at the time of introduction and at a subsequent time when learning from experience should be complete. The preceding discussion implies that, whatever the state of the world, the true post-1962 demand curve will be revealed instantly. This assumption will be carried forward to the empirical work, even though we cannot realistically expect post-1962 demand curves to remain precisely stationary, or, for that matter, can we realistically expect stationary pre-1962 demand curves if the amendments are wrong. Since the demand for new drugs can wax or wane for reasons unrelated to regulation, we will, as a practical matter, have to distinguish between states of the world on the basis of differential growth of pre- and post-1962 demand curves. If pre-1962 demand grows more slowly (declines more rapidly) than post-1962 demand, this differential growth will form the basis for calculating a loss like *HDE*. There is, to be sure, an amendments-are-right bias in this procedure. More rapid post-1962 growth in demand could reflect learning by experience that FDA-sanctioned information was too restricted. Then, the initial post-1962 demand is "too low" in that it entails the sacrifice of genuine benefits. These missed benefits will be assumed nonexistent, in part for procedural simplicity, but, also to impart a conservative (pro status quo) bias to the empirical results. I believe that, given the importance of the policy implications which might be suggested by the empirical results, such a conservative bias is not undesirable. And, wherever a choice of procedure may entail bias, I shall try to make a pro amendments-are-right choice. For example, I will rule out the possibility that the amendments produce slower growth in demand for drugs after initial marketing. If post-1962 growth is, in fact, slower, then this will be attributed to nonregulatory forces, and the initial demand curve will simply be assumed to be the true demand curve for each period.

While the subsequent empirical work can be understood in the context of the simple two-period model outlined above, I shall in fact make use of the following multiperiod model which dispenses with the simplifying assumptions of zero growth in true demand, unchanged prices, and no discount on future benefits. I write the true demand for new drugs (*GHEN* in fig. 2) as

$$p = f^*(q), \tag{5}$$

where p = price and q = quantity. The true net benefit or consumer surplus from consuming new drugs, s, in any year, t, is then

$$s_t = \int_0^{q_t} f^*(q) \, dq - (p_t q_t). \tag{6}$$

The first term on the right-hand side of (6) would correspond to *OGHEC* in figure 2, and the second to *OBDC*. The actual demand at t (e.g., *ADM*) may be written

$$p = f^t(q), \tag{7}$$

so that (6) could be rewritten

$$s_t = \int_0^{q_t} f^*(q) \, dq - [f^t(q_t) \cdot q_t]. \tag{6'}$$

The assumption that f^* is, in the absence of regulation, revealed by experience, leads to the empirical identification of f^* with f^T, where T is the time required for learning. I will assume further that f^T is attained linearly, so that,

$$\frac{\partial f^t}{\partial t} = \frac{1}{T}(f^T - f^0), \tag{8}$$

and

$$f^t = f^0 + t \frac{\delta f^t}{\delta t} = \left(1 - \frac{t}{T}\right) \cdot f^0 + \frac{t}{T} f^T. \tag{9}$$

This permits us to rewrite (6') as

$$s_t = \int_0^{q_t} f^T(q) \, dq - \left[\left(1 - \frac{t}{T}\right) \cdot f^0(q_t)q_t + \frac{t}{T} f^T(q_t) \cdot q_t\right]. \tag{6''}$$

Note that s can be negative, since $f^0 \geq f^T$.

New drugs yield benefits for more than a single year, so the stream of annual benefits must be discounted to yield the present value of that drug's net benefits (S), that is,

$$S_t = \int_0^\infty s_t e^{-rt} \, dt, \tag{10}$$

where r is an appropriate discount rate.

This procedure will be modified in light of postamendment experience. I make the strong assumption that no learning by experience is required for f^* to be revealed when the FDA approves an NDA under the amendments. Instead,

$$F^* = F^0, \tag{11}$$

where F denotes a postamendment demand curve. If F^T happens to be smaller than F^0, this will be attributed to other market forces. Thus, for the post-1962 period, (6'') would be simply

$$s_t = \int_0^{q_t} F^t(q)\, dq - [F^t(q_t) \cdot q_t].$$ (12)

If $F^T \neq F^0$, that fact, along with any associated price changes, will be used to compute the "normal" growth or decline (g) in s:

$$g = \frac{1}{T} \ln \left(\frac{s_T}{s_0} \right),$$ (13)

so that (10) would be, simply,

$$S_t = s_0 \int_0^\infty e^{-(r-g)t}\, dt = \frac{s_0}{r - g}.$$ (14)

Since $s_0 \geq 0$, (14) can never be negative.

If $F^T \neq F^0$ and $F^0 = F^*$, then this implies modification of the identification of f^* with f^T. The modification to be employed will be

$$f^* = \min \left[\left(\frac{f^T}{f^0} \Big/ \frac{F^T}{F^0} \right) \cdot f^0, f^0 \right].$$ (15)

That is, the differential growth in demand between the pre- and post-amendment period will be used to find f^*, if demand did in fact grow more slowly (fall more rapidly) prior to the amendments. The f^* of (15) will then be substituted for f^T in (6″). Since f^* also grows by g, (10) could then be written, for the preamendment period,

$$S_t = \int_0^T s_t e^{-rt}\, dt + e^{-rT} \frac{s_T}{r - g}.$$ (10′)

The 1962 amendments would then confer positive net benefits if the value of S in (14) exceeded that in (10′). This could occur if, for example, there were great losses due to inefficacy, so that the first term on the right-hand side of (10′) was very small or negative. If, on the other hand, the amendments' restriction of privately produced information reduced s_0 in (14) substantially compared with, say, s_T in (10′), then S in (10′) would exceed that in (14), and there would be a net social cost to the amendments.

A. Drug Prices

The preceding discussion has focused on shifts in the demand curve for new drugs. However, shifts in demand may induce sellers to change prices and thus change consumer surpluses. Such demand-induced price changes would tend to increase the surplus produced by the amendments in either State I or State II. If, for example, OB is the seller's profit-maximizing price when the demand curve is $GHEN$, a higher demand would, under appropriate supply conditions, cause sellers to charge more than OB. Therefore, even if the amendments are "wrong," the consumer would, in their absence, have received a net benefit less than ABD, and his loss due to their error is less than $AGHD$. Similarly, in State I, the high initial demand in the absence of the amendments would engender a price above OB, and, therefore, the losses of learning from experience would exceed HDE.

The amendments have, however, also affected the cost of developing and marketing new drugs, and the effects of these costs on prices render the overall impact of the amendments on new drug prices ambiguous. The quantitative limit on seller-provided information would, standing alone, lower marketing costs. The associated price effects would complement those just discussed, again, independently of whether the extra information would have been "good" or "bad." [12] However, the important proof-of-efficacy and clinical testing provisions of the amendments work to increase new-drug development costs and prices. These provisions serve to increase direct expenditures for R & D and increase the uncertainty of their payoff. Since the testing takes time, the capital costs of the investment in new-drug development are also increased. These costs appear to be substantial. [13]

---

[12] Where the extra information would have been worthwhile, the price of a properly defined drug-information bundle is increased by the quantitative restriction, but the price per pill falls. Consumers simply pay a little less for a much inferior product package.

[13] The effects on R & D cost may be estimated from a time series of real R & D (using the GNP deflator) per "NCE equivalent." An NCE equivalent is defined as 1 NCE + .30 new combination product + .16 new dosage form; the weights are Schnee's (1970, p. 77) estimates of the relative R & D cost of different new drug types. Following Schnee's estimates of development time for these types of new drugs, the number of NCE equivalents appropriate to any year's R & D is a 3-year moving average centered about 1 (new combinations and dosage forms) or 2 (NCEs) years later. Prior to 1960, real R & D per NCE equivalent was increasing at 14.8 percent per year (the correlation coefficient with time is +.96). When this rate of increase is extrapolated forward, however, post-1962 values are consistently underpredicted. For 1965–69, the extrapolated values average about half the actual values, that is, the amendments appear to have doubled the R & D costs per NCE. Even with only five observations, this average difference is over 10 times its standard error. These extra R & D costs come to between

We cannot then know a priori the net effect of the amendments on new-drug prices.

There is a similar ambiguity in connection with the effects of the amendments on competition. The proof-of-efficacy requirements and the associated restrictions on drug advertising were designed in part to stimulate price rivalry. If the seller could not "artificially" differentiate his new product, the price he could get for it would be more sensitive to those of close substitutes. The other side of this, though, is that, if the product never gets to the market, a source of new competition for existing sellers is removed. Since the amendments have proved an effective barrier to entry, there is at least the possibility that they have weakened rather than promoted price competition in the drug market generally. I shall therefore investigate the effects of the amendments on prices of both old and new drugs.

B. Summary

The 1962 drug amendments sought to reduce the costs incurred by consumers for ineffective and unsafe drugs. To the extent that this goal has been attained, we would expect to see demand curves for new drugs which are higher and/or rising more rapidly after 1962 than before. We would also expect to see these demand changes complemented by reduced new-drug prices resulting from reduced information expenditures by sellers or increased price rivalry among them. However, the benefits produced by the amendments should not have been costless: some of the drugs and some of the information kept from the market would, unless regulators are omniscient and dealing with them is costless, yield net benefits. These costs (forgone benefits) will be manifested in a smaller difference in the level and rate of growth of pre- and post-1962 new-drug demand curves. Similarly, certain costs imposed by the amendments on new-drug producers and the reduced competition from new drugs facing sellers of old drugs would work to offset any reduction of drug prices. The primary object of the subsequent empirical work is to establish the order of magnitude of the resultant of these forces.

$5 and $10 million per NCE equivalent, or roughly a year's sales for a fairly successful NCE. This then implies an increase in the unit cost of a new drug at least equal to the cost of capital, and each year of delayed payoff to the R & D would inflate that increase by one plus the cost of capital. It appears that the actual delay in payoff due to the amendments is at least 2 years (Peltzman, 1974).

IV. Estimates of the Costs and Benefits of the 1962 Amendments

A. *Consumer Evaluations in the Drug Market*

This section derives demand curves for new drugs and uses them to draw inferences about changes in the consumer surplus generated by new drugs since passage of the amendments.

1. Data Most of the data used in this section are taken from the *National Prescription Audit (NPA)*, and they have been described previously,[14] but some of their shortcomings (for present purposes) deserve mention. The output measure to be used will be number of prescriptions sold and the corresponding price will be average receipts per prescription. Further, since penicillin may be a poor substitute for tranquilizers, the unit of observation is not "the" drug market. However, the relevant submarkets ("therapeutic categories") are defined technologically, by similarity of the chemical properties of the members. The potential for measurement error in these data is, of course, substantial. The more expensive prescription may be the cheaper mode of therapy; some members of one category may be closer substitutes for those in another rather than the same category, and so forth. Much of the measurement error will simply have to be accepted for the sake of empirical implementation. Prescriptions for existing members of a therapeutic category will be treated as perfect substitutes for each other, but as imperfect substitutes for prescriptions for new members. The cross-elasticity of demand and supply for drugs in different categories is assumed to be zero. However, the potential measurement error will be taken into account in interpreting the results and in designing the relevant sample.[15]

The data are sampled from a period spanning the 1962 amendments. The amendments are presumed to have affected the markets for

---

[14] See above, n. 8.

[15] To minimize the effect of errors in categorization, minor therapeutic categories (fewer than a million prescriptions in most years' samples), and minor new drugs (fewer than 1 percent of all category prescriptions or sales) are excluded from the sample. This is done because we wish to examine the behavior of the "typical" new drug within the typical category. Where a new drug gets an unusually small share of a category, it is presumed to be related in demand to only a part of the category, so, for this drug, the category is too comprehensive. If the new drug is related in demand to drugs outside its defined category, the resulting exaggeration of its importance will be most serious if the defined category is small. I also exclude categories where new drugs account for over half of prescriptions or sales in the current or any of the 3 preceding years. This kind of innovation essentially creates a new category, and the new drugs are presumed to have no good substitute or none that are really "old" drugs.

new drugs beginning in 1964, and data on postamendment new drugs are sampled for 1964–70. Since new drug introductions declined after 1962, a similar-sized sample of preamendment new drugs is drawn from only the 3 years 1960–62, just prior to the amendments. (The innovation rate for these 3 years was about 10 percent below the pre-1962 average, so the resulting estimate of pre-1962 demand will be conservative.)

2. *Model* Given the assumption that new-drug prescriptions within a therapeutic category are perfect substitutes,[16] the demand for new drugs may be written

$$q_{nt} = f(p_{nt}, p_{ot}, X_t), \tag{16}$$

where t denotes a particular year, q_n = number of prescriptions for new drugs in a therapeutic category per unit of time, p_n = the price per q_n, p_o = the price of imperfect substitutes for new prescriptions, X = a vector of all other factors affecting the demand for new drugs. For simplicity, p_o is identified with the average price of prescriptions for old drugs in the same category. The vector X is composed of two elements: (1) all of the systematic nonregulatory factors apart from p_n and p_o that might affect the demand for new drugs (e.g., prices of complements, income, "tastes") are assumed to be reflected in total output of prescriptions in the therapeutic category (Q_T); (2) since the 1962 amendments may have changed the demand for new drugs and since our data will span the amendments, the presence or absence of the amendments (A) is included in X. It is assumed that equation (16) is homogeneous of first degree in all nonregulatory arguments and that there are random components of q_n, so (16) may be rewritten:

$$\frac{q_{nt}}{Q_{Tt}} = f\left(\frac{P_{nt}}{P_{ot}}, A_t, u_t\right), \tag{16'}$$

where u_t is a random variable.[17] In the subsequent empirical work (16') is assumed to have the linear form:

---

[16]The prescription priced above (below) average is simply more (less) than a "standard" prescription.

[17]The size-of-market deflator could have been chosen as the output of old drugs in a therapeutic category $(Q_T - q_n)$. The choice of Q_T is made for subsequent computational convenience and to minimize the variance in empirical counterparts to the dependent variable arising from random output shifts between new and old drugs. Since q_n/Q_T and $q_n/(Q_T - q_n)$ are positively and monotonically related, there is no sacrifice of generality with (16'). On the basis of preliminary empirical work, I have not included in (16') a variable for growth of total category demand, though such a variable

$$\frac{q_{nt}}{Q_{Tt}} = a + b \frac{P_{nt}}{P_{ot}} + cA_t + u_t, \tag{17}$$

with a, b, and c constants; $a > 0$, $b < 0$, and the sign of c is uncertain.[18] It is being assumed here that sellers set P_n/P_o in each period and offer to sell indefinitely large amounts at that price during the period. Variation in P_n/P_o is assumed to be determined largely by nondemand-related factors, such as costs, so that any empirical estimate of (16') will largely reflect demand relationships.[19]

3. *Empirical Estimates* Before (17) is estimated, it is instructive to examine some of the underlying data. These indicate that the substantial decline in new drug output following the amendments has not been accompanied by a rise in the relative price of new to old drugs. Table 2 presents data on the mean relative prices and market shares of new chemical entities in the year following introduction for therapeutic categories in our sample and where NCEs were marketed. There is a perceptible decline in NCE market shares from 1960–62 to 1964–70 and a decline in the number of markets penetrated by NCEs. At the same time, the mean relative price of NCEs has, in fact, fallen, though the decrease is insignificant. It is possible that the essentially unchanged relative price of NCEs marks a departure from some trend, but this is unlikely. Table 2 contains data for 1956–57, which had levels of NCE introduction and output comparable to 1960–62; the NCE relative price then is virtually the same as that for both later periods.[20]

These data imply that the amendments have not increased the equilibrium supply price of new drugs, but they are potentially consis-

---

is suggested by the previous analysis of new-drug introductions. The preliminary work included past growth of category output as a demand-growth proxy. While this variable had the expected positive relationship to q_n/Q_T, the effect was insignificant and none of the results derived from the simpler formulation of (16') was materially altered.

[18] The number of good substitutes for a new drug may vary across therapeutic categories, so we would, ideally, like to estimate a different b for each category. However, none of the categories have sufficiently frequent innovation to permit estimation of different relative price coefficients.

[19] Since the amendments may have affected both demand and costs, there is a potential problem in interpreting estimates of c. For example, suppose the amendments have caused P_n/P_o to rise, and q_n/Q_T has, at the same time, fallen partly because of an amendment-induced fall in demand. An empirical estimate of (17) might mistakenly attribute all of the decline in q_n/Q_T to the price increase. However, I shall argue below that this potential problem is empirically unimportant.

[20] Prices of other new drugs (combinations of NCEs and old NCEs marketed under a new trademark) also remain substantially unchanged after 1962. The 1964–69 average price relative is 1.14 versus 1.07 for 1960–62. The small difference is insignificant.

TABLE 2.   Average Market Share and Relative Price for NCEs
            in Year after Introduction

NCEs Introduced in:	Annual Average Number of Therapeutic Categories with NCEs (1)	Average NCE Share of Category Output (2)	Price of NCEs/ Price of Other Drugs in Category (3)
1956–57	11.0	0.132 (0.033)	1.223 (0.063)
1960–62	10.3	0.107 (0.019)	1.263 (0.104)
1964–69	5.4	0.064 (0.012)	1.165 (0.050)

Source: R. A. Gosselin, Inc., *NPA*. (The 1956–57 category classification differs slightly from the later years and the coverage is less comprehensive.)

Note: There are 50 therapeutic categories in the sample. Column 1 indicates the average number of these in which one or more important NCEs were introduced each year per period. Column 2 is the average number of new prescriptions accounted for by NCEs per year as a fraction of total category prescriptions for categories where NCEs were marketed. Column 3 is mean dollar value per NCE prescription divided by dollar value of other prescriptions in category. Standard errors are in parentheses.

tent with several demand effects and demand characteristics that are relevant to this study. For example, such data would be generated in a world where new drugs are essentially no more than high-priced, perfect substitutes for existing drugs, that is, where the demand curve for new drugs is essentially infinitely elastic since varying quantities are purchased at roughly the same price. In such a world, there would be essentially no costs (no consumer surplus lost) offsetting the benefits of the amendments. If the demand for new drugs is not infinitely elastic, then the data imply a post-1962 decline in demand. But the apparent decline might mean that the "true" demand for drugs is unchanged and merely reveals itself without a long and costly learning-by-experience process. Or the decline is "real," and reflects the reduced information content associated with new drugs under the amendments. The data do permit us to rule out the possibility that the amendments have increased the initial demand for new drugs, since that would imply a rise in post-1962 sales at the essentially unchanged price. However, an empirical estimate of (17) and of its temporal behavior is required to distinguish among the potentially valid interpretations of the data.[21]

[21] The unchanged, postamendment new-drug price relative is not necessarily inconsistent with a net increase in new-drug production costs. If new-drug production is subject to diminishing returns, a fall in new-drug demand would have produced a decline in price in the absence of an increase in costs (a leftward shift of supply).

TABLE 3.   Estimated Demand Curve for New Chemical Entities
(NCEs Introduced 1960–62, 1964–69)

Equation and Dependent Variable	Coefficients and SE of:				R^2	SE
	Constant	P_n/P_0	Q_n/Q_T	A		
(E2) (q_n/Q_T)	0.1188	−0.0304	—	−0.0510	.2885	0.0687
	(0.0232)	(0.0132)		(0.0147)		
(E3) (P_n/P_0)	1.6922	—	−2.9084	−0.3772	.8360	0.6721
	(0.1543)		(1.2588)	(0.1501)		
(E4) (q_n/Q_T)	0.3503	−0.1871	—	−0.0903	—	—
	(0.1550)	(0.0810)		(0.0519)		

Source: R. A. Gosselin, Inc., *NPA.*

Note: Sample consists of 58 therapeutic categories; 31 in 1960–62 and 27 in 1964–69. Variable definitions are as follows:

q_n/Q_T = number of new prescriptions for NCEs divided by total number of new prescriptions for all drugs in therapeutic category in year following introduction of NCEs; P_n/P_0 = average price per prescription for NCEs divided by average price per prescription for other drugs in category in year following introduction of NCEs (average price = dollar sales divided by number of prescriptions); A = unity for 1965–70, zero otherwise; Standard errors are in parentheses; R^2 = coefficient of determination; SE = standard error of estimate (both for weighted data). Coefficients of (E4) are simple averages of those in (E2) and those implied by (E3), and their standard errors are approximate upper bounds.

Estimates of equation (17) are in table 3, and they rule out an infinitely elastic new-drug demand curve. The data employed are for the year following introduction for NCEs introduced in 1960–62 and 1964–69. The variable A is unity for each postamendment observation and zero otherwise. Only categories with significant NCE market penetration (1 percent or more of category prescriptions and sales) are employed in the estimates. The categories are of widely varying size, and preliminary estimates revealed heteroskedastic residuals; as might be expected, residual variance decreased with category size. To restore homoskedasticity, table 3 shows weighted regression estimates of (17), with the ratio of total category prescriptions to total prescriptions for all drugs in the year of observation as the weight. Equation (E2) reveals a significant negative relationship between market shares attained by NCEs and their relative price and a significant post-1962 decline in the level of demand. The elasticity of market share with respect to price (at sample means) implied by (E2) is only .7, which indicates that consumers treat new and old drugs as rather poor substitutes. The perceived consumer surplus from new drugs will be larger the less elastic the demand for new drugs, and so too would the perceived loss of surplus due to the postamendment decline in demand. However, in light of the measurement error in the price and quantity variables, it is risky to accept the estimates in (E2) at face value. In particular, measurement error in (P_n/P_0) will lead to downward bias in the estimated demand elasticity. However, it is possible to obtain an upper bound to this elasticity by regressing price on quantity instead of vice versa. This is done in (E3), which implies an elasticity fully 10 times that of (E2). It must be noted that the form of (E3) contains the implausible implicit assumption that sellers of new drugs predetermine output and then find a price which clears the market of this output, so (E2) is probably closer to the "truth" than (E3). However, to keep the relevant estimates of consumer surplus conservative, I will assume that the true values of the demand parameters lie exactly halfway between those in (E2) and those implied by (E3). The resulting parameter estimates are shown in (E4).

Equation (17) was also estimated for new drugs other than NCEs. The counterpart to (E2) was

$$\frac{q_n'}{Q_T} = \underset{(.0357)}{.0515} - \underset{(.0299)}{.0049} \frac{P_n'}{P_o} - \underset{(.0095)}{.0251} A, \tag{E5}$$

where the prime refers to "other new drugs." The coefficients imply a virtually inelastic demand curve which decreased after the amendments. Taken literally, this would imply a far more substantial perceived net benefit loss due to the amendments for "other new drugs" than for NCEs. However, reversing the dependence of quantity on price generates an almost perfectly elastic demand curve which increased after the amendments. This would mean that consumers perceive no net benefits from other new drugs and that all of the value of the post-1962 increased demand is simply appropriated by price increases. That the same data give rise to these conflicting interpretations as to the shape and location of the other-new-drug demand curve, implies rather substantial measurement error. While the true demand curve is surely neither perfectly elastic nor inelastic, the risk of error in using the regression data to estimate demand parameters is much larger here than for NCEs.[22] In light of this risk, I will make what is here the most conservative assumption, namely, that the true demand is perfectly elastic. This amounts to asserting that there is no perceived net benefit to consumers from a class of new drugs with total annual sales comparable to those of NCEs. I leave open the possibility that the 1962 amendments have produced net benefits for consumers of other new drugs; demand may have grown more slowly before 1962. However, given the poor results obtained from the data on other new

[22]The standard error of the average of the two estimated price coefficients is so large that it fails to rule out either essentially perfectly elastic or inelastic demand.

drugs, the most reasonable procedure might be to simply leave these drugs out of the account entirely, and evaluate the amendments and their effects on NCEs. Most of the subsequent work is therefore limited to NCE data.

4. The Perceived Loss of Consumer Surplus Due to the Amendments
The first ingredient in our estimate of the net benefits due to the 1962 amendments will be a gross cost: the decline in consumer surplus perceived by consumers upon their initial evaluation of information about new drugs. The higher pre-1962 evaluation of this information may, of course, reflect ignorance, so this gross cost of the amendments will have to be set off against gross benefits arising from reduced costs of learning from experience. At this stage, though, I am naïvely treating the initial demand, estimated by (E4), as the "true" demand.

The general formula for calculating consumer surplus with linear demand is

$$s = \tfrac{1}{2}(P_n^a - P_n)(q_n),\tag{18}$$

where the a superscript refers to the vertical intercept of the demand curve. In terms of the variables in (E4), equation (18) would be:

$$s = \tfrac{1}{2}\left[\left(\frac{P_n}{P_o}\right)^a - \left(\frac{P_n}{P_o}\right)\right]\left[\frac{q_n}{Q_T}\right] \cdot P_o Q_T.\tag{18'}$$

An approximation to the total of (18') over the whole drug market can then be obtained from the parameters and the appropriate sample means of (E4) and the value of $P_o Q_T$ for categories with NCEs.[23] To provide comparable dollar values, $P_o Q_T$ is measured in terms of the 1970 drug market. Specifically, the aggregate of $P_o Q_T$ for all categories with NCEs is divided by the aggregate for all sample categories in each year, and the subperiod averages of this ratio (.235 before and .231 after the amendments) are multiplied by the 1970 value of $P_o Q_T$ for the whole drug market ($5.2 billion).[24] This permits (18') to be evaluated

[23] The appropriate sample means are the root mean square of q_n/Q_T and its associated P_n/P_o. Use of the simple average of q_n/Q_T understates aggregate surplus; surplus for below average q_n/Q_T is overvalued by less than the undervaluation of surplus for above average q_n/Q_T.

[24] This is essentially the value of prescription sales at retail outlets as estimated from NPA data. The NPA reports estimated sales at the manufacturers' level, which they estimate average 0.48 of retail value. I have excluded drug sales to hospitals, since these data are not used to estimate the relevant demand curve. Such sales are roughly one-third those of manufacturer sales to the retail market, so our surplus estimates may be considerably understated.

as $51.9 million per year prior to the amendments and $9.9 million per year subsequently; the perceived loss in consumer surplus due to the amendments is thus $42.0 million annually for any year's flow of NCEs.[25] Now, since any year's NCEs will yield benefits over many years, the stream of these annual benefits must be converted to present values. For the moment, I will treat the stream of benefits as a perpetuity with an unchanged average annual return. The return is, however, uncertain, since the (growth of) future demand for any set of new drugs and its competitors will fluctuate. The appropriate discount rate for the stream of expected NCE benefits will therefore be the annual rate of return in activities with similarly risky rewards. I will use a 10 percent rate of return, which roughly corresponds to the long-run average rate of return on investment in equities. This discount rate then implies a perceived net loss to consumers of $420 million in each year that the amendments have been effective, or about 8 percent of total annual drug sales.[26]

[25] The data underlying these estimates are as follows: variable $(P_n/P_o)^a = 1.872$ in the preamendments period and 1.390 in the postamendments period; $(P_n/P_o) = 1.199$ and 1.094, respectively; $(q_n/Q_T) = .1259$ and .0554, respectively. These data assume that only the height, and not the slope, of the demand curve has changed. When (E4) was reestimated to allow for change in slope, the resulting difference in surplus estimates increased. However, since the change in slope is insignificant, it is ignored here. To check the sensitivity of the calculations to use of weighted regressions I recomputed surplus from the unweighted analogue to E4:

$$\frac{q_n}{Q_T} = \underset{(.2213)}{.5353} - \underset{(.1385)}{.3399} \frac{P_n}{P_o} - \underset{(.0502)}{.0785} \ D.$$

The demand schedule implies annual surplus of $42.1 million pre-1962 and $14.8 million post-1962. The difference remains substantial, but about one-third less than the estimates from weighted regressions.

[26] The reader should keep clear the distinction between two benefit streams affected by the amendments: (1) benefits derived from the stream of NCEs, and (2) the stream of benefits derived from any 1 year's NCEs. The reduction in (2) is $420 million, and this is repeated every year. This calculation assumes that the decline in new-drug demand leaves unchanged the price and quantity of old drugs for each q_n. However, if the reduced value of information about new drugs leads sellers to increase information provided at each old-drug price-quantity combination, part of the $420 million gross loss on new drugs will be offset. It will be shown subsequently that the amendments have had small effects on prices of old drugs, so a higher old-drug demand should show up in higher old-drug output for a given output of new drugs. To see whether this has occurred, I regressed the annual growth in old-drug prescriptions $(\dot{q}_o)$ from the year prior to the year subsequent to introduction of NCEs on the annual growth of category prescriptions $(\dot{Q}_T)$ in the 4 years prior to introduction of NCEs, the ratio of q_n to $Q_{T,t-2}(q_n')$, and the dummy variable A, of table 3. (Experimentation with a price-change variable for old drugs proved unsuccessful.) This regression is meant to determine whether, holding constant the expected growth in q_o ($\dot{Q}_T$ is a proxy for this) and the encroachment of new drugs (q_n'), the growth of old-drug sales has accelerated

5. *The Reduction in Waste on Inefficacious Drugs* The amendments would be imposing an annual net burden of $420 million on drug consumers only if they never helped save consumers money on ineffective new drugs. But it is precisely such savings that the amendments are designed to produce. To estimate the magnitude of these savings we must examine the behavior of new-drug demand over time. If the amendments have been dealing effectively with what once was an important problem, we should see the difference between pre- and post-amendment new-drug demand narrowing over time, since the preamendment consumers would have been abandoning the ineffective drugs that the amendments now screen out. Some relevant data is presented in table 4. I am assuming that 4 years experience with a new drug is sufficient to reveal its true value. While choice of this period is

---

post-1962. The result of the weighted regression for the therapeutic categories of table 3 is

$$\dot{q}_o = .0035 + .3590 \ \dot{Q}_T - .8636 \ q'_n - .0104 \ A.$$
$$\qquad (.0135) \quad (.0948) \qquad (.1007) \qquad (.0133)$$

The regression implies that, after accounting for the normal effect of new drugs on old-drug sales—an 86 percent replacement of the latter by the former—there has been no acceleration of old-drug sales following the amendments. This, in turn, implies that there is no gain in consumers' surplus on old drugs to offset the loss on new drugs. Finally, the somewhat arbitrary assumptions employed in capitalizing the net benefit streams can be checked by use of observable capital values. One such value is the R & D investment in a new drug, which, as I have shown previously (see n. 17 above), has been increased by the amendments. If one assumes that the higher R & D investment in new drugs post-1962 will be fully recovered by producers (notwithstanding the failure of relative new-drug prices to rise, this assumption is tenable [Peltzman, 1974]) and, generously, that neither any other cost nor the demand for new drugs has been changed by the amendments, then the initial consumer loss (L) from the decline in R & D productivity can be approximated: $L \doteq (C - C^*)[n + \frac{1}{2}(n^* - n)]$, where C = actual post-1962 R & D investment per NCE(n), and the asterisk denotes values expected in the absence of the amendments. This formulation treats producers as "selling" NCEs at a "price," collected over time, but equal in present value to the R & D investment. The post-1962 decline in n is attributed to the post-1962 rise in this price. If this implied demand for NCEs is linear, the present value of consumer loss in any year is the rise in R & D cost for that year's NCEs $[n(C - C^*)]$ plus the surplus forgone on NCEs that are not produced because of the cost increase $[\frac{1}{2}(C - C^*)(n^* - n)]$. To evaluate L, the predicted post-1962 values of the R & D cost regression in n. 17 above are used as estimates of C^*. Since C is measured per "NCE equivalent," the predicted post-1962 values of (E1) are multiplied by 3.03, the pre-1962 average ratio of NCE equivalents to NCEs, to generate n^*. Further, for consistency with C and C^*, n and n^* are 3-year moving averages centered 2 years subsequent to the year in which R & D funds are spent. The 1963–69 averages of these variables are $n = 36.1$, $n^* = 129.9$, $C = \$13.4$ million, $C^* = \$6.9$ million (1970 dollars). I estimated L for each year, 1963–69, and the average estimate (1970 dollars) was $523.0 million, or about $100 million more than the loss I had estimated from new-drug demand curves.

TABLE 4.   Weighted Average Market Shares and Relative Prices
            for New Drugs, 1 and 4 Years after Introduction

Drugs and Subperiod	Market Share (q_n/Q_T)		Relative Price (P_n/P_0)	
	1 Year after Introduction	4 Years after Introduction	1 Year after Introduction	4 Years after Introduction
NCEs introduced				
1960–62	0.083	0.083	1.414	1.327
	(0.017)	(0.020)	(0.144)	(0.124)
1964–69	0.039	—	1.209	—
	(0.008)		(0.045)	
1964–66	0.049	0.038	1.184	1.221
	(0.012)	(0.013)	(0.061)	(0.051)
Other new drugs introduced				
1960–62	0.064	0.077	1.133	1.130
	(0.011)	(0.014)	(0.026)	(0.023)
1964–69	0.024	—	1.206	—
	(0.005)		(0.029)	
1964–66	0.025	0.023	1.231	1.192
	(0.004)	(0.004)	(0.042)	(0.040)

Source: R. A. Gosselin, Inc., *NPA.*
Note: Data are averages for those categories where new drugs were introduced, weighted by category share of total drug prescriptions. Standard errors are in parentheses.

somewhat arbitrary, it is in part forced by the data. A longer period would have left an unreliably small sample of post-1962 drug data.

These data reveal a remarkable stability in the demand for new drugs over time, and, what is most important here, there is no substantial difference in this respect between pre- and postamendment new drugs. None of the intertemporal differences in NCE relative price or market shares is significant for either subperiod. We shall however, have to accept the substantial risk of error in identifying the small differences that are present with changes in population means to attribute any benefits to the 1962 amendments. First I assume that any intertemporal change in demand is one of intercept rather than slope.[27] Then, it will be seen that both pre- and postamendment NCE demand fall slightly over time. In the preamendment period, there is a fall in price with no increase in quantity, while the postamendment decrease in quantity exceeds that expected from the small rise in price.[28] How-

[27]This assumption was tested by reestimating (E4) on year-after-introduction and 4-years-after-introduction data for the relevant subset of data. The resulting difference in the coefficient of price was less than its standard error.

[28]From (E4), a (1.221–1.184) rise in price should have produced only a 0.007 fall in quantity rather than the 0.011 observed fall.

ever, the post-1962 NCE demand curve falls by less than its pre-1962 counterpart. The data imply that the vertical intercept of the former falls by 0.026 versus 0.087 for the latter. This .061 difference can be interpreted as the difference in intercept between the initial and true demand curve for NCEs prior to 1962, since it is assumed that all of the difference is due to the greater incidence of inefficacious drugs prior to 1962. The implied true demand curve can then be used to estimate the true consumer surplus for NCEs (GHB in fig. 2) and the waste due to initial ignorance of their true value (HDE in fig. 2). Since the difference between initial and true demand is so small, it is not surprising that the difference between perceived and true surplus is small and that the waste is trivial. The estimated true surplus for pre-1962 NCEs in the first year after introduction is, in fact, $43.0 million and the estimated waste only $0.4 million. The conclusion to which these data point is that the forgone consumer benefits of NCEs kept from the market by the amendments substantially exceed the waste avoided on inefficacious drugs.

Since ignorance is assumed here to be dispelled by experience, this conclusion can only be strengthened by extending the relevant benefit and cost estimate beyond the first year in which any set of NCEs is marketed. Such estimates were made on the assumption that both the true demand and the pre-1962 gap between initial and true demand decreased linearly for the 4 years after NCEs were introduced. Similarly, prices and quantities for intermediate years were estimated by linear interpolation of the terminal values. The resulting estimates are in table 5. The preamendment surplus, net of waste, actually increases in spite of the small decline in true demand. This increase is due to an increased dispersion of market shares which is not repeated for the post-1962 sample.[29] There is, consequently, a small decline over time in the surplus from post-1962 drugs.

Table 5 also provides estimates of (10') and (14). These are derived by assuming that the pre-1962 growth in s_t ends abruptly at $t = 4$, and that the permanent subsequent growth in s is that of the post-1962 series (about -2 percent per year). If the benefits streams are perpetual, the amendments are imposing a net loss on consumers of roughly $400 million (i.e., $491.0 − $82.4 million) per year. If it is assumed that benefit streams from new drugs last for only 15 years, the estimated net loss is about $330 million annually.[30]

[29] The increased dispersion raises the root-mean-square market share, which is the quantity at which surplus is evaluated, even though average market share is unchanged.

[30] The reduced variability of post-1962 drug demand does confer a benefit which is left out of account in table 5 because it is difficult to measure precisely. The benefit

TABLE 5.   Estimated "True" Net Consumer Surplus for 1 Year's NCEs
in Years Following Introduction

Years after Introduction	Pre-amendment NCEs ($ Millions)	Post-amendment NCEs ($ Millions)
1	42.6	9.9
2	49.1	9.7
3	55.9	9.6
4	63.2	9.4
Present value of surplus stream for		
Perpetual stream	491.0	82.4
15-year stream	397.3	67.3

Note: True net consumer surplus is the estimated consumer surplus for the true demand curve less any waste for ineffective drugs. Waste is assumed zero for postamendment NCEs. See text for method of calculation.

---

arises because inability to perceive true demand immediately imposes a cost regardless of the error of the initial forecast. In the case of an overoptimistic forecast, the consumer buys too much initially, and, as we have seen, his loss is the area *HDE* in figure 2. There is also a similar loss if the initial forecast is too pessimistic. Suppose, for example, that the true demand is, in fact, *ADM* but that the initial demand is only *GHEN*. In this case, the consumer buys too little. With full information he would buy *OC* instead of *OF*, and he therefore sacrifices the surplus on *FC* units until he learns the true value of the drug. This sacrifice is also equal to *HDE*. Since *HDE* increases with the gap between initial and true demand, the consumer will be better off the smaller this gap regardless of its sign. Now, while we have seen that, on the average, initial demand is an essentially unbiased predictor of true demand both before and after 1962, the dispersion about the average (i.e., the average absolute error) is apparently greater before 1962. For pre-1962 NCEs, the standard deviation of the change in market share over the 4 years following introduction is 4.3 percent compared to 3.7 percent after 1962. This difference is statistically insignificant, and factors other than initial consumer ignorance affect both of these dispersions (e.g., discovery of new applications for a drug). However, we must assume that none of these other factors are operative to estimate the value of the reduced post-1962 variability. This estimate entails evaluating *HDE* with *HD* set equal to the standard deviation of market share changes in each period. I assume that the initial error of prediction is revealed and adapted gradually so that the fourth-year error is zero. The resulting estimate is that the 4-year cost of variability for a year's NCEs was $10 million prior to 1962 and $7 million subsequently, or a difference under $1 million annually. It is surprising in this context that, relative to the smaller average market share, variability of post-1962 market-share changes exceeds, though insignificantly, its pre-1962 counterpart. If consumers are made cautious toward all new drugs by the introduction of many ineffective drugs, one might conjecture that the temporal stability of pre-1962 market shares is the resultant of growing use of the effective drugs by cautious buyers and declining use of ineffective drugs. On this argument, the 1962 amendments, by removing uncertainty about product quality, would reduce the need both for caution and gradual discovery of the ineffective drugs. But this argument implies a smaller relative variability in post-1962 market share changes, which we do not observe.

The reader is cautioned against a too literal interpretation of these estimates. They are best regarded as indicators of relevant orders of magnitude. Treated this way, the estimates imply either that the magnitude of the problem of ineffective new drugs prior to 1962 was trivial or that the ability of FDA regulation to reduce the problem is small. At the same time, the reduced flow of new drugs due to the amendments is imposing net losses on consumers which are the rough equivalent of a 5–10 percent excise tax on all prescriptions sold. The general thrust of this conclusion holds up when data on new drugs other than NCEs are examined. Table 4 shows the same temporal stability in relative price and output for these drugs both pre- and post-1962 as for NCEs. [31] These data imply then that any savings on inefficacious drugs due to the amendments would, as with NCEs, not compensate for forgone benefits from drugs kept from the market. Given our conservative assumption that net benefits from other new drugs are zero, these data should strengthen confidence that the estimated net loss from the amendments is not exaggerated.

The conclusion that the 1962 drug amendments have taxed rather than benefited drug consumers is sufficiently startling to require corroboration. I have thus far relied completely on the consumers' own evaluations of drugs to measure benefits and costs. I next examine evaluations of presumably more sophisticated (non-FDA) "experts." The purpose here will not be to develop an alternative "paternalistic" measure of costs and benefits. Nevertheless, the working assumption will be that "expertise" entails the ability to discover the "true" consumer interest. Thus, if there are pervasive differences between expert and consumer evaluations and if these are reduced by FDA supervention for consumers, some doubt will be cast on the magnitude of the net costs we have adduced to the amendments.

B. Expert Drug Evaluations

The effectiveness of new drugs, or their superiority over old drugs, is uncertain. Therefore, in addition to the explicit cost of the drug, the buyer bears a risk cost related to the probability that the drug will be ineffective. This cost is the product of the loss if a new drug is ineffective and the probability that a new drug will be ineffective. I test here the null hypothesis that this probability, which is a proxy for the expected cost of inefficacy per new drug unit, has declined since 1962.

---

[31] If anything, pre-1962 other-new-drug demand increases (quantity rises with price unchanged) while post-1962 demand falls (price and quantity fall) over time. However, given the relevant standard errors, the most prudent conclusion would be that demand is unchanged over time in both periods.

Given the decline in drug innovation, truth of this hypothesis is necessary, but not sufficient, for the amendments to yield net benefits. However, our estimate of the magnitude of reduced inefficacy costs is so small that confidence in it should be weakened by strong evidence for the null hypothesis.

I test the null hypothesis by examining its implications for the behavior of three groups who are presumably more knowledgeable about new drugs than the ordinary consumer: hospitals, expert panels employed by state public-assistance agencies, and the American Medical Association's Council on Drugs.

1. Hospital Drug Purchases Hospitals account for about one-fourth of the value of manufacturer drug shipments. Their drug-purchase decisions will often reflect the prescribing habits of the same physicians who are prescribing for the out-of-hospital market. However, to take advantage of large-scale purchase economies, many larger hospitals limit the bulk of their inventory to a standardized drug list (formulary) developed by a specialized committee. Doctors are then encouraged or required to prescribe from the formulary (Jones and Follman 1971). There is then enough difference in the putative sophistication underlying hospital and nonhospital drug-purchase decisions to make a comparison of the two meaningful. While the difference might be larger in some cases—for example, hospitals affiliated with teaching or research programs—comprehensive data is available only for the hospital universe. These are dollar sales to hospitals of drugs classified into the same therapeutic categories employed for the out-of-hospital market.

If sophisticated hospital purchasers have always been able to discern ineffective drugs more easily than overoptimistic, unsophisticated, ordinary buyers, then we should observe: (1) prior to the amendments, new drugs took a substantially greater share of the nonhospital than the hospital market; (2) after the amendments, this difference narrows or disappears; (3) there is no change in the pre- and postamendment hospital market share of new drugs. The data in columns 1 and 2 of table 6 support all three implications strongly. The same pre-1962 new drugs took over twice their hospital market share in the nonhospital market (col. 1); that difference is substantially eliminated for post-1962 drugs (col. 2); and there is virtually no difference between pre- and post-1962 hospital market shares (row 1, cols. 1 and 2).

Before these data can support the hypothesis of an amendment-induced decline in the incidence of inefficacious drugs, one must, however, examine the implications of consumer learning by experience. If the core of efficacious drugs commands the 4–6 percent share characteristic of the hospital market in both periods (and the nonhospital mar-

TABLE 6.   Weighted Average Percentage of Therapeutic Category Sales Accounted for by NCEs, Hospital and Nonhospital Markets, by Years after Introduction

	1 Year after Introduction		4 Years after Introduction	
	Pre-1962	Post-1962	Pre-1962	Post-1962
Market	(1)	(2)	(3)	(4)
Hospital	5.59	4.87	11.78	6.47
	(0.85)	(1.10)	(2.06)	(3.73)
Nonhospital	14.02	4.67	13.60	4.14
	(2.11)	(0.81)	(2.56)	(1.21)
t-ratio, hospital/nonhospital	−4.67	0.31	−1.03	0.59

Source: R. A. Gosselin, Inc., NPA, nonhospital data; R. A. Gosselin, Inc. (1971), hospital data.

Note: Sample comprises NCEs with sales to both markets (a few NCEs are sold only in one market). Percentages are weighted averages of (NCE sales/total sales in category) × 100 in each market. The weight is the ratio of category to total drug sales in each market. Standard errors are in parentheses. Row 3 is the ratio of the average difference between hospital and nonhospital sales in category (weighted by ratio of category to total drug sales in both markets) to its standard error. Columns 1 and 3 employ NCEs introduced in 1960–62, column 2 those introduced in 1964–69, and column 4 those introduced in 1964–67. The column 2 values for drugs in column 4 are 5.45, 5.06, and 0.24 for row averages in 1–3, respectively.

ket after 1962), then we would expect: (1) the nonhospital market share will gravitate toward this figure over time, as consumers learn from experience, (2) the hospital market share will remain stable over time since the initial judgments by hospital buyers are accurate. The data in columns 3 and 4 of table 6, however, reveal a startlingly different pattern. It is the hospitals rather than the ordinary buyers who are the "slow learners." Pre-1962 NCEs maintained their share of the non-hospital market over time, but fully doubled their share of the hospital market. The net result is that, after 4 years, hospitals were just as enthusiastic buyers of pre-1962 NCEs as ordinary buyers had been all along (the col. 3 difference in market shares is insignificant). And, with the onset of the amendments, hospitals ultimately find themselves about as restricted as ordinary buyers—fourth-year purchases of both groups are about half the pre-1962 level (cf. cols. 3 and 4).

These remarkable results are difficult to understand. Perhaps they reflect risk aversion by large institutions where one wrong decision will inevitably affect many patients and thus be widely publicized, or perhaps they reflect only the slowness of committee decision making. In any case, they surely provide no support for the hypothesis that the amendments have selectively kept inefficacious drugs from the market. Indeed, a most intriguing aspect of the table 6 data is the rather close agreement between the permanent effects of the amendments and the temporary effects of overcautious hospital purchases. In both cases, half the effective new drug sales are kept from the relevant market.

2. *State Public-Assistance-Program Formularies* In recent years, there has been a substantial increase in prescription drug sales which are financed from public funds. Under various state and local general public-assistance and medical assistance programs, pharmacies are reimbursed for prescriptions provided at no or small charge to the program clients. In an effort to control drug expenditures under these programs, several states have developed formularies listing drugs eligible for reimbursement. Reimbursement for drugs not in the formulary is allowed only in unusual circumstances and/or requires extra effort by the physician.[32] While the method by which these formularies are compiled varies considerably, some of the larger states delegate the task to specialized committees employing consultants with pharmacological expertise. Two formularies so compiled, those of California and Illinois will be used here. Their general intent is to provide a list of the cheapest effective remedies for the range of symptoms likely to be encountered by prescribers. As such, they might be expected to screen out Senator Kefauver's bête noir, the high-priced therapeutic equivalent to what is already on the market.

If many drugs introduced before the amendments and few of those introduced subsequently are ineffective, the former should have disproportionately sparse representation in the state formularies. That is, when drugs in the formularies are classified by date of introduction, the preamendment set should constitute a smaller fraction of all preamendment drugs than its postamendment counterpart. (Many drugs introduced in either period will not appear in a formulary because, for example, they treat uncommon conditions.) This hypothesis was tested by a χ^2 test for independence of classification. The question asked is, Does the likelihood of an NCE's appearance in the state formulary depend on its date of introduction? The data in table 7 reveal that, in one case (Illinois), the answer is "no"; in the other it is "yes," but it is the preamendment drugs which are more likely to appear. Some of the "poor" performance of post-1962 NCEs might be attributable to bureaucratic inertia toward the newest drugs, so I replicated the χ^2 test by using only 1964–67 NCEs. The results are basically unchanged: χ^2 for Illinois remains insignificant while that for California declines only

---

[32] For example, Illinois will not grant reimbursal for a nonformulary drug unless the prescriber has secured approval of a written request to the Illinois State Medical Society.

TABLE 7.   NCEs Classified by Date of Introduction and Appearance in State Formularies of California and Illinois

| Date of Introduc-
tion and State | Number of NCEs | | Total |
	Listed in Formulary	Not Listed in Formulary	
Illinois			
1946–62	158	358	516
	(155)	(361)	
1964–70	31	82	113
	(34)	(79)	
Illinois total	189	440	629
California			
1946–62	221	295	516
	(208)	(308)	
1964–70	33	80	113
	(46)	(67)	
California total	254	375	629

Source: Paul de Haen, Inc. (1971), NCEs by date of introduction; Illinois, Department of Public Aid (1971), Illinois; California, Department of Health Care Services (1971), California.

Note: Figures in parentheses are expected number of NCEs with independence of classification. Summary statistics are, for Illinois, $\chi^2 = 0.46$, approximate risk of error $= 0.50$, $df = 1$; for California, $\chi^2 = 7.56$, approximate risk of error $= 0.006$, $df = 1$. "Risk of error" is the risk associated with accepting the hypothesis that the number of NCEs in each cell is dependent on classification by date of introduction.

to marginal insignificance. These data seem to imply that one set of experts (formulary committees) is no more likely to conclude that a drug is effective when it has been defined effective by other experts (FDA) than when it has not.[33] This inability of independent expert groups to improve on the consistency of a random number table might imply that inefficacy is unmanageably difficult to define or that it is empirically trivial. Neither circumstance would be conducive to a major reduction in the incidence of inefficacious drugs since passage of the amendments, and the data in table 7 are inconsistent with any such reduction.

3. *American Medical Association Council on Drugs, Drug Evaluations* The AMA has, since 1905, conducted evaluations of drugs for its

---

[33] Replication of these tests in the future may show more consistency among experts. The National Academy of Sciences is reviewing the efficacy of all pre-1962 drugs, and the FDA is empowered to remove inefficacious old drugs from the market. Illinois, however, alerts physicians that drugs deemed ineffective by the NAS review may be deleted from the formulary prior to any FDA action (Illinois Department of Public Aid 1971).

membership. This is today the largest such program outside government. The evaluations published in *AMA Drug Evaluations* (1971; hereafter *DE*), summarize the existing pharmacological literature on each drug reviewed and make some judgment about the likely effectiveness of the drug in its various indications. I attempted to extract from *DE* some measure of the incidence of ineffective drugs by date of drug introduction. Specifically, I sought to compile, for NCEs introduced in 1960–62 and 1964–70, the longest list of drugs of questionable efficacy. Evaluations were found in *DE* for 80 of all the 111 NCEs introduced in 1960–62 and 94 of the 113 introduced in 1964–70. These are frequently guarded and qualified, but any time *DE* suggested that a drug could be ineffective, it was classified into one of two groups: I, not effective, or II, as or less effective than other drugs. There are relatively few drugs which *DE* will label "not effective" unqualifiedly, so, in addition to these, any drug where, for example, clinical data had not yet established effectiveness or were inconclusive was placed in Group I. Group I is surely too large, since for many of its members, *DE* is willing to recommend use for certain indications.[34] However, the bias is deliberate, since we want here to establish some upper limit to the incidence of inefficacy. A drug was placed in Group II if a less expensive alternative seemed to be available for any important indication.[35] This group is also too large, since it contains drugs which are effective in some indications. I assume pessimistically that doctors prescribe these drugs mainly when a cheaper alternative is available. Table 8 summarizes the resulting classification, and contains the results of a χ^2 test for independence of the classification from time. This test shows that ineffective drugs appear more frequently before 1962. To be sure, the risk of error in accepting the hypothesis of dependence on time is moderately high. However, the data deserve further investigation because none previously encountered are so suggestive of an amendment-induced reduction in the incidence of inefficacy.

[34] The following description of a Group I drug will illustrate the kind of judgments made. "Results of clinical studies to date indicate that [drug] may be useful in treating [list of conditions], but data are insufficient to permit comparison of its effectiveness with that of recommended doses of other [drugs]. The usefulness of [drug] in [list of other conditions] has not been proved." A generous interpretation of this might be that the drug is clearly effective for some conditions and possibly others. I made the pessimistic assumption that doctors are prescribing the drug only for those conditions where usefulness has not been proved, or that the apparently incomplete clinical data are too optimistic.

[35] There are two subclasses of II: (1) those labeled "as effective" as some other specified drug or any other drug in the therapeutic category; (2) those "less effective" than some other drug or group of drugs. A drug labeled "as effective" in *DE* is in Group II if the average cost of a prescription in the year following its introduction exceeds that of the specified alternative; all "less effective" drugs are in Group II.

TABLE 8.   NCEs Classified by AMA Evaluation and Date of Introduction

Date of Introduction	Number of NCEs Evaluated as			Total
	Group I	Group II	Effective	
1960–62	8	8	64	80
	(4.6)	(6.9)	(68.5)	
1964–70	2	7	85	94
	(5.4)	(8.1)	(80.5)	
Total	10	15	149	174

Source: American Medical Association, Council on Drugs (1971).
Note: See text for definition of Group I and Group II and see note to table 7. Summary statistics are: $\chi^2 = 5.53$; approximate risk of error $(df = 2) = 0.067$.

Therefore, I estimated the dollar value of the "waste" entailed by purchase of drugs in Groups I and II in the year following their introduction. All Group I drugs were assumed to have no therapeutic value, so all consumer expenditures on them are pure waste. For those Group II drugs which are as effective as cheaper alternatives, waste is the difference in per-prescription price times the number of prescriptions of the Group II drug purchased. Where a Group II drug is less effective than an alternative, I arbitrarily assumed that equal therapeutic value could have been obtained for half the cost of a prescription for the alternative, and the resulting waste per prescription is then multiplied by number of prescriptions. The resulting average annual bill for waste, adjusted to 1970 drug sales, is $17.3 million for preamendment NCEs and $3.4 million for postamendment NCEs.[36] If these payments continue perpetually, the present value at 10 percent of waste on each year's NCEs is 10 times each figure. These present values, when compared with the counterpart estimate of surplus in table 5, imply that, on an exaggerated estimate, about one-third of surplus is eroded by waste. But, what is relevant for our purposes, this fraction is roughly the same for pre- and postamendment NCEs. Thus, while the amendments seem to have reduced waste, they have not, in spite of the suggestiveness of the table 8 data, reduced its incidence. Therefore, they leave consumers with a net loss. Indeed, the amount of pre-1962 waste is sufficiently small for this last conclusion to have held even if post-1962 waste were eliminated.[37]

[36] Waste each year was divided by total drug sales that year and the quotient multiplied by total drug sales for 1970 to obtain these figures.

[37] Limitation of our sample to NCEs may, however, be important here. DE is extensively critical of combination drugs, typically on the ground that only one component affects a given symptom and that "rational" prescribing requires the physician to select the appropriate component. Any waste calculation for combination products

If consumers learn from experience, it may, moreover, be unreasonable to suppose that this waste continues unabated perpetually. Indeed, it is interesting to find some agreement here between pharmacological experts and the judgment of the market place. The market share of the 16 preamendment drugs in Groups I and II declined an average of 12.9 percent per year from the first to the fourth year after introduction, and this is twice its standard error. Only four of the 16 drugs show increased market shares. Since relative price also declined (by a statistically significant average of 2.4 percent per year), the market-share performance implies a rather substantial decline in demand for ineffective drugs. The drug consumers' ignorance thus seems something less than invincible.[38]

The last result may provide a clue to our difficulty in finding much effect of the amendments on the incidence of inefficacious drugs. Simply put, the effective new drug will be more profitable. The ineffective new drug, to be sure, takes an initial market share and sells at a price roughly equal to that of other new drugs.[39] The effective drugs do not, however, experience the substantial and fairly prompt loss of market share that we find for ineffective drugs. Thus, everything else the same, the likelihood that a seller can recapture his investment in a new drug will increase with its effectiveness. These penalties imposed by the marketplace on sellers of ineffective drugs prior to 1962 seem to have been enough of a deterrent to have left little room for improvement by a regulatory agency. The reduced waste on inefficacious new drugs brought about by the amendments is simply a by-product of their reduction of the flow of all new drugs. Therefore, none of the data we have examined, whether obtained from the evaluations of ordinary consumers or experts, are likely to have been very much different if, instead of detailed regulation, an arbitrary marketing quota had been placed on new drugs in 1962.

The conclusions to which this examination of expert drug evaluation seem to point are:

---

based on *DE*'s conclusions would be extremely difficult. The difference between the cost of the appropriate NCE bought separately and as part of a combination would have to be set off against the cost of more extensive diagnosis and the added cost of separate prescribing where each part of a combination has some expected benefit.

[38] If $17.3 million of waste decreases by something like the 15 percent per year implied here, the present value of the waste issuing from 1 year's NCEs is $69 million [$17.3/(.10 + .15)$] rather than $173 million, and the improvement due to the Amendments is $56 million rather than $139 million.

[39] The 16 "ineffective" pre-1962 drugs in our sample had an average initial market share of 8.7 percent and their average relative price was 1.16. For all preamendment NCEs in our sample, these figures are 7.5 percent and 1.26.

1. The null hypothesis of a post-1962 decline in the incidence of inefficacious drugs cannot be accepted with tolerable risk of error.

2. To the extent that data permit measurement of its size, the costs of inefficacy seem to be small. This is implied by the similarity of new-drug-market shares in sales to buyers of varying pharmacological expertise (hospital versus nonhospital). The implication is confirmed by a direct estimate of what, according to pharmacological experts, consumers are wasting on ineffective new drugs; this is consistently substantially less than half the consumers' surplus generated by new drugs both before and after 1962.

3. These conclusions are similar to those implied by the previous analysis of ordinary-consumer behavior, where we found both a trivial decline in demand for new drugs as they got older and a trivial difference in the rate of decline between pre- and postamendment new drugs.

4. That analysis assumed a gradual learning process that eliminates waste on inefficacious drugs. The market behavior of a sample of new drugs deemed ineffective by experts seems to confirm the usefulness of that assumption. Their decrease in demand and the generally stable demand for new drugs renders the losses from inefficacious drugs trivial next to the surplus generated by other new drugs.

C. The Effect of Drug Innovation on Prescription Drug Prices

An extreme interpretation of the rationale underlying the 1962 amendments would be that most, if not all, new drugs bring no therapeutic improvement over existing drugs. The bulk of the preceding data—on market shares and prices of new drugs over time, expert drug evaluations, and so forth—belies this view, but, for present purposes, I want to accept it. If the consumer "should" but doesn't treat old and new drugs as identical, his presumed gain or loss from regulation of drug innovation will turn completely on the impact of regulation on the prices he pays for drugs. That is, if he pays $1.50 for a new drug rather than $1.00 for a presumably equivalent old drug, he would be saved $0.50 if the new drug were never marketed.

This view might rationalize even the most arbitrary restriction of drug innovation, since we have seen that new drugs sell at a premium over old drugs in the same therapeutic class (see tables 2 and 4). The amendments have not increased this premium, and may even have reduced it.[40] Therefore, simple arithmetic would imply that the amend-

---

[40] Table 4 shows a 20-percentage-point decline in the premium after 1962. This is only barely insignificant. However, the weighted average price relative for the

ments, simply by reducing drug innovation, have saved money for consumers.

Such arithmetic would, however, ignore the effects of competition between producers of new and old drugs. If the latter face a decline in demand, because new substitutes become available, they may be expected to respond by reducing prices so that the new-drug price premium becomes unattractively large for some customers. Thus, even if all of some initial price premium for new drugs is regarded as a waste, the overall effect of reduced drug innovation on consumer drug costs is ambiguous. The corresponding removal of a source of competition for established producers may preempt sufficient price rivalry to offset any savings on high-priced new drugs.

To resolve this ambiguity, I here treat old and new drugs in the same therapeutic category as perfect substitutes and focus on the average price of all drugs in the category. I then seek to measure the net impact of drug innovation on this average. (In the absence of price rivalry engendered by it, more innovation will increase this average.) I first regress a time series of the annual percentage change in average price per drug prescription $(\dot{p}_t)$ in the preamendment period on the number of NCEs introduced in each of the two preceding years $(n_{t-1,t-2})$. Since major initial sales of any of the n_{t-1} are typically attained in t, the coefficient of n_{t-1} will reflect most of the inflationary impact of the new-drug price premium. If there is a lag in response of old-drug producers, the coefficient of n_{t-2} will capture the major deflationary impact of price rivalry. The regression is

$$\dot{p}_t = 8.652 - .003n_{t-1} - .125n_{t-2} \qquad R^2 = .388 \qquad \text{(E6)}$$
$$\phantom{\dot{p}_t = 8.652 - .00}(.006) \qquad (.058)$$

for 11 observations (1952–62).[41] Since the coefficient of n_{t-1} is insignificant and that of n_{t-2} is significantly negative, the regression implies that the dominant effect of reduced drug innovation is reduced price rivalry. Specifically (E6) predicts that a permanent annual decline of 20 NCEs would accelerate the change in drug prices by 2.5 percent per year. However, while that magnitude of NCE decline has been ex-

---

1956–57 NCEs in table 2 is only 1.13. Since this is less than its post-1962 counterpart, it is risky to believe that the premium has been reduced.

[41] Standard errors are in parentheses. The dependent variable is derived from a series on the average retail price of drug prescriptions from *American Druggist*. When the series was deflated by the GNP deflator, the same general result was obtained, though with some loss of explanatory power. This may reflect inaccuracy of the deflator.

perienced since 1962, the predicted price effect has not. Instead, there has been a deceleration from the pre-1962 average of over 1 percent per year. This might mean that the relationship in (E6) is aberrant, or that factors exogenous to that relationship have been holding drug prices down since 1962.

To distinguish among these possibilities, I next examine cross-sectional data for the 3 years preceding the amendments. Exogenous forces are assumed to affect all submarkets equally at any moment, and the dependent variable is redefined as the deviation of the price change for a category from the average price change for all categories in the same time period ($\dot{p}'$). Instead of the number of NCEs, I use q_n/Q_T, as well as the market share of "other" new drugs (q_n'/Q_T), as independent variables. The dependent variable is measured over 2 years spanning the year subsequent to drug innovations, which is the year used to measure the independent variables. In this way, the coefficients of the independent variable reflect both any immediate inflationary impact of the associated innovation and any lagged competitive reaction. The resulting regression is

$$\dot{p}' = .329 - 13.230 \frac{q_n}{Q_T} - 1.216 \frac{q_n'}{Q_T} \qquad R^2 = .036 \qquad (E7)$$
$$\phantom{\dot{p}' = .329 - }(5.625) \phantom{\frac{q_n}{Q_T}} (5.015)$$

for 153 observations (51 therapeutic categories, for 1960–62 innovations). While it is weak, the negative overall effect of NCEs on drug prices persists in the cross-sectional data, and the effect remains significant (non-NCE innovation has a neutral effect on drug prices). The magnitude of the predicted effect of reduced innovation on drug prices is, however, much smaller here than in (E6). The average NCE share of category output has declined by roughly 1.5 percentage points, and in (E7) this translates into an approximate 0.1 percentage point annual acceleration of average drug prices.

The safest conclusions from these data are, I believe: (1) It is difficult to conclude that drug innovation has a net inflationary impact on drug prices, even when innovation is regarded as producing no improvement in drug quality.[42] (2) If innovation has any impact on prices, it is probably deflationary, though the magnitude may be small. (3) Specifically, our estimate of a 0.1 percent annual acceleration of drug prices

---

[42] Such a conclusion would be difficult even using simple arithmetic. The data in table 4 imply that, for 1960–62, the average price of all drugs is 1 percent more than the average price of all old drugs, and the deceleration of average prescription price has exceeded that amount since 1962.

due to the 1962 amendments translates into a permanent annual cost to drug consumers of about $50 million.[43]

V. Summary and Conclusion

The 1962 drug amendments sought to reduce consumer waste on ineffective drugs. This goal appears to have been attained, but the costs in the process seem clearly to have outweighed the benefits. It was shown that the amendments have produced a substantial decline in drug innovation since 1962. This could have produced net benefits if the impact of the decline had been highly selective against ineffective drugs and preamendment expenditures on ineffective drugs had been substantial. Neither condition is consistent with the data. In the context of this study, the decline in innovation translates into a decline in demand for, and hence in the measured consumer surplus from, new drugs. It was then shown that this decline in demand does not reflect a substantially more realistic appraisal by consumers of the genuine worth of new drugs. Pre-1962 demand did not fall substantially after consumers had time to learn the worth of new drugs from experience (nor behave much differently than post-1962 demand), as it would if pre-1962 consumers were made initially overoptimistic by exaggerated claims of effectiveness. Therefore, the cost of any initial overoptimism which is prevented by the amendments proved small next to the surplus forgone due to reduced innovation. That conclusion was corroborated by assessments of "experts" and drug buyers presumably more sophisticated than ordinary consumers. The probability that they will assess a new drug as ineffective is about the same for pre- and post-1962 drugs. An estimate of the waste saved by post-1962 consumers on ineffective new drugs which the amendments keep from the market, based on expert rather than consumer evaluations, proved to be a fraction of the consumer surplus forgone on effective new drugs which otherwise would have been marketed. This waste saving is then simply a by-product of reduced innovation, but it is small enough so that even much more selective regulation would not provide net benefits for consumers. Finally, it was shown that the new competition preempted by the amendments has led to slightly higher prices for all drugs.

The magnitudes of these costs and benefits as of 1970 are:

---

[43] A permanent 0.1 percent increase in drug prices this year costs consumers $5 million this year. Since the price increase is presumably permanent, there will be a perpetual stream of such costs, whose present value is $50 million at 10 percent. A similar $50 million stream of costs is engendered every year that innovation is retarded.

1. The surplus forgone due to reduced innovation is about $300–$400 million annually.

2. Reduced waste on ineffective new drugs is trivial as deduced from the behavior of ordinary consumers or more sophisticated buyers (hospitals). An ungenerous interpretation of the drug evaluations of the AMA Council on Drugs and pessimistic assumptions about prescribing practice yields an estimated annual waste reduction of $100–$150 million. But this must be reduced by more than half in light of the decline in demand experienced by ineffective drugs over time.

3. Reduced price rivalry attributable to reduced innovations costs consumers about $50 million annually.

4. The net effect of the amendments on consumers, then, is comparable to their being taxed something between 5 and 10 percent on their $5 billion annual drug purchases.[44]

This tax might be paying for benefits left out of account here. The preceding analysis is, in fact, inadequate when applied to unusually harmful or beneficial drugs (see Peltzman, 1974), and both are affected by the amendments. Some of each type may be kept from the market for some time by the information requirements of the amendments. However, an analysis of the amendments' effects on the benefits and costs of these unusual innovations indicate that they compound rather than reduce the tax (Peltzman, 1974). The tax might also be partly transferred to drug producers, because of its effects on competition. However, an analysis of this issue indicates that, while the amendments have not hurt drug producers, it is difficult to rationalize them as a crypto-cartelizing device (Peltzman, 1974).

This leaves a paradox: the amendments seem to have harmed their intended consumer beneficiaries. Unlike other regulation which restricts output, there is no partly offsetting transfer to producers. If their net effect is then essentially a deadweight loss, one is tempted to question the amendments' political viability. However, there appears to be no imminent reduction in the political demand for either the amendments or for similarly structured consumer legislation. Clearly, the sources of this political demand require examination.

---

[44] One should mention the direct budgetary cost of implementing the amendments. This appears to be relatively trivial. From 1947 to 1962, the FDA budget, deflated by the price index for general government output, rose 6.6 percent per year. In the 2 subsequent years, this accelerated to 18.0 percent. The 1964–70 growth rate was 4.4 percent. If we assume that the pre-1962 growth rate would have been maintained if the amendments had not been enacted, the 1970 budget would have been about $59 million, or $7 million lower than the actual 1970 budget. Alternatively, if we compound the 1962 budget at the slower post-1964 growth rate, the estimated 1970 budget is $15 million below the actual.

References

American Druggist. Various issues.

American Medical Association, Council on Drugs. *AMA Drug Evaluations.* Chicago: American Medical Assoc., Council on Drugs, 1971.

California, Department of Health Care Services. *Medi-Cal Formulary.* Sacramento, Calif.: California, Dept. Health Care Services, 1971.

Harris, Richard. *The Real Voice.* New York: Macmillan, 1964.

Illinois, Department of Public Aid. *Drug Manual for Physicians.* Springfield: Illinois, Dept. Public Aid, 1971.

Jones, D. D., and Follman, J. F., Jr. *Health Insurance and Prescription Drugs.* New York: Health Insurance Assoc. America, 1971.

Paul de Haen, Inc. *de Haen Nonproprietary Name Index.* Vol. 8. New York: Paul de Haen, 1971.

Peltzman, S. "The Benefits and Costs of New Drug Regulation." In R. Landau, editor, *Regulating New Drugs,* Univ. of Chicago Center for Policy Study, 1974.

R. A. Gosselin, Inc. *National Hospital Audit.* Dedham, Mass.: Gosselin, 1971.

———. *National Prescription Audit: Therapeutic Category Report.* Various issues.

Schnee, J. E. "Research and Technological Change: The Ethical Pharmaceutical Industry." Ph.D. dissertation, Univ. Pennsylvania, 1970.

U.S., Bureau of Labor Statistics. *Employment and Earnings.* Washington: Government Printing Office, various issues. (*a*).

———. *National Survey of Professional, Administrative, Technical and Clerical Pay.* Washington: Government Printing Office, various issues. (*b*).

U.S., Bureau of the Census. *Census of Population.* Washington: Government Printing Office, various issues.

U.S., Office of Business Economics. *National Income and Product Accounts of the United States, 1929–1965.* Washington: Government Printing Office, 1966. (*a*).

———. *Survey of Current Business.* Various issues. (*b*).

U.S., Congress, Senate, Judiciary Committee. *Administered Prices: Drugs.* 87th Congr., 1st sess., June 27, 1961.

Wardell, William. "The Drug Lag: An International Comparison." Mimeographed. Rochester, N.Y.: Univ. Rochester, 1972.

The Effects of Automobile Safety Regulation

11

Sam Peltzman

The attempt to improve automobile safety by regulation of product design is perhaps the trademark of the contemporary "consumerist" movement. The gross and net benefits of this regulation have already been acclaimed.[1] This paper will first review some of the evidence supporting the acclamations and then proceed to an independent evaluation of the effects of auto safety regulation. The main conclusion is that safety regulation has had no effect on the highway death toll. There is some evidence that regulation may have increased the share of this toll borne by pedestrians and increased the total number of accidents.

I. Background

Motor vehicle deaths have long been among the 10 leading causes of death, and they usually comprise between a third and a half of all accidental deaths. However, the specific role of vehicle design was not a major public policy issue until the mid-1960s, when legislation imposing federal regulation of vehicle design was enacted. While it is overly simplistic to attribute this congressional action to a single source, the widespread attention gained by Ralph Nader's allegations of design defects in the Corvair in his *Unsafe at Any Speed* appears to have been an important catalyst. Hearings on automobile design began before Nader came to prominence, but the relevant legislation was passed within a year of the publication of his book.

I am indebted to Paul Evans for diligent research assistance and to Isaac Ehrlich for helpful comments. The support of the Walgreen Foundation for the Study of American Institutions is gratefully acknowledged.

Reprinted with permission from the *Journal of Political Economy* 83, no. 4 (August 1975): 677–725. © 1975 by The University of Chicago

[1] See, e.g., any recent *Annual Report* of the National Highway Traffic Safety Administration and the summary of benefit-cost comparisons in U.S. Office of Science and Technology (1972).

The National Traffic and Motor Vehicle Safety Act of 1966 created what has become the National Highway and Traffic Safety Administration (NHTSA). This agency was empowered to promulgate design standards to which new vehicles sold in the United States had to conform. The first set of these became effective in 1968, and, while they have been subsequently embellished, the 1968 standards remain the most important in terms of their apparent potential for reducing the accident toll. Among the major design changes required by these standards were the following: (1) seat belts for all occupants, (2) energy-absorbing steering column, (3) penetration-resistant windshield, (4) dual braking system, and (5) padded instrument panel. De facto regulation of automobile design apparently preceded these standards, however. Auto producers responded to congressional pressure for legislation by installing many of the devices that became mandatory in 1968. The most significant of these anticipatory moves occurred in early 1964, when front lap seat belts became standard equipment, and in early 1967, when most manufacturers added energy-absorbing steering columns and penetration-resistant windshields, among other items. Since the market acceptance of these items, except seat belts, was almost nil prior to their becoming standard, it seems reasonable to regard the 1968 standards as mainly a codification of a prevailing regulatory framework.

The specific design changes arising from this regulatory framework reflect some judgments, mostly by safety engineers, about the likely productivity of the various devices. Therefore, I begin by reviewing some of the findings of the safety-engineering literature which produced these judgments.

II. The Promise of Safety Regulation

I shall attempt to provide an estimate of the order of magnitude of the (*ceteris paribus*) reduction in the highway death rate which the safety literature would lead us to expect following the mandatory installation of safety devices. This involves nothing more than extrapolating the findings from the samples of accidents studied in this literature to the relevant population. This exercise is intended to convey some of the rationale for the direction of safety regulation and to provide a reference point for comparison with my own estimates of the effects of regulation.

It is worth pointing out the potential straw-man character of these estimates. In the first place, the approach typical of the safety literature takes the probability of an accident as a datum, and seeks only to measure how much the probability of surviving an accident is enhanced by a safety device. I subsequently elaborate on some of the

TABLE 1.   Expected Reduction in Occupant Death Rate due to Selected
Safety Devices, 1972 Device Installation, and Usage Rates

Device	Source of Estimate	Expected Reduction of Death Rate (%)
Lap seat belts	National Safety Council (1967 et seq.)	7–8½
	Huelke and Gikas (1968)	13
	Levine and Campbell (1971)	16
	Kihlberg (1969)	15
	Joksch and Wuerdeman (1972)	13
	U.S. National Highway and Traffic Safety Administration (1968)	13½
	U.S. Office of Science and Technology (1972)*	14
Energy-absorbing steering column	Lave and Weber (1970)	4
	Joksch and Wuerdeman (1972)	5
	U.S. National Highway and Traffic Safety Administration (1968)†	5½
	Levine and Campbell (1971)	6½
Shoulder belt	Bohlin (1967)	1
	Joksch and Wuerdeman (1972)	¼
	Huelke and Gikas (1968)	¼
	U.S. Office of Science and Technology (1972)*	¼
HPR windshield	U.S. National Highway and Traffic Safety Administration (1968)	0
	Joksch and Wuerdeman (1972)	2½
Padded instrument panel	Lave and Weber (1970)	0
Dual braking system	Lave and Weber (1970)	½

Note: See Appendix A for derivation of estimates. Estimates are rounded to nearest ½% for lap seat belts and collapsible steering column, ¼% for others.
* From Cornell Aeronautical Laboratory data.
† From statement by A. Nahum and A. Siegel, University of California, Los Angeles, before U.S. Senate Commerce Committee, April 25, 1968.

biases engendered by this approach. Second, I am going to assume initially that none of the devices required by regulation would have been purchased voluntarily. This is perhaps implausible, even though most devices sold poorly prior to their being required. There was, after all, the important exception of lap seat belts. Moreover, the effect of regulation is overstated if, as I argue subsequently, mandated devices substitute in part for safety which would have been purchased without regulation.

Table 1 shows the percentage reduction in the death rate (deaths per vehicle mile) for motor-vehicle occupants which several studies imply we could expect from a few of the devices mandated under the 1966 act. The expected reduction in the total death rate—that is, including pedestrians[2]—would be about three-fourths the figures in the table. The estimates are based on 1972 device installation and usage rates. Their sources and derivation are left to Appendix A, but they share some common characteristics. Typically, the studies classify a sample of accidents by outcome to occupants and the presence or absence of a particular safety device, and the productivity is estimated by comparison of mean outcomes (sometimes after an allowance for the interaction effects of multiple devices). In some studies, this estimate is based on researcher judgment that some portion of a sample of accident *fatalities* can be blamed on lack of a device.

The main message of the table is that we could expect a reduction of from 10 to 25 percent in the occupant death rate (and 7½–20 percent in the total vehicle death rate) from that which might otherwise have occurred in 1972. The "consensus" estimate is closer to the upper end of this range. These estimates reflect a widespread belief among safety researchers about the importance of ejection from a vehicle and impact from the steering column in producing fatalities, as well as the effectiveness of seat belts and energy-absorbing columns in preventing these. For example, Huelke and Gikas (1968) find that the two events produce over 40 percent of fatalities, and their research and related research of Lave and Weber (1970) imply that fully utilized lap belts and an energy-absorbing column would prevent about 70 percent of these deaths. Indeed, the safety literature implies strongly that all that stands in the way of a tripled or quadrupled saving of lives is public lethargy in using lap and shoulder belts.[3]

Appendix A interprets the relevant data conservatively, so table 1 may understate the effect of these devices. However, even apart from

---

[2] Who for these purposes include bicyclists and motorcyclists.
[3] The possibility that seat belts might themselves sometimes be lethal is acknowledged, but dismissed as empirically trivial.

the possibility that some of these devices may have been produced without regulation, there are grounds for skepticism that the productivity of safety regulation is as great as table 1 implies.

Perhaps the most obvious difficulty with these estimates derives from their purely technological character. The mandatory installation of safety devices does not by itself change the private demand for safety, but it may change some relevant prices the response to which may mitigate some of the technological promise of these devices. To see this, we may focus on the demand for accident risk on the part of a driver. One need not rely on the dominance of a suicidal impulse to derive such a demand. It would be implicit in any technological complementarity between accident risk and other driving outputs—for example, reduced travel time. The typical driver may thus be thought of as facing a choice, not unlike that between leisure and money income, involving the probability of death from accident and what for convenience I will call "driving intensity." More speed, thrills, etc., can be obtained only by forgoing some safety. The terms of this trade are portrayed, for simplicity, as the ray A in figure 1, where the presumed "bad" probability of death is measured vertically and driving intensity horizontally. Looked at in this way, the effect of making safety devices available (let alone mandatory) is to lower the risk price of driving intensity, that is, to lower the probability of death given an accident. The

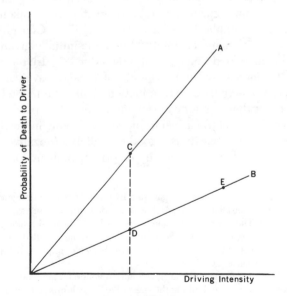

FIGURE 1

estimates of the productivity of these devices in table 1 implicitly hold driving intensity constant, and, if C is the ex-device equilibrium, their magnitude would be represented by CD in figure 1. However, if driving intensity is a normal good, we know that the new equilibrium will be at a point like E rather than D—that is, one at least involving a higher probability of death than at D. Indeed, we cannot rule out a priori a demand for driving intensity so elastic that E involves more risk of death than C.

Such an ambiguity need not, however, derive solely from the belted-milquetoast-turned-daredevil. We have so far ignored another interested party—the pedestrian, or, perhaps, the passenger. There is some complementarity between driving intensity and pedestrian risk, and as long as the new equilibrium entails more driving intensity, we should expect increased risk to pedestrians. This could be offset if the safety devices were designed to reduce all the risks—to drivers and others—of a given level of driving intensity proportionately, but this does not appear to be the case.[4] This implication for pedestrians can be generalized: if sufficiently few accidents are prevented by these devices and they lower the probability of death and injury per accident, the induced increase in driving intensity will increase the total number of accidents. A fortiori, the number of accidents involving harm not to occupants but, for example, to property should increase.

The preceding implications followed from associating regulation with an exogenous reduction in the cost per accident, but that cost is also affected by nonregulatory forces. When these are taken into account, some of the implications have to be modified. Consider first an increased private demand for safety.[5] For some initially given cost per accident, this increased demand will engender less driving intensity. However, the increased "employment" of accident avoidance raises the marginal productivity of loss reduction. Thus, the market demand for, among other things, safer cars will increase. When producers react to this demand, part of the initial reduction in driving intensity will be offset, since driving intensity is a good as well as a (negative) factor in the production of safety. Thus, increased private demand for safety and

---

[4] Most of the important devices mandated by the 1966 act are designed to protect occupants after a crash has occurred, though accident prevention has not been completely ignored. The most notable example is, perhaps, the dual-braking-system requirement. There are, in addition, about 20 standards in the so-called 100 Series (accident prevention) of vehicle safety standards which seek to improve lighting and visibility, tire performance, etc.

[5] The existence of market insurance will not, in general, eliminate a private demand for either self-insurance (limiting the size of loss) or self-protection (limiting the probability of loss). Indeed, market insurance and self-protection are complements (Ehrlich and Becker 1972).

safety regulation will both produce lower cost per accident. The qualitative difference, though, is that regulation, to the extent that it is independent of the private demand for safety, will produce a higher equilibrium driving intensity for the same reduction in cost per accident.

That qualitative difference becomes more tenuous in the case of a joint increase in the demand for safety and intensity. This is perhaps the more relevant case, since it does not require a change of tastes. A rise in real income, for example, would increase the demand for both safety and intensity. While there are different effects, which I discuss later, of wage and time-independent income, there is nothing in general which could lead us to expect a larger income elasticity for either safety or intensity. Therefore, the effects of a rise in income will be similar qualitatively to the effects of mandatory safety devices. There will be a reduced probability of death from any accident as producers respond to the increased demand for safety, and the probability of accidents will increase as drivers respond both to their higher incomes and to the reduced probability of death. For a given reduction in probability of death, different quantitative effects of safety regulation and increased income on death rates would then have to rest on the absence of income-induced intensity in the former case.

Some of the preceding points are made more formally in Appendix B, which develops a simple mathematical model of optimum choice of accident likelihood and severity. Specifically, this model implies that more income and more safety regulation are both consistent with (1) reduced severity of accidents (to drivers) for each level of intensity, (2) increased driving intensity, and so increased probability of accident, the net result being that (3) an equilibrium increase in the expected cost (e.g., deaths) from accidents cannot be ruled out in either case.

The similarity of income and regulation effects forces us to question the exogeneity of regulation. The broad trends of income and the death rate are opposite, and this apparent normality of vehicle safety might be responsible for realization of some of the effects in table 1. Even though the market failed to produce the particular devices listed there, this may be more a difference of form (including a shift from accident prevention to loss prevention) than of substance. Put differently, since safety regulation neither increases income nor reduces the price of voluntarily purchased safety, it will lead to some offsetting reduction of such purchases. Whether the offset is partial, complete, or even more than complete then necessarily becomes an empirical matter.[6]

---

[6]The possibility of a more than complete offset would depend, among other things, on indivisibilities in safety. The basic argument is developed elsewhere (Peltzman 1973) but can be illustrated by an example: Assume that mandated devices yield

In summary, there is no clear theoretical basis for expecting safety regulation to be effective or even for predicting the direction of the effect. Therefore, I try to resolve the ambiguity empirically. Specifically, I explore the following issues:

1. Has safety regulation reduced motor vehicle accident deaths? Since a positive answer is sufficient but not necessary for concluding that regulation is effective, I ask:

2. Have nonoccupant injury and death and property-damage accidents increased relative to vehicle-occupant death and injury, and has the probability of an accident increased? These effects are implied if regulation has indeed affected the cost per accident, and the answer to question 1 depends on the relative magnitudes involved in the answer here. A negative answer would imply that safety regulation has ratified market forces, particularly income effects, pushing in the same direction, and not that particular safety devices are technologically ineffective.

To answer these questions, the next section elaborates a simple model of the demand for auto accidents. The parameters of the model will then be estimated from time-series and cross-section data drawn from the period prior to federal regulation of vehicle design. These parameters and the postregulatory values of the determinants of accidents will be used to project the accident rates that could have been expected in the absence of regulation. These projections will then be compared with observed postregulatory accident rates to answer the questions just set forth.

III. The Determinants of Automobile Accidents

I have chosen to view auto accidents as the by-product of an ordinary consumption activity (driving intensity). Therefore, I seek to explain accident patterns as the resultant of forces which shift the demand for risky driving or change the cost of having an accident. This approach

---

100 units worth of safety at the same time the driver demands 150 units worth. Assume further that the cheapest way to produce these 150 units of safety entails a basic change of, say, vehicle design which, in the extreme, must be bought as a bundle or not at all. Thus, the cost of adding 50 units of safety plus that of the 100 the driver is forced to buy will exceed the cost of the design change alone. Under the circumstances, it is conceivable that utility maximization under regulation will dictate purchase of fewer than 150 units of safety. Indeed, the same sort of choice could emerge even if the mandated devices are provided at zero cost to the driver, since the value of 150 units of safety added to the mandatory 100 will generally be less than that of the 150 standing alone.

involves at least one simplification that should be noted, even if I will ignore it: many accidents involve pedestrians, and the demand for risky walking may differ from that for risky driving.

An analysis of the cost to a driver of having an accident is complicated by the fact that important components of this cost are usually insured. If insurance companies did not adjust premiums in light of particular drivers' accident experience, the insured costs arising from an accident would not deter risky driving. I am, however, going to assume sufficiently accurate and extensive experience rating by insurers for an insured driver to expect to incur some portion of the insured costs associated with his risky driving. If this is so, then the frequency and severity of accidents should be reduced by anything which raises the cost created in an accident. I will represent these costs by an index of direct accident costs (i.e., property damage and medical care) multiplied by an insurance loading factor (the ratio of premiums to benefits paid). That is, if insurance were simply a method of paying for an accident on the installment plan, the "insured" driver would be liable both for the damage inflicted by an accident and for the cost of administering the collection and payment of these damages; I am assuming that some proportion of these costs is in fact levied against insured drivers. To simplify the empirical work, I am going to ignore the fact that some drivers self-insure and that consequently insurance loading charges may be irrelevant to their behavior.

I have previously argued that income has an ambiguous effect on expected accident costs, since it has opposing effects on the probability of accident and on cost per accident. However, the source of income will affect the relative strength of these effects. Time-related income— for example, wages—is affected by driving intensity. Faster driving, more frequent passing of other cars, etc., increase the hours available for work. Therefore, the same increase in wage rates and income from nonhuman capital will have different effects. Both work to increase the consumption demand for safety and intensity, but the former also increases the demand for intensity as a producer good. A similar difference exists between the effects of increased transitory and permanent wage rates. The former may have small pure consumption effects but will raise the current demand for driving intensity as a producer good, since it raises the shadow price of current leisure. Therefore we should see at least a smaller deterrent effect on deaths from increased wage rates, especially the transitory component, as compared to, say, property income.

To incorporate other variables shifting the demand for risky driving into the model, I rely heavily on the conventional wisdom of the safety literature. Empirical testing of the asserted importance of accident-causing factors could easily tax the available degrees of free-dom.[7] However, three factors will almost always receive disproportion-ate attention. These are alcohol, youth, and speed.[8] I elaborate briefly on each here and discuss an important offset—highway design—in the next section.

A. Alcohol

A frequently cited statistic implicates alcohol consumption in over half of fatal accidents.[9] The causal inferences drawn from the incidence of significant blood alcohol concentrations among accident victims usually ignore the possibility that some more basic source of demand for risky driving is involved. Indeed, the belief that reduced inebriation will re-duce highway accidents has become increasingly institutionalized with the recent spread of implied-consent laws to most states.[10]

B. Youth

High relative accident rates among young drivers are as puzzling as they are persistent. If risky driving represents a preference for present as opposed to future consumption, we would expect to find higher acci-dent rates for groups with higher ratios of present to lifetime incomes. Since this ratio generally increases with age, we should find accident rates following the same course. For non-motor-vehicle accidents, this is in fact the case, as the following age distribution of these accidental death rates (per million population) indicates:

[7] Some of the factors which get more than passing attention are men, small cars, the lack of driver education courses, poor highway design, poorly maintained cars, old cars, bad weather, and skimpy tires.

[8] I am, of course, excluding vehicle design here. Some notion of the importance *asserted* for these factors can be gleaned by perusing almost any of the postwar editions of the National Safety Council's *Accident Facts* or the NHTSA *Annual Reports*.

[9] See, e.g., National Safety Council (1972, p. 52). However, North Carolina po-lice reports indicate that less than 15 percent of drivers in accidents had been drinking (Highway Safety Research Center 1973).

[10] Whereby the cost of a driving license implicitly includes consent to a blood alcohol test on demand of a law officer.

Age Group	Average 1962–71 Death Rate
15–24	18.8
25–44	21.0
45–64	31.5
65–74	53.4
75 and older	209.8

The companion distribution of motor vehicle death rates is:[11]

Age Group	Death Rate
15–24	45.4
25–44	27.2
45–64	26.2
65–74	34.2
75 and older	44.0

Only for the very oldest does the motor vehicle death rate approach that for the young, which exceeds that characteristic of the bulk of the population by over half. This peculiar U-shaped distribution is even more pronounced for drivers in fatal accidents; young drivers are represented about three times more frequently than the safest group (age 50–60).

Since it is beyond the scope of this paper to rationalize the disparity between vehicle and other accidental-death-rate distributions, I will have to treat youth as a "taste" factor raising the demand for risky driving.[12]

C. Vehicle Speed

The ubiquity of speed limit signs and the Safety Council's admonition to "slow down and live" testify to the importance attached to speed as a source of accidents. However, crude evidence for this connection is weak. A large proportion of fatal accidents does involve high speed, but so does a large proportion of all driving. For example, by one recent

---

[11] Both distributions are from National Safety Council (1973). It should be noted, though, that nonhighway injuries have a similar age distribution to vehicle deaths.

[12] There is some scattered evidence of interaction between youth and alcohol, in that some surveys have found a higher than average prevalence of significant blood alcohol concentrations among young drivers in fatal accidents (see National Safety Council 1972, p. 52; 1973, p. 52).

estimate (National Safety Council 1972) about 60 percent of rural-area fatal accidents occur at speeds over 50 mph, 30 percent at speeds over 60 mph, and 18 percent at speeds over 70 mph. However, counterpart frequencies of rural driving speeds are on the order of 80, 50, and 15 percent. To be sure, these are biased upward,[13] but they surely give scant support to the notion that increased speeds imply increased accident risk. Nevertheless, this notion so pervades the institutions governing driving that I shall want to test its validity. Since I have argued that income and speed are related, the inclusion of income partially provides such a test. However, some of the variation in speed is independent of income, so a complete test requires that the model include this independent component.

The treatment of such things as alcohol, youth, and speed as exogenous sources of demand for risky driving is purely expedient. Surely the driver who wants to take risks can do so more easily with a faster car or by consuming alcohol, and a more complete model of the demand for accidents would treat these, especially speed, as endogenous. However, my specific purpose of estimating the productivity of safety devices will be served as long as there is some reliable connection between more basic sources of demand for risky driving and the proxies I use. For example, suppose the advent of seat belts is accompanied by an increase in alcohol consumption and a fall rather than a rise in the death rate. In this case, doubt about the implied productivity of seat belts would have to be based on some fortuitous synchronous reduction in the degree of risk that otherwise accompanies drinking. It would appear more reasonable to interpret the increased alcohol consumption as a response which partly offsets the "pure" productivity of seat belts.

It is impractical to treat separately numerous variables which should affect accident rates or severity. Among these would be the state of driver skill, the quality of highways, the private demand and supply of improved vehicle design, the quality of health care, the demand and supply of vehicle maintenance, etc. Some of these factors will respond to driver demand for safety and so should be correlated with income. To the extent that these variables change independently of income, I assume that these can be represented by secular trend. At least the crude death rate data are consistent with a secular increase in safety.

The discussion may now be summarized by writing the reduced

---

[13] They pertain to vehicles on main rural roads in off-peak hours in 1971. For secondary rural roads, these cumulative percentages are 61, 22, and 3 (U.S. Federal Highway Administration, "Traffic Speed Trends," October 10, 1972).

form of the model for unregulated accident rates which will be estimated in the next section. This is

$$R = f(P, Y, T, A, S, K, u),$$ (1)

where R = an accident rate (per vehicle mile) (this will be defined for accidents of differing severity and for all those affected as well as for motor vehicle occupants only); P = the cost component of an accident that is typically insured; Y = income; T = secular trend; A = alcoholic intoxication among the population at risk; S = driving speed; K = driver age; and u = random factors. The expected derivatives are $\partial R/\partial P < 0$, $\partial R/\partial Y(?)$, $\partial R/\partial T < 0$, $\partial R/\partial A > 0$, $\partial R/\partial S > 0$, and $\partial R/\partial K > 0$.

IV. Estimates of the Determinants of Accident Rates and the Effects of Safety Devices

This section presents estimates of the determinants of accident rates in the period before federal regulation of vehicle design and uses these estimates to project, for the subsequent period, the rates that could have been expected without this regulation. The effects of regulation are then inferred by comparing these expected rates with actual rates. The comparison is made for both time-series and cross-section data.

A. Time Series

I developed empirical counterparts to the variables in equation (1) for each year 1947–72. The initial year is chosen to eliminate most of the effects of adjustment from wartime to peacetime driving conditions.[14] Prewar data are unavailable for some of the series. I assume that 1965 is the last year that vehicle design was unregulated. This predates the formal imposition of safety standards and treats the sudden ubiquity of lap seat belts in new cars beginning in 1964 as the de facto result of federal regulation. (An extra year is allowed for measurable effects of this to show up in the car stock.)

The time series used to estimate equation (1) are as follows:

1. Accident rates (R) each are some measure of damage divided by vehicle miles driven. The specific numerators employed are for: TDR, the total death rate—all motor vehicle deaths in the United States in the year (sources: 1947–50, National Safety Council [1973];

---

[14] It is curious that, in light of the reduced vehicle speeds and numbers of young drivers during World War II, there was a temporary interruption of the secular decline in the death rate in this period.

1951–72, National Highway and Traffic Safety Administration [1973]); *VDR*, the vehicle-occupant death rate—total motor vehicle deaths less deaths to pedestrians, bicyclists, and motorcyclists (motorcycles are not treated as "vehicles" because the safety standards we are interested in do not apply to them and their accident rates are atypical of more conventional vehicles; pedestrian deaths typically comprise over 80 percent of those to nonvehicle occupants; source: see *TDR*); *TIR*, the total injury rate—total nonfatal injuries due to motor vehicle accidents (source: National Safety Council [various years]); *VIR*, vehicle-occupant injury rate—total nonfatal injuries less those to pedestrians and bicyclists (source: see *TIR*; separate data for motorcyclists are not reported; *PDR* and *PIR* are nonoccupant death and injury rates, respectively, and are differences between total and occupant rates; *DMGR*, property damage rate—number of vehicles involved in accidents resulting only in property damage (source: see *TIR*).

Most of the empirical work is based on rates standardized for type of driving (urban or rural) and type of road (four-lane limited access or other); these rates are prefixed *A*, for example, *ATDR*. This standardization is motivated by the potential inaccuracy of impounding all left-out variables into a trend term. Accident rates differ widely by area (death rates are higher and injury and damage rates lower in rural areas), but there is no clear trend in the urban-rural composition of driving. To remove the influence of shifts in this composition (and conserve a valuable degree of freedom), the adjusted rates are simple averages of urban and rural rates because the postwar averages of urban and rural vehicle miles are roughly equal. Similarly, accident rates are much lower on multilane limited-access roads than any other type (ranging from roughly half as much for death rates down to a tenth for accident rates). Differences among other types of roads are comparatively trivial. However, the safety benefits of limited-access roads are poorly represented by linear trend. Only with substantial construction of the Interstate Highway System in the 1960s does the proportion of total vehicle miles driven on such roads assume any importance. This bunching suggests that a linear-trend model would be better applied to death rates on more conventional roads.[15] Such rates are available only for a few recent years, but estimates can be derived for all years for both urban and rural driving. These estimates are employed in the adjusted accident rates.[16]

[15]Though this would imply that any gradual improvement in conventional highways was not neglected when the interstates were built.

[16]The estimates are derived as follows. For the years 1967–71, death and injury rates as well as vehicle miles and highway miles on interstates and other highways are

   2. The two major components of the cost of an accident, P, which are typically insured are bodily injury and property damage. Given my assumption that a driver can "buy" an accident only at the cost of paying his insurance company some proportion of these and associated administration costs engendered by the accident, I express P as an index of these costs. Specifically, P is a weighted average of the Consumer

---

available in U.S. Federal Highway Administration, *Fatal and Injury Accident Rates* (various issues). In any year, the adjusted accident rate (AR) for urban or rural driving that we seek is related to the overall rate (R) as follows:

$$AR = R \ \frac{TVM}{k \cdot LVM + OVM} \ ,$$

where TVM = vehicle miles driven on all roads, LVM = vehicle miles on limited-access roads, $OVM = TVM - LVM$, and k = ratio of the rate on limited-access roads to that on other roads. Since k is unavailable prior to 1967, I use the average 1967–71 ratio as an estimate for all years. The components of TVM also have to be estimated. To do this, I assume that the ratio of travel density (VM per highway mile) on limited-access highways to that on all highways in any year equals the average 1967–71 ratio for interstate and all roads; separate ratios are calculated for urban and rural roads (and neither show any obvious trend for 1967–71). The resulting estimate of the limited-access density in any year (the 1967–71 density ratio times the all-road density in that year) is multiplied by limited-access highway mileage to obtain LVM, and by subtraction, OVM. Unfortunately, complete highway mileage data are unavailable, since they are reported by partly overlapping political jurisdictions (state primary systems, Interstate Highway System, and Federal Aid System). For example, a city freeway may be part of the Federal Aid System but neither of the other two, while a toll road may be part of the latter two but not the former. I use the mileage on state primary limited-access roads, since this is usually the largest total. The excluded mileage is bound to be trivial, given the dominant role of the Interstate Highway System, almost all of which is in state primary systems. The data are available from 1956, when such roads covered only about 1,000 miles compared to over 30,000 currently. I assumed arbitrarily that 600 such miles existed at the end of World War II and that this increased linearly to 1956. However, any reasonable alternative assumption would affect the results trivially. The values of k applied to the resulting LVM series are 0.59 and 0.49 for urban and rural death rates, respectively, and 0.30 and 0.36 for injury rates. The Federal Highway Administration does not report property damage experience. However, National Safety Council (1966, 1967) data on several turnpikes for 1965 and 1966 indicate that property-damage accidents occur twice as frequently as injury accidents on these roads, but 10 times as frequently as on all roads. This implies a k for property-damage accidents one-fifth the 0.34 urban-rural average for injury accidents; I round this to 0.07. (By a similar procedure, the implicit k for property damage is about one-eighth the 0.54 average for death, or also about 0.07.) In general, the road-specific accident rates and the crude rates are virtually identical through about 1960 and then diverge gradually though unevenly. By 1965, the two are something like 5 percent apart for deaths and injuries, and this grows to 10 percent by 1971. The corresponding figures for property damage are double these.

Price Indexes for physician and hospital costs and auto repair services deflated by the all-items CPI and multiplied by an insurance loading charge. The weights are the proportions of the insurance premium dollar spent on bodily injury (0.4) and property-damage insurance (0.6) over the sample period.[17] The actual insurance loading charge—the ratio of premiums to benefits—is known only ex post, while the expected load should be relevant to the driver's decision. Instead of assuming that drivers have perfect foresight, I constructed a crude approximation to the expected loading charge by dividing this year's premiums by last year's benefit payments. The assumption here is that insurance is bought at the start of the year, at which time both magnitudes are known. (Sources: for price indexes: U.S. Bureau of Labor Statistics [various issues]; for automobile insurance premiums and benefits, 1947–65: U.S. Bureau of the Census, *Statistical Abstract* [various years]; for auto insurance premiums and benefits, 1966–69: Spectator Co., *Property Liability Insurance Review* [various years], and A. M. Best & Co. [various issues]).

3. Income, Y, is real earned income per adult of working age (15 and over) (U.S. Bureau of the Census, *Survey of Current Business*, various issues). This income concept was chosen after a preliminary investigation of several alternatives, which is discussed subsequently. Earned income is estimated disposable personal income from wages, salaries, business proprietorships, and farms (i.e., it excludes transfers, rents, dividends, and interests)[18] (U.S. Bureau of the Census 1966 and *Survey of Current Business*, various issues).

4. Linear trend is represented by T.

5. Alcoholic intoxication, A, is measured by consumption of distilled spirits per person 15 years and older (Gavin-Jobson Co. 1974). This excludes illegal consumption, which has been estimated at around 15 percent of the total.

6. Vehicle speed, S, is the estimated average speed of motor vehicles on noninterstate rural roads at off-peak hours (U.S. Bureau of the Census, *Statistical Abstract*, various years; U.S. Federal Highway Ad-

---

[17] In preliminary empirical work, it was found, however, that the results are insensitive to a wide range of weights. The medical cost indexes are weighted by relative private expenditures on physician and hospital services averaged over the sample period. The weights are 0.55 for hospital costs and 0.45 for physician fees. The loading charge is earned premiums divided by incurred losses.

[18] For purposes of the estimate, personal tax payments are assumed to be the same percentage of each source of income in any year as the percentage of total personal tax liabilities to total personal income less transfer payments that year. Nominal income is deflated by the deflator for disposable personal income.

TABLE 2.   Regression Estimates, Death Rates, 1947–65

Dependent Variable	Independent Variable						R^2	SE × 100	D-W
	P	Y	T	A	S	K			
ATDR	−0.172	0.884	−0.074	0.359	1.843	0.827	.994	1.585	2.080
	−1.792	4.317	−13.900	2.591	3.863	12.232			
AVDR	−0.045	0.906	−0.068	0.451	2.301	0.594	.978	1.987	1.725
	−0.370	3.528	−10.073	2.592	3.847	7.002			
APDR	−0.432	0.735	−0.092	0.112	1.016	1.274	.995	2.658	2.247
	−2.680	2.140	10.185	0.481	1.271	11.234			

Note: See text for sources and description of series. All variables except T are in natural logarithms. The regression constant is deleted. R^2 = coefficient of determination; SE = standard error of estimate; D-W = Durbin-Watson statistic (none implies significant autocorrelation of residuals). t-ratios are below coefficients. Since, in natural units, $ATDR = AVDR + APDR$, the predicted values of one regression should be, but are not, constrained by those of the other two. However, there is almost perfect correlation (around .99) between the constrained and unconstrained predicted values for each series.

ministration, "Traffic Speed Trends," various issues).[19] Similar data for urban roads are too sparse to be useful.[20]

7. Young drivers, K, is measured by a proxy, the ratio of the 15–25-year-old population to those older (U.S. Bureau of the Census, *Statistical Abstract*, various years [accurate driver-age distributions are available only for a few years]).

1. Death Rates. Table 2 contains estimates of equation (1) for death rates, using earned income per adult as the income concept. Preliminary work with alternative income concepts made it clear that the forces producing a positive relationship between income and the death rate consistently dominated short-run behavior. Every income concept

[19]The available data from 1961 to 1969 (U.S. Federal Highway Administration, "Traffic Speed Trends") are for interstate roads (s_i) and all roads (s_t). The estimate for non-limited-access highways (s_n) is the solution to

$$s_t = \left(1 - \frac{LVM}{TVM}\right)s_n + \frac{LVM}{TVM} \cdot s_i$$

for the single unknown; TVM and LVM are rural vehicle miles and rural vehicle miles on state primary limited-access multilane highways, respectively. For pre-1961, the 1961 ratio (s_n/s_i) is assumed to prevail in all years. The post-1969 data are spliced to the estimated s_n series.

[20]This may not be a serious shortcoming, because the link between accidents and speed is apparently much more important in rural areas. For example, speed is cited as the principal cause on the order of 1½, two, and three times more frequently in rural than in urban fatal, injury, and damage accidents, respectively. See National Safety Council (any recent year).

TABLE 3.   ATDR Regression Results, Various Income Concepts

Income Concept	t-ratio of Income Coefficient	SE of Regression Estimate (× 100)
Per capita permanent income	2.73	1.90
Per capita personal consumption expenditures (proxy for permanent income)	3.26	1.84
Per capita disposable personal income	3.64	1.75
Disposable personal income per working-age adult	3.73	1.72
Earned income per working-age adult (table 2 concept)	4.32	1.59

employed had a positive partial correlation with death rates and was coupled with a strong negative trend effect. Apparently much of this short-run behavior is consistent with driver response to changes in the shadow price of leisure. While the speed variable may pick up part of this response, it specifically ignores most commuting traffic and will not capture all risks induced by a rise in the price of leisure (e.g., more frequent passing of other cars). In consequence, as the income concept becomes more dominated by work-time components, its coefficient tends to become more accurate and the explanatory power of the regression increases. Specifically, for the *ATDR* regression, the results shown in table 3 were obtained. The limited degrees of freedom available made experimentation with much more refined concepts impractical. For example, the table 2 concept implicitly assumes a zero price of leisure for those unemployed or out of the labor force, and does not distinguish permanent from transitory effects. Nevertheless, the foregoing results seem generally consistent with a regime in which the cheapest immediate response to an unexpected increase in income is to increase driving intensity, especially where failure to do so entails a sacrifice of income earning opportunities. (The presumption here is that deviations of income from trend are unexpected.) The strong negative trend effect can then be interpreted as reflecting, in part, a longer-run response to permanent income changes, whereby adjustments of, for example, vehicle design are made to reduce the costs entailed by permanently increased driving intensity. A rationale for such a temporal pattern would be that it simply costs much more relative to the gains to, say, convert immediately a major part of the existing vehicle stock and highway mileage to a safer design than it does to drive the existing stock more intensively.

If the trend term is a partial proxy for permanent income, the regressions seem to imply that the *net* effect of a (permanent) increase in income is to reduce death rates. That is, the average contribution to death rates from the income term in the regressions is on the order of +2 percent annually and is more than offset by the trend effect. Of course, part of that offset need not be connected with lagged income effects, and more precise estimation of the net effect of income must await discussion of the cross-section data. Since cross-section differences in income tend to be persistent, my interpretation of the time series implies that the coefficient of income should be negative in cross-section data. It also implies a narrowing of the difference in explanatory power among income concepts.[21]

The remaining regression coefficients in table 2 (all of which are elasticities) consistently have the predicted signs and are typically significant. The one important exception is the price coefficient, which is significant only for pedestrian deaths. Alcoholism, speed, and youth also appear to contribute differently to occupant and pedestrian deaths. In the case of the first two, their greater elasticity with respect to occupant deaths is consistent with the highway safety literature. However, the (significant) difference between the driver-age elasticities is surprising. The vehicle-occupant elasticity corresponds closely to the crude difference in death rates among age groups, but

[21] The behavior of the various income time series reflects a procyclical pattern of trend-adjusted death rates that cannot be rationalized completely on value-of-time grounds. The residuals from the table 2 regressions tend to be highest and lowest at cyclical peaks and troughs, respectively. Attempts to gain further insight into this cyclical behavior proved unrewarding. Specifically, I examined the following: (1) Travel density: The regressions implicitly assume unit elasticity of deaths with respect to vehicle miles. The probability of accident per vehicle mile may increase with density, and this may in turn behave procyclically. However, when density (vehicle miles per highway mile) was added to the *ATDR* regression, its coefficient was insignificant, though it was positive. (2) New cars: It has been suggested (see "If Economy Crashes, That Could Well Mean Fewer Motorists Will," *Wall Street Journal* [January 22, 1974]) that increased risk of deaths is a cost of driver familiarization with new cars, sales of which are procyclical. However, the new-car/total-car stock ratio had an insignificant negative coefficient when added to the *ATDR* regression. One would like to generalize the argument by examining the response to new drivers, but the required data are unavailable. (3) Error in measuring vehicle miles: A spurious procyclical death rate would be produced if the Federal Highway Administration estimate of vehicle miles is smoother than the actual series. However, residuals from a regression of vehicle miles on gasoline consumption were uncorrelated with cycles in income. (4) Driver age: If access of young drivers to the family car is correlated with income, the high accident risk of these drivers will contribute to a procyclical death rate. However, the population death rate for all age categories behaves procyclically. The cycles are slightly more pronounced for the 15–25-year-old group, but this is hardly sufficient to account for much of the cyclicality of the total death rate.

the much larger pedestrian elasticity implies that young drivers are peculiarly prone to impose risks on pedestrians.[22]

The striking size of the speed elasticities should be interpreted cautiously. Taken literally, they would attribute about 40 percent of all current highway deaths to the increase in postwar vehicle speed, and this is over and above the speed effect implicit in the positive income elasticity.[23] However, the same temporal adjustment process may be at work with speed as with income. That is, increased speed may be the most efficient immediate response to increased demand for risky driving, while the loss-prevention expenditures induced by this demand are spread over time and so get reflected in the trend coefficient. Again, the cross-section data will shed some light on the difference between short- and long-run effects of speed.[24]

The data underlying these regressions may help explain why the political demand for safety legislation increased in the mid-1960s. While the overall trend in the death rate was downward to 1965, the decline slowed in the late 1950s and then reversed itself in the early 1960s. In consequence, 1960–65 constitutes the only period of similar length since the 1920s in which the death rate failed to fall. This fact surely must have contributed to the pressure for safety legislation. In table 4, I try to provide insight into the unique experience of this period just prior to the 1966 act by examining the components of the change in the death rate. Table 4 uses one of the table 2 regressions to partition a change in the death rate among determinants for several subperiods. This partitioning indicates that the most persistent force countering a decline in the death rate was demographic. The favorable effect of a decline in the birth rate in the 1920s and early 1930s had worked itself out by the mid-1950s, and this is sufficient to account for the acceleration of the death rate in the late 1950s. The postwar baby boom then contributed to the subsequent further acceleration of the death rate, so that well over half the acceleration of the death rate from the earliest to the latest postwar subperiod can be attributed to the shift toward a younger driving-age population. However, almost everything else that could have produced an increase in the death rate did so in the early 1960s—the long recovery from the 1960 recession, accelerated growth of alcohol consumption, and accelerated growth of vehicle speeds (the period was marked by popularity of high-horsepower cars).

---

[22] It would be interesting to see whether this reflects a more general difficulty in imposing liability for the costs of these deaths on those with low current incomes.

[23] That is, S will be imperfectly correlated with work-related driving speed because it measures specifically speeds at off-peak hours. I assume that independent variation in work-related speed is correlated with the shadow price of leisure.

[24] More light will be shed by results of the national maximum 55 mph speed limit imposed in late 1973.

TABLE 4.   Annual Rates of Change in Death Rate and Their Composition, 1948–65 and Subperiods

		Subperiod		
Variable	1948–65	1948–54	1954–60	1960–65
ATDR	−1.9%	−4.2%	−3.1%	+2.3%
Contribution due to				
T	−7.4	−7.4	−7.4	−7.4
Subtotal (*ATDR* − contribution of *T*)	+5.5	+3.2	+4.3	+9.7
P	+0.2	+0.2	+0.4	+0.1
Y	+1.9	+2.2	+1.1	+2.6
A	+0.6	+0.3	+0.6	+1.0
S	+2.1	+2.6	+1.3	+1.3
K	+0.6	−2.0	+1.1	+3.2

Note: All percentages are continously compounded annual rates of change. The "contribution" of a variable is its annual growth rate multiplied by its coefficient in the *ATDR* regression in table 2. The sum of contributions may differ from the *ATDR* growth rate due to rounding and random factors. All variables used in the computations are 3-year averages centered about the initial and terminal year of any period. This is done to reduce the importance of random factors.

The early 1960s experience is important for the present purpose because shortly after the auto producers, under the threat of federal regulation, introduced seat belts as standard equipment, the death rate resumed its secular decline. One interpretation, encouraged by the highway safety literature, attributes this conjunction directly to the new devices. An equally facile alternative interpretation is that the recent experience simply marks a return to a norm which had been well established long before these devices were developed. I try to distinguish among these interpretations by asking how closely the post-1965 experience conforms to that which we could expect from the previous experience. Specifically, if the parameters characterizing the response of accidents to their determinants before 1965 are assumed unchanged and any effect of safety devices is thereby assumed away, how well can we explain the recent experience?

The effects of safety devices on death rates.—To answer this, I use the regressions in table 2 and post-1965 values of the independent variables to generate predicted death rates for recent years. These are shown in table 5 (ignore row 1972*a* momentarily). If the evidence from safety studies is taken at face value, we would expect the projected rates to exceed the actual by continually widening amounts until a 1972

TABLE 5.   Actual and Projected Death Rates, 1966–72

| | | | | | Death Rate | | | | | | | |
| | ATDR | | | | AVDR | | | | APDR | | | |
Year	Actual	Projected	Diff	T	Actual	Projected	Diff	T	Actual	Projected	Diff	T
1965	5.83	5.87	−0.6	—	4.54	4.58	−0.6	—	1.29	1.30	−0.6	—
1966	6.04	5.90	+2.4	+1.04	4.68	4.68	0	0	1.36	1.25	+8.4	+2.21
1967	5.83	5.75	+1.4	+0.58	4.51	4.64	−2.8	−0.93	1.32	1.16	+12.9	+3.15
1968	5.78	5.73	+0.9	+0.28	4.51	4.75	−5.2	−1.30	1.27	1.09	+15.3	+2.88
1969	5.67	5.76	−1.6	−0.53	4.49	4.79	−6.5	−1.74	1.18	1.09	+7.9	+1.58
1970	5.37	5.28	+1.7	+0.55	4.16	4.36	−4.7	−1.21	1.21	1.00	+19.1	+3.67
1971	5.11	5.10	+0.2	+0.05	3.91	4.31	−9.7	−2.12	1.20	.92	+26.6	+4.36
1972	5.06	4.83	+4.7	+0.98	3.86	4.14	−7.0	−1.17	1.20	.84	+35.6	+4.45
1972a	5.06	5.08	−0.3	−0.37	3.86	4.24	−9.6	−2.16	1.20	.93	+25.7	+2.53

Note: Projected rates are antilogs of the values obtained by entering 1966–72 values of the independent variables in the table 2 regressions (in deaths per 100 million vehicle miles). Diff is the difference between actual and projected natural logs of death rate × 100, so it can be interpreted as a percentage for continuous compounding. T is the ratio of Diff to the standard error of forecast from the table 2 regression. Row 1972a is obtained from 1947–72 regressions of the same form as those in table 2, except that a variable, the fraction of the vehicle stock of 1964 or later vintage, has been added. Here the projected values are obtained by subtracting the 1972 effect of this variable (its coefficient × 1972 value) from the 1972 predicted value of the regression. Diff is computed from the difference of the 1972 actual and adjusted-predicted value, and T is the ratio of the coefficient of the car stock variable to its standard error. 1965 actual and predicted values of the table 2 regressions are shown for comparison with subsequent years.

gap between them approaching perhaps 20 percent was attained. However, no such gap is evident in the behavior of the total death rate (*ATDR*). Indeed, the projected *ATDR* tracks the actual rate to within around 2 percent up to 1972, when it falls below the actual by around 5 percent. While this last difference hints at a perverse effect of safety regulation, the standard error of the 1972 regression forecast is too large to permit acceptance of this implication. Virtually identical results were obtained by substituting the unadjusted *TDR* for *ATDR* in these calculations (the 1972 *TDR* exceeds its projected value by 4.1 percent). Finally, I estimated the *ATDR* regression on 1947–72 data adding the fraction of the car stock of 1964 and later vintage (i.e., subject to federal safety regulation). The coefficient of this variable yields an estimate of the productivity of regulation which should be biased upward.[25] However, the bias is too small to alter the basic conclusion: the 1972 effect and the *t*-ratio of the coefficient of the pseudo-proxy for safety regulation are reported in row 1972*a* of table 5, and both are nugatory. The implication of all this is that there is essentially nothing in the post-1965 behavior of the total death rate that can corroborate the kind of life-saving impact—indeed, any life-saving impact—of safety devices that are adduced in the safety literature. This experience can be explained entirely by the same forces that explain variation in the death rate before these devices became mandatory.[26]

[25] The regression constrains the pre- and postregulatory coefficients to be equal. However, we cannot expect this to be the case generally. Suppose, for example, that with the mandatory devices every increase in income induces a greater increase in driving intensity than without them. In that case, the direct effect of safety regulation as estimated by the coefficient may be favorable, but this would be offset by a higher income effect. A similar argument would apply if safety regulation were simply a particular manifestation of an income effect. The implication of this and analogous arguments shows up in the expanded regression: it has a larger income and driver-age elasticity and a smaller price elasticity than the table 2 counterparts. However, the alcohol elasticities are roughly equal, and the speed elasticity is lower in the expanded regression. This last result implies that the mandatory safety devices are particularly effective in protecting against the effects of high-speed accidents, though the increased income coefficient casts doubt on this implication. On a similar argument, projection of death rates from preregulation parameters may overstate the productivity of regulation. If regulation induces an increase in speed, for example, the projected death rate will be larger than in a pure "no-regulation" world.

[26] I am told, by representatives of domestic auto producers, that my results may also reflect failure to account for effects of the recent increase in sales of imports. Most studies show that the probability of death in an accident is higher for occupants of small cars, which until recently were dominantly imports (and vice versa). However, the essential point of this paper is that any such differential probability will induce driver responses working in an opposite direction. When I added the fraction of cars which are imports to the regressions, its effect was insignificant, and some crude post-1965 data tend to confirm this. Among the major industrial states, California and, un-

TABLE 6.   Annual Rates of Change in Death Rate and their Composition,
1960–65 and 1965–71

	Subperiod	
Variable	1960–65	1965–72
ATDR	+2.3%	−2.2%
Contribution due to		
T	−7.4	−7.4
Subtotal (*ATDR* − contribution of *T*)	+9.7	+5.2
P	+0.1	−0.7
Y	+2.6	+1.5
A	+1.0	+0.9
S	+2.5	+1.5
K	+3.2	+1.6

Note: See note to table 4. 1972 values of the variables are used in relevant computations.

To elaborate the details of this conclusion, table 6 presents the composition of the 1965–72 change in death rate along with the companion data from table 3 for 1960–65. These indicate that the recent resumption of the decline in the death rate can be attributed, in order of importance, to (*a*) a tapering of the influence of the postwar baby boom on the age distribution of drivers, more normal growth of (*b*) the price of leisure and (*c*) vehicle speed, and (*d*) a rise in the price of accidents (insurance loading fees, health care, and auto repair costs have all increased faster than other consumer prices).

Table 5 also contains data on the distribution of highway deaths among vehicle occupants and pedestrians. These can help distinguish among rival explanations for the overall lack of effectiveness of safety regulation. If this regulation has not merely ratified market forces, we

---

surprisingly, Michigan are at opposite extremes in the receptivity of their drivers toward imports. In the former, the share of imports in total registrations was about 20 percent in 1972 and has grown rapidly in recent years. In the latter, imports account for roughly 5 percent and their share has grown little (the 1972 U.S. average share is about 10 percent). However, no parallel divergence is apparent in recent highway death rate trends. The 1963–65 death rates for the two states are virtually identical (5.1 per 100 million vehicle miles in California, and 5.3 in Michigan), which reflects a basic similarity of driving characteristics. That similarity has apparently dominated their recent experience, because their 1970–72 death rates are still virtually identical (3.9 for California and 4.0 for Michigan). One can also add Illinois to this group, since its drivers have been only a little less hostile to imports than Michigan's. The Illinois death rate closely tracks that of the other two states, falling from 5.0 to 4.0 in the same period. Thus, something like a controlled experiment leaves little room for attributing the lack of effectiveness of safety regulation to the growth of imports.

expect a shift toward nonoccupant deaths, and there is some evidence of this in table 5. Occupant death rates do tend to lie below projected values by increasing amounts over time. If the consistent (though sometimes insignificant) overprojection of AVDR and the significant (biased) coefficient of the regulatory variable in row 1972a lead us to accept the hypothesis that regulation has saved lives of drivers, then the magnitude involved appears to be on the order of half that suggested by a naive reading of the safety literature. At the same time, the preregulation APDR regression consistently underprojects postregulation death rates, and these differences are usually significant. The differences are so large that they engender skepticism, but neither adjustment for growth in bicyclists and motorcyclists (who are included with pedestrians) nor use of a population rather than vehicle-mile death rate changes the basic results.[27]

The time series data then imply that safety regulation has not merely reflected market forces, for then its failure to reduce the highway death rate should have been matched by failure to change the distribution of these deaths. The safest inference from the time series, though, is that there has been a shift in the burden of accident risk toward nonoccupants, which is consistent with optimal driver response to an exogenous reduction of the expected loss from an accident. I will examine injury and property-damage experience and some independent evidence on driver behavior for corroboration of this inference.

2. *Injury and Property Damage.* Effective regulation should also lead to a substitution of less for more severe accidents. Some of these will substitute injury for death, while others will substitute property damage for injury. While one cannot therefore predict the net effect on total injuries, pedestrians should, as with deaths, bear a larger share

[27] Bicycle and motorcycle deaths were a growing portion of nonoccupant deaths prior to 1965. If it were assumed that the ratio of these deaths to other nonoccupant deaths maintained its pre-1965 growth rate (about 3 percent annually), and that none of its recent acceleration was due to substitution for pedestrian deaths, then the 1972 APDR would have been about 5 percent lower than it was. The use of vehicle miles to deflate nonoccupant deaths assumes implicitly that driver action "causes" them. At another extreme, we could assume that pedestrians seek risk independently of driver action, vehicle density, etc. In that case, population, as a proxy for the number of pedestrians seeking risk, would be the more appropriate deflator. However, when the figures in table 5 are obtained from a regression using a population death rate, the underprojection of post-1965 death rates actually becomes more severe (by about 10 percentage points). The reason is that vehicle miles have some effect on pedestrian deaths, and their growth has accelerated relative to population in recent years. Finally, use of unadjusted death rates reveals the same shift in the incidence of risk as the adjusted data. The projected PDR is 26 percent below the actual, and the projected VDR is 5 percent above the actual in 1972.

of the burden of injuries. And we should observe a net increase in property-damage accidents.

Regression estimates of equation (1), with injury and property-damage rates as the dependent variables, are presented in table 7. These are subject to much more measurement error than death rates.[28] However, the regressions almost suspiciously mirror their counterparts in table 2, most notably in their lack of much residual variance. If there are any notable differences between the two sets, they might be the generally lower income elasticity for the less severe accidents and the larger price elasticity of damage accidents.[29] In view of the close correspondence between the different accident series prior to safety regulation,[30] it would be surprising if their behavior differed much subsequently.

The postregulatory injury rate experience does mirror that of death rates. The important exception is injury rates for vehicle occupants. The projections from the *AVIR* regression in table 7 (see table 8) are usually *below* the actual values, though the differences are insignificant. Similarly, the coefficient of the fraction of cars subject to regulation in the expanded form of that regression is insignificant (row 1972a). Therefore, the weak evidence in favor of reduced occupant deaths due to regulation does not hold up for injuries. However, there is evidence for harmful injury effects on pedestrians of roughly the same magnitude as for death rates. However, since the vehicle-occupant series dominates the total, we cannot safely conclude that total injury rates have been adversely affected by regulation.[31]

[28] This is due to the greater degree of underreporting and subjectivity of definition involved with the less severe accidents. The resulting problems are well illustrated by a comparison of the National Safety Council injury series, which I use here, with an alternative series produced by the Travelers Insurance Company: the two are not in remote agreement about either the level or rate of change in motor vehicle injuries. The Travelers estimate of total injuries is currently about 2½ times that of the safety Council, though the immediate postwar excess was only about 30 percent. In recent years, the Federal Highway Administration has also collected injury data, and these run roughly at the geometric mean of the other two series! The Safety Council is the sole source of property accident estimates, but these are bedeviled by sporadically changing reporting requirements, and are consequently rounded generously.

[29] The last result seems reasonable if the fraction of an accident's cost which the insurer imposes on a driver varies inversely with its amount. However, in that case the price elasticity of injury accidents should exceed that for fatalities, but it does not.

[30] The correlation between any pair of accident rates is typically above .95.

[31] Some independent evidence indicates that injury accidents as a whole have become more severe in the aftermath of safety regulation. From 1958 to 1964, a period in which alcohol consumption, speed, and demographic trends were unfavorable, the average paid auto insurance claim for bodily injury deflated by the price index for medical care actually declined by 0.6 percent per annum. From 1964 to 1971, in an environment otherwise less conducive to injury, the average claim increased 2.1 percent per annum. (Data are from Insurance Information Institute [various years].)

TABLE 7. Regression Estimates, Injury and Property Damage Rates, 1947–65

Dependent Variable	Independent Variable						R^2	SE × 100	D-W
	P	Y	T	A	S	K			
ATIR	-0.249	0.524	-0.067	0.295	2.224	0.670	.983	2.190	3.010
	-1.770	1.807	-9.203	1.524	3.473	7.050			
AVIR	-0.220	0.503	-0.064	0.399	2.594	0.469	.957	2.502	2.882
	-1.371	1.516	-7.635	1.803	3.546	4.318			
APIR	-0.290	0.318	-0.096	-0.322	1.624	1.574	.993	4.010	1.738
	-1.128	0.598	-7.147	-0.908	1.386	9.041			
ADMGR	-0.515	0.818	-0.069	0.466	1.663	0.527	.960	2.891	1.473
	-2.938	2.190	-7.070	1.843	1.912	4.271			

Note: See note to table 2 and text.

TABLE 8. Actual and Projected Injury and Property-Damage Rates, 1966–72

Year	ATIR				AVIR				APIR				ADMGR			
	Actual	Projected	Diff	T	Actual	Projected	Diff	T	Actual	Projected	Diff	T	Actual	Projected	Diff	T
1965	217	216	+0.5	—	196	195	+0.5	—	21	21	+0.1	—	1,490	1,475	+1.0	—
1966	221	215	+2.8	+0.88	199	196	+1.5	0.42	22	20	+9.6	1.68	1,491	1,456	+2.4	0.59
1967	215	209	+2.8	+0.80	194	192	+1.0	0.26	21	18	+12.8	2.10	1,466	1,414	+3.6	0.82
1968	217	206	+5.2	+1.16	196	192	+2.0	0.39	20	17	+17.1	2.14	1,500	1,358	+10.0	1.72
1969	208	210	-1.0	-0.23	188	196	-4.2	-0.88	20	17	+16.1	2.19	1,544	1,397	+10.0	1.85
1970	200	191	+4.6	+1.05	181	178	+1.7	0.34	19	15	+21.5	2.76	1,535	1,285	+17.8	3.12
1971	191	185	+3.2	+0.62	173	174	-0.6	-0.10	18	14	+22.9	2.49	1,503	1,208	+21.8	3.25
1972	191	173	+9.9	+1.46	174	163	+6.5	0.84	17	13	+27.8	2.32	1,499	1,107	+30.3	3.48
1972a	191	185	+3.0	+0.15	174	175	-0.5	-0.48	17	13	+27.0	3.00	1,499	1,125	+28.3	3.071

Note: See note to table 5.

Table 8 also compares projected and actual property-damage accident rates. These series behave differently from both death and injury rates, and in precisely the way we would predict if safety regulation has been at all effective: there are significantly more damage accidents after regulation than could have been expected. The size of the gap is startling. Both of the estimates for 1972 imply an excess of on the order of 4 million damage accidents.[32]

The overall thrust of the time-series evidence is then consistent with a regulation-induced reduction in the probability of death per accident, to which drivers have responded with more risk taking. It is this response to which I have attributed the conjunction of (1) an unchanged death rate, (2) an increased risk of death and injury for nonoccupants, and (3) an increased probability of property-damage accidents. I examine next some more direct measures of driver risk taking for consistency with the preceding interpretation.

3. *Driver Risk Taking.* While increased risk taking by drivers can take many forms, the time-series regressions tend to confirm the importance of those associated with alcohol, age, and speed, especially the latter two. Therefore, if safety regulation has led to increased risk taking by drivers, this might be manifested in higher driving speeds, more young drivers, and increased inebriation among drivers. After these conjectures are tested, I shall examine data on accidents to cars of specific model years.

To examine the effect of regulation on driving speed, I first estimated the following regression on preregulation data (1947–65):

$$S = \text{Constant} + 0.013\,T + 0.109\,Y - 0.210\,PG - 1.311\,IM$$
$$\phantom{S = \text{Constant} + }(4.535)\quad(1.262)\quad(-2.819)\quad(-2.618)$$

$$R^2 = .988, \qquad SE = 0.75 \times 10^{-2}, \qquad \text{D-W} = 2.327$$

(*t*-ratios below coefficients), where, in addition to symbols defined previously, PG = log of the consumer price index for gasoline divided by

---

[32] The unadjusted damage rates behave similarly; the actual rate exceeds the projected rate by .264 (natural log units) in 1972. Moreover, there appears to be a subsidiary effect here similar to that encountered with pedestrians: damage accidents have become more damaging. From 1958 to 1964, the average paid auto insurance claim for property damage, deflated by the auto repair price index, rose 2 percent per annum. It will be recalled that vehicle speed, alcohol consumption, and demographic trends in this period were all conducive to increased property damage. Their force abated subsequently, but the increase in the average damage claim accelerated to 6 percent per annum from 1964 to 1971. (Data are from Insurance Information Institute [various years].)

the all-items CPI (per mile gas consumption increases with vehicle speed), and IM = ratio of imports to the total stock of cars (imports typically have lower speed capability than domestic cars). I then projected values of S for the postregulation period, 1966–72, from this regression to see whether they fell short of the actual values. In fact, however, the projected and actual values are consistently within 1 or 2 percent of each other, so we must reject the hypothesis of a regulation-induced increase in vehicle speed. The same result is obtained by adding the fraction of cars subject to regulation to a regression on 1947–72 data. The coefficient of the variable is less than one-tenth its standard error.[33]

Another way that safety regulation may lead to increased probability of an accident is through reduced inhibition of driving by the young. Unfortunately, preregulation data on the age distribution of drivers is sketchy, so they must be interpreted cautiously. However, it is possible to trace the propensities of different age groups to drive through two periods of equal length centered about initiation of safety regulation. This is done in table 9, and the data do imply some reduced restraint on driving by the young after the onset of regulation. Specifically, while driver participation (as measured by the ratio of drivers to nondrivers) among those over 25 increased at roughly the same rate in the two periods, participation among the young accelerated after 1965. This may help explain the substantially increased pedestrian risk which we found for this period, since the regressions in tables 2 and 7 indicate that pedestrians are peculiarly vulnerable to young drivers.

Data on arrests for drunkenness also appear to be consistent with a postregulation increase in driver risk taking. Table 10 compares trends in arrests for drunkenness, drunk driving, and all other "minor" crimes. The series share inaccuracies from changes in coverage, but with the onset of regulation there is a marked departure from the previous conformity of drunk-driving arrests to arrests for other types of drunkenness. Both arrest rates had been declining in tandem, while the arrest rate for other minor crimes remained roughly unchanged. Specifically, the pre-1965 correlation of the two drunkenness arrest series is .91. After 1965, this correlation becomes strongly negative, and arrests for drunk driving grow much more rapidly than for other minor

---

[33] Legal costs may be an important left-out variable here. Speed limits increased little in the 1960s, so that actual driving speeds began to bump against legal limits by the end of the sample period. The average state-noninterstate speed limit has hovered around 60 mph since 1960. In 1960, only 20 percent of all cars were exceeding this speed. This doubled by 1965, but was only about 50 percent by 1972 (see U.S. Federal Highway Administration, "Traffic Speed Trends"). This slowing may reflect the nature of the traffic laws which tax speed only above a critical level which many drivers are beginning to crowd.

TABLE 9.   Ratio of Drivers to Nondrivers by Age, 1958, 1965, 1972

| | Drivers/Nondrivers | | Change of Ratio from Earlier Year (%) | |
| | Under 25 (1) | 25 and Older (2) | Under 25 (3) | 25 and Older (4) |
Series and Year				
National Safety Council				
1958	2.88	2.13	—	—
1965	2.66	2.99	−7.6	+40.3
Federal Highway Administration				
1965	2.91	3.01	—	—
1972	3.42	4.16	+17.5	+38.2

Note: Prior to 1965, the National Safety Council was the sole source of data on the age distribution of drivers. From 1965 on, the Federal Highway Administration had published similar data (see U.S. National Highway Traffic Safety Administration 1973). The figures in col. (1) are adjusted to account for the effects of lower driver participation of those under 20 and shifts in the age composition of those under 25. Specifically, the ratio of drivers to population (p) is calculated separately for the age cohorts 16–19 and 20–24 in each year. These are combined into a weighted average ($\bar{p}$) with fixed weights of .478 and .522, which are the 1958–72 average proportions of these subcohorts in the 16–24 cohort. The figures in col. 1 are $\bar{p}/(1 - \bar{p})$. The unadjusted data for col. 1 would be 2.90, 2.65, 2.86, and 3.46 reading from top to bottom. Percentage changes are for data from the same source.

TABLE 10.   Arrest Rates for Drunkenness, Drunk Driving, and Other Nonserious Crimes, Selected Years

| | Arrest Rates (per 1,000) | | | Change of Arrest Rate in Period (%) | | |
Year	Drunk Driving (per Driver)	Drunkenness (per Person 15 and Older)	Other Nonserious Crimes (per Person 15 and Older)	Drunk Driving	Drunkenness	Other Nonserious Crimes
1953	4.45	23.81	22.20	—	—	—
1959	3.85	21.69	24.59	−13.5	−9.1	+10.7
1965	3.53	16.60	23.11	−8.3	−23.4	−6.0
1971	5.75	13.32	29.30	+62.9	−19.8	+26.8

Note: Data are from U.S. Federal Bureau of Investigation (various years). Prior to 1960, data are available for urban areas only. Therefore, pre-1960 rates are estimates obtained by multiplying reported arrests by the 1960–61 ratio of total to urban arrests. Reported arrests were divided by population in the areas covered by the FBI survey (pre-1960 population is estimated in a manner similar to arrests) and multiplied by the national ratios of population to the relevant subgroup. See source for definition of nonserious crimes. Drunkenness and drunk driving are separate subcategories.

crimes. The divergence between the two drunkenness arrest series can be reconciled by introducing safety regulation. When the drunk-driving arrest rate for the whole 1953–71 period is regressed on that for other types of drunkenness and the fraction of the car stock subject to safety regulation, the partial correlation between the two arrest series (.89) is hardly different from the earlier-period simple correlation (but, of course, much greater than the full-period simple correlation, which is .47), and the partial correlation of drunk driving with regulation is highly significant (.91).

Interpretation of these data as reflecting an increase in the demand for risky driving is, however, subject to an important qualification. The onset of safety regulation coincides with an increased spread of "implied consent" laws, which make it easier for police to obtain evidence of driver intoxication. At the same time it is worth noting that annual growth of alcohol consumption has roughly doubled since 1965, so it risks exaggeration to attribute all of the reported increase in drunk driving to legal changes.

Canada and North Carolina accident data.—Safety regulation in Canada has basically paralleled that in the United States, beginning with "voluntary" introduction of lap belts in 1964. It is therefore possible to use some Canadian data, which classify cars involved in accidents by model year, to test the hypothesis that regulation induces increased driver risk. That hypothesis implies that cars subject to regulation will have above-average accident frequencies.

It will be expedient to focus on the ratio of cars from model year m to all cars reporting involvement in an accident in year t (RA_{mt}).[34] To isolate the impact of regulation on RA, I will take account of the effects of the ratio of cars from m to the total car stock in t (RC_{mt}), and the age of cars from m in t (V_{mt}). The latter variable is included as much to standardize for reporting differences as to measure a true age effect: accidents involving older cars more frequently fail to meet minimum damage criteria for reporting. The basic regulatory variable (SR_m) uses the information from table 1 that lap seat belts produce about 60 percent of the total expected productivity of safety devices. It is defined as zero if m is before 1964, 0.6 for m from 1964 to 66, and 1.0 for 1967 and later vintages. The effect of regulation on any one vintage's share of accident

[34] The data are too fragmentary to permit development of an analogue to the regressions in tables 2 and 7 for each vintage of car. Some relevant independent variables are unavailable for Canada. More important, the model-year breakdown of accidents covers selected provinces, and the coverage is not uniform over time. Therefore, I do not seek to explain the absolute level of accidents in any year's sample, but rather the distribution of accidents among model years. The data are from Statistics Canada (various years).

involvements will become diluted as cars subject to regulation become more common, because of both simple arithmetic[35] and the increased probability that preregulation cars will be struck by postregulation models. As the latter approach ubiquity, the effect of regulation on any one vintage's share of the higher accident total will vanish. To develop a linear approximation to this process, we may let $B \cdot SR_m$ be the partial effect of regulation on RA_{mt}, where B is a coefficient. However, that coefficient should decline as the fraction of the car stock subject to regulation (FR_t) rises; B can then be expressed as $B_0 + B_1 \cdot FR_t$, so that the partial effect of regulation becomes $B_0 \cdot SR_m + B_1 \cdot (SR_m \cdot FR_t)$. We would expect $B_0 > 0$, $B_1 < 0$, and, more precisely, $B_0 = |B_1|$ (so that the partial effect vanishes when $FR = 1$).

The results of the regression on Canadian data fulfill these expectations. The regression is

$$RA_{mt} = 6.65 + 0.59\ RC_{mt} - 0.54\ V_{mt}$$
$$(11.14) \qquad (-13.00)$$

$$+\ 2.07\ SR_m - 2.14\ (SR_m \cdot FR_t)$$
$$(3.24) \qquad (-2.15)$$

$$R^2 = 0.92, \qquad SE = 0.89$$

(t-ratios are below coefficients, RA and RC are in percentage point units). The sample consists of vintages 10 years old and less (which usually comprise about 90 percent of the total stock) for years 1959–72, or 140 observations,[36] of which 45 are subject to regulation. The interesting result, of course, is that the coefficients of the regulatory and interaction variables have the sign pattern and the (virtual) equality of absolute value which is consistent with a regulation-induced increase in driver risk taking. The magnitude of the coefficient of SR is also of interest. It implies that if the sample-average vintage (8.75 percent of the car stock and 9 percent of accidents) is made subject to regulation, its accident frequency increases fully 25 percent. This is sufficient to offset the reduction in deaths per accident claimed by the safety literature for

[35] For example, suppose that the car stock consists of v equal-sized vintages, of which k are regulated. If x is the probability that a car from any of the k will be involved in an accident and y the probability for a preregulatory car, RA will be $x/[kx + (v - k)y]$. This will be $1/v$ if x and y are equal, but it must approach $1/v$ as k approaches v even if x exceeds y.

[36] In some cases, the original accident data were for groups of vintages. For these, I allocated the group total among vintages in proportion to the vintage share of cars. This procedure therefore biases the coefficient of RC toward unity and overstates its accuracy.

mandated safety devices, and it is well within the range of my estimate in table 8 of the regulation-induced excess accident frequency for the United States.

Further corroboration of the time-series results and of increased accident frequency for postregulation cars may be found in North Carolina accident data. Levine and Campbell (1971) use a sample of North Carolina accidents occurring in 1966 and 1968 to cars built in 1964 and after, classified by presence or absence of an energy-absorbing steering column (and implicitly the group of other devices introduced simultaneously; all cars in the sample have seat belts). North Carolina car registration data (R. L. Polk & Co., various years) indicate that no more than 27 percent of all cars eligible for the sample in the 2 years were equipped with this safety device. However, cars so equipped account for 34 percent of all accidents in the sample. That is, the probability of an accident involving cars with the safety devices is 40 percent greater than for cars not so equipped.[37] This is more than sufficient to outweigh the reduced risk of death per accident to drivers of such cars (14 percent in this study), and even suggests that the large estimates of increased accident risk in table 8 are conservative.

In summary, then, the fragmentary evidence is broadly consistent with some increase in driver risk taking since implementation of safety regulation. At the least those data implying such an increase are countered by none showing the opposite. I next examine cross-section death rate data to see whether they reveal the same impact of this increased risk taking on the level and distribution of death rates as the time series.

B. Cross-Section Data

The impact of the Highway Safety Act has been spreading gradually as pre-1964 cars are replaced with subsequent vintages. Because the rate of replacement varies among areas, so will effective enforcement of the act. This cross-sectional variation in effective enforcement of the Safety Act provides an opportunity to test the effectiveness of safety regulation.

Essentially, I will ask whether death rates are lower in areas (states) where cars with safety devices are more prevalent. As with the time series, I will want to account for nonregulatory influences on death rates, so I proceed as follows: Assume that the cross-section distribution of the death rates (D) in a year subsequent to the onset of regulation is generated by

---

[37] But, from the Canadian data, about half of this excess may be due to underreporting of accidents by unequipped, older cars.

$$D_t = aX_t + bR_t + u_t,$$ (2)

where X = matrix of nonregulatory determinants of D, R = matrix of variables serving as indices of the effective degree of enforcement of regulation, a, b = vectors of coefficients, and u = a random variable. In practice, R will be related to the age distribution of cars. For example, in 1970 safety regulation had affected all cars 6 years old or less, so R might be measured by the fraction of all cars of 1964 or later vintage in a state. Now, one wants to allow for the possibility that the age of cars may exert an influence on D independent of regulation.[38] Therefore, it is insufficient merely to estimate equation (2) on data for year t. To disentangle the effects of car age and regulation, then, suppose that in some earlier year, $t - i$, D is given by

$$D_{t-i} = a'X_{t-i} + b'R'_{t-i} + u'_{t-i},$$ (3)

where R' is defined analogously to R. That is, if R_{1970} is the fraction of cars built from 1964 to 1970, then R'_{1960} would be the fraction of cars built from 1954 to 1960. Then, if regulation has no effect, a and b would equal their earlier counterparts (ignoring nonstationarities). If regulation does have an effect, it could change a' as well as b'. By analogy with the time-series tests, we can impose the constraint $a = a'$ and then see if we must reduce b' to successfully explain D_t. That is, if we assume that D_t is generated by the same process as D_{t-i} and regulation has in fact altered the process, we should be overpredicting death rates where R_{1970} is high and *mutatis mutandis*. In general, then, we can define

$$b = b' + B,$$ (4)

where B is a change induced by regulation. So, equation (2) could be rewritten

$$D_t = aX_t + b'R_t + BR_t + u_t.$$ (5)

Then, imposing the constraint on a, compute

$$V_t = (D_t - a'X_t - b'R_t),$$ (6)

and then estimate

---

[38] Though experiments with the time series suggest the effect is weak. In addition to the experiment with the new-car variable reported in n. 21 above, I conducted one using average age of car as an explanatory variable. Its coefficient was insignificant.

$$V_t = BR_t + u_t. \tag{7}$$

If regulation effectively reduces the death rate, an estimate of B should be negative. Equations (3)–(7) summarize the basic procedure I use to test the effects of regulation, though modifications (for example, of the implicit assumption that u' and u are uncorrelated) will be treated.

Since the cross-section data differ in some respects from the time series, it is useful first to summarize the nature and rationale of these differences:[39] the dependent variables are accident losses per capita rather than per vehicle mile (denoted, e.g., $ATDC$ for the total death rate). Accurate state vehicle-mile data are unavailable prior to the last several years, but a fairly good proxy, highway fuel consumption, is available. Rather than constrain the vehicle-mile elasticity of fuel consumption to be one, I make per capita fuel consumption (FC) an independent variable.

Per capita death rates are adjusted to remove effects of interstate highway travel, but not the urban-rural driving mix. Some states have so little driving of one or the other type that a simple average of urban and rural death rates would be unrepresentative of the local experience. However, to account for urban-rural death rate differences, the ratio of urban to rural driving (U/R) is entered as an independent variable. Further, since urban and rural driving conditions are not uniform across states, I employ rural and urban densities (RD, UD)—that is, vehicle miles per highway mile—as independent variables. The effect of density on the death rate is somewhat complex, however. Everything else being the same, we would expect increased density to increase the probability of an accident and thereby death. However, increased density discourages fast driving, passing on two-lane roads, etc., and on this account would reduce deaths.

Estimates of vehicle speed are unavailable for all states, so I use as a proxy the speed limit on main (non-limited-access) rural roads (SL). In preliminary work with a subsample, the residual from the regression of estimated vehicle speed on SL proved uncorrelated with death rates, perhaps in part because these speed estimates sometimes behave erratically over time. Therefore, the characterization of vehicle speed in a state is left to the set of variables SL, U/R, UD, RD.

The price of an accident proved singularly difficult to estimate, primarily because cross-section indices of medical care and auto repair prices are unavailable. I assumed that these were correlated with wage rates for hospital personnel and automechanics, respectively, and employed indices of these as proxies for prices. A weighted average of

---

[39] A detailed description of the sources and methods of constructing these data is available from the author.

these indices multiplied by an insurance load is then used as the cross-section accident price variable (*PA*). One would like to deflate *PA* by a cross-section general price index, but this too is unavailable. In consequence, *PA* will inevitably vary with local wage and salary levels.

The cross-section data permit us to measure both the long-run response of death rates to income and any differences in response to earned and unearned income. Instead of a single income measure, then, I enter disposable personal income per capita (*YD*) and the ratio of earned income per adult to unearned income per capita (*E/N*). If my interpretation of the time-series evidence is correct, *YD*, which would be dominated by permanent cross-section income differences, should have a negative coefficient (or one at least smaller than its time-series counterpart) while the coefficient of *E/N* should be positive.

Both alcohol consumption (*A*) and the age distribution of the population (*K*) are measured as in the time series. The former of these uses local liquor store sales, but tax differentials stimulate considerable interstate movement of liquor purchases, and this introduces measurement error in *A*.

The basic data are for 1961–71, but to reduce the importance of random components, triplets are averaged to yield four cross sections centered about 1962, 1965, 1967, and 1970. The notation X_t, then, always refers to a 3-year average centered about t. To provide a reference point for subsequent work, table 11 presents cross-section regression estimates for the various death rates with regulatory variables excluded. These differ in some respects from the time-series results, so a brief summary of results is useful.

Speed.—The singular importance of this variable carries over to the cross-section data, as does the differential importance for vehicle occupants and pedestrians. In fact, the magnitudes of the time-series and cross-section speed elasticity estimates are almost the same. For fragmentary data on actual vehicle speeds, the cross-section elasticity with respect to *SL* is on the order of 0.3–0.4, and when these are divided into the coefficients in table 11, the implied actual speed elasticities correspond roughly to those in table 2.

Urban-rural driving and densities.—The cross-section data mirror the persistent excess of rural over urban death rates, especially (indeed exclusively) for vehicle occupants. However, strong density effects show up in urban areas and for pedestrians. That is, the discouragement of risky driving provided by high densities appears to dominate the behavior of drivers in rural areas.

Alcohol.—The time-series and cross-section data disagree on both the overall importance of alcoholism and its relative impact on pedestrians and drivers. Indeed, the subgroup alcohol elasticities here are very nearly the reverse of those in table 2.

Youth.—Perhaps the most glaring contradiction between the time-series and cross-section data occurs here. There is virtually no evidence in table 11 of the substantial age differentials in the death rate that show up in crude data and the time-series regressions, nor is there much evidence of a differential impact on pedestrians. Since age differentials in the death rate are pronounced in every state (see Iskrant and Joliet 1968), it is difficult to believe that age is really a proxy for something left out of the regressions, and the cross-section results for age merit skepticism.[40]

Price of accident.—This variable has no significant impact on death rates in any cross section, but this may reflect the peculiar difficulty of measuring cross-section price differences.

Income.—The cross-section results provide a clue to the large negative secular trend terms in the time-series regressions. The income elasticities in table 11 are uniformly negative and significant, in sharp contrast to those in the time series, but consistent with dominance of long-run income effects in the cross sections. If one assumes that the cross-section elasticities measure long-run adaptations while the time-series elasticities capture short-period effects, the difference between the two elasticities would account for something like half of the time-series trend coefficients. The algebraically lower cross-section elasticity for pedestrian as opposed to occupant deaths is also consistent with the time series. Both short- and long-run income changes apparently lead to a substitution of driving for walking. Finally, there is some weak evidence that the differential response to earned and unearned income that was found in the time series is permanent. The coefficient of the ratio of these incomes is persistently positive, though never significant.[41]

---

[40] These results are influenced by interesting cross-section differences in the impact of age. The ratio of the 18–24-year-old to total death rate tends to be lower where that group is relatively large (e.g., the South and West). See Iskrant and Joliet (1968). This may reflect adaptation by localities to the magnitude of the relevant risk through, for example, police enforcement and driver training programs. A successful reconciliation of the cross-section and time-series data would require an explanation of these differences in age-specific death rates.

[41] Attempts to refine measures of the income effect proved unrewarding. For example, I broke each state's per capita income into linear-trend and deviation-from-trend components in a crude attempt to distinguish "permanent" from "transitory" effects. However, there was no significant difference between the coefficients of these components. With similar motivation (and results), I added the interperiod change in income to the regressions. The income effect in the cross sections, like the trend effect in the cross sections, undoubtedly summarizes a number of forces, and, given the larger degrees of freedom, I attempted to measure the effects of some of these separately. However, this attempt was also unsuccessful. It entailed addition of, among others, the following variables to the regression: (1) state highway police expenditures for traffic law enforcement (unfortunately, local enforcement authorities do not account

TABLE 11.   Regression Estimates, Death Rates by State, 1962, 1965, 1967, 1970

Independent Variable and Year	Dependent Variable					
	ATDC		AVDC		APDC	
	Coeff.	t	Coeff.	t	Coeff.	t
FC						
1962	1.11	6.41	1.31	6.87	0.32	1.31
1965	0.94	5.65	1.10	5.91	0.40	1.43
1967	0.70	5.22	0.84	5.58	0.07	0.26
1970	1.00	7.15	—	—	—	—
SL						
1962	0.76	3.42	1.02	4.19	−0.09	−0.29
1965	0.89	3.97	1.07	4.33	0.21	0.55
1967	0.73	4.17	0.89	4.50	0.14	0.41
1970	0.44	2.43	—	—	—	—
U/R						
1962	−0.17	−3.69	−0.21	−4.12	−0.02	−0.33
1965	−0.19	−3.71	−0.22	−3.81	−0.10	−1.15
1967	−0.17	−4.55	−0.21	−5.11	0.00	0.02
1970	−0.09	−2.48	—	—	—	—
UD						
1962	0.23	3.11	0.22	2.68	0.33	3.14
1965	0.16	2.67	0.13	2.04	0.35	3.52
1967	0.15	3.11	0.15	2.71	0.27	2.82
1970	0.16	3.06	—	—	—	—
RD						
1962	−0.09	−1.77	−0.10	−1.94	0.06	0.84
1965	−0.00	−0.04	−0.02	−0.40	0.18	2.28
1967	−0.00	−0.04	−0.02	0.35	0.16	2.06
1970	−0.07	−2.01	—	—	—	—
A						
1962	0.17	2.04	0.10	1.14	0.45	3.87
1965	0.04	0.48	−0.01	−0.10	0.23	1.85
1967	0.04	0.75	−0.02	−0.32	0.35	3.21
1970	0.07	1.18	—	—	—	—
K						
1962	0.21	0.97	0.16	0.67	0.58	1.88
1965	0.12	0.54	0.15	0.61	0.25	0.65
1967	−0.01	−0.03	0.01	0.07	−0.12	−0.33
1970	−0.18	−1.01	—	—	—	—

TABLE 11.   *(continued)*

Independent Variable and Year	Dependent Variable					
	ATDC		AVDC		APDC	
	Coeff.	t	Coeff.	t	Coeff.	t
YD						
1962	−0.81	−3.78	−0.76	−3.24	−1.29	−4.23
1965	−0.66	−3.08	−0.60	−2.50	−1.27	−3.52
1967	−0.75	−4.65	−0.66	−3.67	−1.50	−4.85
1970	−0.92	−5.06	—	—	—	—
E/N						
1962	0.10	0.70	0.11	0.72	−0.01	−0.03
1965	0.06	0.38	0.02	0.11	0.24	0.96
1967	0.13	1.14	0.13	1.04	0.30	1.40
1970	0.17	1.66	—	—	—	—
PA						
1962	0.15	0.89	0.16	0.84	0.07	0.29
1965	0.23	0.93	0.24	0.86	0.35	0.82
1967	0.18	1.00	0.21	1.03	0.26	0.73
1970	0.06	0.34	—	—	—	—
R^2						
1962	0.90	—	0.92	—	0.62	—
1965	0.89	—	0.91	—	0.59	—
1967	0.93	—	0.94	—	0.68	—
1970	0.94	—	—	—	—	—
SE × 100						
1962	11.66	—	12.83	—	16.61	—
1965	11.27	—	12.51	—	18.87	—
1967	8.55	—	9.61	—	16.50	—
1970	8.73	—	—	—	—	—

Note: See text for definitions of variables. All variables are natural logarithms of 3-year averages centered about the year indicated. Constant terms are not shown. Coeff. = coefficient. t = ratio of coefficient to its standard error. *AVDC, APDC* unavailable after 1968. Sample size is 48; data exclude Alaska, Hawaii, and the District of Columbia.

C. The Effect of Safety Regulation

The primary test for the effectiveness of safety regulation entails the addition of a variable like R' in equation (3) to an appropriate table 11

---

separately for this function); (2) state highway department road expenditures; (3) the availability of hospital care, as measured by hospital beds per highway mile; (4) the percentage of cars which are imports; and (5) education, as measured by median years of schooling.

regression, computation of a variable like V in (6), and an estimate of B in (7). Estimates of B, which should be negative if regulation has reduced death rates, are in table 12. The meaning of these estimates can be clarified by focusing on a specific case. In the first line of the table, we want to know if the 1970 death rate was reduced by safety regulation. Now, in 1970 all cars built since 1964 were subject to regulation. However, those built since 1967 had more substantial design changes, substantial enough, table 1 suggests, to improve on the life-saving potential of a 1964–66 model by perhaps two-thirds. Therefore, I define a variable equal to 0.6 × number of 1964–66 cars + 1.0 × number of 1967–70 cars all divided by the total stock of cars as the measure of the impact of regulation (R) in 1970. Since R also measures the age of cars, I then construct an analogue (R') for 1962, and add it to the set of variables in the 1962 $ATDC$ regression in table 11. Data for 1970 are then plugged into this expanded 1962 regression to generate a predicted death rate for 1970. This variable tells us what the 1970 $ATDC$ would be if it had been generated by the same process as the 1962 $ATDC$. When this predicted 1970 $ATDC$ is subtracted from the actual, we obtain a "residual" which includes any impact of regulation. For if regulation in fact altered the 1962 process, this residual should be smaller the larger the variable R; that is, the coefficient of R in a regression of the residual on R should be negative. This coefficient is reported under B in the table (ignore B' momentarily).

Since there is some sampling fluctuation in the table 11 coefficients, we can check for consistency of the regulation effect by generating predicted values of the 1970 $ATDC$ from alternative table 11 regressions, specifically those for 1965 and 1967. Here the R' variable will include some impact from regulation, but always less than R.[42] Therefore, the predicted sign of the R coefficient remains negative if regulation is effective. Similarly, tests can be conducted on 1967 and 1965 death rates by suitably redefining the R variable.

The main conclusion to be drawn from table 12 is the same as from the time series: regulation appears not to have reduced highway deaths. Given the preponderance of positive coefficients, one might be tempted to blame regulation for an increase in deaths, but the general lack of significance of the coefficients and their erratic behavior precludes such a conclusion. The time pattern of the coefficients is also inconsistent with effective regulation. For any year's death rate, the

[42] For example, the numerator of $R'_{1967} = 0.6$ × cars in 1967 built 1961–63 + 1.0 × cars built 64–67. Some of these cars but all of the 1970 counterparts had seat belts; some of these, but many more of the 1970 counterparts, had seat belts plus a set of other devices.

TABLE 12. Effect of Regulation on Death Rates, as Measured by Coefficient of Fraction of Cars in a State Subject to Regulation

Period for DR Residual (Dependent Variable)	Coeffs. for Predicted DR	ATDC			AVDC			APDC		
		B	B'	CHG	B	B'	CHG	B	B'	CHG
1970	1962	0.47	0.56	0.43	—	—	—	—	—	—
		1.49	1.96	1.37	—	—	—	—	—	—
1970	1965	−0.25	−0.19	−0.02	—	—	—	—	—	—
		−0.94	−0.82	−0.09	—	—	—	—	—	—
1970	1967	−0.68	−0.64	−0.24	—	—	—	—	—	—
		−2.71	−3.02	−1.29	—	—	—	—	—	—
1967	1962	1.51	1.60	0.54	1.96	2.03	0.57	0.83	1.01	0.97
		2.78	3.22	1.00	3.23	3.66	0.93	1.10	1.66	1.42
1967	1965	0.65	0.64	0.10	0.88	0.85	0.21	0.45	0.43	0.09
		1.64	2.26	0.30	2.00	2.71	0.59	0.62	1.03	0.21
1965	1962	1.41	1.54	0.74	2.18	2.22	0.64	−0.45	0.30	1.74
		1.40	1.87	0.77	1.96	2.36	0.56	−0.31	0.23	0.85

Note: *DR* residual is the difference between a death rate in the year indicated and the death rate predicted using coefficients from a regression in some prior year. The specific prior year is that in the column headed "Coeffs. for Predicted *DR*." Each column labeled *B* contains the coefficients (and ratios to their standard errors) of a variable constructed from the ratio of cars produced after regulation to the total stock of cars in a regression with *DR* residual as the dependent variable. In the construction of the independent variable, each car with seat belts only (1964–66 models) is weighted 0.6, and 1967 and later models are weighted 1.0. Data are from R. L. Polk & Co. (various years). Each column labeled *B'* contains a counterpart to *B* in a regression which includes the residual from the prior-year regression as an independent variable. The column labeled *CHG* contains counterparts to *B* and *B'* in a regression where the change in death rates is the dependent variable and changes in independent variables in table 11 are included. Coefficients of nonregulatory variables and summary statistics for regressions have been deleted. See text for illustration of variable construction. *AVDC*, *APDC* are unavailable for 1970.

contrast with the earliest alternative year should yield the algebraically smallest regulation coefficient (since the later alternatives are affected by regulation); just the reverse is true for both 1970 and 1967. The generally lower 1970 coefficients hint that the set of devices mandated after 1966 (energy-absorbing column, high-penetration-resistant windshield, etc.) are more effective than the safety literature allows, but closer examination of the data doesn't support this. The R variable can be broken into components—cars with seat belts only and cars with seat belts plus other devices—for 1967 and 1970. When these are employed in tests on $ATDC$ similar to those in table 12, none of the five coefficients of the latter variable is significant (though four are negative).

The failure of regulation to reduce death rates extends to both components of $ATDC$, where data on them are available. This contrasts with the time-series results, in that there is no evidence in table 12 of a shift from occupant to pedestrian deaths. Instead, the overall pattern in table 12 is consistent with an interpretation of regulation as having, at best, mirrored market forces.

Table 12 also presents results of tests on a modified version of the model in equations (3)–(7). The modification is motivated by the tendency of residuals from the separate table 11 regression to keep the same sign. This suggests that there are systematic "state effects" in the death rate, which I assume are some proportion, m, of the residual in (3). Therefore, I express that residual

$$u'_{t-i} = mu'_{t-i} + v'_{t-i}, \tag{8}$$

where v' is a random component. We would then wish to compute, instead of V_t in (6),

$$V'_t = [(D_t - mu'_{t-i}) - a'X_t - b'R_t] = V_t - mu'_{t-i} \tag{9}$$

and estimate the effect of regulation from

$$V'_t = B'R_t + v_t, \tag{10}$$

However, since m is not known, (10) must take the form

$$V_t = B'R_t + mu'_{t-i} + v_t, \tag{11}$$

and m can be estimated by entering u'_{t-i} in a regression estimate of (11). The columns labeled B' in table 12 are estimates of this coefficient in regression estimates of (11). These show that the major effect of the adjustment for state-specific effects is simply to increase the accuracy of the regulation coefficients. None of these differs very much from its counterparts in column B, so their greater precision would only embolden one to conclude that regulation has had perverse effects.

Table 12 also shows coefficients (under CHG) of the regulatory variable in regressions where the change in death rates is the dependent variable and is a function also of changes in the other independent variables. In this variant, any interperiod change in the coefficients in table 11 is permitted to affect the death rate projections, so the change is not attributed to regulation. While this may lead to overstatement of the effect of regulation, the data in the CHG column in table 12 imply that regulation is ineffective.

Finally, one can impose on the model the dubious opposite assumption that coefficients of the other independent variables are the same in all periods. In this variant, the cross sections are pooled, intercept-shift dummies added, and the variables R and R' (see eqs. [3]–[7]) entered separately. The coefficient of the R variable would then measure the effect of regulation. Since residuals from the separate cross sections are correlated, I estimated the pooled regressions by generalized least squares, and derived three alternative values for the coefficient of R. These had the following t-ratios: -2.01 when R is defined for the 1970 $ATDC$ and four cross sections are pooled, $+1.38$ for R_{1967} in a pooling of the first three cross sections, and $+1.72$ for R_{1965} with the first two cross sections pooled. Again, there is no consistent pattern to the regulatory coefficients, though the 1970 result again hints at superiority of the post-1967 devices to seat belts. However, the hint must be tempered by an upward shift of the intercept for 1970, which more than offsets the effect of the regulatory variable. That shift may simply summarize a regulation-induced change in the coefficients of the other variables. A similar pooling procedure for $AVDC$ yields t-ratios of $+1.63$ for the coefficient of R_{1967} and $+2.02$ for that of R_{1965}. For $APDC$, these t-ratios are $+0.56$ and -0.03, respectively. None of these casts doubt on the general conclusion that regulation has failed to reduce death rates.

Nonfatal accidents.—Unfortunately, cross-section data on nonfatal accidents are too skimpy to permit analysis.[43] Some indirect evidence on them is available from automobile insurance data. Even here, though, we are stymied by the fact that auto insurance primarily compensates injury to the party not at fault. Perhaps in consequence, changes in time series of injury accidents and insurance payments for injury loss are uncorrelated, so I eschewed analysis of cross-section

---

[43] Property-damage data do not exist, and injury accident data are available only since 1967.

TABLE 13.   Effect of Regulation on Insurer Payments for Property-
Damage Loss from Auto Accidents

Period for DLC Residual (Dependent Variable)	Coeffs. for Predicted DLC	Coefficient/t-Ratio for Regulatory Variable		
		B	BA	CHG
1970	1962	−0.01	0.07	1.06
		−0.02	0.20	2.80
1970	1965	−0.62	−0.24	0.09
		−2.02	−0.91	0.30
1970	1967	0.35	0.76	0.11
		1.56	3.03	0.59
1967	1962	−0.15	−0.03	0.02
		−0.30	−0.93	0.09
1967	1965	−0.15	−0.03	0.02
		−0.42	−0.08	0.03
1965	1962	0.61	0.69	0.51
		0.57	0.67	0.30

Note: See note to table 12 and text. Sources of *DLC:* Spectator Co., *Insurance by States* (various years); A. M. Best & Co.

injury loss payments. However, property damage is compensated by both first-party and liability insurance, and changes in these compensations are significantly correlated (+.6) with changes in property-damage accidents in the aggregate data. Therefore, I presume that per capita damage accidents in a state are correlated with per capita auto insurer payments for property-damage loss in that state (*DLC*). I then replace death rates with *DLC* and perform the same tests as in table 12 on this variable. The results are in table 13. Since *DLC* will be affected by the cost of accidents and the demand for insurance coverage, the coefficients of the regressions underlying these tests do not always correspond to those for death rates. In particular, the income and accident cost elasticities of insurance losses are positive. Even though this detail does not bias the tests in table 13, I report alternative tests from regressions of *DLC* on a set of variables explaining only the demand for insurance and the cost of property damage repair (these are *FC*, *YD*, the wage of auto mechanics, and the relevant car-age analogues to the regulatory variable). Results of these tests are in the column headed *BA* in table 13. (I have deleted results from the "state-effect" model because these, like those for death rates, are virtually indistinguishable from those under *B*.)

The data in table 13 are consistent with previous cross-section data in their failure to show any effect of regulation. The corresponding time-series results imply significantly *positive* coefficients for the regulatory variables in table 13, but most of them are indistinguishable from zero.

V. Summary and Conclusions

The one result of this study that can be put forward most confidently is that auto safety regulation has not affected the highway death rate. Neither the time-series nor cross-section data permit any other conclusion. However, these data are not as decisive about what underlies this result. On one interpretation, safety regulation has decreased the risk of death from an accident by more than an unregulated market would have, but drivers have offset this by taking greater accident risk. This interpretation is broadly supported by the time-series evidence of a shift of the burden of accidents from drivers to pedestrians, and of an increase in property-damage (and total) accidents. It is also supported by some independent measures of driver risk taking: the growth of both drunken driving and driving by the young appears to have accelerated with the onset of regulation, and cars equipped with safety devices are involved in a disproportionately high share of accidents. Another interpretation of the main result would be that regulation has merely confirmed market forces which had previously produced a long-term decline in the highway death rate. The primary force behind this decline, however, had been a reduction in the probability of accident, not death per accident. Therefore, the alternative interpretation would imply that the only response of drivers to safety regulation has been to have more severe accidents, while continuing to have fewer accidents. This one-sided sort of response is, though, consistent with the cross-section data. These show no effect of regulation on total deaths, on their distribution among drivers and pedestrians, or on the apparent number of property-damage accidents. These conclusions have to be tempered by the lack of a direct measure of damage accidents and of recent data on the distribution of deaths.

However one chooses to interpret them, though, the results of this paper contrast sharply with the apparent intent of safety regulation. It is difficult to imagine that Congress created this regulation either to encourage an increase in accidents or merely to reify market forces. More plausibly, Congress simply failed to give these forces the weight they deserve. This failure may appear more glaring in the next few years than it does now. A naive reading of the safety literature implies that current enforcement of the Vehicle Safety Act will substantially improve safety. The thrust of this enforcement is to require more protective devices—for example, air bags—while simultaneously increasing utilization of existing devices—via, for example, seat-belt

ignition interlocks. Preliminary evidence implies that, had they remained mandatory, ignition interlocks alone would eventually (by the
mid-1980s) have reduced the death rate by something like 20 percent,[44] which is comparable to the total effect of all current devices
listed in table 1. In light of this sort of promise, the NHTSA has established as its goal a mileage death rate of 36 per billion vehicle miles by
1980, which is about 20 percent less than the 1972 rate.

However, nonregulatory forces promise to provide *everything*
the regulators would credit to their own actions. This follows from the
parameters of the *ATDR* regression in table 2, which are from a world
without a NHTSA, and the following assumptions:

1. The recent above-average inflation of medical and car repair
costs will cease, so the relative price of an accident will not change.

2. Earned income per adult will increase at its postwar average,
2 percent per year.

3. Alcohol consumption per adult will also increase at 2 percent
annually, or about ½ percent more than its postwar average.

4. Vehicle speed will increase at its postwar average, 1 percent
per year.

5. The fraction of the driving age population under 25 will remain unchanged, which is the current Census Bureau projection.

6. One-fourth of all traffic will move on limited-access roads,
compared to about one-fifth today.

7. The current urban-rural vehicle mileage ratio will be maintained. The projected 1980 death rate then would be 33 per billion vehicle miles, so we should be disappointed if the NHTSA does not attain
its goal.

Appendix A

Estimates of Expected Reduction in Vehicle Occupant Death Rate

The following sources were used to construct the estimates in table 1: National
Safety Council (various years); Huelke and Gikas (1968); Kihlberg (1969); U.S.
National Highway Traffic Safety Administration (1968); Lave and Weber (1970);
statement by A. Nahum and A. Siegel, University of California, Los Angeles,
before U.S. Senate Commerce Committee, April 25, 1968, cited in U.S. Na-

---

[44]This evidence (in U.S. Office of Science and Technology 1972) is that interlocks double the seat-belt utilization rate. Lap-shoulder belt combinations are now
mandatory, and the safety literature credits them with a full-utilization death rate
reduction in excess of 50 percent. The 70 percent utilization promised by interlocks
therefore implies a 35 percent reduction of deaths, or more than double the current
productivity of seat belts shown in table 1. Congress, however, repealed the interlock
requirement in 1974.

TABLE A1.   Proportion of Car Stock Equipped with
Safety Devices, 1972

Device	Year Standard	Implied 1972 Installation Rate
Lap seat belt	1964	0.95
Energy-absorbing steering column	1967*	0.56
Shoulder belt	1968	0.49
HPR windshield	1967	0.58
Padded instrument panel	1968	0.49
Dual braking system	1967	5.58

*Except Ford, 1968.

tional Highway Traffic Safety Administration (1968); Bohlin (1967); U.S. Office of Science and Technology (1972), data from Cornell Aeronautical Laboratory; Joksch and Wuerdeman (1972); and Levine and Campbell (1971). These studies estimate the reduction in the death rate given complete installation and usage of devices. Since part of the 1972 car stock does not have some or all of these devices, it is first necessary to estimate the fraction equipped with each device. These estimates are based on the age distribution of the 1972 car stock in R. L. Polk and Company (various years) and are summarized in table A1.

Lap Seat Belts

The National Safety Council (1969–72) reports that seat belts are used 40 percent of the time they are available. Coupled with the 1972 installation rate, I take this to imply that they are available in 38 percent of accidents. I then apply the 38 percent usage factor to the following results of safety studies.

The National Safety Council estimates that full usage would save 8,000–10,000 lives annually. The implicit actual saving (3,000–3,800 lives) is roughly 7–8½ percent of the sum of 1972 occupant deaths and the implicit saving.

Huelke and Gikas (1968) estimate that full usage would prevent 40 percent of passenger car deaths (which are 0.86 of all 1972 occupant deaths, i.e., including truck and bus occupants). I assume that no nonauto deaths are prevented by seat belts, though seatbelts have been standard in most trucks since 1966.

Kihlberg (1969) estimates that unbelted occupants are twice as likely to be killed on rural roads as belted drivers. Given the 1972 belt usage rate, this implies a 19 percent reduction in rural deaths, which comprised 79 percent of all occupant deaths in 1972. I assume that no lives are saved by belts in urban accidents.

The U.S. National Highway Traffic Safety Administration (1968) reports Florida and Nebraska data that imply a 56 percent higher probability of death to unbelted occupants. I assume that this applied to all U.S. occupant deaths.

Cornell Aeronautical Laboratory data reported in U.S. Office of Science and Technology (1972) indicate a 37.3 reduction in death rate with full utilization of lap belts.

Joksch and Wuerdeman (1972) survey other studies (including Huelke and Gikas [1968] from the above list) and present "consensus" estimates of the productivity of various devices adjusted for any interaction with other devices. The estimated full-utilization death rate reduction for lap belts is 0.35.

Levine and Campbell (1971) analyze data from North Carolina accidents. The estimated reduction in the probability of serious injury—that is, a fatal injury or one requiring the victim to be carried from the accident scene—is 0.43. I assume that this applies to fatalities.

Energy-absorbing Steering Column

Lave and Weber (1970) cite data from Huelke and Gikas (1968) implying that 5,700 or 15 percent of 1965 occupant deaths are due to impact with the steering column. They estimate, from an examination of photographs of 28 such victims, that half would have survived if the steering column had collapsed (net of those saved by seat belts), which implies a reduction of 7.5 percent in the death rate if the device is installed in all cars.

Nahum and Siegel (cited in U.S. National Traffic Safety Administration [1968]) report that energy-absorbing columns prevent all deaths due to impact with steering column at accident speeds up to 60 mph. They make no estimates for speeds greater than 60 mph, but only about 35 percent of 1965 fatal accidents occurred at those speeds (see National Safety Council 1966). I assume that none of the higher-speed deaths are prevented by the device, and apply the implicit 65 percent reduction in total steering-column-impact deaths to the data in Lave and Weber (1970).

Joksch and Wuerdeman (1972) estimate that the energy-absorbing column reduces the probability of a fatality by 0.10.

Levine and Campbell (1971) estimate a reduction of 0.142 in the probability of serious injury (see lap seat belt section) due to the energy-absorbing column. I assume that this figure applies to the fatality subcategory.

For each of the four estimates, I assume that the energy-absorbing column saves only passenger car occupants, though some trucks have similar devices.

Shoulder Belt

The National Safety Council (1972) reports that shoulder belts are worn less than 10 percent of the time they are available, while the U.S. Office of Science and Technology (1972) cites a Department of Transportation estimate of 4 percent. I use the lower figure and the 1972 installation rate to estimate that shoulder belts are worn in about 2 percent of accidents. The 2 percent usage estimate is then applied to the following results of safety studies.

Bohlin (1967) compares accident survival experience of drivers of Volvo automobiles, all of which were equipped with a combined lap and shoulder belt. Belted drivers perished only 10 percent as frequently as unbelted drivers. This implies a marginal reduction of 50 percent of occupant deaths due to shoulder belts, assuming full utilization, and a 40 percent death rate reduction due to lap belts alone.

Huelke and Gikas (1968) estimate that the marginal reduction over lap belts is 13 percent of occupant deaths.

The U.S. Office of Science and Technology (1972) estimates the marginal reduction at 16.4 percent.

Joksch and Wuerdeman estimate the marginal reduction at 10 percent.

High-Penetration-Resistant (HPR) Windshield

Nahum and Siegel (cited in U.S. National Highway Traffic Safety Administration [1968]) report that penetration of the windshield caused death only at accident speeds of 20–30 mph, and then in only 4 percent of accidents in which windshield penetration occurred. These deaths are eliminated by the HPR windshield. The National Safety Council (1966) reports that 13 percent of 1964 fatal accidents occurred at 20–30 mph. Only if one assumes that all the fatalities were due to windshield penetration would the data of Nahum and Siegel and the HPR windshield installation rate imply a reduction of as much as ¼ percent in the occupant death rate.

Joksch and Wuerdeman estimate that full-installation of the HPR windshield will reduce fatalities 5 percent for unbelted occupants and 3 percent for belted occupants (because more unbelted occupants strike the windshield). I then assume a 0.4 propensity to use seatbelts in cars with HPR windshields, which, together with the HPR installation rate, yields the figure in table 1.

Padded Instrument Panel

Lave and Weber (1970) conclude that this device produces no reduction in fatalities.

Dual Braking System

Lave and Weber (1970) estimate that this device would eliminate all deaths due to brake failure, and that these amounted to about 1 percent of 1965 occupant fatalities. I assume that no deaths to pedestrians are caused by brake failure.

Appendix B

Mathematical Model of Optimal Accident Risk and Loss

This appendix demonstrates two results in the text: (1) that mandatory installation of safety devices, designed to decrease the loss from an accident, have ambiguous effects on the total cost of accidents—the devices will lead to an increase in the probability of an accident, which may offset the reduction in loss per accident; and (2) that a rise in income will lead to similar ambiguity for similar reasons—opposite effects on accident risk and accident loss.

The model is kept extremely simple by ignoring many complications. For example:

1. Effects on nondrivers are ignored.

2. The driver is assumed to receive no direct utility from either safety or risky driving.

3. Instead, the driver is treated as a pecuniary wealth maximizer. Wealth is enhanced by devoting less time to driving a given mileage, and more to work. The cost of this increased speed, passing of other cars, taking of short-cuts, etc., is an increased probability of accident. (The loss from accident may also increase, and this complication is introduced subsequently.)

4. The option of insuring against accident loss in the market is ignored. Instead, the driver may "self-insure" by expenditures on reducing the loss from accident—for example, buying a safer car, voting for better roads. (Again, the complicating detail that such expenditures could also reduce accident risk is considered later.) Alternatively, one may assume availability of actuarially fair insurance, which will induce the driver to insure fully and behave like an expected wealth maximizer (Ehrlich and Becker 1972).

5. The effects of legal restraints and costs (traffic fines) on the driver's decision are ignored.

The driver is assumed to maximize the following expression

$$E = (1 - p) S_1 + pS_2, \tag{A1}$$

where E = expected income or wealth (for a given driving mileage), p = probability of an accident, and S_1, S_2 = income in the nonaccident and accident states, respectively. If the driver avoids any accidents his income is

$$S_1 = I - c - wt, \tag{A2}$$

where I = income in the limit where the time (t) devoted to driving the given mileage is zero, c = the driver's expenditures on reduction of accident losses (e.g., on safer cars), and w = wage rate. I assume that

$$p = p(t) \tag{A3}$$

and $p' < 0$, so that wt is the income forgone to avoid accidents.

In the event of an accident, the driver's income is

$$S_2 = I - c - wt - L, \tag{A4}$$

where L = loss from an accident. This would include loss of income-earning capacity, so that death rather than temporary disability implies a higher L. For simplicity, I assume that

$$L = L'(c), \tag{A5}$$

and $L' < 0$. Combining (1), (2), and (4) and rearranging terms yields

$$E = I - c - wt - pL. \tag{A6}$$

The driver then chooses the t, c combination which maximizes (A6). The first-order conditions for this are

$$E_t = -w - p'(t) \cdot L = 0, \tag{A7}$$

or $-p'(t) = w/L$, and

$$E_c = -1 - p \cdot L'(c) = 0, \tag{A8}$$

or $-L'(c) = 1/p$. Necessary second-order conditions are (subscripts denote partial derivatives)

$$E_{tt} = -p''(t) \cdot L < 0, \tag{A9}$$

and

$$E_{cc} = -p \cdot L''(c) < 0. \tag{A10}$$

These will hold if there are diminishing returns to both accident prevention and loss reduction (p'', $L'' > 0$).

Before proceeding, note the implications of (A7)–(A10): (1) An increase in w or a reduction in L reduces driving time and so increases the risk of an accident. This follows from (A7) and (A9) and is especially important for evaluating safety regulation. (2) Reduced accident risk (increased driving time) reduces the driver's expenditure on accident loss reduction (from [A8] and [A10]).

I now use these results to evaluate the effects of safety regulation designed to mitigate accident losses. To do this, rewrite (A5) as

$$L = L(A, c), \tag{A5'}$$

where A = the loss from an accident when the driver spends nothing on loss reduction, and $L_A > 0$. I assume that the parameter, A, is reduced by mandatory installation of safety devices. (Any parametric change in driver's income due to payment for these devices can be ignored.) We want to determine the total effect of the parametric reduction of A on t and c, and implicitly on the expected loss from accidents to the driver, pL. To get at this, I will assume initially that $L_{cA} = 0$. That is, changes in the "endowed loss," such as are produced by safety regulation, have no effect on the productivity of the driver's own loss-reduction expenditures. The relevant total derivatives, dt/dA and dc/dA, can be obtained by solving

$$\begin{bmatrix} E_{tt} & E_{tc} \\ E_{ct} & E_{cc} \end{bmatrix} \begin{bmatrix} dt/dA \\ dc/dA \end{bmatrix} = \begin{bmatrix} -E_{tA} \\ -E_{cA} \end{bmatrix}, \tag{A11}$$

which yields

$$\frac{dt}{dA} = (-E_{tA} \cdot E_{cc} + E_{cA} \cdot E_{tc})/D, \tag{A12}$$

$$\frac{dc}{dA} = (E_{tA} \cdot E_{ct} - E_{cA} \cdot E_{tt})/D, \tag{A13}$$

where

$$D = \begin{vmatrix} E_{tt} & E_{tc} \\ E_{ct} & E_{cc} \end{vmatrix} > 0 \tag{A14}$$

by the necessary and sufficient second-order conditions for a maximum. Since, from (A7) and (A8),

$$E_{tA} = 1 - p'(t) \cdot L_A, \tag{A15}$$

which is positive for $L_A > 0$, and

$$E_{cA} = -p \cdot L_{cA} = 0. \tag{A16}$$

For $L_{cA} = 0$, the sign of (A12) hinges on that of $-E_{tA} \cdot E_{cc}$. From (A10) and (A15), we deduce that dt/dA is *positive*. That is, a regulation-induced reduction of A reduces driving time and so increases the probability of accident. The sign of (A13) is that of $E_{tA} \cdot E_{ct}$. Since (A7) or (A8) yields

$$E_{ct} = -p'(t) \cdot L_c < 0, \tag{A17}$$

we deduce a negative sign for (A13). That is, regulation increases driver expenditure on loss reduction. This result follows from the combination of reduced driving time and the substitution between driving time and loss-reduction expenditure in (A17). Thus, in general, we can expect regulation to reduce the loss per accident on account of both impact (A falls) and induced (c rises) effects. It is important to note, though, that this result depends on the simplifying assumption that driving time does not affect accident loss. On the more plausible assumption that more reckless driving increases both accident risk and loss, the sign of E_{ct} and thus of (A13) becomes ambiguous: the induced increase in loss-reduction expenses would be opposed by increased loss from faster driving.

In any event, the effect of regulation on the magnitude we are interested in, the *expected* loss from accidents, will be ambiguous because the probability of accident increases.

The ambiguity cannot be resolved if regulation affects the productivity of voluntary loss-prevention expenses. If regulation increases the marginal product of c ($L_{cA} > 0$), the added substitution of c for t that this would engender merely enhances the preceding effects. If regulation reduces the marginal product of c, which is perhaps the more general case, the effects on both t and c become ambiguous ($E_{cA} > 0$ in [A12] and [A13]). The reduced private expenditure thereby engendered (1) discourages fast driving and (2) offsets some or all of parametric loss reduction due to regulation. (This result is especially interesting in light of the empirical results from cross-section data.)

We may now compare the preceding results with the effects of changes in income. In the present model these effects are engendered solely by changes in the wage rate, so we want to evaluate dt/dw and dc/dw. These have the solutions

$$\frac{dt}{dw} = (E_{tw}E_{cc} + E_{cw}E_{ct})/D \tag{A18}$$

and

$$\frac{dc}{dw} = (E_{tw} \cdot E_{tc} - E_{cw} \cdot E_{tt})/D. \tag{A19}$$

From (A7) and (A8), we obtain

$$E_{tw} = -1, \tag{A20}$$

$$E_{cw} = 0. \tag{A21}$$

And these imply that the signs of (A18) and (A19) are negative and positive, respectively. That is, an increase in wages raises the probability of accident and lowers the cost per accident. The direction of these wage effects then corresponds to those of safety regulation, and they have the same ambiguous implications for the expected cost of accidents. If we complicate the model by permitting L to rise with w (because income-earning capacity is diminished by an accident), these effects are only enhanced. A rise in w will then increase the marginal product of loss-reduction expenses (so $E_{cw} > 0$), and the resulting increase in c will stimulate a further reduction in t.

More substantive complications emerge when the preceding results are compared with some broad secular trends. Growth in income has in fact been accompanied by reduced driving time (as measured by vehicle speeds), but not by an increase in the probability of accident. Indeed, that has fallen over time and is the major explanation for the downward trend of the death rate. That is, the $p(t)$ function has shifted over time, and our model does not permit this. A more general model would include driver (and, e.g., highway department) expenditures for accident prevention, and these would likely rise with income. By this route, we could obtain a simultaneous reduction of t and p with increased income. Then, if the reduced t increases the loss per accident sufficiently, we could rationalize the absence of a secular decline in loss per accident. That is, the broad trend of accident behavior seems characterized by a larger income elasticity for expenditures on reducing the impact of speed on accident probability than for expenditures which mitigate the effects of speed on accident loss. Safety regulation has reversed this emphasis, and that provides empirical ground for distinguishing its effects from those of rising income.

References

A. M. Best and Company. *Executive Data Service*. New York, various issues.

Bohlin, N. "A Statistical Analysis of 28,000 Accident Cases with Emphasis on Occupant Restraint Value." In *Proceedings of the 11th Stapp Car Crash Conference*. New York: Soc. Automotive Engineers, 1967.

Ehrlich, I., and Becker, G. "Market Insurance, Self-Insurance, and Self-Protection." *J.P.E.* 80, no. 4 (July/August, 1972): 623–48.

Gavin-Jobson Company. *The Liquor Handbook, 1973*. New York, 1974.

Highway Safety Research Center, University of North Carolina. "Single Variable Tabulations for 1971 and 1972 North Carolina Accidents." Mimeographed. 1973.

Huelke, D., and Gikas, P. "Causes of Deaths in Automobile Accidents." *J. American Medical Assoc.* (March 25, 1968), pp. 1100–1107.

Insurance Information Institute. *Insurance Facts*. New York, various years.

Iskrant, A., and Joliet, P. *Accidents and Homicide*. Cambridge, Mass.: Harvard Univ. Press, 1968.

Joksch, H., and Wuerdeman, H. "Estimating the Effects of Crash Phase Injury Countermeasures." *Accident Analysis and Prevention* 4 (June 1972): 89–108.

Kihlberg, J. *Efficacy of Seatbelts in Injury and Noninjury Crashes in Rural Utah*. Buffalo: Cornell Aeronautical Laboratory, 1969.

Lave, L., and Weber, W. "A Benefit-Cost Analysis of Auto Safety Features." *Appl. Econ.* 2, no. 4 (1970): 215–75.

Levine, D., and Campbell, B. "Effectiveness of Lap Seat Belts and the Energy Absorbing Steering System in the Reduction of Injuries." Mimeographed. Highway Safety Res. Center, Univ. North Carolina, 1971.

National Safety Council. *Accident Facts*. Chicago, various years.

Peltzman, S. "The Effect of Subsidies-in-Kind on Private Expenditures: The Case of Higher Education." *J.P.E.* 81, no. 1 (January/February 1973): 1–27.

R. L. Polk and Company. *Passenger Cars: Registration Counts by Make and Year of Model*. Detroit, various years.

Spectator Company. *Insurance by States*. Philadelphia, various years.

———. *Property Liability Insurance Review*. Philadelphia, various issues.

Statistics Canada. *Motor Vehicle Traffic Accidents*. Ottawa, various years.

U.S. Bureau of the Census. *National Income and Product Accounts of the United States, 1929–65*. Washington, 1966.

———. *Statistical Abstract of the United States*. Washington, various years.

———. *Survey of Current Business*. Washington, various issues.

U.S. Bureau of Labor Statistics. *Consumer Price Index*. Washington, various issues.

U.S. Federal Bureau of Investigation. *Uniform Crime Reports for the United States*. Washington, various years.

U.S. Federal Highway Administration. *Fatal and Injury Accident Rates*. Washington, various issues.

———. "Traffic Speed Trends." Press release. Washington, various issues.

U.S. National Highway Traffic Safety Administration. *Second Annual Report*

on the Administration of the National Traffic and Motor Vehicle Safety
Act. Washington, 1968.

————. Safety '72: A Report on Activities under the National Traffic and
Motor Vehicle Safety Act. Washington, 1973.

U.S. Office of Science and Technology. Cumulative Regulatory Effects on the
Cost of Automotive Transportation (RECAT). Washington, 1972.

Consequences and Causes of Public Ownership of Urban Transit Facilities

12

B. Peter Pashigian

Introduction

Public production of goods and services is somewhat of an embarrassment to most economists. It exists, and will in all likelihood increase in importance, but is difficult to explain. An acceptable theory of public production has not yet appeared. Several hypotheses have been advanced but have not been pursued or subjected to systematic tests. This paper examines the power of these hypotheses to explain the shift from private to public production in the urban transit industry. The urban transit industry is a relative newcomer to the area of public production and for that reason is an interesting industry to study. It has a long history of predominantly private production along with local or state regulation of fares and routes. In the last decade or so a dramatic shift toward public production has occurred. Among the 117 largest cities in 1970, only 10 had publicly owned transit systems in 1949. In the next 10 years, only three more systems became publicly owned. From 1960 to 1969, 31 systems were added to the rolls and 15 more became publicly owned from 1970 to 1971. What has changed to cause this shift after so many years of private production? Section I of this paper reviews several hypotheses of the causes of public ownership. Section II describes the sample and the sources and limitations of the data, and Section III introduces the regulation and ownership variables used in the regression analysis. The effects of the regulation and ownership variables on profitability are studied in Section IV. The com-

This study was partially supported by a grant from the Walgreen Foundation and by a grant from the Center for Management of Public and Nonprofit Enterprise, Graduate School of Business, University of Chicago. I am indebted to the American Transit Association for supplying the data on transit operations and to the referees for suggesting improvements in the paper. Responsibility for errors rests with the author.

Reprinted with permission from the *Journal of Political Economy* 84, no. 6 (December 1976): 1239–59. © 1976 by The University of Chicago.

parative performance of public and private transit systems from 1960 to 1970 is examined in Section V. Section VI quantifies the relationship between changes in the size of selected special interest groups and changes in the profit margin of transit firms. The paper concludes with a summary.

I. Some Explanations of Public Production

Explanations of public production are few, and those that exist are incomplete. This section provides a critical review of some possible candidates.

A. The Regulation Hypothesis

The regulation hypothesis asserts that regulation is an intervening step before public ownership. After a time the regulation of prices and service becomes so stringent that a private firm can no longer earn a normal return. Regulators may not permit fare increases to match cost increases or allow unprofitable routes to be discontinued. Losses caused by more stringent regulation ultimately result in government ownership. Under government ownership the service is provided with costs exceeding revenues but with public subsidy.[1]

The regulation theory lacks an explanation of why regulation becomes more stringent in one city and not in another and, like other theories, assumes but does not explain why net public subsidies for transit will be larger under public ownership than under private ownership. If this were not so, government regulation would be a perfect substitute for public ownership of transit facilities and there would be no need for government ownership.

An extension of the regulation theory requires the identification and measurement of changes in the relative size of groups favoring or opposing more stringent regulation, public ownership, and public subsidies. Increases in automobile ownership reduce the demand for urban transit. The reduced demand for urban transit does not, contrary to common opinion, have to result in unprofitable operations and public ownership if the transit firm is allowed to reduce the number of routes and frequency of service and adjust fares. The increase in automobile ownership increases the relative voting strength of nonusers who will oppose public ownership and subsidies and favor profitable transit operations. If workers with low and middle incomes are the

[1] This view of regulation differs from that of the producer-protection theory, which makes the regulator an agent of the industry (Stigler 1971).

primary users of local transit, increases in the size of these groups would be associated with reduced profitability. Firms located in well-developed central business districts (CBD) would also favor low-cost–high-frequency service to the CBD. This group appears to be better organized in the older cities where well-developed businesses and shopping centers exist.

The regulation theory assumes that users constitute a voting block large enough to use the political power of the state to redistribute wealth from nonusers in the form of a goods-in-kind subsidy. If users constitute too large a share of voters, any gains from a redistribution would be largely offset by the equivalent higher taxes incurred to cover losses (Peltzman 1971). If users are too small a fraction of voters, they would have little political strength to affect the policies of the regulator. Public ownership of transit facilities did occur first in cities where users represented a larger share of all voters.[2] Census data show that the mean proportion of all workers using transit to work in 1960 was 0.28 for systems publicly owned before 1960 and only 0.16 for systems privately owned in 1960.[3] Socialization occurred first in cities where users had greater political strength.

The modern theory of regulation explains the incidence of regulation through an examination of the relative size and relative gains of special interest groups (Stigler 1971). The institutional device used to regulate an industry has in large part been considered a detail. In the transit industry there is some impressive evidence that the political

---

[2] If public ownership first occurred in cities where users represented a smaller proportion of all voters, the special interest theory loses its appeal and one would entertain a charity hypothesis. The general public offers a goods-in-kind subsidy to a small fraction of the population using local transit.

[3] The mean and standard deviation of the proportion of workers using public transit to work in 1960 are shown in the following table:

	Proportion Using Public Transit in 1960	
	Mean	SD
Systems publicly owned before 1960 ($N = 10$)	.284	.157
Systems privately owned in 1960 ($N = 59$)	.163	.083

On the other hand, systems becoming publicly owned since 1959 had a somewhat smaller proportion of workers using public transit in 1960 than systems that remained privately owned from 1960–70. Consequently, the trend to public ownership during the 1960s cannot be simply attributed to the exercise of political strength of users of local transit.

TABLE 1.   Probability of Public Ownership and Type of Agency
Regulating Fares

Type of Agency Regulating Fares	Type of Ownership	
	Private	Public
State commission or agency	38	4
Local agency		
City council or commission	23	29
Transit authority or other metropolitan authority	3	37
Total	64	70

Source: R. L. Banks and Associates (1972, p. 88).

strength of users and nonusers is not independent of the form and type of regulation.[4] The results of a survey of 134 cities are reproduced in table 1 and show that the probability of public ownership is lower when the regulation of fares is by a state public service commission. It appears that state commissions have been less responsive to demands for lower fares or improved service unless state subsidies are provided.[5] State governments have been reluctant to provide subsidies to local transit systems in urban centers because of the opposition of voters in rural and smaller urban and suburban communities.

If the severity of regulation does vary from city to city and depends in part on the regulating agency, government-owned firms will have smaller profit per vehicle mile (or profit margin) than regulated private firms. Under the regulation hypothesis government ownership occurred because regulation did become so stringent that a normal return could no longer be earned.[6] If more stringent regulation occurs when the transit facility is regulated by a local rather than state agency, then profit margins should be higher for firms regulated by state commissions. The equality of profit margins for private and public systems constitutes evidence against the regulation hypothesis. Higher profit margins for private systems regulated by state rather than local agencies would be consistent with the regulation hypothesis but not predicted by the other hypotheses discussed in this paper.

[4]The form and type of regulation may be endogenous and determined by the relative size of the opposing special interest groups. However, the type of regulation in urban transit was often determined prior to the period of analysis.

[5]Systems regulated by state commissions may have experienced smaller autonomous decreases in the demand for urban transit, experienced smaller decreases in profit margins, and therefore remained under private ownership. Evidence presented below rejects this hypothesis.

[6]Privately owned systems are in markets where regulation is less stringent or where the transition to public ownership has not as yet occurred.

The implications of the regulation hypothesis may be summarized as follows: (1) publicly owned systems should have lower profit margins than privately owned systems; (2) more stringent regulation may be expected when the transit facility is regulated by a local rather than a state agency; and (3) profit margins should decrease less over time, and the probability of a change to public ownership should be lower in cities where the relative size of nonusers, for example, auto owners, has increased.

B. The Declining-Industry Hypothesis

A more popular hypothesis is that urban transit is a declining industry and, under recent cost conditions, an unprofitable one under any combination of fares and service levels. The declining-industry hypothesis is an incomplete one, for it only explains why the industry is an unprofitable one and not why government ownership must inevitably follow. The demand for many products has decreased without subsequent government ownership of firms. This hypothesis must be combined with another hypothesis, for example, the presence of externalities, if it is to explain why socialization occurs.

The declining-industry hypothesis could be tested by identifying the demand and cost functions in the respective markets and determining if any combination of fares and service levels would yield a normal return. In principle, one could determine whether a normal return could be earned if a system was allowed to abandon less frequently used routes, service the major arteries and streets of a city, and charge higher fares. Such tests are obviously difficult to conduct, so less comprehensive tests must be relied on to evaluate the declining-industry

TABLE 2.   Ownership, Fare, Wage Rate, and Form of Regulation by Size of City

Group	Percent Public Ownership	Median Date of Public Ownership	Mean Hourly Wage Rate*	Form of Regulation (When Known)		
				State	Authority	City Council
1. Largest 20	70	1958	$3.88(18)	4	11	4
2. Second largest 20	50	1968	3.59(19)	4	8	5
3. Third largest 20	55	1967	2.89(17)	4	5	9
4. Fourth largest 20	55	1967	3.24(16)	4	3	9
5. Fifth largest 20	30	1970	2.99(15)	8	0	6
6. Next 17	41	1967	2.99(10)	7	3	2

Note: Figures in parentheses denote sample size.

*Wage rate is union wage rate for operator of one-man bus with 1 year of experience in 1970.

hypothesis. A reduction in demand is more likely to result in losses if there are economies of scale rather than constant cost in the provision of transit services. If there are economies of scale, public ownership should have first appeared in the smaller markets even before transit firms experienced the large loss of riders because of the growth in auto ownership in the post–World War II period. Table 2 shows the owner-ship status of transit facilities in the 117 most populated cities in 1970. Cities are classified into six groups, and the proportion of cities with public ownership is higher and public ownership occurred earlier in the group with the 20 largest cities. However, cities in this group have higher wage rates, so any cost advantage due to scale may be offset by a higher factor cost. A comparison of groups 3 through 6 shows no sys-tematic variation of the wage rate or in the proportion of cities with public ownership of transit facilities with the size of the city. Some fur-ther confirming evidence is the absence of any economies of scale in a cross-sectional analysis of the operating costs of 58 systems.[7]

One other test clearly distinguishes between the declining-indus-try hypothesis and the regulation hypothesis. The declining-industry hypothesis predicts that a rise in auto ownership will lower the prof-itability of transit firms and increase the probability of change to public ownership, while the regulation hypothesis makes the opposite predic-tion. Hence, the observed relation between the change in profit mar-gin over time and change in automobile ownership provides evidence to distinguish between the competing hypotheses.

C. The Externalities Hypothesis

The trip cost of a transit passenger includes a money and time compo-nent. Even though bus services are produced under constant returns to scale, trip cost per ride will decrease with an increase in the number of passengers if the time between bus arrivals (waiting time) decreases as the number of passengers and buses increases (Mohring 1972). If so, a permanent decrease in the number of riders imposes an external dis-economy on the remaining riders by increasing waiting time.[8] If long-

---

[7] The OLS regression results for 1970 were: $\log C = -1.70(8.2) + 1.16(44.4)$ $\log VM + .12(1.8) \log WAGE - .34 \times 10^{-7}(.8) (VM \log VM) + u$, where C denotes operating expenses and $-.07$ denotes $.0000000$; VM denotes miles, and $WAGE$ de-notes hourly wage of union bus hires with 1 year of experience. The cross-product term determines if the returns-to-scale parameter depends on total vehicle miles supplied. Numbers in parentheses are t-ratios. The results fail to reveal any significant econo-mies of scale. Two-stage results yielded similar results.

[8] Mohring (1972) has presented an extensive discussion of this argument. He shows that waiting time per trip will decrease as the number of passengers and number of buses increase proportionally if the average wait for service is proportional to the time between bus arrivals.

run average cost per trip decreases with the number of passengers (where cost includes time and money costs), marginal cost per trip will be less than average cost per trip. In the absence of any subsidy, the equilibrium number of trips will be determined where the average cost per trip equals the demand price per trip if a uniform fare is charged. If the demand price is to be equated to the marginal cost of a trip, a subsidy is required and may take the form of reducing the fare (the money cost of a trip) below the bus cost per trip. By reducing the fare below bus cost per trip, it may be possible to equate the demand price per trip to the marginal cost (bus plus time cost) of an additional trip. Public ownership could be justified as a method of practicing marginal cost pricing. Why a private transit firm could not be subsidized is unclear.

The externalities hypothesis is an incomplete explanation of socialization of transit firms because it does not explain which cities will offer subsidies. The argument is so general that all systems should be offered subsidies if the goal is to achieve marginal cost pricing. To give content to the hypothesis and explain the shift to public ownership, it is necessary to identify systems where the discrepancy between marginal and average cost per trip may have increased most during the last decade or so. Mohring (1972) suggests that this discrepancy increases with decreases in the number of passengers per mile hour (at least over some range). If the intensity of use of transit facilities decreases with increases in auto ownership or decreases in bus vehicle miles supplied, then cities with larger increases in auto ownership per household or with larger percentage decreases in bus vehicle miles may be expected to have a higher probability of a change to public ownership. In summary, the externalities hypothesis predicts that (1) the profit margin (before subsidy) should be lower for publicly owned than for privately owned systems,[9] and (2) increases in auto ownership should be inversely related to changes in the profit margin and directly related to the probability of a change to public ownership. The predictions of the externalities hypothesis are similar to those of the declining-industry hypothesis and therefore differ from the regulation hypothesis.

II. Selection of Sample

As a starting point, the 117 largest cities in 1970 were selected for study. The ownership status of the transit system in each city at the end of 1971 was determined along with the date of transition to public ownership when applicable. The data base was augmented by including economic and demographic data from current and past issues of the

[9]The profit margin should decline after the system has become publicly owned and a public subsidy is provided.

Census of Population and other sources. Data describing the regulatory agencies were obtained from the study by R. L. Banks and Associates (1972). The definition of variables and sources of data are presented in the Appendix.

Revenue and cost data of transit facilities were supplied by the American Transit Association (ATA). In many cases, the ATA data are incomplete because not all systems provide continuous reports and some report unexpected and unexplained year-to-year differences. These limitations of the ATA data reduced the sample so that 58 systems were used in the 1970 cross sections. Obviously, the sample was not selected by random sampling. While this is a major limitation, the sample is the largest that may be studied with available information. A second sample included 40 of the above 58 systems that reported data in both 1960 and 1970 so that comparisons over time could be made. Not all systems reporting to the ATA use the same accounting conventions or systems of accounts. One limitation of the study is that revenue and cost measures may not be comparable across transit systems. Some tests are formulated in terms of changes over time to reduce the effects of differences in accounting methods between transit systems.[10]

III. Classification by Regulation and Ownership

Each transit system was classified into one of seven groups which identified regulatory agency and ownership form. Systems are regulated by three general forms: (1) state commission (ST; usually a public service commission), (2) local government (CC; often a city council), and (3) a transit authority or district (AU). Publicly owned systems were also classified into two subclasses: (*a*) public ownership occurred before 1960 or (*b*) after 1959.[11] The notation used is summarized below:

[10] Operating revenues and operating costs measure revenues and costs from operations only. Nonoperating revenues are excluded. Operating costs include maintenance, depreciation, taxes, and other standard cost items. This cost measure undoubtedly contains an arbitrary and random component since the depreciation figures will depend on the age and method of depreciation of equipment. However, measurement error in the cost figures may not be serious. Further analysis showed that the change in profit margin from 1960 to 1970 was an important determinant of the change in the probability of public ownership. If there were serious distortions in the revenue and cost figures, such a relationship would not have been observed.

[11] Three exceptions were made: A private transit firm was regulated by a transit authority or district in Buffalo, Nashville, and Washington, D.C. This is considered a temporary arrangement in Buffalo and Nashville since public ownership was anticipated in the near future. The system in Washington, D.C., appeared to have many characteristics of a publicly owned system. Consequently, these three systems were included in the PAUB class even though a privately owned firm was ostensibly operating.

CC = regulated by city council or other form of local government,
PCCA = regulated by city council and publicly owned since 1959,
PCCB = regulated by city council and publicly owned before 1960,
ST = regulated by state commission,
PSTA = regulated by state commission and publicly owned since 1959,
PAUB = regulated by transity authority or district and publicly owned before 1960,
PAUA = regulated by transit authority or district and publicly owned since 1959.

Except for PAUA, each of these variables is introduced as a dummy variable. The PAUA is treated as the base variable. Therefore, the coefficients of the other seven dummy variables represent the effects of regulation and ownership relative to the effects of PAUA. The effect of regulation without public ownership is measured by the coefficients of CC or ST. For example, if private regulated firms receive greater revenue per vehicle mile than do systems in PAUA (publicly owned since 1959 and regulated by a transit authority or district), the coefficients of ST and CC will be positive. If regulation by state commission is less stringent than by city council, the coefficient of ST will be larger than the coefficient of CC. Given the form of regulation, the effect of public ownership is measured by the coefficients of PCCA and PCCB for systems regulated by a city council and by PSTA for systems regulated by state commissions. The variables are defined so that the combined effects of regulation and public ownership are measured by the sum of the coefficients of CC and PCCA (or PCCB) and by the sum of the coefficients of ST and PSTA.[12] If the effects of public ownership are independent of the regulatory agency, the sum of these coefficients should not differ from zero. The coefficient of PAUB measures the effect of public ownership for systems under public ownership before 1960 and regulated by transit authority or district. If the stringency of regulation has increased with the number of years under public ownership, the coefficient of PAUB will be negative. The different tests for measuring the effects of regulation and ownership are summarized in table 3.

IV. Effect of Regulation and Ownership on Profitability

The initial regression results show how the regulation and ownership variables affect (a) revenue per vehicle mile in 1970, RVM, given

[12] The class, PTSB, was empty.

TABLE 3.   Measures of the Effects of Regulation and Ownership

Effect	Coefficient of	Sum of Coefficients of
	Measured by	
Regulation by state government (private ownership)	ST	—
Regulation by state government and public ownership after 1959	—	ST and PSTA
Regulation by local government (private ownership)	CC	—
Regulation by local government and public ownership before 1960	—	CC and PCCB
Regulation by local government and public ownership after 1959	—	CC and PCCA
Regulation by transit authority with public ownership before 1960	PAUB	—

operating expense per vehicle mile in 1970, CVM, and (*b*) the profit margin, PM, given vehicle miles supplied in 1970, VM. The regression equations are of the form:

$$RVM = a_0 + a_1 CVM + \sum_{i=1}^{6} a_i D_i + u$$

$$\ln RVM = b_0 + b_1 \ln CVM + \sum_{i=1}^{6} b_i D_i + v \qquad (1)$$

$$PM = c_0 + c_1 \ln VM + \sum_{i=1}^{6} c_i D_i + w,$$

where D_i denotes the *i*th dummy variable and ln denotes the logarithm of a variable.

Under the regulation hypothesis the coefficients of ST and CC should be positive and significantly different from zero if regulation has been less stringent for privately owned firms. The coefficient of ST should exceed that of CC if regulation is less stringent under state commission. The coefficients of PCCA and PTSA should be negative and significantly different from zero. Finally, the coefficients of PAUB and PCCB may be zero or negative depending on the effect of years of public ownership on RVM.

The results in columns 1 and 2 of table 4 show that the coefficient of ST is positive and statistically significant at the 2.5 percent level.[13]

[13] For a one- (two-) tailed test, a *t*-value of 1.67 (2.00) is significant at the 5 percent level with 60 observations.

TABLE 4.   Revenue per Vehicle Mile and Operating Profit Margin

Variable	RVM, 1970 (1)	Dependent Variable ln (RVM, 1970) (2)	Operating Profit Margin (3)
Constant	0.17	−0.15	−1.09
	(2.2)	(3.0)	(4.6)
Operating expense per VM, 1970 (CVM or ln [CVM])	0.67	1.02	—
	(8.6)	(10.2)	
CC (N = 21)*	0.05	0.11	0.11
	(0.8)	(1.3)	(1.2)
ST (N = 15)	0.11	0.18	0.23
	(2.0)	(2.5)	(2.9)
PCCA (N = 10)	−0.10	−0.18	−0.12
	(1.4)	(1.9)	(1.1)
PSTA (N = 3)	−0.12	−0.24	−0.23
	(1.3)	(2.0)	(1.7)
PAUB (N = 6)	−0.11	−0.18	−0.45
	(1.4)	(1.9)	(4.0)
PCCB (N = 4)	−0.13	−0.23	−0.31
	(1.4)	(2.0)	(2.4)
Log of vehicle miles, 1970	—	—	0.10
			(3.9)
R^2	.668	.734	.461
σ_u	.147	.183	.208
N	58	58	58

Note: Figures in parentheses denote t-ratios.

*For illustration, there were 21 systems regulated by local government of which 10 became publicly owned since 1959 and four were publicly owned before 1960. Thus, seven systems were privately owned and regulated by local government at the end of 1971. Incidentally, the base class PAUA contains 13 observations.

The coefficient of CC is positive, but it is not statistically significant at the 5 percent level. The coefficients of PCCA, PCCB, and PSTA are all negative and significant at the 5 percent level in column 2 but not in column 1. Systems regulated by transit authorities before 1960 received significantly lower RVM than systems regulated by transit authorities after 1959. The dependent variable in column 3 is the operating profit margin, operating revenue less operating cost divided by operating revenue. Similar qualitative conclusions may be drawn of the effects of the regulation and ownership variables.[14]

[14]The direct relationship between vehicle miles and profit margin is surprising. Larger systems would be expected to utilize their equipment more efficiently and obtain higher revenues per dollar of assets and therefore earn a lower profit margin if a normal rate of return is earned. The evidence suggests that larger systems are utilizing their equipment less efficiently than smaller systems.

Knowing the type of regulating agency and the form of ownership is valuable information in predicting the financial position of a transit system. Privately owned systems regulated by state commissions receive higher RVM and earn higher operating margins than publicly owned systems regulated by state commissions. Regulation by state commission appears less restrictive than by local government. Privately owned systems regulated by local government did not receive significantly higher RVM or earn higher profit margins. Systems publicly owned before 1960 have lower RVM and profit margins. Systems publicly owned after 1959 tend to have lower RVM and profit margins than privately owned firms, but the precision of some of the coefficient estimates is low. The evidence does not contradict the regulation hypothesis and in some ways is consistent with it. While the declining-industry and externalities hypotheses are also capable of explaining why the profit margins of publicly owned firms are lower than privately owned firms, they do not explain why privately owned firms under state commission earn significantly higher margins.

A trend toward more stringent regulation can be detected by comparing the coefficients of the dummy variables in successive cross sections. If regulation has become more stringent over time, systems that became publicly owned after 1960 (and possibly for systems which had already become publicly owned) should have experienced larger decreases in RVM relative to CVM from 1960 to 1970. Separate cross-section results are reported in columns 1 and 2 of table 5 for the 40 systems that reported operating data in both years. There is no significant difference between the systems in 1960 except for those systems publicly owned before 1960 and regulated by a transit authority. Hence, systems that were to become publicly owned sometime after 1959 received the same RVM in 1960 (given CVM) as systems that subsequently remained privately owned after 1959. Ten years later, some changes have occurred. Relative to the base group (PAUA), privately owned systems under regulation by state commissions received significantly higher revenues per vehicle mile.[15] Publicly owned systems (except for the one observation in PSTA) received a lower RVM (relative to CVM) and had suffered a relative deterioration in revenue received per vehicle mile. While the significance level of the estimated coefficients of CC, PSTA, and PCCB in the 1970 regression is below the 5 percent level, the direction of change in the value of the coefficient of each dummy variable from 1960 to 1970 suggests a relative improvement in RVM for privately owned systems and a relative deterioration for publicly owned systems. This relative deterioration is not due to, say, a larger autonomous decrease in the demand for transit services in

[15] The coefficient of ST is significant at the 5 percent level given a one-tailed test.

just those cities with systems that became publicly owned after 1959 because the deterioration was also experienced by systems that were publicly owned before 1960. While these results are not inconsistent with the regulation hypothesis, they are weaker because of the reduced significance levels of some of the coefficients.

In columns 3–5, changes between 1960 and 1970 in (1) the profit margin, (2) the log of operating cost, and (3) the log of revenue per passenger are related to the ownership and regulation dummies. The change in the profit margin shows an improvement for the privately owned firms relative to the systems that became publicly owned after 1959 and relative to the systems that were publicly owned before 1960. But, once again, the significance level of the coefficients of the ST and PAUB dummy variables falls below the 5 percent level. The coeffi-

TABLE 5.   Revenue per Mile and Other Operating Characteristics over Time

			Change from 1960 to 1970 in		
Variable	1 RVM, 1960 (1)	1 RVM, 1970 (2)	Profit Margins (3)	Log of Operating Cost (4)	Log of Revenue per Passenger (5)
Constant	0.01	−0.11	−0.20	0.33	0.48
	(0.2)	(2.1)	(3.9)	(8.8)	(7.8)
Log CVM	0.87	0.96	—	—	—
	(12.5)	(8.3)			
CC ($N = 15$)	−0.05	0.11	0.13	−0.12	0.00
	(1.0)	(1.1)	(1.4)	(1.8)	(0.0)
ST ($N = 10$)	0.00	0.13	0.11	−0.01	0.07
	(0.1)	(1.7)	(1.4)	(0.1)	(0.8)
PCCA ($N = 7$)	−0.01	−0.25	−0.31	0.10	−0.24
	(0.1)	(2.6)	(3.2)	(1.5)	(2.2)
PSTA ($N = 1$)	0.04	0.05	0.00	−0.14	−0.35
	(0.4)	(0.3)	(0.0)	(1.0)	(1.8)
PAUB ($N = 5$)	−0.13	−0.24	−0.14	0.17	0.04
	(2.7)	(2.4)	(1.5)	(2.6)	(0.3)
PCCB ($N = 3$)	0.05	−0.18	−0.22	0.17	−0.17
	(0.8)	(1.5)	(1.9)	(2.0)	(1.2)
Change in log of vehicle miles	—	—	−0.22	0.88	−0.09
			(1.8)	(10.1)	(0.6)
R^2	.877	.767	.478	.858	.328
σ_u	.083	.166	.162	.117	.189
N	40	40	40	40	40

Note: Figures in parentheses denote t-ratios.

cients of only PCCA and PCCB are negative and significant at the conventional 5 percent level of significance. The decline in the profit margin for publicly owned systems cannot be attributed to any one cause. Operating cost grew most rapidly for systems in the PAUB class, while revenue per passenger grew less rapidly for systems in the PCCA and PSTA classes.

If public systems raise fares and reduce service by a smaller percentage than private systems do, they would have experienced smaller percentage declines in the number of revenue passengers and in vehicle miles supplied. Cities with public transit systems should experience a smaller percentage increase in automobiles since the money and time price of local transit would have risen less rapidly over time. These hypotheses were tested. The results (not presented) indicated no significant difference between public and private systems in the percentage change from 1960 to 1970 in revenue passengers or in vehicle miles supplied. The growth in autos per household was significantly higher in those cities where transit systems remained privately owned from 1960 to 1970 than in cities where systems became publicly owned. The percentage increase in auto ownership was largest, after controlling for the growth of households, in cities with private systems regulated by state commissions. Publicly owned systems performed less well from 1960 to 1970, but not because they were in markets that experienced unusually large decreases in the demand for urban transit. To review, privately owned systems appeared to have higher revenue per vehicle mile and profit margins in 1970 than publicly owned systems. While the relative profit performance of privately owned systems appears to have improved over time, the precision of these results is clearly lower. The larger growth rate of auto ownership in cities with privately owned systems is consistent with the regulation hypothesis. The evidence also indicates the profit margins are higher when regulation is by state commission rather than a local regulatory agency. The absence of a larger percentage decrease in revenue passengers and vehicle miles for privately owned systems constitutes opposing evidence.

V. Comparative Performance of Public and Private Transit Systems

The comparative performance over time of public and private transit systems will reveal whether publicly owned systems have been more successful than privately owned systems in reducing the diversion of passengers from local transit to the private auto. A comparative analysis of this type also provides additional tests of the competing hypotheses for public ownership. If publicly owned systems charge lower prices or provide more frequent service and require less waiting time, the number of users should have declined less under public than under private ownership.

The performance of a transit system cannot be easily summarized by any one output measure. Nevertheless, policy discussions are often directed at the question of the relative use of local transit. The performance measure chosen for study in this section is the census estimate of the percentage of city workers using public transit to work. While this measure is not without its defects, it is central to current policy issues in urban transit.[16]

Let p_t be the percentage of city workers who use public transit to go to work. This percentage is determined by a vector of independent variables x_t through

$$p_t = \frac{100}{1 + e^{f(x_t) + u_t}},\tag{2}$$

where u_t denotes a disturbance term. The exponent of e may extend from minus infinity to plus infinity, so that p_t is bounded by zero and 100. A transformation of (2) gives

$$y_t \equiv \ln\left[\frac{p_t}{100 - p_t}\right] = -[f(x_t) + u_t].\tag{3}$$

The form of f is given by

$$f(x) = \alpha_0 + \alpha_1 L_t + \alpha_2 M_t + \alpha_3 H_t + \alpha_4 AH_t + \alpha_5 WH_t$$
$$+ \alpha_6 lHO_t + \dots,\tag{3a}$$

where $\alpha_1 < 0$, $\alpha_2 = ?$, $\alpha_3 > 0$, $\alpha_4 > 0$, and $\alpha_5 < 0$; L_t denotes the percentage of families in the city with low family incomes (defined in Appendix); M_t denotes the percentage of families with middle incomes; H_t denotes the percentage with high incomes; AH_t denotes autos per household; WH_t denotes workers per household; and lHO_t denotes the log of the number of households.[17] Since $L_t + M_t + H_t = 100$, equation (2) may be rewritten as

---

[16] A public transit system may increase ridership by providing frequent and subsidized bus service, while a private firm suffers a reduction in ridership because its service is not subsidized. The improved performance of the public system would then be due to the subsidy and not necessarily to public ownership. Other limitations of this measure are (1) the exclusion of users other than workers, and (2) differences between cities in the distribution of jobs in and outside of the central business district.

[17] AH_t, WH_t, and lHO_t are measured over the urbanized area since city data were not readily available.

TABLE 6.   Determinants of the Percentage of Workers Using Public Transit—Logit Model

Variable	1960		1970	
	Coefficient	t	Coefficient	t
Constant	−2.54	2.6	−0.71	0.6
Percent with low income	0.001	0.1	0.04	2.0
Percent with high income	−0.02	1.0	0.02	1.2
Autos per household	−2.88	7.6	−4.63	10.9
Workers per household	1.67	3.2	0.99	1.4
Log of number of households	0.39	7.4	0.42	6.0
CC ($N = 24$)	0.18	1.4	0.22	1.3
ST ($N = 19$)	−0.02	0.2	0.09	0.6
PCCA ($N = 12$)	−0.05	0.3	−0.36	2.0
PSTA ($N = 3$)	0.04	0.2	0.13	0.5
PAUB ($N = 7$)	0.15	0.8	−0.12	0.6
PCCB ($N = 3$)	−0.06	0.3	−0.13	0.5
R^2	.822	—	.845	—
σ_u	.328	—	.396	—
N	70	—	70	—

$$f(x) = \alpha_0 + \alpha_2 \cdot 100 + (\alpha_1 - \alpha_2)L_t + (\alpha_3 - \alpha_2)H_t + \alpha_4 AH_t + \dots \qquad (4)$$

The coefficient of L_t or H_t measures the net effect of a one percent change in the percentage of low- or high-income families on y_t. The regulation and ownership variables are also included in (3a) to test for the effects of ownership and regulation on the percentage using public transit.

Regression results for equation (3) are presented in table 6.[18] The percentage of workers using local transit decreases as the number of autos per household rises and increases as the number of households in the urbanized area rises. The number of workers per household increases transit usage in both regressions, as expected, although the estimated coefficient in the 1970 regression is only statistically significant at the 10 percent level. A one percent point increase in L_t (percent of families with low income), holding the percentage with high income constant, increases the percentage of workers using public transit in the 1970 cross section but has no significant effect in 1960.[19]

The regulation and ownership variables are not significant deter-

[18] Because transit firm operating data were not used in this analysis, a larger sample size was selected and used.

[19] The absence of an effect in the 1960 cross section may be due to the use of the poverty measure as low income in 1970 while $3,000 is the upper bound for the low-income class in 1960.

minants of the percentage of workers using local transit. The market share of local transit in cities with systems becoming publicly owned after 1959 and regulated by CC is significantly lower in 1970. The results for both cross sections do not show a larger percentage of workers using local transit under public ownership. A comparison of the estimated coefficients for 1960 and 1970 for each dummy variable leaves the impression that privately owned systems outperformed the publicly owned systems from 1960 to 1970 (the exception is the PSTA class), even though the coefficients of the individual dummy variables are not significant.[20] The data do reject the hypothesis that publicly owned systems improved their performance from 1960 to 1970 relative to privately owned systems.

If the goal of public ownership is to increase ridership by improving service frequency and, indirectly, reducing trip cost by reducing waiting time, the goal was not realized from 1960 to 1970. If public ownership did not involve significant public subsidies, the apparent failure of publicly owned transit systems to improve relative performance may not be surprising. Subsidization of capital purchases and of operating cost appears to have become more popular in the second half of the decade. Perhaps the full effects of public subsidies have yet to be experienced, and future results may yet reveal an improvement in performance under public ownership. The results of the comparative-performance analysis are also inconsistent with the regulation hypothesis. The regulation hypothesis predicts a larger percentage decline in transit users under private rather than public ownership. These and the earlier tests fail to reveal such an effect.[21]

VI. Determinants of the Probability of a Change to Public Ownership

As reported above, the operating profit margin of many, but not all, systems declined from 1960 to 1970. If the decline in margin was ultimately caused by the increased political strength of groups favoring

---

[20] The coefficient of PAUB and PCCB decreased from 1960 to 1970, which indicates a deterioration in the performance of systems under public ownership before 1960. The deterioration in performance is not limited to systems that only recently came under public ownership. Further tests rejected the hypothesis that the performance of publicly owned systems increases with the number of years under public ownership.

[21] If public ownership occurred because the performance of the transit firm had deteriorated, the coefficients of PCCA and PSTA would have declined relative to CC and ST from 1960 to 1970 and the coefficients of CC and ST should have increased relative to the base group.

public ownership, it should be possible to show a relationship between the change in margin and the change in the size of each special interest group.

Several special interest groups will exert political support for, or opposition to, more stringent regulation, public ownership, and public subsidies to mass transportation. Increases in the number of autos per household will increase the number of nonusers, a majority of which favor profitable operations and oppose subsidies and public ownership. Increases in the number of workers per household increase the number of users, a majority of which will favor lower fares and subsidized service. The effect of increases in the percent of upper-income families in a city is ambiguous. If upper-income families are nonusers, they will favor profitable operations and oppose higher taxes and subsidies to mass transit. If upper-income families are heavy users, they may favor more frequent and subsidized service since the higher the opportunity cost, the higher the family income. Firms located in the central business district would favor low fares and frequent service to the CBD. Given the size of the city, cities with lower growth rates are typically older and have larger well-defined CBDs. Systems in cities with lower growth rates are expected to have larger declines in profit margins. Finally, the size of city is introduced to determine if the cost of organizing political activities is higher in larger cities because of the free rider problem.

The change in the profit margin from 1960 to 1970 for the systems in the 40-city sample was regressed on the change in the size of the special interest groups described above. The results are shown in table 7. After controlling for changes in vehicle miles, smaller decreases in profit margin were experienced by transit systems located in urban areas with (a) larger increases in autos per household, (b) larger increases in the percent of upper-income families, (c) smaller increases in workers per household, and (d) smaller household growth rates. The long-term population growth rate from 1950 to 1970 and the size of urban area have no significant effect on the change in margin.[22]

These results are not easily reconciled with the declining-market or externalities hypothesis. If the fall in profit margin is caused by the decrease in the demand schedule for transit services, an increase in autos per household, a decrease in workers per household, or a de-

---

[22] Additional regression results showed that the change in autos per household was inversely related to the change in the probability of public ownership. Hence, cities with larger increases in autos per household had a lower probability of changing from private to public ownership of transit facilities between 1960 and 1970. For further results, see Pashigian (1975).

TABLE 7.   Change in Profit Margin, 1960–70

Variable	Est.	t	Est.	t	Est.	t
Constant	−0.64	3.2	−0.33	3.8	−0.63	2.9
Δ in autos per household	1.37	3.3	0.67	2.5	1.47	3.7
Δ in workers per household	−0.43	1.7	−0.61	2.4	—	—
Δ in percent with upper income	0.014	2.5	0.013	2.2	0.016	2.6
Δ in log of vehicle miles	−0.28	2.6	−0.32	3.0	−0.23	2.1
Δ in log of households, 1960–70	−0.24	1.7	—	—	−0.28	1.9
Ratio of city population, 1950–70	—	—	−0.039	0.9	—	—
Δ in percent of population between 18–64 years	—	—	—	—	−0.026	1.2
Log of households, 1960	0.031	1.1	—	—	0.016	0.5
R^2	.535	—	.471	—	.517	—
σ_u	.150	—	.158	—	.153	—
N	40	—	40	—	40	—

Note: Δ = difference.

crease in the number of households should have been associated with a decrease in the margin. In this sample of 40 cities, increases in autos per household, decreases in workers per household, and decreases in the number of households are associated with increases in the profit margin. These results are consistent with the hypothesis that nonusers support profitable transit operations and oppose policies which will result in higher taxes and public subsidies.[23] The evidence suggests that automobile owners and high-income groups oppose socialization of transit facilities. The increase in automobile ownership has been the major reason for the decline of urban transit but, at least in recent

[23] It is possible that a decline in ridership reduces capacity utilization (by lowering revenue per dollar of capital invested) and causes the profit margin to rise so that the rate of return on capital does not fall. An increase in autos per household may be directly related to the change in profit margin because of lower utilization of equipment when ridership declines. If the change in margin solely reflected the change in utilization, the change in margin would not be an important determinant of the change in the probability of public ownership (see n. 10 above).

times, has also been an important factor in maintaining profit margins of transit firms and limiting government ownership of transit facilities.

Summary

The results of this paper suggest that the transition from a private regulated transit firm to a government-owned firm is not a mere cosmetic change as far as the financial position of the transit system is involved. In general, government ownership is associated with lower profit margins and lower revenue per vehicle mile. Government ownership of transit facilities yields results which were unattainable under government regulation and explains why there is a demand for government ownership. The deterioration of profit margins and the increase in the number of government-owned systems strongly suggest that private transit firms did not benefit from government regulation during the last 15 to 20 years. With some exceptions, the regulatory agencies have been captured not by the transit firms of the industry but by the riders.

While a final judgment may be premature, the experience of the 1960s should dampen hopes that public ownership of transit facilities will moderate the diversion of transit users to the automobile. Follow-up study is needed, but, for the moment, the results indicate that government-owned facilities have not outperformed privately owned facilities in maintaining ridership.

While the decline in the profit margin of transit systems from 1960 to 1970 was pervasive, it was smaller or negligible in urban areas where the political strength of nonusers increased most. Transit systems with smaller declines in profit margins were located in urban areas with larger increases in autos per household and in the percent of families with upper incomes and smaller increases in workers per household. The evidence appears to contradict the common view that increases in automobile ownership are responsible for unprofitable transit operations. The rise of the automobile is the major cause of the decline of the urban transit industry, but the results of this paper suggest that it is not responsible for unprofitable transit operations and appears to be an important factor inhibiting the expansion of government ownership of transit facilities.

Appendix

Definitions of Variables and Sources of Data

Variable	Source
A. Ownership and regulatory variables	
1. CC = regulated by city council or other form of local government,	
2. PCCA = regulated by city council and publicly owned since 1959,	
3. PCCB = regulated by city council and publicly owned before 1960,	American Transit
4. ST = regulated by state commission,	Association and R. L.
5. STA = regulated by state commission and publicly owned since 1959,	Banks and Associates (1972)
6. PAUA = regulated by transit authority or district and publicly owned since 1959,	
7. PAUB = regulated by transit authority or district and publicly owned before 1960.	
B. Transit system variables	
1. RVM = operating revenue per vehicle mile,	American Transit
2. CVM = operating cost per vehicle mile,	Association (com-
3. PM = operating profit margin,	puter printouts)
4. VM = vehicle miles.	
C. Economic and demographic variables	
1. Percentage of families with low income:	
a) Income less than $3,000 in 1960,	
b) Income less than poverty income in 1970.	U.S. Bureau of the
2. Population of city, 1950, 1960, and 1970.	Census (various)
3. Percentage of families with high income:	
a) Income greater than $10,000 in 1960,	
b) Income greater than $15,000 in 1970.	
4. Autos per household.	
5. Workers per household.	Department of
6. Number of households.	Transportation
7. Percent of workers using public transit.	(1971, 1973)

References

Banks, R. L., and Associates. *Study and Evaluation of Urban Mass Transportation Regulation and Regulatory Bodies.* Springfield, Va.: Nat. Tech. Information Service, 1972.

Mohring, Herbert. "Optimization and Scale Economies in Urban Bus Transportation." *A.E.R.* 62 (September 1972): 591–604.

Pashigian, B. Peter. "Consequences and Causes of Public Ownership of Urban Transit Facilities." Report no. 7536, Center Math. Studies Bus. and Econ., Univ. Chicago, 1975.

Peltzman, Sam. "Pricing in Public and Private Enterprises: Electric Utilities in the United States." *J. Law and Econ.* 14 (April 1971): 109–65.

Stigler, George. "The Theory of Economic Regulation." *Bell J. Econ. and Management Sci.* 2 (Spring 1971): 3–21 (chap. 6 of this volume).

U.S. Bureau of the Census. *U.S. Census of Population.* Washington: Government Printing Office, various.

U.S. Department of Transportation. *Transportation Planning Data for Urban Areas.* Washington: Government Printing Office, 1971, 1973.

Discrimination in HEW: Is the Doctor Sick Or Are the Patients Healthy?

13

George J. Borjas

I. Introduction

Executive Orders No. 11247 and No. 11375[1] require that federal contractors with a contract larger than $50,000 or with fifty or more employees develop and enforce a written plan of affirmative action that guarantees equal employment opportunity. Under these orders and Title IX of the Education Amendments of 1972,[2] the Office of Civil Rights (OCR) at the Department of Health, Education, and Welfare (HEW) has been given the responsibility for carrying out these regulations and ensuring that no employment discrimination exists at the nation's universities.[3] The higher education sector, in turn, has faced the task of convincing HEW that indeed no discrimination exists or it risks losing all federal funds received by the particular universities.

This paper was written while I was a postdoctoral fellow in the Department of Economics at the University of Chicago. The research was partly supported by the Center for the Study of the Economy and the State. Financial support was also received from the National Institute of Mental Health. I am grateful to Jacob Mincer and Sherwin Rosen for encouragement and helpful discussions; to Gary Becker and George Stigler for directing my attention to the analysis of the labor market structure in the federal government; and to D. Gale Johnson for providing me with a large amount of materials concerning the agreements reached between several universities and HEW.

Reprinted with permission from *The Journal of Law and Economics* 21, no. 1 (April 1978): 97–110. © 1978 by The University of Chicago Law School

[1] Exec. Order No. 11247, 3 C.F.R. 348 (1964–65 Compilation), 1 Weekly Comp. of Pres. Doc. 305 (1965); Exec. Order No. 11375, 3 C.F.R. 684 (1966–70 Compilation), 3 Weekly Comp. of Pres. Doc. 1437 (1967); see also 45 C.F.R. § 80 (1977).

[2] As amended, 20 U.S.C.A. § 1681–1686 (1978).

[3] 45 C.F.R. § 86, 1 *et seq.* (1977). In his message to Congress, outlining his Reorganization Plan No. 1 of 1978, President Carter announced that he will issue an executive order on October 1, 1978 consolidating the entire contract compliance program, including OCR's responsibility for discrimination in university employment, in the Department of Labor, Office of Federal Contract Compliance Programs, [1978] U.S. Code Cong. & Ad. News 595.

A surprising development is that HEW is currently "suggesting" that universities perform sophisticated statistical analyses to determine whether or not wage discrimination exists at a particular institution. Thus, for example, the Chicago office of HEW has reviewed affirmative action plans at six universities and has requested detailed statistical analyses from four institutions.[4] These requests are included in the "conciliation agreements" reached between universities and HEW. These agreements ascertain that the affirmative action programs at the institutions are in compliance with the requirements of the executive orders once the universities carry out a detailed list of programs and actions covering its hiring practices of women and minorities. In particular, the conciliation agreements tend to be quite explicit in terms of the statistical analyses the universities must carry out to determine the extent of wage discrimination. For example, in the conciliation agreement between the University of Michigan and HEW the section concerning faculty salaries states that:

> The University is committed to achieving equity in pay between men and women and minority and non-minority employees in every faculty and academic staff category. In order to effect this commitment, the University will analyze its employment records and the qualifications of personnel. Professional job related criteria will be identified as base line variables for use in the analysis. Base line variables shall be quantified and include: department, rank, time in rank, measure(s) of length of professional experience. Other valid base line, quantifiable variables may be included; provided, however, that prior to inclusion the University shall consult with OCR regarding inclusion of these variables.
>
> Upon identifying appropriate base line variables, the University will perform a two tier analysis of faculty and academic staff salaries.
>
> The first tier analysis will consist of a statistical or other empirically verifiable analysis (such as multiple regression) of faculty and academic staff salaries to identify wage discrepancies. The second tier analysis will develop narrative justifications of wage discrepancies located in the first tier analysis and/or develop remedial salary awards. In no case will assertions, verbal or written, unsupported by specific comparative analysis be considered as justification for wage discrepancies.[5]

Thus universities are required to conduct analyses such as multiple regression to determine whether there exist racial or sexual wage differentials. If these are found, and if the university is unable to justify

[4] These facts were made available to me by Mr. Paul Turner, an equal opportunity specialist at the Chicago Office of HEW.

[5] U.S. Department of Health, Education, & Welfare, Office of Civil Rights, Agreement with the University of Michigan 6 (Jan. 9, 1978).

them, the university is required to provide remedial salary awards on current salaries and on two years back pay.[6] This paper is not an attempt to document what these affirmative action programs have done to improve the economic position of minorities and women.[7] It is, instead, an attempt to turn the table around and ask what would happen if HEW were to perform a statistical analysis similar to the ones that universities are currently carrying out. Thus the paper poses the empirical question of whether the doctor swallows his or her own medicine. Put differently, does "discrimination," as defined by the statistical analysis ordered by the conciliation agreements, exist at HEW?

The empirical analysis presented in this paper is based on a one per cent random sample of HEW employees collected by the Civil Service Commission.[8] To be in the sample, the individual had to be a permanent full-time employee of the Department of Health, Education, and Welfare as of July 1977. Moreover, since the salary figures available in the data are full-time salaries, no labor supply differentials exist among individuals and the discrimination coefficients estimated in this paper are for HEW's permanent full-time labor force.

The analysis will use the procedure that has become traditional in estimating wage differentials across sex or race groups after standardizing for skills. The procedure was introduced into the discrimination literature by Oaxaca[9] and is one which causes the residual wage differential—that not explained by differences in observable personal characteristics—to be called "discrimination." It is not my purpose here to defend the procedure since its many drawbacks have been pointed out by Oaxaca and by Polachek.[10] Instead, I will simply inquire into what happens to wage differentials at HEW if the procedure is followed.[11]

---

[6] It is important to note that the conciliation agreements reached between universities and HEW cover not only faculty employees but noninstructional workers as well. Moreover, the universities are also instructed to conduct the same statistical analysis for the latter group.

[7] See Thomas Sowell, Affirmative Action Reconsidered: Was It Necessary in Academia? (Am. Enterprise Inst. 1975).

[8] The original data set is called the Central Personnel Data File and contains a record for each and every federal civil servant.

[9] Ronald Oaxaca, Male-Female Wage Differentials in Urban Labor Markets, 14 Int'l Econ. Rev. 693 (1973).

[10] Solomon W. Polachek, Potential Biases in Measuring Male-Female Discrimination, 10 J. Human Resources 205 (1975).

[11] Note that I am abstracting from the more general question of discrimination in the federal government. Both James E. Long, Employment Discrimination in the Federal Sector, 11 J. Human Resources 86 (1976); and Sharon P. Smith, Equal Pay in the Public Sector: Fact or Fantasy (Princeton Univ., Ind. Relations Section 1977), have studied the problem and have found substantial discrimination, though less than in the private sector. A discussion of programs designed to improve the economic position of women and minorities in several government agencies, including HEW, is provided by

Section II presents a brief descriptive look at HEW and gives the basic wage regressions estimated for the agency. It also presents regressions showing that general schedule ratings differ systematically by sex and race. Section III gives a more detailed accounting of the sex/race wage differentials at HEW and compares them to those found in the total economy and/or the private sector in the major studies in the literature. Section IV summarizes the empirical results and states some policy implications.

II. Basic Results

The Department of Health, Education, and Welfare has the largest budget of any agency in the federal government. In July 1977 its employment of full-time permanent workers was 140,164, an increase of over 100 per cent since 1961. The percentage of black and female employees at various times in the last decade was: [12]

	% Black	% Female
1966	20.3	57.7
1971	22.4	59.5
1976	23.3	61.0

Thus the percentage of women and blacks employed by HEW has always been relatively high but did not increase very much in the last few years.

Table 1 presents estimates of July 1977 wages and wage differentials at HEW. It can be seen that the gross wage differentials are sizable and not very different from those found in the economy as a whole. For example, the chapter on the economic status of women in the 1973 Economic Report of the President reported that the adjusted (for differences in hours worked) female/male wage ratio was 66.1 per cent. [13] At HEW the similar statistic is 64.9 per cent. Similarly, in his analysis of 1970 U.S. Census data for males, Freeman [14] reports a black/white earnings ratio of .64. The respective statistic for HEW is

---

Mary E. Eccles, Race, Sex and Government Jobs: A Study of Affirmative Action Programs in Federal Agencies (1976) (unpublished Ph.D. dissertation at Harvard Univ.).

[12] These data were obtained from various issues of the Federal Civilian Workforce Statistics Monthly Release, Minority Group Employment in the Federal Government, Study of Employment of Women in the Federal Government, and Equal Employment Opportunity Statistics, all published by the U.S. Civil Service Commission.

[13] U.S. President, 1973 Economic Report of the President to the Congress, ch. 4.

[14] R. B. Freeman, Labor Market Discrimination: Analysis, Findings, and Problems, in 2 Frontiers of Quantitative Economics 501 (M. D. Intriligator & D. A. Kendrick eds. 1974) (Contributions to Economic Analysis vol. 87).

TABLE 1.   Mean Wages at HEW[a]

Variable	Male	White Male	Black Male	Female	White Female	Black Female
W	19595.4	20897.3	15333.5	12710.0	13395.8	11642.2
ln(W)	9.782	9.857	9.537	9.387	9.436	9.309
No. of observations	547	419	128	895	545	350

[a]W denotes annual, full-time earnings reported by the agency. Note that the "black" sample includes Negroes as well as members of other minority groups.

.73. Finally, Freeman also reports the female black/white wage ratio to be .86 in 1970, while the HEW statistic for 1977 was .87.

Of course, part of these differentials are due to different characteristics across groups. To standardize for these characteristics in a simple fashion, Table 2 pools the four groups and controls for education, labor-force experience, region, veteran status, retired-military dummy, and health; and then adds dummies indicating the race/sex status of the individual, the omitted group being black females. Columns 1 and 2 of Table 2 present equations with the logarithm of annual full-time earnings as the dependent variable. In column 1, the traditional specification of experience (that is, experience and experience squared) is followed. Column 2 utilizes the additional information given by the data on current job tenure and replaces the experience variable by current job tenure, *CURRENT*, and labor force experience prior to the current job, *PREVIOUS*.[15] It would, of course, be optimal to know whether in the case of women *PREVIOUS* represents labor market experience or time spent in the household.[16] However, information on experience in other jobs or even marital status is not collected in the Central Personnel Data File.

The results are quite interesting. In the simpler equation using total experience (column 1), it can be seen that white males earn about 23 per cent more than white females, 14 per cent more than black males, and a large 31 per cent more than black females even after standardization.[17] Thus wage differentials at HEW are far from trivial. We can go a step beyond these results and standardize for the components of total experience across individuals. These results are presented in column 2. The regressions indicate that white males earn 19 per cent more than white females, 13 per cent more than black males and 28 per cent more than black females. Thus the standardization for current job tenure diminished the unexplained male/female wage differential by only about 3 or 4 percentage points. Therefore, the findings indicate that substantial unexplained race/sex wage differentials exist even at HEW.

The reader might now be wondering exactly how these differ-

---

[15] The exact specification used for these variables is derived in George J. Borjas, Job Mobility and Earnings over the Life Cycle (Nat'l Bureau Econ. Res. Working Paper No. 233, Feb. 1978).

[16] Presumably market experience and time spent in the household have different effects on market earnings. See Jacob Mincer & Solomon Polachek, Family Investments in Human Capital: Earnings of Women, 82 J. Pol. Econ. 576 (March 1974), for a thorough discussion of this issue.

[17] t-tests were carried out on each of these statistics. In every case the estimated test statistic was well over 2.

TABLE 2.   HEW Regressions[a]

Variable	Dependent = ln (W)				Dependent = GS Grade			
	Coeff.	t	Coeff.	t	Coeff.	t	Coeff.	t
CONSTANT	7.9648		7.9317		-6.2501		-6.5982	
EDUC	.0772	(24.01)	.0758	(25.35)	.7603	(23.93)	.7529	(25.45)
EXPER	.0378	(15.88)	—	—	.2751	(12.36)	—	—
EXPER²	-.0006	(-10.56)	—	—	-.0049	(-9.71)	—	—
PREVIOUS	—	—	.0162	(5.83)	—	—	.0888	(3.34)
CURRENT	—	—	.0613	(20.51)	—	—	.4607	(16.99)
PREVIOUS²	—	—	-.0003	(-3.22)	—	—	-.0017	(-2.16)
CURRENT²	—	—	-.0012	(-13.67)	—	—	-.0096	(-12.41)
PREVIOUS X CURRENT	—	—	-.0006	(-5.03)	—	—	-.0062	(-5.40)
NORTH	-.0944	(-3.88)	-.0793	(-3.53)	-.7227	(-3.45)	-.5857	(-3.00)
MIDWEST	-.1001	(-4.21)	-.0989	(-4.53)	-.5965	(-2.91)	-.5339	(-2.80)
SOUTH	-.1072	(-4.74)	-.1024	(-4.92)	-.7489	(-3.79)	-.6362	(-3.45)
WEST	-.0773	(-3.38)	-.0595	(-2.82)	-.6858	(-3.37)	-.4788	(-2.53)
RETIRED MILITARY	.7975	(2.74)	1.0514	(3.90)	—	—	—	—
VETERAN	-.0094	(-.40)	-.0310	(-1.43)	-.2243	(-1.06)	-.4326	(-2.19)
HEALTH	-.0764	(-1.80)	-.0473	(-1.21)	-.7453	(-2.10)	-.4945	(-1.50)
WHITE MALE	.3108	(12.46)	.2778	(12.06)	2.7348	(12.10)	2.5239	(12.01)
BLACK MALE	.1751	(5.43)	.1514	(5.11)	1.6274	(5.22)	1.5771	(5.45)
WHITE FEMALE	.0837	(4.11)	.0889	(4.75)	.7556	(4.33)	.8117	(5.00)
R²	.563		.632		.539		.604	

[a]Key to Variables: EDUC = years of completed schooling; EXPER = age-EDUC-6; CURRENT = years of civilian service in the federal government; PREVIOUS = EXPER-CURRENT; NORTH, MIDWEST, SOUTH, WEST = 1 if individual lives in respective region—left out is District of Columbia area; RETIRED MILITARY = 1 if individual is retired from the military; VETERAN = 1 if individual is a veteran; HEALTH = 1 if agency reported that individual has some kind of handicap.

entials are achieved given the strict civil service pay rules. For example, consider the pay structure facing white collar workers in the federal government. Most of these individuals will be covered by the general schedule (GS) pay system. The GS consists of 18 grades, each of which is defined by law in terms of the skills and responsibilities associated with the job. The data set provides a unique opportunity to establish that indeed discrimination may well work by placing "equally" qualified individuals in lower job categories simply because of sex or race. This is done in columns 3 and 4 of Table 2. Again, column 3 uses total experience whereas column 4 uses current and previous tenure. The sample is restricted to the 1,287 individuals (89.3 per cent of the total sample) who are classified as GS employees. The dependent variable is the GS grade assigned to each employee. As can be seen, women and blacks are systematically assigned lower grades than men and whites. For example, in column 3 the results indicate that white males have a grade that is about one level above that of black males, about 2 levels above that of white females, and 2.7 levels above that of black females! If we standardize for current job tenure (column 4), the results indicate that white males are placed about one level above black males, 1.7 levels above white females, and 2.5 levels above black females. That is, controlling for current job tenure slightly diminishes male-female grade differentials, but does not affect black-white differences. In summary, the results indicate that males are placed about 1.5 to 2 grades higher than females, and that blacks are placed about 1 grade below whites.

III. Decomposition of Wage Differential

Although the simple analysis conducted in the previous section provides convincing evidence that unexplained wage differentials exist at HEW, the methodology can be improved somewhat. In particular, only the intercepts were allowed to vary across sex and race groups when, in fact, slope parameters may also differ. This can be remedied by estimating the equations within each sex/race group. These results can then be used to ask what would males (whites) earn if they faced the female (black) wage structure. These predicted earnings can, in turn, be used to decompose the gross wage differential into that part due to differences in group characteristics and into the unexplained component which has traditionally been identified with "discrimination." Again note that the purpose of the analysis is not to defend the methodology as providing a correct way of estimating discrimination coefficients, but to ask how would HEW fare if it were to conduct its own internal analysis.

The estimated regressions are shown in Appendix Tables A-1 and A-2. Table A-1 provides the regressions using total labor force experience, while Table A-2 presents the regressions holding job tenure constant. Table A-3 gives the average characteristics for each of the four subsamples. The procedure used to decompose the gross wage differential is best understood by means of an example. In particular, suppose one is interested in decomposing the gross 42 per cent wage differential between white males and white females into that part due to differences in characteristics and that part due to discrimination.[18] To do this, one can ask what female earnings would be if they faced the male wage structure (namely, the male regression coefficients). An unbiased estimate of this wage is obtained by predicting female earnings using male regression coefficients and female characteristics. The difference between this predicted wage and the actual female wage is due to differences in structures and is usually attributed to discriminatory practices by the firm. Alternatively, one could have asked what male wages would be if they faced the female wage structure, and again the portion due to "discrimination" is given by the difference of the predicted male wage and the actual male wage. Clearly the answers given by the two methods will not, in general, be identical but they do provide a (hopefully) narrow range for the estimates.

The gross wage differential and the results of the decomposition (using the regressions presented in the Appendix) are shown in Table 3. To provide a detailed and systematic breakdown of the results, Table 3 gives the decomposition separately for each sex and race group, using both available sets of weights, and specifying the regressions either with total experience (columns 1 and 3) or with previous and current tenure (columns 2 and 4). The gross differential between white males and females is .42. Although there are differences in the percentage of this differential that is due to "discrimination" according to the specification of the regression and the set of weights used, it can be seen that at least 40 per cent of the gross differential cannot be explained by observable differences in characteristics and, using the traditional approach, can be attributed to discrimination. The results do not improve if we decompose the wage differentials between black males and females: at least 80 per cent of the gross differential is due to discrimination. Thus the results indicate the strong prevalence of sex discrimination at HEW.

The results concerning race discrimination (shown in parts C and D of Table 3) are not very different qualitatively. In comparing male

[18] The 42 per cent figure is obtained as the difference between the mean logarithm of white male earnings and the mean logarithm of white female earnings.

whites and blacks we find a 32 per cent gross wage differential. The results in Table 3 indicate that about a third of this differential is due to discrimination. Similarly, in comparing female whites and blacks, between half and 75 per cent of the wage differential can be attributed to discrimination.

Perhaps it is best at this point to remind the reader of the dollar magnitudes that can be attributed to discrimination. For example, consider the difference between white males and white females and take the most favorable discrimination coefficient from HEW's point of view. That is, suppose only 39.8 per cent of the wage gap is due to discrimination. The arithmetic dollar wage gap between the two

TABLE 3*.   Decomposition of Sexual and Racial Wage Differences at HEW

	(1)	(2)	(3)	(4)
A. *Sex Differences Between White Males and Females*				
	Male Structure		Female Structure	
Gross Differential	.4208	.4208	.4208	.4208
Due to Characteristics	.2024	.2193	.1840	.2533
% Due to Characteristics	48.1%	52.1%	43.7%	60.2%
% Due to Discrimination	51.9%	47.9%	56.3%	39.8%
B. *Sex Differences Between Black Males and Females*				
	Male Structure		Female Structure	
Gross Differential	.2278	.2278	.2278	.2278
Due to Characteristics	−.0027	−.0093	.0444	.0351
% Due to Characteristics	0%	0%	19.5%	15.4%
% Due to Discrimination	100%	100%	80.5%	84.6%
C. *Race Differences Between Male Whites and Blacks*				
	White Structure		Black Structure	
Gross Differential	.3203	.3203	.3203	.3203
Due to Characteristics	.2095	.2100	.1979	.2102
% Due to Characteristics	65.4%	65.6%	61.8%	65.6%
% Due to Discrimination	34.6%	34.4%	38.2%	34.4%
D. *Race Differences Between Female Whites and Blacks*				
	White Structure		Black Structure	
Gross Differential	.1273	.1273	.1273	.1273
Due to Characteristics	.0321	.0283	.0611	.0489
% Due to Characteristics	25.2%	22.2%	48.0%	38.4%
% Due to Discrimination	74.8%	77.8%	52.0%	61.6%

*See text for explanation of methodology.

groups is $7,501.5, of which approximately $2,986 cannot be explained by observable differences in individual characteristics.

The reader will now be wondering how these estimates compare with those obtained in the private sector and/or the total economy. A brief survey of empirical results in the literature is given in Table 4, which contains information on the gross wage gap (defined as the difference in the logarithm of wages across groups), the sample used, and the percentage of the wage gap which is due to discrimination. By and large, the comparison of men to women or blacks to whites leads to gross wage differentials in the range of 40 per cent, not at all unlike those presented in Table 1 for HEW. The proportions of the wage gap which cannot be explained by observed personal characteristics vary widely across studies of the sex wage differential. For example, consider the Oaxaca study. He finds, after standardizing for a very large set of variables, that about 58 per cent of the white male/female wage gap is due to discrimination.[19] On the other hand, Mincer and Polachek[20] find that by controlling for the fact that women have a discontinuous labor force history (and thus fewer incentives for market-human-capital investments) about two-thirds of the male/female wage differential can be explained by differences in personal characteristics.[21] I find that slightly less than half of the wage gap is due to unexplained differences in HEW. Thus my results are about halfway between the bounds provided by the Mincer and Polachek and Oaxaca studies.

In terms of racial differences, the results are somewhat mixed. It seems that about 80 per cent of the male black/white wage differential in the private sector cannot be explained by differences in individual characteristics, whereas the respective statistic for HEW is about 35 per cent. On the other hand, Smith[22] finds that only about a third of the private female black/white differential is due to discrimination, while in HEW the relevant statistic is between 50 and 75 per cent.

---

[19] Ronald Oaxaca, *supra* note 9. Oaxaca also reports results which exclude occupation and industry dummies. He finds that it is the industrial categories which help to explain a large part of the wage gap and that occupation does not affect significantly the percentage of the wage gap due to discrimination. Since I concentrate the analysis on individuals in the public sector I am already controlling for industry. Moreover by standardizing for job tenure I partly account for the effects of marital status on labor force experience. Thus the regressions are roughly comparable.

[20] Jacob Mincer & Solomon Polachek, *supra* note 16.

[21] Elisabeth M. Landes, Sex-Differences in Wages and Employment: A Test of the Specific Capital Hypothesis, 15 Econ. Inquiry 523 (1977), finds that practically the entire male/female wage gap can be explained by differences in personal characteristics once the regression standardizes for rough estimates of differences in turnover by sex.

[22] Sharon P. Smith, *supra* note 11.

TABLE 4. Estimates of Discrimination from Other Studies[a]

I. Sex Differences

Study	Sample	Gross Wage Gap	% of Gap Due to Discrimination	Variables Held Constant
Oaxaca[b]	SEO	Whites = 43% Blacks = 40%	58.4% 55.6%	Education, experience, class of worker, industry, occupation, health, labor supply, migration, marital status, children, size of urban area, region
Mincer and Polachek[c]	NLS, SEO	White married = 42% White single = 15%	33% 50%	Education, home time, current tenure, other experience, formal training, migration, labor supply, children
Smith[d]	CPS, 1975 private sector	All women = 44%	67.1%	Education, experience, marital status, region, occupation, veteran, size of urban area, union, labor supply, Spanish

II. Race Differences

Study	Sample	Gross Wage Gap	% of Gap Due to Discrimination	Variables Held Constant
Long[e]	Census, 1970 private sector	Males = 38%	88.3%	Education, age, marital status, labor supply, region
Smith[f]	Census, 1970 private sector	Males = 38% Females = 16%	71.1% 36.7%	Education, experience, marital status, Spanish, health, labor supply, occupation, region, urban residence

Notes:

[a] In order to simplify the presentation the estimates from other studies were boiled down to a single summary statistic. In the case where the author reported different results due to the use of different weights, a simple average of the two estimates is reported. Long's study does not report the gross black/white wage differential, only the adjusted one, 33.5%. Smith, using the same data set, reports the gross wage ratio to be .38. The estimate given in the table is calculated from this information.

[b] Ronald Oaxaca, Male-Female Wage Differentials in Urban Labor Markets, 14 Int'l Econ. Rev. 693 (1973).

[c] Jacob Mincer & Solomon Polachek, Family Investments in Human Capital: Earnings of Women 82 J. Pol. Econ. S76 (March 1974).

[d] Sharon P. Smith, Equal Pay in the Public Sector: Fact or Fantasy (Princeton Univ., Industrial Relations Section 1977).

[e] James E. Long, Employment Discrimination in the Federal Sector, 11 J. Human Resources 86 (1976).

[f] Sharon P. Smith, *supra* note d.

438   *George J. Borjas*

IV. Summary and Policy Implications

This paper has documented the existence of large wage differentials in
HEW even after standardizing for skills. These unexplained wage differentials have been attributed to discrimination in studies of the private sector or the economy as a whole. In particular, it was shown that
among HEW employees a wage gap of $2,986 between white men and
women could not be explained by differences in individual characteristics. Similarly, a wage gap of $1,914 between white men and black men
working for HEW remains unexplained.

The question, of course, is whether these differentials truly measure the extent of discrimination. This raises a delicate problem if we
consider the policy implications of one extreme way of interpreting the
wage differential. Suppose, for example, HEW argues that it does not
discriminate against women and blacks and that the whole unexplained
wage gap could be explained if only we could quantify unobserved productivity differences. This may well be true but it certainly raises an important question concerning HEW's handling of observed wage differentials in the higher education sector. Why is it not possible that these
wage differentials *also* are due to unobserved productivity differences?

Let me summarize by restating the purpose of this paper. My
point was not to accuse HEW of discriminatory practices. It was simply
to point out that the statistical procedures universities are currently
carrying out to comply with the conciliation agreements can be easily
applied to HEW wage data. More importantly, this analysis reveals a
wage structure within HEW which follows roughly the same patterns
that the agency is vigorously attacking in the private sector.

Appendix

TABLE A-1.   Earnings Functions by Race and Sex

Variable	White Male Coeff.	t	Black Male Coeff.	t	White Female Coeff.	t	Black Female Coeff.	t
CONSTANT	8.0475		7.9389		8.0011		8.1408	
EDUC	.0783	(15.06)	.0814	(7.78)	.0866	(15.65)	.0698	(9.53)
EXPER	.0601	(11.99)	.0434	(4.79)	.0387	(11.40)	.0202	(4.46)
EXPER^2	−.0009	(−8.10)	−.0004	(−2.39)	−.0007	(−8.96)	−.0002	(−1.66)
NORTH	−.1063	(−2.42)	.0001	(.00)	−.1397	(−4.03)	.0018	(.03)
MIDWEST	−.1783	(−3.78)	.0060	(.04)	−.1252	(−3.74)	−.0038	(−.09)
SOUTH	−.1427	(−3.27)	−.0450	(−.47)	−.1533	(−4.93)	.0141	(.30)
WEST	−.1477	(−3.52)	.1157	(1.54)	−.1656	(−4.36)	.0494	(1.23)
RETIRED MILITARY	.7128	(2.44)	—	—	—	—	—	—
VETERAN	−.0565	(−1.72)	−.1682	(−2.28)	−.0907	(−1.89)	−.0328	(−.27)
HEALTH	−.0297	(−.41)	−.2036	(−1.01)	−.0951	(−1.50)	−.1788	(−2.19)
R^2	.568		.488		.459		.327	

TABLE A-2.   Earnings Functions by Race and Sex

Variable	White Male Coeff.	t	Black Male Coeff.	t	White Female Coeff.	t	Black Female Coeff.	t
CONSTANT	8.0293		7.8172		7.9008		8.1702	
EDUC	.0779	(15.07)	.0783	(7.64)	.0888	(18.51)	.0605	(9.19)
PREVIOUS	.0375	(5.58)	.0282	(2.93)	.0172	(4.54)	−.0049	(−.96)
CURRENT	.0730	(12.68)	.0859	(6.64)	.0650	(15.53)	.0555	(9.30)
PREVIOUS^2	−.0004	(−2.33)	−.0001	(−.34)	−.0004	(−3.92)	.0004	(2.14)
CURRENT^2	−.0013	(−8.40)	−.0017	(−4.74)	−.0013	(−10.89)	−.0011	(−6.16)
PREVIOUS X CURRENT	−.0012	(−4.22)	−.0007	(−1.45)	−.0008	(−5.12)	−.0002	(−.68)
NORTH	−.0954	(−2.23)	.0405	(.37)	−.1201	(−3.98)	.0083	(.19)
MIDWEST	−.1783	(−3.88)	.0414	(.36)	−.1159	(−4.01)	−.0004	(−.00)
SOUTH	−.1428	(−3.35)	−.0097	(−.11)	−.1403	(−5.22)	.0350	(.86)
WEST	−.1427	(−3.49)	.1278	(1.78)	−.1116	(−3.38)	.0327	(.93)
RETIRED MILITARY	.7192	(2.46)	—	—	—	—	—	—
VETERAN	−.0582	(−1.78)	−.2086	(−2.99)	−.0713	(−1.71)	−.1036	(−.98)
HEALTH	−.0177	(−.25)	−.2149	(−1.14)	−.0485	(−.88)	−.1118	(−1.55)
R^2	.593		.564		.601		.486	

TABLE A-3.   Average Characteristics by Race and Sex

Variable	White Male	Black Male	White Female	Black Female
EDUC	15.554	13.520	13.611	12.911
EXPER	19.064	18.262	18.569	16.623
EXPER^2	499.420	501.928	525.547	396.654
PREVIOUS	5.788	6.410	8.662	7.277
CURRENT	13.277	11.852	9.906	9.346
PREVIOUS^2	94.344	104.264	168.774	115.829
CURRENT^2	266.155	225.477	171.928	145.837
$X^{PREVIOUS}_{CURRENT}$	69.461	86.094	92.422	67.494
NORTH	.136	.078	.152	.109
MIDWEST	.112	.070	.169	.154
SOUTH	.136	.125	.213	.126
WEST	.153	.227	.117	.177
RETIRED MILITARY	.002	0.0	0.0	0.0
VETERAN	.456	.508	.062	.014
HEALTH	.041	.023	.033	.031

The Effects of Consumer Safety Standards: The 1973 Mattress Flammability Standard

14

Peter Linneman

I. Introduction

In May 1973, the Consumer Product Safety Commission (CPSC) was established by the Consumer Product Safety Act of 1972.[1] The commission was charged "to protect the public against unreasonable risks associated with consumer products" and empowered to establish mandatory product safety requirements. Several papers have discussed the conceptual problems posed by the phrase "unreasonable risks."[2] However, little effort has been directed to the empirical effects of CPSC standards, and hence there is little evidence on the performance of the CPSC in accomplishing its congressional mandate. This paper presents evidence indicating that the CPSC flammability standard for mattresses has led to a statistically insignificant increase in consumer safety. It demonstrates that any benefits obtained have been at the cost of higher mattress prices as well as notable effects on income redistribution. These latter findings are discussed more fully in the context of recent theories of economic regulation.[3]

I have benefited from helpful comments made by participants of the Industrial Organization Workshop at the University of Chicago and from the comments made at presentations at Bell Laboratories, Claremont Men's College, the Federal Trade Commission, and Tulane University. Daniel Hayes, Stanley Kimer, and Steven Strandberg provided valuable research. I am grateful to The Center for the Study of the Economy and the State, the University of Chicago, for financial support.

Reprinted with permission from *The Journal of Law and Economics* 23, no. 2 (October 1980): 461–79. © 1980 by The University of Chicago Law School

[1] Pub. L. 92-573, 86 Stat. 1207. This act also gave the CPSC the responsibility of administering the Flammable Fabrics Act, the Federal Hazardous Substance Act, the Poison Prevention Packaging Act, and the Refrigerator Safety Act.

[2] See, for example, V. Broussalian, Risk Measurement and Safety Standards in Consumer Products, in Household Consumption and Production 491 (Nestor E. Terlecky ed.) (Nat'l Bureau Econ. Research 1975); H. G. Grabowski & J. M. Vernon, Consumer Product Safety Regulation, 68 Am. Econ. Rev. 284 (May 1978); and Walter Oi, The Economics of Product Safety, 4 Bell J. Econ. & Management Sci. 3 (1973).

[3] See, for example, George J. Stigler, The Theory of Economic Regulation, 2

In Section II the mattress industry and the 1973 flammability standard are briefly described. The third section evaluates the impact of the standard on consumer safety, and Section IV estimates the effect of the standard on mattress prices. Section V describes the effect of the standard on the economic welfare of several specific population groups. Finally, Section VI examines whether the findings for this particular regulation are consistent with existing economic models of the regulatory process. It is argued that developing a data base for testing alternative regulatory models requires a methodology similar to that employed in this paper. Not only would such tests require traditional cost and benefit estimates of regulations but also estimates of the effects of regulation on income redistribution.

II. Industry and Standard Background

The mattress industry employs approximately 32,000 workers in roughly 1,000 firms. Approximately 12 million new mattresses are sold annually, 80 per cent of which are traditional innerspring mattresses. In 1972 annual wholesale sales were $420 million in 1972 dollars. Approximately 25 per cent of industry sales were made by the four largest producers and half by the largest fifty firms.

In the summer of 1973 the CPSC, after a year of hearings and debate, enacted one of its earlier safety standards with the 1973 Mattress Flammability Standard. Simply stated, the standard requires that mattresses not burn (either with or without bedding) when exposed to cigarettes in controlled conditions and establishes record-keeping and testing procedures for manufacturers. The standard was not a new technological standard, and it has been estimated that approximately 80 per cent of the mattresses produced already satisfied its requirements.

III. The Effects on Consumer Safety

The proclaimed purpose of the 1973 Mattress Flammability Standard is "to protect the public against unreasonable risk of the occurrence of fire."[4] This section discusses whether risk is significantly reduced by the standard level, not whether the risk level is "unreasonable."

Fires that start with mattresses impose resource costs in terms of both property and personal damages. The annual resource cost of mat-

Bell J. Econ. & Management Sci. 3 (1971) (chap. 6 of this volume); and Sam Peltzman, Toward a More General Theory of Regulation, 19 J. Law & Econ. 211 (1976) (chap. 7 of this volume).

[4] 38 Fed. Reg. 15095 (June 8, 1973).

tress fires is the sum of the monetary valuations of pain and suffering, loss of life, hospital costs, recovery costs, and property damages. Formally this cost is defined as

$$T = N(c \cdot H + W \cdot H + Q \cdot R + v \cdot P + S) + K \cdot D, \tag{1}$$

where
   T = the total annual resource cost of mattress fires
   N = the number of mattress burn victims (annually)
   c = the average daily hospital cost per day
   H = the average hospital stay (in days)
   W = the average difference between the value of a day when healthy and a day spent in the hospital
   Q = the average difference between the value of a day when healthy and a day spent recovering after leaving the hospital
   R = the average post-hospital recovery period (in full-day equivalents)
   v = the average monetary value of a life
   P = the average probability of death from a mattress burn
   S = the average monetary value of pain and suffering
   K = the annual number of mattress fires which damage property
   D = the average property damage per mattress fire.

To reduce the number of parameters in the system, several simplifying assumptions are employed. First, it is assumed that the post-hospital recovery period is proportional with the length of hospital stay:

$$R = \gamma H, \gamma > 0. \tag{2}$$

The second assumption is that the level of pain and suffering is approximated by a linear combination of the probability of death from a burn and the length of hospital stay

$$S = \alpha H + BP, \tag{3}$$

where α is the proportional increase in the value of pain and suffering as the hospital stay increases and B is the analogous term for the probability of death from a burn.

Since data on property damages from mattress fires are highly questionable due to the purportedly high correlation between mattress fires and arson, it is assumed that the number of property-damaging mattress fires is proportional to the number of mattress-fire burn victims:

$$K = \lambda N, \lambda > 0. \tag{4}$$

Finally, it is assumed that the average property damage (in dollars) from a mattress fire can be expressed as a linear function of the length of hospital stay and the probability of death associated with mattress fires:

$$D = \Theta H + \phi P, \Theta > 0, \phi > 0. \tag{5}$$

Substituting (2), (3), (4), and (5) into (1) and collecting terms yields:

$$T = N(C \cdot H + V \cdot P), \tag{6}$$

where $C = c + W + Q\gamma + \alpha + \lambda\Theta$ = the full resource cost of a day spent in the hospital inclusive of recovery costs, pain and suffering, and property damages associated with increased hospital stay, and $V \equiv v + B + \lambda\phi$ = the full resource cost associated with the loss of a life inclusive of the pain and suffering and property damages associated with dying from burns.

This expression of the total annual resource costs of mattress fires implies that the change in total resource cost brought about by the 1973 flammability standard, L, is

$$\begin{aligned} dT/dL = (C \cdot H + V \cdot P)dN/dL + N \cdot C \cdot dH/dL \\ + N \cdot V \cdot dP/dL, \end{aligned} \tag{7}$$

where it is assumed $dC/dL = dV/dL = 0$. If $dT/dL < 0$, then the standard has improved consumer safety.

To measure the change in resource costs, estimates of C, H, V, P, N, dN/dL, dH/dL, and dP/dL are required. The data used to obtain estimates of these parameters are individual burn records from the public use file of the National Institute for Burn Medicine (NIBM).[5] In the period from 1965 to 1977, approximately 35,000 burn cases were reported to NIBM. Of these, fewer than 1 per cent (269) were identified as caused by beds or bedding. Although the incidence of mattress-related fires was quite low, their severity was very high[6] because

[5] NIBM acts as a clearing house for information on burn victims taken to hospitals (alive or dead). Private correspondence with NIBM officials suggests that their data record between 10 and 35% of all burn cases annually.

[6] For example, the death rate is three times higher than the average (.31 versus .10) and the average hospital stay is about 12% longer.

60 per cent of mattress-burn victims were either sleeping or resting when burned.

Approximately 83 per cent of all mattress-burn victims were either smoking or drinking when they were burned, indicating that cigarettes are a major source of mattress-related fires. It remains, however, an open question whether the CPSC standard for mattress flammability addresses the relevant dimensions of this source of fires.

The CPSC flammability standard may reduce the number of mattress-burn victims for two reasons. First, it addresses a primary source of mattress-related fires; by prohibiting the sale of substandard mattresses, it reduces the stock of "burnable" mattresses held by the population. As the "burnable" stock declines in the poststandard period, so too will the number of burn victims (for a constant burn rate for flammable mattresses).[7]

The flammability standard may also reduce the number of burn victims by informing consumers that they may own potentially flammable mattresses. If consumers did not previously possess this information, either because the benefits of obtaining it were less than its cost or (as many have suggested) because consumers are inherently unable to correctly assess the probability of low probability events, this information will lead to greater care in the use of cigarettes. This informational effect would equal zero if all consumers were fully informed of the flammability risks of their mattresses, unless the standard itself conveys erroneous information.

NIBM data are used to estimate a time-series model with the annual number of burn cases, N, as a function of a linear trend, YR, the total number of burn cases (of all types) in the NIBM file, TOTAL, and a poststandard dummy variable which is equal to one for the years 1974–1977. The total number of burn cases in the NIBM sample is in-

---

[7] A crude estimate of this stock effect on the number of burn victims is obtained by noting that the stock of substandard mattresses in 1973 was somewhat over 20% of the total stock of mattresses, or about 28 million mattresses. If it is assumed that in the prestandard period only substandard mattresses caused burns and the annual average number of burn victims is 25, then the burn rate of substandard mattresses is approximately 1 in a million. If 10% of the stock of burnable mattresses are retired annually, this implies that in the first year after the standard there would be 2 fewer burn victims, in the second year there would be 4 fewer, in the third year there would be 6 fewer, and so on until the tenth year (when the entire burnable stock is replaced by above-standard mattresses) there would be 25 fewer burn cases than the prestandard average. Thus, if one asked what was the average reduction in burn cases over the period 1974–1977, the estimated stock replacement effect would be about −5 cases per year. A higher turnover rate would increase the absolute value of this estimate, whereas a lower burn rate would reduce the estimate. Of course, if the production rate of burnable mattresses was declining even in the absence of a standard, then the estimated stock impact of the standard would be reduced.

cluded to control for increases in the number of hospitals and burn centers which report to the NIBM, while the trend term is included to capture all omitted technological and population characteristics that move smoothly over time. Among these omitted traits are age composition, percentage of the population that smokes, and the flammability of linens.

This model applied to the thirteen annual observations yields

$$N = 100.62 + 1.45YR + 0.0078TOTAL - 9.19L, \tag{8}$$
$$\quad (0.75) \quad (0.70) \quad\quad (1.07) \quad\quad\quad (0.66)$$

$$R^2 = .48$$

where absolute t-values are given in parentheses.[8] The sample reveals an insignificant trend. The share of victims rises roughly in proportion with the total sample, holding constant the effects of the trend and flammability standard. The point estimate of the impact of the standard is a 9-case annual reduction; however, this estimate is significantly different from zero at only the 53 per cent level.[9]

The earlier discussion of the effect of the standard on burn cases suggested that the annual impact would increase over time as the stock of "burnable" mattresses was replaced. To test for the presence of this effect, an alternative specification of the number of burn cases is estimated which allows the impact of the standard to increase over time,

$$N = 117.31 + 1.72\ YR + 0.0070TOTAL$$
$$\quad (0.72) \quad (0.68) \quad\quad (0.80)$$

$$+\ 102.04L - 1.47\ L \cdot YR, \tag{9}$$
$$\quad (0.19) \quad\quad (0.21)$$

$$R^2 = .48$$

where once again absolute t-values are reported beneath the coefficients. The results of this specification are broadly consistent with those reported in (8) both in sign and significance. The estimated re-

[8] Similar specifications of the total number of burn cases in the NIBM sample, TOTAL, indicate that in the poststandard period there has been a marginally significant increase in TOTAL. Thus, not only has there been an absolute decline in mattress burn cases, but also their share has fallen. This result was further substantiated by regressing the share of mattress burns on the trend and law variables.

[9] This point estimate of the standard impact is about 50% greater than the crude estimate of the stock effect on burn cases in note 7 *supra;* however, this differential is not significant at any standard confidence level.

ductions in cases are −6.7 in 1974, −8.2 in 1975, −9.7 in 1976, and −11.2 in 1977. The finding of a 1.5 case reduction annually is consistent with the estimated stock effect of an initial reduction of 5.2 cases (6.7 − 1.5 = 5.2) due to the informational impact of the standard.

The average hospital stay and probability of death for this censored sample of mattress-burn victims is modeled as a recursive system.[10] The data set contains two objective measures of the seriousness of the burn: the percentage of the body burned (% BODY) and the percentage of the body with all three skin layers burned (% THICK). These measures of the seriousness of the burn are modeled as functions of the age and sex of the burn victim, his smoking and drinking status at the time of the burn, a linear trend effect, and L. In turn, the average hospital stay and the probability of death are modeled as functions of the seriousness of the burn, the age and sex of the victim, a trend effect, and L. This specification yields a direct impact of the standard on hospital stay and probability of death and an indirect effect via the effects of the standard on the seriousness of burns.

Table 1 displays the estimates obtained in applying this model to the sample of 269 individual burn cases. The % THICK results (column 1) indicate that males suffer significantly less serious burns, but no significant age pattern is discernible. There is also a positive trend in % THICK. The results suggest that prior to the standard, smoking and smoking/drinking victims suffered more severe burns; none of the smoking or drinking status variables are significant, however, at standard confidence levels. An interesting finding is that no significant impact of the standard is discernible, although the point estimates indicate burn reductions of 5 per cent for the base group, with larger reductions for relatively careless consumers.

The specification of % BODY (column 2) reveals an age pattern in which the young and old are burned more extensively. No significant trend effect is apparent, and males once again are burned about 6 per cent less severely than females. The data suggest that the standard has brought about no significant reduction in the severity of injury for either the base or relatively careless victim categories.

Turning to the recursive specification of the hospitalization regression (column 3, Table 1), no significant trend effect is discernible.

[10] See J. J. Heckman, The Common Structure of Statistical Models of Truncation, Sample Selection, and Limited Dependent Variables and a Simple Estimator for Such Models, 5 Annals Econ. & Soc. Measurement 475 (1976) for a discussion of the estimation biases potentially induced by censored samples. The data used here are not amenable to the selection-bias correction procedure as suggested in that paper, as no exogenous information exists with which the probability of reporting a burn incident to a hospital can be identified.

TABLE 1.   NIBM Burn-Victim Results

	% THICK	% BODY	H	P
Constant	−31.84	−28.64	−10.23	−0.620
	(0.69)	(0.59)	(0.07)	(2.08)
YR	0.73	0.79	−0.07	0.008
	(1.13)	(1.14)	(0.04)	(1.87)
1 if Male Victim	−5.84	−5.95		0.008
	(1.96)	(1.88)		(0.37)
Age of Victim	−0.08	0.61		0.007
	(0.19)	(1.40)		(2.42)
(Age of Victim)^2	0.003	−0.012		-2.5×10^{-4}
	(0.24)	(0.95)		(2.35)
(Age of Victim)^3	-1.2×10^{-5}	7.6×10^{-5}		2.9×10^{-6}
	(0.13)	(0.75)		(2.76)
L	−4.90	−5.87	12.61	−0.043
	(1.00)	(1.13)	(1.90)	(1.48)
1 if Smoking Only	1.94	−0.38		
	(0.44)	(0.08)		
1 if Drinking Only	0.09	−11.25		
	(0.01)	(1.11)		
1 if Both S and D	4.20	−3.47		
	(0.64)	(0.49)		
Smoking · L	−2.77	−2.63		
	(0.47)	(0.42)		
Drinking · L	−10.11	−1.62		
	(0.42)	(0.06)		
Both · L	−17.98	−23.08		
	(0.77)	(0.93)		
% Thick			0.65	0.007
			(1.81)	(5.43)
(% Thick)^2			−0.009	
			(1.56)	
% Body			0.58	0.004
			(1.59)	(2.97)
(% Body)^2			−0.009	
			(1.73)	
Total Sample,			1.16	
Average H for year			(1.41)	
R^2	.038	.051	.103	

Notes: Absolute t-values in parentheses. The P equations are GLS estimates of the linear probability model.

The seriousness of the burn suffered has a nonmonotonic impact on hospital stay, turning negative at % THICK levels greater than 36 and % BODY levels exceeding 32 per cent. These nonmonotonic effects reflect the increased probability of death with more severe burns and the truncation of one's hospital stay. The direct impact of the standard is a significant increase of almost 13 days, which presumably reflects omitted measures of injury severity which result from the standard (for example, smoke-inhalation injuries). The direct effects on hospitalization are partially offset by the poststandard reductions in measured burn severities described earlier, except for the smoking/drinking category, where the indirect impact is sufficiently large to reverse the sign of the effect. The point estimates of the mean total impacts of the standard are: +8 days for the base group, +6 days for smokers, +2.5 days for drinkers, and −8 days for smoker/drinkers. None of these estimates, however, are statistically different from zero at the 90 per cent level.

The estimates of the recursive specification of a linear probability model for the probability of a burn victim dying is presented in column 4 of Table 1.[11] This specification fails to exhibit a significant sex impact, yet, it does reveal a nonmonotonic age effect with young and old victims possessing the highest death probabilities. As expected, the probability of death is an increasing function of both % THICK and % BODY, with the former being roughly twice as deadly. The direct impact of the standard, via omitted severity indicators, is an insignificant −4 per cent. The indirect effects through the measured severity indicators yield total reductions in the probability of death of 10.4 per cent for the base group, 13.6 per cent for smokers, 18.8 per cent for drinkers, and 33.5 per cent for smoker/drinkers; however, once again, none of the results are significantly different from zero.

These estimates of dN/dL, dH/dL, and dP/dL, in conjunction with values of C and V, are used to calculate the change in total resource costs resulting from the flammability standard. C and V are key parameters in this evaluation process. Because of the complex forms of C and V, Table 2 displays the results for an array of joint values of C and V.[12]

---

[11]A logit specification yielded roughly equivalent results; therefore, for ease of interpretation, only the linear model results are reported.

[12]The results reported in Table 2 represent an expanded model of dT/dL. This expansion results from the system:

a) $T = N(CH + VP)$;

b) $H \equiv \sum_{i=1}^{4} H_i s_i$, s_i = the share of consumer category i; H_i = the average hospital stay of consumer category i; $i = 1$ if smoking, 2 if drinking, 3 if smoking/drinking, and 4 if other-victim category;

c) $P \equiv \sum_{i=1}^{4} s_i P_i$ where P_i is the average probability of death in consumer category i. Therefore,

TABLE 2.   Changes in Annual Resource Costs Associated with the
1973 Flammability Standard, Recursive System Estimates,
Contingent on Values of V and C (in Millions)

V Value C Value	$100,000	$200,000	$400,000	$800,000	$1,200,000	$2,000,000	$5,000,000
$ 100	−8	−16	−31	−61	−91	−152	−380
600	−10	−18	−33	−63	−94	−155	−384
1,800	−14	−22	−37	−67	−98	−159	−388
2,500	−17	−25	−40	−70	−101	−162	−391

Note: The numbers shown in this table are dT/dL estimates obtained from the NIBM multiplied by a factor of 10 in order to adjust for the fact that NIBM data cover only between 10 and 35 per cent of all relevant cases.

The positive impact of V on resource savings reflects both the lower death probabilities and fewer victims associated with the standard, whereas the positive impact of C indicates that the effect of a reduced number of victims outweighs the adverse per victim impact on hospital stay.

For a ten-year horizon and 10 per cent discount rate, the present-value resource savings associated with the mattress flammability standard for a set of "reasonable" values of V and C range from $21 million to $1,060 million. At the intermediate values of V = $400,000 and C = $600, the present value savings are estimated at $90 million (or approximately $2.75 per new mattress).[13] However, the estimated resource savings are only about one standard deviation greater than zero.[14]

To summarize, the analysis of safety fails to reject the hypothesis

---

d) $dT/dL = (C \cdot H + P \cdot V)dN/dL + N \cdot C \left(\sum_{i=1}^{4} s_i dH_i/dL \right) + N \cdot V \left(\sum_{i=1}^{4} s_i dP_i/dL \right).$

Reduced form analogues of Table 1 were also estimated and are reported in an earlier draft of this paper, A Case Study of the Impacts of Consumer Safety Standards: The 1973 Mattress Flammability Standard (March 1979) (Working Paper No. 008, Univ. of Chicago, Center for the Study of the Economy and the State). Since the results are consistent with those for the recursive form, only the latter are reported here.

[13]The value of C = $600 seems a reasonable guess, as it assumes c = $300, γ = .5, W = $30, Q = $14, α = $63, λ = 2, and Θ = $100. Similarly, V = $400,000 seems reasonable, as it assumes B = $100,000, λ = 2, ϕ = $50,000 and v = $200,000. The choice of v = $200,000 is consistent (in 1967 dollars) with the value of life estimates obtained by R. Thaler & S. Rosen, The Value of Saving a Life: Evidence from the Labor Market, in Household Production and Consumption, *supra* note 2 at 265; and Glenn Blomquist, Value of Life Saving: Implications of Consumption Activity, 87 J. Pol. Econ. (1979).

[14]The models were also estimated with a quadratic trend term and with no trend terms. Since the results are basically identical, they are not reported but are available upon request.

that the value of the safety improvements associated with the mattress flammability standard is zero. This result may be attributable to: (1) the crude nature of the data, (2) sufficient incentives on the part of the manufacturers, prior to the standard, to voluntarily produce socially desirable fire-resistant mattresses, or (3) the ineffectiveness of the design and policing of the standard.[15] Unfortunately, the present data fail to allow a distinction to be made between these competing hypotheses.

IV. Costs of the Mattress Flammability Standard

The direct costs of the mattress flammability standard are composed of CPSC administrative costs and the increase in mattress prices attributable to the standard. In the absence of accurate intra-agency information on administrative costs, this section concentrates solely on the latter effect.

The price of mattresses may rise as the result of the imposition of the flammability standard for three reasons. First, in the short run the standard will reduce the supply of salable mattresses by prohibiting the sale of substandard mattresses. The prices of above-standard mattresses will then increase as some consumers shift their demand to the available, higher-quality mattresses. As manufacturers make the necessary technological adjustments to satisfy the standard (basically eliminating untreated cotton and including a layer of polyurethane), these quasi rents are eliminated; but competitive equilibrium mattress prices are higher than before due to the costs of satisfying the standard. A third effect on the average mattress price occurs because the distribution of sales shifts toward relatively higher quality mattresses due to the prohibition of the lowest quality sales and because the standard leads to a relatively larger increase in the production costs of low quality producers.

A sample of 1,110 suggested retail mattress prices (in 1967 dollars) and their associated quality vector were obtained from the 1959 through 1977 editions of the Sears Roebuck, J. C. Penney, Montgomery Ward, and Alden customer catalogues. The mean, nonquality-adjusted, prestandard price is $50.75, while the mean poststandard counterpart is $64.49. The average increase in mattress prices after the standard is approximately 25 per cent. This increase can be decom-

---

[15] One possible design flaw is that since polyurethane is relatively resistant to low-grade combustion sources (such as cigarettes), many producers found that the most cost-effective method of satisfying the standard is to pad the mattress with a layer of polyurethane foam. This may, however, actually reduce total safety, given the extreme flammability of polyurethane in the presence of high-grade combustion sources (such as a burning wastebasket).

posed into: (1) the change in mattress prices for a constant quality vector, (2) the change in the quality vector resulting from the altered payoffs to the various quality dimensions associated with the standard, and (3) quality vector changes that are independent of the influences of the standard. In this section the first component is used as a conservative estimate of the total standard-related cost increase.

To quantify the increase in mattress prices associated with the standard for a constant quality set of mattresses, a hedonic price equation for mattresses is estimated as a function of the set of measurable quality dimensions obtained from catalogue descriptions and a dummy variable which is equal to unity in the poststandard period.[16] In general, the estimated hedonic function is consistent with intuition as the desirable quality components command positive premiums. The poststandard dummy variable indicates that the poststandard period is characterized by significantly higher, quality-adjusted prices of almost $2 a mattress. This estimate represents a 4 per cent poststandard increase in the price of a constant quality mattress. For a base annual retail sales of approximately $610 million (in 1967 dollars), this amounts to an increase in mattress expenditures of $24 million annually for constant quality and unchanged quantity.

A more general methodology for evaluating the impact of the standard on constant-quality-mattress prices is to estimate separate hedonic functions for the prestandard and poststandard samples and analyze the difference between the predicted prices for an identical set of mattresses.[17] The mean predicted prestandard price for the sample is $53.06 and the mean predicted poststandard price $53.23. Thus when the hedonic price function is specified with full interaction effects of the standard, the estimated mean increase in mattress prices after the standard (for a constant set of mattresses) is +$.17 or .3 per cent. This would be increased annual retail expenditures of approximately $2 million.

A plot of the predicted price changes using the fully interactive specification suggests that the percentage increase is dependent on the quality of the mattress. This impression is substantiated by estimating the change in predicted prices as a function of the ordinal quality ranking of mattress quality. The ordinal quality of each mattress is established by defining forty-one quality cells, each containing twenty-seven mattresses, in terms of the predicted prestandard price. For

---

[16]The hedonic price estimators described in this section are available upon request and are also available in the earlier draft of this paper, *supra* note 12.

[17]These hedonic results are also available from the author upon request and are reported in *id.*

TABLE 3.   The Predicted Price Change Regressions for a
            Constant Quality Set of Mattresses

	Predicted Postprice Minus Predicted Preprice	(Predicted Postprice Minus Predicted Preprice) Divided by Predicted Preprice
Ordinal quality index (lowest = 1, highest = 41)	0.22 (1.12)	0.0071 (2.22)
(Ordinal quality index)^2	−0.004 (0.90)	−0.00014 (1.93)
Constant	−2.08 (1.15)	−0.068 (2.34)
Ordinal quality value where impact of quality becomes negative	27	26
R^2	.04	.13

Notes: Absolute t-values are in parentheses. The predicted prices are obtained from the fully interactive specifications of the hedonic price equation.

example, quality cell one contains the twenty-seven mattresses with the highest predicted prestandard prices. Applying ordinary least squares to the changes in predicted prices yields the results shown in Table 3. The percentage difference in post- and prestandard prices is significantly and nonmonotonically related to the ordinal quality index.[18] For the lowest twenty-five quality cells, the impact of the standard is to increase the predicted price difference. This is consistent with the expectation that producers of low quality mattresses will be forced to shift to higher cost production methods which are reflected in higher equilibrium mattress prices. This result is also consistent with intermediate quality producers (for example, quality cells 10–25) earning quasi rents, reflected in abnormally high prices, in the poststandard period.

The results presented here indicate that the flammability standard increases prices of constant quality mattresses between .3 per cent and 4 per cent. For a constant quality set of mattresses and constant volume sales, these increases represent present value (for a ten-year horizon and a 10 per cent discount factor) increases on retail mattress expenditures of $5.3 million and $66 million respectively for the fully interactive and dummy variable specifications of the flammability standard effects on mattress prices. These estimates are lower bound estimates of the full costs of the standard as they ignore CPSC administrative costs as well as indirect effects of the standard on changing the quality composition of mattresses (via changes in the implicit quality component prices).

[18]This result is robust with respect to classifications of cell sizes.

V. Redistributive Effects of the Standard

Several authors have recently suggested that regulations are established in order to maximize the political support of the regulator.[19] This hypothesis argues that income distributional effects are key determinants of regulatory action. In this section an attempt is made to determine if any significant income redistributions are associated with the 1973 mattress standard. Largely for reasons of data availability, attention is focused on the intra-industry redistributive effects and the differential value of safety benefits realized by mattress consumers.

As noted earlier, the flammability standard did not require the development of new technology. Most substandard producers obtained the required flame resistance by eliminating untreated cotton and including a layer of polyurethane. Since most large producers had adopted the requisite production technology as the result of an unconstrained profit maximization, it is hypothesized that the standard gave a comparative advantage to relatively large producers. This hypothesis is strengthened by the observation that a large portion of the compliance costs are relatively fixed, such as learning and implementing the testing and record-keeping requirements of the standard. Finally, the profits of all surviving firms would be increased to the extent that the flammability standard establishes an effective barrier to entry.

The hypothesis of the standard imposing a differentially large burden on small producers is substantiated by the results of 1973 and 1974 compliance surveys conducted by CPSC. These surveys reveal that approximately 20 per cent of surveyed manufacturers were not yet in compliance with the standard and its associated testing and record-keeping requirements, with most violations being for the latter reason. Forty-three per cent of these violations were by firms with annual sales less than $100,000 (1973 dollars) and 81 per cent by firms with sales under $500,000, whereas only 5 per cent were by firms with annual sales over $3.5 million. Further, the smaller firms were much more likely to have committed multiple violations of the standard. The ratio of the share of violations to the share of wholesale sales is roughly 6 to 1 for firms with sales under $500,000 annually, and 1 to 3 for firms with sales over $3.5 million.

The hypothesis of large producers being affected differentially by the standard is further substantiated by an examination of the distribution of industry sales and pretax net income.[20] This study is facilitated by an annual survey of mattress producers conducted by the

---

[19] See, for example, Peltzman, *supra* note 3; and Stigler, *supra* note 3.

[20] It is not possible to examine the effect on stock prices, as too few of the products are listed on the major exchanges.

National Association of Bedding Manufacturers (NABM) from 1959 to 1976 which is sent annually to all NABM member producers and returned by approximately 10 per cent.[21]

Table 4 displays estimates of the impact of the standard on the industry distribution of sales and net income (all monetary units are in 1967 dollars), where the industry is divided into four size classifications on the basis of annual sales.[22]

The sign pattern of the shares of sales and net income support the hypothesis that the standard worked to the relative disadvantage of small firms. The greatest decrease for both measures is experienced (significantly) by the second-smallest-size producers (column 2), and the largest increases are realized by the largest producers. The percentage increases for this largest group of producers are 12.2 and 19.0 respectively for shares of sales and pretax net incomes.

The differential distributive hypothesis is further strengthened by a fall in the average sales of the smallest firms by 11 per cent while the sales of the largest two groups of producers rise by 8 and 44 per cent, respectively. Similarly, the average pretax incomes of firms in the smallest group fall by 66 per cent and those in the second category fall by 93 per cent at the same time that, *ceteris paribus*, the same variables of the larger firms rise by 6 and 9 per cent respectively for categories three and four. The present values of the average sale and pretax net income effects for firms in each category are described in Table 5 for a 10 per cent discount factor and ten-year horizon. The per firm present-value changes that result from the standard suggest that the wealth redistributive impacts of the flammability standard are nontrivial and, given the structure of the standard, were *a priori* sign predictable.

The increases in the average net incomes of large firms and decreases for small producers are consistent with the hypothesis that during the poststandard period of adjustment those producers who

[21] I would like to thank NABM and, in particular, Mr. Russell Abolt, for their assistance in developing this data set. Although no evidence of serious sampling bias is discernible, representatives of NABM suggest that the survey tends to overrepresent large producers.

[22] The system of estimating equations yielding these results holds constant the level and distribution of industry (wholesale) advertising, the real value of the size bracket boundaries (in terms of sales), the annual national industrial production index, and a linear trend effect. The impact of the law is captured by a dummy variable which equals unity for 1973 through 1976. The share equations are estimated subject to the restriction that the sum of the change in shares due to any independent variable is equal to zero over the four size categories of producers. Similarly, the total and average effects are identified by the exclusion of redundant equations. The results are not seriously changed when the trend term is omitted or when a quadratic trend is included. All results are available upon request.

TABLE 4. Intraindustry Effects of the 1973 Standard

	Size Categories in Terms of Annual Sales			
	Firms with Sales $0–$548,000	Firms with Sales $548,000–$1,000,000	Firms with Sales $1,000,000–$2,300,000	Firms with Sales Over $2,300,000
Share of sample sales	−.001 (0.15)	−.048 (1.92)	−.015*	.064 (1.30)
Average category sales	−42,000 (0.89)	40,000 (1.20)	120,000 (2.41)	1,900,000 (2.63)
Share of pretax net income	−.013 (0.51)	−.138 (2.79)	.032*	.119 (0.86)
Average category pretax net income	−5,000 (0.82)	−18,000 (2.80)	3,000 (0.15)	18,000 (1.82)

Note: Absolute *t*-values in parentheses.   *Category omitted.

TABLE 5. Present Values of Average Impacts of Standard

	Firms with Sales $0–$548,000	Firms with Sales $548,000–$1,000,000	Firms with Sales $1,000,000–$2,300,000	Firms with Sales Over $2,300,000
Average sales impact	−114,000	109,000	326,000	5,165,000
Average net income impact	−14,000	−49,000	8,000	49,000

initially offered above-standard mattresses realized short-term quasi rents. The rents occurred because the short-term shortage of above-standard mattresses led to price increases exceeding the extra costs associated with the standard. Unless the standard represents an effective long-run barrier to entry, these short-term rents should dissipate. Unfortunately, the available time series does not provide a sufficient number of poststandard observations to test whether these rents are, in fact, eliminated over time.

It is worth noting that the total average sales for the industry sample as a whole rose significantly, by almost $1,000,000 annually (or about 35 per cent). In view of the earlier finding of standard-related price increases, this indicates that the demand for mattresses is own-price inelastic since expenditures rose with price. It is also consistent with the view that the standard conveyed new information to consumers which led to an increase in the demand for new and relatively high quality mattresses. Current data, however, do not allow the identification of the magnitude of these separate effects.

Total industry average net income also rose significantly by $10,400 (or 7 per cent) in the poststandard period. Again, this result may reflect the existence of short-term quasi rents accruing over the period of adjustment as well as long-run rents associated with the standard imposing a successful barrier to entry.

The second income redistribution examined in this section is the differential safety benefits to consumers. Since the standard explicitly protects relatively careless smoker-consumers (from themselves), it seems reasonable to anticipate that careless consumers will realize relatively large safety gains from the imposition of the standard.[23]

The expected value of the per consumer, present-value resource cost associated with mattress fires, $\tau(i)$, is simply the conditional probability of being burned given one is in the ith consumer category, $Pr(\text{BURN} = 1|i)$, times the resource cost associated with being a burn victim in the ith consumer category, $\tau(i|\text{BURN} = 1)$,

$$\tau(i) = Pr(\text{BURN} = 1|i) \cdot \tau(i|\text{BURN} = 1), \tag{10}$$

where i indexes the four consumer categories described in Section III. Using (10), the change in the expected value of the per consumer, present-value resource cost brought about by the mattress flammability standard, L, is

---

[23] Since none of the victim-category results were significant at the 90% level, these results should be viewed only as unbiased point estimates. However, the methodology used here is applicable to a broader range of impact studies.

$$\frac{d\tau(i)}{dL} = \Pr(\text{BURN} = 1|i) \cdot \frac{d\tau(i|\text{BURN} = 1)}{dL}$$

$$+ \tau(i|\text{BURN} = 1) \cdot \frac{d\Pr(\text{BURN} = 1|i)}{dL} \, . \tag{11}$$

If, for simplicity, it is assumed that $\dfrac{d\Pr(\text{BURN} = 1|i)}{dL} = 0$ for all con-

sumer categories, then one can use the results presented in Section III

to estimate $\dfrac{d\tau(i)}{dL}$. For example, the estimates in Section III indicate

that the values of $\dfrac{d\tau(i|\text{BURN} = 0)}{dL}$ when $C = \$600$ and $V = \$400,000$

are $-\$100,000$ for base group victims; $-\$140,000$ for smoking victims; $-\$200,000$ for drinking victims, and $-\$380,000$ for smoking/drinking victims. If it is assumed that $\Pr(\text{BURN} = 1|\text{Neither}) = .5\Pr(\text{Burn} = 1|\text{Smoker}) = \Pr(\text{BURN} = 1|\text{Drinker}) = .25\Pr(\text{BURN} = 1|\text{Both}) =$

$\dfrac{1}{750,000}$, then, from (11), the expected value of the per consumer re-

source savings associated with the standard are 3¢ for base group consumers, 8¢ for smokers, 12¢ for drinkers, and 49¢ for consumers who both smoke and drink. These results support the hypothesis of the standard differentially benefiting relatively careless consumers, as the expected value of the present value savings for the most careless group of consumers is nearly seventeen times larger than that for the most careful group of consumers. In the context of the theory of externalities, this is a perverse result in terms of improving social welfare. Careless consumers tend to impose negative externalities on, for example, neighbors who may suffer damages from a fire started by a careless neighbor smoking in bed. Although the point estimates of the effective subsidies are not significantly different from zero, the pattern of subsidization suggests that regulators should be concerned whether standards provide perverse incentives with respect to raising social welfare.

Finally, recall that the prices of relatively low quality mattresses rose relatively more as the result of the standard. Since the lowest quality mattresses are purchased by low income families, one impact of the standard has been to raise product prices the most for those consumers who can least afford such increases. Further, the price of the highest quality mattresses fell after the establishment of the standard.[24] Since higher quality mattresses tend to be purchased by well-informed higher income consumers, the standard indirectly subsidizes them.

In sum, the evidence presented in this section indicates that large, significant, and predictable income redistributions from small to large producers resulted from the 1973 flammability standard. It was also found that the standard tends to tax low income families and subsidize higher income families. Some evidence of income redistribution from careful to careless consumers was presented but was not statistically significant.

VI. Summary and Conclusions

This paper has presented evidence on the effects of a relatively early CPSC action with respect to consumer product safety, namely the 1973 Mattress Flammability Standard. The primary focus has been the empirical measurement of three types of economic effects. The estimated consumer safety improvements range from $21 to $1,060 million (depending on the value of life used), however the confidence intervals about these figures, for any given value of life, are extremely large. Any safety improvements were obtained at a minimum cost of between $5.5 million and $66 million, or 0.3 to 4.0 per cent increases in mattress prices. In addition to these traditional benefit-cost calculations, the effects of the standard on income redistribution were also estimated. It was shown that the flammability standard induced large and anticipatable income redistributions from small to large producers. It was suggested that these wealth transfers are largely the result of quasi rents being earned in the poststandard market adjustment period. There is also some evidence suggesting the standard improved consumer information. Finally, weak evidence of income transfers from careful to careless consumers was also presented.

One of the primary contributions of this paper is that it presents not only cost-benefit estimates but also examines the income redistribution effects of a product standard. Thus it provides descriptive evidence on perhaps one of the least understood economic phenomena, namely product-quality standards. Of course, a single case study does not allow one to generalize about the effects of quality standards on the determinants of government regulatory action. However, the results of

[24] One explanation of this finding is that the pass/fail nature of the standard has inappropriately led many consumers to believe that all passing mattresses are of the same quality with respect to flammability. Armed with this new misinformation, consumers demand fewer high quality mattresses, which brings about price reductions for these mattresses.

this study of the 1973 Mattress Flammability Standard are weakly consistent with the consumer-welfare-improvement model of regulatory behavior and more strongly consistent with the income-redistribution model. In order to test these alternative models of regulatory behavior, more case studies of specific regulations and quality standards are required. A larger data base will allow the identification of systematic and random regulatory effects on both consumer welfare and wealth redistribution. It is important to stress that to be of use in understanding the behavior of the CPSC and other regulatory agencies, these case studies must measure the costs, benefits, and wealth redistribution effects of the standard in question. This study represents a first step in developing the type of data needed for the empirical testing of theories of regulation.

Insurance, Liability, and Accidents: A Theoretical and Empirical Investigation of the Effect of No-Fault on Accidents

15

Elisabeth M. Landes

Between 1971 and 1976, sixteen states adopted "no-fault" automobile insurance laws.[1] In doing so, they elected to remove or restrict liability for motor vehicle accident injuries. Economists and economic analysts of the law have shown that removing or restricting liability for damages to others permits potential injurers to shift some of the costs of their activity onto potential victims and may result in higher losses from accidents. The principal argument advanced by advocates of no-fault is that savings in administrative costs will outweigh increased losses, if any, from accidents.

This paper investigates the effect on accidents of removing liability for motor vehicle accident injuries. In the first part of the paper I show that compulsory insurance can serve as a substitute for a liability rule, so that no increase in accident losses will occur from restricting liability. This conclusion rests on the assumption that the insurance industry acts as a single competitive firm, either through extensive reinsurance or other cooperative behavior, and thereby induces individuals to internalize all costs of their driving behavior even though they are not legally liable for damage to others. However, if some

An earlier version of this paper was written while I was a research fellow at the Center for the Study of the Economy and the State at the University of Chicago. This paper benefited from the comments and criticisms of George Becker, Dennis Carlton, William Landes, Sam Peltzman, George Stigler, and an anonymous referee, as well as from the members of the Industrial Organization Workshop at the University of Chicago.

Reprinted with permission from *The Journal of Law and Economics* 25, no. 1 (April 1982): 49–65. © 1982 by The University of Chicago. Previously titled "Insurance, Liability, and Accidents: A Theoretical and Empirical Investigation of the Effect of No-fault Accidents."

[1] Massachusetts was the first in 1971. Then came Florida (1972), Connecticut (1973), New Jersey (1973), Hawaii (1973), Michigan (1973), Utah (1974), Kansas (1974), New York (1974), Colorado (1974), Nevada (1974), Pennsylvania (1974), Minnesota (1975), Kentucky (1975), Georgia (1975), North Dakota (1976).

losses are recoverable only if tort suits are permitted—for example, intangible losses such as "pain and suffering"—then this result no longer holds. Even with compulsory insurance provided by a single competitive firm, restricting liability will result in increased accident losses.

The second part of the paper investigates accident losses by state, comparing states that have and have not restricted liability for motor vehicle accident injuries. Here I find that states with tort restrictions have experienced significantly increased fatal accident rates relative to other states. I estimate that states which place relatively moderate restrictions on tort suits have had between 2 and 5 percent more fatal accidents as a result of adopting no-fault, while states with more restrictive laws have had as many as 10–15 percent more fatal accidents.

I find further that the accident effects of no-fault are larger in states in which the insurance industry is less "concentrated" as measured alternatively by the four-firm concentration ratio and the share of direct writers in the voluntary market.

I. Insurance and Liability

To see how compulsory insurance can serve as a substitute for a liability rule, consider the problem of individual choice in the absence of insurance as modeled by Diamond and others.[2]

Accident technology is such that an individual's accident probability is a function of his own level of care, x_i, and the level of care y_j chosen by all other drivers: $P_i(x_i, y_1, \ldots y_n)$ where x and y can be perfectly and costlessly monitored by all participants in the activity—drivers, the courts, and, in this analysis, insurance companies. Assuming that all individuals are identical and that the number of drivers is fixed permits expressing this probability as a function of own care and the average level of care taken by all other drivers: $P_i = P(x_i, y)$ where $P < 1$, $P_x, P_y > 0$, and $P_{xx}, P_{yy}, P_{xy} > 0$. In the absence of a liability rule the individual will choose a level of care to maximize his expected utility: $V = (1 - P)U(c - px) + PU(c - px - L)$, where c is income, L is his own potential loss from an accident, and p is the per unit cost of care. Assuming a linear utility function, an individual will choose a level of care x that satisfies the following relation:

$$-P_x \cdot L = p. \tag{1}$$

[2] See, for example, Peter Diamond, Single Activity Accidents, 3 J. Legal Stud. 107 (1974), and John Prather Brown, Toward an Economic Theory of Liability, 2 J. Legal Stud. 323 (1973).

Since all individuals are assumed to be identical, a no-liability equilibrium will occur for all drivers at x^o where

$$-P_x(x^o, x^o) \cdot L = p.^3 \tag{2}$$

Individual investments in care and the resulting accident losses in the absence of liability present a problem analogous to that of trucks traveling along an unowned road. The marginal cost of an individual's driving, like that of adding another truck to the road, is the sum of his own expected costs plus the additional costs he imposes on all other identical drivers. In the no-liability equilibrium drivers take into account only their own expected accident losses and ignore the expected losses of others.

The efficient individual equilibrium level of care, x^*, minimizes the sum of accident losses and avoidance costs for all drivers, or

$$-P_x(x^*, x^*) \cdot 2L = p, x^* > x^o, \tag{3}$$

where $2L$ is the full cost of an accident.

Diamond shows that introducing a liability rule that holds a driver liable for both his own costs and those of the other driver, if his own level of care falls short of some specified due-care standard and the other driver's does not, results in the following possible equilibria: $x = x^o$ whenever $d \leq x^o$ or $d \geq \hat{d}$; $x = d$ whenever $x^o < d < \hat{d}$, where d is the standard of due care and $\hat{d}$ is a level of care so stringent that all drivers will prefer to be negligent rather than to adopt it.

Thus while x^* is a possible equilibrium, it is achieved only by a liability rule which sets the standard of due care *precisely* equal to x^*. For $d \leq x^*$ or $d \geq \hat{d}$ there will be more accidents than socially optimal. For $x^* \leq d \leq \hat{d}$ the number of accidents will be smaller than the social optimum.

A. *Voluntary Insurance in the Absence of Liability*

For insurance to have a role in this analysis, one must abandon the assumption of risk neutrality. In the absence of a liability rule, the individual will maximize expected utility with respect to both the level of care, x, and the amount of insurance to buy, I:

---

[3] Like Diamond, *supra* note 3, I ignore the question of the activity level. It is intuitively clear, however, that the level of activity in a no-liability equilibrium will be greater than socially optimal.

$$V = (1 - P)U(c - px - qI) + PU(c - px - qI - L + I)$$

$$= (1 - P)U(Y_{NA}) + PU(Y_A),$$

where q is the market price per dollar of insurance coverage (and implicitly depends on x) and Y_A and Y_{NA} denote consumption in the accident and no-accident states, respectively.

The first-order conditions for a maximum are

$$\frac{\partial V}{\partial I} = PU'(Y_A) - [(1 - P)U'(Y_{NA}) + PU'(Y_A)]q = 0, \tag{4}$$

$$\frac{\partial V}{\partial x} = -P_x[U(Y_{NA}) - U(Y_A)] - [(1 - P)U'(Y_{NA}) - PU'(Y_A)] \\ \times \left[p + \frac{\partial(q \cdot I)}{\partial x} \right] = 0. \tag{5}$$

It is clear from inspection of these first-order conditions that if insurance is "fair" (e.g., if $q = P$), then $I = L$ and $x = x^o$, so that the no-liability equilibrium is identical, as one would expect, to that derived in (1) above.

But is $q = P$ an equilibrium price for the insurance industry to charge? The answer depends both on whether insurance is compulsory or voluntary—that is, whether it can serve the dual role of insurance and license to drive or only that of insurance—and on whether insurance firms act cooperatively or noncooperatively.

To see this, assume an insurance industry comprised of m independent identical firms each with a share of the market $\gamma = 1/m$. To any firm the marginal cost of an additional *driver* is $\gamma P \cdot \bar{I}$ if it does not insure him and $P(I + \gamma \bar{I})$ if it does, where γ is the insurer's share of the market of drivers and represents the probability that any accident in which the individual is involved will involve another driver insured by that firm, I is the amount of insurance demanded by the individual, and $\bar{I}$ is the mean value of purchase insurance for all drivers.

The firm's private marginal cost of providing insurance when it acts independently of all other firms in the industry, then, is only $P \cdot I$, since it will bear $\gamma P \bar{I}$ as long as the individual drives, whether or not he is insured. Therefore the competitive price of voluntary insurance cannot exceed P per dollar purchased, ignoring any operating costs. All drivers will purchase full insurance ($I = L$) and will choose the no-liability level of care, x^o. The insurance industry will earn zero profits, since losses paid out per driver will just equal the premium per driver ($= P \cdot L$).

Is this conclusion changed if firms act cooperatively? That is, is there a cooperative zero profit solution that would lead to fewer accidents and lower insurance premiums than the noncooperative solution? With voluntary insurance the answer is no.

To see this, assume that the m firms agree to charge a two-part price for insurance equal to P per dollar of own coverage desired plus a fixed charge equal to $P \cdot \gamma \overline{I}$ to cover the additional expected fixed cost that the individual's driving imposes on the firm. Assuming that insurance companies can perfectly and costlessly monitor the level of care chosen by each driver or the resulting accident probability, the first-order condition (4) still implies that, if they insure at all, all drivers will insure fully ($I = L$), because the marginal price per dollar of insurance remains P. Condition (5) is modified to become

$$p + \frac{\partial(q \cdot I)}{\partial x} = p + P_x(1 + \gamma)L = 0. \tag{6}$$

All insured drivers are induced to choose level of care $x_I(\gamma)x^o$, even in the absence of legal liability.

To assure zero profits, insured drivers must receive a rebate or subsidy equal to $\gamma \overline{P}L$, where $\overline{P}$ is the mean accident probability for the whole class and is not sensitive to any individual's choice of care (although it is clearly the result of the level of care chosen by all drivers).

The final full expenditure on insurance for each driver then is

$$q \cdot L = P[x_I(\gamma), x_I(\gamma)](1 + \gamma)L - P[x_I(\gamma), x_I(\gamma)]L$$

$$= P[x_I(\gamma), x_I(\gamma)]L,$$

which is less than in the noncooperative solution, since $P[x_I(\gamma), x_I(\gamma)] < P(x^o, x^o)$.

At first glance, then, it seems that cooperative pricing by the firms in the insurance industry can reduce both the frequency of accidents and the final price of insurance.

Recall, however, that x^o is the level of care that minimizes $P \cdot L + px$, so that total expected costs are actually lower for a driver who chooses to remain uninsured. Depending upon the degree of risk aversion, every driver may individually wish to remain uninsured and to face expected costs of $P[x^o, x_I(\gamma)]L + px^o$, which are less than $P[x_I(\gamma), x_I(\gamma)]L + px_I(\gamma)$. Therefore, if drivers are not strongly risk averse, the no-liability equilibrium may still be the only possible equilibrium, even when insurance firms act cooperatively.

B. Compulsory Insurance in the Absence of Liability

Compulsory insurance in the absence of a liability rule transforms the road from an unowned resource to a resource held in common by the firms in the insurance industry. Common ownership of a resource will have no allocative effect if the m firms continue to act independently of each other. Since each firm will face the cost γPL of an additional driver whether he is insured by that firm or any of the other identical firms in the industry, the private marginal cost to any firm of offering insurance to any individual remains $P \cdot L$. The noncooperative solution in the case of compulsory insurance then is identical with that in the case of voluntary insurance.

However, with compulsory insurance, *cooperative* behavior by the m firms in the industry can force drivers to take into account the cost they impose on other drivers as well as on themselves, and to drive with greater care.

Consider again the analysis of cooperative behavior in the case of voluntary insurance. The no-liability solution could arise in that case only because all drivers could choose to remain uninsured when faced with any other pricing scheme.

However, by definition, drivers cannot choose to remain uninsured in a regime of compulsory insurance. (Recall that I assume that the number of drivers is fixed.) Compulsory insurance is equivalent to compulsory licensing of drivers where the license fee $[= P(x_i, y)(1 + \gamma) \cdot L]$ forces drivers to choose level of care $x_i(\gamma)$; $1 - \gamma$ is the proportion of total driving costs that individuals do not incorporate in their care decision. The firms in the insurance industry can collectively gain through lower expected accident losses by cooperating until γ effectively equals one, where expected accident losses are minimized ($\gamma = 1$ produces $x_i[1] = x^*$ in eq. [3] above, or the efficient outcome). Stated otherwise, if insurance firms act together so that γ effectively equals one, a no-liability rule coupled with compulsory insurance is equivalent in its effect on accident losses to an efficient liability rule, where the due care standard, d, is set to x^*.

In order to assure zero profits, firms must rebate the excess premiums to their insured. In the real world some of the excess of premiums over loss is absorbed by adjustment and administrative costs. In 1975, for example, the ratio of direct premiums written to losses incurred for private passenger automobile liability insurance was about 1.6.[4] If expense loading is proportional to expected loss, individual drivers face a premium $q = 1.6\ P$ even without cooperation among

[4] Best's Aggregates and Averages, Property-Liability (1975).

firms in the industry. However, most state regulation of insurance permits (and even requires) some cooperative behavior among insurance firms, such as information pooling and cooperative rate setting. This behavior is exempt from federal antitrust sanctions under the terms of the McCarran Act.

Reinsurance is an external force which further acts to discipline and coordinate the actions of the primary insurers. Premiums charged by reinsurers are not subject to state regulation but are part of the cost base of the primary insurers, while commissions paid to the primary insurers by the reinsurers are commonly inversely related to the previously experienced loss ratio.

C. Qualifications

The analysis in Section B demonstrates that a no-liability/mandatory insurance system may be equivalent in its effects on accident losses to a liability rule. A crucial assumption for this result to hold is that all losses are insurable, so that income can be equalized in all states of the world. This assumption is not, however, an accurate description of the insurance market. Partly because of moral hazard, assumed away in Section B, first-party insurance generally carries a coinsurance rate. Even without an explicit coinsurance rate, certain kinds of losses from accidents cannot be recovered except in a tort suit. These are termed "general" or "noneconomic" damages, such as "pain and suffering."

Let the ratio of economic to total losses (= general + economic) equal k, where k is strictly less than one. Then the marginal cost to an insurance firm of offering insurance becomes

$$MC = P \cdot L[(1 + \gamma)k + (1 - \delta)P_N(1 - P_N)(1 + \gamma)(1 - k)], \qquad (7)$$

where $\delta = 0$ when a liability rule is in effect, so that individuals injured may file a tort suit for total damages, $\delta = 1$ under a no-liability rule, $P_N \cdot (1 - P_N)$ equals the probability that the individual would be found liable in a tort suit,[5] and γ again equals the firm's share of the market, or the probability that the accident will involve another individual insured by that firm.

---

[5] $P_N(1 - P_N)$ denotes the probability that a driver involved in an accident will be held liable in a tort suit; that is, it is the product of the probability that the driver will be found to have been negligent (P_N) and the probability that the other party to the accident will be found not to have been negligent ($1 - P_N$); P_N is assumed to be a function of the driver's inputs into safety, or his level of care x; and $(1 - P_N)$ is assumed to be a function of other drivers' inputs into safety, or level of care y.

As before, $(1 - \gamma)$ is the amount of total loss that individuals do not take into account when making their care decisions. But even for $\gamma = 1$, where insurance firms act in concert, the marginal cost of insurance, individual choice of care, and hence accident losses under a liability rule ($\delta = 0$) will differ from those under a system of no-liability and mandatory insurance ($\delta = 1$):

$$\frac{dMC}{d\delta} = -PL(1 + \gamma)P_N(1 - P_N)(1 - k)$$
$$+ \left(P_x \frac{dx}{d\delta} + P_y \frac{dy}{d\delta}\right)\frac{MC}{P}. \tag{8}$$

Assuming for simplicity that $P = \exp[-(x + y)]$ and that all individuals are identical, the second term on the right-hand side of (8) can be derived from individual expected utility maximization. Further, assuming a utility function that is almost linear in income, evaluation of (8) at $\delta = 1$ yields the following:

$$\frac{dx}{d\delta} + \frac{dy}{d\delta} \approx$$
$$\frac{-P_N\left(1 - P_N - \frac{\partial P_N}{\partial x}\right)(1 - \gamma) + (1 - P_N)\left(\frac{\partial P_N}{\partial x} - P_N\right)(1 - \gamma k)}{1 + k} < 0 \tag{9}$$

and

$$\frac{dMC}{MCd\delta} \approx \frac{-P_N(1 - P_N)(1 - k)}{k} - \left(\frac{dx}{d\delta} + \frac{dy}{d\delta}\right). \tag{10}$$

Limiting compensable damages to economic damages, implicit in a no-liability rule, affects the marginal cost of insurance in two ways: it increases the frequency of accidents as individuals reduce their care, thus increasing marginal cost, but reduces the amount of damages for which individuals, and therefore their insurance firms, would be liable, thus reducing marginal cost.

Just as in the case analyzed in Section B above, in which all losses were insurable ($k = 1$), increasing levels of concentration will reduce the positive impact of no-fault on accident rates:[6]

[6] Although the proportional change in marginal cost cannot be signed, it is less positive or more negative, at higher levels of q. This result yields two interesting implications for the adoption of no-fault automobile insurance across states which are not explored here but which were treated briefly in an earlier version of this paper. See

$$\frac{d}{d\gamma}\left(\frac{dx}{d\delta} + \frac{dy}{d\delta}\right) =$$

$$\frac{-2k(1 - P_N)\left(\frac{\partial P_N}{\partial x} - P_N\right) + P_N k\left(1 - P_N - \frac{\partial P_N}{\partial x}\right)(1 - \gamma)}{(1 + \gamma k)^2} > 0. \tag{11}$$

However, even were all firms to cooperate fully so that γ effectively equals one, a no-liability rule would still result in less care and more accidents, as long as the mandatory insurance covers only economic losses ($k \leq 1$):

$$\frac{dx}{d\delta} + \frac{dy}{d\delta}\bigg|_{\gamma=1} = (1 - P_N)\left(\frac{\partial P_N}{\partial x} - P_N\right)\frac{(1 - k)}{(1 + k)} < 0. \tag{12}$$

In the next section I attempt to test these hypotheses with state data on fatal automobile accidents.

II. The Effect of No-Fault on Accident Losses: An Empirical Investigation

Sixteen states enacted no-fault automobile insurance laws between 1971 and 1976. The no-fault plans adopted by these states restrict tort liability for personal injury damages arising from automobile accidents.[7] The degree of restriction placed on tort liability varies among states.[8] For example, in Massachusetts the right to bring a tort suit for damages suffered in an automobile accident is abolished except where the medical expenses involved exceed $500 or where the accident results in "serious injury." At a different point in the spectrum, the law in Michigan prohibits tort suits except where an accident causes the victim's death, serious impairment of bodily function, or serious disfigure-

---

Elisabeth M. Landes, Insurance Liability and Accidents: A Theoretical and Empirical Investigation of the Effect of No-Fault on Accidents (Working Paper No. 017, Univ. of Chicago, Center for the Study of the Econ. & the State, 1980). First, that states in which the insurance industry is effectively more concentrated will experience smaller increased losses from accidents; and second that those same states should be more likely to adopt no-fault automobile insurance because of the smaller expected effect on accident costs.

[7] Details of each state's no-fault law are briefly described in an appendix which may be obtained from the author.

[8] Eight other states have introduced compulsory or voluntary "add-on" no-fault benefits in the form of personal injury protection insurance. The laws in these states are not true no-fault laws, however, because they do not restrict tort liability.

ment, or where the accident was the result of intentional harm or where damages exceed the prescribed limits for economic loss. These limits are 85 percent of lost earnings up to $1,250 per month for up to three years, or, in the case of death, 100 percent of this loss.[9]

These states provide a natural data base for examining the effect of restricting liability on accident losses and for examining the interaction between that effect and industry structure.

The analysis in Section I suggests two hypotheses that I examine in this section. First, laws that restrict liability for injuries arising from automobile accidents will lead to increased automobile accident rates, with more restrictive laws leading to greater increases. Second, the effect on accidents of restricting liability will be lower in states in which the automobile insurance industry is more concentrated because more of the externalities caused by the adoption of no-fault will be internalized. In this section I investigate the effect of restricting tort liability on a single measure of accident losses: fatal accidents. Fatal accidents are chosen as a direct measure of accidents rather than the alternative statistic, injury accidents, because reporting of the latter is likely to be sensitive to differences across states and over time in insurance requirements, which makes them unsuitable for this investigation.[10]

The set of variables used to describe state automobile insurance systems is listed and defined in Table 1. The variables THRESH and RTHRESH are measures of state medical expense tort thresholds. If an accident results in an injury to an individual requiring medical expenses which exceed the value of THRESH, then the injured may bring a tort suit to recover noneconomic damages. The dollar value of THRESH varies from $200 in New Jersey to $2,000 in Minnesota. Because the price of medical and hospital services varies across the states, the same dollar value may reflect different real levels of stringency. To construct RTHRESH, I deflate THRESH for each state by an index of medical care prices in that state, taken from Feldman.[11] A third mea-

---

[9] These limits were the ones in effect at the time of this writing. They may have undergone subsequent changes.

[10] I wish to thank Sam Peltzman for helpful discussions about the appropriate choice of a dependent variable. The variability in reported injury accident rates within states is very large. For example, reported injury accidents in Connecticut increased about 75 percent between 1971 and 1972, while at the same time fatal accident rates increased less than 1 percent. For the same period, the number of reported injury accidents almost doubled in Louisiana, while fatal accidents *fell* in number. In Massachusetts, reported injury accidents fell about 30 percent between 1971 and 1972, while fatal accident rates rose 1 percent.

[11] Roger Feldman, The Supply and Demand for Physicians' Hospital and Office Visits (1976) (unpublished Ph.D. dissertation, Univ. of Rochester).

TABLE 1. Variables Describing State Automobile Insurance Systems

Variable	Description
D2	Dummy variable equal to 1 in any year in which a state has a true no-fault plan in effect, 0 otherwise.
D1	Dummy variable equal to 1 in the first full year in which a no-fault plan is in effect, 0 otherwise.
THRESH	Dollar medical expense threshold (see text).
RTHRESH	Real value of medical expense threshold = THRESH deflated by medical price index.
PCL	The proportion of insurance claims barred from tort recovery by state's tort threshold.
V	Dummy variable equal to 1 if Michigan and no-fault law in effect, 0 otherwise.

Sources: For RTHRESH price index, Roger Feldman, The Supply and Demand for Physicians' Hospital and Office Visits (1976); for PCL, All-Industry Research Advisory Committee (AIRAC), Automobile Injuries and Their Compensation in the United States (1979).

TABLE 2. Measures of Restrictiveness of No-Fault Law in 1976 by State

State	THRESH	RTHRESH	PCL
New Jersey	200	4.08	.2620
Connecticut	400	7.63	.3347
New York	500	7.58	.3238
Kansas	500	7.79	.2389
Massachusetts	500	8.14	.2499
Colorado	500	11.54	.3003
Utah	500	14.71	.1795
Georgia	500	15.57	.2335
Nevada	750	11.33	.2430
Pennsylvania	750	15.54	.3749
Florida	1,000	24.40	.2512
Kentucky	1,000	28.94	.3549
North Dakota	1,000	46.35	.4293
Hawaii	1,500	82.37	.5252
Minnesota	2,000	46.60	.4826
Michigan	—	—	.4053

Sources: For RTHRESH: for expenditure shares, All-Industry Research Advisory Committee (AIRAC), Automobile Injuries and Their Compensation in the United States (1979), vol. 1, table 5-2; for prices, Roger Feldman, The Supply and Demand for Physicians' Hospital and Office Visits (1976) (unpublished Ph.D. dissertation, Univ. of Rochester), tables 14, 15, and 19. For PCL, AIRAC, tables 8-3 and 8-12.

TABLE 3.   Effect of No-Fault on Fatal Accidents: Measure of Stringency
of Tort Threshold; 1967–75

	All States	States Which Passed Laws between 1971 and 1975
A. Stringency Measure = THRESH		
ln (population)	−.013	.443
	(−.29)	(2.82)
Population density	.295	.940
	(5.18)	(1.12)
D1	−.048	−.053
	(−1.53)	(−2.07)
D2	−.334	−.325
	(−1.52)	(−1.81)
ln (THRESH)	.059	.060
	(1.69)	(2.15)
V	.299	.337
	(1.29)	(1.84)
SEE	.00674	.00330
Turning point	$287	$220
Joint F-statistic, legal variables	1.42	1.97
B. Stringency Measure = RTHRESH		
ln (population)	−.014	.411
	(−.30)	(2.59)
Population density	.296	.821
	(5.19)	(1.00)
D1	−.052	−.063
	(−1.64)	(−2.27)
D2	−.079	−.064
	(−1.18)	(−1.17)
ln (RTHRESH)	.049	.053
	(1.83)	(2.46)
V	.046	.085
	(.48)	(1.18)
SEE	.00673	.00327
Turning point	5.02	3.33
Joint F-statistic, legal variables	1.54	2.28*

TABLE 3.   *(continued)*

	All States	States Which Passed Laws between 1971 and 1975
C. Stringency Measure = PCL		
ln (population)	−.008	.656
	(−.18)	(4.40)
Population density	.292	.617
	(5.10)	(.76)
D1	−.035	−.055
	(−1.09)	(−2.10)
D2	.039	−.056
	(.52)	(−1.04)
PCL	.021	.374
	(.09)	(2.18)
SEE	.00068	.00330
Turning point	—	.15
Joint *F*-statistic, legal variables	.50	2.36*

Note: Sample: col. 1 = fifty-one states for nine years; col. 2 = fifteen states for nine years. Numbers in parentheses are *t*-values.
*Significant at a .10 level.

sure of the stringency of state tort thresholds, PCL, is the proportion of insurance claims in a 1979 industry-wide survey in which the injured was barred from tort recovery by the state's tort threshold. Table 2 presents the value of these variables for each of the sixteen no-fault states.

A. The Estimated Effect of No-Fault on Accidents

Table 3 presents results of regressions of fatal accident rates across states for the years 1967–75. The independent variables include those listed in Table 1, state population, and population density. In the equation employing THRESH or RTHRESH as the measure of stringency, a dummy variable V is included to represent Michigan, since Michigan's law does not provide a dollar medical expense threshold. Summary statistics for all variables are presented in Table 4.

In addition to these variables, state and time dummy variables were included to hold constant state and time specific effects. The state dummy variables capture the effect of other important determinants of accident rates which may vary considerably across states, such as the age, race and sex composition of the population. Similarly, the time dummy variables will capture the effect on driving, and therefore on

TABLE 4.   Summary Statistics for Nine-Year Period, 1967–75

Variable		Sample			
		51 States		15 States with Laws	
Name	Definition	M	SD	M	SD
FAC	Annual fatal accidents (N)	880.85	827.93	1,046.99	765.57
POP	Population (000s)	4,107.30	4,542.00	5,397.08	4,671.38
POPDEN	Population per square mile	.36	1.57	.23	.28
D1	See Table 1	.03	.18	.11	.32
D2	See Table 1	.07	.25	.24	.43
THRESH	See Table 1	42.59	188.10	144.81	325.60
RTHRESH	See Table 1	1.02	5.51	3.47	9.77
PCL	See Table 1	.02	.08	.07	.13
Observations (N)		459		135	

accidents, of the dramatic changes in the price of gasoline between 1967 and 1977.

The regressions presented in Table 3 are estimated both for the full sample of fifty-one "states" (including the District of Columbia as a "state") and for the sample of fifteen states which had enacted no-fault laws by 1975.[12] (North Dakota's no-fault law was enacted in 1976.) Fatal accidents, population, THRESH and RTHRESH are all expressed in natural logs in the regressions. Joint F-statistics for the full set of legal variables employed in each regression are reported at the bottom of the table.

The effect of restricting tort liability for motor vehicle accident injuries on fatal accidents is measured by the coefficient on D2 plus the interaction effect with the tort-threshold stringency measure. The effect is nonnegative in the full range of the data except for the extreme low end for all regressions and is increasingly positive with increasing stringency levels. Table 5 presents the estimated effect of no-fault on

[12] I estimated the regressions for the subsample of fifteen no-fault states separately because unobservable differences between the fault and no-fault states could potentially bias the estimates from a full sample regression. For example, if states with relatively increasing accident rates were more likely to adopt no-fault, the full sample regression might show a positive impact of no-fault that merely reflected the choice to adopt it. Note that there is no reason to suspect that the choice of adoption is a function of accident rates. The two major arguments made for no-fault are the resulting reduction in claims costs and the greater "equity" of a no-fault system than a tort-liability system. With respect to the equity of the tort-liability system, see Elisabeth M. Landes, Compensation for Automobile Accident Injuries: Is the Tort System Fair? 11 J. Legal Stud. (1982).

TABLE 5. Estimated Effect on Fatal Accidents of Limiting Tort Liability for Motor Vehicle Accident Injuries by Level of Tort Threshold Stringency

THRESH		Estimated Effect of THRESH on Fatal Accidents (Sample)		RTHRESH		Estimated Effect of RTHRESH on Fatal Accidents (Sample)		PCL		Estimated Effect of PCL on Fatal Accidents (Sample)	
Level ($)	States (N)	51 States (%)	15 States with Laws (%)	Level	States (N)	51 States (%)	15 States with Laws (%)	Level	States (N)	51 States (%)	15 States with Laws (%)
200	1	-2.11 (-.50)	-.59 (-.15)	<5	1	-.02 (.00)	2.18 (.64)	.15-.25	4	2.71 (.84)	1.82 (.53)
400	1	1.98 (.71)	3.66 (1.09)	5-10	3	1.99 (.72)	4.42 (1.32)	.25-.35	5	2.93 (1.11)	5.67 (1.65)
500	5	3.33 (1.25)	5.06 (1.50)	10-15	3	4.56 (1.67)	7.29 (2.03)	.35-.45	3	3.16 (.85)	9.67 (2.24)
750	2	5.83 (1.93)	7.66 (2.05)	15-20	3	6.30 (2.03)	9.23 (2.34)	.45-.55	3	3.39 (.60)	13.82 (2.42)
1,000	3	7.65 (2.09)	9.55 (2.28)	20-25	2	2.03 (2.16)	11.33 (2.54)	—	—	—	—
1,500	1	10.26 (2.13)	12.26 (2.44)	47	1	11.56 (2.24)	15.12 (2.70)	—	—	—	—
2,000	1	12.15 (2.10)	14.21 (2.49)	82	1	14.63 (2.20)	18.59 (2.74)	—	—	—	—

Note: Numbers in parentheses are *t*-values.

TABLE 6.   Interactive Effect of Tort Threshold and Population "Litigiousness" (Population Density) on Fatal Accident Rates: Measure of Tort Threshold Stringency (STRING)

Legal Variables	THRESH		RTHRESH		PCL	
	(1)	(2)	(3)	(4)	(5)	(6)
D1	−.041	−.045	−.045	−.056	−.032	−.048
	(−1.29)	(−1.81)	(−1.42)	(−2.17)	(−.98)	(−1.80)
D2	−.689	−.660	−.201	−.187	.014	−.078
	(−2.38)	(−3.19)	(−2.26)	(−2.92)	(.19)	(−1.37)
STRING	.107	.102	.076	.072	.017	.351
	(2.47)	(3.30)	(2.56)	(3.31)	(.07)	(2.04)
STRING · POPDEN	.024	.035	.080	.122	.096	.275
	(1.87)	(2.81)	(2.08)	(3.33)	(.45)	(1.27)
V	.649	.660	.163	.197	—	—
	(2.18)	(3.11)	(1.47)	(2.57)		
Joint F-statistic, legal variables	1.85*	3.34**	2.12*	4.35**	.43	2.22*

Note: Sample, cols. 1, 3, and 5 = fifty-one states for nine years; cols. 2, 4, and 6 = fifteen states for nine years.
* Significant at a .10 level.
** Significant at a .01 level.

fatal accidents as a function of the tort-threshold stringency measure. Except for states with very low tort thresholds, no-fault has produced both an economically and statistically significant increase in fatal accidents: a medical expense threshold of $500 implies about a 4 percent increase in fatal accident rates; a medical expense threshold of $1,500 implies an increase in fatal accidents of *more than 10 percent!*

The stringency of a tort threshold and its consequent effect on accident losses depends on the proportion of accidents for which tort recovery is barred by the threshold. Clearly, if automobile accidents resulting in medical expenses of less than $500 never gave rise to a tort suit in the absence of a threshold, then a $500 tort threshold would not effectively change liability. The stringency of a tort threshold, then, depends upon the underlying litigiousness of the population.

A 1970 study undertaken by the Federal Judicial Center for the U.S. Department of Transportation concludes that litigiousness—the propensity to file a lawsuit in the event of an accident—is strongly correlated with population density.[13] Table 6 reports results for regressions in which the tort threshold variables are interacted with population density. The results indicate that indeed the effect on accidents of a tort threshold is significantly higher at higher levels of population

[13] U.S. Department of Transportation, Automobile Insurance and Compensation Study, prepared by the Federal Judicial Center through Mitre Corporation (1970).

TABLE 7.   Effect of Market Structure on Fatal Accidents:
Dependent Variable = ln (Fatal Accidents); 1967–75

	All States (1)	States Which Passed Laws between 1971 and 1975 (2)
ln (population)	−.640	.811
	(−3.72)	(4.88)
Population density	.306	−.679
	(.34)	(−.74)
D1	−.038	−.026
	(−1.52)	(−1.00)
D2	.130	.175
	(1.45)	(2.45)
4-firm CR	.002	—
	(.59)	
D2 · 4-firm CR	−.002	—
	(−1.07)	
Share direct writers	—	−.127
		(−.37)
D2 · share direct writers	—	−.302
		(−2.54)
SEE	.0034	.0032

Note: Sample = fifteen states for nine years.

density. Further, with the exception of one specification, the inclusion of the interaction term increases the statistical significance of the legal variables, and the expanded set of legal variables becomes jointly significant at the .10 level in the fifty-one state sample and at the .01 level in the fifteen-state sub-sample.

B. The Interaction between Market Structure, No-Fault, and Fatal Accident Rates

The discussion in Section I concludes that the effect on accidents of restricting tort liability for motor vehicle accident injuries should be smaller in states in which the insurance industry is more concentrated. Here I investigate this hypothesis employing two different measures of market concentration. The first is the four-firm concentration ratio, for which I have data for the years 1967–77, and the second is the share of direct writers in direct premiums written in the voluntary market, for which I have data for the period 1967–78.[14] My conjecture here is that direct writers are more concentrated within states than national com-

[14]These data were provided by A. M. Best Co., Best's Executive Data Service (1975).

panies, which sell through independent brokers. (This conjecture is confirmed by the simple correlation between the share of direct writers and the four-firm concentration ratio for the eleven years in which I have data for both: .79.) In Table 7, I regress fatal accidents (in logs) for the sample of fifteen states which enacted no-fault between 1971 and 1975 on population (in logs), population density, D1, D2, the measure of concentration, and the interaction between D2 and concentration.

In both equations the positive effect of no-fault on fatal accidents is attenuated at higher levels of "concentration." The coefficient on the interaction terms are negative both for the four-firm concentration ratio in column 1 and for the share of direct writers in column 2.

III. Summary and Conclusions

The hypotheses developed in Section I of this paper receive substantial support from the data in Section II. Restricting tort liability for motor vehicle accident injuries substantially increases accident losses, at least as evidenced by comparing the fatal accidents of states which have and have not adopted no-fault, and the pre- and post-no-fault accident rates of those states which adopted it between 1971 and 1975. According to the regression equations in Table 3, those states which adopted no-fault between 1971 and 1975 suffered between 376 and 1,009 additional fatal automobile accidents during the years the laws were in effect as a result.

Efficient Redistribution through Commodity Markets

16

Bruce L. Gardner

Governmental intervention in farm commodity markets often has been evaluated using analytical procedures developed by Nerlove and Wallace to measure deadweight losses. These losses are the costs of obtaining various social and political objectives. The view in this paper is that the central purpose of intervention is to redistribute income to producers from consumers or taxpayers. In this context, the social cost of intervention is the deadweight loss per dollar transferred. This general view is not novel (Dardis, Josling). The purpose here is to treat it more systematically than previously.

The main innovation in this paper is to tie deadweight losses based on consumers' and producers' surpluses explicitly to surplus transfers. This can be important. Consider a p. rticular example: a market with linear supply and demand curves of equal slope. In this situation, the standard approach holds that a production-control program to achieve price $\bar{P}$ (figure 1) at output Q_0 generates deadweight losses equal to area $b + c$. A deficiency-payment program that guaranteed producers price $\bar{P}$ would result in output Q_1, with deadweight losses of area e. Since $e = b + c$, the deadweight losses are equal and there is no way to choose between them on efficiency grounds [Wallace, p. 585, eq. (4)]. However, the deadweight loss per dollar transferred to producers is quite different.

Previously published as Scientific Article No. A-3323 of the Maryland Agricultural Experiment Station. The Center for the Study of the Economy and the State, University of Chicago, supported this research.

Parts of this material have been presented in seminars at the Universities of Chicago, Maryland, Purdue, Illinois, and Texas A&M.

The author is grateful for comments received from participants on these occasions, and from the *AJAE* reviewers.

Reprinted with permission from the *American Journal of Agricultural Economics* 65, no. 1 (May 1983): 225–34. © 1983 by American Agricultural Economics Association.

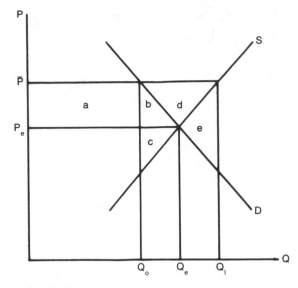

FIGURE 1. Deadweight losses

The amount transferred under the production control is the area *a* (price gain on output Q_o) minus *c* (rents lost on $Q_e - Q_o$). The amount transferred with the deficiency payment is area $a + b + d$. The deadweight loss per dollar transferred with production control is equal to $e/(a - c)$; for the payment program it is $e/(a + b + d)$. Since the latter denominator is larger, the ratio is smaller—the deadweight loss ratio is smaller for the payment program. Thus, payments are a more efficient redistributive mechanism even though the standard triangles are equal for both programs.

I. Quantifying Efficiency in Redistribution

It would be useful to have formulas analogous to those developed by Nerlove and Wallace, but specified to measure efficiency in redistribution. To visualize what is measured by such formulas, a graphical approach can illustrate the tradeoff between consumers' and producers' surpluses (Josling 1974). This surplus transformation curve is analogous to the economy-wide constraint on income redistribution which Bator calls the utility possibilities frontier.

Consider the inverse (price-dependent) demand and supply curves

$$P = D(Q), \tag{1}$$

$$P = S(Q). \tag{2}$$

Let redistribution from consumers to producers occur through production controls. Such intervention results in output $\hat{Q}$, which is less than or equal to the unregulated competitive output, Q_e.

The resulting consumer and producer surpluses (CS and PS, respectively) are defined as

$$CS = \int_0^{\hat{Q}} D(Q)dQ - D(\hat{Q})\hat{Q}, \tag{3}$$

$$PS = D(\hat{Q})\hat{Q} - \int_0^{\hat{Q}} S(Q)dQ. \tag{4}$$

The surplus transformation curve, T, is

$$T = T(CS, PS), \tag{5}$$

where the attainable CS, PS pairs are traced out by variations of the policy variable $\hat{Q}$. For example, consider linear demand and supply functions:

$$P = a_0 + a_1 Q; \ a_1 < 0 \tag{6}$$

$$P = b_0 + b_1 Q; \ b_1 > 0, \ 0 < b_0 < a_0. \tag{7}$$

The surpluses with production controls are

$$CS = -\tfrac{1}{2} a_1 \hat{Q}^2 \tag{8}$$

$$PS = (a_0 - b_0) \hat{Q} + (a_1 - \tfrac{1}{2} b_1) \hat{Q}^2. \tag{9}$$

The surplus transformation curve is obtained by solving (8) for $\hat{Q}$ and substituting in (9), to obtain

$$PS = \frac{(a_0 - b_0)}{\sqrt{-a_1/2}} \sqrt{CS} + \frac{2a_1 - b_1}{-a_1} CS, \tag{10}$$

which is equation (5) for the linear case.

An example of equation (10) is shown in figure 2 as the solid curves to the left of point E, attained when $Q = Q_e$. It is analogous to Bator's endowment point. For given supply and demand curves, E results

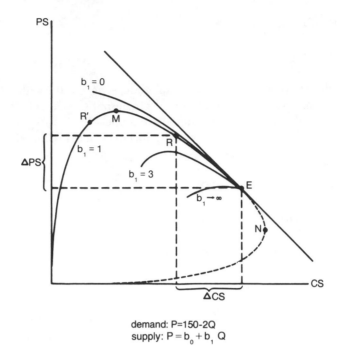

demand: P=150-2Q
supply: $P = b_0 + b_1 Q$

FIGURE 2. Surplus transformation curves: production control

in the maximum sum of consumers' and producers' surpluses. At this point the marginal rate of transformation between PS and CS is -1.[1]

Intervention that favors producers generates points to the left of E. The maximum producers' surplus is obtained at point M. This reflects monopoly production [confirm by differentiating (10) with respect to CS and equating it to zero]. Thus, intervention favoring producers yields points between E and M on the surplus transformation curve, such as R. At this point consumers lose ΔCS and producers gain ΔPS.

Efficiency at the margin is measured by the slope of the surplus transformation curve. If it is -1, then a dollar given up by consumers yields a dollar gained by producers. This could occur (theoretically) through a lump-sum transfer but not market intervention. The greater the slope's departure from -1, the less efficient the redistribution. The general expression for the slope is obtained from equations (3) and (4) as

[1] Derivations of these and following mathematical results are available from the author.

$$\frac{dPS}{dCS} = \frac{dPS/dQ}{dCS/dQ} = \frac{D'(Q)\hat{Q} + D(\hat{Q}) - S(\hat{Q})}{-D'(Q)\hat{Q}}. \tag{11}$$

For an intuitive grasp of this slope's determinants, consider the cases of linear and constant-elasticity (log-linear) demand and supply curves. For the linear case, differentiate equation (10) with respect to PS using equation (8) to replace CS, and substitute $(a_0 - b_0) = Q_e(b_1 - a_1)$ to obtain

$$\frac{dPS}{dCS} = \frac{b_1 - a_1}{a_1}\left(1 - \frac{Q_e}{\hat{Q}}\right) - 1. \tag{12}$$

The slope is negative for $\hat{Q}$ between Q_e and Q_m, the output that maximizes PS. It increases from -1 at Q_e to 0 at Q_m. Thus, the marginal efficiency of redistribution depends on the supply and demand slopes and the extent of production cutback.

For log-linear supply and demand curves, the slope of the surplus transformation curve is

$$\frac{dPS}{dCS} = -\eta[1 - (\hat{Q}/Q_e)^A] - 1, \tag{13}$$

where $A = 1/\varepsilon - 1/\eta$ with η the elasticity of demand (a negative number) and ε the elasticity of supply. The effect of an increase in ε is to make the first term of (13), which is always positive, smaller. Therefore, the slope of the surplus transformation curve, for any given restriction $\hat{Q}$, becomes closer to -1. This means that the marginal deadweight loss per dollar transferred (the "price of redistribution") is reduced. The effect of an absolute increase in η is to make the first term of (13) larger. Consequently, the marginal deadweight loss per dollar transferred is increased. Thus, the social cost of redistribution to producers is reduced by a lower demand elasticity or a higher supply elasticity.

Figure 2 shows the effect of a change in supply elasticity for the linear case from perfectly elastic ($b_1 = 0$) to perfectly inelastic ($b_1 \to \infty$). Equations (11) to (13) each imply that the slope is more sensitive to a change in supply elasticity, the more elastic is the demand function. Note that when $b_1 \to \infty$ (perfectly inelastic supply) in figure 2, it is impossible to redistribute much surplus to producers. This occurs because PS is equal to total revenue and the elasticity of demand is only a little less than 1. For elastic demand curves at E, producers' surplus is reduced by output control when supply is perfectly inelastic. Fixed supply can generate corner solutions at E. The slope of the transformation curve at E is not -1 when $b_1 \to \infty$. Generally, there will be corners in the surplus transformation curve if output restriction is capable of driving supply price to zero.

These are the same qualitative results derived by Wallace. However, we can estimate more readily how sensitive marginal deadweight losses per dollar redistributed are to changes in supply and demand parameters. Note that by setting the derivatives of (11) or (12) with respect to $\hat{Q}$ equal to zero, the size of production cutback that maximizes PS can be found. This quantity (the output sold under pure monopoly) identifies the point at which further production control makes producers and consumers both worse off.

For a given finite change such as E to R, we can analyze the total redistribution, $\Delta PS/\Delta CS$. It is this trade-off, not the marginal redistributions, that is most directly comparable to deadweight losses analyzed by Nerlove and Wallace. Since $D = \Delta PS - \Delta CS$, where D is the deadweight loss, we can estimate $\Delta PS/\Delta CS$ if we have an estimate of ΔPS or ΔCS in addition to D. Rosine and Helmberger estimated that in 1970 $4,829 million was distributed away from consumers and taxpayers in order to give farmers $2,140 million. This implies that $\Delta PS/\Delta CS = .44$, but it does not provide an estimate of the marginal rate of substitution (dPS/dCS) at the restricted equilibrium point.

Analytically, the total redistribution to producers in the linear case is

$$\frac{\Delta PS}{\Delta CS} = \frac{(b_1/a_1)(1 - R) - 2}{1 + R}, \tag{14}$$

where $R = Q_e/\hat{Q}$.

Total redistribution in the constant-elasticity case is

$$\frac{\Delta PS}{\Delta CS} = (1 + \eta) \left[\frac{1}{B} \left(\frac{1 - R^{-B}}{1 - R^{-C}} \right) - 1 \right], (\eta \neq -1) \tag{15}$$

where $B = 1 + (1/\varepsilon)$ and $C = 1 + (1/\eta)$.

An example will clarify these formulas and their relationship to the Nerlove/Wallace results. Suppose a commodity has (constant) elasticities of demand and supply of $\eta = -0.5$ and $\varepsilon = 0.2$, respectively, and that a production-control program reduces output by 20% ($R = Q_e/\hat{Q} = 1.25$). Applying formula (11), $\Delta PS/\Delta CS = -0.75$. For simplicity let $P_e = 1$ and $Q_e = 1$ so that values redistributed are shares of equilibrium total revenue. The constant-elasticity assumption implies that $\hat{P}$ rises to 1.56 when $\hat{Q}$ falls to 0.8. Thus, $\Delta CS = -0.50$; $\Delta PS/\Delta CS = -0.75$, and $\Delta PS = -0.38$. The sum of ΔPS and ΔCS gives the deadweight loss, 0.12, or 12% of total revenue $(P_e Q_e)$. The corresponding formula in Wallace (p. 582) gives the deadweight loss as $\frac{1}{2}(.5)(.45)^2 (1 + .5/.2) = 0.18$. The difference occurs because the Wallace formula is an approximation involving substantial error for large changes. The contribution of equation (15), besides being exact for constant elasticities, is that it ties deadweight losses explicitly to surplus redistribution. The contribution of equation (13), which has no parallel in the Nerlove/Wallace treatment, is to show the marginal costs of further redistribution. In the present example, $dPS/dCS = -.60$. Thus, at the margin, a dollar transferred from consumers results in a 60¢ gain for producers and a 40¢ deadweight loss. A marginal rate of surplus transformation less than the total gain in PS per dollar of CS lost is a quite general result. It follows from the convexity of the surplus transformation curve.

A. Redistribution toward Consumers

An extension of the surplus transformation curve to the right of point E involves intervention to redistribute income from producers to consumers. The mechanism could be a price ceiling below the unregulated market price. Then equations (3) and (4) become

$$CS = \int_0^{\hat{Q}} D(Q)dQ - S(\hat{Q})\hat{Q}, \tag{16}$$

$$PS = S(\hat{Q})\hat{Q} - \int_0^{\hat{Q}} S(Q)dQ, \tag{17}$$

where $\hat{Q}$ is output forthcoming at the ceiling price, $S(\hat{Q})$. The surplus transformation curve for a linear example is to the right of point E in figure 2. It also has a slope of -1 at point E. The maximum consumers' surplus is at point N, the monopsony outcome. Equilibria favoring consumers lie between points E and N.

The producer- and consumer-favoring surplus transformation curves meet with equal slope at point E. They form a continuous, smooth function describing all surplus-distributing possibilities available by output-restricting intervention. The vertical (or horizontal) difference between the surplus transformation curve and its tangent at point E measures the deadweight loss from redistribution. Note that the deadweight loss accelerates with the extent of intervention in either direction from E.

B. Deficiency Payments

There may be more efficient ways of redistributing surpluses than output restriction. In this context, "more efficient" means capable of generating a larger sum of surpluses for a given PS/CS ratio. An intervention mechanism that has been used for some agricultural commodities is to guarantee a "target" price to producers greater than P_e. Payments equal to the difference between the target price and the market-clearing price are made. This approach, equivalent to a subsidy, increases both producers' and consumers' surpluses. But it adds costs to taxpayers who provide the payments, creating a three-group redistribution that defeats graphics like figure 2. It also introduces deadweight losses from additional taxes.

Consider consumers/taxpayers as a single group. They are, of course, the same set of people, but individuals differ in their ratio of food expenditure to tax payments. So there may be significant redistribution within the group if intervention changes from production-control to deficiency payments. This is especially important because the ratio of tax payments to food expenditures changes across income classes, rising from near zero at the lowest incomes to well over one at higher incomes. In this paper, however, taxpayer costs will be subtracted from consumers' surplus to obtain a deficiency-payment income redistribution curve from consumers/taxpayers to producers. The relevant calculation of consumers' surplus plus taxpayers' costs, T, is obtained from equation (16). Producers' surplus comes from equation (17), except that $\hat{Q} > Q_e$ for a deficiency payment. The enforced maximum price has become a guaranteed minimum price. In the linear case, we have

$$CS - T = (a_0 - b_0)\hat{Q} + (\tfrac{1}{2}a_1 - b_1)\,\hat{Q}^2, \qquad (18)$$

$$PS = \tfrac{1}{2}b_1\hat{Q}^2. \qquad (19)$$

These imply the transformation curve,

$$CS - T = \sqrt{\frac{(a_0 - b_0)}{b_1/2}}\,\sqrt{PS} + \frac{(a_1 - 2b_1)}{b_1}\,PS. \qquad (20)$$

Figure 3 compares the surplus transformation curve from figure 2 with that for equation (20), using the same supply and demand functions. The lower dotted curve running northwest from point E shows the trade-off between producers' surplus and consumers' surplus minus taxpayers costs. Between points E and F the production-control approach is relatively efficient, but to the left of F deficiency payments are more efficient. The dotted transformation curve could be extended rightward from point E to generate redistribution favoring consumers. This might involve an all-or-none offer to producers to produce output

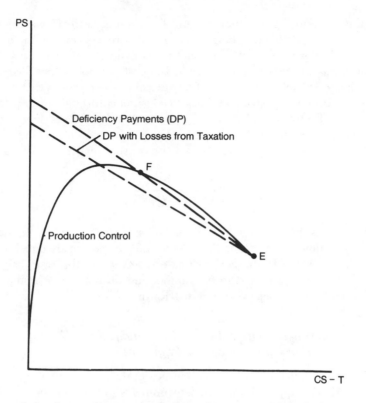

FIGURE 3. Surplus transformation curves for production control and subsidy

$Q'(>Q_e)$ to be sold at a regulated price $P'(<P_e)$. This approach conceivably could be used to redistribute essentially all the producers' surplus to consumers, with relatively small deadweight loss. Stalinist delivery quotas at state-specified prices could approximate such a policy.

With constant elasticities, the slope of the transformation curve for a subsidy generating output $\hat{Q} > Q_e$ is

$$\frac{dPS}{dCS} = \frac{1}{-\varepsilon[1 - (Q_e/\hat{Q})^A] - 1} - \tau. \tag{21}$$

Equation (21) is similar to (13) except for the parameter τ. This parameter is the deadweight loss associated with market distortion when taxes are imposed in order to raise funds for the deficiency payments. This loss is external to the regulated commodity market. It might be approximated by marginal deadweight losses per dollar of federal income tax.

If this were negligible, then τ could be taken as zero. However, this loss is not negligible (Harberger, Layard). Moreover, even if the dead-weight loss per dollar of additional taxes is no more than 15¢ at the margin, as suggested by Harberger, the cost per dollar transferred to producers is likely to be substantially greater. The reason is that part of the tax revenue is distributed back to consumers through lower prices. The net effectiveness of deficiency payments to producers depends on the supply and demand elasticities. (For a clear graphical analysis, see Wallace.) The exact relationship, for the constant-elasticity case, is

$$\tau = D' \Big/ \left\{ 1 - \frac{1}{1 + \eta[1 - B(Q_e/\hat{Q})^{-A}]} \right\}, \tag{22}$$

where D' is the deadweight loss per dollar of taxes raised. Note that if the distortion is very small, $Q_e/\hat{Q} \to 1$, and if ε and $-\eta$ are equal, then $\tau = 2D' - 0.30$ if Harberger's estimate is correct. In this case, half the funds taxed are recycled to consumers and do not reach producers. This doubles the social cost of redistributing income.

C. Comparative Redistribution Efficiency— Production Controls versus Payments

Comparing equation (21) with (13) indicates that the relative size of the demand and supply elasticities determines whether a deficiency payment or production control is most efficient. But exact conditions for preferring one or the other are not obvious. Wallace's result that dead-weight losses are the same when the supply and demand elasticities are equal does not hold. However, while the deadweight loss per dollar transferred is greater for the production control with equal elasticities, this advantage of deficiency payments may be offset by added social cost of raising taxes to finance the payments.[2]

A low demand elasticity or high supply elasticity tends to make production control the preferred alternative. Conversely, a low supply elasticity or a high demand elasticity favors deficiency payments. But the effect is not symmetrical, the demand elasticity being a more important determinant of efficiency for production controls and the supply elasticity more important for deficiency payments.

For linear supply and demand curves, it is even more obvious that there is no simple, general rule for tying supply and demand

---

[2] A reviewer points out that there are administrative costs of production controls that should be taken into account; and there are also administrative costs of payment distribution, albeit probably smaller per dollar transferred than the administrative costs of production controls.

slopes to efficiency. This is illustrated by the crossing of the solid and dashed transformation curves in figure 3. Note also that in the limiting case in which supply is perfectly elastic, deficiency payment can generate no producers' surplus, so production control should always be chosen to aid producers. The transformation curve for deficiency payments is a horizontal line whose length measures the deadweight loss of taxpayer costs over consumers' surplus gains. If supply is perfectly inelastic a subsidy should be chosen, unless the deadweight loss per dollar raised in taxes exceeds $|\eta|$. The qualification is needed because if $\varepsilon = 0$, the benefits of deficiency payments go entirely to producers. Therefore, $D' = \tau$ in equation (22), and $dPS/dCS = -1 + \tau$. For production controls we have $dPS/dCS = -(\eta + 1)$. Therefore, in order for production controls to be more efficient than the subsidy, $|\eta|$ must be less than τ (0.15 in the figure 3 example).

In general, the efficient form of intervention is determined by equations (13) and (21) for specific values of ε, η, τ, and $\hat{Q}/Q_e$.

D. Redistribution with International Trade

Consider the difference it makes for efficient redistribution if the product is exported. Assuming that foreigners have no political power in the United States, their consumers' surplus is ignored. The surplus transformation curves of figure 4 are derived from linear supply and demand curves with own-price elasticities at free-market equilibrium of $-.88$ for domestic demand, -3.5 for export demand, and 1.75 for supply. E' is the market equilibrium without intervention. Production controls generate the solid surplus transformation curve northwest from E'. The sum of producers' surplus and domestic consumers' surplus is no longer maximized at market equilibrium, but at point R. Thus, production controls may be chosen to maximize the sum of surpluses, whereas this could only have been accomplished by laissez-faire in figure 2 or 3.

In the example shown, a deficiency payment program is less efficient in redistributing income, indicated by the upper dotted transformation curve, in figure 4. This is because the lower market prices resulting from payments transfer income to foreign consumers, while production controls transfer income away from them. However, if the demand for exports is sufficiently elastic, this result is reversed, with deficiency payments more efficient. In such cases there is no longer a gain in the sum of surpluses from intervention. The extreme case is the small-country case of perfectly elastic export demand at the world price. In this case, production controls leave price unchanged and reduce producers' surplus, while deficiency payments result in deadweight losses smaller than in figure 4.

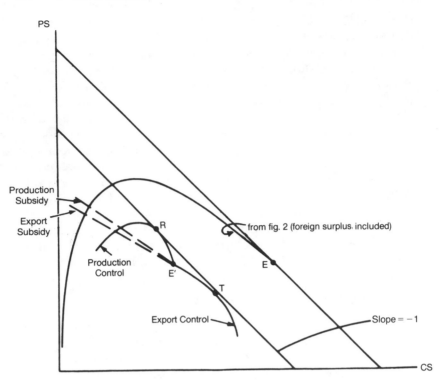

FIGURE 4. Surplus transformation curves (foreigners' surpluses excluded) under four forms of intervention

Trade opens up possibilities for new forms of intervention. Export quotas (or equivalent export taxes) redistribute income to consumers, shown in figure 4 by the solid surplus transformation curve southeast from E'. The sum of surpluses is increased by intervention, reaching a maximum at T, because there is redistribution away from foreign consumers. But the U.S. gainers are now consumers.[3] In such situations, production controls (favoring producers) and export controls (favoring consumers) could yield the same marginal rate of surplus transformation, with a sum of surpluses higher than the free-market equilibrium. Thus, it could be rational to switch, as in the 1970s, quite suddenly from controlling production via "set-asides" to export controls as supply/demand conditions change.

[3] Export restraints could benefit both U.S. consumers and producers if total export demand were less elastic than domestic demand.

Export subsidies are harder to justify. The surplus transformation curve for an export subsidy is the lower dotted curve in figure 4. An export subsidy necessarily causes a greater domestic deadweight loss than a deficiency payment program, while the latter is less efficient than production controls. It is possible that, with domestic demand less elastic than export demand, price discrimination with export subsidies may be an efficient way to redistribute income to producers, but not as efficient as a domestic price floor plus deficiency payments.

Consider the most favorable circumstances for an export subsidy, a perfectly elastic demand function for exports, figure 5. Production controls are not useful because they reduce producers' surplus and leave price unchanged. However, a price floor for domestic consumption, or a tax on processors which is refunded to producers could be a relatively efficient transfer mechanism. A domestic price at P_d would redistribute $(P_d - P_w)\hat{Q}_d$ with the deadweight loss of the hatched triangle. An export subsidy of s per unit would redistribute an additional amount $s(\hat{Q}_s - \hat{Q}_d)$ to producers at the cost of the smaller shaded triangle. However, a deficiency payment program would transfer $s\hat{Q}_s$ to producers for the same deadweight loss. Efficiency in redistribution occurs at domestic price P_d and subsidy s at which the marginal rate of deadweight loss per dollar transferred is the same for both the domestic price floor and the production subsidy. (To be complete, the deadweight losses of raising taxes to pay the subsidy must be added to the

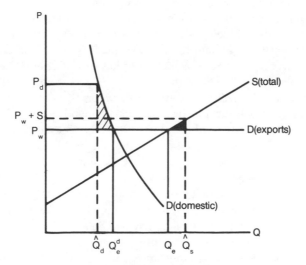

FIGURE 5. Inefficiency of export subsidy (world prices given)

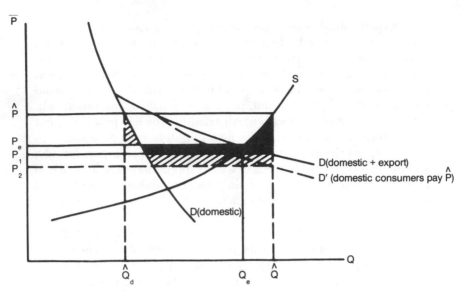

FIGURE 6. Export subsidy (world price influenced by exporter)

shaded triangle, but this cannot make an export subsidy more efficient than deficiency payments.)

If export demand is not perfectly elastic then the efficiency of export subsidies (and deficiency payments) is further reduced because transfers to foreign consumers will occur. The reason is shown in figure 6. Suppose we want producers to have rents attained at $\hat{P}$. This can be achieved with a deficiency payment of $\hat{P} - P_1$. Domestic and foreign consumers both pay P_1, and the deadweight loss is the shaded area. If the same producer price is achieved by an export subsidy, domestic consumers will pay $\hat{P}$. This reduces total demand at all (export) prices below $\hat{P}$ by the horizontal difference between the domestic demand curve and $\hat{Q}_d$, yielding the dashed total demand curve. Now it requires a larger subsidy per bushel, $\hat{P} - P_2$, to boost total demand to $\hat{Q}$. The deadweight loss is increased by the hatched areas. In figure 5, with export demand perfectly elastic at the world price, deadweight losses below P_e disappear.

Export subsidies might be efficient in adjusting to past policy "mistakes." A commodity's support price may lead to an unanticipated buildup of stocks. The stocks may have sufficiently high storage costs that receiving even, say, half the support price for them would reduce taxpayers' costs. In these circumstances, an export subsidy may be efficient. However, domestic consumption subsidies and a move toward production controls also should occur, since these are more efficient adjustment mechanisms.

II. Use and Limitations

The formulas of this paper can be used in two related but distinct ways, one normative and one positive. The positive application is to explore whether policy variations over time and across commodities can be explained in terms of efficiency in redistribution. For example, does the move from production controls to direct payments in cotton and rice during the 1970s reflect changes in efficiency resulting from changes in supply or demand elasticities? Can the general absence of production-control programs for livestock products be explained in terms of efficiency with relatively high demand elasticities?

The normative application is to rank prospective programs for redistributing income. Suppose, for example, that it is the intention of Congress to increase peanut growers' incomes. How should this be accomplished, and what is the marginal cost of alternative redistribution levels? The best available analysis of alternative peanut programs is Nieuwoudt, Bullock, and Mathia. Their work implies an aggregate elasticity of demand for U.S. peanuts of -1.8 and an elasticity of supply of about 4.0. U.S. policy under the Food and Agriculture Act of 1977 involves marketing controls and acreage allotments and so is basically a production-control approach.[4] But there have been continuing proposals, most recently by the Reagan administration early in 1981, to replace this program by a deficiency payment (subsidy) approach. Using the elasticities of -1.8 and $+4.0$, equations (13) and (21) imply a marginal rate of transformation of $-.74$ for a production-control and $-.27$ for a subsidy program, with a 20% quantity reduction or increase. This rough calculation indicates that it is relatively efficient to intervene with marketing controls and that the conclusion of Nieuwoudt, Bullock, and Mathia that "the target price plan would greatly reduce treasury and social costs" (p. 65) is wrong.

A serious limitation of the application just outlined, and of any use of the formulas developed, is that most commodity programs are not simply production-control or payment programs. Often they combine elements of each. However, complex schemes can be simulated for particular values of intervention variables given the values of key behavioral elasticities (or derivatives), and expectations of what such

---

[4]The two-tiered price supports, CCC stocks, and subsidies for crushing "excess" peanuts recently have been introduced. These complicate the program but production control remains the primary redistributive feature.

simulations would show can often be deduced from results in the simpler models. For example, the fact that inelastic demand makes production controls efficient relative to deficiency payments suggests that a higher price in the relatively inelastic fluid milk market is a means of reducing the deadweight loss per dollar transferred to dairy producers.[5]

Further limitations arise when commodity markets are interdependent. For example, the supply of soybeans, given the price of corn, is expected to be quite elastic. If intervention is to be undertaken to aid corn producers specifically (as it has been), because of the high supply elasticity, quantity controls should be more efficient than deficiency payments. The same would be true for soybeans. Yet, if we take corn and soybeans jointly, we have an aggregate commodity substantially less elastic in supply. This suggests that more efficient redistribution might result from intervention of the payment type for both products simultaneously. Indeed, extension of this reasoning suggests the most efficient method of redistributing income to farmers generally might be subsidies applicable to any crop.

Sector-wide intervention implies that the relevant interest group is farmers in total, not splintered commodity groups. Interaction between commodity markets has implications for the formation of political coalitions among commodity groups. The greater the cross elasticities of supply or demand between two commodities, the greater the difference between the partial and total elasticities of supply or demand, and the greater the efficiency gain in income redistribution from a program to protect both commodities jointly. Thus, apart from the political and economic factors that bear on producers' ability to form coalitions, one might expect that coalitions will be more prevalent among closely related commodities because the deadweight losses from intervention are reduced more by joint intervention under these circumstances.

In standard welfare economics the policy optimum is found with a social welfare function,

$$W = W(UP, UC), \tag{23}$$

[5]CCC purchase for price-stabilizing storage between years, like the loan and FOR programs for grains, involves redistributional issues quite different from those discussed in this paper. The point about the dairy program is that it has recently involved simultaneous purchase and subsidized sales, making it equivalent to a subsidy program. In addition, as an *AJAE* reviewer points out, the subsidized consumer prices go to a particular subset of people. Therefore, in the absence of a costlessly functioning secondary resale market for subsidized dairy products, the deadweight losses are even greater than the usual triangle such as *e* in figure 1.

where UP and UC are the aggregate utilities of producers and consumers. Redistributional intervention in a commodity market involves changes in (23) via a regulatory variable, X, such as a level of controlled output, a price floor, or payment per bushel. Changes in UP and UC resulting from a change in X are taken to be changes in producer and consumer surpluses, following Harberger. Therefore, the policy optimum can be found by replacing UP and UC by PS and CS, then differentiating (23) with respect to X and equating to zero, which yields

$$W_p \frac{dPS}{dX} + W_c \frac{dCS}{dX} = 0, \tag{24}$$

where W_p and W_c are the marginal contributions of producers' and consumers' surpluses to the social welfare function. The policy optimum is a point of tangency between a social welfare indifference curve and the highest attainable surplus transformation curve. With equal weights on the utilities of consumers and producers, the policy optimum is the market equilibrium.

The social welfare function is a normative concept. The comparable non-normative concept is a representation of how producers' and consumers' well-being is actually regarded in the political process. Political behavior may involve a bargaining game among interest groups (as in Zusman and Amiad) or a "policy preference function" (Rausser and Freebairn). Becker, in his analysis of the positive economics of redistribution, discusses in detail the properties of the behavioral function that replaces the social welfare function. In this context, W_c and W_p represent the (marginal) political power of consumers and producers. Thus, a point such as R in figure 2 is a political equilibrium in which the political power of producers exceeds that of consumers. The efficient redistribution hypothesis is that the political process places us at points like R, at which resources are used as efficiently as possible given the political preference function.

III. Concluding Remarks and Summary

The deadweight losses caused by governmental intervention in agricultural commodity markets do not tell the whole story about such intervention, nor is desire to redistribute income the sole reason for intervention. Under the assumption that it is an important reason, the deadweight losses can be viewed as a price paid to redistribute through market intervention. This paper develops models for estimating this price—the deadweight loss per dollar redistributed. It also derives for production-control and deficiency-payment programs the relationship between this price and its determinants—supply and demand elasticities, the extent of intervention, and the deadweight loss from raising general tax revenues. Qualitative results are also obtained for intervention when the export market is important.

In general, redistributive efficiency increases as either the supply or the demand function becomes less elastic. The efficient method of intervention depends on which function is less elastic. Inelastic demand favors production controls, and inelastic supply a deficiency payment approach. If demand is inelastic enough, less than about -0.15 in the cases considered in this paper, production controls are more efficient even than lump sum transfers to producers. This is because of deadweight losses associated with the taxes necessary for payments.

For intervention with an exported product, it is shown that deficiency payments are generally preferable to an export subsidy. Yet if the exporter is not a price taker in world markets, production controls may be more efficient than either type of subsidy. Moreover, under shifting economic conditions or political power, it may be efficient to shift between production controls (favoring producers) and export controls (favoring consumers).

The usefulness of the exact results generated by the formulas developed in the paper depends on having reliable estimates of supply and demand elasticities. These are often lacking. Nonetheless, it may still be of value to know exactly how much difference it makes for efficiency in distribution if the supply elasticity, say, is ½ or 1½. And the formulas can also be informative about the value of better information on elasticities. If costs of redistribution are sensitive to potential error in elasticities, it will be worthwhile to make the econometric effort necessary to sharpen our estimates. And if data do not permit accurate estimation, we can at least assess more exactly the range of likely errors in our redistributive analyses.

References

Bator, Francis M. "The Simple Analytics of Welfare Maximization." *Amer. Econ. Rev.* 47(1957): 22–29.

Becker, Gary S. "A Positive Theory of the Redistribution of Income and Political Behavior." CSES Work. Pap., University of Chicago, Oct. 1980.

Dardis, Rachel. "The Welfare Cost of Grain Protection in the United Kingdom." *J. Farm Econ.* 49(1967): 597–609.

Harberger, A. C. "On the Use of Distributional Weights in Social Cost-Benefit Analysis." *J. Polit. Econ.* 86(1978): S87–S120.

Josling, T. E. "Agricultural Policies in Developed Countries: A Review." *J. Agr. Econ.* 25(1974): 220–64.

———. "A Formal Approach to Agricultural Policy." *J. Agr. Econ.* 20(1969): 175–91.

Layard, Richard. "On the Use of Distributional Weights in Cost-Benefit Analysis." *J. Polit. Econ.* 88(1980): 1041–47.

Nerlove, Marc. *The Dynamics of Supply.* Baltimore MD: Johns Hopkins University Press, 1958.

Nieuwoudt, W., J. B. Bullock, and G. Mathia. "Alternative Peanut Programs: An Economic Analysis." North Carolina Agr. Exp. Sta. Tech. Bull. No. 242, May 1976.

Rausser, G. C., and J. W. Freebairn. "Estimation of Policy Preference Functions: An Application to U.S. Beef Import Quotas." *Rev. Econ. and Statist.* 56(1974): 437–49.

Rosine, J., and P. Helmberger. "A Neoclassical Analysis of the U.S. Farm Sector, 1948–1970." *Amer. J. Agr. Econ.* 56(1974): 717–29.

Wallace, T. D. "Measures of Social Costs of Agricultural Programs." *J. Farm Econ.* 44(1962): 580–94.

Zusman, P., and A. Amiad. "A Quantitative Investigation of a Political Economy—The Israeli Dairy Program." *Amer. J. Agr. Econ.* 59(1977): 88–98.

Environmental Regulation: Whose Self-Interests Are Being Protected?

17

B. Peter Pashigian

Economists have had marginal success in applying the self-interest hypothesis to explain legislation. Though an assessment may be premature, supporters of the self-interest hypothesis must be concerned over the difficulty of successfully applying the hypothesis to explain legislation. Even the usefulness of the self-interest hypothesis has been called into question. This reassessment is partially motivated by the apparent difficulty of the self-interest theory to explain the social legislation passed during the seventies. It is conceded by many that the self-interest hypothesis is more useful in explaining the regulation of specific industries. But, skeptics question whether the self-interest hypothesis can explain social legislation which typically affects many groups and imposes costs and benefits on a large number of industries and occupations.

The epitome of social legislation is environmental regulation. Just how the self-interest hypothesis would help explain environmental legislation remains to be seen. Most economists rely on the established theory of externalities to explain the reason for environmental regulation. Self-interest or rent-seeking is seldom mentioned when the subject is pollution control. The infatuation of economists with the theory of externalities to the exclusion of the self-interest hypothesis is not

This research was supported by the Center for the Study of the Economy and the State, University of Chicago, the Graduate School of Business, University of Chicago, and the National Science Foundation, Regulation and Policy Analysis, NSF SES 8308909. I would like to thank Rodney Smith for a careful and detailed review of the manuscript and for the many suggested improvements in content, style and organization of the paper. I have also received helpful comments from participants of seminars at the University of Chicago, Center for the Study of Business Regulation, Duke University, University of Florida, Center for the Study of American Business, Washington University, Rochester University and Stanford University. Andrew Weiss and Alan Frankel served as able research assistants.

Reprinted with permission from *Economic Inquiry* 23 (October 1985): 551–84.
© 1985 by Western Economic Association International

difficult to understand. The theory of externality is well known and firmly embedded in the economists' arsenal of economic analysis. By and large, the profession accepts the notion that social welfare and not private interest is the guiding principle for environmental legislation and regulation. This easy acceptance of the externalities hypothesis is nevertheless disquieting because the literature on the self-interest hypothesis, beginning with Stigler's (1971) classic paper, is considerable, and the evidence from regulated industries suggests private interests have benefited from regulation. Yet, when it comes to explaining environmental legislation, a substantial number of economists believe the regulatory program has been largely untouched by the special interest considerations and has been successful in improving social welfare. Indifference to the self-interest hypothesis is not the sole province of economists, but is shared by many political scientists.

Though a majority of economists and political scientists question the value of the self-interest hypothesis, a few economists, political scientists and lawyers have argued rent-seeking permeates environmental legislation as well. Buchanan and Tullock (1975) have claimed the frequent use of direct controls rather than pollution taxes could be explained as means of raising rents. Maloney and McCormick (1982) have shown how mandated cost increases could increase short run profits by reducing industry output, and they report that the cotton dust standard raised the stock price of the companies involved. Crandall (1983) has suggested that votes on environmental issues are better explained by the growth rate of income than by the level of air quality. Ackerman and Hassler (1981) have described how the SO_2 standard was the product of an alliance between environmental groups and eastern high sulfur coal producers and forced the use of scrubbers and high sulfur content coal. Pashigian (1984) reports small plants have been harmed relative to large plants by compliance with environmental regulations. Though often ignored, the results of these studies suggest that the externalities hypothesis is too simple to explain important features and consequences of environmental policy.

This paper seeks to elevate the role of self-interest in explaining the regulation of stationary sources. An important part of environmental legislation becomes comprehensible under the self-interest hypothesis and not under hypotheses based on a taste or political preference for environmental protection. The paper focuses on the policy of prevention of significant deterioration (PSD), a policy that is largely unfamiliar to all but specialists in environmental policy. This policy prohibits areas with air quality superior to the *minimum* national standards from permitting a significant deterioration of local air quality by placing limits on economic development. Environmental policy also requires all areas to meet the minimum national standards. While areas with unduly low air quality are ordered to improve air quality and to attain the minimum standards, other areas with air quality superior to the minimum standards must prevent a significant deterioration of air quality.

Environmental policy has fostered a curious set of multiple standards. On the one hand, minimum national standards are supposed to be met in all air control regions. On the other hand, areas with air quality superior to these minimum standards are required to control economic development and prevent air quality from deteriorating beyond a prescribed amount, even if the resulting air quality is still superior to the minimum standard. Environmental policy has given a stamp of approval for industrial-urban locations to merely achieve the minimum standards while imposing higher than minimum standards on areas with superior air quality.

Why these implicit multiple standards became an integral part of environmental policy is the central focus of this paper. The major premise advanced and tested is that PSD policy was developed to attenuate the locational competition between developed and less developed regions and between urban and rural areas. The votes cast in the House on PSD policy are examined and show opposition to PSD policy comes from the South, the West, and rural locations, areas with higher growth rates and with generally superior air quality. PSD policy is opposed in these areas because it places limits on growth. The strongest supporters of PSD policy are northern urban areas, many of which have lower air quality and are not directly affected by PSD policy. It is argued that federal PSD policy raised the cost of factor mobility and thereby allowed northern locations with lower air quality to improve local air quality without as large a loss of factors to areas with superior air quality.

Other hypotheses could and have been advanced to explain this North-South/West voting dichotomy. The regional differences in voting position might be due to differences in political representation or philosophy or to tastes for environmental regulation. A considerable part of the modeling effort is designed to separate the locational competition hypothesis from a taste or cultural-political heritage interpretation. This is done by first comparing the votes on PSD policy with votes on auto emission policy, another important environmental issue. A comparative vote analysis shows greater regional differences for votes cast on PSD policy than on auto emission policy. This finding is interpreted to mean that the votes on the PSD issue do not simply reflect regional differences in the taste for environmental protection. Otherwise, the regional patterns of votes on the two issues would be similar. Second, a comparison of the votes on environmental policies with the votes cast on a portfolio of economic issues once again shows greater regional differences in the votes cast on environmental issues than on the economic issues. If the votes cast on environmental issues reflect differences between regions in liberal-conservative political philosophy, these differences are simply too small to explain the regional differences in the votes on environmental issues. The weight of the evidence indicates that PSD policy cannot be explained solely by regional differences in political philosophy or tastes for environmental regulation. Finally, the paper examines per unit pollution abatement costs and shows that higher per unit pollution costs are incurred in the South and the West where the strongest opposition to PSD policy is found. The vote and cost evidence suggest that at least some parts of the environmental protection program have been shaped by self-interest.

Section I presents the basic hypothesis, describes the legislative history of the Nondegradation Amendments, examines the likely economic effects of PSD policy, and explains the reasons for comparing the votes cast on PSD policy with those cast on auto emission policy and on economic issues. Section II presents the logit specification for the analysis of the votes cast on PSD and auto emission policy. Section III shows the votes by region and by population density and presents the logit results. The results for PSD policy are compared with these results for auto emission policy and then with the results for a representative sample of economic issues. The difficulty of reconciling the results with the implications of alternative hypotheses is also discussed here. Section IV investigates the effect of party on voting position in more detail. The votes on PSD policy cast by newly-elected freshmen in the House are compared to the votes cast in the previous year by defeated incumbents to determine if party turnover causes a change in voting position. Section V displays per unit pollution abatement costs by region and shows that political support for PSD policy is greater in regions where per unit pollution abatement costs have been relatively low. The conclusions are presented in the last section.

I. Legislative History and Economic Effects of PSD Policy

One objective of the 1970 Clean Air Act was "to protect and enhance the quality of the nation's air resources so as to promote the public health and welfare and the productive capacity of its population." This general language highlights the twin objectives of environmental legislation. The enhancement language was directed at improving air quality in nonattainment areas, *i.e.*, in the industrial cities located in the north and in cities with pollution problems caused primarily by mobile sources. Superior air quality in less developed rural areas and smaller cities and towns was to be protected from industrial development and not allowed to deteriorate toward the minimum standards. The protection language did satisfy the demands of environmental groups who opposed the spread of environmental pollution from urban to rural areas and of residents in northern cities who feared factors would leave to escape the cost of compliance.[1]

The Environmental Protection Agency (EPA) was assigned the unenviable task of translating this language into regulatory policy and throughout the early seventies issued several preliminary interpretations of PSD policy in hopes of navigating through a thicket of opposition. These cautious efforts failed to satisfy the objections raised by industry and environmental groups. Efforts by the EPA to define a PSD policy were constantly frustrated by legal challenges. In 1976 the 94th Congress attempted to resolve this and other impasses when it considered a major overhaul of the Clean Air Act. Votes were cast on three amendments dealing with PSD policy, but the final conference bill was killed by a filibuster. The next congress repeated the ritual. Two more PSD amendments were voted on in 1977, and a comprehensive bill was finally passed in 1977. The votes cast in 1976 and 1977 on the Non-degradation (PSD) Amendments offer the first opportunity to render a comprehensive accounting of the sources of Congressional support for PSD policy. The amendments are briefly reviewed below.

A. The 1976 Amendments

In 1976 the Senate Public Works Committee reported Senate Bill S3219. This bill declared the intent of Congress to prevent clean air from deteriorating even if it remained above minimum standards. Two types of clean air areas were defined. Class I areas include national parks, wilderness areas, and other areas added by the states, and would be allowed the smallest increment in pollution levels. The remaining areas were included in Class II. States would issue construction permits to all major new pollution sources—plants emitting over 100 tons per year—and require new plants to use "best available control technology" (BACT). The permit system would be used to enforce the incremental limits and encourage planned growth in Class II areas.

The House bill gave the states and local government more powers and set aside fewer pristine areas. Both bills allowed certain increments from existing baseline emissions for sulfur dioxide and particulates. Under the House bill, most clean air areas would begin in Class II,

[1] For a representative statement, see the testimony of Lawrence Moss, President of the Sierra Club [U.S. Congress, Senate, 93rd Congress].

where pollution increments of up to 25 percent would be allowed. Class I listing was reserved for national parks and wilderness areas in excess of 25,000 acres. Class III, to which areas could be transferred, would allow pollution increment levels of up to 50 percent. States could reclassify lands after public hearings, assessments of the economic, environmental and energy impact, and the approval of the legislature. Once the bill reached the House floor, two amendments by Chappel of Florida and Carter of Kentucky to delay or weaken and one by Maquire of New Jersey to strengthen the Nondegradation section were defeated. The vote on each of the 1976 Nondegradation Amendments is described in Appendix A.

B. The 1977 Amendments

The House bill established three classes: Class I areas included national parks in excess of 25,000 acres, national memorial parks and wilderness areas in excess of 5,000 acres; Class II included all other clean air areas; Class III areas would be designed after hearings and studies. Increments for particulates and sulfur dioxide above baseline levels were 2 percent for Class I areas, 25 percent for Class II and 50 percent for Class III. Areas could be reclassified (except Class I areas) after hearings were held. New or modified stationary sources emitting in excess of 100 tons per year were required to obtain permits. The House considered two amendments by McKay of Utah and by Breaux of Louisiana to weaken the Nondegradation section. It adopted the one submitted by Breaux which allowed state governors to permit Class I and Class II areas to exceed pollution levels for 18 days per year. The 1977 Nondegradation Amendments are summarized in Appendix B. Altogether, the House voted on five Nondegradation Amendments in 1976 and 1977, and these votes serve as the basic input for the vote analysis.

C. Economic Effects

The economic effects of adopting a PSD policy may be analyzed by comparing the effects of two federal policies: one with just a *minimum* air quality standard, and the other with a minimum air quality standard *and* a PSD requirement. For simplicity, assume I is a measure of air quality in each locality. In Figure 1, air quality is measured on the horizontal axis and increases as I increases. The percent distribution of the population living in local areas with air quality of I is measured on the vertical axis. Let MM' be the resulting distribution of the population when federal environmental policy merely establishes a minimum

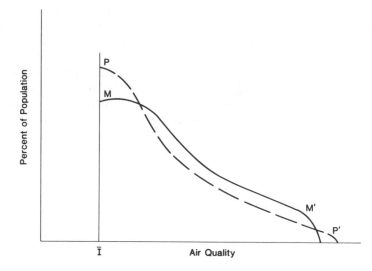

Figure 1

standard of I. All locations with I lower than $\bar{I}$ would become non-attainment locations and would have to introduce compliance policies that raised air quality to $\bar{I}$. Cities with $I < \bar{I}$ would comply by imposing limits on industrial expansion and by requiring more demanding technology for new plants and plant expansions. Some plants would relocate rather than comply with these more stringent regulations. If a federal program includes a PSD requirement along with a minimum standard, the cost of moving a plant from a location with $I < \bar{I}$ to locations with $I > \bar{I}$ is higher because limits are placed on the number of new plants that can enter each location. The resulting distribution would look something like PP'. More individuals would live in locations that were closer to the minimum standard. The reason for this is that *each* location with I in excess of $\bar{I}$ would be permitted only a percentage reduction in the baseline (existing) I, e.g., k percent reduction from the existing I before the federal program was implemented. Once the bank of permitted air quality decrements was exhausted, further development would be restricted. Fewer plants would be permitted to locate in that community under a PSD policy. Since the PSD requirement applies to each location with I in excess of $\bar{I}$, it would increase the percent of the population that lives at locations where air quality is near the minimum standard compared to a federal policy with just a minimum standard. Under PSD policy some locations with pristine air would achieve air quality levels not achievable under a minimum standard policy (because fewer plants could enter these locations under

TABLE 1.   Ten Leading States in Tons of Emissions Per Square Mile, 1972[a]

State	Particulates and Sulfur Dioxides	State	All Other Emissions[b]
1. Ohio	211	1. New Jersey	875
2. Delaware	180	2. Rhode Island	750
3. Pennsylvania	156	3. Massachusetts	660
4. New Jersey	149	4. Connecticut	498
5. Indiana	128	5. Indiana	363
6. Massachusetts	126	6. Maryland	355
7. Illinois	102	7. Delaware	323
8. Rhode Island	98	8. Ohio	311
9. Kentucky	90	9. New York	265
10. West Virginia	87	10. Pennsylvania	256

Source: J. Golden, et al. (1979)
[a] Areas used as federal and state parks are excluded.
[b] Includes hydrocarbons, carbon monoxide and other oxides.

PSD policy). Hence, the PP' curve will cut through the MM' curve at two points.

PSD policy did not develop in isolation but was a consequence of more fundamental shifts in the demand for improved environmental conditions. Air quality has been lower throughout the North, particularly in northern cities, than in many parts of the South and the West. Of course there are many exceptions to this generalization. Table 1 shows tons of emissions of particulates and sulfur oxides per square mile in 1972 (excluding federal and state parks) and tons of all other pollutants per square mile for the ten leading states in 1972. Northern industrial states have had more severe problems with particulates and sulfur emissions while Massachusetts, Connecticut, and New Jersey face more severe problems due to hydrocarbon and carbon monoxide emissions. In addition, virtually all studies have shown air quality in cities is inferior to air quality in rural areas.[2]

There is some evidence of an increased demand for a cleaner environment by residents living in northern cities with lower air quality. During the sixties, individual cities made efforts to improve environmental conditions. If the rents of the remaining factors specific to a location declined when factors moved as a consequence of the cost of complying with more stringent local regulations, the owners of the location specific factors would support federal policies that reduced mo-

[2] Data published by the Environmental Protection Agency shows suspended particulate concentrations at 18 nonurban locations were about one-third of the concentration levels at 95 urban locations from 1960 to 1971 [U.S. EPA, 1973].

bility. They would favor more demanding performance standards for new than for existing plants and no significant deterioration of air quality in clean air areas. By raising the cost of mobility, any improvement in local air quality could be achieved but with a smaller reduction in the rents of factors specific to the locality. PSD policy begins to make sense in a world where there is a selected demand for an improvement in local environmental conditions and where there are location specific rents. The evolution of a multiple standard policy is then a product of a demand for improved environmental conditions by residents in cities with lower air quality, the (potential) loss of factors caused by local independent clean up programs, and the collective political strength of states with lower air quality. Efforts to prevent a reduction in location specific rents will be less successful when there is interjurisdictional competition. But rent-seeking efforts promise to be more successful when regulation is shifted to the federal government. Federal regulation should raise the net benefits from rent-seeking behavior and therefore should increase the amount of rent-seeking activity.

D. Other Explanations

Regional differences in the support for environmental policy and PSD policy in particular could be due to regional differences in taste for environmental protection or political philosophy. The recorded votes indicate residents of northern urban locations were more desirous of preserving relatively pristine environments for future generations than were other constituencies. A stronger taste for environmental protection by residents of northern urbanized areas might also explain the votes. The taste hypothesis can be challenged on several grounds but, more importantly, tested. The taste hypothesis does not explain just why the environmental concerns of northern residents extend beyond the Class I areas (national parks and wilderness areas) and include all undeveloped areas throughout the country, whether scenic or unsightly. The taste hypothesis merely postulates, but does not explain, why residents of northern urbanized areas alone have these tastes for the preservation of environmental conditions and why similar concerns are not expressed by residents of southern and western states. Just why residents in northern cities express more concern about the consequence of industrial development on air quality in other regions of the country than do the residents of those regions has not been explained.

If there are regional taste differences in political support for environmental protection and if these taste differences explain the votes on environmental policy, then the pattern of regional voting support should be similar for PSD policy as for auto emission policy, the other major environmental issue considered by Congress in 1976 and 1977. If the votes cast on PSD policy were affected more by how PSD policy would affect locational competition, then the regional differences in voting support will be even greater on PSD policy than on automobile emission policy. The effects of locational competition should be a more important determinant of the votes cast on PSD policy than on auto emission policy. If locational competition considerations play a more prominent role in explaining votes cast on environmental issues, regional differences in support for legislation should also be greater on environmental issues than on economic issues. Regional differences in support of economic legislation have already been documented by Peltzman (1983). These regional differences on economic issues may serve as a benchmark. If these economic issues usually involve less of an element of locational competition among regions, then the regional differences in political support will be greater on environmental issues than on economic issues. Hence, votes on different issues can be compared to determine if regional differences in the votes on PSD policy merely mimic regional differences in the votes on auto emission policy or on economic issues. This methodology will be used to show that locational competition considerations did play a more prominent role in determining the votes on PSD policy.

II. Statistical Model of Legislative Voting

The statistical analysis will be limited to House votes because there are larger differences in the economic and demographic characteristics between Congressional districts than between states. A preliminary examination of Senate votes indicated the regional pattern of Senate votes did not differ substantially from House votes. The statistical analysis will rely on a logit model to explain 1,905 votes cast in 1976 and 1977 on *five* Nondegradation Amendments and 1,607 votes cast on *four* Automobile Emission Amendments.[3] However, it may be helpful to proceed first by just considering the Nondegradation Amendments. Let P_{ij} be the ith vote by the representative in district j. For each Nondegradation Amendment $P_{ij} = 1$ if the representative voted for a more stringent PSD policy.[4] The probability of supporting a more stringent

---

[3] The 1976 Automobile Emission Amendments and CQ numbers were Waxman (D, California) Amendment [556] and the Dingell (D, Michigan) Amendment [557]. In 1977 Congress voted on the Preyer (D, North Carolina) Amendment [266] and the Dingell (D, Michigan) Amendment [267]. The numbers in the brackets represent numbers assigned by the Congressional Quarterly.

[4] Except for one amendment, it was easy to determine if an amendment tightens or relaxes a standard. The McKay Substitute Amendment [262] is a weaker relaxation

policy will depend on l economic, demographic, industry and party variables in the district. X_{ijl} is the observation for one of the l independent variables in Congressional district j. These independent variables are augmented by eight dummy variables representing the eight Census regions (New England is the suppressed dummy variable). R_{ijm} equals 1 if the Congressional district j is in region m and zero otherwise. Because there are 5 Nondegradation Amendments, i is indexed from one to five. The log of the odds ratio can be represented by

$$\ln \{P_{ij}/(1 - P_{ij})\} = \sum_l B_l X_{ijl} + \sum_{m=2}^{9} V_m R_{ijm}$$

(1)

$$i = 1, \ldots , 5$$
$$j = 1, 2, \ldots .$$

Equation (1) may be considered a reduced form equation. The independent variables describe the economic, demographic, industry and party characteristics of the district and thereby determine the net benefits or losses from a more stringent PSD policy. The independent variables can be grouped into four classes. First are the economic and demographic variables. The most important of these are the variables distinguishing between urban and rural districts (population density and percent urbanized) and between growing and stagnating districts (population growth). Greater support for PSD policy is expected from urban rather than rural districts and from declining rather than growing districts. Per Capita Income and Capital, the percent of household income received from interest, dividends and net rental income, are used to control for the effects of income. Percent Senior controls for any effect of the age distribution. The income and age variables are used here simply as control variables. Generally, environmental quality might be expected to be a superior good, but it is less clear how income of residents should affect the vote when the issue is air quality in other areas.

The effect of the party of the representative is captured through a dummy variable which equals one if the vote was cast by a Democrat.

_____

than incorporated in the Breaux Amendment [263]. The vote on 262 attracted considerable support from representatives of districts located in the Northeast and Middle Atlantic regions as a means of staving off a favorable vote on 263. In this case, a yes vote on 262 was interpreted as favoring a more restrictive PSD policy. While there may be disagreement over this interpretation, there can be little disagreement over the interpretations given the other amendments.

The party variable is introduced to try and separate out the effect of party from the effect of region. However, party and region are not independent since Democrats represent northern urban and some southern constituencies; hence, the coefficient of the party variable may capture some of the effects of region as well as party.

The next group of independent variables measures the relative importance in the district of industries affected by environmental policy. Selected three digit industries were included because the industries had incurred relatively high pollution abatement costs or because they had testified on or had been affected by environmental legislation. The share of district employment in each industry is used as the independent variable. These industry variables are measured with error since they are based on *employment* and not on residence in the Congressional district. The industry variables are included to determine if the composition of industry in a district affected the vote cast on the two environmental issues. The last group of independent variables includes the Census regions as dummy variables. The definition of each variable is presented in Appendix C.

The taste or political philosophy hypothesis may be distinguished from the locational competition hypothesis by analyzing the votes on PSD policy and on auto emission policy simultaneously. The methodology will pool the votes on the two issues and introduce an issue dummy variable, Z_R. $Z_R = 1$ if the vote is on one of the five Nondegradation Amendments and zero otherwise. By interacting Z_R with each independent variable, it is possible to determine if each independent variable had a different effect on the auto emission votes than on the PSD votes. The full specification becomes

$$\ln \{P_{ij}/(1 - P_{ij})\} = \sum_l (B_l + B_l' Z_R) X_{ijl} + \sum_{m=2}^{9} (V_m + V_m' Z_R') R_{ijm}$$

$$(2)$$

$$i = 1, \ldots, 9$$
$$j = 1, 2, \ldots .$$

$P_{ij} = 1$ if the representative voted for a more stringent PSD or auto emission policy. B_l''s are the interaction coefficients for the economic, demographic, party and industry variables. If a B_l' is statistically significant, the effect of the independent variable is different on the PSD vote than the auto emission vote. Some of the B_l' coefficients will be of special interest. For example, districts with employment related to the automobile industry are more likely to oppose any strengthening of auto emission controls because of the likely effect on auto prices and output, while they could be indifferent or supportive of PSD policy.

Hence B_l' would be expected to be positive for the new car industry variable. Particular interest will be focused on the sign and significance of the interaction coefficients of the regional variables, i.e., V_m'. If the votes cast on PSD policy by representatives from the South and West were affected more by locational competition considerations, the interaction coefficients for these regions will be negative and statistically significant. If these coefficients are found to be negative and statistically significant, the results would indicate greater regional variation in support for PSD policy than for auto emissions policy. Hence, more than just a regional variation in the taste for environmental protection or in political philosophy would be needed to explain the votes on PSD and auto emission policies.

III. Results of Vote Analysis

The percent of the votes on the five Nondegradation Amendments in support of a more stringent PSD policy is shown by Census region in column 1 of Table 2. The region's percentage relative to New England's percentage is shown in column 2. Political support for PSD policy does vary across regions. The strongest support for a more stringent PSD policy has come from the New England, Middle Atlantic, Pacific, and East North Central regions, while the regions mounting the strongest opposition to PSD policy are the East South Central, West South Cen-

TABLE 2.   House Votes on Nondegradation and Auto Emission Amendments by Census Region[1]

Area	Percent of Votes in Favor of More Stringent Policy			
	Nondegradation Amendments		Auto Emission Amendments	
	Percent	Region Percent Relative to New England Percent	Percent	Region Percent Relative to New England Percent
United States	46.1	.59	36.8	.54
New England	78.8	1.00	67.7	1.00
Middle Atlantic	72.0	.91	57.8	.85
East North Central	50.7	.64	23.0	.34
West North Central	40.4	.51	30.1	.44
South Atlantic	29.9	.38	32.5	.48
East South Central	10.0	.13	12.5	.18
West South Central	11.5	.15	9.2	.14
Mountain	38.0	.48	27.1	.40
Pacific	58.3	.74	60.2	.89

[1] Votes were cast in 1976 and 1977 and include paired votes.

tral and South Atlantic. The results in Tables 1 and 2 suggest that House members from areas with relatively dirty air were staunch defenders of the relatively clean air in *other* parts of the country. Congressmen from New England and other northern states demonstrated more concern about degrading air quality in Oklahoma and South Carolina than did the Congressmen from these states.

Table 3 shows the percent of votes supporting a more stringent PSD policy by population density and by degree of urbanization in the Congressional district for the nation and for selected Census regions. The locational competition hypothesis predicts greater support for PSD policy by Congressmen representing urban constituencies. Political support for PSD policy increases with population density in and degree of urbanization of the Congressional district. These simple comparisons of the raw votes suggest that PSD policy has been supported

TABLE 3. Percent of Votes Supporting More Stringent PSD Policy by Urbanization and Population Density in Congressional District[1]

Area	Percent of Population Within Urbanized Area in Congressional District			
	0–34%	35–62%	63–98%	>98%
United States	26.6	34.0	50.8	75.3
	(110)	(109)	(104)	(112)
Middle Atlantic	51.2	45.5	67.2	92.5
	(10)	(17)	(17)	(35)
East North Central	33.9	51.2	53.3	67.0
	(23)	(19)	(19)	(25)
South Atlantic	16.5	16.0	45.8	62.5
	(20)	(18)	(19)	(8)
Pacific	35.3	48.9	56.7	67.3
	(5)	(12)	(15)	(25)

	Population Density in Congressional District		
	0–500	500–2,135	>2,135
United States	30.5	58.0	76.5
	(251)	(75)	(109)
Middle Atlantic	49.6	58.2	90.7
	(26)	(14)	(39)
East North Central	40.4	56.4	70.0
	(47)	(14)	(25)
South Atlantic	19.4	67.3	52.4
	(48)	(12)	(5)
Pacific	44.7	60.4	68.1
	(20)	(13)	(24)

[1] Numbers within parentheses represent the number of Congressional districts.

by urban constituencies and opposed by rural constituencies. The votes cast on the Nondegradation Amendments may be compared with the votes cast on the Automobile Emission Amendments where regional conflicts are expected to be less pronounced. Columns 3 and 4 of Table 2 show the percent of votes supporting a more stringent automobile emission policy and the region's percentage relative to New England's percentage. Among the faster growing regions of the country, the South Atlantic, East South Central and Pacific regions deviate more from New England on PSD policy than on automobile emission policy. This comparative assessment will be strengthened below to include the West South Central region after the effects of other economic and demographic variables are taken into account. Among the faster growing regions, only the West North Central and the Mountain regions do not deviate more from New England on the PSD issue than on the automobile emission issue. The second interesting finding in column 3 is the opposition to tighter auto emission controls by the East North Central region. This region deviates substantially more from New England on the automobile emission policy than on PSD policy. This is not surprising since the automobile and related industries are located throughout the East North Central region. This casual review of the raw votes suggests that voting position on the two environmental issues changes as the self-interest of the region changes.

A more systematic logit analysis is needed to isolate the effects of region from the effects of other independent variables. The estimated regression coefficients of the determinants of the auto emission votes are presented in column 1 of Table 4 and the associated chi-square values are in column 2. The estimated interaction coefficients measure the difference between the effect of each independent variable on the nondegradation votes and auto emission votes and are presented in column 3 (the chi-square values in column 4). By adding the estimated coefficients in columns 1 and 3, the implied coefficients for the Nondegradation Amendments can be obtained. The interaction coefficients are insignificant except for the fuel and new car industries and for four regional variables representing the South and the Pacific regions. So the slope coefficients of many of the variables are the same for the two environmental issues. Urbanized and high population density districts have supported more stringent PSD and auto emission policies. Residents of metropolitan areas are stronger supporters of environmental policy than are residents of nonmetropolitan areas. A second interesting finding is that faster growing districts (Population Growth) opposed both the Nondegradation and Automobile Emission Amendments.[5]

---

[5]Crandall (1983) also found faster growing states opposed most environmental legislation.

TABLE 4.   Combined Logit Analysis of Votes on Automobile Emission
           and Nondegradation Amendments

Variable	Automobile Emissions Estimated Coefficient (B_l or V_m) (1)	Chi Square[1] (2)	Difference Between Nondegradation and Auto Emission Estimated Coefficient (B'_l or V'_m) (3)	Chi Square[1] (4)
Intercept	−2.031	8.8**	.822	a
Population Density, 1980	$.566 \times 10^{-4}$	9.1**	$-.246 \times 10^{-4}$	a
Percent Urbanized 1980	$.752 \times 10^{-2}$	4.9**	$.362 \times 10^{-2}$	a
Population Growth Rate	−.020	12.5**	.006	a
Capital	.312	16.6**	−.027	a
Per Capita Income, 1980	$.115 \times 10^{-3}$	2.3	$-.020 \times 10^{-3}$	a
Percent Senior	−.134	8.2**	.001	a
Democrat	1.969	121.2**	.053	a
Industry Variables				
Coal	.089	12.2**	−.001	a
Fuel	−.467	19.9**	.274	5.3**
Mining	.065	a	.050	a
Paper	.109	6.8**	−.029	a
Chemical	−.082	2.7	.029	a
Petroleum	.085	a	−.019	a
Cement	.071	a	.181	2.4
Foundries	−.229	7.8**	.168	3.1
Smelters	−.330	9.8**	.065	a
Rolling Mills	−.011	a	.022	a
New Cars	−.053	7.3**	.071	9.1**
Used Cars	.088	a	−.002	a
Census Region Variables				
Middle Atlantic	−.729	5.7**	.052	a
East North Central	−1.729	29.7**	.360	a
West North Central	−1.469	17.7**	−.265	a
South Atlantic	−1.526	24.2**	−1.084	6.0**
East South Central	−1.882	19.8**	−1.343	5.1**
West South Central	−1.796	14.6**	−1.374	4.7**
Mountain	−.639	a	−1.010	2.3
Pacific	−.459	a	−1.166	6.3**
−2 Log Likelihood	3230			
Model Chi Square	1545			
Number of Votes	3512			

[a]Denotes chi square less than 2
[1]One asterisk indicates chi square significant at the 5 percent probability level and two asterisks indicate the chi square value significant at the one percent probability level.

The younger, less developed but faster growing districts opposed PSD and auto emission policy as did districts with a larger percentage of senior citizens. A disappointing finding is that faster growing districts did not oppose PSD policy more than auto emission policy. Support for a more stringent environmental policy also came from districts where dividends, rents and interest income make up a larger share of total income.[6] The results also highlight the solid support by Democrats for PSD and auto emission policies. Similar party effects have been reported before by other researchers and are discussed in more detail below.

Few of the coefficients of the industry variables are significant. Districts where the coal and paper industries were important supported both policies. Support by the coal industry is probably due to the success of the eastern and midwestern high sulfur coal industry in securing the use of scrubbers and high sulfur coal during the revision of the Clean Air Act. Opposition by the fuel industry (which includes the crude oil industry) and the new car industry was greater to the Automobile Emission Amendments than to the Nondegradation Amendments. Among the remaining manufacturing industries only the foundries and the nonferrous smelter industries opposed both the Automobile Emission and the Nondegradation Amendments.

The pattern of coefficients for the regional variables is of special interest. The coefficients of the regional variables are all negative because New England was the strongest supporter of more stringent PSD and auto emission policies and is the excluded regional variable. After taking account of the economic, demographic, party and industry effects, the Mountain and the Pacific regions supported the Automobile Emission Amendments to the *same* degree as did the New England region. The strongest opposition came from the East North Central, West South Central and the East South Central regions. There is a significant realignment of the regional coefficients for the Nondegradation Amendments. For PSD policy, the Middle Atlantic and the East North Central regions are closer to New England in their support for PSD policy. The interaction coefficients are all negative for the six remaining and faster growing regions of the country, and four of these coefficients are significantly different from zero. There is greater regional variation in the support for Nondegradation Amendments than for the Automobile Emission Amendments. Support for PSD policy is more

---

[6]This finding indicates the PSD policy received more support in districts where capital's share of income is high. Owners of property in declining areas would presumably favor PSD policy. On the other hand, owners of physical capital would not prefer restrictions on the location of the capital.

concentrated in the northern regions of the country. The younger and less developed regions of the country offered more active opposition to the Nondegradation Amendments than to the Automobile Emission Amendments. This changing pattern of the regional coefficients lends some support to the locational competition hypothesis. Locational competition considerations help explain why the southern and western regions deviated more from New England on PSD policy than they did on auto emission policy.

Other results also suggest that the pattern of regional coefficients on the two environmental issues reflects the effects of self-interest and not tastes. As noted above, the regional coefficients of the Pacific and the Mountain regions on the auto emission issue are close to the regional coefficient for New England. California has a state auto emission policy that is more stringent than the federal policy. A more stringent federal auto emission policy would place California at less of a competitive disadvantage and would explain why the California delegation supported a more stringent federal auto emission policy. The support for a more stringent auto emission policy by the Mountain region is less easily explained even though several cities in this region have severe auto emission problems, e.g., Denver. Still, the voting position of the Mountain region appears to be a departure from the implications of the locational competition hypothesis.[7]

Still other results indicate voting position changes from one environmental issue to another as the perceived net benefits change. This is well illustrated by the votes cast in districts with a large share of district employment connected with the automobile industry (new car). Not surprisingly, these districts strongly opposed the Automobile Emission Amendments and supported or were neutral on the Nondegradation Amendments. Support for a less stringent auto emission policy after a neutral stance on PSD policy indicates voting position changes as the interests of the district change. Another result is consistent with the self-interest hypothesis. Rural and less densely populated districts opposed a tightening of auto emission standards. Since average air quality in rural areas is superior to that in urban areas, the reluctance of rural residents to support more stringent emission controls and to pay higher automobile prices so that the lower air quality in central cities can be improved is understandable. These different results all suggest that more is at work here than simply regional differences in the taste for environmental protection.

The differences between the regional coefficients on the two envi-

---

[7]A referee pointed out tourism and not economic development may be more important throughout the Mountain region.

ronmental issues suggest that votes change when regional self-interest changes. However, the pattern of regional coefficients for environmental legislation may not be that unusual. A similar pattern is often found when the issue is economic or regulatory policy. In recent times the North has been more supportive of redistribution and regulatory policies than the South and West. While the regional coefficients differ across environmental issues, the significance of these differences would diminish if the pattern of regional coefficients for the environmental issues was found to be similar to the pattern of regional coefficients on economic and regulatory issues. Such a similarity could imply the votes on all issues, environmental or other, were determined more by a liberal-conservative division across regions. A reasonable inference would be that political philosophy, and not locational competition, was the main cause for the variation in regional coefficients.

It would be both useful and informative to determine if the variance of the regional coefficients on PSD policy is greater than on the representative economic issue. Peltzman (1983) has found systematic regional differences in support for legislation on economic issues. His results will be used as a standard of comparison. Peltzman was interested in quantifying the regional departure from the support given by northern Democrats (liberal position). He adopted the following methodology. He let p equal one if a House member voted the same way as the majority of northern Democrats did on an economic issue and zero otherwise. Peltzman estimated the following linear regressions:

$$p - \bar{p} = \sum_i B_i R_i \tag{3}$$

and

$$p - \bar{p} = \sum_i B_i R_i + a(P - \bar{P}) \tag{3a}$$

where $\bar{p}$ is the mean of p, R_i denotes a dummy variable for region i, P equals one if the vote is cast by a Democrat and zero otherwise and $\bar{P}$ is the mean of P. Equation (3) only includes region effects while equation (3a) adds a party effect to determine if all of the votes in a region were more or less liberal than the votes cast by all northern Democrats. A northern Democrat was defined broadly by Peltzman and included all Democrats outside of the South Atlantic (excluding Delaware and Maryland), East South and West South Central regions.

Because the primary interest here is in comparing the regional coefficients on environmental issues in the nineteen seventies with those on economic issues, only the results reported by Peltzman on

TABLE 5.   Average of Regional Coefficients on Economic Issues,
PSD Policy and Automobile Emission Policy

	Economic Issues		Nondegradation Amendments		Auto Emission Amendments	
	Without Party (1)	With Party (2)	Without Party (3)	With Party (4)	Without Party (5)	With Party (6)
New England	.213	.183	.308	.327	.309	.322
Middle Atlantic	.132	.127	.226	.224	.188	.185
East North Central	−.024	.053	.047	.086	−.122	−.086
West North Central	−.058	−.007	−.067	.174	−.076	−.040
South Atlantic	−.129	−.197	−.137	−.158	−.040	−.060
East South Central	−.136	−.130	−.308	−.294	−.220	−.206
West South Central	−.100	−.210	−.304	−.359	−.257	−.308
Mountain	−.157	−.077	−.088	−.049	−.090	−.053
Pacific	.088	.070	.077	.067	.204	.195
Standard Deviation of Regional Coefficients	.133	.141	.214	.235	.199	.203

Source: Regional Coefficients on economic issues were kindly supplied by Sam Peltzman.

House votes cast in 1970, 1976 and 1980 are relevant and are reproduced here. Peltzman estimated the coefficients of (3) and (3a) for *each*
bill or amendment. The average of the estimated regional coefficients
(B_i) on economic issues is reported in columns 1 and 2 of Table 5.
These averages of regression coefficients show just how much more or
less liberal each region is compared to the voting position of northern
Democrats. For example, all House members from New England were
about 21 (column 1) percent more liberal compared to northern Democrats when party effects are excluded and 18 percent more liberal when
party effects are included (column 2). In contrast all representatives
from the West South Central region were 30 percent less liberal (compared to northern Democrats) on economic issues.

The average regional coefficients on the portfolio of economic
issues serve as a benchmark. The Peltzman procedure was repeated for
each of the five Nondegradation Amendments and each of the four Automobile Emission Amendments. If the regional coefficients reported
by Peltzman reflect the typical liberal-conservative division on economic issues, and if the votes on environmental issues are determined
primarily by the same liberal-conservative philosophical division, then
the regional coefficients for the five Nondegradation Amendments and
the four Automobile Emission Amendments will be similar to the re-

gional coefficients reported by Peltzman.[8] If the locational competition considerations played a more important role in determining the votes on the environmental issues, there should be even greater differences between the regional coefficients on the environmental issues. Northern regions should be even more liberal and southern and western regions should be even more conservative on environmental issues.

The (average) regional coefficients for the Nondegradation Amendments are shown in columns 3 and 4 and for the Automobile Emission Amendments in columns 5 and 6 of Table 5. New England and the Middle Atlantic are more liberal on the environmental issues than on the economic issues while the East South and West South Central regions are even less liberal on the environmental issues than on the economic issues. Compared to economic issues, the East North Central region appears more liberal on PSD policy and more conservative (than northern Democrats) on auto emission policy. Compared to economic issues, the Mountain region appears more conservative on economic issues than on environmental issues. The Pacific region is much more liberal on auto emission policy and not much different on PSD policy compared to economic issues.

These comparisons do suggest that the votes on environmental issues cannot be explained solely by reference to a liberal-conservative division across regions. There appear to be greater differences among regions on environmental issues than on economic issues. This is reflected in the larger standard deviation of the regional coefficients (last line of Table 5) for the Nondegradation Amendments and the Automobile Emission Amendments than for the economic issues. These findings do suggest that locational competition considerations play a more important role in determining the votes on environmental issues than on economic issues. An important implication is that political or ideological differences across regions are not capable of explaining the votes cast on environmental issues.[9]

---

[8] Ideally, one would like to control for variables other than region and party, as is done in Table 4. However, the purpose of Peltzman's study was to show long run changes in a region's support for liberal legislation. Data were unavailable in earlier decades for many of the other variables, so Peltzman did not include other variables.

[9] Suppose northerners are more liberal on PSD votes than on economic votes, while southerners and westerners are more conservative on PSD votes than on economic votes. If the regional coefficients on PSD policy are regressed on the regional coefficients on economic issues, they should yield a slope coefficient greater than one. The estimated slope of this regression was 1.44, which is significantly different from one at the 14 percent probability level (when party effects are included), and was 1.54 (when party effects were excluded) which is significantly different from one at the 6 percent probability level. Hence, the regression coefficients do appear to vary more across regions for PSD policy than for economic issues.

IV. The Importance of Political Party

Table 4 shows Democrats supported PSD policy in relatively greater numbers than did Republicans. A natural question to ask is whether the party variable is capturing the effect of party or whether it is merely a proxy for other effects, e.g., ideological preference for environmental regulation or the effects of region. This type of cross-sectional vote analysis just does not clearly reveal what the party variable stands for. These ambiguities over interpretation led to a different and perhaps superior test of the effect of party. The turnover of House membership can be exploited to isolate the effect of party while holding location constant.

Recall that the votes on the Nondegradation Amendments were cast in 1976 and in 1977. In some districts the incumbent was defeated in the elections in the fall of 1976 and replaced in 1977 by a freshman from the other party. The effect of party can be identified by comparing the votes cast in 1976 by the defeated incumbents with those cast in 1977 by freshmen representatives. If the votes on PSD policy were determined solely by locational competition considerations, a change in party of representatives would have no effect on the vote cast. Democrats and Republicans would be swayed by the same locational considerations. On the other hand, each party could represent the interests of a different constituency and not the interest of the median voter. If Democrats represent different constituencies than do Republicans, and if these constituencies differ on PSD policy, turnover of representatives will change the voting position on PSD policy. Peltzman (1984) has found Democrats represent different constituencies than do Republicans. If the constituency interests within a Congressional district are disparate, the turnover of representative will be signaled by a change in vote on PSD policy.

Table 6 shows the vote in 1976 and 1977 for districts where the incumbent was reelected and for districts where the party of the representative changed. The top panel shows the percentage of votes for PSD policy in districts with a Democrat in both 1976 and 1977 (column 4) and in districts with a Democrat in 1976 and a Republican in 1977 (column 8). The bottom panel reports comparable percentages in districts with a Republican representative in 1976. In districts with a Democrat in both 1976 and 1977, 59.1 percent of votes cast in 1976 favored a stricter PSD policy and 55.0 percent did in 1977. In districts where the Democratic incumbent was defeated in 1977, 44.8 percent of votes cast by Democrats in 1976 favored a stricter PSD policy. Defeated Democrats may have represented less liberal constituencies than did reelected Democrats and were less supportive of a stricter PSD policy in 1976. They were replaced by Republicans whose sup-

TABLE 6. Change in Party of Representative and Vote on PSD Policy

Party in 1976	Year of Vote	Same Party Holds Seat in 1977				Other Party Holds Seat in 1977			
		Party of Rep. (1)	R (2)	N (3)	P (4)	Party of Rep. (5)	R (6)	N (7)	P (8)
Democrat	1976	Democrat	406	281	59.1%	Democrat	13	16	44.8%
	1977	Democrat	293	240	55.0%	Republican	3	24	11.1%
Republican	1976	Republican	101	230	30.5%	Republican	10	13	43.8%
	1977	Republican	37	207	15.2%	Democrat	15	9	62.5%

R = Total votes in favor of more stringent PSD policy.
N = Total votes against more stringent PSD policy.
P = Percent of total votes favoring more stringent PSD policy.

port for a stricter PSD policy dropped to just 11.1 percent. The defeated Democrats cast decidedly different votes in 1976 than did their Republican replacements in 1977. In 1977 Republican freshmen voted just like reelected Republicans. Where Republicans were replaced by Democrats, the freshman Democrats were more supportive of PSD policy than the defeated Republicans and were, if anything, even more supportive of PSD policy than were the reelected Democrats.

This alternative way of looking at the effects of party suggests that Democrats and Republicans represent different constituencies. As the size of these different constituencies changes, party turnover occurs and voting position changes. The Democratic and Republican *newcomers* voted differently than the defeated incumbents did in the previous year and more closely matched the position of their respective parties in 1977. An implication of these results is that House Democrats in districts that would have lost factors in the absence of PSD policy represent the political interests of factors with location specific investments, while Republicans represent the interests of factors with more general investments.

As mentioned above, the most likely reason for the change in voting position is that parties represent different constituencies and not the median vote. However, two other explanations should also be considered. Freshmen have little personal brand name capital and could be more dependent on the brand name of the party and on campaign funds received from the party. They support the party position as a lower cost way of increasing their own political capital with the voters. This hypothesis could be tested by showing that deviations from party position increase with tenure and that party share of a Congressman's total campaign funds decreases with tenure. It is also possible defeated House members did not well represent the interests of voters in their districts and were replaced. It is interesting that defeated incumbents were Democrats that were less supportive of PSD policy in 1976 than were reelected Democrats, or they were Republicans that were more supportive of PSD policy in 1976 than were reelected Republicans. If either of these two explanations has merit, it implies the results of the turnover test overestimate the effects of party.

V. Pressure Groups, Abatement Costs and Support for PSD Policy

The vote analysis relied on the economic, demographic, industry and party characteristics, and regional location of the district to explain the vote cast by its representative on PSD policy. This specification is lacking in some respects because the voting position is not directly related to measures of direct benefits and costs of PSD policy. Direct measures of the benefits and costs are not easily gathered and are not available by Congressional district. This limitation can be partly remedied if the state is used as the unit of measurement. State data are available for membership in environmental organizations, per unit pollution abatement costs, and state air quality. This section tries to tie the votes cast on the Nondegradation Amendments more closely to the perceived benefits received and costs incurred from a more stringent PSD policy. A second and no less important objective is to show that per unit pollution abatement costs were higher in the faster growing parts of the country than in the developed regions, even though air quality was on average superior in the faster growing parts of the country. Such a finding is not only surprising but would be difficult to reconcile with the externalities hypothesis.

The analysis begins by relating the vote on PSD policy to the relative size of political pressure groups that support a more stringent environmental policy, the per unit state pollution abatement cost, and average air quality in the state. If voting position is not solely determined by locational considerations, then support for PSD policy also should be directly related to the importance of political pressure groups supporting a more stringent environmental policy. Support will also be related to the cost of compliance with environmental regulation. States that expected a larger increase in per unit pollution abatement costs under PSD policy would register greater opposition.[10] Indeed, an im-

---

[10] Under the locational competition hypothesis, political support for PSD policy will be inversely related to the *increase* in per unit pollution abatement costs before and after the federal PSD program is introduced and to state air quality. Let $V = \log P/(1 - P)$, the log of the odds ratio. Under the locational competition hypothesis, V will be directly related to the change in per unit pollution abatement costs caused by the program, $C_{post} - C_{pre}$ and nonattainment status, N, (a proxy for air quality)

$$V = \alpha + \beta(C_{post} - C_{pre}) + \gamma N \quad \text{where } \beta < 0 \text{ and } \gamma > 0. \tag{4}$$

However, data are unavailable for C_{pre}. The actual regression run is

$$V = a + bC_{post} + CN. \tag{4a}$$

Because C_{pre} is left out, the estimated coefficients of (4a) will be biased. In particular the expectation of b and C equal $E(b) = \beta + W_1(-\beta) = \beta(1 - W_1)$ and $E(C) = \gamma + W_2(-\beta)$ where W_1 and W_2 are coefficients of the regression of the left out variable, C_{pre}, on C_{post} and N.

$$C_{pre} = W_0 + W_1 C_{post} + W_2 N \tag{4b}$$

Without knowledge of the sign and magnitude of W_1, it is impossible to tell whether the estimated value of b will be biased and in which direction. Several special cases are

plication of the locational competition hypothesis is that PSD policy will raise per unit compliance cost more in the clean air areas than in dirty air areas. Under the locational competition hypothesis, support for PSD policy should be greater in states with lower air quality. States with lower air quality would have a larger demand for improved air quality, and they would support a federal environmental policy that was expected to increase per unit compliance costs more in clean air areas than in dirty air areas.

Membership in environmental groups per 1,000 residents of a state is used to proxy the relative importance of political pressure groups in a state supporting more stringent federal environmental policies. Some members join these organizations to acquire useful information about outdoor activities and not with any expectation or aspiration of influencing legislation. Others join in part to support environmental policies, including PSD policy, that impede the development of rural and scenic areas *within* the state and thereby preserve scenic, hunting, and fishing areas. Still others join because of a deep concern for the preservation of environmental conditions throughout the country for reasons other than narrow rent-seeking. While these different motivations are present, this analysis assumes that support for PSD policy does increase with increases in membership rates. Membership data have been kindly supplied by the National Wildlife Federation, National Audubon Society, the Sierra Club and the Wilderness Society.[11] This is not a complete canvass or even a random sample of such organizations. The National Wildlife Federation is one of the largest organiza-

---

of interest. Suppose the federal environmental protection policy merely raised each state's per unit abatement costs by the same amount so that $W_0 < 0$, and $W_1 = 1$. Then the expected value of b is zero. So, the log of the odds ratio would not be related to C_{post} in (4a) even though $\beta < 0$. On the other hand, suppose the federal regulatory program raised the per unit abatement cost in states with higher per unit costs before regulation by more than in states with lower per unit costs before regulation. Then, $W_0 < 0$ and $0 < W_1 < 1$. The expected value of b will be biased toward zero but will still be less than zero. If the coefficient of C_{post} turns out to be negative and significant in (4a) it can be inferred the true coefficient, β, is still more negative than the estimated coefficient. In the actual regressions run PACVA, the per unit pollution abatement costs, is used as a measure of C_{post}. A significant negative coefficient for PACVA implies the regulatory program increased the coefficient of variation in state per unit abatement costs (since $0 < W_1 < 1$). If $W_1 > 1$, the expected value of b is positive and the log of the odds ratio would be directly related to PACVA. The regression results reject this case.

[11] The Wildlife Federation supplied membership data for 1983, while the other organizations supplied membership data for 1976. The membership data were adjusted for resident population in 1976 except for membership data supplied by the Wildlife Federation which was adjusted for resident population in 1982 (latest available information).

TABLE 7.   Membership in Environmental Organizations and Per Unit
            Pollution Abatement Costs (1974–1977)

	Membership in Environmental Organizations Per 1000 Residents (1)	Pollution Abatement Operating Costs Per $1,000 of Value Added (2)	Air Pollution Abatement Operating Costs Per $1000 of Value Added (3)
United States	5.75	8.32 (45)[2]	3.40 (45)[2]
New England	7.62	4.18 (6)	1.16 (6)
Middle Atlantic	5.81	7.81 (3)	3.41 (3)
East North Central	5.72	7.42 (5)	2.85 (5)
West North Central	6.20	5.36 (6)	1.97 (6)
South Atlantic	4.71	9.12 (8)	3.18 (8)
East South Central	2.65	9.74 (4)	3.93 (4)
West South Central	3.24	15.09 (4)	6.30 (4)
Mountain	7.23	10.66 (6)	7.12 (6)
Pacific	8.92	8.33 (3)	3.85 (3)

[1] In each year the weighted average ratio was calculated for each region. A simple yearly average of these ratios is reported in this table.

[2] Number of states used to calculate mean in parentheses. Deleted states were Alaska, Hawaii, New Mexico, South Dakota and Wyoming.

Source: Membership data supplied by organizations. Cost data from U.S. Bureau of Census, *Pollution Abatement Costs and Expenditures*, Current Industrial Reports, MA-200 (74–77)

tions and may be more representative of state interest in environmental questions. The Sierra Club's strength lies mostly in the West. Total members in these four organizations per 1,000 residents for each of the Census regions is shown in column 1 of Table 7. These membership figures show the highest membership rates in the Pacific, New England and the Mountain regions. The three regions with the lowest membership rates are East South Central, West South Central, and the South Atlantic regions.[12]

Opposition to PSD policy will be greater in states that expect to incur larger increases in per unit pollution abatement costs because of PSD policy. Gross pollution abatement costs incurred by manufacturing plants per $1,000 of value added (PACVA) are available by state.[13]

[12] Membership rates were found to increase with per capita income and to decline with the degree of urbanization of state population and state growth rate. The effects of region and party were small.

[13] The Bureau of Census has sampled manufacturing establishments since 1973 and collected annual pollution abatement costs and capital expenditures for air, water and solid waste. Only manufacturing plants are sampled. The respondents are asked to estimate gross pollution abatement annual costs (payments to government for water and solid waste, depreciation on equipment, labor, equipment leases and materials

Column 2 of Table 7 shows the annual average of PACVA for the United States and for each region. *Air* pollution abatement costs per $1,000 of value added are shown in column 3. A surprising and in some ways amazing finding is that the industrial and more developed regions of the country incurred *lower* pollution abatement costs per $1,000 of value added between 1974 and 1977 than did the more rapidly growing areas. New England and the East and West North Central regions are well below average, and the Middle Atlantic region is slightly below average, while the East and West South Central and Mountain regions are well above average. If the purpose of regulating manufacturing plants and other point sources is to improve air quality and public health in those states with more severe air quality problems, then one would have expected higher per unit compliance expenditures by plants located in the North, than in the South.[14]

Two measures serve as imperfect proxies for state air quality. The first is the simple average of the nonattainment percentage across all air quality control regions in the state in 1976. The EPA reported the 1976 attainment status in each air quality control region for five pollutants—suspended particulates, sulfur dioxide, carbon monoxide, oxidants and nitrogen dioxide. A nonattainment percentage was calculated for each state by weighting each pollutant and each air quality control region in the state equally.[15] Another imperfect measure of air quality is the total tons of pollutants (particulates, sulfur dioxide, nitrates, hydrocarbons and carbon monoxide) per acre.[16] The share of total tons of pollutants made up of particulates and sulfur dioxide is used to measure the relative importance of industrial pollutants.

---

purchased). These data are reported by type, industry, region, state and for selected SMSA's and these data serve as the raw material of the analyses of pollution abatement costs.

[14] A possible explanation is that there are economies of scale in pollution abatement. If plants located in the North are larger, they will have lower per unit abatement costs. However, the variance in state abatement costs per unit of output is explained better by the variance in state tons of pollutants removed per unit of output than by the variance in abatement costs per ton of pollutant removed. Hence, states differ more in the amount of pollutant removed per unit of output than in the per ton cost of removing a pollutant. There is little evidence of economies of scale in pollution abatement. The higher per unit pollution abatement cost in the South and West is because tons of pollutants removed per unit of output is higher in these regions and not because the cost per ton removed is higher.

[15] Every violation of an applicable National Ambient Air Quality Standard was counted in the calculation of nonattainment status even though no revisions of a State Implementation Plan was called for.

[16] Tons of emissions in 1972 by type of pollutant are reported in J. Golden, R. Quellette, S. Saari and P. Cheremisinoff (1979).

TABLE 8.   Gains and Losses and Political Support for PSD Policy[a]

Variable	Estimated Coefficients		
	(1)	(2)	(3)
Constant	−3.047	−3.046	−2.027
	[98.2]	[141.9]	[47.2]
Membership Rate in Environmental Organizations	.236	.235	.285
	[67.6]	[69.4]	[95.8]
State Pollution Abatement Costs Per $1,000 of Value Added	−27.04		−46.45
	[3.1]		[9.9]
State Air Pollution Abatement Costs Per $1,000 of Value Added		−72.40	
		[7.6]	
State Nonattainment Percentage	.046	.047	
	[114.6]	[125.2]	
Tons of State Emissions Per Acre			.0030
			[109.5]
Particulates and Sulfur Emissions as Share of Total Emissions			−1.027
			[4.0]
−2 Log L	2,182	2,177	2,173
Model Chi Square	357.4	362.2	366.3
N	1,838	1,838	1,838

[a]Chi square value in brackets

These independent variables are used to determine if state support for the Nondegradation Amendments is directly related to the state membership rate in environmental organizations and inversely related to PACVA and to state air quality. Columns 1–3 of Table 8 display the regression results for the state logit analysis. States with higher membership rates in environmental organizations supported a more stringent PSD policy. If membership rate is an exogenous variable, these results indicate the environmental organizations reflect the strength of an effective political pressure group.[17] After accounting for the effects of the political strength of environmental groups, there is evidence that the votes were influenced by locational competition con-

[17] However, membership rates may not be exogenous. They tend to be higher in states with lower air quality and in states with lower per unit pollution abatement costs. The simple correlation between membership rate and nonattainment percentage is .35, between membership rate and PACVA is −.31, and between membership rate and air PACVA is −.20. So the relative size of environmental organizations appears to be larger in states with lower air quality and states that did not incur relatively high per unit pollution abatement costs.

siderations. States with higher nonattainment percentages (lower air quality) were stronger supporters of the Nondegradation Amendments. The state *air* pollution abatement costs per $1,000 of value added is inversely related to support for PSD policy and explains more of the vote on PSD policy than does *total* pollution abatement costs per $1,000 of value added. In column 3 the nonattainment proxy for air quality is replaced by two other measures of air quality, total tons of emissions (particulate, sulfur dioxide, nitrates, hydrocarbons and carbon monoxide) per mile and particulates and sulfur emissions as a share of total emissions. States with more tons of emissions per square mile supported a stricter PSD policy. An unexpected result is that support for PSD policy decreases as the share of particulates and sulfur emissions increases. This contradictory finding is probably due to the high share of particulate and sulfur emissions in selected states in the South and the West, *e.g.*, Kentucky, Nevada and Arizona.[18] These same independent variables were also used to explain the votes on the Automobile Emission Amendments, and they explained less of the variation of votes cast on Automobile Emission Amendments than on the Nondegradation Amendments. Since the effects of location are expected to play a more important role on PSD policy than on auto emission policy, this finding indicates the air quality and cost variables, for all their admitted imperfections, are nevertheless proxies for the likely gains and costs of a more stringent PSD policy.

Support for PSD policy in states with relatively more members in environmental organizations indicates the votes were not determined

[18]The particulate and sulfur share variable could be capturing the effect of location as well as the effect of type of pollutant. Suppose that sulfur and particulate share is higher in some southern and western states. The simple correlation between membership rate and the share of particulate and sulfur emissions is −.31. Since membership rate is lower in the southern states, this indicates particulate and sulfur share is typically higher in the South. The coefficient of the share variable is capturing the effect of location and the effect of pollutant type on the probability of voting for the Nondegradation Amendments. The higher the share of particulants and sulfur emission is, the higher the probability is of supporting the Nondegradation Amendments. However, the effect of location works in the opposite direction, and the results in Table 8 indicate the net effect is negative. There is some support for this explanation. The same variables were also used to explain the votes on the Automobile Emission Amendments. The coefficient of the share variable in automobile emission regression (not presented) is −3.908 compared to −1.027 in the PSD regression, or roughly four times larger in absolute value. The higher the share of particulate and sulfur emissions is, the lower is the share of emissions due to automobile emissions, and the lower the probability is of voting for a more stringent automobile emissions policy. In the automobile emission regressions the effects of location and pollutant type work in the same direction and produce a coefficient for the share variable that is even more negative than the comparable coefficient in the PSD regression.

solely by locational considerations. Even so, locational considerations continue to play a role. Opposition of southern and western states to PSD policy is partly grounded on the higher per unit pollution abatement costs these areas incurred between 1974 and 1977 under federal environmental policy. Undoubtedly, these regions did not expect to fare better if a more stringent PSD policy was adopted. Similarly, the support for PSD policy by states with lower air quality is consistent with the locational competition hypothesis. The urban residents in these states would have been even more interested in local environmental improvement and hence would have favored a federal PSD policy that reduced the flight of factors while local air quality was improved.

The regression results show support for PSD was lower in states that incurred higher per unit pollution abatement costs. This finding raises the question of whether state per unit abatement costs under the federal environmental program was directly related to the growth rate of the state before the federal environmental program began. If so, it would be difficult not to conclude that federal environmental policy has penalized the faster growing states. Under the locational competition hypothesis, per unit abatement costs should increase more in the less developed areas of the country under the federal environmental program. Unfortunately, this implication cannot be tested because state abatement cost data are unavailable for before 1973. Table 7 shows per unit pollution abatement costs were higher in less developed than in developed regions between 1974 and 1977. It is impossible to tell if this regional pattern is merely a continuation, or is substantially different from the regional pattern prior to environmental regulation.

Because time series comparisons cannot be made, the analysis focuses on explaining state differences in per unit abatement costs. The major determinants of the logarithm of state per unit pollution abatement costs are assumed to be (1) the relative importance of industries with more serious emission or water discharge problems, (2) the relative use of dirty fuels, (3) the relative use of water in the production process, and (4) the growth of manufacturing value added prior to the federal environmental regulation program. The growth rate in state manufacturing during the pre-regulatory period, 1963–1972, is expected to raise per unit state abatement costs under the federal program if faster growing states are penalized under the federal regulatory program.

The definitions of the variables and the regression results are presented in Table 9. Only the regional dummy variables are included in the first regression. Column 1 shows that the South, the Mountain, and the Pacific regions had higher pollution abatement costs relative to New England. The effects of industry composition, fuel and water use, and growth rate are included in column 3. Per unit costs are higher in states where the chemical, petroleum and primary metals industries are relatively more important. The more intense use of water relative to output raises per unit costs, but the more intense use of dirty fuels does not have a statistically significant effect on per unit abatement costs. Perhaps, the most interesting result is that states with higher growth rates between 1963 and 1972 incurred higher per unit abatement costs between 1974 and 1977. To check on the validity of this interesting finding, the regression was rerun after the state growth rate between 1963 and 1972 was replaced by the state growth rate between 1972 and 1977. The state growth rate between 1972 and 1977 proved not to be a statistically significant determinant of per unit abatement costs. Per unit state abatement costs between 1974 and 1977 depend on how fast the state was growing before the federal program began and not on the state growth rate between 1972 and 1977. This finding combined with the earlier finding that faster growing states opposed PSD policy suggest that per unit abatement costs have probably increased more rapidly under the federal regulatory program in the faster growing regions than in the rest of the country.

VI. Conclusions

The self-interest hypothesis gives a more complete understanding of why northern-urban constituencies are for, and southern, western and rural constituencies against, PSD policy. Other hypotheses that relate the votes on PSD policy to party or political philosophy or to tastes for environmental protection are lacking in one or another dimension and are unable to explain the interesting and subtle variations in votes across environmental issues or between environmental and economic issues. These findings suggest that self-interest has played a prominent role even in environmental legislation, a prime example of social legislation.

There is a temptation to misinterpret the locational competition hypothesis as simply a contrived opportunity to impose costs on less developed regions by the developed regions of the country. Such an interpretation is misguided since it ignores the important role played by northern residents demanding improved environmental conditions. The source of strength of the environmental movement is this constituency and not merely the membership in environmental organizations. PSD policy is the product of this increase in demand for improved environmental conditions and the desire to reduce the potential loss in rents caused by compliance with environmental regulations.

The locational competition hypothesis, while unquestionably useful in understanding PSD policy, has its limitations as well. It has difficulty explaining the relatively strong support for PSD policy by House members from the Mountain region. The importance of party and the

TABLE 9. Determinants of the Logarithm of Pollution Abatement Costs
Per $1,000 of Value Added (Weighted Regression)

Independent Variable	Regression Coefficient (1)	t (2)	Regression Coefficient (3)	t (4)
Constant	−5.51	28.5	−4.96	8.6
Paper			1.03	.9
Chemical			3.99	3.6
Petroleum			14.69	2.5
Primary Metal			2.37	1.9
Dirty Fuel			.03	.2
Water Use			.25	4.2
Value Added Growth			.41	3.0
Regional Dummies				
Middle Atlantic	.59	2.6	.33	3.0
East North Central	.60	2.8	.27	2.5
West North Central	.27	1.0	.18	1.3
South Atlantic	.66	2.8	.18	1.3
East South Central	.87	3.2	.24	1.4
West South Central	1.26	5.0	−.08	.3
Mountain	.90	2.4	.53	2.4
Pacific	.70	2.9	.63	5.0
R^2	.471		.916	
Mean Square Error	1141		226	

Definition of Variable

I. Dependent Variables:
  1. Log of mean of state pollution abatement costs per $1,000 of value added from 1974–77.

II. Independent Variables:
  1. Composition of Industry in State:
     a) Paper: Mean share of total state manufacturing employ-
     ment in S.I.C. 26, Paper and Allied Products, 1974–77.
     b) Chemical: Mean share of total state manufacturing employ-
     ment in S.I.C. 28, Chemicals and Allied Products, 1974–77.
     c) Petroleum: Mean share of total state manufacturing employ-
     ment in S.I.C. 29, Petroleum and Coal Products, 1974–77.
     d) Primary Metal: Mean share of total state manufacturing employ-
     ment in S.I.C. 33, Primary Metal Industries, 1974–77.
  2. Use of Dirty Fuel: Log of total BTUs consumed in state manufactur-
     ing less BTUs from natural gas, hydroelectric and purchased electricity per million dollars of value added, 1974–77.

TABLE 9.   *(continued)*

	Definition of Variable
3. Water Use:	Log of millions of gallons of water intake in state manufacturing per million of value added, 1972–77.
4. Value Added Growth:	Proportionate growth rate of value added in manufacturing, 1963–72.
5. Regional Dummy:	Nine Census regional dummy variables.

Sources: U.S. Bureau of Census Pollution Abatement Cost and Expenditure, Current Industrial Reports MA-200.

U.S. Bureau of Census, Census of Manufactures, 1963, 1972, 1977.

U.S. Bureau of Census, Annual Survey of Manufactures 1970–80, (non-Census years)

U.S. Bureau of Census, County Business Patterns, 1974–77.

U.S. Energy Information Agency, State Energy Data Report, 1981.

effect of membership rates in environmental organizations show that a more complete understanding of the votes cast on PSD policy requires a mutual consideration of the locational competition hypothesis and other hypotheses. While the competition among locations was a major determinant of the vote on PSD policy, it was not the only determinant. The basic point is that the self-interest hypothesis need not take a back seat to hypotheses based on other motives.

The underlying self-interest of regions changes at a glacial pace. The distribution of political power among regions also changes slowly. Hence, drastic or major changes in PSD policy appear unlikely. Current PSD policy reflects the current distribution of political power among regions and locations. Over the longer run, the continued shift of the population to the South and the West and out of northern cities into smaller cities and towns implies the political support for PSD policy, new performance standards, and other restrictions on factor mobility will gradually decline. It would be ironical but not unexpected if the growing political strength of the South and West not only weakened PSD policy but raised demands for a stricter enforcement of the minimum environmental standards in the nonattainment areas of the North.

Appendix A

Summary of 1976 Nondegradation Amendments*

A. House Amendments
   1. Amendments to Weaken the Nondegradation Section of House Bill:
      a. Chappell (D, Florida) Amendment to delete from the bill provisions to require protection of pristine air and direct the National

Commission on Air Quality to conduct a one-year study of the issue. Rejected 156–199 (R 77–38; ND 20–142; SD 59–19) [530].
b. Carter (R, Kentucky) Amendment to set less stringent overall pollution limits in clean air areas covered by the nondegradation provisions. Rejected 100–183 (R 53–481; ND 5–116; SD 42–19) [538].
2. Amendment to Strengthen the Nondegradation Section of the House Bill:
a. Maquire (D, New Jersey) Amendment to delete Class III nondegradation category from the bill, thus requiring more stringent protection of air in areas where it had not deteriorated to the minimum air quality levels required by national standards. Rejected 107–247 (R 18–98; ND 79–80; SD 10–69) [528].

*Number in square brackets represents number assigned by the Congressional Quarterly.

Appendix B

Summary of 1977 Nondegradation Amendments*

A. House Amendments
1. Amendments to Weaken the Nondegradation Section of the House Bill:
a. McKay (D, Utah) Amendment (substitute) for the Breaux (D, Louisiana) Amendment to allow sulfur dioxide pollution to exceed permissible levels for 18 days of the year in high terrain Class II areas. Rejected 170–237 (R 17–115; ND 132–56; SD 21–66) [262].
b. Breaux (D, Louisiana) Amendment to allow state governors to permit Class I and Class II areas to exceed pollution levels for 18 days in a year. Adopted 237–172 (R 112–23; ND 56–131; SD 69–18) [263].

*Number in square brackets represents number assigned by Congressional Quarterly.

Appendix C

Definition of Variables in Table 4*

1. Population Density, 1980 = population per square mile in 1980.
2. Percent Urbanized, 1980 = Percent of population of district living in urbanized areas in 1980.
3. Population Growth Rate = Percentage change in population, 1970–1980 for boundaries in effect from 1973–1982.
4. Capital = Percent of aggregate household income received from interest, dividends and net rental income in 1979.
5. Per Capita Income, 1980 = Per capita income in 1979.

6. Percent Senior = Percent of population aged 65 or more in 1980.
7. Democrat = Dummy variable equal to one if vote was cast by Democrat.
8. Coal = Percent of district employment in anthracite mining [111] and bituminous coal mining [112].
9. Fuel = Percent of district employment in crude petroleum and natural gas [131], natural gas liquids [132] and oil and gas field services [138].
10. Mine = Percent of district employment in iron ores [101], copper ores [102], lead and zinc ores [103], gold and silver ores [104], bauxite [105], ferroalloy ores [106], metal mining services [108], miscellaneous metal ores [109], dimension stone [141], crushed stone [142], sand and gravel [144], chemical minerals [147], non-metallic minerals [148], and miscellaneous non-metallic minerals [149].
11. Paper = Percent of district employment in pulp mills [261], paper mills except building paper [262], paperboard mills [263].
12. Chemicals = Percent of district employment in industrial inorganic [281], industrial organic [286], agricultural chemicals [287], and miscellaneous chemical [289].
13. Petroleum = Percent of district employment in petroleum refining [291].
14. Cement = Percent of district employment in cement [324], concrete, gypsum and plaster [327], and miscellaneous non-metallic mineral [329].
15. Foundries = Percent of district employment in iron and steel foundries [332] and non-ferrous foundries [336].
16. Smelters = Percent of district employment in primary non-ferrous metals [333].
17. Rolling Mills = Percent of district employment in blast furnaces and basic steel [331] and non-ferrous rolling [335].
18. New Car = Percent of district employment in motor vehicles and equipment [371] and new and used car dealers [551].
19. Used Car = Percent of district employment in auto and home supply retail stores [553] and automobile repair shops [753].

*Numbers in square brackets are S.I.C. industry numbers.

Sources:
Economic Information Systems, *Congressional District Business Patterns*, U.S. Bureau of Census, 1980.
U.S. Bureau of Census, 1980, *Census of Population Advance Reports*, U.S. Summary, Table 2 (COP 80).
U.S. Bureau of Census, *Congressional District Data Book for the 93rd Congress* (and revisions for 94th Congress for California, New York and Texas).

References

Ackerman, B. and Hassler, G., *Clean Coal/Dirty Air*, Yale University Press, New Haven 1981.
Buchanan, J. M. and Tullock, G., "Polluters' Profits and Political Response:

Direct Controls Versus Taxes," *American Economic Review*, March 1975, 139–47.

Crandall, R. W., *Controlling Industrial Pollution*, Brookings Institution, Washington, D.C. 1983.

Golden, J., Quellette, R., Sarri, S., and Cheremisinoff, P., *Environmental Impact Data Book*, Ann Arbor Science Publishers, Ann Arbor 1979.

Maloney, M. and McCormick, R., "A Positive Theory of Environmental Quality," *Journal of Law and Economics*, April 1982, 25, 99–124.

Pashigian, B. P., "The Effects of Environmental Regulation on Optimal Plant Size and Factor Shares," *Journal of Law and Economics*, April 1984, 1–28.

Peltzman, S., "An Economic Interpretation of the History of Congressional Voting in the Twentieth Century," Center for the Study of the Economy and the State Working Paper 028, University of Chicago, August 1983 (chap. 4 of this volume).

Peltzman, S., "Constituent Interest and Congressional Voting," *Journal of Law and Economics*, April 1984, 181–210.

Stigler, G., "The Theory of Economic Regulation," *Bell Journal of Economics and Management Science*, Spring 1971, 3–21 (chap. 6 of this volume).

U.S. Congress, Senate Subcommittee on Air and Water Pollution on the Committee of Public Works, *Nondegradation Policy of the Clean Air Act*, 93rd Congress, 1st Session, 46–51.

U.S. Environmental Protection Agency, *The National Air Monitoring Program: Air Quality and Emission Trends*, Annual Report, Vol. I, 1973.

U.S. Environmental Protection Agency, *State Air Pollution*, Implementation Plan Progress Report, January 1 to June 30, 1976.

CORRECTIVE
POLICIES

4

Crime and Punishment: An Economic Approach

18

Gary S. Becker

I. Introduction

Since the turn of the century, legislation in Western countries has expanded rapidly to reverse the brief dominance of laissez faire during the nineteenth century. The state no longer merely protects against violations of person and property through murder, rape, or burglary but also restricts "discrimination" against certain minorities, collusive business arrangements, "jaywalking," travel, the materials used in construction, and thousands of other activities. The activities restricted not only are numerous but also range widely, affecting persons in very different pursuits and of diverse social backgrounds, education levels, ages, races, etc. Moreover, the likelihood that an offender will be discovered and convicted and the nature and extent of punishments differ greatly from person to person and activity to activity. Yet, in spite of such diversity, some common properties are shared by practically all legislation, and these properties form the subject matter of this essay.

In the first place, obedience to law is not taken for granted, and public and private resources are generally spent in order both to prevent offenses and to apprehend offenders. In the second place, conviction is not generally considered sufficient punishment in itself; additional and sometimes severe punishments are meted out to those convicted. What determines the amount and type of resources and

I would like to thank the Lilly Endowment for financing a very productive summer in 1965 at the University of California at Los Angeles. While there I received very helpful comments on an earlier draft from, among others, Armen Alchian, Roland McKean, Harold Demsetz, Jack Hirshliefer, William Meckling, Gordon Tullock, and Oliver Williamson. I have also benefited from comments received at seminars at the University of Chicago, Hebrew University, RAND Corporation, and several times at the Labor Workshop of Columbia; assistance and suggestions from Isaac Ehrlich and Robert Michael; and suggestions from the editor of the *Journal of Political Economy*.

Reprinted with permission from the *Journal of Political Economy* 76 (March/April 1968): 169–217. © 1968 by The University of Chicago

punishments used to enforce a piece of legislation? In particular, why does enforcement differ so greatly among different kinds of legislation?

The main purpose of this essay is to answer normative versions of these questions, namely, how many resources and how much punishment *should* be used to enforce different kinds of legislation? Put equivalently, although more strangely, how many offenses *should* be permitted and how many offenders *should* go unpunished? The method used formulates a measure of the social loss from offenses and finds those expenditures of resources and punishments that minimize this loss. The general criterion of social loss is shown to incorporate as special cases, valid under special assumptions, the criteria of vengeance, deterrence, compensation, and rehabilitation that historically have figured so prominently in practice and criminological literature.

The optimal amount of enforcement is shown to depend on, among other things, the cost of catching and convicting offenders, the nature of punishments—for example, whether they are fines or prison terms—and the responses of offenders to changes in enforcement. The discussion, therefore, inevitably enters into issues in penology and theories of criminal behavior. A second, although because of lack of space subsidiary, aim of this essay is to see what insights into these questions are provided by our "economic" approach. It is suggested, for example, that a useful theory of criminal behavior can dispense with special theories of anomie, psychological inadequacies, or inheritance of special traits and simply extend the economist's usual analysis of choice.

II. Basic Analysis

A. *The Cost of Crime*

Although the word "crime" is used in the title to minimize terminological innovations, the analysis is intended to be sufficiently general to cover all violations, not just felonies—like murder, robbery, and assault, which receive so much newspaper coverage—but also tax evasion, the so-called white-collar crimes, and traffic and other violations. Looked at this broadly, "crime" is an economically important activity or "industry," notwithstanding the almost total neglect by economists.[1]

---

[1] This neglect probably resulted from an attitude that illegal activity is too immoral to merit any systematic scientific attention. The influence of moral attitudes on a scientific analysis is seen most clearly in a discussion by Alfred Marshall. After arguing that even fair gambling is an "economic blunder" because of diminishing marginal utility, he says, "It is true that this loss of probable happiness need not be greater than the pleasure derived from the excitement of gambling, and we are then thrown back upon the induction [*sic*] that pleasures of gambling are in Bentham's phrase 'impure'; since

TABLE 1.   Economic Costs of Crimes

Type	Costs (Millions of Dollars)
Crimes against persons	815
Crimes against property	3,932
Illegal goods and services	8,075
Some other crimes	2,036
Total	14,858
Public expenditures on police, prosecution, and courts	3,178
Corrections	1,034
Some private costs of combatting crime	1,910
Over-all total	20,980

Source: President's Commission, (1967*d*, p. 44).

Some relevant evidence put together by the 1967 President's Commission on Law Enforcement and Administration of Justice (the "Crime Commission") is reproduced in Table 1. Public expenditures in 1965 at the federal, state, and local levels on police, criminal courts and counsel, and "corrections" amounted to over $4 billion, while private outlays on burglar alarms, guards, counsel, and some other forms of protection were about $2 billion. Unquestionably, public and especially private expenditures are significantly understated, since expenditures by many public agencies in the course of enforcing particular pieces of legislation, such as state fair-employment laws,[2] are not included, and a myriad of private precautions against crime, ranging from suburban living to taxis, are also excluded.

Table 1 also lists the Crime Commission's estimates of the direct costs of various crimes. The gross income from expenditures on various kinds of illegal consumption, including narcotics, prostitution, and mainly gambling, amounted to over $8 billion. The value of crimes against property, including fraud, vandalism, and theft, amounted to almost $4 billion,[3] while about $3 billion worth resulted from the loss of

experience shows that they are likely to engender a restless, feverish character, unsuited for steady work as well as for the higher and more solid pleasures of life" (Marshall, 1961, Note X, Mathematical Appendix).

[2] Expenditures by the thirteen states with such legislation in 1959 totaled almost $2 million (see Landes, 1966).

[3] Superficially, frauds, thefts, etc., do not involve true social costs but are simply transfers, with the loss to victims being compensated by equal gains to criminals. While these are transfers, their market value is, nevertheless, a first approximation to the direct social cost. If the theft or fraud industry is "competitive," the sum of the value of the criminals' time input—including the time of "fences" and prospective time in prison—plus the value of capital input, compensation for risk, etc., would approxi-

earnings due to homicide, assault, or other crimes. All the costs listed in the table total about $21 billion, which is almost 4 per cent of reported national income in 1965. If the sizeable omissions were included, the percentage might be considerably higher.

Crime has probably become more important during the last forty years. The Crime Commission presents no evidence on trends in costs but does present evidence suggesting that the number of major felonies per capita has grown since the early thirties (President's Commission, 1967a, pp. 22–31). Moreover, with the large growth of tax and other legislation, tax evasion and other kinds of white-collar crime have presumably grown much more rapidly than felonies. One piece of indirect evidence on the growth of crime is the large increase in the amount of currency in circulation since 1929. For sixty years prior to that date, the ratio of currency either to all money or to consumer expenditures had declined very substantially. Since then, in spite of further urbanization and income growth and the spread of credit cards and other kinds of credit,[4] both ratios have increased sizeably.[5] This reversal can be explained by an unusual increase in illegal activity, since currency has obvious advantages over checks in illegal transactions (the opposite is true for legal transactions) because no record of a transaction remains.[6]

B. The Model

It is useful in determining how to combat crime in an optimal fashion to develop a model to incorporate the behavioral relations behind the costs listed in Table 1. These can be divided into five categories: the relations between (1) the number of crimes, called "offenses" in this essay, and the cost of offenses, (2) the number of offenses and the punishments meted out, (3) the number of offenses, arrests, and convictions and the public expenditures on police and courts, (4) the number of convictions and the costs of imprisonments or other kinds of punishments, and (5) the number of offenses and the private expenditures on

---

mately equal the market value of the loss to victims. Consequently, aside from the input of intermediate products, losses can be taken as a measure of the value of the labor and capital input into these crimes, which are true social costs.

[4] For an analysis of the secular decline to 1929 that stresses urbanization and the growth in incomes, see Cagan (1965, chap. iv).

[5] In 1965, the ratio of currency outstanding to consumer expenditures was 0.08, compared to only 0.05 in 1929. In 1965, currency outstanding per family was a whopping $738.

[6] Cagan (1965, chap. iv) attributes much of the increase in currency holdings between 1929 and 1960 to increased tax evasion resulting from the increase in tax rates.

protection and apprehension. The first four are discussed in turn, while the fifth is postponed until a later section.

1. Damages Usually a belief that other members of society are harmed is the motivation behind outlawing or otherwise restricting an activity. The amount of harm would tend to increase with the activity level, as in the relation

$$H_i = H_i(O_i),$$

with   (1)

$$H_i' = \frac{dH_i}{dO_i} > 0,$$

where H_i is the harm from the ith activity and O_i is the activity level.[7] The concept of harm and the function relating its amount to the activity level are familiar to economists from their many discussions of activities causing external diseconomies. From this perspective, criminal activities are an important subset of the class of activities that cause diseconomies, with the level of criminal activities measured by the number of offenses.

The social value of the gain to offenders presumably also tends to increase with the number of offenses, as in

$$G = G(O),$$

with   (2)

$$G' = \frac{dG}{dO} > 0.$$

The net cost or damage to society is simply the difference between the harm and gain and can be written as

$$D(O) = H(O) - G(O). \tag{3}$$

If, as seems plausible, offenders usually eventually receive diminishing marginal gains and cause increasing marginal harm from additional offenses, $G'' < 0$, $H'' > 0$, and

---

[7] The ith subscript will be suppressed whenever it is to be understood that only one activity is being discussed.

$$D'' = H'' - G'' > 0, \tag{4}$$

which is an important condition used later in the analysis of optimality positions (see, for example, the Mathematical Appendix). Since both H' and $G' > 0$, the sign of D' depends on their relative magnitudes. It follows from (4), however, that

$$D'(O) > 0 \text{ for all } O > O_a \text{ if } D'(O_a) \geq 0. \tag{5}$$

Until Section V the discussion is restricted to the region where $D' > 0$, the region providing the strongest justification for outlawing an activity. In that section the general problem of external diseconomies is reconsidered from our viewpoint, and there $D' < 0$ is also permitted.

The top part of Table 1 lists costs of various crimes, which have been interpreted by us as estimates of the value of resources used up in these crimes. These values are important components of, but are not identical to, the net damages to society. For example, the cost of murder is measured by the loss in earnings of victims and excludes, among other things, the value placed by society on life itself; the cost of gambling excludes both the utility to those gambling and the "external" disutility to some clergy and others; the cost of "transfers" like burglary and embezzlement excludes social attitudes toward forced wealth redistributions and also the effects on capital accumulation of the possibility of theft. Consequently, the $15 billion estimate for the cost of crime in Table 1 may be a significant understatement of the net damages to society, not only because the costs of many white-collar crimes are omitted, but also because much of the damage is omitted even for the crimes covered.

2. *The Cost of Apprehension and Conviction* The more that is spent on policemen, court personnel, and specialized equipment, the easier it is to discover offenses and convict offenders. One can postulate a relation between the output of police and court "activity" and various inputs of manpower, materials, and capital, as in $A = f(m, r, c)$, where f is a production function summarizing the "state of the arts." Given f and input prices, increased "activity" would be more costly, as summarized by the relation

$$C = C(A)$$

and   (6)

$$C' = \frac{dC}{dA} > 0.$$

It would be cheaper to achieve any given level of activity the cheaper were policemen,[8] judges, counsel, and juries and the more highly developed the state of the arts, as determined by technologies like finger-printing, wire-tapping, computer control, and lie-detecting.[9]

One approximation to an empirical measure of "activity" is the number of offenses cleared by conviction. It can be written as

$$A \cong pO, \tag{7}$$

where p, the ratio of offenses cleared by convictions to all offenses, is the over-all probability that an offense is cleared by conviction. By substituting (7) into (6) and differentiating, one has

$$C_p = \frac{\partial C(pO)}{\partial p} = C'O > 0$$

and $$\tag{8}$$

$$C_o = C'p > 0$$

if $pO \neq 0$. An increase in either the probability of conviction or the number of offenses would increase total costs. If the marginal cost of increased "activity" were rising, further implications would be that

$$C_{pp} = C''O^2 > 0,$$

$$C_{oo} = C''p^2 > 0, \tag{9}$$

and

$$C_{po} = C_{op} = C''pO + C' > 0.$$

A more sophisticated and realistic approach drops the implication of (7) that convictions alone measure "activity," or even that p and O have identical elasticities, and introduces the more general relation

$$A = h(p, O, a). \tag{10}$$

---

[8] According to the Crime Commission, 85–90 per cent of all police costs consist of wages and salaries (President's Commission, 1967a, p. 35).

[9] A task-force report by the Crime Commission deals with suggestions for greater and more efficient usage of advanced technologies (President's Commission, 1967e).

The variable a stands for arrests and other determinants of "activity," and there is no presumption that the elasticity of h with respect to p equals that with respect to O. Substitution yields the cost function $C = C(p, O, a)$. If, as is extremely likely, h_p, h_o, and h_a are all greater than zero, then clearly C_p, C_o, and C_a are all greater than zero.

In order to insure that optimality positions do not lie at "corners," it is necessary to place some restrictions on the second derivatives of the cost function. Combined with some other assumptions, it is *sufficient* that

$$C_{pp} \geq 0,$$

$$C_{oo} \geq 0,$$

(11)

and

$$C_{po} \cong 0$$

(see the Mathematical Appendix). The first two restrictions are rather plausible, the third much less so.[10]

Table 1 indicates that in 1965 public expenditures in the United States on police and courts totaled more than $3 billion, by no means a minor item. Separate estimates were prepared for each of seven major felonies.[11] Expenditures on them averaged about $500 per offense (reported) and about $2,000 per person arrested, with almost $1,000 being spent per murder (President's Commission, 1967a, pp. 264–65); $500 is an estimate of the average cost

$$AC = \frac{C(p, O, a)}{O}$$

of these felonies and would presumably be a larger figure if the number of either arrests or convictions were greater. Marginal costs (C_o) would be at least $500 if condition (11), $C_{oo} \geq 0$, were assumed to hold throughout.

---

[10] Differentiating the cost function yields $C_{pp} = C''(h_p)^2 + C'h_{pp}$; $C_{oo} = C''(h_o)^2 + C'h_{oo}$; $C_{po} = C''h_o h_p + C'h_{po}$. If marginal costs were rising, C_{pp} or C_{oo} could be negative only if h_{pp} or h_{oo} were sufficiently negative, which is not very likely. However, C_{po} would be approximately zero only if h_{po} were sufficiently negative, which is also unlikely. Note that if "activity" is measured by convictions alone, $h_{pp} = h_{oo} = 0$, and $h_{po} > 0$.

[11] They are willful homicide, forcible rape, robbery, aggravated assault, burglary, larceny, and auto theft.

3. The Supply of Offenses Theories about the determinants of the number of offenses differ greatly, from emphasis on skull types and biological inheritance to family upbringing and disenchantment with society. Practically all the diverse theories agree, however, that when other variables are held constant, an increase in a person's probability of conviction or punishment if convicted would generally decrease, perhaps substantially, perhaps negligibly, the number of offenses he commits. In addition, a common generalization by persons with judicial experience is that a change in the probability has a greater effect on the number of offenses than a change in the punishment,[12] although, as far as I can tell, none of the prominent theories shed any light on this relation.

The approach taken here follows the economists' usual analysis of choice and assumes that a person commits an offense if the expected utility to him exceeds the utility he could get by using his time and other resources at other activities. Some persons become "criminals," therefore, not because their basic motivation differs from that of other persons, but because their benefits and costs differ. I cannot pause to discuss the many general implications of this approach,[13] except to remark that criminal behavior becomes part of a much more general theory and does not require ad hoc concepts of differential association, anomie, and the like,[14] nor does it assume perfect knowledge, lightening-fast calculation, or any of the other caricatures of economic theory.

This approach implies that there is a function relating the number of offenses by any person to his probability of conviction, to his punishment if convicted, and to other variables, such as the income available to him in legal and other illegal activities, the frequency of nuisance arrests, and his willingness to commit an illegal act. This can be represented as

$$O_j = O_j(p_j, f_j, u_j), \tag{12}$$

where O_j is the number of offenses he would commit during a particular period, p_j his probability of conviction per offense, f_j his punish-

---

[12] For example, Lord Shawness (1965) said, "Some judges preoccupy themselves with methods of punishment. This is their job. But in preventing crime it is of less significance than they like to think. Certainty of detection is far more important than severity of punishment." Also see the discussion of the ideas of C. B. Beccaria, an insightful eighteenth-century Italian economist and criminologist, in Radzinowicz (1948, I, 282).

[13] See, however, the discussions in Smigel (1965) and Ehrlich (1967).

[14] For a discussion of these concepts, see Sutherland (1960).

ment per offense, and u_j a portmanteau variable representing all these other influences.[15]

Since only convicted offenders are punished, in effect there is "price discrimination" and uncertainty: if convicted, he pays f_j per convicted offense, while otherwise he does not. An increase in either p_j or f_j would reduce the utility expected from an offense and thus would tend to reduce the number of offenses because either the probability of "paying" the higher "price" or the "price" itself would increase.[16] That is,

$$O_{p_j} = \frac{\partial O_j}{\partial p_j} < 0$$

and   (13)

$$O_{f_j} = \frac{\partial O_j}{\partial f_j} < 0,$$

which are the generally accepted restrictions mentioned above. The effect of changes in some components of u_j could also be anticipated. For example, a rise in the income available in legal activities or an increase in law-abidingness due, say, to "education" would reduce the incentive to enter illegal activities and thus would reduce the number of offenses. Or a shift in the form of the punishment, say, from a fine to

---

[15] Both p_j and f_j might be considered distributions that depend on the judge, jury, prosecutor, etc., that j happens to receive. Among other things, u_j depends on the p's and f's meted out for other competing offenses. For evidence indicating that offenders do substitute among offenses, see Smigel (1965).

[16] The utility expected from committing an offense is defined as

$$EU_j = p_j U_j(Y_j - f_j) + (1 - p_j)U_j(Y_j),$$

where Y_j is his income, monetary plus psychic, from an offense; U_j is his utility function; and f_j is to be interpreted as the monetary equivalent of the punishment. Then

$$\frac{\partial EU_j}{\partial p_j} = U_j(Y_j - f_j) - U_j(Y_j) < 0$$

and

$$\frac{\partial EU_j}{\partial f_j} = -p_j U_j'(Y_j - f_j) < 0$$

as long as the marginal utility of income is positive. One could expand the analysis by incorporating the costs and probabilities of arrests, detentions, and trials that do not result in conviction.

imprisonment, would tend to reduce the number of offenses, at least temporarily, because they cannot be committed while in prison.

This approach also has an interesting interpretation of the presumed greater response to a change in the probability than in the punishment. An increase in p_j "compensated" by an equal percentage reduction in f_j would not change the expected income from an offense[17] but could change the expected utility, because the amount of risk would change. It is easily shown that an increase in p_j would reduce the expected utility, and thus the number of offenses, more than an equal percentage increase in f_j[18] if j has preference for risk; the increase in f_j would have the greater effect if he has aversion to risk; and they would have the same effect if he is risk neutral.[19] The widespread generalization that offenders are more deterred by the probability of conviction than by the punishment when convicted turns out to imply in the expected-utility approach that offenders are risk preferrers, at least in the relevant region of punishments.

The total number of offenses is the sum of all the O_j and would depend on the set of p_j, f_j, and u_j. Although these variables are likely to differ significantly between persons because of differences in intelligence, age, education, previous offense history, wealth, family upbringing, etc., for simplicity I now consider only their average values, p, f, and u,[20] and write the market offense function as

[17] $EY_j = p_j(Y_j - f_j) + (1 - p_j)Y_j = Y_j - p_j f_j$.

[18] This means that an increase in p_j "compensated" by a reduction in f_j would reduce utility and offenses.

[19] From n. 16

$$\frac{-\partial EU_j}{\partial p_j} \frac{p_j}{U_j} = [U_j(Y_j) - U_j(Y_j - f_j)]\frac{p_j}{U_j} \gtrless \frac{-\partial EU_j}{\partial f_j}\frac{f_j}{U_j} = p_j U_j'(Y_j - f_j)\frac{f_j}{U_j}$$

as

$$\frac{U_j(Y_j) - U_j(Y_j - f_j)}{f_j} \gtrless U_j'(Y_j - f_j).$$

The term on the left is the average change in utility between $Y_j - f_j$ and Y_j. It would be greater than, equal to, or less than $U_j'(Y_j - f_j)$ as $U_j'' \gtrless 0$. But risk preference is defined by $U_j'' > 0$, neutrality by $U_j'' = 0$, and aversion by $U_j'' < 0$.

[20] p can be defined as a weighted average of the p_j, as

$$p = \sum_{j=1}^{n} \frac{O_j p_j}{\sum_{i=1}^{n} O_i},$$

and similar definitions hold for f and u.

$$O = O(p, f, u). \tag{14}$$

This function is assumed to have the same kinds of properties as the individual functions, in particular, to be negatively related to p and f and to be more responsive to the former than the latter if, and only if, offenders on balance have risk preference. Smigel (1965) and Ehrlich (1967) estimate functions like (14) for seven felonies reported by the Federal Bureau of Investigation using state data as the basic unit of observation. They find that the relations are quite stable, as evidenced by high correlation coefficients; that there are significant negative effects on O of p and f; and that usually the effect of p exceeds that of f, indicating preference for risk in the region of observation.

A well-known result states that, in equilibrium, the real incomes of persons in risky activities are, at the margin, relatively high or low as persons are generally risk avoiders or preferrers. If offenders were risk preferrers, this implies that the real income of offenders would be lower, at the margin, than the incomes they could receive in less risky legal activities, and conversely if they were risk avoiders. Whether "crime pays" is then an implication of the attitudes offenders have toward risk and is not directly related to the efficiency of the police or the amount spent on combatting crime. If, however, risk were preferred at some values of p and f and disliked at others, public policy could influence whether "crime pays" by its choice of p and f. Indeed, it is shown later that the social loss from illegal activities is usually minimized by selecting p and f in regions where risk is preferred, that is, in regions where "crime does not pay."

4. *Punishments* Mankind has invented a variety of ingenious punishments to inflict on convicted offenders: death, torture, branding, fines, imprisonment, banishment, restrictions on movement and occupation, and loss of citizenship are just the more common ones. In the United States, less serious offenses are punished primarily by fines, supplemented occasionally by probation, petty restrictions like temporary suspension of one's driver's license, and imprisonment. The more serious offenses are punished by a combination of probation, imprisonment, parole, fines, and various restrictions on choice of occupation. The Commission survey estimated for an average day in 1965 the number of persons who were either on probation, parole, or institutionalized in a jail or juvenile home (President's Commission 1967*b*). The total number of persons in one of these categories came to about 1,300,000, which is about 2 per cent of the labor force. About one-half were on probation, one-third were institutionalized, and the remaining one-sixth were on parole.

The cost of different punishments to an offender can be made comparable by converting them into their monetary equivalent or worth, which, of course, is directly measured only for fines. For example, the cost of an imprisonment is the discounted sum of the earnings foregone and the value placed on the restrictions in consumption and freedom. Since the earnings foregone and the value placed on prison restrictions vary from person to person, the cost even of a prison sentence of given duration is not a unique quantity but is generally greater, for example, to offenders who could earn more outside of prison.[21] The cost to each offender would be greater the longer the prison sentence, since both foregone earnings and foregone consumption are positively related to the length of sentences.

Punishments affect not only offenders but also other members of society. Aside from collection costs, fines paid by offenders are received as revenue by others. Most punishments, however, hurt other members as well as offenders: for example, imprisonment requires expenditures on guards, supervisory personnel, buildings, food, etc. Currently [1967] about $1 billion is being spent each year in the United States on probation, parole, and institutionalization alone, with the daily cost per case varying tremendously from a low of $0.38 for adults on probation to a high of $11.00 for juveniles in detention institutions (President's Commission, 1967b, pp. 193–94).

The total social cost of punishments is the cost to offenders plus the cost or minus the gain to others. Fines produce a gain to the latter that equals the cost to offenders, aside from collection costs, and so the social cost of fines is about zero, as befits a transfer payment. The social cost of probation, imprisonment, and other punishments, however, generally exceeds that to offenders, because others are also hurt. The derivation of optimality conditions in the next section is made more convenient if social costs are written in terms of offender costs as

$$f' \equiv bf, \tag{15}$$

where f' is the social cost and b is a coefficient that transforms f into f'. The size of b varies greatly between different kinds of punishments: $b \cong 0$ for fines, while $b > 1$ for torture, probation, parole, imprisonment, and most other punishments. It is especially large for juveniles in detention homes or for adults in prisons and is rather close to unity for torture or for adults on parole.

---

[21] In this respect, imprisonment is a special case of "waiting time" pricing that is also exemplified by queuing (see Becker, 1965, esp. pp. 515–16, and Kleinman, 1967).

III. Optimality Conditions

The relevant parameters and behavioral functions have been introduced, and the stage is set for a discussion of social policy. If the aim
simply were deterrence, the probability of conviction, p, could be
raised close to 1, and punishments, f, could be made to exceed the
gain: in this way the number of offenses, O, could be reduced almost at
will. However, an increase in p increases the social cost of offenses
through its effect on the cost of combatting offenses, C, as does an increase in f if $b > 0$ through the effect on the cost of punishments, bf. At
relatively modest values of p and f, these effects might outweigh the
social gain from increased deterrence. Similarly, if the aim simply were
to make "the punishment fit the crime," p could be set close to 1, and f
could be equated to the harm imposed on the rest of society. Again,
however, such a policy ignores the social cost of increases in p and f.

What is needed is a criterion that goes beyond catchy phrases and
gives due weight to the damages from offenses, the costs of apprehending and convicting offenders, and the social cost of punishments. The
social-welfare function of modern welfare economics is such a criterion,
and one might assume that society has a function that measures the social loss from offenses. If

$$L = L(D, C, bf, O) \tag{16}$$

is the function measuring social loss, with presumably

$$\frac{\partial L}{\partial D} > 0, \quad \frac{\partial L}{\partial C} > 0, \quad \frac{\partial L}{\partial bf} > 0, \tag{17}$$

the aim would be to select values of f, C, and possibly b that minimize L.

It is more convenient and transparent, however, to develop the
discussion at this point in terms of a less general formulation, namely,
to assume that the loss function is identical with the total social loss in
real income from offenses, convictions, and punishments, as in

$$L = D(O) + C(p, O) + bpfO. \tag{18}$$

The term $bpfO$ is the total social loss from punishments, since bf is the
loss per offense punished and pO is the number of offenses punished (if
there are a fairly large number of independent offenses). The variables
directly subject to social control are the amounts spent in combatting
offenses, C; the punishment per offense for those convicted, f; and the
form of punishments, summarized by b. Once chosen, these variables,

via the D, C, and O functions, indirectly determine p, O, D, and ultimately the loss L.

Analytical convenience suggests that p rather than C be considered a decision variable. Also, the coefficient b is assumed in this section to be a given constant greater than zero. Then p and f are the only decision variables, and their optimal values are found by differentiating L to find the two first-order optimality conditions,[22]

$$\frac{\partial L}{\partial f} = D'O_f + C'O_f + bpfO_f + bpO = 0 \tag{19}$$

and

$$\frac{\partial L}{\partial p} = D'O_p + C'O_p + C_p + bpfO_p + bfO = 0. \tag{20}$$

If O_f and O_p are not equal to zero, one can divide through by them, and recombine terms, to get the more interesting expressions

$$D' + C' = -bpf\left(1 - \frac{1}{\varepsilon_f}\right) \tag{21}$$

and

$$D' + C' + C_p \frac{1}{O_p} = -bpf\left(1 - \frac{1}{\varepsilon_p}\right), \tag{22}$$

where

$$\varepsilon_f = -\frac{f}{O}O_f$$

and

$$\varepsilon_p = -\frac{p}{O}O_p. \tag{23}$$

The term on the left side of each equation gives the marginal cost of increasing the number of offenses, O: in equation (21) through a reduction in f and in (22) through a reduction in p. Since $C' > 0$ and O is assumed to be in a region where $D' > 0$, the marginal cost of increas-

---

[22] The Mathematical Appendix discusses second-order conditions.

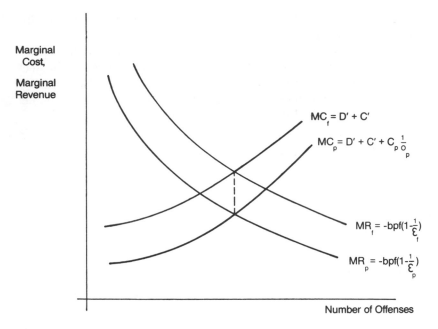

FIGURE 1

ing O through f must be positive. A reduction in p partly reduces the cost of combatting offenses, and, therefore, the marginal cost of increasing O must be less when p rather than when f is reduced (see Fig. 1); the former could even be negative if C_p were sufficiently large. Average "revenue," given by $-bpf$, is negative, but marginal revenue, given by the right-hand side of equations (21) and (22), is not necessarily negative and would be positive if the elasticities ε_p and ε_f were less than unity. Since the loss is minimized when marginal revenue equals marginal cost (see Fig. 1), the optimal value of ε_f must be less than unity, and that of ε_p could only exceed unity if C_p were sufficiently large. This is a reversal of the usual equilibrium condition for an income-maximizing firm, which is that the elasticity of demand must exceed unity, because in the usual case average revenue is assumed to be positive.[23]

Since the marginal cost of changing O through a change in p is less than that of changing O through f, the equilibrium marginal revenue from p must also be less than that from f. But equations (21) and

[23] Thus if $b < 0$, average revenue would be positive and the optimal value of ε_f would be greater than 1, and that of ε_p could be less than 1 only if C_p were sufficiently large.

(22) indicate that the marginal revenue from p can be less if, and only if, $\varepsilon_p > \varepsilon_f$. As pointed out earlier, however, this is precisely the condition indicating that offenders have preference for risk and thus that "crime does not pay." Consequently, the loss from offenses is minimized if p and f are selected from those regions where offenders are, on balance, risk preferrers. Although only the attitudes offenders have toward risk can directly determine whether "crime pays," rational public policy indirectly insures that "crime does not pay" through its choice of p and f.[24]

I indicated earlier that the actual p's and f's for major felonies in the United States generally seem to be in regions where the effect (measured by elasticity) of p on offenses exceeds that of f, that is, where offenders are risk preferrers and "crime does not pay" (Smigel, 1965; Ehrlich, 1967). Moreover, both elasticities are generally less than unity. In both respects, therefore, actual public policy is consistent with the implications of the optimality analysis.

If the supply of offenses depended only on pf—offenders were risk neutral—a reduction in p "compensated" by an equal percentage increase in f would leave unchanged pf, O, $D(O)$, and $bpfO$ but would reduce the loss, because the costs of apprehension and conviction would be lowered by the reduction in p. The loss would be minimized, therefore, by lowering p arbitrarily close to zero and raising f sufficiently high so that the product pf would induce the optimal number of offenses.[25] A fortiori, if offenders were risk avoiders, the loss would be minimized by setting p arbitrarily close to zero, for a "compensated" reduction in p reduces not only C but also O and thus D and $bpfO$.[26]

There was a tendency during the eighteenth and nineteenth centuries in Anglo-Saxon countries, and even today in many Communist and underdeveloped countries, to punish those convicted of criminal offenses rather severely, at the same time that the probability of cap-

---

[24] If $b < 0$, the optimality condition is that $\varepsilon_p < \varepsilon_f$, or that offenders are risk avoiders. Optimal social policy would then be to select p and f in regions where "crime does pay."

[25] Since $\varepsilon_f = \varepsilon_p = \varepsilon$ if O depends only on pf, and $C = 0$ if $p = 0$, the two equilibrium conditions given by eqs. (21) and (22) reduce to the single condition

$$D' = -bpf\left(1 - \frac{1}{\varepsilon}\right).$$

From this condition and the relation $O = O(pf)$, the equilibrium values of O and pf could be determined.

[26] If $b < 0$, the optimal solution is p about zero and f arbitrarily high if offenders are either risk neutral or risk preferrers.

ture and conviction was set at rather low values.[27] A promising explanation of this tendency is that an increased probability of conviction obviously absorbs public and private resources in the form of more policemen, judges, juries, and so forth. Consequently, a "compensated" reduction in this probability obviously reduces expenditures on combatting crime, and, since the expected punishment is unchanged, there is no "obvious" offsetting increase in either the amount of damages or the cost of punishments. The result can easily be continuous political pressure to keep police and other expenditures relatively low and to compensate by meting out strong punishments to those convicted.

Of course, if offenders are risk preferrers, the loss in income from offenses is generally minimized by selecting positive and finite values of p and f, even though there is no "obvious" offset to a compensated reduction in p. One possible offset already hinted at in footnote 27 is that judges or juries may be unwilling to convict offenders if punishments are set very high. Formally, this means that the cost of apprehension and conviction, C, would depend not only on p and O but also on f.[28] If C were more responsive to f than p, at least in some regions,[29] the loss in income could be minimized at finite values of p and f even if offenders were risk avoiders. For then a compensated reduction in p could raise, rather than lower, C and thus contribute to an increase in the loss.

Risk avoidance might also be consistent with optimal behavior if the loss function were not simply equal to the reduction in income. For example, suppose that the loss were increased by an increase in the ex post "price discrimination" between offenses that are not and those that are cleared by punishment. Then a "compensated" reduction in p would increase the "price discrimination," and the increased loss from this could more than offset the reductions in C, D, and $bpfO$.[30]

---

[27] For a discussion of English criminal law in the eighteenth and nineteenth centuries, see Radzinowicz (1948, Vol. I). Punishments were severe then, even though the death penalty, while legislated, was seldom implemented for less serious criminal offenses.

   Recently [1968] South Vietnam executed a prominent businessman allegedly for "speculative" dealings in rice, while in recent years a number of persons in the Soviet Union have either been executed or given severe prison sentences for economic crimes.

[28] I owe the emphasis on this point to Evsey Domar.

[29] This is probably more likely for higher values of f and lower values of p.

[30] If p is the probability that an offense would be cleared with the punishment f, then $1 - p$ is the probability of no punishment. The expected punishment would be $\mu = pf$, the variance $\sigma^2 = p(1 - p)f^2$, and the coefficient of variation

IV. Shifts in the Behavioral Relations

This section analyzes the effects of shifts in the basic behavioral relations—the damage, cost, and supply-of-offenses functions—on the optimal values of p and f. Since rigorous proofs can be found in the Mathematical Appendix, here the implications are stressed, and only intuitive proofs are given. The results are used to explain, among other things, why more damaging offenses are punished more severely and more impulsive offenders less severely.

An increase in the marginal damages from a given number of offenses, D', increases the marginal cost of changing offenses by a change in either p or f (see Fig. 2a and b). The optimal number of offenses would necessarily decrease, because the optimal values of both p and f would increase. In this case (and, as shortly seen, in several others), the optimal values of p and f move in the same, rather than in opposite, directions.[31]

An interesting application of these conclusions is to different kinds of offenses. Although there are few objective measures of the

---

$$v = \frac{\sigma}{\mu} = \sqrt{\frac{1-p}{p}} \; ;$$

v increases monotonically from a low of zero when $p = 1$ to an infinitely high value when $p = 0$.

If the loss function equaled

$$L' = L + \psi(v), \qquad \psi' > 0,$$

the optimality conditions would become

$$D' + C' = -bpf\left(1 - \frac{1}{\varepsilon_f}\right) \tag{21}$$

and

$$D' + C' + C_p \frac{1}{O_p} + \psi' \frac{dv}{dp} \frac{1}{O_p} = -bpf\left(1 - \frac{1}{\varepsilon_p}\right). \tag{22}$$

Since the term $\psi'(dv/dp)(1/O_p)$ is positive, it could more than offset the negative term $C_p(1/O_p)$.

[31] I stress this primarily because of Bentham's famous and seemingly plausible dictum that "the more deficient in certainty a punishment is, the severer it should be" (1931, chap. ii of section entitled "Of Punishment," second rule). The dictum would be correct if p (or f) were exogenously determined and if L were minimized with respect to f (or p) alone, for then the optimal value of f (or p) would be inversely related to the given value of p (or f) (see the Mathematical Appendix). If, however, L is minimized with respect to both, then frequently they move in the same direction.

damages done by most offenses, it does not take much imagination to conclude that offenses like murder or rape generally do more damage than petty larceny or auto theft. If the other components of the loss in income were the same, the optimal probability of apprehension and conviction and the punishment when convicted would be greater for the more serious offenses.

Table 2 presents some evidence on the actual probabilities and punishments in the United States for seven felonies. The punishments

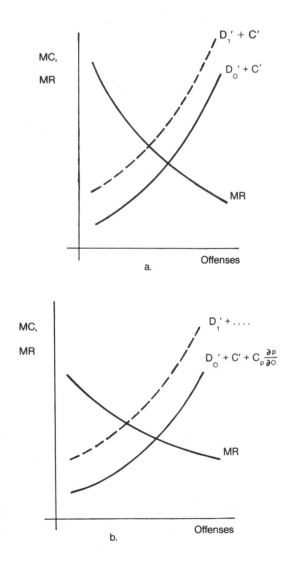

FIGURE 2

TABLE 2.   Probability of Conviction and Average Prison Term for Several Major Felonies, 1960

	Murder and Non-negligent Manslaughter	Forcible Rape	Robbery	Aggravated Assault	Burglary	Larceny	Auto Theft	All These Felonies Combined
1. Average time served (months) before first release				Months				
a) Federal civil institutions	111.0	63.6	56.1	27.1	26.2	16.2	20.6	18.8
b) State institutions	121.4	44.8	42.4	25.0	24.6	19.8	21.3	28.4
2. Probabilities of apprehension and conviction (per cent)				Per Cent				
a) Those found guilty of offenses known	57.9	37.7	25.1	27.3	13.0	10.7	13.7	15.1
b) Those found guilty of offenses charged	40.7	26.9	17.8	16.1	10.2	9.8	11.5	15.0
c) Those entering federal and state prisons (excludes many juveniles)	39.8	22.7	8.4	3.0	2.4	2.2	2.1	2.8

Source: 1, Bureau of Prisons (1960, Table 3); 2 (*a*) and (*b*), Federal Bureau of Investigation (1960, Table 10); 2 (*c*), Federal Bureau of Investigation (1961, Table 2), Bureau of Prisons (n.d., Table A1; 1961, Table 8).

are simply the average prison sentences served, while the probabilities are ratios of the estimated number of convictions to the estimated number of offenses and unquestionably contain a large error (see the discussions in Smigel, 1965, and Ehrlich, 1967). If other components of the loss function are ignored, and if actual and optimal probabilities and punishments are positively related, one should find that the more serious felonies have higher probabilities and longer prison terms. And one does: in the table, which lists the felonies in decreasing order of presumed seriousness, both the actual probabilities and the prison terms are positively related to seriousness.

Since an increase in the marginal cost of apprehension and conviction for a given number of offenses, C', has identical effects as an increase in marginal damages, it must also reduce the optimal number of offenses and increase the optimal values of p and f. On the other hand, an increase in the other component of the cost of apprehension and conviction, C_p, has no direct effect on the marginal cost of changing offenses with f and *reduces* the cost of changing offenses with p (see Fig. 3). It therefore reduces the optimal value of p and only partially compensates with an increase in f, so that the optimal number of offenses increases. Accordingly, an increase in both C' and C_p must increase the optimal f but can either increase or decrease the optimal p and optimal number of offenses, depending on the relative importance of the changes in C' and C_p.

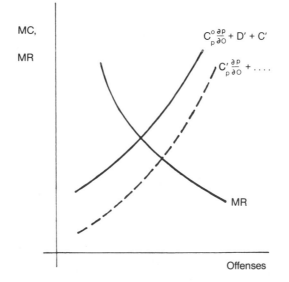

FIGURE 3

The cost of apprehending and convicting offenders is affected by a variety of forces. An increase in the salaries of policemen increases both C' and C_p, while improved police technology in the form of fingerprinting, ballistic techniques, computer control, and chemical analysis, or police and court "reform" with an emphasis on professionalism and merit, would tend to reduce both, not necessarily by the same extent. Our analysis implies, therefore, that although an improvement in technology and reform may or may not increase the optimal p and reduce the optimal number of offenses, it does reduce the optimal f and thus the need to rely on severe punishments for those convicted. Possibly this explains why the secular improvement in police technology and reform has gone hand in hand with a secular decline in punishments.

C_p, and to a lesser extent C', differ significantly between different kinds of offenses. It is easier, for example, to solve a rape or armed robbery than a burglary or auto theft, because the evidence of personal identification is often available in the former and not in the latter offenses.[32] This might tempt one to argue that the p's decline significantly as one moves across Table 2 (left to right) primarily because the C_p's are significantly lower for the "personal" felonies listed to the left than for the "impersonal" felonies listed to the right. But this implies that the f's would increase as one moved across the table, which is patently false. Consequently, the positive correlation between p, f, and the severity of offenses observed in the table cannot be explained by a negative correlation between C_p (or C') and severity.

If $b > 0$, a reduction in the elasticity of offenses with respect to f increases the marginal revenue of changing offenses by changing f (see Fig. 4a). The result is an increase in the optimal number of offenses and a decrease in the optimal f that is partially compensated by an increase in the optimal p. Similarly, a reduction in the elasticity of offenses with respect to p also increases the optimal number of offenses (see Fig. 4b), decreases the optimal p, and partially compensates by an increase in f. An equal percentage reduction in both elasticities a fortiori increases the optimal number of offenses and also tends to reduce both p and f. If $b = 0$, both marginal revenue functions lie along the horizontal axis, and changes in these elasticities have no effect on the optimal values of p and f.

The income of a firm would usually be larger if it could separate,

---

[32] "If a suspect is neither known to the victim nor arrested at the scene of the crime, the chances of ever arresting him are very slim" (President's Commission, 1967e, p. 8). This conclusion is based on a study of crimes in parts of Los Angeles during January, 1966.

at little cost, its total market into submarkets that have substantially different elasticities of demand: higher prices would be charged in the submarkets having lower elasticities. Similarly, if the total "market" for offenses could be separated into submarkets that differ significantly in the elasticities of supply of offenses, the results above imply that if $b > 0$ the total loss would be reduced by "charging" *lower* "prices"—that is, lower p's and f's—in markets with *lower* elasticities.

Sometimes it is possible to separate persons committing the same

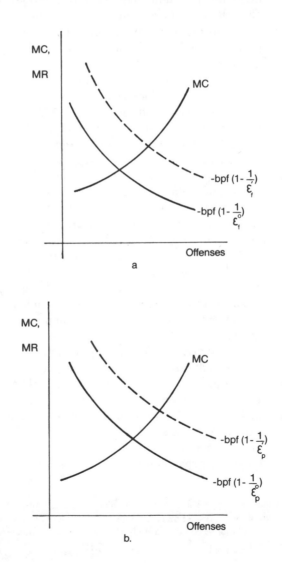

FIGURE 4

offense into groups that have different responses to punishments. For example, unpremeditated murderers or robbers are supposed to act impulsively and, therefore, to be relatively unresponsive to the size of punishments; likewise, the insane or the young are probably less affected than other offenders by future consequences and, therefore,[33] probably less deterred by increases in the probability of conviction or in the punishment when convicted. The trend during the twentieth century toward relatively smaller prison terms and greater use of probation and therapy for such groups and, more generally, the trend away from the doctrine of "a given punishment for a given crime" is apparently at least broadly consistent with the implications of the optimality analysis.

An increase in b increases the marginal revenue from changing the number of offenses by changing p or f and thereby increases the optimal number of offenses, reduces the optimal value of f, and increases the optimal value of p. Some evidence presented in Section II indicates that b is especially large for juveniles in detention homes or adults in prison and is small for fines or adults on parole. The analysis implies, therefore, that other things the same, the optimal f's would be smaller and the optimal p's larger if punishment were by one of the former rather than one of the latter methods.

V. Fines

A. Welfare Theorems and Transferable Pricing

The usual optimality conditions in welfare economics depend only on the levels and not on the slopes of marginal cost and average revenue functions, as in the well-known condition that marginal costs equal prices. The social loss from offenses was explicitly introduced as an application of the approach used in welfare economics, and yet slopes as incorporated into elasticities of supply do significantly affect the optimality conditions. Why this difference? The primary explanation would appear to be that it is almost always implicitly assumed that prices paid by consumers are fully transferred to firms and governments, so that there is no social loss from payment.

If there were no social loss from punishments, as with fines, b would equal zero, and the elasticity of supply would drop out of the optimality condition given by equation (21).[34] If $b > 0$, as with im-

---

[33] But see Becker (1962) for an analysis indicating that impulsive and other "irrational" persons may be as deterred from purchasing a commodity whose price has risen as more "rational" persons.

[34] It remains in eq. (22), through the slope O_p, because ordinarily prices do not affect marginal costs, while they do here through the influence of p on C.

prisonment, some of the payment "by" offenders would not be received by the rest of society, and a net social loss would result. The elasticity of the supply of offenses then becomes an important determinant of the optimality conditions, because it determines the change in social costs caused by a change in punishments.

Although transferable monetary pricing is the most common kind today, the other is not unimportant, especially in underdeveloped and Communist countries. Examples in addition to imprisonment and many other punishments are the draft, payments in kind, and queues and other waiting-time forms of rationing that result from legal restrictions on pricing (see Becker, 1965) and from random variations in demand and supply conditions. It is interesting, and deserves further exploration, that the optimality conditions are so significantly affected by a change in the assumptions about the transferability of pricing.

B. Optimality Conditions

If $b = 0$, say, because punishment was by fine, and if the cost of apprehending and convicting offenders were also zero, the two optimality conditions (21) and (22) would reduce to the same simple condition.

$$D'(O) = 0. \tag{24}$$

Economists generally conclude that activities causing "external" harm, such as factories that pollute the air or lumber operations that strip the land, should be taxed or otherwise restricted in level until the marginal external harm equals the marginal private gain, that is, until marginal net damages equals zero, which is what equation (24) says. If marginal harm always exceeded marginal gain, the optimal level would be presumed to be zero, and that would also be the implication of (24) when suitable inequality conditions were brought in. In other words, if the costs of apprehending, convicting, and punishing offenders were nil and if each offense caused more external harm than private gain, the social loss from offenses would be minimized by setting punishments high enough to eliminate all offenses. Minimizing the social loss would become identical with the criterion of minimizing crime by setting penalties sufficiently high.[35]

Equation (24) determines the optimal number of offenses, $\hat{O}$, and the fine and probability of conviction must be set at levels that induce offenders to commit just $\hat{O}$ offenses. If the economists' usual theory of

---

[35] "The evil of the punishment must be made to exceed the advantage of the offense" (Bentham, 1931, first rule).

choice is applied to illegal activities (see Sec. II), the marginal value of these penalties has to equal the marginal private gain:

$$V = G'(\hat{O}), \tag{25}$$

where $G'(\hat{O})$ is the marginal private gain at $\hat{O}$ and V is the monetary value of the marginal penalties. Since by equations (3) and (24), $D'(\hat{O}) = H'(\hat{O}) - G'(\hat{O}) = 0$, one has by substitution in (25)

$$V = H'(\hat{O}). \tag{26}$$

The monetary value of the penalties would equal the marginal harm caused by offenses.

Since the cost of apprehension and conviction is assumed equal to zero, the probability of apprehension and conviction could be set equal to unity without cost. The monetary value of penalties would then simply equal the fines imposed, and equation (26) would become

$$f = H'(\hat{O}). \tag{27}$$

Since fines are paid by offenders to the rest of society, a fine determined by (27) would exactly compensate the latter for the marginal harm suffered, and the criterion of minimizing the social loss would be identical, at the margin, with the criterion of compensating "victims."[36] If the harm to victims always exceeded the gain to offenders, both criteria would reduce in turn to eliminating all offenses.

If the cost of apprehension and conviction were not zero, the optimality condition would have to incorporate marginal costs as well as marginal damages and would become, if the probability of conviction were still assumed to equal unity,

$$D'(\hat{O}) + C'(\hat{O}, 1) = 0. \tag{28}$$

Since $C' > 0$, (28) requires that $D' < 0$ or that the marginal private gain exceed the marginal external harm, which generally means a smaller number of offenses than when $D' = 0$.[37] It is easy to show that equation (28) would be satisfied if the fine equalled the sum of marginal harm and marginal costs:

[36] By "victims" is meant the rest of society and not just the persons actually harmed.
[37] This result can also be derived as a special case of the results in the Mathematical Appendix on the effects of increases in C'.

$$f = H'(\hat{O}) + C'(\hat{O}, 1).^{38}$$ (29)

In other words, offenders have to compensate for the cost of catching them as well as for the harm they directly do, which is a natural generalization of the usual externality analysis.

The optimality condition

$$D'(\hat{O}) + C'(\hat{O}, \hat{p}) + C_p(\hat{O}, \hat{p})\frac{1}{O_p} = 0$$ (30)

would replace equation (28) if the fine rather than the probability of conviction were fixed. Equation (30) would usually imply that $D'(\hat{O}) > 0$,[39] and thus that the number of offenses would exceed the optimal number when costs were zero. Whether costs of apprehension and conviction increase or decrease the optimal number of offenses largely depends, therefore, on whether penalties are changed by a change in the fine or in the probability of conviction. Of course, if both are subject to control, the optimal probability of conviction would be arbitrarily close to zero, unless the social loss function differed from equation (18) (see the discussion in Sec. III).

C. The Case for Fines

Just as the probability of conviction and the severity of punishment are subject to control by society, so too is the form of punishment: legisla-

---

[38] Since equilibrium requires that $f = G'(\hat{O})$, and since from (28)

$$D'(\hat{O}) = H'(\hat{O}) - G'(\hat{O}) = -C'(\hat{O}, 1),$$

then (29) follows directly by substitution.

[39] That is, if, as seems plausible,

$$\frac{dC}{dp} = C'\frac{\partial O}{\partial p} + C_p > 0,$$

then

$$C' + C_p\frac{1}{\partial O/\partial p} < 0,$$

and

$$D'(\hat{O}) = -\left(C' + C_p\frac{1}{\partial O/\partial p}\right) > 0.$$

tion usually specifies whether an offense is punishable by fines, probation, institutionalization, or some combination. Is it merely an accident, or have optimality considerations determined that today, in most
countries, fines are the predominant form of punishment, with institutionalization reserved for the more serious offenses? This section
presents several arguments which imply that social welfare is increased
if fines are used *whenever feasible.*

In the first place, probation and institutionalization use up social
resources, and fines do not, since the latter are basically just transfer
payments, while the former use resources in the form of guards, supervisory personnel, probation officers, and the offenders' own time.[40]
Table 1 indicates that the cost is not minor either: in the United States
in 1965, about $1 billion was spent on "correction," and this estimate
excludes, of course, the value of the loss in offenders' time.[41]

Moreover, the determination of the optimal number of offenses
and severity of punishments is somewhat simplified by the use of fines.
A wise use of fines requires knowledge of marginal gains and harm and
of marginal apprehension and conviction costs; admittedly, such knowledge is not easily acquired. A wise use of imprisonment and other punishments must know this too, however, and, in addition, must know
about the elasticities of response of offenses to changes in punishments.
As the bitter controversies over the abolition of capital punishment
suggest, it has been difficult to learn about these elasticities.

I suggested earlier that premeditation, sanity, and age can enter
into the determination of punishments as proxies for the elasticities of
response. These characteristics may not have to be considered in levying fines, because the optimal fines, as determined, say, by equations
(27) or (29), do not depend on elasticities. Perhaps this partly explains
why economists discussing externalities almost never mention motivation or intent, while sociologists and lawyers discussing criminal
behavior invariably do. The former assume that punishment is by a
monetary tax or fine, while the latter assume that non-monetary punishments are used.

Fines provide compensation to victims, and optimal fines at the
margin fully compensate victims and restore the status quo ante, so

---

[40] Several early writers on criminology recognized this advantage of fines. For
example, "Pecuniary punishments are highly economical, since all the evil felt by him
who pays turns into an advantage for him who receives" (Bentham, 1931, chap. vi), and
"Imprisonment would have been regarded in these old times [*ca.* tenth century] as a
useless punishment; it does not satisfy revenge, it keeps the criminal idle, and do what
we may, *it is costly*" (Pollock and Maitland, 1952, p. 516; my italics).

[41] On the other hand, some transfer payments in the form of food, clothing, and
shelter are included.

that they are no worse off than if offenses were not committed.[42] Not only do other punishments fail to compensate, but they also require "victims" to spend additional resources in carrying out the punishment. It is not surprising, therefore, that the anger and fear felt toward ex-convicts who in fact have *not* "paid their debt to society" have resulted in additional punishments,[43] including legal restrictions on their political and economic opportunities[44] and informal restrictions on their social acceptance. Moreover, the absence of compensation encourages efforts to change and otherwise "rehabilitate" offenders through psychiatric counseling, therapy, and other programs. Since fines do compensate and do not create much additional cost, anger toward and fear of appropriately fined persons do not easily develop. As a result, additional punishments are not usually levied against "ex-finees," nor are strong efforts made to "rehabilitate" them.

One argument made against fines is that they are immoral because, in effect, they permit offenses to be bought for a price in the same way that bread or other goods are bought for a price.[45] A fine *can* be considered the price of an offense, but so too can any other form of punishment; for example, the "price" of stealing a car might be six months in jail. The only difference is in the units of measurement: fines are prices measured in monetary units, imprisonments are prices measured in time units, etc. If anything, monetary units are to be preferred here as they are generally preferred in pricing and accounting.

Optimal fines determined from equation (29) depend only on the marginal harm and cost and not at all on the economic positions of offenders. This has been criticized as unfair, and fines proportional to the incomes of offenders have been suggested.[46] If the goal is to mini-

[42] Bentham recognized this and said, "To furnish an indemnity to the injured party is another useful quality in a punishment. It is a means of accomplishing two objects at once—punishing an offense and repairing it: removing the evil of the first order, and putting a stop to alarm. This is a characteristic advantage of pecuniary punishments" (1931, chap. vi).

[43] In the same way, the guilt felt by society in using the draft, a forced transfer *to* society, has led to additional payments to veterans in the form of education benefits, bonuses, hospitalization rights, etc.

[44] See Sutherland (1960, pp. 267–68) for a list of some of these.

[45] The very early English law relied heavily on monetary fines, even for murder, and it has been said that "every kind of blow or wound given to every kind of person had its price, and much of the jurisprudence of the time must have consisted of a knowledge of these preappointed prices" (Pollock and Maitland, 1952, p. 451).

The same idea was put amusingly in a recent *Mutt and Jeff* cartoon which showed a police car carrying a sign that read: "Speed limit 30 M per H—$5 fine every mile over speed limit—pick out speed you can afford."

[46] For example, Bentham said, "A pecuniary punishment, if the sum is fixed, is in the highest degree unequal. . . . Fines have been determined without regard to the profit of the offense, to its evil, or to the wealth of the offender. . . . Pecuniary punish-

mize the social loss in income from offenses, and not to take vengeance or to inflict harm on offenders, then fines should depend on the total harm done by offenders, and not directly on their income, race, sex, etc. In the same way, the monetary value of optimal prison sentences and other punishments depends on the harm, costs, and elasticities of response, but not directly on an offender's income. Indeed, if the monetary value of the punishment by, say, imprisonment were independent of income, the length of the sentence would be *inversely* related to income, because the value placed on a given sentence is positively related to income.

We might detour briefly to point out some interesting implications for the probability of conviction of the fact that the monetary value of a given fine is obviously the same for all offenders, while the monetary equivalent or "value" of a given prison sentence or probation period is generally positively related to an offender's income. The discussion in Section II suggested that actual probabilities of conviction are not fixed to all offenders but usually vary with their age, sex, race, and, in particular, income. Offenders with higher earnings have an incentive to spend more on planning their offenses, on good lawyers, on legal appeals, and even on bribery to reduce the probability of apprehension and conviction for offenses punishable by, say, a given prison term, because the cost to them of conviction is relatively large compared to the cost of these expenditures. Similarly, however, poorer offenders have an incentive to use more of their time in planning their offenses, in court appearances, and the like to reduce the probability of conviction for offenses punishable by a given fine, because the cost to them of conviction is relatively large compared to the value of their time.[47] The implication is that the probability of conviction would be systematically related to the earnings of offenders: negatively for offenses punishable by imprisonment and positively for those punishable by fines. Although a negative relation for felonies and other offenses punishable by imprisonment has been frequently observed and deplored (see President's Commission, 1967c, pp. 139–53), I do not know of any studies of the relation for fines or of any recognition that

---

ments should always be regulated by the fortune of the offender. The relative amount of the fine should be fixed, not its absolute amount; for such an offense, such a part of the offender's fortune" (1931, chap. ix). Note that optimal fines, as determined by eq. (29), do depend on "the profit of the offense" and on "its evil."

[47] Note that the incentive to use time to reduce the probability of a given prison sentence is unrelated to earnings, because the punishment is fixed in time, not monetary, units; likewise, the incentive to use money to reduce the probability of a given fine is also unrelated to earnings, because the punishment is fixed in monetary, not time, units.

the observed negative relation may be more a consequence of the nature of the punishment than of the influence of wealth.

Another argument made against fines is that certain crimes, like murder or rape, are so heinous that no amount of money could compensate for the harm inflicted. This argument has obvious merit and is a special case of the more general principle that fines cannot be relied on exclusively whenever the harm exceeds the resources of offenders. For then victims could not be fully compensated by offenders, and fines would have to be supplemented with prison terms or other punishments in order to discourage offenses optimally. This explains why imprisonments, probation, and parole are major punishments for the more serious felonies; considerable harm is inflicted, and felonious offenders lack sufficient resources to compensate. Since fines are preferable, it also suggests the need for a flexible system of instalment fines to enable offenders to pay fines more readily and thus avoid other punishments.

This analysis implies that if some offenders could pay the fine for a given offense and others could not,[48] the former should be punished solely by fine and the latter partly by other methods. In essence, therefore, these methods become a vehicle for punishing "debtors" to society. Before the cry is raised that the system is unfair, especially to poor offenders, consider the following.

Those punished would be debtors in "transactions" that were never agreed to by their "creditors," not in voluntary transactions, such as loans,[49] for which suitable precautions could be taken in advance by creditors. Moreover, punishment in any economic system based on voluntary market transactions inevitably must distinguish between such "debtors" and others. If a rich man purchases a car and a poor man steals one, the former is congratulated, while the latter is often sent to prison when apprehended. Yet the rich man's purchase is equivalent to a "theft" subsequently compensated by a "fine" equal to the price of the car, while the poor man, in effect, goes to prison because he cannot pay this "fine."

Whether a punishment like imprisonment in lieu of a full fine for offenders lacking sufficient resources is "fair" depends, of course, on the length of the prison term compared to the fine.[50] For example, a

---

[48] In one study, about half of those convicted of misdemeanors could not pay the fines (see President's Commission, 1967c, p. 148).

[49] The "debtor prisons" of earlier centuries generally housed persons who could not repay loans.

[50] Yet without any discussion of the actual alternatives offered, the statement is made that "the money judgment assessed the punitive damages defendant hardly seems comparable in effect to the criminal sanctions of death, imprisonment, and stigmatization" ("Criminal Safeguards . . . ," 1967).

prison term of one week in lieu of a $10,000 fine would, if anything, be "unfair" to wealthy offenders paying the fine. Since imprisonment is a more costly punishment to society than fines, the loss from offenses would be reduced by a policy of leniency toward persons who are imprisoned because they cannot pay fines. Consequently, optimal prison terms for "debtors" would not be "unfair" to them in the sense that the monetary equivalent to them of the prison terms would be less than the value of optimal fines, which in turn would equal the harm caused or the "debt."[51]

It appears, however, that "debtors" are often imprisoned at rates of exchange with fines that place a low value on time in prison. Although I have not seen systematic evidence on the different punishments actually offered convicted offenders, and the choices they made, many statutes in the United States do permit fines and imprisonment that place a low value on time in prison. For example, in New York State, Class A Misdemeanors can be punished by a prison term as long as one year or a fine no larger than $1,000 and Class B Misdemeanors, by a term as long as three months or a fine no larger than $500 (*Laws of*

---

[51] A formal proof is straightforward if for simplicity the probability of conviction is taken as equal to unity. For then the sole optimality condition is

$$D' + C' = -bf\left(1 - \frac{1}{\varepsilon_f}\right). \tag{1'}$$

Since $D' = H' - G'$, by substitution one has

$$G' = H' + C' + bf\left(1 - \frac{1}{\varepsilon_f}\right), \tag{2'}$$

and since equilibrium requires that $G' = f$,

$$f = H' + C' + bf\left(1 - \frac{1}{\varepsilon_f}\right), \tag{3'}$$

or

$$f = \frac{H' + C'}{1 - b(1 - 1/\varepsilon_f)}. \tag{4'}$$

If $b > 0$, $\varepsilon_f < 1$ (see Sec. III), and hence by eq. (4'),

$$f < H' + C', \tag{5'}$$

where the term on the right is the full marginal harm. If p as well as f is free to vary, the analysis becomes more complicated, but the conclusion about the relative monetary values of optimal imprisonments and fines remains the same (see the Mathematical Appendix).

New York, 1965, chap. 1030, Arts. 70 and 80).[52] According to my analysis, these statutes permit excessive prison sentences relative to the fines, which may explain why imprisonment in lieu of fines is considered unfair to poor offenders, who often must "choose" the prison alternative.

D. Compensation and the Criminal Law

Actual criminal proceedings in the United States appear to seek a mixture of deterrence, compensation, and vengeance. I have already indicated that these goals are somewhat contradictory and cannot generally be simultaneously achieved; for example, if punishment were by fine, minimizing the social loss from offenses would be equivalent to compensating "victims" fully, and deterrence or vengeance could only be partially pursued. Therefore, if the case for fines were accepted, and punishment by optimal fines became the norm, the traditional approach to criminal law would have to be significantly modified.

First and foremost, the primary aim of all legal proceedings would become the same: not punishment or deterrence, but simply the assessment of the "harm" done by defendants. Much of the traditional criminal law would become a branch of the law of torts,[53] say "social torts," in which the public would collectively sue for "public" harm. A "criminal" action would be defined fundamentally not by the nature of the action[54] but by the inability of a person to compensate for the "harm" that he caused. Thus an action would be "criminal" precisely because it results in uncompensated "harm" to others. Criminal law would cover all such actions, while tort law would cover all other (civil) actions.

As a practical example of the fundamental changes that would be wrought, consider the antitrust field. Inspired in part by the economist's classic demonstration that monopolies distort the allocation of resources and reduce economic welfare, the United States has outlawed conspiracies and other constraints of trade. In practice, defendants are

---

[52] "Violations," however, can only be punished by prison terms as long as fifteen days or fines no larger than $250. Since these are maximum punishments, the actual ones imposed by the courts can, and often are, considerably less. Note, too, that the courts can punish by imprisonment, by fine, or by *both* (*Laws of New York*, 1965, chap. 1030, Art. 60).

[53] "The cardinal principle of damages in Anglo-American law [of torts] is that of *compensation* for the injury caused to plaintiff by defendant's breach of duty" (Harper and James, 1956, p. 1299).

[54] Of course, many traditional criminal actions like murder or rape would still usually be criminal under this approach too.

often simply required to cease the objectionable activity, although sometimes they are also fined, become subject to damage suits, or are jailed.

If compensation were stressed, the main purpose of legal proceedings would be to levy fines to[55] the harm inflicted on society by constraints of trade. There would be no point to cease and desist orders, imprisonment, ridicule, or dissolution of companies. If the economist's theory about monopoly is correct, and if optimal fines were levied, firms would automatically cease any constraints of trade, because the gain to them would be less than the harm they cause and thus less than the fines expected. On the other hand, if Schumpeter and other critics are correct, and certain constraints of trade raise the level of economic welfare, fines could fully compensate society for the harm done, and yet some constraints would not cease, because the gain to participants would exceed the harm to others.[56]

One unexpected advantage, therefore, from stressing compensation and fines rather than punishment and deterrence is that the validity of the classical position need not be judged a priori. If valid, compensating fines would discourage all constraints of trade and would achieve the classical aims. If not, such fines would permit the socially desirable constraints to continue and, at the same time, would compensate society for the harm done.

Of course, as participants in triple-damage suits are well aware, the harm done is not easily measured, and serious mistakes would be inevitable. However, it is also extremely difficult to measure the harm in many civil suits,[57] yet these continue to function, probably reasonably well on the whole. Moreover, as experience accumulated, the margin of error would decline, and rules of thumb would develop. Finally, one must realize that difficult judgments are also required by the

[55] Actually, fines should exceed the harm done if the probability of conviction were less than unity. The possibility of avoiding conviction is the intellectual justification for punitive, such as triple, damages against those convicted.

[56] The classical view is that $D'(M)$ always is greater than zero, where M measures the different constraints of trade and D' measures the marginal damage; the critic's view is that for some M, $D'(M) < 0$. It has been shown above that if D' always is greater than zero, compensating fines would discourage all offenses, in this case constraints of trade, while if D' sometimes is less than zero, some offenses would remain (unless $C'[M]$, the marginal cost of detecting and convicting offenders, were sufficiently large relative to D').

[57] Harper and James said, "Sometimes [compensation] can be accomplished with a fair degree of accuracy. But obviously it cannot be done in anything but a figurative and essentially speculative way for many of the consequences of personal injury. Yet it is the aim of the law to attain at least a rough correspondence between the amount awarded as damages and the extent of the suffering" (1956, p. 1301).

present antitrust policy, such as deciding that certain industries are "workably" competitive or that certain mergers reduce competition. An emphasis on fines and compensation would at least help avoid irrelevant issues by focusing attention on the information most needed for intelligent social policy.

VI. Private Expenditures against Crime

A variety of private as well as public actions also attempt to reduce the number and incidence of crimes: guards, doormen, and accountants are employed, locks and alarms installed, insurance coverage extended, parks and neighborhoods avoided, taxis used in place of walking or subways, and so on. Table 1 lists close to $2 billion of such expenditures in 1965, and this undoubtedly is a gross underestimate of the total. The need for private action is especially great in highly interdependent modern economies, where frequently a person must trust his resources, including his person, to the "care" of employees, employers, customers, or sellers.

If each person tries to minimize his expected loss in income from crimes, optimal private decisions can be easily derived from the previous discussion of optimal public ones. For each person there is a loss function similar to that given by equation (18):

$$L_j = H_j(O_j) + C_j(p_j, O_j, C, C_k) + b_j p_j f_j O_j. \tag{31}$$

The term H_j represents the harm to j from the O_j offenses committed against j, while C_j represents his cost of achieving a probability of conviction of p_j for offenses committed against him. Note that C_j not only is positively related to O_j but also is negatively related to C, public expenditures on crime, and to C_k, the set of private expenditures by other persons.[58]

The term $b_j p_j f_j O_j$ measures the expected[59] loss to j from punishment of offenders committing any of the O_j. Whereas most punishments result in a net loss to society as a whole, they often produce a gain for the actual victims. For example, punishment by fines given to the actual victims is just a transfer payment for society but is a clear gain to victims; similarly, punishment by imprisonment is a net loss to

---

[58] An increase in C_k—O_j and C held constant—presumably helps solve offenses against j, because more of those against k would be solved.

[59] The expected private loss, unlike the expected social loss, is apt to have considerable variance because of the small number of independent offenses committed against any single person. If j were not risk neutral, therefore, L would have to be modified to include a term that depended on the distribution of $b_j p_j f_j O_j$.

society but is a negligible loss to victims, since they usually pay a negligible part of imprisonment costs. This is why b_j is often less than or equal to zero, at the same time that b, the coefficient of social loss, is greater than or equal to zero.

Since b_j and f_j are determined primarily by public policy on punishments, the main decision variable directly controlled by j is p_j. If he chooses a p_j that minimizes L_j, the optimality condition analogous to equation (22) is

$$H'_j + C'_j + C_{jp_j} \frac{\partial p_j}{\partial O_j} = -b_j p_j f_j \left(1 - \frac{1}{\varepsilon_{jp_j}}\right). ^{60} \qquad (32)$$

The elasticity ε_{jp_j} measures the effect of a change in p_j on the number of offenses committed against j. If $b_j < 0$, and if the left-hand side of equation (32), the marginal cost of changing O_j, were greater than zero, then (32) implies that $\varepsilon_{jp_j} > 1$. Since offenders can substitute among victims, ε_{jp_j} is probably much larger than ε_p, the response of the total number of offenses to a change in the average probability, p. There is no inconsistency, therefore, between a requirement from the optimality condition given by (22) that $\varepsilon_p < 1$ and a requirement from (32) that $\varepsilon_{jp_j} > 1$.

VII. Some Applications

A. Optimal Benefits

Our analysis of crime is a generalization of the economist's analysis of external harm or diseconomies. Analytically, the generalization con-

---

[60] I have assumed that

$$\frac{\partial C}{\partial p_j} = \frac{\partial C_k}{\partial p_j} = 0,$$

in other words, that j is too "unimportant" to influence other expenditures. Although usually reasonable, this does suggest a modification to the optimality conditions given by eqs. (21) and (22). Since the effects of public expenditures depend on the level of private ones, and since the public is sufficiently "important" to influence private actions, eq. (22) has to be modified to

$$D' + C' + C_p \frac{\partial p}{\partial O} + \sum_{i=1}^{n} \frac{dC}{dC_i} \frac{dC_i}{dp} \frac{\partial p}{\partial O} = -bpf \left(1 + \frac{1}{\varepsilon_p}\right), \qquad (22')$$

and similarly for eq. (21). "The" probability p is, of course, a weighted average of the p_j. Eq. (22') incorporates the presumption that an increase in public expenditures would be partially thwarted by an induced decrease in private ones.

sists in introducing costs of apprehension and conviction, which make the probability of apprehension and conviction an important decision variable, and in treating punishment by imprisonment and other methods as well as by monetary payments. A crime is apparently not so different analytically from any other activity that produces external harm and when crimes are punishable by fines, the analytical differences virtually vanish.

Discussions of external economies or advantages are usually perfectly symmetrical to those of diseconomies, yet one searches in vain for analogues to the law of torts and criminality. Generally, compensation cannot be collected for the external advantages as opposed to harm caused, and no public officials comparable to policemen and district attorneys apprehend and "convict" benefactors rather than offenders. Of course, there is public interest in benefactors: medals, prizes, titles, and other privileges have been awarded to military heroes, government officials, scientists, scholars, artists, and businessmen by public and private bodies. Among the most famous are Nobel Prizes, Lenin Prizes, the Congressional Medal of Honor, knighthood, and patent rights. But these are piecemeal efforts that touch a tiny fraction of the population and lack the guidance of any body of law that codifies and analyzes different kinds of advantages.

Possibly the explanation for this lacuna is that criminal and tort law developed at the time when external harm was more common than advantages, or possibly the latter have been difficult to measure and thus considered too prone to favoritism. In any case, it is clear that the asymmetry in the law does not result from any analytical asymmetry, for a formal analysis of advantages, benefits, and benefactors can be developed that is quite symmetrical to the analysis of damages, offenses, and offenders. A function $A(B)$, for example, can give the net social advantages from B benefits in the same way that $D(O)$ gives the net damages from O offenses. Likewise, $K(B, p_1)$ can give the cost of apprehending and rewarding benefactors, where p_1 is the probability of so doing, with K' and $K_p > 0$; $B(p_1, a, v)$ can give the supply of benefits, where a is the award per benefit and v represents other determinants, with $\partial B/\partial p_1$ and $\partial B/\partial a > 0$; and b_1 can be the fraction of a that is a net loss to society. Instead of a loss function showing the decrease in social income from offenses, there can be a profit function showing the increase in income from benefits:

$$\Pi = A(B) - K(B, p_1) - b_1 p_1 aB. \tag{33}$$

If Π is maximized by choosing appropriate values of p_1 and a, the optimality conditions analogous to equations (21) and (22) are

$$A' - K' = b_1 p_1 a \left(1 + \frac{1}{e_a}\right) \tag{34}$$

and

$$A' - K' - K_p \frac{\partial p_1}{\partial B} = b_1 p_1 a \left(1 + \frac{1}{e_p}\right), \tag{35}$$

where

$$e_a = \frac{\partial B}{\partial a} \frac{a}{B}$$

and

$$e_p = \frac{\partial B}{\partial p_1} \frac{p_1}{B}$$

are both greater than zero. The implications of these equations are related to and yet differ in some important respects from those discussed earlier for (21) and (22).

For example, if $b_1 > 0$, which means that a is not a pure transfer but costs society resources, clearly (34) and (35) imply that $e_p > e_a$, since both $K_p > 0$ and $\partial p_1/\partial B > 0$. This is analogous to the implication of (21) and (22) that $\varepsilon_p > \varepsilon_f$, but, while the latter implies that, at the margin, offenders are risk *preferrers*, the former implies that, at the margin, benefactors are risk *avoiders*.[61] Thus, while the optimal values

[61] The relation $e_p > e_a$ holds if, and only if,

$$\frac{\partial EU}{\partial p_1} \frac{p_1}{U} > \frac{\partial EU}{\partial a} \frac{a}{U}, \tag{1'}$$

where

$$EU = p_1 U(Y + a) + (1 - p_1)U(Y) \tag{2'}$$

(see the discussion on pp. 545–48). By differentiating eq. (2'), one can write (1') as

$$p_1[U(Y + a) - U(Y)] > p_1 a U'(Y + a), \tag{3'}$$

or

$$\frac{U(Y + a) - U(Y)}{a} > U'(Y + a). \tag{4'}$$

But (4') holds if everywhere $U'' < 0$ and does not hold if everywhere $U'' \geq 0$, which was to be proved.

of p and f would be in a region where "crime does not pay"—in the sense that the marginal income of criminals would be less than that available to them in less risky legal activities—the optimal values of p_1 and a would be where "benefits do pay"—in the same sense that the marginal income of benefactors would exceed that available to them in less risky activities. In this sense it "pays" to do "good" and does not "pay" to do "bad."

As an illustration of the analysis, consider the problem of rewarding inventors for their inventions. The function $A(B)$ gives the total social value of B inventions, and A' gives the marginal value of an additional one. The function $K(B, p_1)$ gives the cost of finding and rewarding inventors; if a patent system is used, it measures the cost of a patent office, of preparing applications, and of the lawyers, judges, and others involved in patent litigation.[62] The elasticities e_p and e_a measure the response of inventors to changes in the probability and magnitude of awards, while b_1 measures the social cost of the method used to award inventors. With a patent system, the cost consists in a less extensive use of an invention than would otherwise occur, and in any monopoly power so created.

Equations (34) and (35) imply that with any system having $b_1 > 0$, the smaller the elasticities of response of inventors, the smaller should be the probability and magnitude of awards. (The value of a patent can be changed, for example, by changing its life.) This shows the relevance of the controversy between those who maintain that most inventions stem from a basic desire "to know" and those who maintain that most stem from the prospects of financial awards, especially today with the emphasis on systematic investment in research and development. The former quite consistently usually advocate a weak patent system, while the latter equally consistently advocate its strengthening.

Even if A', the marginal value of an invention, were "sizeable," the optimal decision would be to abolish property rights in an invention, that is, to set $p_1 = 0$, if b_1 and K[63] were sufficiently large and/or the elasticities e_p and e_a sufficiently small. Indeed, practically all arguments to eliminate or greatly alter the patent system have been based either on its alleged costliness, large K or b_1, or lack of effectiveness, low e_p or e_a (see, for example, Plant, 1934, or Arrow, 1962).

If a patent system were replaced by a system of cash prizes, the elasticities of response would become irrelevant for the determination

---

[62] These costs are not entirely trivial: for example, in 1966 the U.S. Patent Office alone spent $34 million (see Bureau of the Budget, 1967), and much more was probably spent in preparing applications and in litigation.

[63] Presumably one reason patents are not permitted on basic research is the difficulty (that is, cost) of discovering the ownership of new concepts and theorems.

of optimal policies, because b_1 would then be approximately zero.[64] A system of prizes would, moreover, have many of the same other advantages that fines have in punishing offenders (see the discussion in Sec. V). One significant advantage of a patent system, however, is that it automatically "meters" A', that is, provides an award that is automatically positively related to A', while a system of prizes (or of fines and imprisonment) has to estimate A' (or D') independently and often somewhat arbitrarily.

B. The Effectiveness of Public Policy

The anticipation of conviction and punishment reduces the loss from offenses and thus increases social welfare by discouraging some offenders. What determines the increase in welfare, that is "effectiveness," of public efforts to discourage offenses? The model developed in Section III can be used to answer this question if social welfare is measured by income and if "effectiveness" is defined as a ratio of the maximum feasible increase in income to the increase if all offenses causing net damages were abolished by fiat. The maximum feasible increase is achieved by choosing optimal values of the probability of apprehension and conviction, p, and the size of punishments, f (assuming that the coefficient of social loss from punishment, b, is given).[65]

Effectiveness so defined can vary between zero and unity and depends essentially on two behavioral relations: the costs of apprehension and conviction and the elasticities of response of offenses to changes in p and f. The smaller these costs or the greater these elasticities, the

---

[64] The right side of both (34) and (35) would vanish, and the optimality conditions would be

$$A' - K' = 0 \qquad (34')$$

and

$$A' - K' - K_p \frac{\partial p_1}{\partial B} = 0. \qquad (35')$$

Since these equations are not satisfied by any finite values of p_1 and a, there is a difficulty in allocating the incentives between p_1 and a (see the similar discussion for fines in Sec. V).

[65] In symbols, effectiveness is defined as

$$E = \frac{D(O_1) - [D(\hat{O}) + C(\hat{p}, \hat{O}) + b\hat{p}\hat{f}\hat{O}]}{D(O_1) - D(O_2)},$$

where $\hat{p}, \hat{f},$ and $\hat{O}$ are optimal values, O_1 offenses would occur if $p = f = 0$, and O_2 is the value of O that minimizes D.

smaller the cost of achieving any given reduction in offenses and thus the greater the effectiveness. The elasticities may well differ considerably among different kinds of offenses. For example, crimes of passion, like murder or rape, or crimes of youth, like auto theft, are often said to be less responsive to changes in p and f than are more calculating crimes by adults, like embezzlement, antitrust violation, or bank robbery. The elasticities estimated by Smigel (1965) and Ehrlich (1967) for seven major felonies do differ considerably but are not clearly smaller for murder, rape, auto theft, and assault than for robbery, burglary, and larceny.[66]

Probably effectiveness differs among offenses more because of differences in the costs of apprehension and conviction than in the elasticities of response. An important determinant of these costs, and one that varies greatly, is the time between commission and detection of an offense.[67] For the earlier an offense is detected, the earlier the police can be brought in and the more likely that the victim is able personally to identify the offender. This suggests that effectiveness is greater for robbery than for a related felony like burglary, or for minimum-wage and fair-employment legislation than for other white-collar legislation like antitrust and public-utility regulation.[68]

C. A Theory of Collusion

The theory developed in this essay can be applied to any effort to preclude certain kinds of behavior, regardless of whether the behavior is "unlawful." As an example, consider efforts by competing firms to collude in order to obtain monopoly profits. Economists lack a satisfactory theory of the determinants of price and output policies by firms in an industry, a theory that could predict under what conditions perfectly competitive, monopolistic, or various intermediate kinds of behavior would emerge. One by-product of our approach to crime and punishment is a theory of collusion that appears to fill a good part of this lacuna.[69]

[66] A theoretical argument that also casts doubt on the assertion that less "calculating" offenders are less responsive to changes in p and f can be found in Becker (1962).

[67] A study of crimes in parts of Los Angeles during January, 1966, found that "more than half the arrests were made within 8 hours of the crime, and almost two-thirds were made within the first week" (President's Commission, 1967e, p. 8).

[68] Evidence relating to the effectiveness of actual, which are not necessarily optimal, penalties for these white-collar crimes can be found in Stigler (1962, 1966), Landes (1966), and Johnson (1967).

[69] Jacob Mincer first suggested this application to me.

The gain to firms from colluding is positively related to the elasticity of their marginal cost curves and is inversely related to the elasticity of their collective demand curve. A firm that violates a collusive arrangement by pricing below or producing more than is specified can be said to commit an "offense" against the collusion. The resulting harm to the collusion would depend on the number of violations and on the elasticities of demand and marginal cost curves, since the gain from colluding depends on these elasticities.

If violations could be eliminated without cost, the optimal solution would obviously be to eliminate all of them and to engage in pure monopoly pricing. In general, however, as with other kinds of offenses, there are two costs of eliminating violations. There is first of all the cost of discovering violations and of "apprehending" violators. This cost is greater the greater the desired probability of detection and the greater the number of violations. Other things the same, the latter is usually positively related to the number of firms in an industry, which partly explains why economists typically relate monopoly power to concentration. The cost of achieving a given probability of detection also depends on the number of firms, on the number of customers, on the stability of customer buying patterns, and on government policies toward collusive arrangements (see Stigler, 1964).

Second, there is the cost to the collusion of punishing violators. The most favorable situation is one in which fines could be levied against violators and collected by the collusion. If fines and other legal recourse are ruled out, methods like predatory price-cutting or violence have to be used, and they hurt the collusion as well as violators.

Firms in a collusion are assumed to choose probabilities of detection, punishments to violators, and prices and outputs that minimize their loss from violations, which would at the same time maximize their gain from colluding. Optimal prices and outputs would be closer to the competitive position the more elastic demand curves were, the greater the number of sellers and buyers, the less transferable punishments were, and the more hostile to collusion governments were. Note that misallocation of resources could not be measured simply by the deviation of actual from competitive outputs but would depend also on the cost of enforcing collusions. Note further, and more importantly, that this theory, unlike most theories of pricing, provides for continuous variation, from purely competitive through intermediate situations to purely monopolistic pricing. These situations differ primarily because of differences in the "optimal" number of violations, which in turn are related to differences in the elasticities, concentrations, legislation, etc., already mentioned.

These ideas appear to be helpful in understanding the relative success of collusions in illegal industries themselves! Just as firms in legal industries have an incentive to collude to raise prices and profits, so too do firms producing illegal products, such as narcotics, gambling, prostitution, and abortion. The "syndicate" is an example of a presumably highly successful collusion that covers several illegal products.[70] In a country like the United States that prohibits collusions, those in illegal industries would seem to have an advantage, because force and other illegal methods could be used against violators without the latter having much legal recourse. On the other hand, in countries like prewar Germany that legalized collusions, those in legal industries would have an advantage, because violators could often be legally prosecuted. One would predict, therefore, from this consideration alone, relatively more successful collusions in illegal industries in the United States, and in legal ones in prewar Germany.

VIII. Summary and Concluding Remarks

This essay uses economic analysis to develop optimal public and private policies to combat illegal behavior. The public's decision variables are its expenditures on police, courts, etc., which help determine the probability (p) that an offense is discovered and the offender apprehended and convicted, the size of the punishment for those convicted (f), and the form of the punishment: imprisonment, probation, fine, etc. Optimal values of these variables can be chosen subject to, among other things, the constraints imposed by three behavioral relations. One shows the damages caused by a given number of illegal actions, called offenses (O), another the cost of achieving a given p, and the third the effect of changes in p and f on O.

"Optimal" decisions are interpreted to mean decisions that minimize the social loss in income from offenses. This loss is the sum of damages, costs of apprehension and conviction, and costs of carrying out the punishments imposed, and can be minimized simultaneously with respect to p, f, and the form of f unless one or more of these variables is constrained by "outside" considerations. The optimality conditions derived from the minimization have numerous interesting implications that can be illustrated by a few examples.

If carrying out the punishment were costly, as it is with probation, imprisonment, or parole, the elasticity of response of offenses with respect to a change in p would generally, in equilibrium, have to exceed its response to a change in f. This implies, if entry into illegal

---

[70] An interpretation of the syndicate along these lines is also found in Schilling (1967).

activities can be explained by the same model of choice that economists use to explain entry into legal activities, that offenders are (at the margin) "risk preferrers." Consequently, illegal activities "would not pay" (at the margin) in the sense that the real income received would be less than what could be received in less risky legal activities. The conclusion that "crime would not pay" is an optimality condition and not an implication about the efficiency of the police or courts; indeed, it holds for any level of efficiency, as long as optimal values of p and f appropriate to each level are chosen.

If costs were the same, the optimal values of both p and f would be greater, the greater the damage caused by an offense. Therefore, offenses like murder and rape should be solved more frequently and punished more severely than milder offenses like auto theft and petty larceny. Evidence on actual probabilities and punishments in the United States is strongly consistent with this implication of the optimality analysis.

Fines have several advantages over other punishments: for example, they conserve resources, compensate society as well as punish offenders, and simplify the determination of optimal p's and f's. Not surprisingly, fines are the most common punishment and have grown in importance over time. Offenders who cannot pay fines have to be punished in other ways, but the optimality analysis implies that the monetary value to them of these punishments should generally be less than the fines.

Vengeance, deterrence, safety, rehabilitation, and compensation are perhaps the most important of the many desiderata proposed throughout history. Next to these, minimizing the social loss in income may seem narrow, bland, and even quaint. Unquestionably, the income criterion can be usefully generalized in several directions, and a few have already been suggested in the essay. Yet one should not lose sight of the fact that it is more general and powerful than it may seem and actually includes more dramatic desiderata as special cases. For example, if punishment were by an optimal fine, minimizing the loss in income would be equivalent to compensating "victims" fully and would eliminate the "alarm" that so worried Bentham; or it would be equivalent to deterring all offenses causing great damage if the cost of apprehending, convicting, and punishing these offenders were relatively small. Since the same could also be demonstrated for vengeance or rehabilitation, the moral should be clear: minimizing the loss in income is actually very general and thus is *more useful* than these catchy and dramatic but inflexible desiderata.

This essay concentrates almost entirely on determining optimal policies to combat illegal behavior and pays little attention to actual policies. The small amount of evidence on actual policies that I have examined certainly suggests a positive correspondence with optimal policies. For example, it is found for seven major felonies in the United States that more damaging ones are penalized more severely, that the elasticity of response of offenses to changes in p exceeds the response to f, and that both are usually less than unity, all as predicted by the optimality analysis. There are, however, some discrepancies too: for example, the actual tradeoff between imprisonment and fines in different statutes is frequently less, rather than the predicted more, favorable to those imprisoned. Although many more studies of actual policies are needed, they are seriously hampered on the empirical side by grave limitations in the quantity and quality of data on offenses, convictions, costs, etc., and on the analytical side by the absence of a reliable theory of political decision-making.

Reasonable men will often differ on the amount of damages or benefits caused by different activities. To some, any wage rates set by competitive labor markets are permissible, while to others, rates below a certain minimum are violations of basic rights; to some, gambling, prostitution, and even abortion should be freely available to anyone willing to pay the market price, while to others, gambling is sinful and abortion is murder. These differences are basic to the development and implementation of public policy but have been excluded from my inquiry. I assume consensus on damages and benefits and simply try to work out rules for an optimal implementation of this consensus.

The main contribution of this essay, as I see it, is to demonstrate that optimal policies to combat illegal behavior are part of an optimal allocation of resources. Since economics has been developed to handle resource allocation, an "economic" framework becomes applicable to, and helps enrich, the analysis of illegal behavior. At the same time, certain unique aspects of the latter enrich economic analysis: some punishments, such as imprisonments, are necessarily non-monetary and are a cost to society as well as to offenders; the degree of uncertainty is a decision variable that enters both the revenue and cost functions; etc.

Lest the reader be repelled by the apparent novelty of an "economic" framework for illegal behavior, let him recall that two important contributors to criminology during the eighteenth and nineteenth centuries, Beccaria and Bentham, explicitly applied an economic calculus. Unfortunately, such an approach has lost favor during the last hundred years, and my efforts can be viewed as a resurrection, modernization, and thereby I hope improvement on these much earlier pioneering studies.

Mathematical Appendix

This Appendix derives the effects of changes in various parameters on the optimal values of p and f. It is assumed throughout that $b > 0$ and that equilibrium occurs where

$$\frac{\partial D}{\partial O} + \frac{\partial C}{\partial O} + \frac{\partial C}{\partial p}\frac{\partial p}{\partial O} = D' + C' + C_p \frac{\partial p}{\partial O} > 0;$$

the analysis could easily be extended to cover negative values of b and of this marginal cost term. The conclusion in the text (Sec. II) that $D'' + C'' > 0$ is relied on here. I take it to be a reasonable first approximation that the elasticities of O with respect to p or f are constant. At several places a sufficient condition for the conclusions reached is that

$$C_{pO} = C_{Op} = \frac{\partial^2 C}{\partial p \partial O} = \frac{\partial^2 C}{\partial O \partial p}$$

is "small" relative to some other terms. This condition is utilized in the form of a strong assumption that $C_{pO} = 0$, although I cannot claim any supporting intuitive or other evidence.

The social loss in income from offenses has been defined as

$$L = D(O) + C(O, p) + bpfO. \tag{A1}$$

If b and p were fixed, the value of f that minimized L would be found from the necessary condition

$$\frac{\partial L}{\partial f} = 0 = (D' + C')\frac{\partial O}{\partial f} + bpf(1 - E_f)\frac{\partial O}{\partial f}, \tag{A2}$$

or

$$0 = D' + C' + bpf(1 - E_f), \tag{A3}$$

if

$$\frac{\partial O}{\partial f} = O_f \neq 0,$$

where

$$E_f = \frac{-\partial f}{\partial O}\frac{O}{f}.$$

The sufficient condition would be that $\partial^2 L/\partial f^2 > 0$; using $\partial L/\partial f = 0$ and E_f is constant, this condition becomes

$$\frac{\partial^2 L}{\partial f^2} = (D'' + C'')O_f^2 + bp(1 - E_f)O_f > 0, \tag{A4}$$

or

$$\Delta \equiv D'' + C'' + bp(1 - E_f)\frac{1}{O_f} > 0. \tag{A5}$$

Since $D' + C' > 0$, and b is not less than zero, equation (A3) implies that $E_f > 1$. Therefore Δ would be greater than zero, since we are assuming that $D'' + C'' > 0$; and $\hat{f}$, the value of f satisfying (A3), would minimize (locally) the loss L.

Suppose that D' is positively related to an exogenous variable α. The effect of a change in α on $\hat{f}$ can be found by differentiating equation (A3):

$$D'_\alpha + (D'' + C'')O_f \frac{d\hat{f}}{d\alpha} + bp(1 - E_f)\frac{d\hat{f}}{d\alpha} = 0,$$

or

$$\frac{d\hat{f}}{d\alpha} = \frac{-D'_\alpha(1/O_f)}{\Delta}. \tag{A6}$$

Since $\Delta > 0$, $O_f < 0$, and by assumption $D'_\alpha > 0$, then

$$\frac{d\hat{f}}{d\alpha} = \frac{+}{+} > 0. \tag{A7}$$

In a similar way it can be shown that, if C' is positively related to an exogenous variable β,

$$\frac{d\hat{f}}{d\beta} = \frac{-C'_\beta(1/O_f)}{\Delta} = \frac{+}{+} > 0. \tag{A8}$$

If b is positively related to γ, then

$$(D'' + C'')O_f \frac{d\hat{f}}{d\gamma} + bp(1 - E_f)\frac{d\hat{f}}{d\gamma} + pf(1 - E_f)b\gamma = 0,$$

or

$$\frac{d\hat{f}}{d\gamma} = \frac{-b_\gamma pf(1 - E_f)(1/O_f)}{\Delta}. \tag{A9}$$

Since $1 - E_f < 0$, and by assumption $b_\gamma > 0$,

$$\frac{d\hat{f}}{d\gamma} = \frac{-}{+} < 0. \tag{A10}$$

Note that since $1/E_f < 1$,

$$\frac{d(p\hat{f}O)}{d\gamma} < 0. \tag{A11}$$

If E_f is positively related to δ, then

$$\frac{d\hat{f}}{d\delta} = \frac{E_{f\delta}bpf(1/O_f)}{\Delta} = \frac{-}{+} < 0. \tag{A12}$$

Since the elasticity of O with respect to f equals

$$\varepsilon_f = -O_f\frac{f}{O} = \frac{1}{E_f},$$

by (A12), a reduction in ε_f would reduce $\hat{f}$.

Suppose that p is related to the exogenous variable r. Then the effect of a shift in r on $\hat{f}$ can be found from

$$(D'' + C'')O_f\frac{d\hat{f}}{dr} + (D'' + C'')O_p p_r + C_{pO}p_r$$
$$+ bp(1 - E_f)\frac{\partial\hat{f}}{\partial r} + bf(1 - E_f)p_r = 0,$$

or

$$\frac{d\hat{f}}{dr} = \frac{-(D'' + C'')O_p(1/O_f)p_r - bf(1 - E_f)p_r(1/O_f)}{\Delta}, \tag{A13}$$

since by assumption $C_{pO} = 0$. Since $O_p < 0$, and $(D'' + C'') > 0$,

$$\frac{d\hat{f}}{dr} = \frac{(-) + (-)}{+} = \frac{-}{+} < 0. \tag{A14}$$

If f rather than p were fixed, the value of p that minimizes L, $\hat{p}$, could be found from

$$\frac{\partial L}{\partial p} = \left[D' + C' + C_p\frac{1}{O_p} + bpf(1 - E_p) \right]O_p = 0, \tag{A15}$$

as long as

$$\frac{\partial^2 L}{\partial p^2} = \left[(D'' + C'')O_p + C_p' + C_{pp}\frac{1}{O_p} + C_{pO} + C_p\frac{\partial^2 p}{\partial O \partial p} \right. $$
$$\left. + bf(1 - E_p) \right]O_p > 0. \tag{A16}$$

Since $C_p' = C_{pO} = 0$, (A16) would hold if

$$\Delta' \equiv D'' + C'' + C_{pp}\frac{1}{O_p^2} + C_p\frac{1}{O_p}\frac{\partial^2 p}{\partial O \partial p} + bf(1 - E_p)\frac{1}{O_p} > 0.$$
(A17)

It is suggested in Section II that C_{pp} is generally greater than zero. If, as assumed,

$$D' + C' + C_p\frac{1}{O_p} > 0,$$

equation (A15) implies that $E_p > 1$ and thus that

$$bf(1 - E_p)\frac{1}{O_p} > 0.$$

If E_p were constant, $\partial^2 p/\partial O \partial p$ would be negative,[71] and, therefore, $C_p(1/O_p)$ $\times (\partial^2 p/\partial O \partial p)$ would be positive. Hence, none of the terms of (A17) are negative, and a value of p satisfying equation (A15) would be a local minimum.

[71] If E_p and E_f are constants, $O = kp^{-a}f^{-b}$, where $a = 1/E_p$ and $b = 1/E_f$. Then

$$\frac{\partial p}{\partial O} = -\frac{1}{ka}p^{a+1}f^b,$$

and

$$\frac{\partial^2 p}{\partial O \partial p} = \frac{-(a + 1)}{ka}p^a f^b < 0.$$

[72] The term $(1 - E_p)\Delta$ would be greater than $(1 - E_f)\Sigma$ if

$$(D'' + C'')(1 - E_p) + bp(1 - E_f)(1 - E_p)f_o$$
$$> (D'' + C'')(1 - E_f) + bf(1 - E_f)^2 p_o,$$

or

$$(D'' + C'')(E_f - E_p) > -\frac{bpf}{O}(1 - E_f)\left[(1 - E_p)\frac{f_o O}{f} - (1 - E_f)\frac{p_o O}{p}\right],$$

$$(D'' + C'')(E_f - E_p) > -\frac{bpf}{O}(1 - E_f)[(1 - E_p)(E_f) - (1 - E_f)E_p],$$

$$(D'' + C'')(E_f - E_p) > -\frac{bpf}{O}(1 - E_f)(E_f - E_p).$$

Since the left-hand side is greater than zero, and the right-hand side is less than zero, the inequality must hold.

The effects of changes in different parameters on $\hat{p}$ are similar to those already derived for f and can be written without comment:

$$\frac{d\hat{p}}{d\alpha} = \frac{-D'_\alpha(1/O_p)}{\Delta'} > 0,$$ (A18)

$$\frac{d\hat{p}}{d\beta} = \frac{-C'_\beta(1/O_p)}{\Delta'} > 0,$$ (A19)

and

$$\frac{d\hat{p}}{d\gamma} = \frac{-b_\gamma pf(1 - E_p)(1/O_p)}{\Delta'} < 0.$$ (A20)

If E_p is positively related to δ',

$$\frac{d\hat{p}}{d\delta'} = \frac{E_{p\delta'} bpf(1/O_p)}{\Delta'} < 0.$$ (A21)

If C_p were positively related to the parameter s, the effect of a change in s on $\hat{p}$ would equal

$$\frac{d\hat{p}}{ds} = \frac{-C_{ps}(1/O_p^2)}{\Delta'} < 0.$$ (A22)

If f were related to the exogenous parameter t, the effect of a change in t on $\hat{p}$ would be given by

$$\frac{d\hat{p}}{dt} =$$

$$\frac{-(D'' + C'')O_p f_t(1/O_p) - bf(1 - E_p)f_t(1/O_p) - C_p(\partial^2 p/\partial O\partial f)f_t(1/O_p)}{\Delta'} < 0$$ (A23)

(with $C_{pO} = 0$), since all the terms in the numerator are negative.

If both p and f were subject to control, L would be minimized by choosing optimal values of both variables simultaneously. These would be given by the solutions to the two first-order conditions, equations (A2) and (A15), assuming that certain more general second-order conditions were satisfied. The effects of changes in various parameters on these optimal values can be found by differentiating both first-order conditions and incorporating the restrictions of the second-order conditions.

The values of p and f satisfying (A2) and (A15), $\hat{p}$ and $\hat{f}$, minimize L if

$$L_{pp} > 0, \ L_{ff} > 0,$$ (A24)

and

$$L_{pp}L_{ff} > L_{fp}^2 = L_{pf}^2. \tag{A25}$$

But $L_{pp} = O_p^2\Delta'$, and $L_{ff} = O_f^2\Delta$, and since both Δ' and Δ have been shown to be greater than zero, (A24) is proved already, and only (A25) remains. By differentiating L_f with respect to p and utilizing the first-order condition that $L_f = 0$, one has

$$L_{fp} = O_f O_p[D'' + C'' + bf(1 - E_f)p_O] = O_f O_p\Sigma, \tag{A26}$$

where Σ equals the term in brackets. Clearly $\Sigma > 0$.
    By substitution, (A25) becomes

$$\Delta\Delta' > \Sigma^2, \tag{A27}$$

and (A27) holds if Δ and Δ' are both greater than Σ. $\Delta > \Sigma$ means that

$$D'' + C'' + bp(1 - E_f)f_O > D'' + C'' + bf(1 - E_f)p_O, \tag{A28}$$

or

$$\frac{bfp}{O}(1 - E_f)E_f < \frac{bpf}{O}(1 - E_f)E_p. \tag{A29}$$

Since $1 - E_f < 0$, (A29) implies that

$$E_f > E_p, \tag{A30}$$

which necessarily holds given the assumption that $b > 0$; prove this by combining the two first-order conditions (A2) and (A15). $\Delta' > \Sigma$ means that

$$D'' + C'' + C_{pp}p_O^2 + C_p p_O p_{Op} + bf(1 - E_f)p_O \\ > D'' + C'' + bf(1 - E_f)p_O. \tag{A31}$$

Since $C_{pp}p_O^2 > 0$, and $p_O < 0$, this necessarily holds if

$$C_p p p_{Op} + bpf(1 - E_p) < bpf(1 - E_f). \tag{A32}$$

By eliminating $D' + C'$ from the first-order conditions (A2) and (A15) and by combining terms, one has

$$C_p p_O - bpf(E_p - E_f) = 0. \tag{A33}$$

By combining (A32) and (A33), one gets the condition

$$C_p p p_{Op} < C_p p_O, \tag{A34}$$

or

$$E_{p_O,p} = \frac{p}{p_O} \frac{\partial p_O}{\partial p} > 1. \tag{A35}$$

It can be shown that

$$E_{p_O,p} = 1 + \frac{1}{E_p} > 1, \tag{A36}$$

and, therefore, (A35) is proven.

It has now been proved that the values of p and f that satisfy the first-order conditions (A2) and (A15) do indeed minimize (locally) L. Changes in different parameters change these optimal values, and the direction and magnitude can be found from the two linear equations

$$O_f \Delta \frac{\partial \tilde{f}}{\partial z} + O_p \Sigma \frac{\partial \tilde{p}}{\partial z} = C_1$$

and $\qquad\qquad\qquad\qquad\qquad\qquad\qquad\qquad\qquad$ (A37)

$$O_f \Sigma \frac{\partial \tilde{f}}{\partial z} + O_p \Delta' \frac{\partial \tilde{p}}{\partial z} = C_2.$$

By Cramer's rule,

$$\frac{\partial \tilde{f}}{\partial z} = \frac{C_1 O_p \Delta' - C_2 O_p \Sigma}{O_p O_f (\Delta\Delta' - \Sigma^2)} = \frac{O_p(C_1 \Delta' - C_2 \Sigma)}{+}, \tag{A38}$$

$$\frac{\partial \tilde{p}}{\partial z} = \frac{C_2 O_f \Delta - C_1 O_f \Sigma}{O_p O_f (\Delta\Delta' - \Sigma^2)} = \frac{O_f(C_2 \Delta - C_1 \Sigma)}{+}, \tag{A39}$$

and the signs of both derivatives are the same as the signs of the numerators.

Consider the effect of a change in D' resulting from a change in the parameter α. It is apparent that $C_1 = C_2 = -D'_\alpha$, and by substitution

$$\frac{\partial \tilde{f}}{\partial \alpha} = \frac{-O_p D'_\alpha (\Delta' - \Sigma)}{+} = \frac{+}{+} > 0 \tag{A40}$$

and

$$\frac{\partial \tilde{p}}{\partial \alpha} = \frac{-O_p D'_\alpha (\Delta - \Sigma)}{+} = \frac{+}{+} > 0, \tag{A41}$$

since O_f and $O_p < 0$, $D'_\alpha > 0$, and Δ and $\Delta' > \Sigma$.

Similarly, if C' is changed by a change in β, $C_1 = C_2 = -C'_\beta$,

$$\frac{\partial \tilde{f}}{\partial \beta} = \frac{-O_p C_\beta' (\Delta' - \Sigma)}{+} = \frac{+}{+} > 0, \tag{A42}$$

and

$$\frac{\partial \tilde{p}}{\partial \beta} = \frac{-O_f C_\beta' (\Delta - \Sigma)}{+} = \frac{+}{+} > 0. \tag{A43}$$

If E_f is changed by a change in δ, $C_1 = E_{f\delta} bpf$, $C_2 = 0$,

$$\frac{\partial \tilde{f}}{\partial \delta} = \frac{O_p E_f bpf \Delta'}{+} = \frac{-}{+} < 0, \tag{A44}$$

and

$$\frac{\partial \tilde{p}}{\partial \delta} = \frac{-O_f E_f bpf \Sigma}{+} = \frac{+}{+} > 0. \tag{A45}$$

Similarly, if E_p is changed by a change in δ', $C_1 = 0$, $C_2 = E_{p\delta'} bpf$,

$$\frac{\partial \tilde{f}}{\partial \delta'} = -\frac{O_p E_{p\delta'} bpf \Sigma}{+} = \frac{+}{+} > 0, \tag{A46}$$

and

$$\frac{\partial \tilde{p}}{\partial \delta'} = \frac{O_f E_{p\delta'} bpf \Delta}{+} = \frac{-}{+} < 0. \tag{A47}$$

If b is changed by a change in γ, $C_1 = -b_\gamma pf(1 - E_f)$, $C_2 = -b_\gamma pf$ $\times (1 - E_p)$, and

$$\frac{\partial \tilde{f}}{\partial \gamma} = \frac{-O_p b_\gamma pf[(1 - E_f)\Delta' - (1 - E_p)\Sigma]}{+} = \frac{-}{+} < 0, \tag{A48}$$

since $E_f > E_p > 1$ and $\Delta' > \Sigma$; also,

$$\frac{\partial \tilde{p}}{\partial \gamma} = \frac{-O_f b_\gamma pf[(1 - E_p)\Delta - (1 - E_f)\Sigma]}{+} = \frac{+}{+} > 0, \tag{A49}$$

for it can be shown that $(1 - E_p)\Delta > (1 - E_f)\Sigma$.[72] Note that when f is held constant the optimal value of p is decreased, not increased, by an increase in γ. If C_p is changed by a change in s, $C_2 = -p_0 C_{ps}$, $C_1 = 0$,

$$\frac{\partial \tilde{f}}{\partial s} = \frac{O_p p_0 C_{ps} \Sigma}{+} = \frac{C_{ps} \Sigma}{+} = \frac{+}{+} > 0, \tag{A50}$$

and

$$\frac{\partial \bar{p}}{\partial s} = \frac{-O_f p_O C_{ps} \Delta}{+} = \frac{-}{+} < 0.$$ (A51)

References

Arrow, Kenneth J. "Economic Welfare and Allocation of Resources for Invention," in National Bureau Committee for Economic Research. *The Rate and Direction of Inventive Activity: Economic and Social Factors.* Princeton, N.J.: Princeton Univ. Press (for the Nat. Bureau of Econ. Res.), 1962.

Becker, Gary S. "Irrational Behavior and Economic Theory," *J.P.E.*, Vol. LXX (February, 1962).

———. "A Theory of the Allocation of Time," *Econ. J.*, Vol. LXXV (September, 1965).

Bentham, Jeremy. *Theory of Legislation.* New York: Harcourt Brace Co., 1931 reprint.

Bureau of the Budget. *The Budget of United States Government, 1968, Appendix.* Washington: U.S. Government Printing Office, 1967.

Bureau of Prisons. *Prisoners Released from State and Federal Institutions.* ("National Prisoner Statistics.") Washington: U.S. Dept. of Justice, 1960.

———. *Characteristics of State Prisoners, 1960.* ("National Prisoner Statistics.") U.S. Dept. of Justice, n.d.

———. *Federal Prisons, 1960.* Washington: U.S. Dept. of Justice, 1961.

Cagan, Phillip. *Determinants and Effects of Changes in the Stock of Money, 1875–1960.* New York: Columbia Univ. Press (for the Nat. Bureau of Econ. Res.), 1965.

"Criminal Safeguards and the Punitive Damages Defendant," *Univ. Chicago Law Rev.*, Vol. XXXIV (Winter, 1967).

Ehrlich, Isaac. "The Supply of Illegitimate Activities." Unpublished manuscript, Columbia Univ., New York, 1967.

Federal Bureau of Investigation. *Uniform Crime Reports for the United States.* Washington: U.S. Dept. of Justice, 1960.

———. *Ibid.*, 1961.

Harper, F. V., and James, F. *The Law of Torts*, Vol. II. Boston: Little-Brown & Co., 1956.

Johnson, Thomas. "The Effects of the Minimum Wage Law." Unpublished Ph.D. dissertation, Columbia Univ., New York, 1967.

Kleinman, E. "The Choice between Two 'Bads'—Some Economic Aspects of Criminal Sentencing." Unpublished manuscript, Hebrew Univ., Jerusalem, 1967.

Landes, William. "The Effect of State Fair Employment Legislation on the Economic Position of Nonwhite Males." Unpublished Ph.D. dissertation, Columbia Univ., New York, 1966.

Laws of New York, Vol. II (1965).

Marshall, Alfred. *Principles of Economics.* 8th ed. New York: Macmillan Co., 1961.

Plant, A. "The Economic Theory concerning Patents for Inventions," *Economica,* Vol. I (February, 1934).

Pollock, F., and Maitland, F. W. *The History of English Law.* Vol. II. 2d ed. Cambridge: Cambridge Univ. Press, 1952.

President's Commission on Law Enforcement and Administration of Justice. *The Challenge of Crime in a Free Society.* Washington: U.S. Government Printing Office, 1967(a).

———. *Corrections.* ("Task Force Reports.") Washington: U.S. Government Printing Office, 1967(b).

———. *The Courts.* ("Task Force Reports.") Washington: U.S. Government Printing Office, 1967(c).

———. *Crime and Its Impact—an Assessment.* ("Task Force Reports.") Washington: U.S. Government Printing Office, 1967(d).

———. *Science and Technology.* ("Task Force Reports.") Washington: U.S. Government Printing Office, 1967(e).

Radzinowicz, L. *A History of English Criminal Law and Its Administration from 1750.* Vol. I. London: Stevens & Sons, 1948.

Schilling, T. C. "Economic Analysis of Organized Crime," in President's Commission on Law Enforcement and Administration of Justice. *Organized Crime.* ("Task Force Reports.") Washington: U.S. Government Printing Office, 1967.

Shawness, Lord. "Crime *Does* Pay because We Do Not Back Up the Police," *New York Times Magazine,* June 13, 1965.

Smigel, Arleen. "Crime and Punishment: An Economic Analysis." Unpublished M.A. thesis, Columbia Univ., New York, 1965.

Stigler, George J. "A Theory of Oligopoly," *J.P.E.,* Vol. LXXII (February, 1964).

———. "The Economic Effects of the Antitrust Laws," *J. Law and Econ.,* Vol. IX (October, 1966).

Stigler, George J. and Friedland, C. "What Can Regulators Regulate? The Case of Electricity," *J. Law and Econ.,* Vol. V (October, 1962).

Sutherland, E. H. *Principles of Criminology,* 6th ed. Philadelphia: J. B. Lippincott Co., 1960.

Law Enforcement, Malfeasance, and Compensation of Enforcers

19

Gary S. Becker and George J. Stigler

The new economic approach to political behavior seeks to develop a positive theory of legislation, in contrast to the normative approach of welfare economics. The new approach asks why certain industries and not others become regulated or have tariffs imposed on imports or why income transfers take the form and direction they do, in contrast to asking which industries *should* be regulated or have tariffs imposed, or what transfers *should* be made.

Both the normative and positive approaches to legislation, however, generally have taken enforcement of laws for granted, and have not included systematic analyses of the cost of enforcing different kinds of laws. In separate studies[1] we recently formulated rules designed to increase the effectiveness of different laws. We proposed that offenders convicted of violating laws be punished by an amount related to the value of the damages caused to others, adjusted upwards for the probability that offenders avoid conviction.

In and of itself, this rule says nothing about appropriations for enforcing laws, or the diligence and honesty of enforcers. We did discuss optimal enforcement through the introduction of enforcement cost functions, but did not seek to explore the detailed content of these functions. The purpose of the present essay is to inquire more closely into the enforcement problem.

Part I discusses the general circumstances that influence the vigor of enforcement and the frequency of violations. Part II considers

Our research has been supported by a grant from the National Science Foundation to the National Bureau of Economic Research.

Reprinted with permission from the *Journal of Legal Studies* 3, no. 1 (January 1974): 1–18. © 1974 by The University of Chicago

[1] See Gary S. Becker, Crime and Punishment: An Economic Approach, 76 J. Pol. Econ. 169 (1968) (chap. 18 of this volume); George J. Stigler, The Optimum Enforcement of Laws, 78 J. Pol. Econ. 526 (1970).

the consequences of weak enforcement for the operation of the legal system. Part III makes two suggestions for improving the incentives given enforcers. Both utilize the price mechanism in related, yet somewhat different, ways: one penalizes malfeasance and other signs of weak enforcement; the other, which we think is preferable, rewards successful enforcement.

I. The Market in Enforcement

There is a powerful temptation in a society with established values to view any violation of a duly established law as a partial failure of that law. Even economists long trained in the harsh realities of a world in which wishes far outstrip resources will be found lamenting the moral laxity that leads to widespread violation of law. Yet it surely follows from basic economic principle that when some people wish to behave in a certain way very much, as measured by the amount they gain from it or would be willing to pay rather than forgo it, they will pursue that wish until it becomes too expensive for their purses and tastes. And in general it will not be inexpensive for society to make prohibited behavior expensive for the potential violator.

Thus the prohibitions of prostitution, gambling, and narcotics are widely held to be failures or at least very meager triumphs of enforcement. There is an obvious economic reason why violations should be extensive. These so-called victimless crimes are highly remunerative, if undetected, when entry into their performance is restricted by law. It is worth perhaps $500 a week to practice one of these trades in a neighborhood, and we must ask: to whom is it worth $500 a week to suppress the traffic? Indeed, a somewhat more effective enforcement of the prohibition would serve to increase the potential earnings. Unless the society has a preoccupation with this one goal to the exclusion of all others, it will not—it cannot—completely drive out the illegal activity, "whatever the cost."

Or reverse the viewpoint: how will the violator conduct himself? If a person violates a law carrying a punishment equivalent to[2] a fine of $10,000 he would be willing to spend up to $10,000 to avoid apprehension and conviction. He could, for example, bribe, intimidate, harass or cultivate the police to avoid apprehension, and prosecutors or judges to avoid conviction if apprehended.

The same problem is encountered in the enforcement of noncrimi-

---

[2] We say "equivalent to" because the punishment may be in the form of imprisonment, loss of business, probation, etc., instead of a fine.

nal policies which bear heavily on particular people or enterprises. The much publicized episode of International Telephone and Telegraph's endeavors to obtain permission to remain merged to Hartford Insurance is a striking, but perhaps widely misinterpreted, illustration of our argument. ITT deployed extensive resources to obtain consent for the merger—clearly the company would have been delighted to spend $10 million in a legal manner to obtain the consent. To whom was it worth this sum to prevent the merger? (As an aside, we do not believe it was worth anything to society to prevent it.) The common misinterpretation, we suspect, is to assign a special significance to the episode: we are prepared to predict that an equally complex and expensive set of negotiations has dwelt behind the process of every major governmental decision of comparable consequence to a large company or labor union. Another illustration is the Knapp Commission's report of significant corruption in the New York City police department, a corruption which we confidently predict is not unique to the largest city's police department.

In fact the problem is encountered throughout the private sector. Every employer of a person who will have the opportunity to serve his own interests at the cost of his employer faces the problem of fidelity. The employee may commit torts for which there are legal remedies, as when the purchasing agent receives subsidies from a favored supplier. The employee may simply engage in nonfeasance: shirking or under-performing tasks which cannot be completely supervised.[3] (Even the professor must determine whether the term paper he is grading was written or purchased by the student!)

We should abandon all thoughts of judging enforcement of laws and rules as simply successes or failures, even if these categories are "realistically" defined. The society (or a person) buys the amount of enforcement which it deems appropriate to the statute or rule: more will be bought if the statute serves a more valuable goal (protects us from murder rather than assault) and if a given increase in enforcement is less expensive. So it is with all prudent conduct.

The level of enforcement will depend upon a variety of factors in addition to the effort (i.e., the amount of resources) that the society is prepared to devote to enforcement as a function of the amount of enforcement (reduction in probability of successful commission of the offense) that is obtained. There is, first of all, the degree of honesty of the enforcers: for a given bribe, some men will condone offenses that other

[3] See Armen A. Alchian & Harold Demsetz, Production, Information Costs, and Economic Organization, 62 Am. Econ. Rev. 777 (1972); Gary S. Becker, Economic Theory 122–23 (1971).

men would prosecute. The honesty of enforcers will be dependent not only upon the supply of honesty in the population, but also on the amount spent to ascertain how honest a given person is. With an increasingly thorough and expensive investigation, one can determine with increasing precision the probable behavior of a given person.

There is, second, the structure of incentives to honesty embedded in the remuneration of enforcers. The correlation between the gain to enforcers from enforcing laws and the gain to violators from successful violation is almost certainly positive. But the variation in the gain to violators is often much greater than that to enforcers from preventing or punishing violations, so that the quality of enforcement would tend to decline as the gain to violators increased. This is one reason why effective enforcement against petty larcenists, muggers, or minor smugglers (once apprehended) is more common than it is against major antitrust or SEC violators, or wealthy murderers. The ITT case is in fact one illustration of this relation.

We do not mean that a highly profitable violation that is also flagrant and politically conspicuous can be committed without fear of apprehension and punishment. The penalty incurred by the enforcer—be he President, mayor, prosecuting attorney, or patrolman—from connivance would be sufficient to make it in his interest to enforce the law. Even so, would Leopold and Loeb, for example, have escaped the death penalty if their parents had been paupers?

The quality of enforcement depends, thirdly, on the temporal pattern of violations. It is difficult to bribe or even intimidate the enforcers who would be involved in a nonrepetitive violation. They are not easy to identify in advance—whose prowl car will be going by?—and not easy to negotiate with—how can negotiation be distinguished from entrapment? Repetitive violations, such as gambling, prostitution, or the sale of drugs, are otherwise. The substantial transactions costs of ascertaining that the other party is reliable (abides by contracts) become manageable for both violators and enforcers. In fact, the particular enforcers are no longer an independent variable: if the police chief is an unyielding saint, the mayor may be in greater need of cash.

This expectation of mutually profitable contracts between repetitive violators and enforcers is part of the logic behind the widely held view that prostitution or the regular sale of consumer goods cannot be successfully prohibited. It also helps explain the development of organized crime: an organization is engaged more continually in violations than its individual members are, and can, therefore, make arrangements with judges or police that would not be feasible for these members.

The quality of enforcement depends, fourthly, on whether a violation has a "victim," *i.e.*, a particular person who largely bears the cost of the violation. The customer of the numbers game or of the prostitute or of the marijuana peddler is not, in his opinion, a loser by these activities, as contrasted (say) to the person who is burglarized or charged more than the permissible rent. Enforcement is generally more effective against violations with victims because victims have a stake in apprehending violators, especially when they receive restitution (as the recovery of a stolen television set or the excess paid over the legal rental). Consequently, victims, in effect, often do the enforcing themselves. The role of victims in enforcement is discussed more extensively in Part III.

II. The Quality of Enforcement and the Effectiveness of Laws

We have argued that the quality of enforcement depends on the magnitude and regularity of violations, and the interests of victims, but have not considered the relation between the quality of enforcement and the effectiveness of laws. We do this now for corruption, an extreme manifestation of apparently poor enforcement; a related analysis can be developed for intimidated or lackadaisical enforcement.

Consider enforcers with sufficient evidence to convict a person of a violation that is punishable by a $5,000 fine. The violator would be willing to bribe enforcers as much as $5,000 to ignore the evidence. If a $5,000 bribe were paid,[4] the violation would be punished as fully as it would be if the violator paid the fine; consequently, the deterrent effects of the bribe and the fine would be the same. Moreover, if the enforcers anticipated the bribe (and had no fear of detection), they would be willing to work for $5,000 less than they otherwise would. Then the state, rather than the enforcers, would in essence be collecting the bribe. The transaction between the violator and the enforcers is equivalent to the violator's paying the state $5,000 for his violation; *i.e.*, it is equivalent to honest and diligent enforcement.

Effectiveness could actually be improved if a bribe of $5,000 were the alternative to punishment by a prison term with a monetary equivalent of a $5,000 fine. Again, one can show that the deterrence to violators would be the same, but with a bribe the state would collect as punishment not a prison term, but, in effect, a $5,000 fine. Since fines are preferable to other kinds of punishments,[5] the monetization of pun-

---

[4] A bribe would not be less than the value to an enforcer of enforcing a law, nor would it be greater than the cost to a violator of punishment. Its location between these extremes is determined by bargaining between the parties. We are indebted to William M. Landes for comments on this point.

[5] See Gary S. Becker, *supra* note 1, at 193–98; George J. Stigler, *supra* note 1, at 530–31.

ishments by bribery would improve the operation of the punishment system.

Effectiveness is reduced if the amount paid in bribes is significantly less than the monetary equivalent of the punishment. Bribes may be less because competition among enforcers (for example, alternative examiners for auto licenses) lowers the market price of bribes, or because the marketable resources of violators are less than the monetary value of punishments. In these cases, bribery reduces punishment and thus deterrence.[6]

Whether a reduction in effectiveness is desirable or not obviously depends on whether laws are passed in the "social" interest or to reward special interest groups, to revert to the theme of the opening paragraph of this essay. For example, bribes that reduced the effectiveness of many housing codes,[7] of the laws in Nazi Germany against Jews, or of the laws restricting oil imports, would improve, not harm, social welfare (although not as defined by the legislature). Some of the opposition we have encountered to our proposals (in Part III) to improve the quality of enforcement argues that more effective enforcement is often undesirable. Presumably, this is based on the belief that many laws or the way they can be interpreted do not promote social welfare.

III. How to Improve Enforcement

A. Punishing Malfeasance

In this part we make two proposals for improving the quality of enforcement, our assumption being that better enforcement, on the whole, does more good than bad. The first proposal concerns punishment of enforcers for taking bribes or other acts of misfeasance or nonfeasance. We assume that enforcers discovered committing such acts are simply dismissed. Although occasionally imprisonment and fines are imposed on enforcers discovered in the most flagrant bribe-taking, by far the most common sanction, if any, is dismissal.

If the state knew with certainty whenever enforcers did not perform adequately, and if dismissal always resulted, enforcers could be induced to perform adequately simply by being paid what they could get in other jobs requiring comparable skills, risk, effort, etc. To achieve certainty of detection, however, is extraordinarily expensive, partly because enforcers try to prevent detection. Since the state has its own

---

[6] Again, however, by monetizing punishments, bribery reduces the social cost of punishments.

[7] This is apropos of the recent [1974] revelation in the *New York Times* of significant bribery in the enforcement of these codes in New York City.

enforcement budget constraint, the effective probability of detection is invariably less than unity. How then can corrupt enforcement be discouraged when detection is uncertain?

The fundamental answer is to *raise* the salaries of enforcers above what they could get elsewhere, by an amount that is inversely related to the probability of detection, and directly related to the size of bribes and other benefits from malfeasance. A difference in salaries imposes a cost of dismissal equal to the present value of the difference between the future earnings stream in enforcement and in other occupations. This cost can more than offset the gain from malfeasance.

To develop the analysis formally in a simple model, let p be the probability of detecting malfeasance during any single time period. Although p is taken as given, it depends on the amounts spent by the state on detection. Let b be the monetary value of the gain to enforcers from bribery and other malfeasance; b is also taken as given, although it depends on p and other variables. Let r be the discount rate, and v_i the earnings that could be obtained by enforcers (aged i) in other occupations. The problem is to find the minimum salary (w_i) to enforcers, in each time period, that would discourage them from malfeasance.

We start from the final period of employment of a given enforcer, n, and work backwards. He can either receive w_n with certainty, or, by engaging in malfeasance during this period, have the probability p of receiving v_n (he is dismissed at the beginning of the period and forfeits his gain from malfeasance), and $1 - p$ of receiving $b + w_n$. If he is risk neutral and maximizes expected wealth, the minimum w_n that would discourage malfeasance is determined from the equation

$$w_n = pv_n + (1 - p)(b + w_n), \tag{1}$$

or

$$w_n = v_n + \frac{1 - p}{p} b. \tag{2}$$

Consider now his position at the beginning of period $n - 1$. With no malfeasance in periods $n - 1$ and n, the present value of his income stream would be $w_{n-1} + w_n/(1 + r)$. With malfeasance in period $n - 1$, he has the probability p of receiving a present value equal to $v_n + v_n/(1 + r)$,[8] and a probability $1 - p$ of receiving $b + w_{n-1} + w_n/$

---

[8] We assume that if he is fired for malfeasance in any period, he cannot return in any future period.

$(1 + r)$.[9] By equating these present values, the minimum w_{n-1} can be determined:

$$w_{n-1} + \frac{w_n}{1 + r} = p\left(v_{n-1} + \frac{v_n}{1 + r}\right)$$

$$+ (1 - p)\left(b + w_{n-1} + \frac{w_n}{1 + r}\right);$$

(3)

hence by using equation (2),

$$w_{n-1} = v_{n-1} + \frac{(1 - p)b}{p} \frac{r}{1 + r}.$$

(4)

Similarly, by continuing to go backwards in time one can derive the general expression

$$w_i = v_i + \frac{(1 - p)b}{p} \frac{r}{1 + r}, \qquad i = 1, \ldots, n - 1.$$

(5)

The income as an enforcer in the first $n - 1$ periods is higher than elsewhere by an amount that is inversely related to the probability of detection, and directly related to the gain from malfeasance and (approximately) to the interest rate. The term $(1 - p)b/p$ can be considered a measure of the "temptation" of malfeasance.[10] The cost of dismissal is the present value of the excess income stream that would be forgone. The income in the last period is still higher to offset the increasing attractiveness of malfeasance as retirement nears because of the decline in the number of years of future income that must be forgone.

The excess of the premium in the last period over that in other periods can be considered the capital value of the "pension" at the beginning of the last period:

$$P = \frac{(1 - p)b}{p} - \frac{(1 - p)b}{p} \frac{r}{1 + r} = \frac{(1 - p)b}{p} \frac{1}{1 + r}.$$

(6)

[9] Equation (1) insures that his expected income in period n equals w_n both when he does and when he does not engage in malfeasance in that period.

[10] We assume that enforcers plan their behavior using the expected value of the gain from malfeasance. Therefore, they would not be tempted to engage in malfeasance if the expected value did not justify it, even if an unexpected good opportunity for malfeasance came along, because they would not have planned their behavior ("covered their tracks") for malfeasance. We are indebted to Arnold Harberger for raising this point.

The prospect of losing the pension is an increasingly important deterrent to malfeasance as one gets closer and closer to retirement. The forgone interest on this capital value, $r P$, the pension "income," equals the annual premium in the first $n - 1$ years:

$$r P = \frac{(1 - p)b}{p} \frac{r}{1 + r}.$$ (7)

Consequently, the pension income is also directly proportional to the gain from malfeasance and inversely proportional to the probability of detection. The ratio $r P/w_i$, of pension income to salary, clearly ranges from 0 to 1[11] and would be larger the more tempting malfeasance is relative to the incomes available elsewhere. Therefore, this ratio can serve as an indirect measure of the relative importance of bribes and other temptations available.

The present value of the lifetime salary to an enforcer is

$$V_w = \sum_{i=1}^{n} \frac{w_i}{(1 + r)^{i-1}} = \sum_{i=1}^{n} \frac{v_i}{(1 + r)^{i-1}}$$ (8)
$$+ \sum_{i=1}^{n-1} \frac{(1 - p)b}{p} \frac{r}{(1 + r)^i} + \frac{(1 - p)b}{p} \frac{1}{(1 + r)^{n-1}},$$

$$= V v + \frac{(1 - p)b}{p}.$$ (9)

This present value would exceed the present value of salaries available elsewhere by the temptation of malfeasance. Consequently, the payments to each enforcer could be reduced by charging an "entrance fee"

equal to $\frac{(1 - p)b}{p}$; then enforcement would pay as well as the best

alternative, no more and no less, and an appropriate number of persons would be available for employment as enforcers.

Malfeasance can be eliminated, therefore, even when the probability of detection is quite low, without lifetime payments to enforcers that exceed what they could get elsewhere. The appropriate pay structure has three components: an "entrance fee" equal to the temptation of malfeasance, a salary premium in each year of employment approxi-

---

[11] It approaches 1 as v_i gets smaller and smaller relative to $r P$.

[12] This pay structure follows from our assumption that dismissal is the only punishment for malfeasance. However, if enforcers detected in malfeasance were fined, their salary should be equal to what they could get elsewhere, if fines equalled the

mately equal to the income yielded by the "entrance fee,"[12] and a pension with a capital value approximately equal also to the temptation of malfeasance. As it were, enforcers post a bond equal to the temptation of malfeasance, receive the income on the bond as long as they are employed, and have the bond returned if they behave themselves until retirement. Put differently, they forfeit their bond if they are fired for malfeasance.[13]

As the probability of detecting malfeasance, p, is made smaller, resources spent on detection would be reduced with no effect on malfeasance if salaries and the entrance fee adjust according to equations (2), (5) and (9). Consequently, the optimum would appear to be a probability of detection arbitrarily close to zero, and earnings and the entrance fee indefinitely high. Then malfeasance would be discouraged at zero cost to the state!

As entrance fees become larger, the state appears to have more incentive to fire enforcers without cause since it could then pocket these fees. But if the probability, i, of being fired without cause (that is, if he is honest) were known to enforcers, their salaries would have to rise to take account of this, according to the formulas:

$$w_i = v_i + \frac{(1 - p)b}{p - i} \frac{(r + i)}{1 + r},$$

$$(10)$$

$$w_n = v_n + \frac{(1 - p)b}{p - i}.$$

As i increased, the salaries that must be paid enforcers to discourage them from malfeasance would also increase; hence, the state would not gain from increasing i.[14] (Note that i could also be viewed as includ-

---

temptation of malfeasance. The minimum value of the fine, F, that would just discourage malfeasance is given by:

$$(1 - p)(w_i + b) + p(v_i - F) = w_i,$$

or

$$F = (v_i - w_i) + \frac{(1 - p)b}{p}.$$

Then

$$F = \frac{(1 - p)b}{p} \quad \text{if} \quad v_i = w_i.$$

[13] The analysis is generalized somewhat in the Appendix at the end of this paper.

[14] For any undesired behavior, the efficiency argument against punishing innocent persons is that behavior depends on the *difference* between p and i, the proba-

ing the probability that innocent enforcers would voluntarily quit their jobs.)

It is, however, costly to determine whether someone is being fired with or without cause. The greater their salary, the greater the stake of enforcers in litigating efforts to fire them by proving their innocence: they would try to arrange for compulsory hearings on dismissals, appeals procedures, and the like. The extent of the procedures, and hence their cost, would rise as the probability of detection went down and salaries went up. When these costs of litigation are included, the optimal probability of detecting malfeasance is not necessarily arbitrarily close to zero, but would depend on the increase in litigation expenditures as salaries rose (*i.e.*, as the probability of detection fell). Of course, the optimal probability would not be zero if enforcers were unable to borrow a sufficiently large entrance "bond" because lenders were uncertain about being repaid.

Since eliminating malfeasance by raising salaries may not be costless, it may be preferable simply to permit malfeasance. If enforcers anticipate engaging in malfeasance they will be willing to accept a lower salary than they can get elsewhere: their gain from malfeasance is a "compensating differential." If their gain equals the loss to the state, the state would not suffer a net loss nor would enforcers obtain a net gain—by net is meant after account is taken of the compensating differential—from malfeasance. The gain to enforcers is likely, however, to be less than the loss to the state because of the time and effort that enforcers spend on malfeasance, because of transactions costs in disposing of stolen merchandise, and because of the other reasons discussed in Part II. Then if enforcers did not obtain a net gain from malfeasance, the state (and society) would suffer a net loss.

Formally, we have

$$v_i = w_i + b, \tag{11}$$

where $v_i - w_i = b$ is the compensating differential to enforcers, and

$$w_i + \alpha b = w_i^s, \tag{12}$$

where w_i^s is the total "wage" rate paid by the state, and α is the loss to the state for each dollar-equivalent received by enforcers from malfeasance. Then, by substitution,

---

bilities of punishing guilty and innocent persons respectively. Any increase in i relative to p would increase the undesired behavior, even if p itself was also increasing.

$$w_i^s - v_i = b(\alpha - 1). \tag{13}$$

The net cost to the state from malfeasance, the difference between w_i^s and v_i, is greater the greater the gain to enforcers (b), and the greater the net "social" or dead-weight loss ($\alpha - 1$) per dollar of gain to enforcers.

Therefore, whether salaries should be raised and malfeasance eliminated (or lowered) and whether malfeasance should be permitted depend on the cost of the optimal probability of detecting malfeasance, and the dead-weight loss from malfeasance. The higher the latter—the less that malfeasance resembles a transfer payment—the more likely that malfeasance should be eliminated.

Our analysis of malfeasance is applicable not only to enforcers but to all public and private employees who must be "trusted." By "trust" is meant the following. Assume that employees must choose between several actions, say, for simplicity, two, A and B: A makes *them* better off whereas B makes their employers better off. Employers could ensure that action B would be chosen if they always knew when A occurred, simply by paying employees as much as they could get elsewhere, and by firing them whenever A occurred. If, however, A could be detected only some of the time, employees would have to be "trusted" to take the appropriate (that is, B) action. They would do so if the pattern of compensation we developed for enforcers were adopted: a salary premium, pension, and "entrance fee" all determined by the temptation of malfeasance.

Clearly, therefore, the temptations seducing enforcers are also available to purchasing agents, sales personnel, soldiers, physicians, lawyers, managers, and persons in many other occupations.[15] Trust calls for a salary premium not necessarily because better quality persons are thereby attracted,[16] but because higher salaries impose a cost on violations of trust.

---

[15] Robert J. Barro analyzes these temptations for politicians in The Control of Politicians: An Economic Model, 12 Public Choice (Spring 1973). Truth is perhaps no stranger than fiction:

> It appeared that the firms [makers of safes] were fully alive to the possibility of fraud or theft on the part of their men. For this reason only old hands who had been with them for many years, and of whose honesty they were completely satisfied, were entrusted with the fitting of the keys. *These men, moreover, were paid a high rate of wages, so as to reduce temptations as far as possible.*

Freeman Willis Crofts, Crime at Guildford (1935).

[16] Adam Smith believed that occupations requiring trust paid higher wages in order to attract better quality persons. "Such confidence [*i.e.*, trust] could not safely be reposed in people of a very mean or low condition. Their reward must be such, therefore, as may give them that rank in the society which so important a trust requires." The Wealth of Nations 105 (Modern Library ed.).

The extent of control by the stockholders over the conduct of the officers of large corporations has been a much debated subject at least since the celebrated study by Berle and Means, *The Modern Corporation*. [17] The focus of attention has gradually shifted away from their main concern, the difficulties in using the proxy fight and the stockholders' suit to protect stockholder interests. The recent focus has been upon the takeover bid and the merger as devices to eliminate inefficient or corrupt management.

Throughout the period of discussion, however, one assumption of Berle and Means has been almost unquestioned: when one or a few stockholders have a controlling holding of voting stock, there is no serious problem of ownership control. Yet the incentives to malfeasance and nonfeasance are obviously present in all employment and agency arrangements, and these incentives are presumably important in the management of all large enterprises. There is no entry in a corporate income statement, "profits that would have been attained with superb management," to guide even the single owner of all the stock of a corporation.

The cases of diffused and concentrated ownership of a corporation's stock differ in certain respects: the dominant owner has a larger incentive to monitor the performance, and offers a more accessible market to others with information to sell on the performance of management, than each of numerous part owners. These differences may not be very important, however, if specialists ("takeover artists" and merger-seeking companies) undertake the task of searching for mismanaged enterprises.

As we already indicated, the role of trust in an employment contract is larger, the less easily and quickly the quality of performance can be ascertained. The more diverse the activities of the enterprise, the more rapidly it is growing or declining, the more unstable the industries in which it is operating—in each case the greater the role for trust in one's managers. We would therefore expect to find the pattern of compensation we developed for enforcers to be especially prominent for managers in companies with these characteristics.

B. *Rewarding Enforcement*

Although the compensation structure we have developed could eliminate malfeasance, it would not automatically result in optimal enforcement. No guidance is provided to the optimal number of enforcers (or more generally to the optimal total expenditure on enforcement), as

---

[17] Adolf Berle & Gardner Means, The Modern Corporation and Private Property (1933).

opposed to the optimal expenditure per enforcer. Moreover, considerable resources may be spent by the state in detecting malfeasance, by enforcers in hiding it, and, more generally, by the state and enforcers in protecting their own interests.

A highly promising method of compensating enforcers is suggested by the market in private transactions, which also has innumerable "rules" to be enforced. It is a rule that I am not to take a quart of milk from a store unless I pay 40 cents, or that I am not to receive wages from my employer unless I work 40 hours. Of course, there are reciprocal rules: the 40 cents is not paid unless the quart of milk is received; the wages must be paid if I have performed the work. The "rules"—which are what contracts embody—are enforced extensively and effectively: the escape rate on murders is higher than on 20 cent pencils in a variety store. The enforcement is good precisely because the incentives to enforcers are as large as the incentives to prospective violators.

The same method is often used, almost inadvertently, to enforce public statutes—namely, in the widespread reliance on victim enforcement. Persons charged in excess of the legal ceiling on rents report their landlords because they anticipate a reduction in their rents. Laws against shoplifting are enforced primarily by stores, often using private police, because the shopkeepers are the immediate beneficiaries. Similarly, libel laws are enforced by those libeled because they anticipate compensation. Private triple damage suits have become the only effective sanction of the antitrust laws. In the great electrical equipment conspiracy, General Electric was fined $400,000, and paid several hundred million dollars in damages. The recently developed class action suits extend victim enforcement to include many situations where the damage is so widely diffused that no one victim alone has much incentive to enforcement.

The amount of victim enforcement would be optimal if successful enforcers were paid the amount that they had suffered in damages, excluding their enforcement costs, divided by the probability that they are successful (this assumes that victim enforcers are risk-neutral). If this amount were levied in fines against convicted violators, so that, in effect, violators compensated victims, the gain to victims from enforcement would be the same as the punishment to violators; hence these enforcers could not be corrupted.

Of course, most victims would not literally become enforcers: they would hire lawyers, private investigators, and other specialized "enforcement firms" to gather evidence and argue their cases. Free competition among these firms would insure that enforcement was provided at cost. Moreover, these firms would not wait passively until contacted by victims, but would seek out evidence and bring it to the attention of victims.[18]

The essence of victim enforcement is compensation of enforcers on performance, or by a "piece-rate" or a "bounty," instead of by a straight salary. Why not then generalize this system, and let *anyone* enforce statutes and receive as compensation for performance the fines levied against convicted violators? Specialist enforcement firms would develop and would either compensate victims *en masse* (by appropriate division of penalties with, *e.g.*, the motor vehicle fund), or retain all awards for themselves. Where victim cooperation aids enforcement, we would expect that, whatever the formal distribution of awards, victims would receive a share. Where victims had little to contribute to detection and conviction, it seems more appropriate to allow the enforcers, whoever they be, to retain the awards. The rule that *anyone* could enforce a statute would basically achieve this distribution.

Free competition among enforcement firms may seem strange, even terrifying, and much more radical than the method of compensation proposed earlier to eliminate malfeasance by salaried enforcers. But society does not pretend to be able to designate who the bakers should be—this is left to personal aptitudes and tastes. Why should enforcers of laws be chosen differently? Let anyone who wishes enter the trade, innovate, and prosper or fail. The method by which ditch diggers, professors, and Senators are obtained surely should supply us with health inspectors, antitrust inspectors, rent-control investigators, and even tax collectors.

The case for allowing rules to be enforced by normal market methods of recruitment is not simply a mechanical generalization of the case for competition, for it corrects a major error of the theory of rules. This error—or omission—is to assume that rules provide any guidance or incentive to their enforcement: on the contrary, rules usually provide neither the slightest hint of where to look for violations nor the incentive to convict violators. Nothing in the Sherman Act tells us where to look for collusion; nothing in the motor vehicle laws tells us who will be a speeder; nothing in a pure food law tells us who will be an adulterator. Moreover, as we have been arguing, often there is little incentive to convict the colluder, speeder, or adulterator.

Consider some additional advantages of this proposal. Society would use fewer resources to detect malfeasance because payment for performance reduces the gain from malfeasance. Moreover, society is more likely to use fines equal to damages divided by the probability of

[18] Some law firms now take the initiative in proving antitrust violations in class action suits.

conviction [19] to punish offenders if it must pay this amount to successful enforcers. Although private enforcement of rules need not change the rules, we predict that they would gain currency and relevance because enforcement would then be much more efficient and transparent. In addition, the right amount of self-protection by potential victims is encouraged, not the excessive (wasteful) self-protection that results when victims are not compensated, or the inadequate self-protection that results when they are automatically compensated. Further, the rewards of innovation will spur technical progress in private enforcement as in other economic callings.

Capricious or arbitrary enforcement is always possible, and is much encouraged under our present system by the policy of not compensating acquitted persons for the costs (of all sorts) that they had borne. If a man is falsely charged with a crime, or a federal regulatory body erroneously denounces a company, at present neither victim is compensated in general, and we consider this a shameful flaw in our system of enforcement. The proposed system would have full compensation of persons acquitted of charges paid by the enforcement firms bringing these charges. This proposal is equally relevant to public enforcement but is more easily adopted in a regime of private enforcement because of the legal tradition of governmental immunity.

As with our proposal to eliminate malfeasance, innumerable complications would be encountered by private enforcement in a world full of variety and ingenuity (and just a little fraud). Impoverished violators would pose a problem in restitution: where violators have no legally merchantable skills the state would be compelled to use nonmonetary punishments, such as imprisonment, and to compensate the persons apprehending them. Impoverished enforcers also pose a problem in restitution: perhaps enforcement firms should be required to post a bond or its equivalent ("malpractice" insurance) to guarantee their solvency if they are required to pay damages to persons they have falsely accused or harassed. [20] The state also would be compelled to assess more accurately the damage of numerous violations (adultery, assault, sale of a stock or commodity off an organized exchange, driving a truck without an ICC license), but one need not apologize for retracing Bentham's steps after almost two centuries. Violence unfortunately must often be met by violence; so it will be necessary to face the question of who should be permitted to use force in enforcing laws. At least limited use of licensed firms seems desirable here.

---

[19] The optimality of these fines is discussed in Gary S. Becker, *supra* note 1, at 191–93, and George J. Stigler, *supra* note 1, at 531.

[20] We owe this point to Melvin Reder.

Since different enforcement firms would compete to eliminate any particular malfeasance, the concept of double jeopardy would need elaboration and rules would be needed to determine the docket order in courts of different enforcers, and, more generally, to determine the distribution of compensation when several enforcers were involved in a conviction.

If the probability of conviction implicit in the punishment levied against convicted violators and paid to successful enforcers were less than the actual probability, the state could eliminate the difference in probabilities by lowering the fines on offenders (rewards to enforcers). This would lower the actual probability because enforcers have less to gain from enforcement. By lowering fines sufficiently, the implicit and actual probabilities could be equalized. Similarly, if initially the implicit probability exceeded the actual one, fines could be raised until they were equalized.

One might question whether the equilibrium probability of conviction thus obtained with private enforcement would be socially optimal, for since the apprehension and conviction of violators consume real resources, society can conserve its resources by raising punishments and lowering probabilities.[21] Perhaps public enforcement could more readily achieve an optimal combination of punishments and probabilities, but note that the temptation of malfeasance by public enforcers and thus the cost of policing them would rise as the punishment rose, and that an appropriate tax on private enforcement could lower its equilibrium probability of conviction to any desired level.

Conclusion

We conclude by emphasizing that the view of enforcement and litigation as wasteful in whole or in part is simply mistaken. They are as important as the harm they seek to prevent, and are really only names for the orderly ascertainment of facts, resolution of doubts, and reduction of conflicts. In any event, the amount of enforcement is determined ultimately by the rules to be enforced and the quality of enforcement.

We have discussed different methods of improving the quality of enforcement. One discourages malfeasance by raising the salaries of public enforcers, whereas the other encourages results by paying private enforcers for performance, or on a piece-rate basis. Both methods have considerable advantages over much contemporary enforcement procedure, and the latter method in particular would unleash the powerful forces of competition.

[21] See the discussion in Gary S. Becker, *supra* note 1, at 183–84, 193.

Appendix

The analysis can be generalized by assuming that (1) the probability of detection depends on the experience of enforcers and other variables; (2) the income available at any age in other occupations depends on the age of entry into these occupations; (3) expected utility rather than expected wealth is maximized; and so forth. We here analyze the relation between the gain from malfeasance and the experience of enforcers; that is, the bribes and other gains available are assumed to increase as enforcers become more experienced and have more authority.

Let b_i be the monetary equivalent of the gain from malfeasance at age i. Then the minimum salaries that discourage malfeasance can be shown to be

$$w_n = v_n + \frac{(1 - p)b_n}{p}, \tag{A.1}$$

$$w_i = v_i + \left[\frac{(1 - p)b_i}{p} - \frac{(1 - p)b_{i+1}}{p(1 + r)} \right], \quad i = 1 \ldots n - 1 \tag{A.2}$$

and the difference in present values is

$$V_w - V_v = \frac{(1 - p)b_n}{p}. \tag{A.3}$$

For the equivalent of equation (3) is

$$w_{n-1} + \frac{w_n}{1 + r} = p\left(v_{n-1} + \frac{v_n}{1 + r} \right)$$
$$+ (1 - p)\left(b_{n-1} + w_{n-1} + \frac{w_n}{(1 + r)} \right), \tag{3'}$$

which implies by using equation (A.1) that

$$w_{n-1} = v_{n-1} + \frac{(1 - p)b_{n-1}}{p} - \frac{(1 - p)b_n}{p(1 + r)}; \tag{4'}$$

similarly for the other w_i. Moreover,

$$V_w = \sum_{i=1}^{n} \frac{w_i}{(1 + r)^{i-1}} = V_v + \sum_{i=1}^{n} \frac{\left[\dfrac{(1 - p)b_i}{p} - \dfrac{(1 - p)b_{i+1}}{p(1 + r)} \right]}{(1 + r)^{i-1}}$$
$$+ \frac{(1 - p)b_n}{p(1 + r)^{n-1}}, \tag{8'}$$

which implies equation (A.3).

If b increases over time, the earnings of enforcers would begin *below* alternative earnings, *equal* alternative earnings when b rises at the interest rate, and remain *above* alternative earnings thereafter. The effect is similar to that resulting from investment in human capital; indeed, analytically the problems are very close, with the growth in earnings due to the growth in the gain from malfeasance being akin to the growth in earnings due to the accumulation of human capital. For equation (A.2) can be written as

$$w_i = v_i + \frac{r(1-p)b_i}{p} - \frac{(1-p)}{p}\left(\frac{b_{i+1}}{(1+r)} - (1-r)b_i\right),$$

$$\cong v_i + \frac{r(1-p)b_i}{p} - \frac{(1-p)}{(1+r)p}(b_{i+1} - b_i), \text{ if } \frac{1-r}{1+r} = 1.$$

(A.4)

The term $\dfrac{r(1-p)b_i}{p}$ is the income yielded by the malfeasance "capital" accu-

mulated to period i, and $\dfrac{(1-p)}{(1+r)p}(b_{i+1} - b_i)$ is the amount invested in addi-

tional capital in period i; the latter is subtracted from earnings capacity to arrive at "net" earnings.[22] The stock of malfeasance capital in period $i+1$ is then the stock in i plus the value in $i+1$ of the net investment in i or

$$C_{i+1} = \frac{(1-p)b_i}{p} + (1+r)\frac{(1-p)}{(1+r)p}(b_{i+1} - b_i)$$

$$= \frac{(1-p)}{p}b_{i+1}.$$

(A.5)

Equation (A.1) indicates that the pension is largely determined by the temptation of malfeasance in the terminal year of employment, not the average temptation during the whole employment period. This may help explain why pension incomes are often geared to earnings shortly before retirement instead of average earnings during the whole employment period. The "entrance fee" (given by equation (A.3)), on the other hand, equals the temptation in the initial year of employment. Since this fee results from considering the difference between life-time earnings streams, the initial temptation is important not because of myopia, but rather because enforcers pay for the growth in the gain from malfeasance through appropriate reductions in earnings.

Consequently, the "entrance fee" and the capital value of the pension are no longer similar when the gain from malfeasance grows with experience. Indeed, the fee might be only a small fraction of the pension or extra earnings. For example, if the gain (b) grew 20 fold from the initial to terminal year of employment—say from $500 to $10,000—, and if the pension's capital value were 5 times average earnings, the entrance fee would only be about ¹⁄₂₀ of the pension, and ¼ of average earnings.

[22] See the related equations for human capital in Gary S. Becker, Human Capital chs. 2, 3 (1964).

The Impact of Product Recalls on the Wealth of Sellers

20

Gregg A. Jarrell and Sam Peltzman

I. Introduction

This paper has a simple goal: to estimate the losses borne by owners of a firm that recalls a defective product from the market. While we stick close to the "facts," we hope they will shed some light on an important issue in consumer protection regulation. This is the extent to which information about product quality is sufficient to deter production of faulty products. We focus on two products—drugs and autos—where extensive regulation of product quality occurs before marketing of the product. One rationale for such premarket regulation would be that mere disclosure of any defects after a good is marketed does not impose sufficient costs on the seller to deter optimally the production of defective products. Suboptimal deterrence could occur if, for example, consumers were insufficiently sophisticated in assimilating information about defects or the tort liability system insufficiently compensated them for resulting damages.

While we do not address these normative issues directly, we hope that our results will be useful in assessing the magnitude of the potential problem. Accordingly, we compare our estimates of losses to owners with independent estimates of some elements of direct costs to firms of recalling defective products. These would include the costs of destroying contaminated batches of drugs, the costs of repairing defec-

We thank James Frieden, Michael Ryngaert, Thaddeus Niemira, and Monica Noether for their assistance. Jarrell was a research fellow at the University of Chicago, Center for the Study of the Economy and State, when the project began. An earlier version of this paper was presented at a Federal Trade Commission Conference on Consumer Protection in 1984. We gratefully acknowledge the support of the FTC, the Center, and the Lilly Endowment, Inc. Nothing herein should be construed to reflect the views of the SEC or FTC.

Reprinted with permission from the *Journal of Political Economy* 93, no. 3 (June 1985): 512–36. © 1985 by The University of Chicago

tive cars, and so on. An obvious question—and a test of capital market efficiency—would be whether the capital market internalizes these costs. If it fails to do so, any presumption of suboptimal deterrence would be strengthened: some cases involve potentially large indirect costs for consumers—for example, health damages from a dangerous drug—and for these cases, optimal deterrence would require a penalty greater than the direct costs we are able to estimate.

We chose to focus on recalls of automobiles and drugs (prescription, over-the-counter, and medical devices) because each yields a good-sized sample of recalls and because we could obtain associated data on some elements of the direct costs of most of these recalls. The products also differ in an interesting dimension: drug recalls occur much less frequently (per firm) than auto recalls. Important examples of the latter occur every few weeks or months, while the former occur once or twice in a decade.

Our primary finding is that the capital market in fact penalizes producers of both recalled drugs and autos far more than the direct costs. Indeed, the capital market penalty seems so great that it may even exceed a plausible independent estimate of the relevant social costs. We do not press this point, because we have only the most fragmentary data on the relevant indirect costs. But to the empirical question, "How much deterrence does the capital market provide against the sale of faulty products?" the answer implied by our data must be, "Considerable."

We also find that competitors of drug and auto firms with recalled products are not helped by their rival's travail. In fact, in both cases they bear substantial losses.

The next section sketches the theoretical link between a regulatory event, like a recall, and the capital market's response to it.[1] The two following sections describe this response to recalls of drug and auto products, respectively.

II. How "Should" the Stock Market React to News of a Product Recall?

The extent to which the stock market reacts to some event that entails a cost to shareholders depends on how well the event is anticipated. Thus, wage payments impose costs on stockholders, but stock prices do not decline on payday. Recalls do not occur with quite the same predictable regularity as wage payments, but neither are they a complete surprise. In such cases, the stock market response to the event will

[1] See Schwert (1981) for a fuller treatment.

understate the total costs borne by stockholders. To see this, let any uncertainty be resolved within a "month," and suppose that only one of two things can happen to a firm next month: either a product is recalled at some cost (K) to shareholders or there is no recall. So, the firm's month-end stock price (S_1^i) will be either

$$S_1^{NR} = V, \tag{1}$$

if no recall occurs, or

$$S_1^R = V - K, \tag{2}$$

if a recall occurs, where V = present value of the firm's profits, including all expected recall costs except those occurring next month, and where we assume independence of successive monthly events. The firm's stock price at the beginning of the month is the present value of future profits, or

$$S_0 = p(V - K) + (1 - p)V = V - pK, \tag{3}$$

where p = probability that a recall occurs next month. Thus, if a recall occurs next month, the stock price will change by $(2) - (3)$ above, or

$$S_1^R - S_0 = -(1 - p)K, \tag{4}$$

that is, by the unexpected component $(1 - p)$ of the recall cost. Only if the recall is entirely unexpected $(p = 0)$ will $(4) = K$. In months where recalls do not occur, stockholders get a capital gain of $(1) - (3)$, or

$$S_1^{NR} - S_1^0 = pK. \tag{5}$$

So, to get the full loss to stockholders, we would need to divide (4) by $(1 - p)$ or subtract (5) from (4).

In practice, (4) and $(4) - (5)$ will be about equal if p is small. This is the case with drugs where no company in our sample has been involved in more than two distinct recalls in nearly a decade. For this sample, then, we use conventional "event study" methodology, more fully described below, in which we in effect estimate just (4). But for the more frequent auto recalls we also provide estimates of $(4) \div (1 - p)$ and $(4) - (5)$.

III. The Stock Market Response to Drug Recalls

A. *Drug Recall Sample*

When a drug product is found to be defective, the manufacturer is required to remove it from the market. This recall can be initiated by either the manufacturer or the Food and Drug Administration (FDA), and it can involve anything from a few bottles of contaminated or mislabeled product to the permanent removal of a product from the marketplace. Several hundred recalls occur in a typical year, and most involve minor health or financial consequences. Our sample comes from those recalls reported in the trade press.

Specifically, we consulted the weekly reports of FDA Recalls and Court Actions in the *Food, Drug and Cosmetic Reporter,* an industry newsletter commonly called the "Pink Sheets." Recalls were included in our sample if the Pink Sheets report gives an estimate either of the direct costs of the recall or, more commonly, of the number of units recalled. We also include those recalls where direct cost estimates are reported in the *Wall Street Journal* (*WSJ*). Our sample period runs from 1974 through 1982. We exclude cases without stock returns data for the manufacturer.

Our sample overrepresents large and hazardous recalls (because these are always reported in either the Pink Sheets or *WSJ*). For example, the FDA uses a three-level classification of recalls in which Class I recalls involve the most serious potential health hazard. Class I recalls account for over half of our sample, while Block (1980) reports that they account for less than 2 percent of the over 3,000 FDA recall citations issued between 1973 and 1978. Many of our cases received considerable publicity. Over half were covered by the *Wall Street Journal.* Five of these cases were serious enough so that the recalled products were withdrawn indefinitely from the market. Table 1, which is elaborated below, summarizes this sample. It shows the names of the manufacturers of the recalled drugs in our sample, the event dates and estimates of the stock market response, and direct costs incurred by these manufacturers as a result of the recalls.

B. *Choosing Event Dates*

For each recall, we sought to identify the earliest date at which news of a recall might have become public. For most of the cases reported by the *WSJ*, this is the date that the recall begins. Sometimes, however, the first hint of a recall appears in a story preceding the recall date—for example, a story implicating a drug in a serious health problem. In these cases, we use the date of the earliest *WSJ* story on the troubled

TABLE 1.   Sample of Drug Recalls, Selected Characteristics

Case No.	Firm Name	Event Date	Direct Cost as Percentage of Market Value (%)	Recall Firm's CER Percentage −4 to +5	Estimated Direct Dollar Cost ($ Thousands)
1.	Abbott (N)*	4/28/76	.00	−1.91	5
2.1	Am. Hospital (N)	11/26/74	.03	−4.26	172
2.2	Am. Hospital	1/13/75	.05	−7.10	430
3.	Block	6/11/79	2.33	−7.76	2,330
4.	Bolar	12/24/80	2.34	−10.63	1,600
5.	Lilly (V-Cillin)	12/5/77	.05	−1.42	1,150
6.	Lilly (Oraflex)†	8/3/82	.66	−10.46	30,400
7.	Johnson (Tylenol)†	10/1/82	1.35	−15.88	100,000
8.1	Mallinckrodt (N)	11/14/74	.00	3.55	10
8.2	Mallinckrodt	12/10/74	.57	−8.43	1,300
9.	Merck (N)	8/8/80	.01	−2.76	353
10.1	Milton Roy (N)	7/15/76	.05	3.64	12
10.2	Milton Roy	8/25/76	.05	−1.98	12
11.	Morton Norwich	11/23/79	.06	−2.75	250
12.	Johnson (Ortho)	10/13/75	.13	2.65	6,500
13.	Parke Davis	8/13/76	.04	−.63	1,000
14.	Procter-Gamble (Rely)†	9/18/80	2.46	−5.29	150,000
15.	Richardson	10/1/78	1.68	−8.18	11,500
16.	Richardson (N)	9/26/80	1.78	−2.35	9,530
17.	Robins (N)	4/28/76	.77	−.33	2,100
18.	Searle Labs (N)	11/17/76	.09	−6.56	600
19.	Searle Labs (N)	6/9/81	.07	−1.00	1,000
20.	SmithKline	4/26/79	.13	−8.93	3,700
21.	Squibb	1/16/75	.24	−9.40	3,500
22.	Squibb (N)	11/28/77	.05	−12.11	560
23.1	Sterling (N)	1/14/76	.55	−18.20	6,000
23.2	Sterling	2/18/76	.55	−18.84	6,000
23.3	Sterling (N)	4/14/76	.03	−2.15	270
24.	Sterling (N)	4/5/78	.02	−6.77	200
25.	American Home Prod.	3/4/82	.05	−.69	3,044
26.1	Robins (Dalkon Shield)†	5/29/74	.47	−18.12	2,550
26.2	Robins (Dalkon Shield)†	6/28/74	.47	−11.16	2,550

*N = Recall *not* reported in *WSJ*.
† = Recalled products were withdrawn from the market.

product. For cases covered only in the Pink Sheets, our event date is the earliest date on which the FDA notified the manufacturer to recall the product.[2]

Sometimes news about essentially the same product defect is spread out over time. For example, two defective batches of a product are found several weeks apart (cases 2.1 and 2.2) or a product defect is found a month before the firm decides that a recall is necessary (26.1 and 26.2). We treated these related episodes as separate events (and split direct costs evenly among them) if more than 3 weeks elapsed between the events. These are identified by case numbers with decimals in the table. (We treat related events less than 3 weeks apart, like the rest, as a single event beginning on the earliest date of adverse news.)

C. Direct Costs of Recalls

For most recalls, we estimate the "direct cost" by assuming that all of the defective units become worthless on recall. Specifically, where the Pink Sheets report the number of units of the recalled batch that are in distribution channels, we multiply this figure by the wholesale price of the product as reported in the appropriate yearly issue of the *American Druggist's Blue Book* and the *Drug Topics Red Book* to estimate "direct costs."

For some of the more publicized recalls (cases 6, 7, 14, and 26), direct cost estimates were available from news stories, because the companies took an extraordinary charge to their income. For instance, the *WSJ* reported on October 29, 1982, that it would cost Johnson and Johnson about $50 million to recall and destroy 22 million units of Extra-Strength Tylenol capsules. It also reported that new tamper-proof packaging, additional television advertising, and related efforts to rebuild consumer confidence would cost another $50 million. Therefore, our estimated direct cost to Johnson and Johnson of the Tylenol recall is $100 million.

We make no allowance for tax benefits due to recall costs. Where we use reported extraordinary charges, we use the pretax figure, and we ignore any tax savings from inventory losses. Accordingly, our direct cost estimates may be overgenerous.

For each recall, table 1 gives the estimated direct cost in dollars (last column) and as a percentage of the market value (just before recall) of the respective manufacturer's common stock. In both dollar and

---

[2]Sometimes the Pink Sheet story implies that the initial FDA communication is private. For these cases, we use the publication date of the Pink Sheet story—usually a week or so later.

percentage terms, the recall of Procter and Gamble's Rely tampon (14) entails the largest estimated direct cost ($150 million, 2.5 percent of market value) in our sample, while the Class I recall of Abbott Laboratories' Plasmatein (1) is the least costly ($5,000, 0.0005 percent).

D. Capital Market Returns

The full cost to manufacturers of recalled drugs is measured by net-of-market (or excess) stock returns in the period surrounding public announcement of the recall. These excess returns are obtained from the Scholes excess return file at the University of Chicago's Center for Research in Security Prices (CRSP).[3] We cumulate excess returns for each manufacturer over several "event windows" of different intervals to allow for pre-event leakage or post-event revision. The narrowest event window is 6 days, from $t = -2$ to $t = 3$, where $t = 0$ is the formal event date of the recall. The widest event window is from $t = -49$ to $t = 50$.[4]

Table 2 presents mean cumulative excess returns (CER) for various event windows. These are negative for every window from 1 week to 5 months around the event date. But the 2-week window, CER$(-4, 5)$, yields a loss roughly within a percentage point of that for any wider window. This means that essentially all of the market response to the event is compressed into the 2 surrounding weeks. In addition, there are no systematic "mistakes"—that is, there is no systematic recovery of some of these losses in the 50 days after the event date, or else the CER$(-49, 50)$ would be smaller than CER$(-4, 5)$. Finally, fully nine-tenths of the sample suffers a loss in the 2 weeks surrounding a recall. (This proportion is indistinguishable from 0.5 in all the other 2-week subperiods.) So there can be little doubt that recalls constitute adverse news for stockholders and that most of the uncertainty about them is resolved in the 2 weeks surrounding public disclosure of the recall.

Table 2 splits this 2-week CER into its prerecall, CER$(-4, 0)$,

[3] For cases 3, 4, 8.1, and 8.2, stock returns are unavailable from this source. So we constructed excess return series for these cases by subtracting the return to the New York Stock Exchange Index from returns to these firms' stocks.

[4] Some of the wider event windows result in overlap of the related events denoted by decimal case numbers in table 1. In these cases, we (1) arbitrarily split the time between events in half and attributed the excess return for any day to the event closest in time and (2) set the remaining excess returns to zero. For example, cases 26.1 and 26.2 occur 22 trading days apart. Excess returns for the first 11 days after May 29, 1974, are attributed to 26.1, and all subsequent excess returns are set equal to zero for that case. Excess returns for the 11 days ending June 28, 1974, are attributed to 26.2, and all preceding excess returns are set equal to zero for that case. In this way, we avoid double counting of the same excess return.

and postrecall, CER(1, 5), components. Both are negative. So, if our event date is the earliest date of public information, these data imply some prior leakage of public information.

Perhaps the most striking result in the table is the magnitude of the capital losses due to recalls. In particular, they are much larger than our generous estimate of direct costs. The mean CER(−4, 5) is −6.13 percent, which is fully 12 times the mean relative direct cost of 0.53 percent (and over 50 times the median). We never fully succeed in explaining this enormous gap.

TABLE 2.   Means and Dispersion Measures for CER to Drug Recall Firms (Various Intervals), Direct Cost and CER to Drug Portfolio

Variable Name*	Mean (%)	t(Mean)†	Percentage of All CERs Negative	t(%)‡
CER(−49, 50)	−6.742	−2.17	62.5	1.46
CER(−29, 30)	−5.479	−2.27	71.9	2.76
CER(−14, 15)	−7.147	−3.63	71.9	2.76
CER(−9, 10)	−6.563	−4.71	84.4	5.36
CER(−4, 5)	−6.132	−6.23	90.6	7.87
CER(−2, 3)	−2.832	−4.07	84.4	5.36
CER(−4, 0)	−2.36	−3.72	71.9	2.76
CER(1, 5)	−3.78	−5.95	81.3	4.54
BDRUG(−4, 5)	−1.170	−3.49	81.3	4.54
Relative direct cost	.534	3.95	—	—

*CER(−X, Y) is the cumulative excess return (from Scholes's Excess Returns Tape, University of Chicago, CRSP) from X trading days before to Y trading days after the recall event. BDRUG(−4,5) is the cumulative excess return to an equal-weighted portfolio of all NYSE or ASE drug manufacturers having an SIC of 2834, 2840, or 2841 (about 50 firms). The cumulative excess return to this drug portfolio is computed from $t = -4$ to $t = 5$ for each date on which there was a drug recall that is included in our sample. The drug firm subject to the recall is excluded from the drug portfolio when computing BDRUG for each particular recall event. Relative direct cost is the estimated direct loss expressed as a percentage of the market value of the equity of the recall firm 40 trading days before the recall event date.

†Ratio of mean to its standard error. The standard error of the mean CER(−X, Y) is computed as:

$$\sigma(-X,\ Y) = \frac{\left(\sum_{i=1}^{N} \sigma_i^2 \right)^{1/2}}{N},$$

where σ_i^2 is the variance of the ith recall firm's excess stock return and $N = 32$ recalls. σ_i^2 is estimated for each firm by using daily excess returns from $t = -49$ to $t = -5$ to $t = 50$. Let S_i^2 be the variance of the above-defined time series of daily excess returns. Then σ_i^2 is computed by multiplying S_i^2 by T, where T is the number of trading days in the particular event window. T is 10 for CER(−4, 5), 20 for CER(−9, 10), and so on. These standard errors are virtually identical to the standard errors of the sample mean CERs.

‡Fraction of all CERs negative minus 0.5 divided by standard error from binomial distribution. S.E. = $(PQ/N)^{1/2}$, where p = proportion of CERs negative, $Q = (1 - p)$.

Table 2 also shows the CER(−4, 5) for an equally weighted port-folio of drug firms not involved in the recall. Our motive here is to see if competitors benefit from the adversity visited on the seller of the re-called product. Instead, the spillover seems negative. All other drug stocks suffer a (significant) mean loss of just over 1 percent in the 2 weeks surrounding a recall. This cannot be explained by any tendency for re-calls to be bunched (in which case one recall would beget expectations of others).[5]

E. Direct Costs and Capital Market Losses

The large difference between the capital market losses and our esti-mate of direct costs led us to see if the capital losses are related to the degree of publicity surrounding the recall or whether there was a complete product withdrawal. These may be proxies for costs that we cannot estimate. For example, a withdrawal may engender losses to specific assets (e.g., research and development, past advertising) that are not written off. For the 14 recalls in our sample that neither were covered by the *WSJ* nor involved a withdrawal, the mean CER(−4, 5) is −3.76 percent, while it is −6.36 percent for the 13 nonwithdrawal cases covered by the *WSJ*. The mean CER for the five withdrawals (all were covered by the *WSJ*) is −12.18 percent. So the crude data imply that both extra publicity and withdrawal are costly. But the remaining cases still entail an enormous discrepancy between the capital loss and direct costs.

The relationship between capital market losses and direct costs is shown more formally in table 3. Part A contains regressions of CERs on direct costs and dummies for publicity (= 1 if there was a *WSJ* story) and withdrawal and the CER(−4, 5) to the portfolio of other drug firms. This last variable is not really exogenous, given the previously documented spillover effect of recalls. But we include it to account crudely for the industry-specific component of the total loss (as well as "other" industry-specific news). These regressions confirm the ten-dency for both publicity and product withdrawal to be costly, though some of the standard errors are large enough to caution against pushing these conclusions too hard. The main new result is the negative coeffi-

[5]We have 26 unrelated events in the 9 years 1974–82, or about three per year. If recalls were being generated by a Poisson process with a mean of (26/9) per year, the standard deviation would be 1.7. This differs insignificantly from the sample standard deviation of 1.45, so the distribution of recalls seems essentially random. These data, of course, could hide some more complicated interdependencies—e.g., one recall could signal an increase in all firms' quality control expenditures.

TABLE 3.   Regressions of Stock Returns, Direct Cost, and Recall Characteristics for Sample of 32 Drug Recalls

	Independent Variables					Summary Statistics	
Dependent Variable	Constant	Direct Cost as Percentage of Market Value	WSJ Dummy	Withdrawal Dummy	CER(−4, 5) Drug Portfolio	Adj. R^2 / F	Mean of Dependent Variable (%)
A. Recall co. CERs:							
1. CER(−14, 15)	−1.2	−3.9	−4.0	−4.5	.74	.25	−7.1
	(.5)	(2.0)	(1.3)	(1.1)	(1.6)	3.6	
2. CER(−9, 10)	−1.4	−3.5	−2.2	−4.0	1.09	.25	−6.6
	(.6)	(1.9)	(.8)	(1.1)	(2.7)	3.6	
3. CER(−4, 5)	−2.4	−2.0	−1.6	−5.8	.69	.25	−6.1
	(1.3)	(1.4)	(.8)	(2.0)	(2.1)	3.6	
B. Direct cost as percentage of market value	.25	—	.38	.45	—	.09	.53
	(1.2)		(1.4)	(1.2)		2.6	
C. CER(−4, 5) of drug portfolio	−1.8	1.4	.8	.6	—	.03	−1.3
	(1.7)	(1.8)	(.7)	(.4)		1.3	

Note: All variables, except dummies, are in percentage points (1.0 = one percent).

cient of the relative direct cost variable: it says that an extra dollar of direct cost adds $2.00–$4.00 to the stockholders' loss. This implies that even our generous estimates of direct losses are systematically low but correlated positively with the "true" cost of a recall.

Part B of table 3 tells us that direct costs are higher for publicized recalls and for withdrawals. The relevant coefficients are statistically weak, but they are large relative to the mean direct cost. This implies that part of the extra costs of publicity and product withdrawals shown in table 3 are due to the tendency for these recalls to have larger direct costs.

The larger message suggested by both the crude data and table 3 is that stockholder losses from recalls go beyond costs that can be attributed to the specific product. Part C of table 3 shows that the CER to competitors is much more weakly related to the case-specific variables than is the recall firm's CER. This means that any recall, regardless of "size," engenders a roughly similar industry-wide asset loss. Further, even after allowing for a multiple of direct costs (as in part A of table 3), we do not come close to rationalizing the 6 percent average loss of a recall. That is, the regressions imply that an unpublicized recall that does not result in a withdrawal and has trivial direct costs still entails a loss of over 3 percent, based on CER(−4, 5).

We have so far not dealt explicitly with one potentially important product-specific cost: expenses for product liability suits. But these cannot amount to much for a case involving a small defective batch of an otherwise safe product. We suspect that the major impact of product liability costs is showing up in the large coefficient of direct costs and in the extra losses due to product withdrawals. Every withdrawal in our sample has engendered well-publicized product liability suits.

For one of these we have a long profile of product liability costs. Though samples of one yield notoriously noisy estimates, it seems worth exploiting these data to get a sense of the likely magnitude of this specific cost. The case involves the Dalkon Shield, an intrauterine birth control device that was implicated in the deaths of some users. The two events in our sample (26.1 and 26.2) emanating from this product withdrawal generated CER(−4, 5) values of −18 and −11 percent, or a total loss of around $150 million to the manufacturer, A. H. Robins. Robins took a pretax charge in 1974 of $5.1 million for the costs directly related to withdrawing the product and destroying inventory, and these are shown in table 1. The company also agreed with the SEC to break out all expenses (extra legal fees and uninsured liability payments) related to litigation over this product in its financial statements. It has done this in every annual report from 1976 to date. The total of the pretax charges reported for 1976–82 is $29 million, or a 1974 present value of $17 million using a 10 percent annual discount rate. A simple regression of the log of the annual elements of this expense stream against time implies a mean increase in these expenses of 21 percent (S.E. = 11 percent) per year. We then assumed that expenses would continue to be incurred for another 5 years and would equal the predicted values from this regression in each year from 1983 through 1987. These assumptions imply an additional $21 million of liability costs in 1974 present value, bringing the total to $38 million.

This exercise tells us that, in (partial) hindsight, a reasonably complete independent estimate of the full product-specific costs of the recall to Robins is on the order of under one-third of the stock market loss. (Since Robins has had an average tax rate of over 40 percent in recent years, even this is too high.) So, if the product liability component of this cost is anything like the consumer cost of the product defect, the stock market loss would exceed the "social loss." While we hesitate to push these fragmentary data this far,[6] they, like the preceding data, show how substantially the stock market losses can exceed those costs specifically attributable to the recall of a specific drug.

Another way of putting this is that the stock market is imposing a substantial goodwill loss on a firm over and above the product-specific costs. The stock market appears to expect that news of a recall will reduce consumers' demand (or raise costs) for other products sold by the firm and thereby impose additional losses on the firm. We tested this conjecture by adding the market value of the firm to the regressions in table 3. A single product typically accounts for a smaller fraction of a firm's profits the larger the firm. Thus, the percentage loss due to recall of a single product should be smaller for larger firms, if there is no spillover to other products. But the coefficient of the firm's market value was never as much as one-tenth of its standard error, and this implies that losses do spill over to the firm's other products (just as they seem to spill over to other firms in the same industry).

This goodwill element of the recall loss poses a challenge to further research, because there seems to be no easily apprehensible basis for expecting one product failure to beget others. As nearly as we can tell from our recall data, product failures occur randomly. However, whatever their source, it seems clear that the costs to drug firms of a recall are so large that they must exert a powerful deterrent effect on the production of defective products.

---

[6] A fuller treatment would require us to see if announcement of the liability costs affected the returns to Robins's stock. For example, if the initial reaction overestimated these costs, subsequent announcements of the actual costs would engender positive excess returns.

IV. Auto Recalls

Since the late 1960s, the National Highway Traffic Safety Administration of the Department of Transportation (DOT) has been empowered to order manufacturers to recall and repair autos with defects that compromise safety. We use a sample of 116 "major recalls" that occurred in 1967–81 to analyze the stock market's response to the news of this form of product defect. Our analysis recognizes a problem we raised in Section II: auto recalls occur too frequently to be entirely surprising to the stockmarket, so the market's response to the news of a recall can understate the full costs it imposes on producers of recalled cars.

A. Recall Sample

Each recall is initiated by an order from DOT specifying which particular group of cars are to be recalled and what is to be done to fix the cars. The distribution of the number of cars per recall is highly skewed. Some involve a few hundred cars or even less, and a few involve millions of cars. Our sample is designed to exclude many obviously trivial cases while retaining enough variety to permit analysis of the effects of recall size. It is drawn from all recall announcements reported in the *WSJ* involving the domestic Big 3 (GM, Ford, and Chrysler) for 1967–81 that exceeded 50,000 cars for GM, 20,000 for Ford, and 10,000 for Chrysler.[7] These cutoffs are crudely consistent with the relative market shares (and stock market values) of these firms, and they result in roughly equal representation of each firm in our sample. The sample is described more precisely in table 4. Even after excising the small recalls, there is a very broad range of recalls in our sample. Our sample remains highly skewed to the right; every relevant coefficient of variation comfortably exceeds one. Chrysler has the smallest recalls, GM the biggest, but these ranks are reversed when recalls are measured relative to market value.

B. Stock Market Response to Auto Recalls

For each recall in our sample we computed CERs for various periods around the event date—the date of the *WSJ* story about the recall. We used the same source and procedure as for drug recalls. The basic results are in panel 1 of table 5: Average CERs are significantly negative for every event window, and the average gets larger absolutely

---

[7] We have no stock market data for foreign producers, and American Motors has too few recalls to permit reliable comparisons with the others.

TABLE 4.   Major Auto Recalls, 1967–81 Descriptive Statistics

Sample	No. of Recalls	Cars per Recall (Thousands)				Cars per $ Million of Market Value	
		Mean	S.D.	Minimum	Maximum	Mean	S.D.
1. All recalls	116	717.8	1,552.8	14	12,000	158.8	342.7
A. GM	41	1,244.7	2,352.0	50	12,000	70.5	141.0
B. Ford	44	567.2	859.8	50	2,700	128.0	179.0
C. Chrysler	31	234.6	391.1	14	1,300	320.0	582.0
2. All 1967–74 recalls	53	612.7	1,320.8	14	6,700	72.0	132.0
3. All 1975–81 recalls	63	806.1	1,729.6	19.6	12,000	231.9	437.4

as the windows widen. We did not go beyond the 2-week window, CER(−5, 5), because recalls are so numerous that much wider windows would have created serious overlap problems.[8] That window yields a mean CER of −1.60 percent. About half this total is realized in the 3 days surrounding the event (−1, 1), another one-third in the subsequent 4 days, CER(2, 5), with the one-fifth or so remaining leaking out prior to the day before the event. Also, there is a significantly above-average frequency of negative recalls for every window, though these do not begin to approach the near unanimity in the corresponding data for drugs.

Panels A, B, and C of table 5 break out results by company. Every firm suffers a negative average CER and an above-average frequency of negative CERs for every event window. That unanimity tends to support a conclusion that recalls are costly, even though many of the individual statistics in panels A–C are not significant. The rather wide standard errors on some of these make us cautious about pushing comparisons among firms too hard, but it appears that GM loses about half as much per recall as either of its competitors, based on CER(−5, 5). This difference is due mainly to GM's smaller recalls per dollar of market value (see tables 4 and 7).

1. Does the CER Understate the Cost of a Recall? Our discussion in Section II implies that the CER for recall periods is an estimate of $-(1-p) \times K$, where K = the cost of a recall to a company and p = probability of a recall. So one way to estimate K would be to esti-

---

[8] As it is, four of our 116 cases overlap. We left the overlaps in our sample, but no result would change very much if the overlapping cases were deleted or if we had made the same adjustments as for drug-recall overlaps.

TABLE 5.   Mean CER for Auto Stocks: Various Intervals
             Around Day of Recall, 1967–81

Sample (No. of Recalls)	Event Window				
	$(-5, 5)$ (%)	$(-3, 3)$ (%)	$(-1, 1)$ (%)	$(-5, 1)$ (%)	$(2, 5)$ (%)
1. Total (116)					
Mean	−1.60	−.96	−.81	−1.07	−.53
t	3.40	2.56	3.30	2.85	1.87
Percentage negative	61.2*	62.1*	64.7*	62.1*	60.3*
A. General Motors (41)					
Mean	−.97	−.80	−.88	−.48	−.49
t	1.64	1.70	2.86	1.02	1.38
Percentage negative	56.1	58.5	65.9*	56.1	56.1
B. Ford (44)					
Mean	−2.03	−1.58	−.63	−1.51	−.52
t	3.50	3.42	2.08	3.26	1.49
Percentage negative	63.6	68.2*	61.4	63.6	54.5
C. Chrysler (31)					
Mean	−1.83	−.28	−.98	−1.24	−.59
t	1.37	.26	1.40	1.16	.73
Percentage negative	64.5	58.1	67.7*	67.7*	74.2*

Note: See text for description of sample, and see note to table 2 for method of computing t.
* = $t > 2.0$ (see note to table 2).

mate p directly and divide the CER by $(1 - p)$. To see where such a procedure would lead, note that every company in our sample experienced an average of 2–3 major recalls per year in the 1967–81 period, or about 1 in every 10 2-week periods. If uncertainty is resolved within 2 weeks, $p \approx .1$, and this implies an estimated average loss due to a recall (K) of around 1.8 percent of market value rather than the 1.6 percent in table 5.

However, this procedure would be biased if "other" news during recall periods was systematically favorable or unfavorable on average. That possibility needs to be taken seriously for the auto industry in 1967–81, a period in which adverse effects of foreign competition, pollution regulation, and so on cannot have failed to affect the industry's stock market performance. If nonrecall surprises in 1967–81 were indeed systematically unfavorable for auto stocks, then (1) the mean CER for nonrecall periods would be less than pK, the capital gain due to absence of a recall, and (2) the mean loss in recall periods would exceed $-(1 - p)K$. But, if the average effect of adverse "other" news is the same in recall and nonrecall periods, we can still estimate K by subtracting the mean CER in recall periods from the mean CER in non-

TABLE 6.   Mean CERs for Auto Recalls: Adjusted for Nonrecall News:
            1967–81 and Subperiods

Sample and Number of Recalls (in Parentheses)	Adjusted Mean CER(−5, 5)		Unadjusted Mean CER(−5, 5)	
	Mean (%)	t	Mean (%)	t
1. All 1967–81 (116)	−1.38	2.83	−1.60	3.40
A. General Motors (41)	−.60	.91	−.97	1.64
B. Ford (44)	−2.05	3.51	−2.03	3.50
C. Chrysler (31)	−1.46	1.06	−1.83	1.37
2. All 1967–74 (53)	−.60	.77	−.55	.73
A. GM (18)	−.56	.57	−.57	.63
B. Ford (17)	−.44	.63	−.44	.60
C. Chrysler (18)	−.81	.40	−.64	.33
3. All 1975–81 (63)	−2.04	3.35	−2.48	4.19
A. GM (23)	−.64	.71	−1.28	1.45
B. Ford (27)	−3.07	3.88	−3.02	3.79
C. Chrysler (13)	−2.37	1.29	−3.48	1.99

Note: See text for description of adjusted mean CER(−5, 5). Unadjusted mean CER(−5, 5) is
computed as in table 5.

recall periods.[9] This procedure is implemented in table 6 in the column
labeled "adjusted mean CER": For each year we compute the mean
CER(−5, 5) for every nonrecall period for each of the three firms.[10]
Then we subtract this year- and company-specific nonrecall mean CER
from the CER(−5, 5) for each recall experienced by the company in
the same year. For ease of comparison, we repeat the unadjusted
CER(−5, 5) from table 5, and we provide the added detail of a subperiod breakdown.

    None of the results in table 5 are much affected by our adjust-
ment. The adjusted mean CER(−5, 5) for 1967–81 remains significantly negative. It is a bit (0.2 percent) smaller than the unadjusted
mean, but some of this may be due to a conservative bias stemming
from subsequently documented negative spillovers of recalls.[11] The
main innovation in table 6 is in the subperiod data of panels 2 and 3,
not in how the CERs are calculated. These reveal a sharp difference in
the impact of recalls between periods. The average recall costs less
than 1 percent of market value before 1975 (for every firm) regardless
of how the CER is measured, and it costs more than 2 percent after

    [9]Call this common average effect of adverse news $(-X)$. Then, the nonrecall
period mean CER is $(pK - X)$, the recall period mean CER is $[-(1 - p)K - X]$, and
the difference between them is just K.
    [10]More precisely, we compute $11 \times$ mean daily ER for nonrecall periods.
    [11]So, e.g., Ford's non-recall-period mean CER is capturing negative spillovers
from GM recalls. This means that "other" news, including news of other companies'
recalls, is more adverse on average during nonrecall periods than in recall periods.

1975. This difference is mainly attributable to Ford and Chrysler whose average recall period CERs in this post-1975 period range from around −2.5 to −3.5 percent.

The next section, however, shows that the substantial difference between the stock market response to pre- and post-1975 recalls is more apparent than real.

2. The Relation between Stock Market Losses and Recall Size. We cannot compare the direct cost of auto recalls with the stock market loss, as we did for drugs, because we have no estimates of the former. We know only how many cars were involved in each recall and, from fragmentary press reports, that the firms' estimates of their repair costs per car range widely from something like $10 to $1,000. Perhaps because of the "measurement error" entailed by this wide range, efforts to extract the per car stock market cost by regressing CERs on the number of cars (per dollar of market value) across recalls proved singularly unrewarding.[12]

It proved more rewarding to aggregate over subgroups of recalls and thereby iron out some of the variability across recalls in the cost per car. Table 7 summarizes (1981) dollar losses per recall (= CER[−5, 5] × market value/GNP deflator) and per car for various groups of recalls. While we report a mean loss per car, we have little confidence that the high dollar amounts are meaningful. These means are dominated by a few extremely small recalls that generate extremely large losses per car. Accordingly, we show two other measures less affected by these extreme values—the median and the mean dollar loss per mean number of cars in a recall (labeled mean per mean).[13] This last datum is equivalent to aggregate losses in a sample divided by aggregate cars, so it comes closest to summarizing the experience of these firms over long periods. What is perhaps most interesting about this figure is its stability over time and between companies: in any large sample of recalls, the loss per car seems to be around $200.

How much of the $200 figure is attributable to direct costs and how

---

[12]The regression coefficients were usually within one standard error of zero and often of the wrong sign. We tried some crude adjustment for differences in response rates (car owners often do not respond to recall notices) and repair cost across a subsample of recalls. Specifically, we allowed the regression coefficient to depend on the response rate and a dummy equal to one if the recall order mandated a repair procedure for all recalled cars (and equal to zero if repair was required only if inspection revealed a defect). Neither variable sharpened our result.

[13]To illustrate the problem entailed by very small recalls, remember that losses and cars are essentially uncorrelated. So, suppose losses in a 1-car recall and a 100-car recall are each $100. The mean loss per car = ½(100/1 + 100/100) = $50.50, but the total loss from both recalls is only 200 = $1.98 per car. This last figure is our mean per mean for this sample.

TABLE 7.   Estimated Dollar Losses Per Recall and Per Car, 1967–81
            (Constant 1981 Dollars)

Sample (No. of Recalls)	Loss/Recall (Million $)		Loss/Car ($)			Mean/ Mean
	Mean	t	Mean	t	Median	
1. All 1967–81 (116)	141.1	2.2	813.3	1.5	185.7	196.6
A. GM (41)	235.5	1.4	477.5	.6	46.6	189.2
B. Ford (44)	128.6	3.7	694.2	2.3	198.2	226.7
C. Chrysler (31)	34.0	1.0	1,426.4	.9	95.7	144.9
2. All 1967–74 (53)	110.1	.9	1,092.9	1.0	64.7	179.7
3. All 1975–81 (63)	167.2	2.7	578.1	2.0	189.0	207.4

Note: Loss/recall is estimated by multiplying CER(−5, 5) for each recall period by the market value
of the firm in that period. Mean loss/car is the mean of (loss/recall)/cars involved in the recall.
The last column (mean/mean) is obtained by dividing the mean of loss/recall, as shown in the
first column, by the mean of cars/recall from table 4. Each loss/recall is deflated by the GNP
deflator set to a base of 1981 = 1.0.

much to lost goodwill? The skimpy data suggest that, as with drugs, the
latter dominates. If there were no indirect costs, the $200 figure would
imply pretax direct costs of around $400 per car (since direct costs are a
deductible expense). This would be in the high end of the range of per
car costs that have appeared in press reports about specific recalls.[14]
We know of only one publicly available piece of data that permits an
estimate of the cost per car in a large sample of recalls: GM disclosed
that it spent $33 million on recalls in 1982 (*Detroit Free Press*, May 22,
1983). This amounts to about $35 per GM car recalled that year. If this
is anywhere close to being typical, then the bulk of the stock market
loss represents indirect costs: lost sales, liability suits, and so on.[15, 16]

[14] For example, a *Detroit Free Press* series on recalls states that a 1983 recall of
240,000 GM cars "is thought to be the most expensive per-car recall ever." GM's estimate of its total direct cost for the recall is $30 million, or $125 per car (*Detroit Free
Press*, May 24, 1983).

[15] In this connection, Crafton, Hoffer, and Reilly (1981) and Reilly and Hoffer
(1983) show that sales of recalled models appear to decline when the recall is announced. The latter article estimates that sales of a domestic recalled "line" declined
about 5 percent in the month of a recall announcement in the 1977–81 period, but
there is no indication that the decline lasted more than a month. A single-month sales
decline of this magnitude could not account for very much of the typical stock market
loss. There are about 60 domestic "lines" with average monthly sales of around 10,000
cars. Reilly and Hoffer exclude lines with fewer than 8,000 cars per month. If the
average line in the sample has 20,000 monthly sales, a 5 percent decline represents
1,000 cars, or roughly $10 million sales. The loss pretax profits on these sales would
amount to under $2 million, based on the industry's margin of sales over material and
labor costs.

[16] We also found no serial correlation in recalls. For example, the correlation of
the number of recalls in successive 3-month periods is .03 for Chrysler, .08 for Ford

Table 7 also sheds light on the very large discrepancy between pre- and post-1975 CERs. The first column (lines 2 and 3) shows a much smaller discrepancy when the loss per recall is converted to constant dollars, and the discrepancy in the last column (loss per car) is smaller still. So, most of the discrepancy in CERs is due simply to the decline in the real value of auto stocks in the late 1970s: it took a bigger percentage of a smaller market value to generate the same dollar loss per recall. Most of the remaining discrepancy is attributable to the larger size of post-1975 recalls (see table 4).

3. *How Are Competitors Affected by Auto Recalls?* The result that competitors lose rather than gain during a drug recall holds for auto recalls as well. And, as with drugs, the spillover effects are substantial. The data are summarized in table 8. The upper-left corner shows mean CERs to equal-weighted "portfolios" of the two competitors during recall periods (e.g., a Chrysler-Ford portfolio during GM recalls). On average, competitors lose about 1 percent during a 2-week recall period, or about two-thirds as much as the recall company loses. All of this is attributable to 1975–81 recalls, where the competitors' loss (−2.40 percent) virtually matches the recall company's loss.[17] The remainder of the table provides the company detail behind these averages in terms of (1) all competitors' response to a specific company's recalls (upper right), (2) a specific competitor's response to both its rivals' recalls (lower left), and (3) a specific competitor's response to a specific rival (lower right). With due respect given to the large standard errors, this detail reveals a considerable heterogeneity in the spillover. For example: (*a*) GM loses more during its rivals' recalls (1.59 percent) than it does during its own recalls (0.97 percent); the reverse is true for both Chrysler and Ford. (*b*) The most damaging recalls for competitors are GM and Ford recalls, particularly in 1975–81 (−2.61 percent and −2.77 percent, respectively). (*c*) By contrast, the relatively small Chrysler recalls cost rivals about half (−1.25 percent) as much as GM

and GM, and .17 for the aggregate of all three firms. None of these is significant; auto recalls, like drug recalls, appear to occur randomly.

[17] This difference between subperiods is less intelligible than the similar sort of difference we found for recall company CERs (see table 6). In that case, we saw that the apparently weak negative CERs for 1967–74 were plausibly masking negative real dollar losses roughly comparable to those in the later period. In table 8 we find similarly weak but positive CERs for competitors in 1967–74. These would be consistent with nontrivial real dollar gains to competitors, a result that would excite no surprise. But the post-1974 data clearly describe a much different world.

TABLE 8. Mean CER(−5, 5) of Competitors during Recall Periods by Company and Subperiod, 1967–81

	All Recalls of Other Companies in Various Years			Recall Company		
	1967–81 (%)	1967–74 (%)	1975–81 (%)	GM (%)	Ford (%)	Chrysler (%)
All Competitors						
1. 1967–81						
Mean	−1.01	—	—	−1.03	−1.54	−.23
t	2.46	—	—	1.24	2.64	10.33
Percentage negative	59.5*	—	—	56.1	63.6	58.1
N	116	—	—	41	44	31
2. 1967–74						
Mean	—	.64	—	1.00	.42	.50
t	—	1.09	—	.87	.45	.50
Percentage negative	—	41.5	—	38.9	41.2	44.4
N	—	53	—	18	17	18
3. 1975–81						
Mean	—	—	−2.40	−2.61	−2.77	−1.25
t	—	—	4.65	2.39	4.22	1.47
Percentage negative	—	—	74.6*	69.6*	77.8*	76.9*
N	—	—	63	23	27	13
Competitor Company						
A. GM						
Mean	−1.59	−.09	−2.92	—	−2.13	−.83
t	3.49	.13	5.34	—	4.02	1.04
Percentage negative	66.7*	45.7	85.0*	—	75.0*	54.8
N	75	35	40	—	44	31
B. Ford						
Mean	−.48	.86	−1.81	−1.11	—	.36
t	.8	1.11	2.24	1.34	—	.47
Percentage negative	54.2	50.0	58.3	53.7	—	54.8
N	72	36	36	41	—	31
C. Chrysler						
Mean	−.94	1.16	2.41	−.94	−.94	—
t	1.27	1.12	2.44	.83	.95	—
Percentage negative	54.1	37.1	66.0*	53.7	54.6	—
N	85	35	50	41	44	—

Note: Each entry shows the mean CER(−5, 5) of the competitor (or group of competitors) listed in the left margin during recalls of cars produced by the company (or group) described at the top. The "all competitors" CER in the top half is the CER to an equal-weighted portfolio of the two nonrecall companies—e.g., Ford and Chrysler in the case of a GM recall. The table provides more details as it is read either down columns or across rows. To illustrate: Reading down the first column says: "The typical competitor lost 1.01% during a recall; more specifically, GM lost −1.59% during Ford and Chrysler recalls, etc." Reading across the first row says: "The typical competitor lost 1.01%; more specifically, GM's competitors lost 1.03%, etc."

and Ford recalls and only about one-third what they cost Chrysler itself in this 1975–81 period. So Chrysler recalls seem to be treated mainly as idiosyncrasies without strong implications for industry wealth.

The large size of the spillover relative to the company-specific CER raises the question of whether there is any company-specific effect of recalls at all. Or does a recall engender only an industry-wide loss, which is shared equally by the three firms? Table 8 gives a hint: there is no general tendency for companies to respond identically to their own recalls and those of competitors. A more formal answer is given by regressing a recall company's CER(−5, 5) on the CER to the portfolio of its competitors during recall periods. The regression coefficient here gives the company's average share in any industry-wide effects of recalls, and the intercept gives the average company-specific component. We computed the regression for each of the three companies and obtained a mean intercept of −1.12 percent ($t = 2.98$).[18] So there is a significant company-specific component to recall losses over and above a company's share in the industry-wide loss.[19]

V. Summary

Drug and auto recalls have strikingly similar effects on the wealth of shareholders. Both are much more costly than the direct costs of recalling the defective product. In both types of recalls a more general loss of goodwill seems to be a large component of the total loss. This result is not unique to this form of regulation. One of us (Peltzman, 1981) has found similarly large goodwill losses for FTC false advertising cases. Just what lies behind these goodwill losses remains something of a mystery, which we leave for future research. Our attempts, mainly with drugs, to find answers in costs of product liability suits and in time dependence of recalls succeeded only in deepening the mystery.

Another similarity between drug and auto recalls—and the source of another mystery—lies in the response of competitors. Their owners lose substantially when a rival product is recalled. Any favorable effects

---

[18] The average regression coefficient is 0.69 ($t = 7.46$). This implies that the typical company share in an industry-wide recall loss of 1 percent is under 1 percent. The proximate reason for this is that Chrysler has more volatile returns than the others, so when Chrysler loses 1 percent the others lose less.

[19] Since auto stocks generally had negative CERs during our sample period— especially in 1975–81—we also have to wonder whether there really is a spillover. That is, could the so-called spillover just be the result of other bad news? This is unlikely. For 1975–81, the average company CER(−5, 5) during all periods when it had no recalls was −0.5 percent. But, in the subset of these periods when its competitors have recalls, the mean CER is, as table 8 shows, over four times as large. So recalls to competitors were clearly especially bad news.

on the demand for substitutes from a recall are swamped by a more general negative effect on the industry. This is another piece of evidence that something much more is involved in a recall than failure of a specific product.

It is difficult to compare the magnitudes of the losses in drug and auto recalls, because both the frequency of recalls and the number of firms involved differ. Per recall, the percentage loss is much greater for drug recalls (6 percent vs. 1.5 percent). But auto recalls occur over twice as often and involve only three companies versus 19 for drugs (in our samples). So per company per year, auto recalls are considerably more costly. The average loss to rivals is roughly the same (1 percent) for auto and drug recalls, but with about 50 rivals in the case of drugs versus two for autos, the drug recalls clearly have the more substantial cross-firm effects.

Our results help shed light on the degree to which the capital market might suboptimally deter production of faulty products. They show that, in the simple sense of the market's not internalizing even the direct costs, suboptimal deterrence is no problem. Our results also show that to make a suboptimal deterrence story credible requires very generous estimates of the indirect social costs. The only source of such large costs we have found is in the cross-company effects. They are large enough to suggest a larger scope for industry cooperation in product design and inspection that economists have heretofore imagined.

Finally, we hope that our results have begun defining a new research agenda. They suggest that recall costs are like an iceberg whose easily visible part hides most of what is important. The challenge for future research is to discover just what form—for example, reduced sales, increased quality costs, lost "political capital"—these large, currently amorphous costs take.

References

Block, Lawrence H. "An Evaluation of Drug Product Citations in the FDA Weekly Reports between 1970 and 1978." *Contemporary Pharmacy Practice* 3 (Summer 1980): 171–79.

Crafton, Steven M.; Hoffer, George E.; and Reilly, Robert J. "Testing the Impact of Recalls on the Demand for Automobiles." *Econ. Inquiry* 19 (October 1981): 694–703.

Peltzman, Sam. "The Effects of FTC Advertising Regulation." *J. Law and Econ.* 24 (December 1981): 403–48.

Reilly, Robert J., and Hoffer, George E. "Will Retarding the Information Flow on Automobile Recalls Affect Consumer Demand?" *Econ. Inquiry* 21 (July 1983): 444–47.

Schwert, G. William. "Using Financial Data to Measure Effects of Regulation." *J. Law and Econ.* 24 (April 1981): 121–58.

Index